ISBN 978-0-428-19718-6
PIBN 10297190

IN THE

District Court of the United States

FOR THE

Northern District of California

SECOND DIVISION

SPRING VALLEY WATER COMPANY, Plaintiff, vs. CITY AND COUNTY OF SAN FRAN-CISCO, ET AL., Defendants.	Nos. 14,735, 14,892, 15,131, 15,344, 15,569, Circuit Court of U. S., Ninth Judicial Circuit, Northern District of California, and 26 and 96 District Court of U. S. Northern District of California, Second Division.

ABSTRACT OF TESTIMONY TAKEN BEFORE HONORABLE H. M. WRIGHT, STANDING MASTER IN CHANCERY FOR THE DISTRICT COURT OF THE UNITED STATES IN AND FOR THE NORTHERN DISTRICT OF CALIFORNIA, SECOND DIVISION, IN THE PROCEEDING ENTITLED SPRING VALLEY WATER COMPANY vs. THE CITY AND COUNTY OF SAN FRANCISCO, ET AL., IN EQUITY NOS. AS ABOVE.

For Defendants:
PERCY V. LONG, ESQ.
JESSE H. STEINHART, ESQ.
ROBERT M. SEARLS, ESQ.

EDWARD J. McCUTCHEN, ESQ.,
WARREN OLNEY, JR., ESQ.,
A. C. GREENE, ESQ.,
Solicitors for Plaintiff.

NEAL PUBLISHING COMPANY, PRINTERS, SAN FRANCISCO

C

IN THE

District Court of the United States

FOR THE

Northern District of California
Second Division

SPRING VALLEY WATER COMPANY, Complainant, vs. CITY AND COUNTY OF SAN FRANCISCO, Et Al., Defendants.	Nos. 14,735, 14,892, 15,131, 15,344, 15,569, Circuit Court of U. S., Ninth Judicial Circuit, Northern District of California, and 26 and 96 District Court of U. S. Northern District of California, Second Division.

ABSTRACT OF TESTIMONY TAKEN BEFORE HON. H. M. WRIGHT, STANDING MASTER IN CHANCERY FOR THE DISTRICT COURT OF THE UNITED STATES IN AND FOR THE NORTHERN DISTRICT OF CALIFORNIA, SECOND DIVISION, IN THE PROCEEDING ENTITLED "SPRING VALLEY WATER COMPANY vs. THE CITY AND COUNTY OF SAN FRANCISCO, Et Al., IN EQUITY Nos. AS ABOVE.

ABSTRACT OF TESTIMONY OF COMPLAINANT

FIRST HEARING.   JULY 12, 1915.

Appearance by counsel.   1

Argument over understanding as to valuations to be proved as   1-2
of Dec. 31, 1913; capital expenditures deducted prior thereto and
added since.

Judges' order refers eight cases to Master beginning fiscal year   2
July 1, 1914, then back for eight years.

SPRING VALLEY WATER CO. VS. CITY AND COUNTY OF SAN FRANCISCO

3-7   Discussion of stipulation to effect adjustment as between calendar years and fiscal years. Counsel state that they will attempt to agree by stipulation later.

Witness JOHN JOSEPH SHARON.

DIRECT EXAMINATION BY MR. OLNEY.

            Am Assistant Engineer of the Spring Valley Water Company.
8   Have been employed over seventeen years by Spring Valley Water
8-9   Company and its predecessor. I began as time-keeper during construction of San Andres pipe line, and during installation of Millbrae Pumping Station, pipe line, and auxiliaries of Millbrae Pumping Station, and during construction of Sunol Aqueduct and filter beds at Sunol and a part of Alameda pipe line.

            Was one year in Water Division as flume tender; six years in Engineering Department as clerk; five years as Assistant Superintendent of the City Distributing System, and last year as Assistant Engineer.

            I have had charge of the Statistical Department, and am familiar
9   with the various properties of the company, and of the demands of the service upon the company's properties. Am acquainted with the operating side of the company as well as the engineering side.

            Identifies topographical map of the region surrounding the Bay of San Francisco, modeled by Mr. F. F. Kelsey. It is accurate for all practical purposes for a map of that size. Shows the lands and the
10   locations of some of the conduits and reservoirs of the Spring Valley Water Company. The property which is either enclosed in red or is colored in a solid red is the property that is owned in fee. I think that that map represents the property that the company owned as of December 31, 1913. Riparian rights are indicated in
11   yellow, water sheds by green lines. Map admitted as "Plaintiff's Exhibit 1" without the printed matter upon it above the word "Legend".

12   Map introduced made up of various sheets of United States Geological Surveys covering the district in and about San Francisco Bay. The land of the Spring Valley Water Company is portrayed thereon in red. Yellow indicates the riparian rights of the company, green the boundaries of the water sheds. Reservoir sites are indicated in blue. Map admitted as Complainant's "Exhibit 2". Also indicates
13   the main conduits of the company in red.

            Introduces a map of district, including San Francisco and the region about San Francisco. The lands and the riparian rights owned by the company all indicated in red and yellow. Main conduits for bringing water into San Francisco indicated in yellow, red
14   and green, marked "Complainant's Exhibit 3".

            The Lake Merced source of supply located almost wholly within the City and County of San Francisco. The water is delivered by a

2

pumping station located on easterly shore of the south lake, forced through the Merced Filter Plant, through a 23-inch force pipe to top of hill known as Daly Hill or Daly City; the water flows by gravity through a 30-inch pipe line flumed for a short distance, a 44-inch pipe and through a brick lined tunnel. It is delivered into the Lake Honda reservoir at San Francisco at an elevation of about 365 feet above the city base. The pumping station is marked by a blue spot on Lake Merced, and the conduit from there to top of Daly City Hill is marked in deep green.

The next nearest source of supply is the San Andres reservoir, elevation 446 feet, supplied, in addition to its own water shed, from the drainage area reservoir known as Pilarcitos Reservoir. The water flows from San Andres reservoir to San Francisco through conduit colored light green on "Exhibit 3". First portion of conduit   15 is brick lined tunnel. Water leaves this at an elevation of 368 feet above high tide, and flows through a 44-inch wrought iron pipe as far as the Town of Baden. (Indicated on "Exhibit 3" as Baden Station.) Here 44-inch pipe has two branches; one 30-inch, colored green, runs from Baden Station to back of cemetery, in through Colma, around base of the hill at Daly City, and through Ocean View, follows along San Jose Avenue and ends at College Hill Reservoir at elevation of 255 feet above city base. The other branch, from Baden Station northward is called the Baden-Merced Pipe Line. (Indicated on "Exhibit 3" in carmine). It is 30-inches in diameter, and delivers water to the city pumps located on the east shore of the South Lake Merced. Also delivers water to the Central pumping station, located on Sloat Boulevard about Twenty-third Avenue, which forces the water to the Baden-Merced pipe line through a 30-inch pipe (also colored carmine) following Corbett Avenue to the junction of the pipe line indicated on this map as Pilarcitos Pipe Line, being the pipe described in connection with the water from city pumping station at Lake Merced to Lake Honda Reservoir. The water then from this connection runs into Lake Honda Reservoir.

The City pumps pump the water into the pipe line which is used to take water from Lake Merced into Lake Honda, and by that means the City pumps supply water to Lake Honda as well, which is one of the distributing reservoirs in the city.

The light green conduit on the map is actually used for taking   16 the water to the city pump; the conduit used for taking the water out is colored deep green.

The elevations of the reservoirs in San Francisco are usually referred to the city base or datum line established years ago, which datum is always referred to in city elevations. That base is 6.7 feet above ordinary high tide. The elevation at the collection works, such as the Peninsula System, and in the Alameda System, is the datum plane established by the Spring Valley Water Company, and is known as the "Crystal Springs base," which corresponds with the elevation of ordinary high tide as it was determined at Coyote Point (marked San Mateo Point on "Exhibit 3") by the Spring Valley Water Company about 1890. "Crystal Springs Base" is the elevation referred to in the properties and reservoirs of the company in the Peninsula and Alameda system, and is 4.984 ft. below the city base. The water from San Andres gets into the city in this way, some goes to Lake Honda, and some to College Hill Reservoir. In the water which comes from San Andres is also included the water which comes from Pilarcitos, and from the stone dam on Pilarcitos Creek below Pilarcitos Dam, which is conducted by tunnels and flumes from stone dam and Pilarcitos Dam into Lake San Andres.

The next source of supply is the Crystal Springs Reservoir. It has a capacity of 22,600 million gallons; it has an elevation of 288 feet and controls the flow from 22½ square miles of water shed. The water is delivered into San Francisco through a 44-inch wrought iron pipe (indicated on "Exhibit 3," as Crystal Springs 44-inch pipe line), colored light red, taking approximately the following route: Down the San Mateo Canon parallel with San Mateo Creek to a point about a mile west of the Town of San Mateo, then enters the County Road at the Town of Burlingame, along the County road to the Town of San Bruno, follows the old Bay Road up into the University Mound Reservoir, located in the Southeastern part of the City of San Francisco, at an elevation of 165 feet above city base. At a pumping station known as the Millbrae Pumps (indicated by a dark blue circle on "Exhibit 3") there is a connection between the 44-inch Crystal Springs pipe line to the pumping station. The pumping station is supplied with the Crystal Springs water and also with the water from Alameda, which is connected with the Crystal Springs pipe line. The Millbrae pump forces the water into the San Andres 44-inch pipe (light green on "Exhibit 3"). Crystal Springs and Alameda water is thus delivered into the College Hill Reservoir or to the Central pumping station. The Crystal Springs water by being pumped into the San Andres pipe line can fill either of those conduits. The water in the Merced-Baden pipe line can also be sent to the Merced pump and into Lake Honda. The Crystal Springs pumps perform two functions; to pump water from the Crystal Springs reservoir into a flume line ("Exhibit 3," Crystal Springs Pump flume), which water flows by gravity into the San Andres Reservoir, at an elevation of 446 feet; the object of that is to get a greater head on the water, San Andres being in a higher elevation than Crystal Springs. The other function is to take water from the Crystal Springs Reservoir when it is less than full, force that water into Crystal Springs 44-inch pipe line, and thus give a larger supply than would otherwise flow into that pipe line by gravity. It is a booster station.

4

There are two sources of supply in Alameda County, one at Pleasanton and the other at Sunol. The Pleasanton source is an artesian well supply. The water comes from wells to the pumping station ("Exhibit 3" Pleasanton Pump No. 1 & 2). These pumps force the water into pipe line (light yellow marked "Pleasanton Pipe Line") and water flows to point (indicated on "Exhibit 3" as Water Temple) where Pleasanton water meets water from Sunol filter beds, and combined water flows through Sunol Aqueduct and Alameda pipe line (indicated in yellow "Exhibit 3"), that pipe line delivering water to Belmont pumping station (indicated on "Exhibit 3" by dark circle) and designated Belmont Pump, which is located near the Town of San Carlos. The water arrives there at about 12 feet above high tide and is forced to an elevation sufficiently high to deliver water with the Crystal Springs water to the University Mound Reservoir at San Francisco at an elevation of 165 feet. The Alameda pipe line is connected with the Crystal Springs pipe line at the Millbrae pumping station. By means of this connection the water can be sent either to the University Mound or to College Hill, or to Lake Honda in the same 21 manner that the Crystal Springs water goes there. This pipe line from Alameda crosses underneath the bay at Dumbarton Point by means of four sub-marine pipe lines. At the westerly end of this submarine pipe is located the "Ravenswood Pump" which is a booster for increasing the head in the Alameda pipe line from Ravenswood Pump to Belmont, thus accellerating the flow through the pipe line and increasing the supply. The Pleasanton pumps put pressure in the conduits and also draw water from the wells. These wells flow probably two or three million gallons daily without the aid of the pumps. The Alameda pipe line is not all pipe line. The upper end is a series of tunnels and flumes 22 from the Sunol filter beds to a screen tank east of the Town of Niles. From there to Belmont pumping station the conduit is a 36-inch pipe all the way, except at the crossing of the bay, where there are two 16-inch and two 22-inch sub-marine pipes. From Belmont Pumping Station to Burlingame this is 36-inch pipe and from Burlingame to Millbrae pumping station the pipe line is 54 inches in diameter. The length of the sub-marine pipe across the bay is about 6300 feet, and the character of the conduit from the Pleasanton wells to the water temple is wrought iron pipe 30 inches in diameter. The water is collected at the Sunol filter beds as follows: The filter bed is a large gravel deposit located at the easterly end of the Niles Canon at the confluence of the Arroyo de Laguna, San Antonio and Alameda Creeks. The waters from Calaveras Creek, Alameda Creek, San Antonio and Arroyo de Laguna supply the gravel beds; in those gravel beds is located a series of concrete lined tunnels, perforated with small pipes 1½ and 2 inches in diameter. The water flows into the concrete galleries known as the Sunol Filter Galleries through these small pipes, thence through a con- 23 crete lined tunnel under the Sunol Valley down to the Sunol Dam, and

there enters the Sunol Aqueduct and Alameda pipe line. The Arroyo de Laguna comes from the Pleasanton Valley down to Sunol. The Alameda Creek is usually known as that part of the stream which runs to Sunol and down to the bay, and also from Sunol up to the confluence of the upper Alameda and the Calaveras Creek. Some times the portion of the stream from Sunol up to the confluence is called Calaveras Creek, and some times Alameda Creek, and above that confluence we have the confluence of the tributaries known as Upper Alameda Creek
24   coming in from the east, while Calaveras Creek is a tributary which comes in on the west side. Calaveras Creek also has a tributary known as Arroyo Honda. The San Antonio comes into the Calaveras or some times Alameda about a mile above the Sunol Dam.

    Introduces map entitled "Water District Map" of the distribution system, City of San Francisco. It is intended to show the pipe system in the city with particular relation to the sources from which the water is distributed, the distribution pipes being indicated in black lines. It is accurate in that respect. Map admitted in evidence as "Complainant's Exhibit 4". The district colored yellow is that por-
25   tion of San Francisco which is supplied through the distribution pipe leading from University Mound Reservoir at an elevation of 165 feet above city base, and is known as the low service, being low in elevation. College Hill Reservoir, the next highest portion in San Francisco in elevation is shown in pink, elevation 255 ft. above city base. Lake Honda Reservoir, elevation 365 feet, supplies the next highest elevation in San Francisco, district served indicated in light blue. Next highest elevation is supplied from the Clay Street tank and Presidio Heights tank at an elevation of 400 feet above city base. Districts
26   supplied colored brown. The Black Point pumps draw their supply from University Mound Reservoir, and then pump it into the Clay Street tank and Presidio Heights tank. Highest source of supply is known as the Clarendon Heights District, colored purple, and is supplied by the Clarendon Heights tank, located on easterly slope of the Twin Peak Ridge at an elevation of 600 feet above city base. This tank is supplied with water by Clarendon Heights pumping station located at Seventeenth and Pond Streets. The pumping station is supplied in turn by a pipe line from the low service indicated yellow and supplied by the University Mound Reservoir. The elevation of the pump at Clarendon Heights is about 100 feet. The water is forced to 600 feet above city base. The color deep blue is the district supplied from the Potrero Heights Reservoir, which is supplied from the Lake Honda Reservoir through pipe line over Twenty-first and Twenty-second Streets. The Potrero Heights Reservoir is located at Twenty-
27   second and Wisconsin Streets at an elevation of 300 feet. A small district adjoining the Potrero Heights Reservoir colored orange is supplied by a small wooden tank, which is in turn supplied from the Potrero Heights Reservoir by means of a small electric centrifugal

SPRING VALLEY WATER CO. VS. CITY AND COUNTY OF SAN FRANCISCO

pump. Light green represents district supplied from Lombard Street Reservoir connected with Lake Honda system, and supplied from the Lake Honda Reservoir. Water flows by gravity into the Lombard Street Reservoir at an elevation of 303 feet, and from there is delivered by gravity to the district colored green. The light green district is really a part of the Lake Honda system. The University Mound district is known in the company's water records as the low service and is indicated in yellow. Pink indicates College Hill District because supplied by College Hill Reservoir. Blue indicates Lake Honda District, and in the company's records comprises the district shown in brown, supplied from the Clay Street and Presidio Heights tank; comprises the district supplied by the Lombard Street Reservoir is indicated in green and it comprises the district colored dark blue, being supplied from the Potrero Heights Reservoir. The district colored orange is supplied also from the Potrero Heights Reservoir. The dark blue district bordering on Pacific Ocean is supplied from the pipe system of the Lake Honda District. Water is delivered into two wooden tanks, one at Forty-sixth Avenue and Anza Street, known as Meyer tank, elevation about 120 feet above tide; the other as Ocean Side tank, located Forty-first Avenue and Lincoln Way. These tanks break the pressure which would be excessive on these low districts.

Identifies "Plaintiff's Exhibit 5" called pavement map showing distributing system in the City of San Francisco. This is a correct map. The pipe lines of the S. V. W. Co. are indicated by black lines, the other colors indicate the different kinds of pavement; blue indicates basalt on sand pavement; yellow basalt on concrete pavement; vermillion basalt with grout pavement; dark yellow bitumen on concrete; red bitumen on concrete with binder pavement; sepia indicates oiled macadam; brown indicates macadam; green indicates cobble pavement; purple indicates brick pavement. Pipe lines indicated without any coloring is evidence there is no pavement on the street.

Witness introduces sub-soil map, which is a map of the distribution system, and likewise shows the pipe lines of the company in small black lines. The various colors show the different characters of the soil, formation in which the pipes of the distribution system are laid. This map was prepared in conjunction with the city officials. It has been agreed to by Mr. Ransom of the City Engineer's office for the city, and by Mr. Elliott for the Spring Valley Water Company, marked as "Plaintiff's Exhibit 6". The colors on this map entitled as sub-soil map of distribution system, etc., indicate the different characters of soils. The soil known as sandy soil is indicated in yellow. The sandy clay soil is indicated in green; the hard clay in brown; the soft rock in red; the hard rock in blue.

Witness introduces traffic map. This map graphically portrays the difference between the various streets, in the difficulty of con-

28

29-30

30-31

32
33

struction, owing to the obstruction of congested traffic, other conduits and matters of that sort. This map was prepared by Mr.
M. M. O'Shaughnessy, City Engineer, in December, 1913. The data
that is presented here with reference to districts 1, 2 and 3 were
agreed to by Mr. Ransom, of the City Engineer's office, for the city,
and Mr. Elliott for the Spring Valley Water Co. As to the traffic conditions, the city was divided into three districts known as
districts 1, 2 and 3. District 1 is indicated on the map in solid dark
lines; that is the heavy traffic and numerous underground obstructions, and includes the most congested portions of the commercial
and business districts. District No. 2 shown on the map in broken
lines as the lighter traffic, and not many underground obstructions,
and represent conditions more favorable than district 1, and less
favorable than district 3. As regards the laying of water mains, the
remaining portion of the City of San Francisco was not symbolized
at all as regards traffic conditions, and is known as District 3. District 3 has light or no traffic, and no underground obstructions, and
includes the outlaying residence districts of the city, marked as
"Plaintiff's Exhibit 7". There are sewers and pipes in some of District 3.

34   Introduces volume of maps headed "Maps of Real Estate, Rights
of Way, and Riparian Rights, Spring Valley Water Co., December
31, 1913". These maps were prepared under my supervision. They
correctly set forth the properties of the Spring Valley Water Co.,
which they purport to cover. These maps are furnished to the city.
The lands are sub-divided and indicated by colors, also each subdivision is numbered. The sub-divisions represent the parcels of
land acquired by the company from different owners, and each parcel was acquired from different owners at different times. Offered
in evidence as "Plaintiff's Exhibit 8".

Introduces volume entitled "Plans of some important structures,
excluding distribution pipe system, Spring Valley Water Co., December 31, 1913". This volume was prepared under my supervision,
35   and is correct, and purports to set forth the plans of the important
structures of the Spring Valley Water Co. outside of the distribution
system.

These plans were furnished to the city's representatives, but in
larger scale. This volume offered in evidence as "Plaintiff's Exhibit
9". Introduces profile of the works of the Spring Valley Water Co.
showing the various elevations of the reservoirs and pipe lines. This
composite profile represents the relative distances in miles, and the
elevations above sea level in feet, of the different city reservoirs; the
routes of the various pipe lines leading into the city of San Francisco of the supply reservoirs, and the diversions and the control
36   works in the Peninsula and Alameda systems, including in the elevation the proposed reservoirs of San Antonio, Calaveras, and Arroyo

8

Valle. Arroyo Valle height of proposed reservoir 800 feet; 650 feet height of the proposed dam site; Calaveras altitude 800 feet for the surface of the reservoir when completed. The Pleasanton gravels at a height of about 320 feet. The Pleasanton 30-inch pipe line has the relative elevations and distances along it indicated by a black line. Height of the reservoir at San Antonio 450 feet. The Pilarcitos supply from the west side comes in at something over 800 feet. Height of Pilarcitos Dam is just below 700   37 feet; offered in evidence as "Plaintiff's Exhibit 10". An inventory of the properties of the company has been prepared as of December 31, 1913, and checked with the representatives of the city, and agreed to. It includes the quantities which were computed by the representatives of the city, and also by the representatives of the company, also includes structures and lands. This volume offered in evidence. Referring to the inventory   38-39 and to the maps of real estate, rights of way, etc., explanation is made of the connection between the paging in this volume of maps and the number of the particular parcels of land with the inventory as printed. Explanation is also made as to how to run from one of these volumes to the other to establish the connection between them. Introduces a bound volume headed "Normal capacities of plant,   40 population, vital statistics, water consumption, pumping station equipment, assessed valuation, etc., Spring Valley Water Co., December 31, 1914". I prepared this volume, and it correctly sets forth the matters that are therein set forth, offered separately as "Exhibit 12-a, 12-b, 12-c, etc. The first page is a schematic diagram showing the relative locations and capacities and elevations of the storage reservoirs at Pilarcitos, San Andres, and Crystal Springs, and of the proposed reservoir Calaveras, San Antonio, Arroyo Valle, the pumping stations at Pleasanton and their connections with the system by a 30-inch pipe line to Sunol as shown, as well as the connection between the Sunol filter beds, with the Niles aqueduct and screen tank; the Niles screen tank is shown with reference to the pipe line leaving the Belmont pumps, and from Belmont pumps to its connection with the Crystal Springs pipe line at Millbrae pumps. The pipe line from Crystal Springs Reservoir is also shown and followed through to its connection with the Alameda pipe at Millbrae pumps. Briefly, this is a diagram of the system showing the various sources of supply and conduits leading from them to the main distribution reservoirs within the City of San Francisco. It shows the pumping station and the size of the conduits and the inter-connection between the various pipes of the system. The single circle represents the reservoirs that are at present developed. The double circle represents the proposed reservoirs. There is no connection between Portola and Crystal Springs Reservoir. The Portola Reservoir is not used in connection with San Francisco. Admitted as "Plaintiff's Exhibit   41 12-a".

The sheet on the second page is entitled "Peninsula Pipe Lines". It is a schematic profile of the pipe lines from the Peninsula reservoirs into the City of San Francisco. It shows in profile what is shown in plan on exhibit 12-a, admitted as "Plaintiff's Exhibit 12-b". Sheet 3 is a photographic reproduction of lithographic print of a map entitled "Map of property of the Spring Valley Water Co., August 14, 1914"; the properties, real estate holdings, and riparian rights, and the reservoirs are shown on this map. The second part of the legend crossed out, offered in evidence as "Plaintiff's Exhibit 12-c", and marked "Plaintiff's Exhibit 12-c". The next page is a small blue print entitled "Drainage areas Spring Valley Water Co." Offered as "Plaintiff's Exhibit 12-d". This map was prepared by Mr.

42
43
I. E. Flaa. I did not prepare it myself. It is a convenient map on a small scale, indicating the boundary lines and the areas of the various drainage areas. Those drainages are also shown on these other maps and were introduced this morning, for instance, Exhibit 2. The drainage of the area tributary to the Pleasanton, Livermore Valley is stated in this small map as 258.34 square miles, that is not shown in figures in Exhibit No. 2, the boundaries of the drainage however, are shown on Exhibit 2. Marked "Plaintiff's Exhibit 12-d".

44
The next map is a map entitled "Rainfall Distribution, Alameda System, Spring Valley Water Co., April 14, 1914". The map itself was compiled from United States Geological Survey Topographic Sheets, simply for the purpose of indicating on this map the boundaries of watershed lines and the creeks. The dark, heavy lines and the dotted lines represent isohyetose or lines of equal rainfall, as was determined from a number of gauging stations which are shown on the map and numbered. From the records of these rainfall stations the computations were made which indicated in our judgment the lines shown on the map. Some of the gauging stations, at Mt. Hamilton, maintained by the Lick Observatory, and others, viz., at railroad stations of the Southern Pacific Company. Base stations were sta-

44-45
tions from which there were the longest records of seasonal rainfall obtainable which were used in connection with the San Francisco rainfall. Example: Rainfall was kept at San Francisco, and record is available for over sixty years. At Lick Observatory, Livermore, San Jose and other places, rainfall records kept from thirty to forty years, perhaps. Found a certain relation existed in the forty years rainfall of these various stations, with the rainfall for corresponding forty years at San Francisco and for running back records of the other rainfall stations to see how many dry years, and when they did occur, applied that ratio which we found to exist in the forty years to the San Francisco record in order to expand the Lick Observatory, Livermore, and other records back to a sixty period.

Gauging stations maintained by the company are indicated by solid circles surrounded by a ring, and the stream gauging station, indicated by a solid circle, stream gauging station having automatic recording gauge indicated by star. 45

This map was prepared from data obtained from all these stations.

Offered in evidence as "Plaintiff's Exhibit 12-e".

CROSS-EXAMINATION BY MR. STEINHART.

The gauging taken at the primary station at San Francisco is not shown in and of itself. The gaugings taken at these recording stations, for instance, Town of Livermore, is shown on the table to have extended from 1871-72 to 1913-14, that is 43 years. Station No. 2 is at Pleasanton, about where Pleasanton pumping station is. Explains designations Al. (Alameda), A. C. (Alameda Creek), S. A. (San Antonio), A. P. (Arroyo Positos), A. M. (Arroyo Mocho), 46-47 T. C. (Tassajero Creek).

Station 2 located about where Pleasanton pumping station is, is kept by Spring Valley Water Co., records there consecutively for fifteen years from 1899-1900 to 1913-14.

Station 3 is down by Niles, maintained by Southern Pacific Railroad Company. Records published in U. S. Weather Bureau 48 reports, and extend from 1886-87 to 1913-14. These figures are not checked, but simply taken as reported by United States Weather Bureau.

Station 4 is at Sunol, maintained by Spring Valley Water Co., record extends from 1889-90 to 1913-14. Station 5 at Town of Livermore maintained by Southern Pacific Company, record obtained from U. S. Weather Bureau, not checked by Spring Valley Water Co.; record there from 1871-72 to 1913-14. Station No. 6, I don't see that now, I do not run across Station No. 6. Station No. 7, located at Calaveras. Maintained by Spring Valley Water Co. Record extends from 1874-75 to 1913-14. Station No. 21 located at 49 Mt. Hamilton, Lick Observatory. Figures obtained from U. S. Weather Bureau Reports. Records extend from 1881-2 to 1913-14. Station 101 is near headwaters of Alamo Creek. A farmer reports to the Company weekly the rainfall record there. Record extends over period of two seasons only, 1912-13 and 1913-14. No check made of these records. The company has accepted the reports of the observer. Station 102 is in the Tassajero Region. Records obtained same as at Alamo. Reports accepted without checking. The other stations shown are kept by farmers or other persons, the data of which is accepted by the Spring Valley Water Co. and not checked 50 against the gaugings. These gauging stations are on the different streams tributary to the gravel beds, and tributary to the different streams about there.

Explanation of column headed "65 year expanded mean" represents: By comparison with the secondary base stations we extended the records of these stations that are shown here, numbered from 1 up to 24, but not consecutively, back to the 65 year mean, for the purpose of determining annually the periods of drought and execs-sive winters, to see whether in making an analysis of what the probable yield of the sources would be, about when the drought would occur, as indicated from the rainfall record.

The secondary base stations covered about 40 years from 1871 to 1913, that is 43 years. This was extended over a 65 year period by comparison with the rainfall in San Francisco, and then each one of these streams, gauging or rainfall stations the data was taken from for a limited period of time and extended over the same period on the same type of average, using the average of the six recording stations in the immediate vicinity here. I should have said seven secondary stations. The Isohyetose lines represent the average rainfall as determined from these stations for the 65 year mean, and are represented in column 4.

The report of 1914 and 1912, whatever difference would exist there would be because the two years added to the report of 1912 made the average a little bit different. At many of these stations we have observations for only two years, accordingly when comparison is made of the average of those two years with the 65 years expanded mean, you may get quite a difference.

The legend in the lower left hand corner, "Watershed Sub-divisions; Calaveras, San Antonio, Arroyo Valle, Upper Alameda, Sunol Drainage, Livermore total catchment area"; was determined from the topographic maps published by the U. S. Geological Survey, and was measured off by employees of the Spring Valley Water Co. in the Engineering Department, for the purpose of checking.

The meaning given to "Catchment Area" in determining the extent of the Catchment Area was from the crest of the mountains or the dividing lines which would afford drainage to the reservoirs or to a common point or outlet of a valley.

The second column, entitled "1914, Areal Rainfall Column", is deduced from the records of the various rainfall stations had for the year 1914. To get at that figure we chose all the rainfall stations shown in the legend on the top of the page where we had those records for the year 1914.

In determining the rainfall record for Calaveras other stations would be used than for determining the rainfall in San Antonio, but which ones are not indicated on this map. I have not the record with me to show what stations were actually used, but take for instance Calaveras; the records of the stations would be taken from those in the vicinity of the drainage area, either within or in close proximity to the drainage area.

The two series of isohyetose lines, one solid, and the other broken, shows the difference in the area rainfall or the equal distri-

SPRING VALLEY WATER CO. VS. CITY AND COUNTY OF SAN FRANCISCO

bution of rainfall due to the introduction into the table of two dry
years.

Offered in evidence as "Plaintiff's Exhibit 12-e'".

(Objected to as immaterial, irrelevant, and incompetent, and as   55
hearsay). Went in with that objection appearing on its face.

DIRECT EXAMINATION CONTINUED BY MR. OLNEY.

Only method of checking reports sent in by farmers is only in a   56
general way by comparison with reports that come in from adjoining
stations, and that was done, or to actually make the gauging a second
time as a check after the observer had reported it and that cannot
be done after the rain has fallen and has passed away.

The next map is entitled "Run Off Distribution, Alameda System, S. V. W. Co., 1914." Similar to other map just referred to
entitled the rainfall distribution, except that tabulations shown here
show seasonal runoff measured at the various stations recorded in the
table and for the years shown, the observations being made by employees of the Spring Valley Water Company and in recent years
checked by engineers from the City Engineer's Office, to extent of
determining the proper factors or rating curves to be used in determ-   57
ining the flow through the season.

CROSS-EXAMINATION BY MR. STEINHART.

The Brightside Weirs are on aqueduct leading from the Sunol
Dam down the Niles Canyon to the screen house at Niles, and are
about half way down the canyon at the outlet of the first long tunnel
from Sunol Dam about 7500 feet west thereof. It measures the
water delivered through the Alameda pipe line to Belmont pumps.
I never heard of any discussions as to the correctness of that weir   58
measurement. I think the conditions there are ideal.

The records over the Sunol Dam were based upon a rating curve
made during the two years 1913 and 1914 of the flow in Alameda
Creek just upstream from the dam. The rating curve was calibrated
with the discharge in Alameda Creek, as determined by the current
meter measurements. We have a complete record of the gage heights   59
over the Sunol Dam, and by applying to those gage heights the quantity of water as found or determined by this rating curve, we got the
quantity of water that corresponds to those gage heights. The
record as to discharge of Alameda Creek extends over a period from
1900 to 1914. We have the actual records of the gage heights and
the heads on the weir from this period 1900 to 1914 at both points.

By gage heights, I mean the gage as corresponding to a certain
reference point. The rating curve established by current meter
measurements for two years 1912-1913 is used to determine the quantity of water at those gage heights. The quantity of water at that

13

60   gage height determined at that time was found by determining with the current meter the velocity of water in various sections in the creek and applying the mean velocity to the mean area and thus determining the cubical contents. I think the company used a Price current meter; the results were checked by Mr. Bartel of the City Engineer's Office. We determined from those current meter measurements of 1912 and 1913 the rating curve which applied to the flow over the dam corresponding to certain gage heights. It was merely a matter of applying the gage heights to the rating table to determine the quantity and it is as accurate as may be had. In 1912 the City Engineer was making some investigations of various water

61   supplies for the City of San Francisco and in the final report which is made on the various systems which had been investigated some doubt was cast upon the accuracy of the records of the quantities of water which actually wasted down the Alameda Creek from the 621 square miles of the Alameda drainage area; for the purpose of checking the correctness of the rating table which the Spring Valley Water Co. had used prior to 1913 when these measures were taken the City Engineer's Office co-operated with the Engineering Department of the Spring Valley Water Company in actually taking these current meter measurements for the purpose of determining the quantity of water that went over the Sunol Dam at certain gage heights on the dam. In checking those and adopting the rating curve which was made in co-operation with the Engineering Department of the City, we found that the total runoff extending from the year 1900 up to 1914 was about 4 or 5 per cent in excess of that claimed by the company in 1912. Rating curve was made in conjunction with city officials.

The city officials and the Spring Valley Water Company agreed on a rating curve to be applied to the Sunol Dam. Rating was determined from observations taken for two years. Measured the torrential flow coming down the Alameda Creek by means of the gauge height. 1910-11 was a very wet year.

63   The rating curve was actually made under the direction of Mr. M. M. O'Shaughnessy, City Engineer, and F. C. Hermann, who was Chief Engineer of the Spring Valley Water Company. Mr. Grunsky, or Prof. Marks and Prof. Hyde, had nothing to do with this rating curve. They made a report in 1912 to the City of San Francisco. The legend in the lower left-hand corner (Exhibit 12-f) indicates the

64   quantity of water that flowed in the Arroyo Valle Station No. 2 for the year 1906-07, to the years 1913-14. Also of the quantity of water that was measured at Arroyo Mocho, Station No. 1, for the year 1911-12, 1913-14 inclusive.

The areas marked A, B, C, D, E, & F, are drainage areas tributary to the various reservoirs, to the Livermore Valley, and the Sunol filter beds. The subdivision marked "A" is the Calaveras Water-shed,

14

98.3 square miles. That drainage area is tributary to Calaveras Reservoir. The Arroyo Valle Water-shed, that would be the upper portion, the 140.8 square miles shown as capital "C" in the sub-division here, is an entirely separate watershed.

The Arroyo Mocho is a portion of the drainage to Livermore Valley. Arroyo Positas is a portion of the drainage to the Livermore Valley. Upper Alameda watershed is included in drainage "D".

SECOND HEARING.   JULY 13, 1915.

Witness: J. J. SHARON.

DIRECT EXAMINATION BY MR. OLNEY.

The page entitled "Approximate Normal Capacities of Plant of   68
Spring Valley Water Co. as of December 31, 1913," and headed in
the upper righthand corner, "Lands Owned, in use and out of use",
was prepared under my supervision and shows the acreages owned in
the various counties. This table consists of two pages, and correctly   69
sets forth the acreage of lands owned, out of use and in use. I have
compared the lands of the company with the lands which the city
sought to condemn, as shown in their complaint, and found that to
be also correct. The page which covers riparian rights and rights
of way is also correct.

Offered and admitted as "Plaintiff's Exhibit 12-g".   70

The page headed "Approximate Normal Capacities of Plant of
Spring Valley Water Co., San Francisco, California, Sources of Supply", shows in the upper righthand corner, "Approximate Normal
Capacities of Plant". This page sets forth in tabulated form the
physical details with reference to elevations, capacities and depths of
water in the storage reservoirs; it also sets forth the mean runoff and
safe yield in million gallons daily from the various sources set forth.

Referring to item "3c", "Proposed Future Level", the elevation
shown there of overflow, 300 feet, is an error, and should be 333
feet. The acreages are also in error, the 1770 acres will change with   71
the change of elevation of the overflow as will also the capacity in
million gallons. The item "3c", "Proposed Future Levels", is correct, however, if the elevation of 300 feet is taken as the ultimate
elevation, but if increased to 333 feet, then the acreage and depth
would be correspondingly changed. With this exception, the tabulation is correct.

Offered in evidence as "Plaintiff's Exhibit 12-h".

CROSS EXAMINATION BY MR. STEINHART.

This table was set up by Metcalf from data furnished by me.
The data in column 1, "Tributary Drainage Area, Square Miles",
was obtained by making computations of the area as shown on the
United States Topographical Map. The seasonal rainfall was ob-

tained from records kept by the Spring Valley Water Co. at the various stations shown there. These I can give only approximately, as I have not the records. At Pilarcitos records were kept from about 1865 up to date, at San Andres from about 1868 to date, at Crystal Springs

72 these records were kept at the upper dam from about 1875, and at the cottage from about 1896 or 7, to date. From the lower dam the records have been kept from 1890 up to date. The record which is indicated as San Francisco record, and shown for Merced Lakes, is from the U. S. Weather Bureau. The Calaveras record was kept by the Spring Valley Water Co. from 1874 up to date, and has been kept at all times. This is the company's oldest record there. The San Antonio records are taken from an average of a series of stations in that vicinity, but I do not remember what stations were used. The City has agreed with us in regard to some of these records, but not for the entire length of time. I agreed with Major Dockweiler on the rainfall at San Francisco.

73   The Sunol gravels are the Sunol filter beds, and the Livermore gravels constitute the artesian supply in the Livermore Valley at

74 Pleasanton. The seasonal rainfall is reached by taking the record of Sunol for the Sunol filter beds, and the rainfall record at Livermore for the Livermore gravels. Thus there are two sub-divisions in that single item 8, of underground sources; one is the source at Sunol, the filter beds, the other is the artesian basin at Pleasanton. The seasonal rainfall estimated in the Sunol gravels is 22.11, and in Livermore 15.49. The estimate for this latter is made at the Town of Livermore.

Referring to the next column, the elevation of overflow, and of the bottom of reservoir, indicates Pilarcitos to be the high-water, or overflow elevation; stone dam is taken from actual figures as they exist at the present time; San Andres the same; the tunnels the same; but the Crystal Springs is 280 feet, which is the crest of the overflow. The level of the high-water mark maintained by bulkheading the waste-way, is 288.85 feet. By proposed future level is meant the level to which the dam can be increased in height, thereby increasing the storage capacity of the Crystal Springs Reservoir. The dam has been built with extra foundations, and extra width in the foundations and throughout, so as to be able to increase its height.

The actual flow at the Merced Lakes at present is shown there. The Calaveras is a proposed reservoir. In taking the elevation of overflow and bottom of reservoirs, the dam-site is taken at the point

75 where the present dam is being constructed. There have been other proposed dam-sites, the elevation of overflow, and bottom of reservoirs, of which is the same as in the present dam-site. This means that the dam, lower down, would have to be a few feet higher to make up in the slope of the creek between the present dam-site and one of the lower site.

The San Antonio is also a proposed reservoir site. It is to be constructed at a point a little up-stream from the location of the present gaging station, and at a site that has already been explored. This is indicated on "Exhibit 2". The Arroyo Valle is also a proposed dam-site, which is shown on "Exhibit 2". There is also another dam-site further down-stream, which is indicated on "Exhibit 2" at about Cresta Blanca, being between 3½ and 4 miles below the present proposed dam-site.

76

The depth in feet overflow to bottom is just the vertical distance between the flow line and the bottom of the reservoir. These computations I made myself. The bottom of the reservoir means the outlet, or just at the base of the dam, or low elevation; it may be within a few feet of the bottom of the dam. In calculating unavailable water, I mean the water that could be taken out by pumping, if needed. Generally speaking, the outlets are pretty low in the reservoirs.

The next column "Water Surface Full, Reservoir in Acres", represents the area in acres flooded by water when the reservoir is full at the overflow elevation shown in the third column. The capacity in million gallons is figured from actual surveys of the reservoir site, and the cubical contents determined. The surveys were all made by the Spring Valley Water Co., but I had nothing to do with them. The areas shown in the previous column of "Water surface full, Reservoir in acres", were checked over recently under my direction, by means of the planimeter.

77

Referring to the next column, "Capacity in Million Gallons", further data than what has preceded is needed to determine cubical contents. That is ordinarily determined by making a topographical survey indicating the contours. In all of these cases this was done at five foot intervals, and interpolating the contents for each foot between each of these contours. Those surveys are shown in "Exhibit 9".

The next column, "Mean Run-off Million Gallons Daily, Approximate," was determined from the records kept by the Spring Valley Water Co., and includes the run-off for the entire drainage area at Pilarcitos. At San Andres it would include the run-off for the entire San Andres, and the tributary drainage area, which includes the Davis Tunnel. The same is true in Crystal Springs. In this case the run-off was determined from a number of years actual service of the reservoir, and these are net after a deduction for evaporation has been made. It is the net result obtained through a long series of years in the operation of the reservoir. A quantity of water drawn from the reservoirs and added to the loss or gain in the storage during the year, indicated the net run-off for that year. This was the method of measurement used.

78

The quantity run-off from the reservoirs was measured by drawing it off into San Francisco and measuring it by weirs. At Pilarcitos

79

17

the water was measured in the San Mateo Creek in the flume and weir box between the outlet of tunnel No. 1 and inlet of tunnel No. 2. At San Andres the water taken from that reservoir is measured by a weir at the outlet of the San Andres, or Bald Hill Tunnel, the outlet of the tunnel being the inlet of the San Andres 44-inch pipe which delivers the water to San Francisco. At Crystal Springs the water is measured at the weirs before it enters the University Mound Reservoir. At Calaveras the water was measured by run-off measurements and gaugings taken in the stream during the time that water was flowing at a point about the site of the dam in the gorge just below the present dam-site. This was taken for a period beginning in 1898, and ending 1914, and is shown on "Exhibit 12-f" in the table appearing in the upper righthand corner. The measurements were made partially with current meter measurements in the streams, and other measurements were made with what is known as the float measurement method in order to determine surface velocity. The float measurement method is to determine the surface velocity by means of some buoyant substance which will float on top of the water, and the time necessary to travel
80 a certain distance is then computed, and in that way the velocity of the surface of the water is determined. This method is not so accurate as current meter measurement. A method of this kind is subject to changes due to the change in the bed of the stream caused by floods, but I would not say that that would apply with such great force to Calaveras for the reason that the stream bed is not so likely to change very materially, as there is quite a good deal of rock and on the sides the bed-rock crops out to the sides of the creek; there are small changes in the bottom, but they are not so very material.
81 It is true that this method of float measurement is inaccurate, due to the fact that it depends entirely upon surface conditions, upon the expertness of the man handling it, and to the fact that the computations depend entirely upon the nature and size of the bed of the stream, and that the size and nature of the bed of the stream are constantly changing, but if the difference in the area of the cross section of the stream was noted, then the error is not so great as it would be if you did not take that into consideration. It can be noted constantly with a reasonable degree of accuracy, but it has not been noted in all instances. A number of records have been kept for the last two or three years showing the change in the character of the bed of the stream, and also the size of the stream. These were taken in conjunction with the City Engineer's Department. I think we have some of Calaveras for the years 1910-11 and 1912.

  The San Antonio and Arroyo Valle are given together for the
82 reason that I think that those reservoirs might be combined by a tunnel through the hills from Arroyo Valle to San Antonio, or they could be operated independently; the combined run-off of the two

SPRING VALLEY WATER CO. VS. CITY AND COUNTY OF SAN FRANCISCO

is approximately thirty million gallons daily. The only idea in combining them was that the reservoirs might be combined by tunnels or by pipe lines or something of that sort. The data for this was taken from some measurements of Arroyo Valle which we had, as shown on "Exhibit 12-f" for the years 1904-5 to 1913-14, and at San Antonio for the years 1911-12 to 1913-14. The records of the run-off measurements at Arroyo Valle from 1904-5 to 1907-8 were float measurements and from 1911-12 to 1913-14 the measurements were made with current meters located at Cresta Blanca. The accuracy of this measurement, I think, is subject to some correction, owing to the gravelly nature of the creek, and the existence of the bridge near which the meter was located, and the fact that it is at an angle. I don't know that it has ever been proven that the existence of the bridge there and the fact that it is at an angle materially effected the accuracy of those measurements.

83

Mr. Herrmann, Chief Engineer of the Spring Valley Water Co., had charge of the matter of those measurements in November, 1914.

The method of measurement on the San Antonio was from the years 1911-12 to 1913-14 the current meter measurement. The station, I think, was a satisfactory one for measurements, and I do not remember all the details in connection with the fact that the representatives of the city, and of the Spring Valley Water Co., reported that that station should be changed, owing to the location of trees thereon.

In order to determine the amount of water that was in the reservoir, a topographical survey was made of the reservoir site, and the contents computed from that survey; by the use of these figures in connection with that survey, we made a table of the capacity corresponding with each foot on the gage board of the reservoir. To determine the heights of the water in the reservoir in any one year, in order to get the mean run-off from the catchment area, we have a gauge board in the reservoir which is read once each day. This, I should say, was not so very inaccurate, although the measurement would be affected by any wind or any disturbance of the surface. A mistake in reading that gauge measurement would not make a great difference in our total computations; a mistake of an inch, for example, on the gauge board at Pilarcitos reservoir, would make a difference, possibly, of two and one-half million gallons, which, divided by 365 days is a very small item; I think we neglected that in the third or fourth decimal place in this table. We take the readings of January 1 in one year, and of January 1 in the succeeding year, and the difference in the level is the difference for the entire year, so that the one inch, if there were a mistake of that kind, would show up in the total record. In this particular case the determination is made by comparing it from July 1 to July 1.

84

·

85

Referring to column "Safe Yield in Million Gallons Daily", the figure 18.5 represents the safe yield from those reservoirs after deduc-

19

tions from the previous column has been made for waste in very wet
years from the reservoir. In the case of Crystal Springs, the amount
that is supplied from the Crystal Springs pipe line would be deducted
from the safe yield of the Crystal Springs reservoir. In the case of
the San Andres and the Pilarcitos the measurements have been made
86   at the reservoirs so that the withdrawals along the line are accounted
for in the measurements there. I should have said that from the
Crystal Springs pipe line should be deducted from the preceding
column in Crystal Springs, and not from the safe yield, as the safe
yield is actually the measurements of the water delivered into San
Francisco, except from the Pilarcitos and San Andres line, and those of
very small quantities aggregating, I think, fifty-thousand gallons a day.

Merced Lakes have no outside consumers.

The Daly City distribution is in the City and County of San
Francisco. The present development of the underground sources includes the amount distributed from Sunol and Livermore gravels,
and I think that is the net distributed to San Francisco, and does not
include the amount distributed to outside consumers. That measurement was taken at Brightside weirs. That present development includes the development made possible by the booster pumps at Ra-
87   venswood. That booster pump increased the carrying capacity of
the pipe line from seventeen million gallons daily to twenty-one and
a half to twenty-two million gallons daily. There is no measuring
box at Ravenswood, and the total present development is forty million gallons a day.

Our assumed economic development in the future was prepared
by Mr. Metcalf.

(Admission of exhibit objected to as immaterial, irrelevant, and
incompetent.)

Discussion between attorneys in relation to Mr. Steinhart's objection as to the items, capacity in million gallons, and, the capacity of
reservoirs, and suggested by Mr. Olney that Spring Valley Water Co.
would have to produce the surveys, but it was decided to be unneces-
88   sary unless upon consultation it is deemed relevant, and at that time
89   it could be easily checked up without having the surveys brought into
court.

"Plaintiff's exhibit 12-h" was admitted with the right to re-open
the matter as regards the matter of capacity in million gallons for
required proof of the original surveys, if the City wants it.

90   DIRECT EXAMINATION BY MR. OLNEY.

The reading of gauges at the reservoir are taken year after year,
and in the course of years any inaccuracy in these readings due to
wave action, or anything of that sort, tend to compensate themselves,
such as the records do in this case. The records at Pilarcitos reservoir were taken by Mr. Ebright for about forty years; at San Andres

SPRING VALLEY WATER CO. VS. CITY AND COUNTY OF SAN FRANCISCO

they were taken by Mr. Sole for, I think, over thirty years, and at
the lower Crystal Springs dam they were taken by a man who is
there now, and who has been there since 1890. If a man had an incorrect method of taking measurements, I think he would be just as
apt to read one inch lower one year, and one inch higher the next.

The next page which appears in the volume is simply a detail
of the previous page, and those areas are all represented on the exhibits which were put in yesterday, "Exhibit 1" and "Exhibit 2".

Offered in evidence "Plaintiff's Exhibit 12-i".

Referring to the next page, that also includes the detail of some   91
of the previous pages that have already been admitted in evidence.

Offered in evidence as "Plaintiff's Exhibit 12-j".

(Here follows discussion by attorneys of various inaccuracies in
certain exhibits).

Spring Valley Water Co. states its storage for future development in Calaveras is fifty-three million gallons a day, whereas in
"Plaintiff's Exhibit 12-h" the capacity is given as fifty-five million
gallons a day. It is to be determined which is the correct figure.

A difference in area is also noted; under 3-b in "Exhibit 12", the
present water surface in Crystal Springs Reservoir is 1443.14 acres.
This figure is a Spring Valley computation, in "Exhibit 12-i" the area
for the same height is 1492.16 acres; this is the computation made by
the City Engineer.

Then follows a discussion between attorneys on the question of
which figure is correct. Mr. Olney insisting that it is a point that
ought to be worked out and settled and that it is a point capable of   92
accurate determination. Reference is then made to a discrepancy in
the San Andres in relation to the totals there as between the first three
items, Pilarcitos, San Andres, and Crystal Springs, wherein they
differ 115.69 acres. This has reference to area high-water mark acres
"Exhibit 12-j". It was explained that the entire table in this exhibit
was worked up either by or under the direction of Mr. Herrmann,
whose initials are shown on the top of the page, and that the witness
had nothing at all to do with that table.   93

"Exhibit 12-j" withdrawn.

Referring to table entitled "Capacities Filter Plant, Flumes and
Conduits"; this was made by Mr. Metcalf from figures submitted by
me, and is correct. It shows capacities of the filter plant, and of the
various flumes and conduits of the company.

Offered in evidence as "Plaintiff's Exhibit 12-j".

CROSS EXAMINATION BY MR. STEINHART.

This tabulation is intended to show the capacity of the pipes,
conduits and flumes. In the Alameda System, Sunol to Niles screen
flume, is intended to show the capacity of the flume in the Sunol aque-   94
duct between the tunnels. The pipe running from that flume is a 36-

21

inch pipe, but at the present time has not a capacity of thirty-five to forty million gallons a day. I have never made the computation to ascertain whether the pipe is strong enough to carry that much water. In computing the total capacity I would not compute into that total capacity the capacity given from Sunol to the Niles screen flume, from thirty-five to forty million gallons a day; that was not entered in the total capacity for the entire line. So far as the entire line is concerned in its supply of water to the Belmont Pumping Station, or to the City of San Francisco, that supply is limited by the capacity of the Alameda pipe line, shown on this table 21,000,000 gallons daily.

95

The capacity of the Sunol to Niles screen flume was determined at thirty-five to forty million gallons a day by measurements made in the flume of the velocity of the water. The capacity of the Alameda system at the present time is twenty-one million gallons a day. The capacity from the San Andres Reservoir is the carrying capacity of the 44-inch pipe line shown up near the top of the page on this table as twenty-five million gallons daily. Our present safe yield is only eighteen million gallons from the Sunol and Livermore gravels. The first item of the Peninsula system is upper Pilarcitos to San Andres flume, tunnel and pipe; capacity eighteen million gallons a day; this is the total capacity of that conduit measured by flume measurements made in the flume of the velocity of the water. According to the method of preparing this table, the velocity of the water is one of the things to know. The area of the water in the flume is multiplied by the velocity of the water which gave the cubical contents, in cubic feet, which reduced to gallons gave gallons per minute or per second, or some other unit of time. It was reduced in this case to a million gallons daily.

96

The velocity is determined by float measurements, not surface float, but thin slits of wood that were weighted to carry them down near the bottom; we submerged them at different levels in the flume and thereby got a very close approximation to the mean velocity of the flow. I did that personally, and I think put in five across, and I had strings tied along the caps to guide the channel of the float so that they would not cross, or interfere with one another in the path.

97

The San Andres 44-inch steel pipe to Baden was determined by a pitometer measurement to show the coefficient which would be applied to that pipe; that coefficient was applied to the ordinary formula for determining the velocity of the water in the pipe. That was a purely mathematical calculation; the coefficient that was applied to the formula was deduced from a series of tests made with a pitometer by Prof. LeConte, of the University of California, to determine the velocity of water in a pipe. When I say that the pitometer test was made, I meant all the paraphernalia that went with it, taking the loss of head in the flow of water through the pipe. Referring to the two Baden pipes, one of these leaves Baden, as shown on "Exhibit 1 and 2", and

22

runs into College Hill Reservoir; the other one leaves Baden, as indicated on "Exhibit 1 and 2", and is known as the Baden-Merced pipe, and runs to the Central pumping station at Twenty-third Avenue and Sloat Boulevard, with connections from the pipe, as indicated on "Exbibit 1 and 2", to the Ocean View pumping station, and to the Lake Merced pumping station. The waters that are put in there run through those pipes, going to the Ocean View pump, and from there to Lake Honda.

That capacity would be determined by the capacity of the Ocean View pump and Lake Honda by the 23-inch, 16-inch and 30-inch pipe and flume, which is given lower down as ten million gallons a day, and then some of the water that is taken out of the Baden-Merced pipe, or eight million gallons at Central pump, is also forced into the 44-inch pipe just south of the Lake Honda tunnel, that has a capacity much greater than ten million gallons daily. 98

By the item Crystal Springs on full reservoir without pumping, twenty-two million gallons a day, I mean that with the reservoir about full it gives the water a head sufficient to force twenty-two million gallons daily through the pipe line to University Mound. The pipe line is capable of carrying more than that, and by pumping it can be increased.

(Mr. Olney here interjected that the safe daily yield is much below that, and that this has no reference to the safe daily yield.)

The summary showing total approximate conduit capacity to College Hill, eight millions, means that through the 30-inch pipe line 99 to College Hill there can be taken eight million gallons daily, at the same time that there are eighteen million gallons daily taken through the 30-inch branch to the Central pumping station by the 30-inch pipe line known as the Baden-Merced pipe. That is based upon the figure, Baden 30-inch steel pipe to College Hill eight million gallons a day.

On "Exhibit 3" there is shown in light green, from the Town of Baden, the 30-inch pipe to College Hill, through which eight million gallons daily can be supplied at the same time that eighteen million gallons can be supplied through the 30-inch Baden-Merced pipe to the Central pumping station, Ocean View pumps, or to Lake Merced pumps. That would make below the junction point of the 30-inch Baden pipe, and the 30-inch Baden pipe to College Hill, twenty-five million gallons a day. The item of eighteen million gallons should be seventeen million gallons, and the two together should be twenty-five million gallons, as the total capacity of the 44-inch pipe line, shown in light green on "Exhibit 3" from the San Andres Reservoir to the Town of Baden.

The Ocean View pumps are located about at the crossing of the Baden-Merced pipe line over the suction line to the Lake Merced pump, and the force line from the Lake Merced pump. They are fed by the Baden-Merced line. The statement of the capacity of the Baden pipe 100 has reference to its delivery capacity to those points. The Baden 30-inch pipe to Ocean View, the Ocean View pump to Lake Honda, and the Central pump to Lake Honda, are different pipes. The capacity from Ocean View and the Lake Merced pump may not be all of the water that is supplied by the Baden-Merced pipe for the reason that the Lake Merced pumps pump water also out of Lake Merced, and force it into the pipe line shown in this "Exhibit 12-j" as Ocean View pump to Lake Honda by 23-inch, 16-inch, and 30-inch, and flume ten million gallons a day. The capacity for the Lake Merced Reservoir is about three million gallons a day, but for the pumping station is seven and a half million gallons. This table has not reference to sources of supply, but only to the carrying capacity of the conduit.

101   Admitted as "Plaintiff's Exhibit 12-j".

The next sheet is entitled "Capacities Pumping Stations". I am acquainted with the matter as set forth in that table, and it is correct. Under the second heading, "From Low Service", is meant delivery at low services in the city, and it is the same district which I described yesterday, and which is called in the Spring Valley Water Co. records, the University Mound District. The pumps which occur under that heading take the water from the low service distributing system and pump it into the reservoirs that are subsequently stated.

102   Offered in evidence as "Plaintiff's Exhibit 12-k".

Under the heading "In Pleasanton Valley", the pumping stations 1, 2 and 3, have been indicated on the maps, "Plaintiff's Exhibit 2". The Pleasanton pump, Station No. 1, is shown, and it is also designated; the other two pumping stations are designated only by two small circles colored in solidly. These are immediately to the north of the pumping station marked "Pleasanton Pump No. 1", and are connected with it by a red line indicating the conduit line. The No. 3 pump is the westerly pump, and No. 2 pump is the easterly pump of those two without a name.

THIRD HEARING.   JULY 14, 1915.

Witness J. J. SHARON.

103-104   (Certain corrections noted on the face of the record)

CROSS EXAMINATION BY MR. STEINHART.

"Exhibit 12-k" was set up by Mr. Metcalf from data furnished by me, which is the data that is shown by the displacement of the pump operating at maximum speed for which it was designed. I did not allow for slippage, although there is a small loss. The loss through slipping does not increase, as the period of time during which the pump has been used increases, for the reason that we replaced the valves in the pumps at intervals, so that the working order is maintained at as high a state of efficiency as possible. This loss

24

through slippage is likely to amount to from 4 to 5% the first year that the pump is in use, and continue at probably that rate during all the time that it is in use.

The column headed "Combined Capacity Million Gallons Daily, 21.5'', was inserted there for the reason that in item 2 there are five units aggregating twenty-two million gallons daily; that meant the combined capacity at the station. Where there is only one unit it refers to that one unit.   106

The column "Actual Average Pumpage Million Gallons Daily 1913, 2.42 Millions'', means that the pumps were in operation but for a short time during the year, and the total pumpage was divided by the number of days in the year, thus reducing it to million gallons daily for the year 1913. The Belmont and Millbrae pumps were also used during the year 1913. The purpose of showing that pumpage in the other was because they are used only at intervals, and in 1913 to assist in getting more water into the city. The Belmont pumping station has a capacity of twenty-two million gallons daily, and pumped in 1913 only 13.1 million gallons daily. That figure comes in on an exhibit later on in this book. It should have been entered in on this sheet before us, as should also Millbrae. I have not the record for the pumpage at Millbrae.

These pumps are all operated below full capacity. Slippage has not been deducted from the total of the column, "Combined Capacity Million Gallons''. The correction for slippage should also be made for the 4.25 in the last column, in other words, in neither column has there been any correction for slippage. The actual average pumpage Million Gallons Daily column, is not the actual amount delivered, but the computed amount, without deduction for slippage.   107

DIRECT EXAMINATION BY MR. OLNEY.

It is not advisable to run the pumps at any higher speed than accords with the totals shown here, although they do occasionally, and it is possible to run them at a higher rate of speed for short intervals, and this is also done.

CROSS EXAMINATION BY MR. STEINHART.   108

The last column, "Actual Average Pumpage Million Gallons Daily'', was prepared from the logs kept at the various pumping stations, showing the number of revolutions that the pumps make, and the quantity of water was computed by multiplying the number of revolutions made by the displacement in gallons per revolution. The total pumpage during the year 1913 was not at the combined capacity of the pumping station; there were days in the year when they worked at the maximum capacity, and an average such as is given here would be realized if the pumps worked to full capacity a certain number of days, twenty or thirty days, and the amount arrived at in that way were divided by 365. We have the record for

109   every day showing the actual working of these pumps, which is accessible to you, and the most of which records Major Dockweiler has seen. This column is put in there simply to show the average throughout the year.

The combined capacity million gallons a day in the second column is the combined capacity of the different stations and pumps under the conditions under which they actually pump; these pumps were designed for certain purposes, and the capacity is in accordance with the operation under those conditions. I think this includes all the pumps.

The Millbrae pump is so arranged that the water has first to go from the pumping station into the 44-inch pipe, into College Hill or Baden, and then about four miles north of the location of the Millbrae station at the Town of Baden, the 44-inch pipe has two 30-inch
110   branches. There is only one San Andres pipe line and that is the 44-inch pipe at the Millbrae pumping station. The force pipe from Millbrae pumps is 30 inches from the pumps out to the 44-inch, and that is a short distance of 100 or 200 feet; but the capacity of the pump is not limited by that in any way, as the 30-inch pipe may carry a good deal more than the pump can deliver to it. We take the speed at which these pumps were designed to operate and then multiply that by the displacement of the pump, which gives a result obtained here. The combined capacity million gallons includes the units that are connected up and actually in use.
111   Admitted as ''Plaintiff's Exhibit 12-k''.

DIRECT EXAMINATION BY MR. OLNEY.

The next page, ''Pipe Distribution System'', is a summary of the pipes of various diameters in the city distribution system, the lengths of which have been agreed upon by Mr. Ransom, of the City Engineer's Office, and Mr. Elliott, of the Spring Valley Water Co. This is all set forth in the inventory in detail, and is simply a summation of the results of the inventory. There is no steel pipe in the system.

Offered and admitted as ''Plaintiff's Exhibit 12-l''.

The next sheet is a summary of statistics which have a bearing on the population of San Francisco from 1850 to 1915. These figures
112   were obtained from the Municipal Reports of the City and County of San Francisco, and include in the first column the United States census for 1860, and for each decade thereafter down to 1910. In column 2 is an estimate for a portion of that time, from 1872 to 1903 inclusive, made by the San Francisco Health Board. The figures for the years 1904, 1908, 1910, 1913 and 1914 were not published in the Municipal Reports. The reports for 1913 and 1914 are not published to my knowledge. In the case of the previous years they were not shown in the Municipal Report.

The third column, "Estimate by Spring Valley Water Co., 1913", is an estimate of the population for each year from 1867 to 1915, based primarily on the United States Census for the decades 1870, 1890 and so on, and for the inter-censal years the population has been interpolated between those points as shown by the Census in connection with the study of the other statistics that are shown in column 4, "Registered Voters", column 5, "School Children", column 6, "Average Daily School Attendance", column 7, "Births", column 8, "Deaths". I do not know that the births and deaths had very much to do with it, but they were put in simply as an independent summary, to show some vital statistics.

The data which appears in the column headed "From Municipal Reports", was obtained from the Municipal Reports, but in the last five columns there is some data which was obtained from the Spring Valley Water Co.'s records of live bills which are live accounts. The next column shows the new services added during the year. The third 113 column shows the dwellings at the end of each year, but this record is not complete. No account has been kept from 1906 to 1910. This incompleteness is due to the fact that some of the data was lost in the fire, and the next column, which shows families at the end of the year, is likewise incomplete from the early beginning, for the same reasons. It is possible to get the data from 1906 to date, but it had not been actually summarized, and I did not put it in. There is enough data to show the general trend of the increase of families during the later years. The last column shows the vacant houses, and is the average during the year. This record has not been maintained since the fire. These last columns, under the heading "From Spring Valley Water Co.'s Records" were so derived, and all of these columns, with the exception of the third, correctly represent the result of the records from which they were taken.

Offered in evidence as "Plaintiff's Exhibit 12-m".

(Discussion between attorneys as to admissability of statistical 113-114 information of character as offered by Municipal Reports).

Objected to by Mr. Steinhart, and objection overruled.

Admitted as "Exhibit 12-m".

CROSS EXAMINATION BY MR. STEINHART.   115

I do not know the method of estimating the second column "Estimates by San Francisco Health Board", as that appeared in their report, which was published in the Municipal Report, and I took those figures from that report without knowing who made them or how they made them.

The third column is an estimate made by Spring Valley Water Co. in 1913, to which I added the years 1914 and 1915 a few days ago. This estimate I made from the United States Census primarily, 116 and for the purpose of getting the population for the inter-censal years, I was aided in the increase from 1870 to 1880, and from 1880 to 1890, and so on, by the data as shown in the other columns, particularly the columns headed, "Registered Voters", "School Children", and "Average Daily School Attendance", which I took for the reason that in 1910 the school children census was abolished, and there is a record only of the average daily school attendance from 1911 to 1914 or 1915. The number of live accounts headed, "Live Bills End of Each Year", aided me in the determination of that line, by the new services added during the year, and also by the dwellings and families at the end of the year. I did not use any data other than the data that appears upon this record to get my conclusions in column 3, and the correctness of my conclusions can be estimated from the data upon this record. I did not use the estimate as given by Mr. Schussler, nor anything except the data that is shown on this table.

The columns "Registered Voters", and "School Children", were taken from the Municipal Reports, and the average daily school at-

117

tendance was also taken from the Municipal Reports up to the year 1911 or 1912, and since that time I have obtained the information from the School Board. Births and deaths were taken from the Municipal Reports, except the last two years, which I obtained from the Health Board.

The "Live Bills" at the end of each year includes all the bills to business places and residences. New services also include business places and residences.

The record in the column, "Dwellings at the end of the year", is taken from the water company's books, in which are classified the various buildings in San Francisco, to which it supplies water; for example, business buildings and dwellings which are houses, or flats, or apartments in which families live. This column does not include business places.

The column, "Families at the end of the year", was taken from the records of the company, showing the dwellings, and also the vacancies occurring in those dwellings, and has a bearing on the population, for if the families increase, we assume that the population increases. I presume this is an estimate in part taken from occupied

118

and unoccupied dwellings. The company keeps a record in which it has the number of dwellings to which it supplies water, and to which it submits bills each month. When a family moves out, the company is notified, and makes an inspection to see that the place is not occupied, and if not, it is entered as vacant. If it is not vacant, it is taken to be occupied. This gives the number of families in San Francisco supplied by the Spring Valley Water Co., and is estimated by the occupancy of dwelling houses. It is taken for granted that a certain number of dwelling houses, if occupied, contain a certain number of families, and the dwelling, for example, is sometimes classified as a flat; two flats as one dwelling, and there may be two families living in it if they are both occupied. In ascertaining the number of families to the dwelling, if the records of the company show it was occupied, it was simply considered one family. This is an actual record, except that it may be an estimate at the end of the year, for the reason that it has been assumed, unless a vacancy has been reported, that a flat is occupied, whereas, at the end of the year it might have been vacant, and might not have been reported to the company. In that way, the figures are not exactly right. If the dwelling is a flat, the figures would include one family. If there were two flats, both occupied, there would be two families, and so on. I do not know who actually compiled these figures of families at the end of the year; it was done in the Water Sales Department, under the direction of Mr. Wallace, for a number of years from 1908 to 1914, and under the direction of Mr. Crawford for the year 1915.

DIRECT EXAMINATION BY MR. OLNEY.

In reaching the estimated population, as contained in the third column, I platted the curve represented by the figures in the other columns so that I had the assistance of a diagramatic scheme. That is shown two or three sheets further on in this book.

Referring to the next sheet, headed "Table showing the number of services and live bills 1858-1913, at end of each year, and the number of new services added for each year since 1865 to November 1, 1913", that should be changed to December 31, 1914. This table was computed from the records of the Spring Valley Water Co., and the first column contains the year, the next column, headed "New Services", means the new services which the company puts in each year for supplying water, except the first figure of 7,144, which is the total number of services from 1858 to 1865. From 1866 to 1914, the figures in the second column represent the new services added annually by the company.

The column headed "Cumulative Total", was made up by adding the new services added annually, to the total of the year before, these being taken from the preceding column. The third column is the sum of the second column down to that year.

The fourth column, "Total live bills at the end of the year", is the record of the live accounts as shown in the previous exhibit, and is the number of accounts that are active at the end of the year shown.

Offered as "Plaintiff's Exhibit 12-n".

Questioned by Master.

The difference of 25,000 services in vacant houses, between the cumulative total of 89,000 and 64,000 odd, means that some of them are inactive, and some of them gone out of use, and this cumulative total 89,624 does not represent the total active services. It represents some that have been abandoned. The total live accounts, 64,000, in-

119

120

121

cludes those actually operative at the end of the year; there are others temporarily inactive. The active services are not shown here, but the services in use are stated in the inventory, and there is an allowance made for such of these services as are shown in the third column that are abandoned or out of use.

Admitted as "Exhibit 12-n".

DIRECT EXAMINATION BY MR. OLNEY.

The company has a record of the active services, meaning by that, services in use, though possibly not at the time having water flowing through them. This would include services to vacant houses. There is a list of these shown on page 342 of the printed inventory. The total active services for the year 1913 being 66,224, and that includes services to vacant houses.

122   Table headed "Basis for estimated population of San Francisco, California, Spring Valley Water Company, June 22, 1915", introduced as "Plaintiff's Exhibit 12-o".

The next sheet headed "Population of Greater San Francisco as estimated by Marx, 1911, and Freeman, 1912", is a diagramatic representation, and was prepared by Prof. Marx, of Stanford University, and John R. Freeman, of Providence, R. I., an hydraulic engineer, who was engaged in an investigation of the water situation here in 1912.

The heavy, solid line, as shown on the sheet entitled "Estimated Population of District Served by Spring Valley Water Company, San Francisco, California", and running from the year 1867 up to the year 1913, represents the actual growth as estimated, and as shown in "Exhibit 12-o". The dotted lines which branch out from this line at the year 1910, headed "At Chicago Rate", "Cleveland Rate", "St. Louis Rate", "Boston Rate", "Pittsburg and Alleghany Rate", and "Baltimore Rate", indicate the rate of increase and the growth of population of those various cities from the time when their population

123   was the same as San Francisco's was in 1910. I took the rate of increase in Chicago beginning with the time at which it had a population slightly over 400,000, and then platted the rate of increase of Chicago from that time on, and that is the same with the other cities. In each case I have taken as a starting point for the dotted line the time at which the city under consideration had a population of close to 400,000 people.

The dotted line marked "Manson, 1910, Freeman Report", represents data that was taken from a report made by Mr. Marsden Manson, City Engineer, in which he estimated probable future population of the City of San Francisco.

The line marked "Estimate Schussler, 1913, Marx 1906, Herrmann, Spring Valley Water Co., 1913, Grunsky 1901", indicates estimates made by these gentlemen of the probable increase in population.

Mr. Schussler and Mr. Herrmann were engineers for the Spring Valley Water Co., and Mr. Grunsky was City Engineer, I believe, at 124 the time he made those estimates. The dates which appear opposite the names of these gentlemen are the dates at which they made their estimates.

Admitted as "Plaintiff's Exhibit 12-p".

The data on the sheet headed "Vital Statistics", all came from the Municipal Report, except the estimate of population, and the computations that were made per thousand population, both according to the Spring Valley Water Co. records. The computation under the heading "Deaths from Typhoid Fever, according to Spring Valley Water Company's Estimate of Population", came from the Spring Valley Water Co.'s estimates of population. The other records are from the Municipal Reports, and that table should read "Vital Statistics, San Francisco, 1866 to 1915", instead of 1913. 125

Offered and admitted as "Plaintiff's Exhibit 12-q".

The next tabulation contained on the following sheet, is continued on sheet 2, so that this tabulation is made up of two sheets, and is a summary of water consumption statistics of the Spring Valley Water Co., made up from the records of the company, with the exception of the population, which is an estimate.

Offered in evidence as "Plaintiff's Exhibit 12-r".

CROSS EXAMINATION BY MR. STEINHART.

The second column, "Acre Feet", is the equivalent of the million gallons per day in acre feet, but I do not remember now what figure we used for the purpose of transmuting it from million gallons to acre 126 feet, but I think we used the figure 3.06.

Questioned by Master.

This is the consumption as shown by the water measured through the town through weirs and pumps, and includes leakage.

Admitted as "Exhibit 12-r".

The next sheet is a statement showing the monthly water consumption of the City and County of San Francisco in million gallons per month and per day from Spring Valley Water Co. plant. The data extends from 1909 to and inclusive of 1914. These records were checked over by Major Dockweiler for the City and found correct, except as to the estimated population, and the average gallons per capita per day, as indicated just before his signature on the end. We both agreed to the statement which is on that sheet, and entitled "Total Water Consumption in San Francisco is measured by weirs 127 and pumpage records. No deductions were made for slippage in these pump records".

Offered and admitted as "Exhibit 12-s".

The next table shows the water consumption in San Francisco by districts, which corresponds with those described from "Exhibit 4".

31

The "High Service" district is the one which I described as the Clarendon Heights District, supplied by the Clarendon Heights Reservoir, at an elevation of 600 feet. The district headed "Upper Service", elevation 365 feet, is the district which I described on "Exhibit 4" as embracing the portion of San Francisco supplied by what is called the Lake Honda Reservoir. The middle service is the portion of the city supplied by College Hill Reservoir, and the elevation is shown as 255 feet. The low service previously described on "Exhibit 4" as the University Mound District, is supplied by University Mound Reservoir at an elevation of 165 feet.

This tabulation was agreed to by Major Dockweiler and myself. Offered and admitted as "Plaintiff's Exhibit 12-t".

128   The next sheet is a summary showing the water draft from different sources, of the Spring Valley Water Co., in million gallons per year from the year 1907 to 1914, and in the last column showing the average for the years 1907 and 1914. The second portion of the table shows the million gallons per day, which is the same as the above figures except that the above figures are divided by 365 days, or in the case of a leap year by 366 days. Per-cent of total draft is a mathematical computation based upon the preceding figures; the water draft from the Alameda system during the irrigation season, in million gallons daily, from the year 1906 to 1914, showing the mean, and also, as in the last two columns, the maximum months in the irrigation season showing the largest quantity of water received during those years. The irrigation season, made up from the months extending from May to October inclusive, is taken from the records of the Spring Valley Water Co.

Offered in evidence as "Plaintiff's Exhibit 12-u".

CROSS EXAMINATION BY MR. STEINHART.

The records showing the water draft from the Alameda system are from the Brightside weirs. I believe that most all of the record as to the Alameda system are taken from the Brightside weirs, and
129   that where we have not the record at Brightside weirs, we used the pump displacement at the Belmont pump, indicating the quantity drawn from the Alameda system. This would be subject to deduction as to slippage, but what the normal allowance for slipping of pumps, such as the Belmont pumps is, I do not know positively; possibly 4 or 5% should be deducted for slippage. Measurements at Brightside weirs would include water distributed between Brightside weirs and distributing centers of San Francisco to suburban consumers, and would also include waters wasted at the Niles screen house. I do not know that the waste water at the Niles screen house is very considerable during certain seasons of the year, but think the waste occurs there when they are making changes in the quantity of water that is required at the Belmont pump. I do not know of any record being

32

SPRING VALLEY WATER CO. VS. CITY AND COUNTY OF SAN FRANCISCO

kept as to the waste at Niles. Waste is water, wasted from the top of   130
the screen tank in flowing down into the creek. I have seen waste
there myself but it was due to a change in the operations of the quantity of water that was actually wanted at Belmont; the regulation
takes place at the Sunol dam.

Other than deductions for the Belmont pump slippage, waste at
Brightside and distribution to suburban consumers, there are no other
to my knowledge. The Crystal Springs measurements were taken at
University Mound at the weir. There should be no deductions made
from that. The measurements at University Mound do not include
all the water from the Crystal Springs Reservoir. There is water
taken from there and supplied, for example, to San Mateo, about three
hundred thousand gallons a day, and other places along the line.
Water for San Mateo is supplied at the San Mateo screen house. The
water is really measured at University Mound Reservoir. San Andres   131
water is measured at the outlet of the San Andres or Bald Hill tunnel, just before the water enters the 44-inch pipe line to be delivered
into San Francisco. It is a weir measurement. It is subject to a
slight deduction made for uses along the line which aggregates possibly about 50,000 gallons a day. Lake Merced is not subject to any
deduction. That water is all supplied within the city. It is measured
at the Lake Merced pumping station. The same methods of measurement were resorted to during all the period of time from 1907 to
1914, except at San Andres, we increased the weirs from two weirs to
four; the method is the same, but there are a different number of   132
weirs. The measurements are recorded every day. The data given
here are the sum totals of those daily measurements. I did not make
them all myself. They were made by different people in different
years. I might say that they have all been made under my direction
while I was in the Operating Department and the Engineering Department. I know that the computations are correct. Major Dockweiler and I checked the data that are shown on the first table;
the water draft in million gallons per year; we went over the records.
There was no agreement between Major Dockweiler and myself as to
the one set forth on that table, but on the succeeding table there was
—the same figures appear. The million gallons per day is a matter
of computation from the first figures there. The per-cent of total
draft is a computation. The draft from the Alameda system is given   133
only during the irrigation period, just to show the water that is drawn
during those months. They are not the heavy rain months. They are
the summer months. The measurements for that water draft for the
Alameda system during the irrigation season were taken from the same
place as indicated above, either at Brightside or Belmont pumps, when
the Brightside weirs were not in operation.

"Plaintiff's Exhibit 12-u" admitted.

SPRING VALLEY WATER CO. VS. CITY AND COUNTY OF SAN FRANCISCO

DIRECT EXAMINATION BY MR. OLNEY.

The next tabulation is made up of three sheets, which follow in consecutive order. They represent water drawn monthly from different sources of the Spring Valley Water Co. in the years 1907 to 1914 inclusive, in million gallons. Those figures are monthly details of the figures set up in the yearly totals, as shown in "Exhibit 12-u", which we have just discussed. This table has been agreed upon between Mr. Dockweiler and myself.

Offered as "Plaintiff's Exhibit 12-v", and admitted.

134   The next tabulation is likewise made up of three sheets. These three sheets are the same as the exhibit immediately preceding, with the exception that this is upon the basis of million gallons per day instead of million gallons per month.

Offered as "Plaintiff's Exhibit 12-w", and admitted.

The next tabulation is headed "Water Stored in the Different Sources at the end of each month, Spring Valley Water Co., in million gallons", and it purports to set out the amount stored in these various reservoirs. The data was obtained in the Spring Valley Water Co.'s records of the gauge heights of the various reservoirs, and of the table of contents of storage capacity tables. The tabulation is correct. It was made by me, or under my supervision. It consists of three pages.

Offered as "Plaintiff's Exhibit 12-x".

CROSS EXAMINATION BY MR. STEINHART.

These measurements were made in the same way that I testified yesterday concerning the reservoir measurements in "12-h", and are subject to any objection that that method has. These objections are very small. We did not carry these out only to the nearest million gallons.

134½   Admitted as "Plaintiff's Exhibit 12-x".

DIRECT EXAMINATION BY MR. OLNEY.

The next sheet, headed "Boilers" purports to set out certain data in regard to boilers, and is correct.

Offered as "Plaintiff's Exhibit 12-y".

135   CROSS EXAMINATION BY MR. STEINHART.

Commencing with the columns "Heating Surfaces Square Feet", and "Rated Horse Power Each"; that is data that appears on the boiler itself, and is also taken from the size of the boiler. The rated horse power is based on the size of the boiler. That is the rating of the manufacturer. The steam pressure is the maximum allowed by the insurance company which carried the boiler insurance. The average steam pressure there is the average pressure that is carried in the

34

actual operation of the boilers in pounds and is the normal average during the operation of the boiler, which is taken from the records of the plant itself every day. For a certain period of time those records are taken and averaged up. There is a slight fluctuation, for example, from 109 to 111, and we call that 110.

136

DIRECT EXAMINATION BY MR. OLNEY.

The average is the pressure that is normally carried in the operation of the plant, and it fluctuates a little. In the first case from 109 to possibly 111; 110 being the average. We carry boiler insurance which is written by the Maryland Casualty Co. The inspection is made by the American Casualty Co. The Underwriters, 1910, report on conditions was made under the direction of Mr. Clarence Goldsmith, who is a hydraulic engineer for the Board of Fire Underwriters, and is the printed published report of the Fire Underwriters. (Last column objected to by Mr. Steinhart). Objection sustained.

DIRECT EXAMINATION BY MR. OLNEY.

137

The next sheet headed "Pumping Stations—Equipment Pumps", purports to set forth a lot of data concerning the various pumps of the company and is correct as set forth.

Offered in evidence as "Plaintiff's Exhibit 12-z".

CROSS EXAMINATION BY MR. STEINHART.

The data in the column "Slip Per-Centage", was obtained through pitometer tests of the flow of water through the force pipe connected with the pumps, and from that was deduced the slippage, that being the actual delivery of water as compared with the delivery based upon the plunger displacement. Where there are no data as to slippage, we did not make experiments on the tests to get that. There is slippage on a centrifugal pump. As I recall it now, those are the only slip tests that were made, I am quite positive of that. The slip tests were made at different times in the operation of the plant, and those are the records that were obtained. The one at Millbrae station shown first there, was made, I think, in 1912 or 1913. I am not positive about the exact dates of these. The one at Belmont was made at about the same time.

138

Ocean View was made, I think, about 1911. Black Point was made first in 1909, and also a number of times since. Clarendon Heights, I think, was made about 1911 or 1912. The one at Central pumps was made in 1914. The next column means the labor shifts; three eight hour shifts. They are from our own records.

139

The water Horse Power corresponds with the horse power of the pumps, and is stated as water horse power.

"Plaintiff's Exhibit 12-z" admitted.

35

DIRECT EXAMINATION BY MR. OLNEY.

As regards the per-centages of slippage, the slippage has reference to that particular pump and only to the extent the measurement of water coming into the city are determined by pump measurements, would these percentages of slippages have any bearing on the amount of water delivered into the city. A correction would have to be made for slippage. It may not be exactly this amount, because it would fluctuate slightly. This does not appear on weir measurements, as there is no deduction to be made. The percentage of slippage bears only on the net capacity of the particular pump.

CROSS EXAMINATION BY MR. STEINHART.

I do not mean to say that where no data is given as to the other pumps that there is no slippage on those pumps. There is slippage on all pumps, as a matter of fact, even when they are new. It is mechanical imperfection.

DIRECT EXAMINATION BY MR. OLNEY.

The next sheet is headed "Statement of Assessed Value of Property, Rate of Taxation, and Amount of Taxes Levied from 1850 to 1912 and 1913 inclusive, San Francisco, California, copied from the report of Auditor of San Francisco, contained in Municipal Reports 1911 and 1912, pages 156-157". It is a correct abstract of what appears in the Municipal Reports as regards to those matters, except that for the years 1913 and 1914, and 1914 and 1915, which are added at the bottom of the second sheet, those figures were obtained from the Assessor of the City and County of San Francisco, and did not appear in the Municipal Reports as shown. This particular tabulation is made up of two pages, and it is the assessed value of all property in the City and County of San Francisco.

A discussion by Master and Mr. Olney, regarding the term "operative".

"Plaintiff's Exhibit 12-aa" admitted.

(Objected to. Objection overruled.)

Referring to "Exhibit 12-v", relative to pumps, and also to the exhibit concerning water consumption, the slipping of the pump would have very little effect on the total water brought into the city, for the reason that the only pumping station where the pump displacement is entered as a factor in the total supply of the town, is the Lake Merced pumps. The daily pumpage through the Lake Merced is about three and one-half million gallons, or less than one-tenth of forty million gallons, the total daily supply. A slippage of five per-cent in Lake Merced pumps would amount to about a half per-cent of the total supply.

CROSS EXAMINATION BY MR. STEINHART.

I did not state that the measurements of the Crystal Springs source were made through the pumpage measurements at University Mound, but that the water entering University Mound was measured over the University Mound weirs.

The San Andres was measured over a weir for water coming from San Andres Reservoir; that is to say, the water delivered into San Andres, and measured out of San Andres Reservoir. The water from Pilarcitos is brought into San Andres, and is measured over the same weirs as is the water from San Andres. We do not separate the supply, it is mixed. The water from Pilarcitos is delivered to the San Andres Reservoir and is mixed with the water in that reservoir, and we take that water then out of the San Andres reservoir. The Alameda water is measured at the Belmont pumps, so far as Belmont was concerned, but the water as delivered into San Francisco was delivered into University Mound Reservoir and was measured at the University Mound weir. This water enters the Crystal Springs pipe line at Millbrae pumps, and from Millbrae pumps into the University Mound; it is an admixture of both waters, and the waters thus combined are measured before they enter the University Mound Reservoir over the University Mound weir, which gives the combined output from the Alameda and Crystal Springs source.

The separate Alameda system source is measured over the Brightside weirs, where we have not the measurement at the Belmont pumps, and so far as the computation is concerned, if there is slippage in the pumps, we deduct the total amount as registered by the pumps from the total supply from the Crystal Springs pipe line, as measured over the University Mound weirs. Thus, any deficiency from Alameda would actually increase the supply from Crystal Springs. Applying to the Alameda system, alone, there is an inaccuracy in-so-far as that is founded upon the pumpage at Belmont, as there should be a deduction made for slippage when the pump records are used.

DIRECT EXAMINATION BY MR. OLNEY.

The Belmont pumps are relied on for measurement, in order to get the amount of water coming from the Alameda system, for a very short period of time. It occurs occasionally during repairs to the Brightside weirs. This is also possibly true when in the regulation of the supply from Sunol there is a waste over the screen tank at Niles, and instead of measuring the water there, some of which is wasted, the record is taken at the Belmont pumping station as being more nearly the amount supplied than would be recorded at the Brightside weirs. Generally, however, the measurement is taken over the Brightside weirs.

143

144

145

CROSS EXAMINATION BY MR. STEINHART.

We have complete data of the Belmont pumps, at Belmont, and also here in the city.

DIRECT EXAMINATION BY MR. OLNEY.

The tabulation, "Bond and Stock Holders Actual Cash Investment in Spring Valley Water Company, Excluding Allowance for Deficiencies in Return", was prepared by Mr. Metcalf and I, and the first column simply gives the year, the second, third and fourth columns come under the heading "Amount paid in by Bond Holders". The fifth, sixth and seventh columns come under general heading "Amount paid by Stock Holders". The figures in regard to amount paid by bond holders represent the actual money derived from the sale of bonds; column 3 is headed "Actual", and column 6 headed "Amount paid by Stock Holders", represents the actual amount paid by stock holders. Column 8 is the sum of the figures

146   appearing in column 3 and column 6, and column 9 represents the total amount of cash paid in by bond holders and stock holders up to the particular year which is indicated. Columns 10 and 11 are headed "Interest for six months at assumed fair rate upon combined payments"; column 10 being the interest for six months on the combined amounts paid in by stock and bond holders, as shown in column 8, while column 11 is the cumulative total of column 10. The interest was taken for six months on the theory that the payments were made more or less regularly, and that the total amount was actually paid in and in use for an average of about six months. The interest rate is shown in column 18, headed "Assumed fair cost of money without profit, Metcalf, rate per-cent". Column 12 is the sum of the annual amount paid in, as shown in column 8, plus the interest on that amount, as shown in column 10, being interest for six months. The sum of those two items represents the sum shown in column 12. Column 14, headed "Actual Return", represents the coupon interest paid on the bonds by the Spring Valley Water Works, and the Spring Valley Water Co.

147   Column 15 represents dividends paid annually by the Spring Valley Water Co. and the Spring Valley Water Works.

Column 16 is the total of columns 14 and 15, and column 17 is the rate per-cent of column 13 divided into column 16, or, in other words, it is the rate per-cent which column 16 bears to column 13.

The amounts actually paid in by the bond holders and stock holders were obtained from the minutes of the San Francisco City Water Works, the Spring Valley Water Works, and from an analysis, made by Mr. George Reynolds, an accountant who offered testimony in the 1903 and 1904 rate cases, of his analysis made of these matters from the Spring Valley and San Francisco Water Works books. The original books of account of the Spring Valley are not in existence,

SPRING VALLEY WATER CO. VS. CITY AND COUNTY OF SAN FRANCISCO

having been lost in the fire of 1906. The figures in these tables are taken off correctly from the sources of information which I had, and the calculations which are deduced from these figures are also correct. Offered in evidence as "Plaintiff's Exhibit 12-bb".

CROSS EXAMINATION BY MR. STEINHART.

148

The date 1858 in the first column was taken because the first company organized for supplying water to San Francisco was the San Francisco Water Works Company, organized in 1858, and afterward consolidated with the Spring Valley Water Works in 1865. The date from 1858 to 1865 covers the San Francisco Water Works and also the Spring Valley Water Works from 1860 to 1865. The actual amount as shown in column 6 from 1860 down is the actual amount contributed by the stock holders of the two companies, and added together here. The deduction at the end of the table takes care of refunded bonds as shown in column 3, for the years 1877 and 1880; the sum of these two refundings aggregate $895,137.00, and are indicated by minus signs in the column.

CROSS EXAMINATION BY MR. STEINHART.

The first item in column 2, headed "Face of Bond $320,000", I got out of the minutes of the company, or out of the analysis made by Mr. Reynolds. I got that entry from the minutes shown under date of April 12, 1867, April 26, 1867, and June 15, 1867. The minutes were not the original copies of the minutes, but I think possibly were the copies obtained from Mr. Dockweiler; I got the copy that I had from Mr. Behan, the Secretary of the Spring Valley Water Co. The second item, $180,000, I got from the minutes, and also from Mr. Reynolds' analysis; Mr. Reynolds' analysis also covered the first item that I gave, $320,000, being $500,000 for the total bond issue of 1867 and 1868, which I segregated into two items. I don't know where the reference is to the minutes from which I got the $180,000, but I have the minutes here in reference to that total bond issue of $500,000, under the dates I gave you, namely, April 12, 1867, April 26, 1867, June 15, 1867, and March 21, 1868.

149

I cannot recall the exact phraseology of the minutes, but it had reference to the sale of those bonds; that is to the issuance of them, the sale being authorized by the Directors of the company.

150

Questioned by the Master.

Mr. Reynolds was the accountant who made an examination of the Spring Valley Water Co.'s books, and the San Francisco Water Works Co.'s books in the 1903 and 1904 case.

CROSS EXAMINATION BY MR. STEINHART.

I do not know whether Mr. Reynolds is alive or not, as I have not seen him for a number of years.

I have a record of the next item, "1870, $500,000", from the minutes of the company as of date March 26, 1870.

(It was here suggested that Mr. Dockweiler and Mr. Sharon get together and see if the document is in such shape so that it can be checked up in so far as this column is concerned, and also columns 3, 5 and 6. The Master decided that that could be done after adjournment).

151   Referring to column 3, item "1867, $320,000"; this is also in the minutes, and it was stated that the bonds were sold at par, so I put down the par value of the bonds. I checked it up from the records shown by Mr. Reynolds, and also from an analysis made by Mr. Wenzelberger, of the actual amounts paid for coupon interest, and those accorded very closely with the records I had. They did not do so exactly, for the reason that I did not know for how long a period the bonds had been issued during the year when the coupon interest was paid. I had, in a way, a check on the actual sale of the bonds from the coupon interest that was paid. The analysis that was made by Mr. Reynolds, and also by Mr. Wenzelberger, who went over the Spring Valley books for the City and County of San Francisco in the 1903 and 1904 cases, showed that the coupon interest amounting to $24,515, was paid in the year 1867. That item appeared in the profit and loss account, or income account, I have forgotten just what the name was, and showed the actual expenditures for interest, dividends, operating expenses, and all other financial matters, as well as the total receipts from the sale of water and other

152   receipts of the company. The coupon interest was stated as coupon interest, and was a separate item. The rate of the coupon interest on the amount issued in 1867 was ten-per-cent. The bonds, $320,000, issued in 1867, were ten year bonds bearing interest at the rate of ten per-cent. The next item, $180,000, were the same bonds, and of the same series. They were called in the minutes, and in the statements appearing in the analysis made by Mr. Reynolds, and also in the income and profit and loss account made by Mr. Wenzelberger for the City, the second series bonds of the Spring Valley Water Works. The first series were issued in 1863, and were five-year bonds bearing interest at the rate of twelve per-cent per annum, interest payable quarterly. They were issued, but they were issued in payment for stock, and as I had taken account of the amount in the stock, I did not take an additional account of it as bonds. We will get that in the stock column. The next item, $505,137, I got from the minutes, March 26, 1870, and also from the testimony given by Mr. Reynolds, at pages 4634 and 4636 of his testimony. The minutes show that the bonds were authorized to be issued, and dated April 1, 1870, for a ten-year period, and bearing interest at the rate of nine

153   per-cent, payable semi-annually, interest payable April 1st, and October 1st. The minutes show that these bonds were sold, and the

testimony of Mr. Reynolds shows that the cash was received for them. The bonds were sold at a premium, which on the $500,000 amounted to $5,137. The face value in the column is shown as $500,000 and the actual amount received is shown as $505,137. They were ten-year bonds running from 1870.

The next item is an issue of bonds, face value one million dollars, issued in 1875, the actual amount received for those being one million dollars. The entry as to the issuance of these bonds I got from the minutes of August 2, 1875, and also from the testimony of Mr. Reynolds, page 4636. My note simply shows that the bonds were issued, rate of interest seven per-cent, interest payable semi-annually. I don't seem to have the record of the term of the bonds here. These bonds were issued for property, and to pay debts incurred in construction of the works. I did not make any analysis as to which of these bonds were issued for property, because they came in to pay debts that had already been incurred by the company by the purchase of property, and in the construction of works. The bonds issued in 1875 were issued in exchange for property, but as to the previous bonds, I don't know the details of that. I know that they were issued for debts incurred by the company, for the reason that the company had a construction account extending over all of these years, as shown by exhibits in the 1903 case, prepared by Mr. Reynolds for the company, and by Mr. Wenzelberger for the City. I had no means of checking whether the money actually went into property or structures. I simply exhibited the figures as shown by those two accountants as having come from the books of the company, and showing the construction costs, and these matters which I have already detailed. During the period we are speaking of here, when the face of the stock aggregated $8,000,000, I think it was held by a number of people. These debts that were paid, or for which stock or bonds were issued, were not debts appearing as due to individuals interested in the company. For the years 1858 and 1859, and earlier years, it was true that in the San Francisco City Water Works, the stock that was issued to Bensley and Von Schmidt, and Chabot, was issued to them for accounts purporting to have been incurred by them in behalf of the company, but I thought your questions related now to bond issues of which we had been speaking, from 1867 down to 1875. That appears in the testimony of Mr. Reynolds and Mr. Wenzelberger that small amounts were paid to those men named. They were $6,000 and $8,000 at a time. For example, in the year 1858 the total amount, including those payments, was $185,000 that was put into the plant.

To go back to the bonds, those bonds appear to have been issued in exchange for property, and in payment of debts. I thought that from the records made by Wenzelberger and Reynolds that it was for the cost of the property, the cost to the company of the properties,

154

155

41

156   and the structures which they had put in. The inference is from the exhibit which he placed in evidence. I think it was called Exhibit 101, which is the new construction and general construction figures of the company. They are taken from the company's books. I cannot show from the Exhibit 101, wherein it appears that the $320,000 worth of bonds were issued for property at its actual cost, not to the company from the individual, but to the individual, for the reason I have no statement of what the company actually owed on borrowed money at the time these bonds were issued. That is not shown in the exhibit. I did not assume or deduce from the fact that the bonds were issued fully paid up that the value of the property was equal to the value of the bonds at par, because the company has always owed money, and has owed money in excess of its bond issues. I did not make any examination to enable me to say that the property was worth the value of these stocks and bonds each year since 1865 to date. I only know in a general way what the nature of the debts was in payment of which the bonds were issued, and that it was property bought, and

157   for structures put in by the company. It does not appear to what particular individual those bonds were issued. I got the item of $65,500 from the minutes, November 15, 1876. That is an entry showing that sixty-nine bonds of the first mortgage bond issue were paid for property bought at Lake Merced. The bonds were sold at $95.00—$69,000 of bonds sold at $95.00, showing $65,550. The minutes state that these bonds were exchanged for Lake Merced property. It was an exchange of bonds for property. Those were first mortgage bonds, dated September 1, 1876, term 30 years, interest six per-cent, payable semi-annually, interest payable March 1st, and September 1st each year.

DIRECT EXAMINATION BY MR. OLNEY.

I have not a note that shows to whom the bonds were issued. I don't remember that it did show that. The people were not interested in the company. I think they were people who owned property in Lake Merced which the company wanted to buy.

CROSS EXAMINATION BY MR. STEINHART.

I do not know that for a fact, only from the minutes. I infer that it is so from the minutes.

158   (Discussion by attorneys as to the original ownership of Lake Merced properties).

The next item of $480,000 is a minus quantity there, and was deducted from the investment because of the fact that those bonds which were issued in 1867, called the second series bonds, were redeemed between May 1st and August 30th, 1877, and as they were no longer in existence, I made the deduction from that total amount. They were redeemed at par, $500,000,—but there was an additional bond issue of the first mortgage bonds, which left this net result of $480,000. The $320,000 par value bonds were not redeemed at that time, but in the two years 1867 and 1868, that was a redemption of $500,000. That did not mean an issue of $500,000 first mortgage bonds; there was no issuance at all in that year of first mortgage bonds, nor did it mean an exchange, for the reason that the total bond issue outstanding was reduced by $480,000. These were probably redeemed in cash, but I don't know how they were redeemed. There were no bonds sold for the purpose. The company may have borrowed the money from someone to redeem these, and afterwards paid it. I don't know that the company made the money. That is a lot of money to make. I find in 1877 from the minutes that there was $250,000 borrowed from the Savings & Loan Society; $150,000 borrowed from John Parrott; $50,000 borrowed from G. W. Granniss; $40,000 borrowed from N. Luning; $36,-000 borrowed from Wm. Sharon; $50,000 borrowed from O. Eldrich; $50,000 borrowed from Jerome Lincoln; $50,000 borrowed from the Security Savings Bank; $50,000 borrowed from John L. Gardner; $20,000 borrowed from H. W. Halleck; $75,000 borrowed from the Masonic Savings Bank; $36,000 borrowed from William Sharon. Those are all running through the year of 1877. The minute entries show the Savings & Loan Society, the first item I read, as April 16, 1877. The list of others is as follows: April 16, 1877, May 1, 1877, May 13, June 1, June 25, August 15, September 17, November 15. I think those are all the references in the minutes. I endeavored to get them all out and I think I got them all out. The next item, $2,536,833, I had a little difficulty in establishing the amount for that year, due to the fact that the minutes, and the testimony of Mr. Reynolds straddled over a period, and while I had the total amount as shown in 1880, I did not quite know about the distribution, or the sale of those first mortgage bonds as of the year 1879. I had a little difficulty in getting the exact year. Some of them may have been bought in 1878. There was a period there that was straddled over and I could not account for it. They were the thirty-year six percent mortgage bonds. The items began in the minutes of November 1st, 1877, and some were in exchange for other bonds.

This record was not very complete. It is fragmentary. This item that I just read of November 1, 1877, shows that the President was authorized to purchase back 103 of the bonds issued in 1875; that was the $1,000,000 bond issue. Those bonds bore interest at the rate of seven per-cent, and the company from 1877 on to 1881 or 1882 redeemed those as opportunity afforded, by exchanging them for first mortgage bonds bearing six per-cent. The minute entry is November 1, 1877. The President was authorized to purchase 103 Calaveras bonds, paying for them at the rate of 90 cents on the dollar. The bonds that were redeemed there were the bonds that were known as the Calaveras bonds. It was the $1,000,000 purchase in 1875. They

160

161

43

were issued for the purchase of Calaveras and Vallejo Mills property. It included part of the Calaveras property, the Vallejo Mills and whatever lands were down the Alameda Creek; there was an acreage in them. It included the Vallejo Mills aqueduct.

162

DIRECT EXAMINATION BY MR. OLNEY.

I do not think that the people from whom this Calaveras and Vallejo Mills property were purchased were people who were interested in the company. I think it was a separate concern.

CROSS EXAMINATION BY MR. STEINHART.

Yes, the entry of November 1, 1877, shows that the President was authorized to buy the $103,000 worth of bonds at 90 per-cent on the dollar. In figuring up the amount actually received of $2,536,833, I did not take that on a basis of 90 cents on the dollar. First mortgage bonds were issued at par for the other bonds bought back at a discount. If the company issued a bond of $1,000 for another bond for 90 cents, I included the $1,000 expenditure as of that year. If the bonds were selling for 50 cents on the dollar, and they were issued at par, I would nevertheless have entered under colum three, par, for the reason that they bought back the bonds that were carrying seven per-cent and exchanged therefor bonds on which they had to pay six per-cent. The President did not sell them at 90 cents on the dollar. The other bonds were issued at 100 cents on the dollar. He bought back the Calaveras bonds at 90 cents on the dollar. If he issued $1,000 worth of first

163

mortgage bonds, he got more than $1,000 worth face value of the older mortgage back again. The other items entering into that $2,536,833 is an item of January 15, 1879, an exchange at par for 470 of the first mortgage bonds. That was another exchange of the Calaveras bonds on June 16th. Because of the fact that it was an exchange at par, I allowed the full amount under column 3. The next item of June 16, 1879, in the minutes state, that to that date 3,600 of the first mortgage bonds had been issued. They had been sold up to the date June 16, 1879. This is one of the items I did not get. I said things were a little fragmentary and straddled over a period there, but it is in the minutes of June 16, 1879. The minutes show the issuance of parts of these bonds. The minutes authorize that 7,000 bonds of the corporation be issued in sums of $1,000 each, payable thirty days after date, with interest at the rate of six per-cent, and states that only 3,600 of these

164

bonds have been issued, and provides that the President proceed to have the other bonds printed and issued. I took that as one of the evidences that they were. In the San Francisco "Bulletin" of June 18, 1879, I saw a record which stated that the company had recently authorized and sold $3,000,000 worth of first mortgage bonds at 95. They did not know just what the rate was. Taking all these various records that I have indicated together with the statement as shown of the actual discount which the company had suffered on the issuance of these bonds from the Reynolds exhibit—I have not the number of it, but it is an exhibit entitled "Bonds outstanding" in which is shown the distribution of the first mortgage, second mortgage, third mortgage, and general mortgage bonds of the Spring Valley Water Co.,—Major Dockweiler informs me that that is Reynold's Exhibit 105; from all, of those evidences, and also from the amount of coupon interest that was paid, which I got from the Reynold's exhibit, and also from Wenzelberger's exhibit, I arrived at the conclusion that those bonds were outstanding as of date December 31, 1879; I was not certain as to whether they were all issued in 1879, or some of them were issued in 1878. They could not have been issued in 1879. The record shows that they were sold in 1879. For example, the minutes that you refer to, and the discount item as shown by Reynolds and Wenzelberger, show that the discount occurred in 1879, and it was entered up in 1879. In Reynold's Exhibit 105 there is a discount shown there of $377,167.30. I have not the page reference here, but Reynolds shows 165 in his testimony that the discount was as follows: July, $256,864.20; August 1879, $20,303.20; October, $40,000; November, $60,000. These are on pages 4787 and 88 of Reynold's testimony. The next item was a redemption of the bonds issued in 1870, $500,000. Reynolds, on page 4634 and 4636, states that they were redeemed and paid for in cash, and that the redemption took place between February 27, 1880, and April 26, 1880. I have not in this list of money borrowed, anything for 1880. I don't know that there is anything in the minutes. I will investigate and see if I can find anything. The minus sign in both columns 2 and 3 is a reduction of the face value of bonds outstanding, and also of the actual contribution. There is a deduction made in both columns; $500,000 of those bonds were issued in 166 1870, the aggregate bond issues show that $10,000 more had been redeemed. During this period, as I stated before, the company was actually redeeming some of the Calaveras bonds in 1875. It would be possible that $10,000 of those bonds that were redeemed were Calaveras bonds; I don't know that it was that way.

(Witness admits a discrepancy in the second column where the minus $480,000 should not be carried into the second column instead of the $20,000.)

FOURTH HEARING.　　　JULY 16, 1915.

Witness Mr. JOHN JOSEPH SHARON.

CROSS EXAMINATION BY MR. STEINHART.　168

I think it is a fact that the item appearing in "Exhibit 12-bb", under year 1876, under column "Face of Bonds $69,000" and the item in third column under "Actual" $65,550 were bonds issued for the purchase of stock of the Clear Lake Water Co. I had in mind another tran-

45

169 saction with the Clear Lake Water Co., the purchase of riparian rights at Merced. This particular company was a corporation owning rights and property at Clear Lake. That property was never put into use.

(Objection by Mr. Steinhart to "Exhibit 12-bb").

170 These minute books are not the original minute books of the Spring Valley Water Works, or the San Francisco Water Works Co.

(Discussion by attorneys over the admission of minute books into the records).

174 DIRECT EXAMINATION BY MR. MCCUTCHEN.

In former testimony Mr. Wenzelberger and Mr. Reynolds agreed within $9,003 as to the total investment of $28,000,000.

(Discussion by attorneys regarding Reynolds' and Wenzelberger's testimony).

Questioned by the Master.

178 Besides Reynolds' testimony and the minute book, I referred also to Mr. Wenzelberger's exhibit from which I deduced from his charges or statement, showing coupon interest paid,—I made certain deductions from that as to the outstanding issue of bonds of these various issues.

(Ruling on Steinhart's objection reserved).

179 CROSS EXAMINATION BY MR. STEINHART.

In minute book "C", page 68, date November 16, 1876, appears the following statement with reference to the 69 first mortgage bonds "On motion of Mr. Norris, seconded by Mr. Forbes, it was resolved "that the action of the president in purchasing 9,134 shares of the "capital stock of the Clear Lake Water Co., and paying therefor 69 "of the first mortgage bonds of this company at 95 cents, amounting "to $65,550, and the accrued interest thereon, amounting to $839.50, "and the interest on said accrued interest for 108 days at one per "cent per month, $30.24"—the total of the two latter items being $869.74—"also check to order of Clear Lake Water Co. for $270.50. "Together with cash amounting to $41,505. And the notes of the "company in favor of A. Hayward, dated the 8th and 13th instant "respectively, one payable four months after date at 10% per annum "for $37,986.49, and the other payable on or before 12 months after "date, with interest at 10% per annum for $12,000, be approved". The total of those columns being $158,181.73. "Carried unanimously".

Referring to table "bb" there are no bonds appearing prior to 1867. The bonds issued prior to that date, amounting to $69,500 were issued by the Spring Valley Water Works, and were redeemed May 1 180 to May 4, 1868. Turning to minute book "B", page 249, the following appears as to the security of the bonds of 1867. "Resolved, that "in the opinion of this board it is not necessary or expedient that pay-

"ment of said bonds should be secured by mortgage upon the property
"of the corporation".

The bonds that appear on page 251 were sold at a premium, and
page 252 there were a number that sold at par, and the difference in
the total, 205, was so small that I thought possibly the expense incurred in the sale of them would at least have amounted to that much,
and I rounded it off by dropping the $205 premium in this issue of
$155,000, and later on, at the sale of other bonds, aggregating, as I
have it, $320,000 in the year 1867 (column 2), there was no evidence
that any of the other bonds, the difference between $155,000 and $320,-
000, had been sold except at par.

Turning to page 263, minute book "B", under date of June 15,
1867, the following appears: "Gentlemen: Our receipts last year
"were $536,374.16 against $468,754.28 in the year previous, say 1865
"and 1866, showing excess in favor of the year 1866 and 67 of $67,-
"619.88; our general expenses have been about $60,000. We paid in   181
"dividends to stockholders $360,000, leaving a balance of $116,374.16.
"We had in the city June 1, 1866, 337,868 feet of pipe laid; during
"this year we have laid 50,805 feet, making a total of 388,724 feet, of
"about 75 miles, besides pipes laid outside of the city.

"Gentlemen: You will remember that at your last meeting you
"authorized the board of trustees to borrow on the Co. credit $500,000
"to complete all our projected works, we have issued our bonds for
"$162,000, which with the separate income of the year, was employed
"in the payment of our works now in construction. These bonds cer-
"tainly present the best and surest investment for widows' and or-
"phans' money. They yield a good percentage, and have a long num-
"ber of years to run. Our income and its slow but steady increase
"are the best proofs of my assertion".

These $162,000 of bonds are part of the bonds contained in my
item of 1867, and I want to say in connection with that item of $320,-
000 that in going over the records with Major Dockweiler I found he
had some data from the books of the company which I did not have in
making my analysis. I believe I stated the other day in talking about
these bond issues, that there was some uncertainty in my mind as
to the year in which they were issued, and I made certain deductions
from the charges shown by Mr. Wenzelberger and Mr. Reynolds
for coupon interest paid. In this particular case, the bonds may have
been issued close to the end of the year 1867 or the beginning of the
year 1868, and I divided it in the way that appeared. Major Dockweiler let me have a list yesterday showing the date when these bonds
were issued, and they were all issued during the year 1867, so that
that column should be $500,000 for 1867, and there should not be any-
thing appearing for 1868. Referring to (column 2), $1,000,000 face   182
of bonds, and in (column 3) $1,000,000 actual, I think I said I did
not know, the other day, the terms of these bonds, but they were 20

year bonds with the privilege of exchange within two and one-half years for six per cent, thirty year gold bonds of the company.

Referring to bonds of 1877, that should be minus $480,000, the same figure as appears in the second column. This does not affect the total at the bottom of the column, because they were bonds that were redeemed and did not go into the total of those outstanding. Taking the bonds of 1879, I got that item from several sources. The minutes of 1877 showed that $470,000 of the first mortgage bonds were exchanged for $470,000 of the fourth series of Calaveras bonds, and in 1879 $393,000. The minutes state $375,000, but Reynolds, page 4789, and also page 4640, states that there were $393,000 redeemed by the first mortgage bonds. I had a statement furnished by the former secretary of the Spring Valley Water Co., Mr. Ames, which showed the outstanding stock and bond issues from 1880 to 1903, and at the end of 1880 the bond issue outstanding at that time was $3,969,000; so I deducted from the $3,969,000 the first mortgage bonds issued in 1876, amounting to $69,000; the first mortgage bonds issued in 1877, $20,000, and the first mortgage bonds issued in 1877 to redeem the Calaveras bonds, $103,000, and the first mortgage bonds issued January, 1879, to redeem Calaveras bonds of $470,000, also the first mortgage bonds issued December, 1879, to redeem Calaveras bonds of $393,000, making a total of the first mortgage bonds issued for those purposes of $1,055,000, which deducted from the $3,969,000 outstanding of 1880, left a net figure of $2,914,000 for the year 1879. Mr. Reynolds, in his testimony, shows, pages 4787 and 4788, that the discount on the bonds issued in 1879 occurred in July, August, October and November, the total discount being $377,167.30. I also had a reference to an old newspaper record, which showed in the "Bulletin" of June, 1879, that the company had recently placed $3,000,000 of bonds, 6% first mortgage, in New York at the reported figure of 90 net. Taking the first computation that I had, of $2,914,000 and applying the discount as shown by Mr. Reynolds, I find an equivalent selling price of 87 as against 90 as shown in the "Bulletin". I have not any other information than that, except in the way of coupon interest that was paid according to Mr. Wenzelberger's testimony, but that coupon interest may have included interest that was brought forward from the other bond issues, so that it did not check out quite exactly, within about $100,000. I did not use the "Bulletin" as a basis, but simply as an assumption.

Mr. Ames' report was a statement furnished to Mr. Schussler in 1903 and 1904, showing the outstanding bonds and stock issue. This was in the engineering record files of the company but I have not it here with me. I will arrange to let Major Dockweiler see it.

These were the first mortgage bonds issued in 1876, dated September 1, 1876, 30-year bonds, that bore interest at the rate of 6%, interest payable semi-annually, March 1 and September 1 of each year.

For the issuance of the $69,000, I refer to minute entry of November 15, 1876; for the $20,000, I refer to the minute entry October 15, 1877. On page 100, minute book "C", under date of October 15, 1877, the following appears:

"On motion of Colonel Mayne, seconded by Colonel Granniss, "Resolved that this board ratify the action of the president on the "purchase from Mr. J. M. Wilson of about 40 acres near Laguna "Merced for 20 of the first mortage bonds of this company, carried." I have a minute entry also as of date November 1, 1877, which is the minute entry for the purchase of certain of the Calaveras bonds at 90 cents on the dollar. At page 103, minute book "C", under date November 1, 1877, the following appears:

"Resolved that the president be authorized to purchase 103 of 185½ "the Calaveras bonds amounting at par to $103,000, he paying for "the same 90 cents on par and he be further authorized to borrow "such amount thereon as he may deem advisable." In the income account or profit and loss account of Mr. Wenzelberger in his exhibit 101, the discount is shown of $10,300.

The next minute entry, I think, on page 145 of book "C", minutes of January 15, 1879, reads as follows:

"Resolved: that the action of the president in exchanging 470 186 "first mortgage bonds value par $1,000 each, bearing 6% interest— "for 470 fourth series (Calaveras bonds) value par $1,000 each, "bearing 7% interest, be ratified by this board".

The next item is 1880. That shows in column 2 face of bonds minus $510,000, and refers to the redemption of the bonds issued as shown in the year 1870, known as the third series bonds. These bonds were dated April 1, 1870, term 10 years, interest 9%, payable semi-annually, on April 1, and October 1 of each year. Mr. Reynolds' testimony, pages 4634 to 4636, stated that they were redeemed between February 27 and April 26, 1880, so that I made a deduction of these $500,000 bonds in that year. I have not a note here showing in what way that redemption was made, but my recollection is that they were paid off in cash. I will explain why if there is a redemption of $500,000 bonds how I got the figure $510,000. From the redemption of the Calaveras bonds of $103,000 in 1877, 187 and the $470,000 in January 1879, and of the $375,000 which I took as $393,000 because of Reynolds' testimony, showing that as appearing in the ledger, the total redemption up to the end of 1879 was $966,000 of the Calaveras bond issue, leaving $34,000 outstanding as of the end of 1879, or beginning of 1880, and from this statement of Mr. Ames that I have already referred to in 1880, there was only $24,000 of these Calaveras bonds outstanding. The difference between the 34 and the 24 being the 10 which I account for here.

49

Questioned by Master.

The next column, $515,137, is an error, for the reason that the deduction was made of the actual amount received for these bonds in 1870; the bonds were sold for $505,137 at a premium, and in this table the deduction was made for that; that should be minus $510,000 in column 3 for 1880.

The next item in column 2, face of bonds 1884, shows the issuance of $500,000 of bonds. That was obtained from minute book "C", pages 435 to 437, as showing an increase as between October 1 and October 15 of the year 1884 of the $500,000 bond issue. Mr. Reynolds, on page 4595, states that those bonds were sold October 30, 1884, for $565,000, also he states on page 4788 that ledger F, page 462, shows a premium of $65,000 less debit by cash $2,500, leaving a net premium of $62,500. I entered the $500,000 face value in column

188   2, and the actual amount received $562,500 in column 3. These were first mortgage 6% bonds dated September 1, 1876.

Referring to the minutes of August 3, 1885, which show an exchange of 18 Calaveras bonds for 18 first mortgage bonds; this does not appear in my records. The face value of the bonds, and the actual amount received do not differ. This would not account for the fact that I do not find apparently the instance of the redemption of these additional $10,000 bonds, as the redemption was in 1880 from 34 Calaveras to 24, and some time between then and 1881 or 82, the bonds had been further reduced to 18 bonds, and in the year that you speak of they were wiped out entirely, which was the final consummation of the matter, being the exchange of 18 Calaveras bonds for 18 first mortage bonds.

The next item is 1887, and refers to the second mortgage bond. Turning to the minutes of 1886, December 1st, page 18 of minute book "D", the following appears:

"Whereas, it has become and innecessary in the judgment of "this board that this corporation should proceed without delay to "construct the lower Crystal Springs Reservoir and to provide a

189   "supply of water equal to the capacity of the same by procuring the "necessary property and water rights and connecting the said reser-"voir with the water sheds of the San Francisquito, Pescadero, San "Gregorio, Calaveras and other sources, a work involving large ex-"penditures of money and more than quadrupling the capacity of the "works of the company:

"Now, therefore, resolved: that in the judgment of this board "it is for the best interests of the company that the funds neces-"sary to meet this extraordinary expenditure and to pay off the "present floating indebtedness of the corporation should be raised by "the issue of bonds of the corporation from time to time as funds "are needed; and to that end be it further resolved that the execu-"tive officers call a meeting of the stockholders of this corporation,

"giving the notice thereof required by law, at which there shall be
"submitted to the stockholders a proposition to authorize the board
"of trustees to prepare and cause to be executed 10,000 bonds of this
"corporation in the sum of $1,000 each, bearing date on a given date
"to be therein named, and payable 30 years after date, with the privi-
"lege of redemption at any time after the 1st day of September, 1906,
"with interest at the rate of 3% per annum, payable semi-annually,
"with proper interest coupons thereto attached, and as security for
"the payment of said bonds and the interest coupons thereto attached
"to make, execute and deliver and to cause the same to be duly re-
"corded as mortgage upon the property of the corporation held and
"used in connection with and as a part of its system of works."

That interest rate was changed to 4% payable quarterly and
the authorization was reduced from $10,000,000 to $5,000,000, so
that the rate of interest that those bonds bore was 4%, interest   190
payable quarterly. The item as to issuance of those bonds I got
from the minutes of April 25, 1887, page 97 of minute book "D",
wherein appears the following:

"The balance of bonds to be placed in the hands of the finance
"committee, being in number $513,000, for sale, not to be disposed
"of at a less premium than one-half of one per cent." These bonds
were sold at a premium 60 one-hundredths percent, as shown on
page 97 of minute book "D". I have another list that evidently anti-
dates that—my date must be wrong—showing the sale of the following bonds:

   60 bonds at 1.00½
   20 bonds at 1.00¼
    5 bonds at 1.00½
   80 bonds at 1.00⅝
   45 bonds at 1.00 3-16
    5 bonds at 1.00¼
   12 bonds at 1.00⅛
    7 bonds at 1.00¾
    3 bonds at 1.01
  100 bonds at 1.00 1-20
  100 bonds at 1.00 1-10
   50 bonds at 1.00 3-20

which I got from minutes of April 25, 1887. That is evidently a
wrong date. It came out of the minutes though, and it just pre-   191
ceded that item of $513,000, and that makes up the total of the bonds
together with an issue as shown August 1, 1887, of $530,000. I de-
duced that from Mr. Reynolds' testimony, page 4798-99, in which he
stated that there had been issued from April 1887 to March 1888,
$1,582,000 worth of second mortgage bonds; there were also shown
on the minutes of the company, in the tabulation showing the out-

standing indebtedness, an increase in the first mortgage bond from $4,493,000 to $4,975,000; that is, by a face amount of $482,000.

The next item is $1,875,000, which I find in the minutes as of September 17, 1888, were sold at $95, netting $1,776,500.

192   The next item is from the minutes of August 7, 1890, and refers to the $90.

The next issue is November 12, 1891, $100,000 sold at $90, less 1% commission. The $83,000 I find in Wenzelberger's exhibit, which showed that in addition to the discount there was a commission and expense of net $83,000 instead of $89,000, as would be shown from the price less commission. The nature of those expenses I do not know. The reference to the minutes as of November 12, 1891, is as follows:

"Resolved that the action of the president in selling to the "San Francisco Savings Union 100 of the second mortgage bonds for "the sum of $90,000, less $1,000 paid as commission, be ratified by "the board."

193   The next item appears on pages 485 and 486 of minute book "D" under date of April 14, 1892, and in this case I also deducted the commission. Those were likewise sold at $90 at 1% commission.

The following quotation from the letter referred to there, was read by Mr. Steinhart:

"I will pay to the Spring Valley Water Works Company at the "rate of $90 and accrued interest, one percent, for commission, for all "of the remaining Spring Valley Water Works second mortgage "bonds which the company still holds and I obligate myself to take "and pay for each month, at least fifty of the Bonds, I reserve to "myself the right to take as many more and pay for the same, as I "may require. I will pay interest to the company at the rate of 5% "per annum on amount due from this date.

"For the fullfillment of any contract I will deposit with the "Company ten of the Spring Valley Water Works, Second Mort- "gage Bonds, and leave the same in the possession of the company, "until I have paid for all the Bonds as above specified.

(Signed) "Phil Barth."

194   The next item is the issuance of the third mortgage bonds; I refer now to the minutes of June 2, 1898. The issue is for $4,000,000; the rate was 4% per annum, payable quarterly; the date of the bonds was September 1, 1898, and the term was 8 years. The first evidences as to the issue is as of June 3, 1898. I have a statement that at page 4800 of the Reynolds testimony, he shows that there were sold $1,300,000 mortgage bonds from September to December, 1898, but I have not any further notes or evidences of that sale than

195   that. The $1,300,000 face value was taken from Reynolds' testimony, and the deduction was made for the bond expense and discount as

charged by both Reynolds and Wenzelberger for that year, so that the net amount is the difference between the total as shown by that and the face value of $1,300,000. Those bonds were not sold at par, as the company received $1,232,147 for a face value of $1,300,000. I could tell by reference to Wenzelberger's testimony whether they were sold at par less commission, or whether it was discount or commission, but I have not it here. Referring to page 462, minute book "E" under date of August 6, 1898, there appears a letter from The Bank of California, signed by Thomas Brown, Cashier, in which it is stated:

"We will take at par less 5% commission, $1,000,000 deliver-"able during the year 1898, $500,000 deliverable during the year 1899; "$500,000 deliverable during the year 1900, provided that with your "acceptance of this offer we are to receive an option to be availed of "on or before July 1st, 1900, to purchase the remaining $2,000,000 at "par less 2½% commission, upon terms as to time and delivery similar "to those offered above as may be agreed upon."

Mr. Steinhart then stated that that offer provided that the right should be given them to take the remainder at par less 2½% commission, and that the minutes showed an acceptance, stated as follows, on pages 462-3 of minute book "E": 196

"Resolved that the proposal now made by the Bank of Cali-"fornia as contained in their letter dated August 6, 1898, for the "purchase of 4 percent, third mortgage bonds, the issue of which has "been duly authorized, be and is hereby accepted."

The next item is $700,000 face of bonds, column 2, opposite the year 1899, and was taken from the minutes of May 11, 1899, when 200 bonds were sold at $95; September 14, 1889, when 200 bonds were sold at $95; November 16, 1899, when 200 bonds were sold at $95, being a total of $700,000. The $665,000 is 95% of $700,000. I think that is the way in which I arrive at the former figure. I find in Wenzelberger's exhibit that he had not set out that much money as chargeable to that bond issue, and I think possibly it may have been in some other item; so that I took the amount as shown in the minutes rather than to use Wenzelberger's figures.

Referring to page 525 of minute entries, it was stated in the offer of the Bank of California as of August 6, 1898, that they would take $500,000 deliverable during the year 1899, at par, less 5% commission. The minute book reference is page 525 of minute book "E", and reads: 197

"Resolved, that the president and secretary be and they are "hereby authorized and instructed to deliver to the Bank of Cali-"fornia on the 31st inst. 200 mortgage bonds, namely, 1301 to 1500, "of $1,000 each, under the same terms and conditions as have gov-"erned such bonds already sold and delivered to said bank." Each one of the sales referred to under this last item were made under the same type of resolution.

The next item of $800,000 face of bonds in the year 1900, I found in the minutes as of May 24, 1900, and November 8, 1900. These bonds were sold at 2½% commission, and the deduction made by me was the deduction of the commission. On page 199 of Wenzelberger's report he also shows for both of those that the commission was actually paid. The item as to the deduction of the commission, I got in two ways; by taking the commission of 2½% on $400,000, or $10,000, which checked with the commission as shown by Mr. Wenzelberger in his report.

198 Referring to page 111 of minute book "F", and to this letter of the Bank of California, that is a letter in which they availed themselves of the option expressed in the previous letter.

The next item is $900,000, face of bonds, in the year 1901, and was obtained from the minutes of April 25, 1901, when 300 bonds were sold; August 29, 1901, when 300 bonds were sold; and November 21, 1901, when 300 bonds were sold. The discount was for commission. In other words, they were a part of that option still with the Bank of California. (See minute book "F", page 197) These bonds, beginning with the year 1898, were all the third issue of 4% eight-year bonds.

The next item is "Face Value of bonds, $300,000, in the year 1902", which I obtained from the minutes as of date May 22, 1902, when $300,000 worth of bonds were sold at 2½% commission. At page 301 of minute book "E", under date of May 22, 1902, I find the following:

"Resolved that the president and secretary be and they are "hereby authorized and instructed to deliver to the Bank of California "on the 31st inst. 300 third mortgage bonds, Nos. 3701 to 4000, of the

199 "par value of $1,000 each, in accordance with an option given to said "bank on August 11, 1898, and referred to in their letter to this com- "pany dated May 18, 1900."

The next item is an issue of 1903, of a face value of $1,000,000, of the general mortgage bonds, authorized December 3, 1903, minutes of December 3, 1903, and which are the general mortgage bonds that are now outstanding. The term is 20 years; the interest is 4% per annum, payable semi-annually. I don't know whether that discount is a commission or not, I have the figure $95.

DIRECT EXAMINATION BY MR. OLNEY.

I did not include in columns 2 or 3 any items of bonds issued prior to 1865, although bonds had been issued, because bonds issued in 1863 were issued in part payment for full paid non-assessable stock that had been redeemed, and as I included the total actual value in the stock, I did not want to make a double entry by adding the bonds in.

CROSS EXAMINATION BY MR. STEINHART.

It was full paid stock that was issued to Ensign and Pioche, and others, who were the incorporators of the Spring Valley Water   200
Works for property and rights utilized by the company in supplying water to the City of San Francisco. The par value of the stock was $1,000, which was issued in 1860, and in 1863 it had been redeemed on the basis of $450 for each $1,000 share. The $450 were paid partly in bonds, of which the $69,000 is the total, partly in cash, and partly in the issuance of assessable stock on which $280 per share had been credited.

Referring to "Exhibit 104" introduced by Mr. Reynolds in the 1903-4 rate case, the stock issued in 1858 it was stock of the San Francisco Water Works, and I have checked these figures, I think in their entirety, with the minutes of the San Francisco Water Works. The reference to the minutes from which I obtained that is September 29, 1858. In the minute book is shown assessment No. 1, Bensley $45,000; Chabot $45,000; Von Schmidt $45,000. The following letter was then read from page 11 of the minutes of the San Francisco   201
Water Works:

"To the President and Trustees of the San Francisco City Water Works. Gentlemen:

"The undersigned, owning and representing the entire capital "stock of the San Francisco City Water Works, in the following "proportions, namely, John Bensley, 1000 shares, A. W. Von Schmidt "1000 shares and Anthony Chabot 1000 shares, and having received "certificates for the following shares, namely, John Bensley 600 "shares, A. W. Von Schmidt 600 shares, and Anthony Chabot 600 "shares, have hereby agreed and stipulated one with the other that "the balance of 1200 shares shall be placed to a fund designated and "called the construction fund. You are therefore hereby ordered "and empowered to place the said 1200 shares to the debit of said "construction fund on the books of your corporation to be used "by your board for the purpose of carrying on operations and con- "struction of the works of the corporation as shall in your judgment "be deemed most proper until otherwise ordered."

CROSS EXAMINATION BY MR. STEINHART.   202

I don't remember that the 3000 shares of stock issued by the San Francisco Water Works Co. were fully paid. As I understand it, the shares were issued to Von Schmidt, Bensley and Chabot, and later on they paid assessments on the shares.

I received the data for the first item in column No. 6 and No. 7, being $185,000, from page 7 of exhibit 104, which is a summary of the actual contribution of property and cash by stockholders of the San Francisco City Water Works and Spring Valley Water Works. This was submitted by Mr. Reynolds in the 1903 case; on page 8 of that same exhibit there is shown assessment No. 1, J. Bensley, $45,000, assessment No. 1, Von Schmidt, $45,000, assessment No. 1, Chabot, $45,000, total, $135,000. On March 15, 1858, there is shown 100 full paid shares of stock to J. Bensley $50,000. The $50,000 and the $135,000 total $185,000. I cannot identify the record here as shown by Mr. Reynolds, as to the last entry, as to whether it refers to the minutes or some other book—he has some page numbers, and it

203   is under date of March 15, 1858. I don't remember now that I did find any record in the minutes concerning that, but it is shown in Reynolds' testimony, page 4001. Referring to the first assessment, I said that I put these totals down from pages 7 and 8 of Mr. Reynolds' exhibit 104 in the 1903-4 case. My recollection is that I did find some of these entries in the minutes, but I don't know that I found all of them. My recollection is that I found a reference to an assessment, and that the assessment was a credit on the shares issued to these gentlemen for cash and materials which they had supplied to the San Francisco City Water Works Co. in the construction of its works. I read from the entry as it appears on Reynolds' exhibit, but it might also refer to page 13 of the minute book of the San Francisco Water Works, and also to the statement showing the accounts presented, which appears on page 14. On page 13, minute book of San Francisco City Water Works, under date September 27, 1858, the following appears:

204   "On motion of A. Chabot and seconded by A. W. Von Schmidt, "that an assessment of 15 per cent shall be ordered on 1800 shares, "or $900,000 capital stock now issued, payable on or before the 4th "day of October next." I credited this assessment on my account as paid in cash. On page 14 of the minutes of the San Francisco City Water Works, under date September 29, 1858, I find the following:

"On motion of A. Chabot, and seconded by A. W. Von Schmidt, "that the account of John Bensley, Esq., amounting to $40,091.34, "be hereby approved and allowed.

"Motion being put, received a unanimous vote in the affirmative.

"The accounts of A. Chabot were next presented, amounting "to $48,911.10, which were also approved and allowed.

"The accounts of A. W. Von Schmidt were next presented, "amounting to $38,069.97, which were also approved and allowed.

"The above accounts having been passed by an unanimous vote, "the secretary was directed to have the respective amounts entered "to the credit of each of the above-named parties." I think that is all the evidence in the minutes of the payment of that first assessment as I see no further references here by Mr. Reynolds to that.

On page 8, the minute book of San Francisco City Water Works, under date May 25, 1858, I find: "On motion of A. Chabot, and "seconded by A. W von Schmidt, that the salaries of the different "officers of the company shall be as follows, to-with: 205

"The president shall receive the sum of $500 per month; and "John Bensley, as treasurer, shall receive the sum of $500 per "month; and that the superintendent and engineer shall each receive "the sum of $1000 per month for their services from date; and for "their services heretofore rendered from the 6th day of August, "1857, up to date, shall be at the rate of $1000 per month each, "to-wit, John Bensley, A. Chabot and A. W. Von Schmidt, motion "being put a unanimous vote was received in the affirmative."

The president at that time was Mr. John Bensley, but I do not remember whether Mr. Chabot was an officer or not, although he was one of those whose salary is fixed here. The only amount I find credited on the minutes to the account of Bensley, Chabot and Von Schmidt is $127,072.41 provided those three items add up that amount. I find another item for 100 full paid shares of stock to J. Bensley under date March 15, 1858, of $50,000. I don't know that it is in the minutes; it is from the exhibit. 206

The next item is $221,825, in column 6, in the year 1859. I found that figure on page 7 of Mr. Reynolds' exhibit 104 and the details for it on page 8 of exhibit 104. It has, under date here of January 15, 1859, 50 full paid shares of stock to Perkins, $25,000. I find on page 18 of the San Francisco City Water Works minutes, the following

"On motion of Mr. Chabot, seconded by Mr. Bensley, it was "resolved and carried unanimously, that the president and secre- "tary of the company be authorized and directed to issue to A. B. "Perkins 50 shares of the capital stock of the San Francisco City "Water Works, the same to be issued as full paid stock, and re- "ceived by him as full payment of his interest in the Lobos Creek "ranch, pursuant to contract made between A. Chabot of the second "part, and John Bensley, A. B. Perkins and James Gordon, party "of the first part, dated May 15, 1856, and in full satisfaction "thereof." I do not know anything about the value at that time of the property that was exchanged for that 50 shares of stock.

The shares of stock issued to the law firm of Shafter, Park & Heydenfeldt, is not included in the year 1859; it is not in the exhibit at all. 207

I don't know whether the minutes correspond to these dates or not that are shown on here, but the date as shown here for the first item after that $25,000 is one dated January 28, 1859, in which assessment No. 2 had been credited to Bensley, Chabot, and Von Schmidt, $7,500 each, making $22,500 for that assessment. There is another assessment June 9, 1869, to these three gentlemen amounting to $12,500. On June 9, 1859, assessment 3, Bensley, $7,500, Von Schmidt, $7,500, Chabot $7,500, total $22,500. October 19, 1859, 525 shares sold to Parrott, Low Brothers & Co., and Birdseye & Co., $52,500; 35 shares sold to Simpkins, $3,150. November 26, 1859, assessment on 138 shares to Simpkins, $12,420. December 20, 1859, extra assessment $71,255.

208   The references to those assessments; on page 19 of the minute book, San Francisco City Water Works, under date January 28, 1859, I find the following:

"On motion of Mr. Chabot, seconded by Mr. Bensley, that a sec-"ond assessment be called on 1800 shares of the capital stock of the "San Francisco Water Works, now issued, and that said assessment "be 2½ per cent on the par value of said 1800 shares, viz., $900,000, "payable on or before the 31st instant".

On page 29 of the San Francisco City Water Works minutes, under date of June 8th, 1859, I find the following:

"Mr. A. Chabot presented a bill of $6,000 for sundry expenses "and services rendered, said account not included in any previous "settlement with said company, and asked to have the same placed to "his credit on the books of the company.

A. W. Von Schmidt moved, and seconded by Mr. Bensley, that "said amount is just, and that it be ordered paid. Motion put and "carried.

"Mr. John Bensley presented his account for services rendered "and expenses paid, not included in any previous settlement, amount-"ing to $5,000, and asked to have the same acted upon and passed to "his credit. On motion of Mr. Chabot, and seconded by A. W. Von "Schmidt that said account is just and the same ordered paid. Motion "put and carried.

"A. W. Von Schmidt presented his account for the sum of $1,500, "paid by Etting Mickle to Van Tyne for the purchase of Lobos Creek "ranch and asked the same to be placed to his credit and paid. On "motion of Mr. A. Chabot, and seconded by Mr. Bensley, that said "account is just and to order it paid".

209   Mr. Reynold's exhibit is entitled "Investment of Stockholders, San Francisco City Water Works", and he shows under these various dates these assessments, but he refers to the minutes for his authority, and he also has page numbers of an assessment book, a column headed "Cash Book", a column headed "Journal", and a column headed "Ledger".

210   The next entry in the minutes appears at page 35 under date of September 26, 1859, and is as follows:

"President Bensley called the meeting to order. Minutes of the "previous meeting read and approved. The president stated the ob-"ject of the meeting to be as follows:

"That in consideration of the sale of 525 shares of the capital "stock of the said San Francisco City Water Works, being stock re- "maining unpaid. The proceeds of which sale are required to meet "payments of the company now due, and for the purpose of continu- "ing the works. Mr. Chabot moved that said sale of the reserved stock "be approved, and that the president and secretary be desired to issue "said stock to the respective parties who have purchased, to-wit, John "Parrott, 175 shares; Low Bros. & Co., 175 shares; and Birdseye & "Co., 175 shares".

Questioned by the Master.

The money amount is $52,500, $100 per share.

CROSS EXAMINATION BY MR. STEINHART.

I got the item 8 of the Exhibit 104. It is entered here under date October 19, 1859, and that is the only point of information I have as to that.

The next entry is under date of October 19, 1859, being 35 shares sold Simpkins, payment I think of $3,150, and which is from Rey- nold's Exhibit 104 showing the investment of stockholders. The entry on pages 37 and 38 of the minutes of October 18, 1859, reads as follows:

"The president stated the object of the meeting to be, to take into "consideration the issuance of stock to Charles H. Simpkins, in con- "formity with contract dated the 4th day of April, 1859, for the sup- "ply of pipe. Mr. Chabot moved to issue 35 shares for the present, "until the exact amount can be ascertained. Motion seconded. Mo- "tion put and carried by unanimous vote". That stock was issued for pipe, and my recollection is that later on in the minutes there is a bill presented by Simpkins for pipe. I do not know upon what basis that was settled.

There is another item under date November 26, 1859, assessment on 138 shares to Simpkins, $12,420, going to make up the item $221,- 825. That is probably on page 42 of the minutes, the reference that I gave was probably an error; I do not see anything in the minutes that would indicate that exact reference of 138 shares. Refer to the item of December 20, 1859, reading as follows:

"Resolved, that all assessable stock now issued be assessed at a "rate sufficient to make all the stock 25 per cent on its par value. "Carried unanimously". That resolution probably has reference to the item which is on Reynold's Exhibit 104, under date of December 20, 1859, assessment extra $71,255 for the year 1859, but I have not any evidence of the payment of that assessment.

That is all that goes to make up my total of $221,825. On page 30 there appears the following in the minutes of the San Francisco City Water Works: "Mr. Chabot moved that the stock of said company "not heretofore issued, and being placed at present to the credit of the "construction account, shall be issued to each of the above-named "parties, in proportion of their accounts as passed upon, and at such "valuation as shall hereafter be put upon said stock by the board of "trustees".

I have 50 shares of stock issued to Bensley, $5,000, which corresponds with the amount of the account as presented by Mr. Bensley, $5,000, and I have an account of 15 shares of stock issued to Von Schmidt on page 8 of Exhibit 104, which corresponds with an account presented by Von Schmidt for the sum of $1,500 for the purchase of a portion of the Lobos Creek ranch, and I have 60 shares of stock issued to Chabot, $6,000, on Exhibit 4, the $6,000 corresponding with the bill presented by Mr. Chabot for expenses and services rendered.

215

DIRECT EXAMINATION BY MR. OLNEY.

So far as my account goes, I entered up the stock issued in the same amount as the bills presented by these various men.

CROSS EXAMINATION BY MR. STEINHART.

The next item 1860, $281,685, was made up of two items, a contribution by the stockholders of the San Francisco City Water Works, amounting to $125,175, and by the Spring Valley Water Works for the remainder. On page 7 of Reynold's Exhibit 104 he has the contribution by the Spring Valley Water Works in 1860 at $442,500, and at the end of this tabulation he shows a credit repaid to stockholders $210,000. That repayment was in the purchasing from the stockholders the full paid shares issued in 1860, so that in making up the tabulation, as it appears in column 6, for 1860, I entered up the amount actually credited to the stock in 1863 rather than the full amount as Mr. Reynolds showed in 1860. In this exhibit of Reynolds, on page 3, in the column headed "Record Book", there are several references, and possibly those references are to the minutes, pages 31 and 32. The amount credited to the Spring Valley Water Works was $256,500 of the amount that enters into the $281,675. Up to the present time I find no reference in the minutes showing the payment or the credit of

216   that amount.

The following is read from page 6 of the minutes of the Spring Valley Water Works, minute book "A", being a portion of Article 2 of The Articles of Incorporation of the Spring Valley Water Works: "The property and works of said company shall be held and deemed of the value of $60,000, represented by capital stock to that amount, divided into 300 shares of $200 each, and each share shall entitle the holder thereof to the undivided one-three hundredth part of said property and works and the profits and proceeds thereof".

The date of the articles of incorporation are June 19, 1858. With regard to the remainder of the amount going to make up the figure of $281,675, page 11 of Exhibit 104 under date of August 20, 1860, shows 200 full paid shares, issued to Ensign, $200,000, October 18,

1860, 200 full paid shares, issued to Pioche, De Boom, Cobb, et al, $200,000. The shares were for $1,000 each, and I took the $550, which was the difference between the $450 and the $1,000 in the first instance; the shares were bought back in 1863 and I made the correction in the first year rather than in 1863. To describe that operation a little more fully, the shares were issued in 1860 and were full paid non-assessable. They ran along until 1863, when they were bought back by the Spring Valley Water Works from the holders on the basis of $450 per share. There was then issued to the holders new shares, assessable, on which there was a credit allowed of $280, being the amount of the assessment on the stock up to that time. There was also issued to the holders, bonds to the amount of $69,000 and cash; the cash, as I remember it, was about $68,000. This I got from Mr. Reynolds' testimony, so that the value then in 1863 of the stock as issued in 1860 was the value that I attach to it as of 1860 rather than the $1,000 value as shown by Reynolds on pages 7 and 11 of his exhibit because he makes a credit at the end, at the time of the consolidation of the companies, for that difference. I have a list here which shows the disposition of $69,500 of bonds, which list Major Dockweiler had, and is entitled "Excerpt from Spring Valley's book marked Stock Issued". That shows the disposition and the parties who received the $69,000 worth of bonds, and so far as any of the stockholders who received those bonds were concerned, I credited that to them under the term "Stockholders", without particular reference to any names, and my payment of cash I got from Reynolds' testimony. I consider that the value was not the full paid shares, but the value as of 1863. The stock was issued by the company to these people, Pioche, De Boom and Ensign, for property and rights from which the company got its supplies; out in Islais Creek was one place, and also, I think, a holding in Crystal Springs.

Page 31 of minute book "A" Spring Valley Water Works, under date of May 18, 1860, shows that the capital stock of the Spring Valley Water Works Co. be increased from $60,000 to $3,000,000, namely, 3,000 shares of $1,000, and that the necessary notice be published in the "Evening Telegram" and "Daily Times", two newspapers printed in the City and County of San Francisco. On page 31 there appears the following statement:

"The president stated that in pursuance of an agreement made "with A. W. Von Schmidt as to the terms and conditions upon which "new stockholders are to be permitted into this company are sub-"stantially as follows, to-wit: That the president of said Spring Val-"ley Water Works, George H. Ensign, in consideration of $300,000 "worth of property by him assigned, transferred and delivered to said "company shall receive $2,000 cash in hand and 10 percent. of all the "capital stock of the said company, whatever the amount of capital "stock may be, not to exceed $300,000, of non-assessable stock, and "shall be the owner of one-tenth of all the stock of said company to

217

218

219

61

"be issued and delivered to him as preferred full paid or unassessable
"stock".

That was issued to him as full paid stock. It is so recorded by
Mr. Reynolds. On page 78 minute book "A", Spring Valley Water
Works, under date October 20, 1860, I find the following:

"Resolved, that the president and secretary be authorized to sign
"the certificates of stock in conformity with the by-laws of the com-
"pany and to issue the same forthwith to the respective holders of the
"assessable stock; also to George H. Ensign 100 of the 200 shares full
"paid stock to be paid him in conformity with contract, and that that
"200 shares unassessable stock to be paid to F. L. A. Pioche and others
"composing the late Islais and Salinas Water Works Company pur-
220   "suant to the contract to that effect dated the 14th day of August,
"1860, be issued as soon as the attorney of this company shall have
"reported that the said Islais and Salinas Water Works Company
"have disincorporated according to law".

   That all relates to item, 1860, that I have charged up as of the
value given upon the purchase or exchange in 1863, and the remainder
of that item I got from Exhibit 104 page 11 whereon under date September 1, 1860, there is shown assessment No. 1, collected $21,250,
and on December 1, 1860, there is shown assessment 2, collected $21,-
250. The reference in the minutes to those, may be on page 51. Page
51 minute book "A", Spring Valley Water Works, under date of
August 15, 1860, produces the following:

"Mr. Tillinghast proposed an assessment to meet current and
"coming outlays and suggested $7.00 as about the sum requisite; after
"mature deliberation it was unanimously decided to call in an in-
"stallment of $10 per share on all assessable stock, payable within ten
"days from this 15th August, 1860". I have no evidence that that
was collected, only as stated here in Reynolds' Exhibit 104. That
makes up the complete item as given in 1860.

221   The next item for the year 1861, $237,075, is made up of two items
taken from pages 7, 8 and 11 of Reynolds' Exhibit 104; San Francisco Water Works $36,575, and Spring Valley Water Works $218,500.
The item $36,575 I find on page 8, under date July 12, 1861, in Ex-
hibit No. 104, assessment No. 4, of 15 per cent less dividend credited
on above, and I also found reference to it in the minutes on page 77
of the San Francisco City Water Works. The amount credited on this
assessment, $213,750 less earnings, $177,175, leaving $36,575.

   On page 77 of the minutes of the San Francisco City Water Works
appears:

"Resolved, that an assessment be levied on the assessable stock of
"the company, of 15%, said assessable stock amounting to 2,850 shares,
"representing $1,425,000. Resolved, that no call be made on the stock-
"holders but that the said assessment be paid out of the surplus profits
"of the company which have been expended in the construction of the

"work". That, and the statement shown, are the only knowledge that I have of that item from the records of the company.

   . I have the following items: On page 11 of Reynolds' Exhibit 104, there is shown under date February 1, 1861, assessment No. 3, collected $20,750. On February 9, 1861, 25 full paid shares, issued to Parsons, Pioche, for Lake Honda, $25,000. On April 1, 1861, assessment No. 4, collected $20,750. On April 9, 1861, ten full paid shares issued to Wilkins for San Gregorio, $10,000. On June 1, 1861, assessment No. 5, collected $20,750. On June 6, 1861, sold 100 shares of stock, less paid out, $5,000. That item shows two figures, $6,000 and $1,000 under it, leaving a net amount out in the column, of $5,000. The item reads as follows: June 6, 1861, sold 100 shares of stock, less paid out. Then there are two figures, $6,000 and underneath that $1,000, and out in the column is shown $5,000, that being the investment or contribution. On June 8, 1861, assessments 1, 2, 3, 4 and 5, on 25 shares of stock, $1,250. On July 23, 1861, 5 full paid shares, issued McMahan, Pilarcitos, $5,000. August 1, 1861, assessment No. 6, collected $22,000. September 1, 1861, assessment No. 7, collected $22,000. October 1, 1861, assessment No. 8, collected $22,000. November 1, 1861, assessment No. 9, collected $22,000. December 1, 1861, assessment No. 10, collected $22,000.

   I made a correction there also for the purchase for the full paid shares that are shown on this list that I have just read, and entered in this column in this exhibit "Plaintiff's Exhibit 12-bb", only the value in 1863 under the date 1861. I gave the credit then of the value of the stock in 1863 in the year 1861—in this case. Under date of February 9, 1861, 25 full paid shares, issued to Parsons and Pioche, for Lake Honda, $25,000. I included in 1861 $11,250 as a contribution to the Spring Valley Water Works, being a payment for property at Lake Honda. That was the issue of 25 shares fully paid for property at Lake Honda, and may be found on page 94 of the minute book. On page 94 of minute book "A", Spring Valley Water Works, February 15, 1861, I find the following:

   "The action of the president in issue of certificates for the 25 full "paid shares representing $25,000 stock of the company in payment "of the purchase money of Lake Honda and property thereto attached "was unanimously approved".

   Page 104 of minute book "A" of Spring Valley Water Works, shows the following:

   "Resolved, that the president be fully empowered to conclude "purchase of certain water rights offered by Henry Wilkins for the "use of the company to the following named streams in the County of "San Mateo. Arroyo de San Gregorio; Arroyo Honda or Tunitas "Creek, and the Corte Madera Creek and all the sources of the same, "etc., together with the right of way through the lands known as the "San Gregorio Rancho, all as fully specified in the deeds of convey-

"ance, and that after examination and approval of title deeds by Mr.
"S. W. Holiday, attorney of the company, the president be authorized
"to issue in payment of said water rights, etc., full paid stock of the
"company to the amount of $10,000, or say a certificate or certificates
"for the aggregate number of ten fully paid stock". These sources of
supply have not been used.

225   Page 110, minute book "A" Spring Valley Water Works, of
date June 4, 1861, contains the following:

"Stock sold. Sale of 100 shares of stock of the company stand-
"ing on the books to account reserve stock, sold at $60 with $50 paid
"in, corresponding to the first, second, third, fourth and fifth install-
"ments, sold to the following parties:

    "50 shares to Louis McLean, Jr.

    "10 shares to Samuel Knight.

    "20 shares to Henry A. Fox.

    "20 shares to Henry Hudson.

"Sale approved and president authorized to issue the stock in
"conformity". The number of shares outstanding would be 2,200
"shares, the assessment having been $10 a share, and netted $22,000".

Questioned by Mr. McCutchen.

I got the figures of the amount from the minutes, and I also
have the amount from Reynolds' exhibit 104, and I have a pencil
note of 2200 shares on the margin.

CROSS EXAMINATION BY MR. STEINHART.

These sales of stock that I have referred to were of the Spring
Valley Water Works, as also were assessments Nos. 3 to 10, which I
have already detailed.

On page 7 of minute book "B", appears the following:

226   "Stock to Owen and Patrick McMahan for water rights; the
"issuance of 5 shares of full paid stock to Owen and Patrick
"McMahan in payment of water rights on Pilarcitos Creek as per
"resolution of this board 14th ultimo, approved." That I credited
on the basis of the exchange in 1863, as it was full paid stock.

On page 30, minute book "B", Spring Valley Water Works,
April 8, 1862, reserve stock. "On motion of Mr. Johnson, seconded
"by Mr. Roxby, resolved that the president be authorized to sell
"any number of shares, not to exceed 300, of the stock standing on
"the books of the company to account reserved stock for contingent
"purposes at prices not less than $10 per share advance over and
"above the amount paid in; unanimously adopted."

Page 48, minute book "B", Spring Valley Water Works, under
date of June 21, 1862, presents the following:

"Resolved that the board of trustees of the Spring Valley
"Water Works be requested to sell, issue and dispose of for cash
"at the highest price they can obtain for the same all of the re-

"maining shares of the capital stock of said company yet remaining
"unissued and undisposed of.

"W. F. Farwell, substitute: W. B. Farwell offered the follow-
"ing as substitute:

"Resolved that the board of trustees be instructed to divide
"the shares of stock now on hand pro rata among the assessable
"stockholders of the company, and to cause the same to be issued
"without delay and that the same shall be assessed from the time
"of issuance as other assessable stock. After debate the substitute   227
"being duly seconded was adopted by the following vote, the ayes
"and noes having been called for". Minute book "B", page 61,
September 26, 1862: "The following resolution was offered by Mr.
Carlton and seconded by Mr. Woodworth:

"Resolved that the president be authorized to negotiate for the
"purchase of the full paid stock of the company at prices not to
"exceed $350 per share. Resolution adopted unanimously."

Page 70, minute book "B", under date of April 1, 1863, present
the following:

"The President submitted to the board the terms of a proposed
"agreement with certain holders of full paid stock for the redemp-
"tion of certificates outstanding under said denomination and the
"following resolution was offered by Mr. Woodworth and seconded
"by Mr. Carlton:

"Resolved that the outstanding certificates of stock issued by
"this company under the denomination of full paid be redeemed and
"the terms stated in the proposal above referred to, namely, the
"sum of $450 per share, to be paid partly in assessable stock with
"$280 credited thereon as paid assessment, partly in cash and partly   228
"in bonds of the company payable in five years and bearing one
"percent, per month interest, payable quarterly, according to the
"separate terms stipulated respectively by the several owners of
"such full paid stock. Adopted unanimously; subject to the ratifi-
"cation of majority of the stockholders to be called together for the
"purpose on Monday the 13th inst., at 2 P. M. by notification of the
"secretary in the form prescribed by the bylaws."

I have the amount of these different assessments per share, from
page 3 to page 11 a statement concerning the assessment number and
the amount collected for the year 1861. I have the amount for
assessment No. 4 of April 1, 1861. That is $10 a share. I have the
amounts of assessment 5, $20,750, which would be $10 a share. Nos.   229
6, 7, 8, 9 and 10 are each $22,000, and I have a note here as to $10
a share, which I took from the minutes. Assessment No. 11 is entered
on exhibit No. 104, page 11, under date January 1, 1862, in the
amount of $22,000. The dates for 1862 are as follows, in addition to
the one I have just read as of January 1, 1862: February 1, 1862,

assessment No. 12, collected $24,000. The total figures that I give, and which I have set out in column 6, are taken from the Reynolds exhibit, with the modification that I have explained about the full paid stock. The next one was assessment No. 14 of April 1, 1862, at

230   $20. The next one, April 26, 1862, 15 full paid shares, issued to Mezes, for Pilarcitos, $15,000. The next assessment is May 1, 1862; June 1, 1862; July 1, 1862; August 1, 1862; August 11, 1862; that is a special here; $3,000 is all that I have. Assessment No. 19, September 1, 1862, the shares must have been increased then, because the amount is increased to $12,725. I mean it has increased solely in proportion to the $10 as shown previously, and my evidence as to that is taken solely from the Reynolds testimony. Assessment 19 is $5.00 a share. I stated that the amount here had increased, so the number of shares had increased. Up to this time we had been talking about 2200 shares. Now the number of shares have in-

231   creased. Assessment 20, of $25,450, was paid October 1, 1862, $10 a share. Assessment 21 for $10 is of date November 1, 1862. Assessment 22, date December 1, 1862, is $15 a share, minutes page 62. Assessment 23, minutes page 63, is of date January 1, 1863, $15 a share. Assessment 24, February 1, 1863, $15 a share. Assessment 25, minutes page 67, is of date April 25, 1863, $10 a share. Assessment 26, dated December 15, 1863, minutes page 93, $15 a share.

232   These check out assessments that were paid in 1863.

There are no items that I have computed in the amount $281,675 for 1860 other than those to which I have testified. The item of 1861, $237,075, is made up from the figures taken from pages 7, 8 and 11 of exhibit 104, showing contributions in 1861 to the San Francisco City Water Works $36,575, and to the Spring Valley Water Works in 1861, of $218,500, and that reference, I think, is page 77 of the minutes of the San Francisco City Water Works. I did not include this in the item in 1860; that was in 1861, and $218,500 is the contribution in that year by the Spring Valley Water Works, and the $36,575 was the contribution in 1861 to the San Francisco City Water Works. In 1862 on pages 7, 8 and 11 of exhibit 104, there is shown under the San Francisco City Water Works a contribution of $141,625, and for 1862 the contribution of the Spring Valley Water Works is shown as $404,375.

233   My figures do not check there, by the difference between the full paid shares and the credit which I allow for those full paid shares which were issued in 1862, and which we have just read. The same computations extend to the year 1862 as to the years previously where the issuance of the full paid stock entered into the totals as I have given them to you. The item of $141,625, San Francisco City Water Works, I got on exhibit 104, page 8, under date April 15, 1862, assessment No. 5, $71,250, and under date June 15, 1862, assessment No. 6, $70,375; those two items aggregate $141,625.

On page 91, minutes of the San Francisco City Water Works, under March 13, 1862, the following appears:

"On motion of Mr. Bensley, it was unanimously resolved that "an assessment of 5% on the capital stock of the company be and "is hereby levied. Payable on or before the 15th day of April next, "the same being assessment No. 5." I have no knowledge as to the payment of that, except the entry as shown by Reynolds in exhibit 104, as a contribution by stockholders.

On page 95 of the minutes of the San Francisco City Water Works, under date of May 12, 1862, the following appears:

"On motion of Mr. Sneath an assessment of 5 percent on the "assessable capital stock of the company, payable on or before the "14th day of June next, be and is hereby levied, said assessment "being No. 6; voted unanimously." I have no evidence of knowledge from the minutes of the company, or from the books of the company as to the payment of that amount.

234

FIFTH HEARING.   JULY 19, 1915.

Witness MR. JOHN JOSEPH SHARON.

CROSS EXAMINATION BY MR. SEARLS.

The payments for year 1863 were based upon figures which I obtained from Mr. Reynolds' exhibit 104, on page 7, of which is shown $84,450 for the San Francisco City Water Works, and $140,515 for the Spring Valley Water Works. These represent assessments 23, 24, 25 and 26.

235

Questioned by Master.

These were assessments for the Spring Valley Water Works, whereas the San Francisco City Water Works appear on Page 7 of assessment No. 8, $84,450.

I know only in a general way that this assessment money was put into the construction of works of the San Francisco City Water Works, and also into property. This property consisted of property out at Lobos Creek. From Lobos Creek the water was taken by conduit along the shore of the Golden Gate and delivered to a pumping station at the foot of Van Ness Avenue, about where the present Black Point pumping station of the Spring Valley Water Co. is located, and from that station the water was pumped to two reservoirs, one the Francisco Street Reservoir, and the other the Lombard Street Reservoir. From these reservoirs pipe was laid in the city distribution system, and water was sold through those pipes to consumers.

236

CROSS EXAMINATION BY MR. SEARLS.

Q. Do you find anything in these records showing whether the San Francisco City Water Works or the Spring Valley Water Works were at that time competing companies?

A. I think that that was mentioned in the minutes, and I also had some notice of that also from the daily newspapers of the time.

237   When the Spring Valley Water Works took over the San Francisco City Water Works, I do not think that there was any duplication of plant, as where there was duplication of plant, I find from Mr. Wenzelberger's exhibit that the duplicated pipes were all sold to the San Francisco Gas Company, and I think there was not very much in the way of duplication, as the San Francisco City Water Works were supplying the north-eastern portion of the town, while the Spring Valley Water Works was supplying out in the Mission, and in the Western Addition, and that where the duplication did exist was about at the limits of the San Francisco City Water Works and the Spring Valley Water Works.

On page 39 of minute book "B", Spring Valley Water Works, under date May 6, 1862, I find the following:

"The president reported that the indenture made the 4th of "April, 1862, between Francois L. A. Pioche, Soledad Ortega de Ar- "guello, Jose Ramon Arguello and S. M. Mezes and this company "had been duly executed and placed on record in the Recorder's "office, Redwood City, San Mateo County, said indenture conveys "to this company certain land and water rights on the Domingo "Feliz Ranch in San Mateo County, etc. Document ordered on file "and the president authorized to issue, in conformity with the terms "of agreement the fifteen full paid shares of the stock of the com- "pany standing on the books as reserved stock."

238   I accounted for that stock as of April 26, 1862, being 15 full paid shares issued to Mezes. We are now talking about the year 1863, and the figures that I gave were for 1863, as I understood you to say 1863. Referring to these assessments, of which I have just spoken, I have compared the amount of the various levys with the minutes in each case, and it is my impression now that the figures that are shown on "Exhibit 104" compare with those that are shown in the minutes.

239   The following dates of assessment levys was read into the records, with the understanding that it could be checked later; Assessment No. 24, December 12, 1862, $15 per share; Assessment No. 25, February 24, 1863, $10 per share; Assessment No. 26, Octo-
240 ber 31, 1863, $15 per share; (the next assessment will show as paid during 1864) Assessment No. 27, December 4, 1863, $15 per share; Assessment No. 28, January 6, 1864, $15 per share. Assessment of January 15, 1864, of $90 per share, to pay up all the company's indebtedness is not given a number in the minutes, but is subsequently recognized as Assessment No. 29; Assessment No. 30, July 11, 1864, $10 per share; Assessment No. 31, September 1, 1864, $25 per share; Assessment No. 32, November 4, 1864, $10 per share; Assessment 33, January 11, 1865, $30 per share.

The contribution as shown on page 7 of Reynolds' exhibit 104 for the San Francisco City Water Works in 1864, is shown as $95,631.45; Spring Valley Works for 1864 is shown as $450,945. I have no number for the assessments of the San Francisco City Water Works, but for the Spring Valley Water Works, the assessments for 1864 are 27, 28, 29, 30, 31 and 32.

Question by the Master.

The figures for the Spring Valley Water Works is made up of these assessments; I do not see in Mr. Reynolds' exhibit, any number for the assessment corresponding to the $95,631.45 for the San Francisco City Water Works.

CROSS EXAMINATION BY MR. SEARLS.

I cannot identify that payment from the Reynolds exhibit 104.

The following was read from page 118 of the minutes of the San Francisco City Water Works, being under date of February 8, 1864:

241

"On motion of Mr. Low, seconded by Mr. Thomas, resolved that "an assessment of 6 percent on the capital stock be and is hereby "levied, payable by the stockholders on or before the 15th day of "March, 1864, in gold coin of the United States. Carried unani- "mously."

Mr. Reynolds' exhibit shows just the year 1864 on this table from which I was reading, and he has a lot of details on the preceding pages 1 and 2, exhibit 104, in which are shown references to record books, assessment books, cash book and ledger, and other books of the company, and giving the page numbers, so I don't know whether that corresponds with the data he has for 1864 or not. There is nothing to show whether that was the amount received from that assessment or not, unless it is shown in the minutes, and I do not remember whether it is.

DIRECT EXAMINATION BY MR. McCUTCHEN.

I mean that there is nothing in the minutes so far as I am now advised, but I will say that there is nothing on this exhibit 104 to show that. It does show that there was that amount contributed by the stockholders of the San Francisco City Water Works in the year 1864, but it is not tied up with any assessment number, so I cannot identify it in that respect.

Questioned by Master.

Assessment No. 8, 6%, amounted to $84,450, and back assess- ment collected under date of August 1, 1864, was $11,181.45.

242

DIRECT EXAMINATION BY MR. McCUTCHEN.

In view of that discovery I would like to correct the answer to conform with the data that I see here on page 9, exhibit 104, showing the two items aggregating $95,000 odd that I read there. That assessment No. 8, is under date of April 1, 1864, and the back assessment collected is under date August 1, 1864.

CROSS EXAMINATION BY MR. SEARLS.

On page 125 of the minutes of the San Francisco City Water Works, annual meeting on May 25, 1864, appears the following resolution:

"Resolved that a stock dividend of one-third or 33 1-3% be "made to each stockholder, and certificates for the same be issued "to the stockholders as they stand on the books of the company on "the 20th day of June, and that no dividend shall at any time be "declared on any fractional share of stock."

243
The only consideration for that stock that I entered in my paid column was the amount of assessment, and if there was no assessment, it is not shown. That was a dividend. The dividends that are shown in column 15 of "exhibit 12-bb" are taken from Reynolds' exhibit 104, on page 10; there is shown the dividends paid by the San Francisco City Water Works, beginning with July 1, 1864, the last dividend is shown as dividend No. 7, March 1, 1865. There is no notation of a stock dividend stated on the exhibit. The consolidation between the San Francisco City Water Works, and the Spring Valley Water Works took place in 1865, and the capital stock is shown as $6,000,000 on the exhibit.

244
Questioned by Master.

Exhibit 104 does not show the $6,000,000 of that year as par or face value, but it is referred to on pages 144, 145 to 150 of the record book.

CROSS EXAMINATION BY MR. SEARLS.

On page 148 of minute book "B", December 28, 1864, it appears that the capital be formed of $6,000,000 in 6000 shares of $1,000 each, of which capital 3200 shares shall be awarded to the San Francisco City Water Works, and 2800 shares to the Spring Valley Water Works, the stockholders of each to be entitled to a distributive share pro rata.

Taking up the paid column for 1865, that amount is shown on page 7 of exhibit 104 to March 1, 1865, $100,459.51, and on page 14 is shown under date March 6, 1865, cash from James Ludlow for 10 shares, $5,000, making a total of $105,000.

DIRECT EXAMINATION BY MR. MCCUTCHEN.

Exhibit 104 is an exhibit as filed by Mr. Reynolds in the 1903 rate case.

245
There is only one number for the assessment upon which the 1865 payments were based. The other was a purchase of stock. Page 12 of exhibit 104 shows under date March 1, 1865, assessment

No. 33, collected $83,700, and under date January 11, 1865, received from the estate of Doon, back assessment, $16,759.51. On page 14 is shown, March 6, 1865, cash from James Ludlow for ten shares, $5,000. The next entry is 1868, showing 20,000 shares—$2,000,000. Page 14 of exhibit 104 shows April 20, 1868, 20,000 shares sold, on which was collected at this date $400,000. On August 1, 1868, 20,000 shares were sold, on which was collected at this date $400,000. Those are dittoed in the exhibit here, so it does not mean an additional 20,000 shares, but 20,000 shares for the entire year. On October 1, 1868, collected to this date $360,000, making a total of $1,160,000.

Questioned by Master.

The reference to the minutes there is page 278 to page 302.

CROSS EXAMINATION BY MR. SEARLS.

Resolution appearing on page 283 of minutes "B" Spring Valley Water Works, under date March 18, 1868, is as follows:

"Resolved that if the stock be increased then the directors be "requested to issue the new stock to the stockholders pro-rata upon "the stock held at the rate of $58 per share."

Page 284 of the minutes of March 20, 1868, shows the following resolution:

"On motion of Mr. Babcock, seconded by Mr. Walker, resolved: "that the payment to be made on the new stock shall be made in "the following manner, $20 on or before 20th of April, interest on "payment to commence May 1st; $20 payable on or before August "1st, and $18 payable 30 days after notice by publication. Scrip to "be issued for the payments so made."

I multiplied the amount of stock issued by $58 a share, the sum at which it was sold, and received the total $1,160,000, which total was also shown in exhibit 104. It is stated in the minutes that there was a resolution to increase the capital stock to $18,000,000, which was subsequently amended to $16,000,000, as shown on page 48 of minute book "C". That seems to be an error for 1883; it should be 1884. On page 18 of exhibit 104 it shows, under date of November 15, 1884, sales 10,000 shares, and collected $860,000, which is at $86. Minute book "C", page 374, as of date April 1, 1884, shows the following resolution:

"On motion of Mr. Fry, seconded by Captain Eldridge, it was re-"solved that the president and secretary of this company be and they "are hereby authorized to issue and sell 20,000 shares of the unissued "stock of this corporation at $87.50 per share; and they are hereby "instructed to cause notice to be given by publication in the 'San "Francisco Chronicle' and the 'Evening Bulletin' to the effect that "upon application at the office of the company on or before the 30th "April the stockholders will be entitled to purchase one share of

246

247

"stock for every four shares which they now own, upon paying there-
"for in cash the said $87.50 per share."

By resolution of date September 26, on page 433 of the minutes,
the price was reduced to $86 per share, as follows:

"Resolved that the price of said stock be and the same is hereby
"fixed at the sum of $86 per share, that being in the judgment and
"opinion of this board as near the present market value of the stock
"of the corporation as the same can be fixed, having regard to uni-
"formity."

Page 439 of the minutes of November 3, 1884, shows the following resolution

"On motion of Mr. Goodman, seconded by Colonel Fry, resolved
"that the finance committee—(Mr. Bigelow and Mr. Mayne) be au-
"thorized to negotiate for the sale of the remaining unsold stock
"which was authorized to be sold by resolution of the board Septem-
"ber 26, 1884, namely, 15,966 shares (4034 shares having been sold)
"at a price not less than $86 per share. Carried.

248   Page 444, minutes of December 8, 1884, shows the following
resolution:

"On motion of Colonel Fry, seconded by Mr. Beaver, resolved
"that the sale by the committee of 4458 shares of Spring Valley
"Water Works stock to Sutro & Company at $86 per share, payable
"at the company needs money, and when the stock is issued, inter-
"est to be charged from the 1st day of each month up to the time of
"issue at 6 percent per annum, and with the understanding that the
"further issues of the company's stock shall be made before the 1st
"day of July, 1885, and said 4458 shares of stock are to be issued as
"payments are made in not less than 500 share lots be ratified by
"the board. Carried unanimously."

I should not say that the minutes would indicate that the entire
10,000 shares were sold during 1884. Mr. Reynolds shows that the
10,000 shares were sold and collected.

(Mr. Searls then advised the Master that the sum of these was
about 8900 shares out of 10,000, and that these minutes are as of
December 8, and as the witness has just said, authorized the sale of
4,458 shares to Sutro & Company, and that he could find nothing
249   else in the minutes). There was some stock sold in 1885, and it may
be that the last resolution under date of December 8, 1884, had reference to the sale of some of that stock. I have already noted the
correction for the year 1884 on the exhibit. Exhibit 104, under date
December 31, 1885, shows 10,000 shares sold and $953,521 collected.
The following resolution appears on page 496 of minutes "C" under
date of November 23, 1885:

"On motion of Mr. Goodman, duly seconded it was resolved
"that the president and secretary of this corporation are authorized
"and instructed to issue and sell 10,000 shares of the capital stock

"of this company at $95 per share, and they are hereby instructed
"to cause notice to be given by publication in the daily papers that
"upon application at the office of the company on or before the 31st
"of December the stockholders of record on the 1st of December will
"be entitled to one share of stock for every nine shares which they
"own on that date, upon payment therefor the sum of $95 per share,
"with interest at the rate of 6% per annum from the 1st of December
"to date of payment."

That is slightly in excess of $95 per share, and the interest would
probably take care of the difference, as it is a small amount, $3,000.

DIRECT EXAMINATION BY MR. MCCUTCHEN.

The date of that is November 23, 1885. The interest was to be 250
calculated from December 1st, and my record shows the date of
payment to be made December 31, 1885.

Questioned by Master.

The rate of interest was 6 per cent.

CROSS EXAMINATION BY MR. SEARLS.

The next sale that appears from exhibit 104, page 18, under date
May 9, 1891, shows 10,000 shares and collected $931,723.75. The fol-
lowing was read from page 411 of minute book "D", under date of
March 26, 1891:

"On motion of Mr. Borel, seconded by Mr. King, it was resolved
"that this corporation will sell 10,000 shares (in bulk or in lots) of
"its increased capital stock for the purpose of paying on account of
"its current indebtedness other than bonds, and that the secretary
"is hereby directed to advertise for bids for the purchase thereof,
"but subject to the condition that all such bids shall be reported
"to this board and be subject to its approval or rejection; and that
"if approved (or as to such as may be approved) the president and
"secretary upon receiving payment are authorized to issue and sell
"such shares. Carried."

Page 419 of minute book "D", under date of April 25, 1891, 251
shows the following resolution:

"On motion of Mr. Beaver, seconded by Mr. Bigelow, it was
"resolved that all bids for the new issue of stock made today for the
"price of $93 per share and upwards be accepted and bids made at a
"lower price than $93 be rejected and that the secretary be author-
"ized to receive applications for stock which shall be considered at
"the next regular meeting. On motion adjourned."

On page 491, being minutes of May 7, 1891, appears the following
resolution:

"On motion of Mr. King, duly seconded, resolved that the stock
"remaining unsold of the issue of May 5, 1891, being 485 shares, be

"awarded 100 shares at $94.50 per share to Allen McLane and 385
"shares at $94.50 per share to J. C. & E. Coleman.'"

(Mr. Searls stated to the Master that he had made calculations
based on the reports in the minutes for the year 1891, and that said
reports show that under resolution of April 25th, page 419, that at
least $116,529 should have been realized, and from the resolution
read on page 421, of May 7th, $45,782 should have been realized,
making a total of approximately $162,000.)

DIRECT EXAMINATION BY MR. McCUTCHEN.

252
The amount received in fact, according to this statement, was
$931,723.75. I don't know that I checked this from Mr. Wenzel-
berger's testimony, in fact I don't know that his testimony or that
his exhibit shows that. His exhibit covers mostly construction accounts, and I do not remember now that he sets forth any place in
his exhibit the receipt from sale of stocks or bonds.

On page 20, Exhibit 104, under date November 1, 1893, appears
sold 10,000 shares and collected $656,848.29, which is the basis for my
receipts in that year.

Page 44 of minute book "E", of date November 1, 1893, shows
the following resolution:

"The bids for the purchase of stock 7,000 shares under adver-
"tisement of October 19, were opened. On motion, duly seconded, it
"was resolved that all bids of $93 and upwards be accepted and that
"the secretary be instructed to advertise in the daily papers for new
"bids for the 2025 shares not allotted under this resolution. Bids re-
"ceived in accordance with advertisement to be opened at the com-
"pany's office at 11 a. m. on Monday the 6th inst".

253
The total number of shares, as appearing under the advertisement of October 19, 4,975, and the average price figuring a little over
93 is correct, assuming this addition to be correct.

On page 46, minute book "E", November 6, 1893, appears:

"The bids for 2025 shares of stock advertised in November 1,
"were opened. On motion. duly seconded, it was resolved that S. P.
"Drexler and C. H. Kaufman be allotted 92½ shares of stock each
"at 95 1/12 per share and that all of the bids received which were over
"95⅛ amounting to 1840 shares be accepted". There were 2,025
shares sold at 95½ approximately. The previous price being slightly
in excess of 93 for 7,000 shares. This last will make about $193,000,
which, added to the amount previously received, would give a $200 dif-
ference. Mr. McCutchen just called my attention to the fact that
there is a statement on Exhibit 104 showing 10,000 shares sold, and
collected $656,848.29, which should read 7,000 shares if that amount
checks with the figures that you have. That price would bring up the
total.

SPRING VALLEY WATER CO. VS. CITY AND COUNTY OF SAN FRANCISCO

The figure $596,478 in the year 1895 is shown on page 20 of Exbibit 104 under date September 11, 1895, sold 6,000 shares and collected $596,477.70.

254

Page 168 of minute book "E", September 6, 1895:

"The president stated that the object of the meeting was to open "all bids made for the 6,000 shares of stock advertised for sale by the "company. The trustees awarded to the following bidders the 6,000 "shares of stock as being the best bids that was made for the same". There follows an award of the entire 6,000 at a figure slightly in excess of 99.

The allotment for 1896 I have shown as page 20, Exhibit 104, under date of September 8, 1896, 5,000 shares sold and collected $486,-600.12. On page 244, minute book "E", there was an allotment of 25 shares at 99 on June 1, 1896, and on page 280 an allotment of 4,975 shares at $97. There are some few shares here sold at $96. Taking these last two allotments, the price is a little in excess of $97, and against that figure Reynolds has, in Exhibit 104, the sum of $486,000.

255

On page 20, of Exhibit 104, under date September 8, 1897, appears sold 5,000 shares and collected $497,500. That checks exactly with the allotment made on page 352 of the minute book "E", of date September 2, 1897.

For the year 1898 I have, on page 20, Exhibit 104, sold 7,000 shares and collected $693,000. I find on page 397 of minute book "E" of February 10, 1898, that they sold the 7,000 shares at $99 per share, and the remaining item in 1906 was the assessment levied subsequent to the fire. The basis for that figure was 280,000 shares of capital stock at $3 per share.

The minutes of the Spring Valley Water Works, as they appear from minute book "B", page 366, of May 16, 1870, show that the bonds were being sold on that date at 1¾ and 1⅜ premium, and that those bonds which were dated April 1, 1870, term 10 years, bore interest at 9 per cent, payable semi-annually. They are known as third series bonds.

256

The reason for the computation of interest for six months at an assumed fair rate as shown in columns 10 and 11, was that the rate of interest used was the rate as shown in column 18, headed "Assumed fair cost of money without profit, Metcalf". In the computations that I made for the interest, I assumed that the money would be in operation about a half year; that is, the entire amount would be in use for that time, and so I took that rate as shown in column 18, and applied it to the actual contribution at a six months rate. It was not my idea that the money invested would not begin to earn any return until at least six months had expired, but I meant by that that the stockholders had contributed through the year a certain amount of money, as shown in columns 3 and 6, and that in addition to the actual contribution,

257

75

they also had contributed the loss in interest on that money during that year, which would correspond in a measure to interest during construction. I assumed that the money was in use from the moment that it was put into the system; the stockholders though were not getting any return on it supposedly until toward the end of the year, at which time they had to actually invest it—the money shown in column 3 and 6—and in addition to that, had lost the interest on that amount for a period of about six months. The loss of interest was due to the fact that they had paid it into the company and had not earned the interest they otherwise would earn if it had been in a bank, or in a corporation that was actually paying. It would correspond to inter-

258   est during construction.

The figures as to coupon interest and dividends, columns 14 and 15, I derived mostly from Mr. Wenzelberger's Exhibit 101, showing the coupon interest in the earlier years that had been charged to new construction. I do not remember the year, but there was a change made, and the coupon interest is shown in the profit and loss and income account. Those were taken from Wenzelberger's exhibit of the year 1904, and from the company's records since that time. My recollection is that I checked Mr. Wenzelberger's exhibit with Mr. Reynolds', and they both checked. My recollection also is that I checked them as to the dividend columns with the minutes, and found that it compared with the figures as shown by Mr. Reynolds and Wenzelberger.

Referring to column 18, the assumed fair cost of money was entirely computed by Mr. Metcalf, and constitutes his opinion, and is not based upon any opinion of mine.

I have not the details with me showing how I arrived at the figure 6.93 per cent as the actual cost of the money at the time of sale of the gold notes bearing 5½ per cent interest, as shown in the bond column, year 1913, but it was arrived at by taking the expense incurred in issuing the notes, and dividing the actual amount of money received

259   by the company. It may possibly be that there is an error there; I will look up those figures.

Objection made to the introduction of "Exhibit 12-bb" upon the ground that the evidence is immaterial, irrelevant and incompetent, and not the best evidence and mere hearsay. This objection is made subject to any future stipulation, if any such is made, between counsel as to the propriety of admitting the Reynold's exhibit.

259-260   Mr. McCutchen here stated that every effort had been made to locate Mr. Reynolds through every possible channel, and that no one seems to know his whereabouts. ''I take it that if Mr. Reynolds is actually alive, and is living out of this jurisdiction, we would be entitled to use his testimony. I would like to know from you whether you desire us to put that information in the form of an affidavit, and whether you will also require us to have a subpœna issued and placed in the hands of the Marshal and returned. I am satisfied that Mr. Reynolds cannot be found''.

Mr. Searls then stated that there was no intention on the part of counsel for the City to put counsel for the complainant to any unnecessary trouble in this matter, but that outside any question of law he felt that they should properly insist upon some information as to why Mr. Reynolds cannot be produced. Ruling was suspended.

The paper following the one which has been marked ''Exhibit 12-bb'' is an exhibit identical with ''12-bb'' up to and including column 18, with the addition of columns 19, 20, 21, 22, 23 and 24. I mean up to and including column 18, the remaining and additional columns 19 to 24 have the heading ''Including allowance for deficiency in return''. In detail, column 19 is intended to show the amount on the capital sum in column 13 at the ''Assumed fair cost of money without profit, Metcalf'', as shown in column 18. Column 20 gives the excess in the actual return over that which was assumed as a fair return in column 19. Column 20 gives the deficiency in the actual return as measured by the assumed fair amount of return in column 19. Column 22 gives cumulative deficiency, being the sum of the figures shown in columns 20 and 21. The capital sum cumulative is shown in column 13, plus cumulative deficiency in column 22. Column 24 shows the actual rate per cent return upon capital sum, and is the result of dividing column 16 by column 23. I have established from time to time a new principal and upon that have calculated interest at the assumed fair rate of return, and have in all cases charged the investment with the amount of dividend and coupon interest. The cumulative sum shown in column 23 for the year 1914, is $40,192,201.

Column 24 is intended to show the actual per cent returned upon the capital sum in column 23 divided into the actual return as shown in column 16, column 16 being the actual coupon interest paid the company plus the actual dividend paid by the company, and in this column is shown the rate of return which the aggregate of the coupon interest paid, and the dividends paid is upon the new principal established from time to time.

This table is based upon Mr. Metcalf's opinion as to fair return, and I would like to say in connection therewith that the same errors will appear in this new table as have been shown to appear in the previons exhibit, and it will have to be modified in accordance with the modifications on the sheet marked ''Exhibit 12-bb''. My preparation of this table was solely one of computation.

(Marked for identification ''Exhibit 12-cc'', and its admission objected to upon the same grounds as were made against exhibit marked for identification ''Exhibit 12-bb''. It was decided not to offer it in evidence until some understanding could be arrived at between counsel.)

DIRECT EXAMINATION BY MR. McCUTCHEN.

Mr. Metcalf in making up that column of "Assumed fair cost of money without profit", considered interest rates and also the interest of savings banks.

This table was gotten up by Mr. Metcalf almost entirely independently. I was with him part of the time, and furnished him some data, but his final analysis was made when I was not with him.

264

CROSS EXAMINATION BY MR. SEARLS.

265   Referring to "Exhibit 1"; the scale is shown in the lower lefthand corner, the horizontal scale is 1 inch equals 1 mile; the vertical scale is 1 inch equals 2600 feet. In a general way this model shows the ravines to the same extent as the topographical map "Exhibit No. 2", except for the fact that where the contours are close together, the material used in that model is welded together, so that you do not see all the details as clearly as you would in the contour map shown on "Exhibit 2". The water shed area of Lake Merced is not shown on this exhibit. The water that supplies Lake Merced comes from the water shed surrounding the lake, and that water shed area is shown on "Exhibit 12-h" as 7.61 square miles. The water for Lake Merced comes from springs in the lake itself, but the springs are supplied from the water that falls on the watershed.

A large part of the watershed has considerable sand on the surface, and a strata of hardpan underneath that surface of sand. I do not remember now what other geological formations are there. I think the drainage system built around Lake Merced goes down to hardpan in the Colma Gulch, but as to the rest of the drainage system, I think it simply intercepts surface flow.

266   The area tributary to the lake is 7.61 square miles, and it is partly occupied in the southern end of San Francisco County, and the northerly end of San Mateo County by people in the towns known as Ocean View, Daly City, and smaller places further down, for instance Vista Grande. The portion which is occupied in both counties lies east of the Junipero Serra Boulevard.

There is a ravine which goes down to the ocean north of the Lake Merced Reservoir, and which carries the drainage from the territory north of Sloat Boulevard, but as to the area that the company owns, there are no buildings thereon to any extent. There are gardeners there who raise potatoes and cabbages and vegetables of that kind, but I do not know what area is actually leased to these parties for agri-

267   cultural purposes. Mr. Roeding, Superintendent of Agriculture, could give that information.

The water gets into the lake through percolation into these springs. This is possible as the hardpan may be broken. I do not know just what the geological formation is. Underneath that hardpan there may

SPRING VALLEY WATER CO. VS. CITY AND COUNTY OF SAN FRANCISCO

be still other porous materials through which the water would flow. I think all that underground percolation would come from all the drainage area both inside and outside of the company's holdings, and I think it could come from Ocean View and the heights there above Ingleside. I do not remember of any surface streams running into the lake, as it has been the policy of the company to divert the surface water outside of the property through the drainage works into the Pacific Ocean, in order to prevent polution of the water of Lake Merced. I do not know how far vertically the filtration of such surface water, that falls on the watershed goes before it reaches this hardpan, except from the hearsay evidence of persons who have made excavations there. I believe the hardpan in places is from 15 to 25 and 30 feet below the surface of the ground.

DIRECT EXAMINATION BY MR. MCCUTCHEN.   268

I think it is not of uniform depth.

CROSS EXAMINATION BY MR. SEARLS.

Apparently that depth is sufficient to properly filter the surface drainage, as is also the character of the soil through which the water would percolate, as that water is good potable water, and we use it a good deal.

Certain corrections were suggested by counsel, on page 15, tenth   269
line from the bottom, change "place" to "pipe"; page 18 on first line next to last word on that line, change "Mission" to "Bay"; on page 24, sixth line, change "San Antonio" to Arroyo Honda"; on page 24, sixth line from bottom, change the figures "168" to "165"; on page 36, fifth line from the top of the page, change "San Antonio" to "Arroyo Valle"; page 77, eleventh line from the bottom, after the word "Contents", insert "for each foot"; page 101, about the middle of the page, in a question by Mr. Olney, change "Steinhart" to "Sharon".

CROSS EXAMINATION BY MR. STEINHART.

Q. Mr. Sharon, on page 221, I asked you the question, "That   270
"is the only knowledge you have of that item?
"A. That and the statement shown".
The statement shown you was the Reynolds' statement, was it not?
A. I think it had reference also to the statement shown in the minutes, as I recall it.
Q. But I mean outside of that, the only other statement was the Reynolds' statement? A. Yes.
Q. Now, Mr. Sharon, I questioned you also as to the assessments being assessments as the same appear on page 222 of the record, being

assessments Nos. 1, 2, 3, 4, 5, 6, 7, 8, 9, 10 and so forth. I, myself, made the statement, I notice, and you did not answer on the record, that all that the minutes show was a levy of assessment of $5 or $15, or whatever the amount might be per share, and the total you gave was the total taken from Reynolds' estimate. That is correct, is it not?

271   (Mr. McCutchen here stated to Mr. Steinhart what had taken place at the morning session regarding the presentation with reference to Mr. Reynolds, with the purpose in view that his suggestion might possibly postpone any further examination of Mr. Sharon on this subject. He also asked that Mr. Steinhart advise as to what he desired counsel for the Spring Valley Water Co. to do, that is to say, whether counsel for the City wished the Water Co. to make a formal showing of these facts, or if they would accept that showing as sufficient. He asked the following question: "Do you desire us to put in the form of an affidavit the facts which I have stated to the Court, and do you desire us to have a subpœna issued and placed in the hands of the Marshal"? Counsel for the City would give an absolutely definite answer tomorrow morning.)

Referring to "Exhibit 2"; the Overacker Tract is shown about three-quarters of the distance between Niles and Centerville, and is shown on map 19 and known as parcels A 269 and B 269 on Exhibit 8.

272   The Beard Tract is shown on Exhibit 2 in pink west of the Town of Niles, and on Exhibit 8, page 19, comprises the following parcels: I, J, K, L, M, 268. This tract is at present being subdivided and sold.

The Stone Tract is the large tract colored pink just west of the Town of Sunol. It is shown on Exhibit 8, page 12, as H, 239.

The Poorman property is west of the Beard property on Exhibit 2, near the east shore of the Bay of San Francisco, in Alameda County, and is shown on map 19 as parcel 259. It is the red tract over the word "Potrero".

The West Union property are parcels of long strips running from the creek at the south end of upper Crystal Springs Reservoir, and from there practically up to the top of the ridge between the Crystal Springs Reservoir and the Pacific Ocean.

Questioned by the Master.

They are west of the Crystal Springs.

CROSS EXAMINATION BY MR. STEINHART.

Certain portions of them are outside of the Crystal Springs watershed.

DIRECT EXAMINATION BY MR. McCUTCHEN.

They are southwest of Crystal Springs, and are shown on map 5 as part of parcel 194, 195, 205, 211, 210 and part of 208, on Exhibit 8.

SPRING VALLEY WATER CO. VS. CITY AND COUNTY OF SAN FRANCISCO

The Searsville property is in San Mateo County; it surrounds the Searsville Lake, and is near the Town of Woodside.

(Discussion between counsel as to whether that property is referred to in any of the bills of complaint.)

Searsville properties are all shown on map 6 in Exhibit 8.

The Ravenswood property is in San Mateo County, on the west shore of the Bay of San Francisco, and is about where the submarine pipes cross the Bay of San Francisco. The Ravenswood lands are in San Mateo County only, and north of San Francisquito Creek. The properties around the south edge of the bay in Santa Clara County are known as the Alviso Lands, and are contiguous with the Ravenswood property. Taken together they constitute the portion around the southerly end of San Francisco Bay, as shown on Exhibit 2. The Ravenswood lands are shown on map 7, Exhibit 8, as parcels 157, 154, 201, 156, 213 and 155. The Alviso lands are shown on maps 21 and   274
22 in Exhibit 8. No waters have been taken from the Searsville, Alviso, or Ravenswood lands in supplying San Francisco.

The Nusbaumer Tract is shown in pink between the Towns of Sunol and Pleasanton, and lies west of the Pleasanton 30-inch pipe line as shown on Exhibit 2. It is shown in Exhibit 8, map 12, as parcel 290.

The Polhemus Tract is shown a little south of San Mateo Creek, and east of the ridge forming the watershed line in the Crystal Springs Reservoir, Crystal Springs drainage area. It is to the east of this Crystal Springs drainage area, and is shown on Exhibit 8, map 8, as parcel 204.

The Chinese Cemetery lots are not shown on Exhibit 2, but they are a little north of the Town of Baden, and opposite Holy Cross Cemetery. These lots were formerly on the line of the Pilarcitos pipe line. They are shown on map 8 in Exhibit 8, as parcels 135, 136, 137.

The Pescadero lands are shown at the southwesterly corner of   275
Exhibit 2; there are two tracts, one of 640 acres, and the other of 40 acres. They have not been used in distributing and supplying water to San Francisco. They appear on map 9 of Exhibit 8, as parcels 75, 76 and 190.

Stevens Creek is shown down near the lower margin of Exhibit 2, a little southwest of the City of San Jose. The Stevens Creek property is shown on map 20 in Exhibit 8, as parcel 326.

The Coyote properties are not shown on Exhibit 2. They are in the drainage area of the Coyote River, and are located a few miles east of the Town of Gilroy. They are shown on Exhibit 8, page 20, by parcels B 348 and A 348. It takes up practically the entire half of that page, excepting parcels 342 and 326.

The Tequesquito properties are not shown in Exhibit 2. They are located on the Pajaro River south of the Town of Gilroy, between Santa Clara and San Benito Counties, and are shown on map 20, parcel 342, Exhibit 8.

276   The San Francisquito properties, as shown on Exhibit 2, are those shown in yellow, between the Searsville Lake and the Bay of San Francisco; they are riparian rights, but have not at any time been used in supplying water to San Francisco. The yellow boundaries mark the boundaries of the separate parcels of land from which the company obtained riparian rights. The San Francisquito riparian rights and properties are marked on page 62 of Exhibit 8.

The San Gregorio properties on Exhibit 2 are indicated in yellow. They are riparian lands, and are just north of the Pescadero properties in the southwest corner of this Exhibit 2. They are shown on

277   map 61 of Exhibit 8. These lands have not been used, nor these rights in the supply of water to San Francisco.

The Locks Creek property is shown on Exhibit 2, southwest, and over the ridge from the Crystal Springs Reservoir; the properties are indicated in pink, northeast of Half Moon Bay, and are not used in supplying water to the City of San Francisco. Shown on Exhibit 8, map 3, as parcels 33, 128, 29, 60 and a small part of parcel 5.2, and 138. I cannot give the amount of property owned by the Spring Valley Water Co. in the drainage area marked out as the Arroyo Valle drainage area, as I have not the acreage with me, but I think it is in the neighborhood of 4200 acres.

The acreages marked in Exhibit 12-d is intended to give the square miles in the watershed.

DIRECT EXAMINATION BY MR. McCUTCHEN.

I said that I did not have the acreage in the Arroyo Valle watershed owned by the company, but that I think it is about 4200 acres. I have no record here that will enable me to state that acreage.

I have not any figures here from which I could tell the areas in the upper Alameda drainage area, Calaveras drainage area, San Antonio drainage area and the Livermore drainage area. I can get those

278   figures. (Question reserved until tomorrow.)

The little dots running along the Calaveras Creek on Exhibit 12-d are intended to show approximately the location of the Sunol filter beds and the gravel area.

The same type of dotting at the Laguna Creek opposite Pleasanton pump, is intended to show the gravel beds at the lower end of the Livermore Valley, from which the company is drawing a supply now. The Livermore drainage is supplied from the Mocho, which comes in from the southeast, and is indicated here on exhibit 2 as the north-easterly strip coming down and pointing toward the town of Livermore.

The Tasajero comes into the Livermore drainage about due north of the town of Pleasanton.

The Positas starts in the easterly end of the watershed, and comes in north of the town of Livermore; it follows along the southerly foothills of the ridge lying north of the town of Livermore and the town of Pleasanton, and finally gets into the Laguna Creek. 279

The Arroyo Valle starts in the south-easterly corner of exhibit 2, and follows a northwesterly direction through the property here shown, and to the reservoir here indicated as the Arroyo Valle Reservoir. Then it leaves the property of the Spring Valley Water Co. and follows down the Arroyo Valle Creek; it finally emerges from the mountains at the northerly slope of the ridge, just south of the town of Livermore, and follows along the base of the foothills south and west of Livermore, and empties into the Arroyo Laguna near the town of Pleasanton. Formerly the waters from Livermore were brought down through the Laguna Creek to the neighborhood' of Sunol; that is the natural flow was down there. I don't know that it has stopped yet; it still goes on. It was taken into the pipe line in 1909, when the Pleasanton 30-inch pipe line shown on exhibit 2 was constructed, and since that time, the waters from Livermore 280 are brought down to Sunol by that 30-inch pipe line. The junction point between the Laguna Creek and the Alameda Creek as shown here, is near the Sunol water temple. On exhibit 9, map F, 268, it is just a little west of the Sunol water temple, and is marked "Laguna Creek".

DIRECT EXAMINATION BY MR. McCUTCHEN.

The two creeks are distinctly marked, the Laguna Creek in one case, and the Calaveras, or Alameda, or whatever the name is, in the other.

CROSS EXAMINATION BY MR. STEINHART.

The confluence of the Laguna Creek and the Alameda Creek is west of the temple.

The Hadsell ditch is not shown on exhibit 2. It was constructed in about the year 1901, and was used in diverting the flow of Laguna Creek at about the station Bonita, on the Western Pacific, through an open ditch and short tunnel, so that the water from Laguna Creek would enter the Sunol filter beds at the easterly end. It was used up to the time that the Pleasanton 30-inch pipe line was laid in 1909, but it is not used at the present time. Only a portion of it was used as an excavation in which to lay the 30-inch pipe. The 281 Bonita Station referred to is north of the town of Sunol, between Sunol and Pleasanton.

The filter galleries at Sunol are not laid in clay, but the conduit that carries the water from the water temple down to the Sunol dam, and which is a concrete conduit, is in clay. It was not intended for filtration. There are no galleries along the point where the clay is. The beginning of the clay is not shown on this exhibit. That is a conduit carrying the waters from the filter galleries down to the Sunol dam.

DIRECT EXAMINATION BY MR. McCUTCHEN.

When I say they are one structure, I mean one runs into the other; they join together, and that is the only sense in which they are one structure.

CROSS EXAMINATION BY MR. STEINHART.

282 . I mean by that, that where the gallery is pierced by pipes, it serves as a filter gallery, and where it is not pierced by pipes it serves as a conduit.

San Mateo Creek, as shown on exhibit 2, runs from the western arm of the Crystal Springs Reservoir, which is in San Mateo Creek, and continues in a north-westerly direction right up to the summit line on the north-westerly corner of the properties owned by the Spring Valley Water Co. San Mateo Creek runs into the Crystal Springs Lake, and its initial point is known as Sweeney Ridge, and it runs along in a canyon between Sawyer Ridge, on the east, and Fifield Ridge and Cahill Ridge on the west.

The Pilarcitos Creek is southwest of the San Mateo Creek, and lies between the Fifield and the Cahill Ridge, and Montara mountains.

283 The dotted lines on the Peninsula system, exhibit 12-d, ought to be the same, as the dotted lines in my segregation on exhibit 2. They are on a little smaller scale, and may not show all the kinks and curves that are shown on a larger scale map. There is a further sub-division here. In the upper San Mateo Creek, there is an area shown as Davis Tunnel, 1 square mile; that means that 1 square mile of the upper San Mateo Creek is diverted through the Davis Tunnel into San Andres Reservoir, and is not allowed to run down into Crystal Springs Reservoir.

Refer to exhibit 12-h: The top of the dam at Calaveras is taken at 800 feet above high tide, and the flow line is shown as 795 feet. This corresponds with my column, "Overflow in bottom of reservoir", and in connection with the building of these reservoirs or
284 dams, and in the operation of the present dams, there is a certain amount of leeway allowed between the top of the dam and the overflow, to take care of freshets that come along in the Winter season. As the Winter season advances, and the rains become less, it is possible to bulk-head up the overflow a few feet, and increase the elevation of the reservoirs, so that the water may be carried at a few feet higher than the actual overflow as shown. We do that at

Crystal Springs. There might be slight discrepancies of a foot or two, but they are immaterial in that respect.

To explain more fully the difference that exists between the totals in the column "Mean Run-off" and "Present Development"; in the actual operation, of the Pilarcitos, San Andres and Crystal Springs Reservoirs, we find that from time to time there is a slight waste over the dam at Crystal Springs, and also over the dam at San Andres, and going down into Crystal Springs Reservoir, and then from Crystal Springs Reservoir wasted into San Mateo Creek, and thence into San Francisco Bay; so that the actual run-off is slightly in excess of that which is taken to the City of San Francisco. In the case of the Crystal Springs, the Crystal Springs Reservoir is shown as having a mean run-off of approximately 10.1 million gallons daily, and out of that 10.1 million gallons daily there is the supply that is taken along the Crystal Springs pipe line and delivered to the San Mateo water works and other places along the line.

The column, "Mean Run-off, million gallons, approximate", means mean run-off million gallons daily, approximate, as impounded and wasted over the reservoir. The mean run-off, million gallons, approximate, as figured by me, is not equivalent in amount to the total rainfall upon the entire drainage area contributing to that reservoir, because the total rainfall that comes over that drainage area does not run down into the reservoir. Some of the water that falls in the form of rain upon the drainage area enters the ground and supplies plant life, and is afterwards evaporated from the surface of the soil; a certain part of it runs into the reservoir and is evaporated from the surface thereof, so that the figures that we show there of the total Peninsula system, "Mean approximate run-off 19.6 million gallons" is the net run-off that we are able to catch, and the waste slightly, in certain big years. It is due in the Peninsula to the fact that we have not drawn the actual 18½ million gallons every day. There is a fluctuation. There was not any need for it. One year we may draw 20 million gallons a day from the reservoirs, and the next year we may draw only 16 million gallons, so that if two or three such years occur, we would be in the position of accumulating some storage in the reservoir that would not be there if we were drawing the average amount of 18 million gallons daily from it. It is impossible to regulate the system so that the reservoir is empty, necessarily, at the time the flows come. That comes in the practical operation of the system, and is not due to any fault in the construction of that system. That is a very completely developed drainage system; I think that the Peninsula is one of the most completely developed drainage systems in the world.

Refer to "Exhibit 12-j": Under heading "Peninsula System", appears "same with pumping at Belmont through 36 and 54-inch to

285

285½

286

85

Millbrae, and 44-inch to city, 26 million gallons daily''. That means that the Crystal Springs pipe line which has a capacity on full reservoir without pumping, as shown in the line above the one you just read, of 22 million gallons a day, has a capacity from the Millbrae pumping station into the University Mound of 26 million gallons when the Belmont pumps are running.

Refer to "Exhibit 12-f": The Brightside weirs are on the Sunol aqueduct, and are also below the point where the waters from Sunol and Livermore have entered the Sunol aqueduct, and the measurement at that point also includes the measurement of water from Livermore as well as from Sunol.

Refer to "Exhibit 12-h": The method used to measure rainfall was the common method of measuring the water caught in a graduated glass.

287   Refer to "Exhibit 12-e": The Isohyetose lines there, showing 24 to 26 inches, are the lines between station 107 and 116. In sketching out those lines I think in a general way all the station rainfalls were used. It was matter of judgment. We did not exclude anything in the way of rainfall records, in the way of making up those lines; we used everything we could get. We considered the topographical features as well in connection with the rainfall station, and also considered that the rainfall on one side of the ridge would necessarily be different than the rainfall on the other side of the ridge, and we tried to make allowance for that, in drawing the Isohyetose lines. To what extent allowance was made, I could not say, except to get those lines to follow generally the topographical features with reference to the crest of the mountains; there may be an error due to wind gaps on valleys, and things of that sort. Those are not intended to be very accurate; matters of that kind are not subject to any great precision, but they are simply a general indication of our judgment from the study of the rainfall as shown at the various stations located thereabouts, as to what the rainfall was.

288   Refer to "Exhibit 12-u": The figures at the bottom, "Water draft from Alameda system", include the water drawn and distributed to suburban consumers of the Spring Valley Water Co.

Refer to "Exhibit 12-bb": For the year 1903 there is shown "Face of bonds $1,000,000, actual amount received $941,000". That amount of $941,000, or the difference between $941,000 and $1,000,-000 includes discounts, commissions, and expenses, and the item of $500,472.26 for the year 1904 includes discounts, commissions and expenses. The same with the item for 1905, and the same with the item for 1906. In the item for 1906 there was a considerable expense involved in redeeming the first mortgage bonds by the present general mortgage bonds, so that the $357,000 as shown in column 3, was not actually the receipts from $884,000 worth of bonds. The receipts from the $884,000 worth of bonds were something less than

$884,000; in addition to them there were certain other expense incurred in redeeming the first mortgage bonds dated September 1, 1876, and redeemed in 1906 by the present general mortgage bonds; the net amount there, $357,000 is what was actually received by the company. The difference between $884,000 and $357,098 includes the expenses, commissions and amounts incurred in redeeming the first, second and third mortgage bonds, and also the discounts or expenses incurred in selling that year the $884,000 worth of bonds. Throughout this entire column 3, wherever I find discounts, or commissions, or expenses incurred in connection with a bond issue, I deducted that amount in getting at the actual amount received. The 13th item, for the year 1913, gold notes $1,000,000, and in the third column, $971,425, includes in the difference between those two sums the discounts, commissions and expenses.

In regard to column 15, in the year 1867, I remember reading from page 263, minute book "B" of the Spring Valley Water Works.

My recollection is (page 212 of J. J. Sharon's testimony) that there was a bill presented by Simpkins to the Spring Valley Water Works, and that such a bill is in the minutes, but I have not looked at it since. I will look that up.

Concerning my testimony regarding water measurements, I have a letter with me dated November 5, 1914, signed by Mr. Lawrence, and by Mr. Bartell, which is addressed to Mr. S. P. Eastman, Manager of the Spring Valley Water Co. It reads as follows:

"Dear Sir:—

"Regarding the hydrography of the Alameda Creek System for "the coming winter Mr. Bartel and myself have gone over the "various stations used last year, and recommend that the station "be changed for the reasons stated as follows:

"Mocho The present station is located at a bridge. It has been "found that the cross section of this bridge has changed some five "feet during the high waters, consequently, our gauge height, ex- "cept by constant gauging at the rise and fall of flood waters would "be of very little value and it is recommended that this station be "changed to a mile and a half up stream where there is a compara- "tively long, straight channel with evidence of very little change in "the creek bottom which would naturally result in a more reliable "cross section. The cost of this station installed would be $200.00.

"Arroyo Valle The present station is located at what is known "as the Cresta Blanca bridge. It has been found that the cross sec- "tion of this changes with every high water. The conditions are "further complicated by the fact that the bridge is at an angle with "the stream, consequently, it would be necessary to do constant "gauging to obtain any result as our gauge height would be of little

"value. We recommend that this station be located about one quar-
"ter of a mile down stream where there are two available locations.
"To build a gauging station at either one of these points it will be
"necessary to obtain permission from the Cresta Blanca people (Wet-
"more Bowen Co.) and L. C. Cross. The cost of installing this sta-
"tion would be about $450.00.

"Laguna Creek at Road 2000 This is a very good place to
"make stream measurements but the bridge is not at right angles

291 "with the stream, consequently, it will be necessary to install a new
"bridge somewhat to the north in order to obtain satisfactory re-
"sults. The cost of changing the station will be about $150.00.

"San Antonio This station is at a good location but there are
"two trees to be removed in order to obtain satisfactory results, also
"a bridge installed. This cost would be about $150.00.

"Upper Alameda Creek Mr. Espy went over this with Mr.
"Bartel and it was agreed to locate this gauging station about one
"mile up stream where there is a satisfactory location. The present
"station is in a narrow rocky gorge and interfered with by large
"boulders and trees. The cost of this installation will be about
"$250.00.

"Calaveras Creek It was agreed by Mr. Espy and Mr. Bartel
"to locate this station below the concrete culvert of the dam a suffi-
"cient distance so that the velocity from the culvert will not affect
"it. The cost of the installation of this station will be about $350.00.

"The locations here recommended are believed to be the best
"available, and the equipment necessary for the results sought.

"By making these installations it is believed that very satisfac-
"tory results will be obtained. It is believed that this expenditure
"will result in a very material saving of labor both in field and
"office and will give records not only of value during the present
"year but will permit of considerably less cost for future main-
"tenance which was not possible with the locations as previously.

"Very truly yours,
"W. B. LAWRENCE,
"M. J. BARTEL."

292 I believe those changes were made.

SIXTH HEARING.   JULY 20, 1915.

Witnesses JOHN JOSEPH SHARON and A. S. BALDWIN.

294 Witness JOHN JOSEPH SHARON.

DIRECT EXAMINATION BY MR. OLNEY.

There was made under my supervision the computation of the
acreages of the various parts of the Lake Merced tract, into which
Mr. Baldwin has divided the property for the purpose of valuation,
and the results of these computations were correct and were fur-

nished to Mr. Baldwin. The watersheds of Pilarcitos, San Andres and Crystal Springs, were divided into sub-divisions for the purposes of valuation, according to the tracts in which they were originally purchased, and some of them were partly under water and partly watershed lands.

Computation was also made under my supervision of the acreages of these particular sub-divisions which were under water and which were in the watershed. These I also furnished to Mr. Baldwin, and the acreages so given him were correct.

295

Witness A. S. BALDWIN.

Baldwin

DIRECT EXAMINATION BY MR. OLNEY.

Am a real estate agent in San Francisco, and have been about thirty years. I am president of the corporation of Baldwin & Howell, and have been associated in business with several other gentlemen, Mr. R. R. Hammond and Mr. McAfee. I was first with the firm of McAfee Bros., being a partner of the firm for seven or eight years, and following that the firm was changed to McAfee, Baldwin & Hammond in 1891 or 92, and continued under that name for about two or three years; in 1898 I took in Mr. Howell, and the firm has been Baldwin & Howell ever since 1897 or 1898.

296

I have had experience in dealing in real estate for thirty years in the City and County of San Francisco, and my dealings covered any section of the city wherever we could do business; in fact practically every portion of it. I have been employed by the Spring Valley Water Co. to make a valuation of its properties in San Francisco, and have made such a valuation of the properties, exclusive of the Lake Merced tract. In making that valuation I have ignored the presence of any structures in the way of tanks, buildings or reservoirs, or any improvements of that character. I have not considered in my valuation any improvements on the properties whatever. In the case of a reservoir I assumed in making the value that attaches to any property in which there is a reservoir, that the reservoir was not there, and that the land was substantially on the level of the grade surrounding the reservoir, or as near as it has been possible to figure the property in its natural condition.

297

I was endeavoring to determine simply the fair market value as of December 31, 1913, and these valuations were made about a year ago, and have been modified or changed slightly within the last month. This appraisement was a contemporaneous appraisement as of the date December 31, 1913. With regard to the properties of the company in San Francisco, exclusive of the Lake Merced lands, I compared my valuation with persons employed in behalf of the City. In many instances we were almost identically the same, in

298

298-299 others we differed slightly, but the valuations which are now on the various properties, or which I have submitted, or will submit, are the same, so I understand, as those which have been made by the City appraisers. (It was here suggested by the Master that if the exhibit were in such shape as would permit of its being offered in bulk, that it could be so admitted and thus save the recital of each particular tract; that it would thus save the record and also the time of reading it over. Counsel for the City could then specify the properties that should be excluded).

A list of the properties in San Francisco, with the valuation, excluding the Lake Merced lands, that have been put upon them by Mr. Baldwin was then offered in evidence as "Plaintiff's Exhibit 13".

Objected to upon the ground that it was immaterial, irrelevant and incompetent, and that certain of the items are not used and useful. It was received and marked as "Plaintiff's Exhibit 13" with the reservation that counsel for the City objects to certain of the items as being not used and useful.

DIRECT EXAMINATION BY MR. OLNEY.

300
301
302
The total of that list is $1,166,685.10, and the parcels thereon are numbered according to the map.

Here discussion ensued between the Master and counsel as to the correctness of the record on the proposition that the properties are in use and useful.

Counsel for the City stated his reason for considering it irrelevant and immaterial, in that the question involves an investigation, in so far as the properties are concerned, as to whether or not the property is used or useful, and the condemnation proceedings, in so far as they omitted property would show that at least in the opinion of the City, that property was not used and useful, but the inclusion of property in the condemnation suit is not evidence as to its being used and useful. The City may have taken it for entirely different reasons, or for entirely future use.

Counsel for Plaintiff stated that he would offer the complaint in the condemnation suit as evidence, and have further proof, also, in regard to the character of these properties. Suggested by the Master that Mr. Sharon or any qualified witness testify as to what was the fact, and that in regard to the question whether a particular piece of property is used and useful, after such evidence of a prima facie character was introduced, it would be for the City to deduce the facts to support their opinion that it was not used or useful.

303
DIRECT EXAMINATION BY MR. OLNEY.
I am acquainted with the Lake Merced properties of the Spring Valley Water Co., and have handled a good deal of property in that particular neighborhood. In buying—one particular instance was the Sutro tract. A syndicate was organized which purchased that

over three years ago, and sold it off to other parties who are now sub-dividing it. That involved in round numbers in the original purchase $1,500,000 and subsequent sales amounting to probably $1,000,000 more. I think I am acquainted with the value of land in that locality, and I have made as careful an appraisement of the Lake Merced lands of the Spring Valley Water Co. as I know how.

I made three sales out of the Sutro tract; one tract 82 acres, which is now Forest Hill, another of about 173 acres, which includes St. Francis Wood and the proposed addition, and another of 142 or 143 acres taking in what is known as Claremont Court, El Portal, and I think Hawkins' Sub-Division, and Forest Hill Annex.

304

A portion of the Sutro tract is just across the way from the Lake Merced property, but the Sutro tract is in many portions steep and rugged; there is proportionately, I think, more waste land on the Sutro property than there is on the Lake Merced tract. It lies on the western slope of hills there looking toward the Lake Merced property, and a part of it is immediately across the Junipero Serra Boulevard from the Lake Merced lands.

We sold a 15 acre tract in that immediate neighborhood in 1912, known as the German General Benevolent Society tract, which fronts on Junipero Serra Boulevard adjoining St. Francis Wood. This is across the way from the north-easterly corner of the Lake Merced tract.

We have not sold any other acreage property there. We had 305 cooperated with the Mason McDuffie Co. in the handling of St. Francis Wood, but only as associated sales agent. We have been concerned with retail sales in that neighborhood only in the St. Francis Wood tract. I am acquainted with purchases and sales in that neighborhood which I have from information from time to time received from people who are handling those tracts.

Park Side District is immediately opposite the Lake Merced tract, facing on the Sloat Boulevard, and extends from there northerly; the Ingleside Terraces are on the Junipero Serra Boulevard, opposite the Lake Merced property.

I have been over the Lake Merced lands numerous times and examined it carefully for the purpose of determining what the value of it is, but I did not take into consideration the fact that the land has a value for water producing property. I valued them just as I would any other property. My valuations are upon the basis of 306 what the entire tract would sell for wholesale, in its entirety, and for the purpose of reaching a total value I graded it into various parcels, not with particular reference to the quality of the land, but for determining the value with reference especially to portions of the property which had the highest valuation and the lowest value. I started at one point in the property that I think is the most valuable and then worked from that. I have those various parcels into which I so sub-divided the property shown on the map.

Offered in evidence as "Plaintiff's Exhibit 14".

Objected to upon the ground that it was immaterial, irrelevant and incompetent; the test is the value of the land as a whole, and it is immaterial as to what these sub-divisions are worth. Objection overruled and map marked "Plaintiff's Exhibit 14".

307
308-309

Here is presented the tabulation of valuations on the San Francisco lands, which will be marked "Plaintiff's Exhibit 13".

310

I have numbered these various parcels (speaking of Lake Merced) into which I have sub-divided the lands consecutively 1, 2 and 3, and have lettered some of them as well. Objected to upon the ground that it is irrelevant, immaterial and incompetent. Objection is overruled.

Q. Now, what was the value, market value, of the Lake Merced lands of the company December 31, 1913, exclusive of the lakes?

A. $6,718,250, or an average of $2,691.68 an acre.

Q. Now, how do you get at that value, Mr. Baldwin, that figure?

A. I get at it by—

Objected to as immaterial, irrelevant and incompetent and cross examination of the Plaintiff's own witness, and that it comes within the case of Neal vs. San Diego, 88 California. Objection overruled.

The market value of the Lake Merced lands of the Spring Valley Water Co. December 31, 1913, exclusive of the lakes is $6,718,250, or

311

an average of $2,691.68 an acre. That value I got at by arranging the property in various tracts, according to the map, and then graded it by valuation in what I conceived to be the best and most conservative method. Also as regards the topography of the tract; I have a description of each one of these tracts with regard to topography.

Counsel for the City: It may be stipulated that our objection goes to this entire line of testimony.

The Master: Yes.

Tract No. 1, situated at the intersection of Sloat and Junipero Serra Boulevard immediately west of St. Francis Wood, and Balboa Terrace, all level land, 26 acres, $6,000 an acre, $156,000.

Tract No. 2, immediately west of tract 1, fronting on Sloat Boulevard, including area covered by Central Pumping Station, also including home place or nursery tract, which is situated in the extreme westerly portion of tract 2. All of this tract is practically

312

level. The 25 or 30 acres included in the home place, by reason of the fine growth of trees, have in my opinion a somewhat greater value per acre than the balance of the tract. 235 acres at $5,000 per acre, $1,175,000.

Tract No. 3 at the intersection of the Great Highway and Sloat Boulevard. About seven acres is situated on the northerly line of Sloat Boulevard. The balance, about 100 acres, is broken and uneven and is in parts low and covered to some extent with the seepage from the lakes. The property has great potential value because it is the only property in San Francisco privately owned having a frontage on the Pacific Ocean with the exception of a small area owned by the Sutro estate at Lands End. It is especially adaptable for use as an out-of-doors resort, and it is more than likely that with the growth and development of the city the tract will be utilized at some time in the near future for this purpose. 107 acres at $4,500, $481,500.

The land immediately to the north, and across Sloat Boulevard, indicated by the same coloring as the tract marked 3, is included in my acreage valuation. There is about seven acres of that and about 100 in the other, making about 107 acres.

I will make a revaluation which will eliminate this 7 acres which lies north of the Sloat Boulevard, at $5,000 an acre that property is worth more per acre than this, and is about the same value as the property on the opposite side of Sloat Boulevard. I will eliminate on account of the 7 acres $35,000 in valuation, making my net valu-   313 ation $481,500 less $35,000.

DIRECT EXAMINATION BY MR. McCUTCHEN.

My net valuation is $446,500. Tract No. 4, fronting on Junipero Serra Boulevard, opposite Ingleside Terrace. About 100 acres of this tract is level, and the balance of about 90 acres consists of two swales or depressions, a large portion of which, however, could be utilized by methods of terracing for residential purposes. These portions of the swales or depressions which were not so used could be made particularly attractive as parking strips, which would add to the value of the adjacent lands enough to offset the loss of acreage so used. 100 acres at $5,000 per acre, $500,000, and 90 acres at $3,000, $270,000.

The 100 acres is the level portion of the tract and is near the center, and the 90 acres, I think, is about 60 acres in the northerly part, and about 30 acres in the southerly part. They are in a hollow which runs up into the level land.

Tract No. 5; this is a very fine tract fronting on Junipero Serra Boulevard, immediately south of tract 4. Total area about 471 acres. Of this area about 177 acres constitutes the plateau or peninsula   314 between the northerly and southerly lake. With the exception of 8 or 10 acres the entire tract is level. The 8 or 10 acres is indicated in the south-westerly corner. There is quite a growth of trees, and a slight depression there. The valuation of the 471 acres is $4,000 per acre, or $1,884,000.

Tract No. 6, situated on the westerly side of the Junipero Serra Boulevard, immediately north of the boundary line between the City of San Francisco and the County of San Mateo, practically all level land. 143 acres at $3,000 an acre, $429,000.

Tract No. 7, on the westerly line of Junipero Serra Boulevard, immediately south of the county line. This tract contains several large swales or depressions, which, however, are not by any means waste land. The total area in these depressions is about 114 acres. The northerly depression being about 60 acres, and the southerly one 64. The balance of the tract containing 294 acres is practically level. The Ocean Shore Railroad extends through the easterly and southerly portions of this property. 294 acres at $2,000, $588,000, 114 acres at $1,000 per acre, $114,000.

Tract No. 8, this tract constitutes all of the balance of the land owned by the Spring Valley Water Co. in the County of San Mateo within the limits of the Merced Ranch, except about 48 acres in and around the settling pond or basin. With the exception of about 55 acres near the center of the tract which contains some steep slopes and is somewhat broken, and with the exception of about 43 acres of precipitous lands, constituting the cliffs which front on the Pacific Ocean, the entire tract is either level or the slopes are moderate and give, if anything, a somewhat added value to the property. The Ocean Shore

315 Railroad extends through the southerly portion of this tract. 271 acres at $1,500 an acre, $406,500; 98 acres at $500 an acre, $49,000.

Tract No. 9; situated on the westerly slope of the southern lake immediately north of Tract 8, sloping from the 50 to the 150 foot contour, a particularly well sheltered portion of the property. 65 acres at $1,750 per acre, $113,750.

Tract No. 10; fronting on the Pacific Ocean, and constituting all of the land between the Pacific Ocean and the 50 foot contour above the southerly lake. Somewhat broken in character, but commanding panoramic view in all directions; 206 acres at $1,250 an acre, $257,500. Strip along the easterly side of Junipero Serra Boulevard, 20 feet wide, the value of which is largely strategic, because it prevents adjacent owners access to the boulevard, about 6 acres; that extends nearly the entire length of the land; 6 acres at $4,000 per acre, $24,000.

Questioned by Master.

This strip is along the easterly side of Junipero Serra Boulevard, and was reserved by the company at the time the boulevard was laid out.

CROSS EXAMINATION BY MR. STEINHART.

As to the northerly and southerly limits; it is in front of Ingleside Terraces, and I think it runs to the southern line of the ranch.

316 It does not make any difference whether it runs to the end of the ranch or not, because I am only valuing it by the acre, unless it might have

more value in front of some particular property than in front of some other property.

Tract A, the canyon between Tracts 5 and 6, extending from Junipero Serra Boulevard to the southerly lake, is about 62 acres.

Tract B, settling pond or basin, with adjacent land, in the northerly part of San Mateo County, and partly in San Francisco County, about 48 acres. Marginal land, a strip around the northerly and southerly lakes, varying in width according to the contour of the land, about 160 acres; the total of those is 270 acres, which I put at $1,000 an acre, $270,000. I value altogether 2,496 acres, which includes the piece north of Sloat Boulevard, and the total result I have already testified to is $6,718,250, which, in my opinion, was the market value of the land, which I have valued as a whole, on December 31, 1913. 317

(This table marked "Plaintiff's Exhibit 15", subject to the objections which the Defendant has made. The exclusions of the strip on the north of the boulevard should be taken into consideration.)

Whether there are 7 or 12 acres in that land to be excluded, in my judgment it would be excluded at the rate of $5,000 an acre, that is the market price of that portion of the land, whatever its acreage may be. The value which I have put upon the tract as a whole is not subject to the Twin Peaks Tunnel assessment; this assessment is not considered because it had not been paid, or any portion of it paid as of December 31, 1913. I think it would have been possible to have sold the tract on December 31, 1913, for the figures which I have mentioned, taking a reasonable time to make a sale, subject to the Twin Peaks Tunnel assessment.

The Twin Peaks Tunnel project has increased values to some extent, certainly to the extent of any assessment that exists for construction of the tunnel. I think the property is worth, or was worth on December 31, 1913, the value that I put on it, plus the Twin Peaks Tunnel assessment if it had been paid at that time. My value does not include anything by reason of the proximity of the lakes. 318

The following answer is objected to upon the ground that it is immaterial, irrelevant and incompetent. The question was permitted to be answered with the understanding that any authorities which the defendants might later submit would be considered at that time. 318-319

If the lakes were considered in conjunction with the lands, that is, if the owner of the property were not only the owner of the lakes, but of both the lands and the lakes, and if they were free of any public trust or dedication to a public use, so that the owner was perfectly free to dispose of them together, and to use or dispose of the lakes or the rights in the lakes in such a manner as to assist the sale of the lands, I think it would add at least 10 per cent to my value of the property. If 2,496 acres were worth $6,718,250, the 336 acres constituting the two lakes, being thrown into the property, that is, selling with or without the lakes, would give an added value to the property of at least 10 per cent.

Questioned by the Master.

In the first valuation that I made of $6,718,250, I had in mind that the lakes are there, but I have not given any value to the property by reason of their presence, and this additional value does not mean that I am adding 10 per cent by reason of the fact that the lakes are there, but because they are thrown into the pot, as it were, in selling the 2,496 acres.

320

DIRECT EXAMINATION BY MR. OLNEY.

My reason for thinking the value of the land would be increased if the lakes were thrown in with the rest of the land, is that they might be used as a water supply for the land in question, and if there was any reason for not being able to use them, the lakes could be utilized for boats and other purposes. They could be devoted exclusively to the property owners within the boundaries of that tract for either purpose.

I have handled property in San Mateo County off and on for more than 20 years. My first experience of any consequence was in the development of the Burlingame property. I represented the Sharon Estate, which owned the property, and we began operations, I think, in 1893. The Sharon Tract is at Burlingame in what is known as Burlingame and Hillsboro. It includes the better portion of those towns, the more valuable property, and ran from the County Road up to the foothills. Portions have been subdivided into small lots that I think are within the corporate limits of Burlingame, while other portions of it constitute what is known as Hillsboro and Burlingame.

321 The company owned, I think, 500 or 600 acres there altogether. We sold quite a lot of it, and what was left was subsequently sold to a syndicate which Lyon & Hoag were interested in. They cut it up into small tracts.

We also sold considerable property for the Bowie Estate, in what was known as El Cerito, and we laid out the property known as San Mateo Park in about 1901 or 2, which was about 300 acres. It has since been sold off. That was not the Hayward property, that was the property owned by the Clark Estate. It lies north of San Mateo, and is now a part of San Mateo City, I think. I sold the property now known as Uplands to Colonel Crocker, which formerly belonged to W. H. Howard. I sold Mr. Irwin the Carolan place in Burlingame.

The Clark Tract, or San Mateo Park, is about the only property outside of some Hayward tracts, which we purchased for several syndicates, in which I have had any experience in the purchase or sale of large undivided tracts in San Mateo County. I think we have been either directly or indirectly connected, perhaps, with all the principal sales around the neighborhood of San Mateo and Burlingame within the past 20 years.

We had nothing to do with the sale of the Horace Hawes Tract in Redwood City, known as the Dingee Tract, in its original shape, but we subsequently sold a number of lots in Dingee Park, and then afterwards sold to the Geo. H. Irving Co. the remaining lots, which they took over wholesale, and which they are now developing.

I do not think that we had anything to do with the sale of any of the Hooper property back of Redwood City. I have frequently been over the so-called watershed land of the Spring Valley Water Co. in San Mateo County around the reservoirs of Pilarcitos, San Andres and Crystal Springs. I have known these lands in a general way, I suppose, during the last 15 or 20 years, and I have gone down there very frequently. I have made an examination of these lands for the purpose of ascertaining the value of them, and I have been over them all. I have, in a general way, been fairly familiar with the values of adjacent properties and have endeavored in determining the value of these lands to obtain information bearing upon the value of similar lands in the nearby vicinity, and I finally reached a result as to what they were worth. The total value which I have placed on the 22,982.45 acres of the so-called watershed lands of the Spring Valley Water Co. in San Mateo County is $3,000,363.90. As far as I know it does not include any of the lands in the reservoir. Two maps offered and admitted and marked "Plaintiff's Exhibits 16 and 17". The smaller map will be marked "Plaintiff's Exhibit 17".

I got this value of $3,000,363.90 by placing a value on each of the parcels according to the company's maps, guided by that contour map which was of considerable aid in determining the contours of the property and similar locations.

Q. I think we had better go through this parcel by parcel. It is going to be somewhat long but it is the right way, I think, of doing it. Will you take up parcel by parcel, Mr. Baldwin, these pieces, and describe them, and state to the Court the value you put upon them?

Mr. Steinhart: It is stipulated, is it not, that all this testimony is open to the objections we have made heretofore and that we are making them now and that the same ruling is made?

Mr. Olney: What is the objection, Mr. Steinhart?

Mr. Steinhart: The objection is that Mr. Baldwin's evidence of valuation is immaterial, irrelevant and incompetent because it is a special value, and furthermore, because it is a segregated value.

Mr. Olney: We have no objection to that stipulation.

The Master: Very well. The objection will be overruled.

I valued it as a whole, I simply arrived at that value by taking the different parcels. I did not give any special value by reason of the fact that it was water producing. I valued them as a tract of

97

326   22,000 or 23,000 acres, not having in mind any special value as attaching to the property by reason of a water supply any more than the normal or any other water supply that there would be on other lands in San Mateo County. I have not considered the water element in any way. I did not consider the lake. I valued this property—the watershed—just as if the lake were not there, and it was a valley instead of a lake. I did not investigate the water features of any particular tract. There might be some of the tracts which by reason of water would have a greater value than I put on them. I considered

327   that just as I would any other lands there, that a buyer would have the same chance of getting water for domestic, or for any other purpose, that he would if he bought any other land in San Mateo County. There are lands being sold in many places around Woodside and elsewhere that are being sold with no assurance that they can get water; sometimes you get it in considerable quantities, and sometimes you don't get it at all. I do assume that the purchaser of the land would have the right to put down wells. I assume that a man would have the right to do with that land just as he would do with any other land he were buying there, and to the extent to which the ownership of the land gave him the right to use the water for domestic purposes, or irrigation, or anything else on the land. I would assume that he would get whatever rights went with the land, and in the nature of things,

328   the water.

    I did not consider as an element of value the possibility of water being gathered on these lands and taken elsewhere and supplied to another community. In making the valuations, I have already said I simply ignored the water elements in the land as I did with Lake Merced. I have assumed that the purchaser of these pieces would have the right to use whatever water there was on the land or in connection with it for domestic purposes or for irrigation, or whatever use he might have the right to put the water to on the land, and that he certainly would not be restricted in the use of the land by any unreasonable objections; that there would be no conditions attached to the land that would have a tendency to depreciate the value of it. In other words, I treated it as if it was not being dedicated to a public use at all.

329   Questioned by the Master.

    I was not treating it from the point of view of its value to the water company, but to the general public.

330   (Citation of authorities by Mr. Steinhart in re speculative values of lands.)

    Argument by Mr. Olney against citations as cited by Mr. Stein-

334   hart.

335   The Master: I will examine the citations and announce a ruling later.

DIRECT EXAMINATION BY MR. OLNEY.

The subdivisions as shown on the map were not made by me. They were given to me. The acreage almost always corresponds with the map, for the reason that I have only valued the land outside of the lakes, and to begin with, in parcel 2 on maps 2 and 3, which is up near Pilarcitos, and has 40 acres, I have only valued 20.41 acres. The balance of 19.60 acres is under water.

336

CROSS EXAMINATION BY MR. STEINHART.

I valued them in a measure separately, but with a view of ascertaining the value of the entire property. In some instances the valuation separately is not by any means of advantage to the company, for the reason that in a few instances they are in very bad shape, probably they had been bought, I assume, as they were owned for many years, in triangular shape. Now, perhaps, the adjoining land is better situated for boundary purposes, or not being at a disadvantage by reason of the shape, may be valued at a higher rate than these small parcels are; if that is your idea, with a view of determining the value of the property by subdivision, because this method of subdivision is not of advantage to the property at all; it does not add in any way to the value of the property, if that is what you want to get at.

337

I valued these parcels on the basis of what I considered the property worth by reason of sales, perhaps, in as near as you could get to that particular property. I took the market value of the particular parcel, I take what would be considered the salable value of that property as of December 31, 1913, and when I valued another parcel, I would take the market value of that other parcel, then to get the total I added the market value of these separate parcels together.

Objection to the testimony of Mr. Baldwin.

DIRECT EXAMINATION BY MR. OLNEY.

I made my valuation upon these separate parcels with the idea that the land was subdivided in this manner, and I was placing a value upon the land as subdivided. I do not think that the sum of the subdivided property exceeds the value of it as a whole by any means. My valuation is as a whole arrived at by the total of these various parcels which were purchased from time to time. The only reason for my valuing the parcels has been simply that the matter has been submitted to me in that way with the parcels shown.in that method. I think the property could have been sold, and would have been salable then (December 31, 1913) or even now at that price as an entirety.

338

339

I testified in regard to the valuation of the Lake Merced lands in the former case before Judge Farrington. The basis of my valuation was made entirely on the subdivision proposition, as I was requested to make it, but not as a whole. I have not made any of these valua-

340

tions on any such basis as that at all. The valuation was formerly made on what the property would retail for. The total retail selling price of the land. I did not subtract the cost of subdivision, surveys, laying out streets and so on. I had no instructions to do that. Those costs were to be ascertained, and were to be submitted by the engineers.

341   Argument by Steinhart against the admission of Mr. Baldwin's testimony. Objection made and overruled.

343   DIRECT EXAMINATION BY MR. OLNEY.

Regarding parcel No. 2, appearing on maps 2 and 3, I have my notes in regard to its character. The only thing is that my description of each parcel, I have already explained, in some instances, takes in the whole parcel, and only a portion of it may be included in the appraisal. The acreages to which I will testify are the acreages outside of the reservoir sites. Parcel No. 2, on maps 2 and 3, 20.40 acres. That acreage is wholly watershed. It was given me by the company as watershed land. I value it at $50 an acre, $1,020. The whole parcel contains 40 acres, about one-half of it in Pilarcitos Reservoir, the other half on east slope of saddle between Fifield Ridge and Cahill Ridge. Quite steep. These two pieces connected by strip running over end of Cahill Ridge. Elevation runs from 700 to 1000 feet. I place a valuation of $50 an acre on that. Map 3, parcel 3, 41.75 acres, at $60 an acre, $2,505. East of Scarper Peak, and north of Ox Hill. Very steep,
344 heavily wooded, ravine runs northeast through piece. Both sides slope, steep and wooded. Elevation, 700 to 1300 feet. Map 3, parcel 4, 4 acres, $50 an acre, $200. There are two pieces. One piece on east slope of north end of Cahill Ridge steep. Second piece half down easterly slope to Sawyer Ridge, very steep and rugged. Constitutes the two portals to Pilarcitos Tunnel. Map 3, parcel 5, 23.60 acres, at $60 an acre, $1,416. On the west slope of Cahill Ridge, very steep, about half of it in Pilarcitos Reservoir. Elevation, 700 to 900 feet. There are 23.60 acres in the watershed, and there are forty acres in the whole piece. Parcel 5-1, is on the west slope of the north end of Cahill Ridge. Includes saddle between Cahill and Fifield Ridge. Fronts on east arm of Pilarcitos Reservoir. Very steep except saddle. Elevation, 700 to 900 feet. It is partly in the reservoir. It is on the east side of Pilarcitos just at the north edge of the map. This last piece 5-1 contains 28.33 acres at $90, $2,945.70. Parcel 5-2 overlaps 2 and 3. Runs part on one map and part on the other. It is 2852.82 acres in watershed, at $100 an acre, $285,282. It includes most of Pilarcitos beautifully wooded canyon, running from top of Cahill Ridge on east, including Scarper Peak and top of Montara Mountains on west side of valley. South end of this piece is quite steep and rugged. Central part not so steep, with several prominent knolls. Top of Montara Mountains nearly level. The north end of piece includes large part of Pilarcitos Reservoir, with slopes on both sides.

The Cahill Ridge is a ridge between San Mateo Creek on the east and   345
Pilarcitos Creek on the west.

Map 3, parcel 6, 80 acres at $50, $4,000. North slope of Ox Hill.
Quite steep on sides, not so steep in center. Elevation, 900 to 1500
feet.

Map 2, parcel 7, 160.40 acres, at $40 per acre, $6,416. East end
of Whiting Ridge, including north slope, which is quite steep and
rugged, and south slope which is not so steep.

Map 2, parcel 8, 160 acres at $30 an acre, $4,800. Whiting
Ridge runs north-easterly through this ridge; both slopes quite steep
and cut up with ravines. Elevation from 800 to 1200 feet.

Map 2, parcel 9, 58.25 acres, at $20 an acre, $1,165. Part of top
of Montara Mountains and its northerly slope which is quite steep.
Elevation from 1200 to 1600 feet.

Map 2, parcel 12, 102.79 acres, at $100 an acre, $10,279. That
portion is in the bed of the reservoir, prominent circular knoll which
is the spur of the Sweeney Ridge, with uniform steep slopes. Includes
part of San Andres Lake. Elevation from 400 to 900 feet. The difference between 102.79 acres and 181.09 acres is in the reservoir. In
each case where that comes in I have not appraised the portion that
is in the reservoir.

Maps 2 and 3, parcel 13, are in three pieces. 332.74 acres, at $100
an acre, $33,274. 15.15 acres at $175, $2651.25. 27.41 acres at $200
an acre, $5482. By reference to the map on Exhibit 8, parcel 13 is
composed of three tracts, and one of those tracts contains a water-   346
shed of 332.74 acres. The parcel on the map referred to is the one
marked 13 with the acreage underneath of 369.49 acres. This is what
is left of that, outside of the reservoir. The second parcel, 15.15 acres
is what is left of the piece that contained 59.95 acres, and is on the
westerly end of San Andres Lake. The other piece of 27.41 acres is
what is left of the 102.61 acre piece.

Map 2, parcel 14, 175.26 acres, at $125 an acre, $21,907.50. This
is a portion of a larger tract containing 234.56 acres on the easterly
slope of northerly end of Sawyer Ridge. Three prominent points, the
slopes of which are steep. Some live oak and madrones, or manzanitas.
Includes part of San Andres Lake and dam; elevation from 500 to
900 feet.

Map 2, parcel 15, 143.35 acres, at $300 an acre, $43,005; part of
the tract containing 153.75 acres on westerly slope of northerly end
of Buri Buri Ridge. Includes part of San Andres Lake. Gentle
slopes. Fine sites for villas. Fine view of bay from top of ridge.
Keeper's cottage surrounded by pines and eucalyptus trees.   347

Map 2, parcel 16, 67.61 acres, at $300 an acre, $20,283. A portion
of tract containing 96.11 acres at south end of San Andres Lake. Contains some of the meadow land below the dam, and westerly slope of
Buri Buri Ridge. This is a mistake, dam and keeper's cottage—the

cottage is on the tract that I described last. This is another keeper's cottage. There is one at the upper end, and one down at the lower end.

Map 2, parcel 17, 17.39 acres, at $300 an acre, $5217. It is part of tract containing 31.69 acres; takes in top of Buri Buri Ridge, which is level on top. Westerly slope to San Andres Lake. About one-half the piece in lake. Elevation about 500 feet.

DIRECT EXAMINATION BY MR. GREENE.

The amount of watershed land in my total, 17.39 acres, at $300, $5,217.

DIRECT EXAMINATION BY MR. OLNEY.

Map 2, parcel 18, 30.19 acres, at $300 an acre, $9,057. There are two pieces in 18, Nos. 1 and 2. The first piece of 30.19 acres is a portion of the 52.35 acre piece on the easterly side of San Andres Lake, and the westerly slope of the Buri Buri Ridge; that is $300 an acre. The other is 53.36 acres, and is part of the tract containing 66.90 acres, at the northerly arm of the San Andres Lake; that is valued at $250 an acre, making $13,340.

348

Map 2, parcel 19, of 43.12 acres, at $300 per acre, $12,936; that is a portion of the tract containing 66.92 acres, and runs from the top of Buri Buri Ridge down gentle western slope, composed of two knolls to San Andres Lake, which comprises about half of the piece. Elevation about 500 feet.

Map 2, parcel 20, of 16.90 acres, at $300 an acre, $5,070. Portion of the tract containing 36.60 acres. It runs from top of Buri Buri Ridge down gentle western slope of San Andres Lake, which covers about two-thirds of the piece.

DIRECT EXAMINATION BY MR. GREENE.

The acreage of the watershed in parcel 20 is 16.90 acres.

Map 2, parcel 21, of 20.72 acres, at $300 an acre, $6,216. A portion of tract containing 34.52 acres, running from the top of the Buri Buri Ridge, and steep western slope to San Andres Lake, which covers about one-half of the piece.

Map 3, parcel 25, of 27.23 acres, at $25 an acre, $680.75. Very steep on western slope of the Cahill Ridge. Elevation from 400 to I think 1000 feet.

Map 3, parcel 27, of 67.49 acres, at $30 an acre, $2024.70. Those are six small triangular pieces just over the top of Cahill Ridge on the western slope. Very steep. They are little pieces bought to square up the ownership.

349

Map 2, parcel 28, of 396.16 acres, at $25 an acre, $9,904. Top of Montara Mountains running east and west; very badly cut up, and spur running north-easterly, the slopes of which are steep and cut up with ravines; elevation 1100 to 1600 feet.

Map 3, parcel 29, of 824.56 acres, at $30 an acre, $24,736.80. Basin between Montara Mountains and Coral de Tierra and ridge adjoining these two ranges; steep slopes cut up with many wooded ravines.

Map 3, parcel 33, of 153.50 acres, at $30 an acre, $4605. East slope of Coral De Tierra including part of Lock's Creek, nearly all steep.

Map 2, parcel 34, of 58.84 acres, at $20 an acre, $1176.80. Top of Montara Mountains and very steep slope both north and south. Elevation 1200 to 1600 feet.

Map 3, parcel 36, of 103.14 acres, at $500 an acre, $51,570. Spur at northerly end of Pulgas Ridge. Northerly slope very precipitous to San Mateo Creek. Westerly slope to Crystal Springs Lake. Includes part of the lake. Fine site. Wooded knolls. Elevation 200 to 500 feet.

Map 4, parcel 37, of 350.43 acres, at $175 an acre, $61,325.25. Part of a tract that contained 516.43 acres. On the westerly and south-westerly slopes of Pulgas Ridge, sloping gently at top and bottom and steep between. Includes part of Crystal Springs Lake. Elevation from 300 to 500 feet.

DIRECT EXAMINATION BY MR. OLNEY.

Referring to parcel 36; it is at the southerly end of the dam. It is to my mind the finest piece of property of the whole tract.

Map 3, parcel 38, of 23.82 acres, at $200 an acre, $4764. Portion of the tract containing 95.14 acres, foot of spur on easterly spur of Cahill Ridge, gently sloping to Crystal Springs Lake, which comprises about three-quarters of this piece.

350

Map 3, parcel 39, of 2094.05 acres, at $150 an acre, $314,107.50. Portion of a tract containing 2162.25 acres. Sawyer Camp site in northeast corner. Beautifully wooded. The southerly half of Sawyer Ridge comparatively flat on top, both east and west slope quite steep. Includes arm of Crystal Springs Lake.

Map 3, parcel 40, of 9.33 acres, at $125 per acre, $1166.25. Portion of tract containing 13.23 acres. Spur on the east slope of Sawyer Ridge. Includes part of Crystal Springs Lake. Elevation from 300 to 700 feet.

Map 3, parcel 41, of 42.45 acres, at $150 an acre, $6367.50. Portion of tract containing 44.95 acres on the easterly slope of Sawyer Ridge, sloping toward lake. Includes small part of Crystal Springs Lake. Elevation 300 to 800 feet.

Map 2, parcel 42, of 22.38 acres, at $300 per acre, $6714. Top of Buri Buri Ridge and west slope, level land at bottom below San Andres dam. Elevation 400 to 600 feet. There are two pieces. One is 312.69 acres, and the other 80 acres, making 391.69 acres. There is a discrepancy of 1 acre in the description and in the map, but I think 391.69 is correct. The two pieces have been valued by me at $40 an acre, making $15,667.60. The first portion of the property, 312.69 acres, is on the northerly end of Fifield Ridge, and very steep ravine on its west slope; east slope not so steep to San Mateo Creek. Part of Sweeney Ridge with steep western slope, and precipitous eastern ridge cut up with two big ravines. Elevation 500 to 1200 feet.

351

The 80 acres is at the southerly and south-westerly slope of Fifield Ridge; elevation 400 to 800 feet.

Map 4, parcel 44, of 9.46 acres, at $200 an acre, $1892. Portion of a tract of land containing 21.86 acres. Island in upper Crystal Springs Lake, and level bottom land, a portion of which is now in the lake.

Map 4, parcel 45, of 147.47 acres, at $250 an acre, $36,867.50. Portion of tract containing 154.17 acres, foot of spur on north-easterly slope of Cahill Ridge, very gentle slope.

Map 4, parcel 46, of 150.43 acres, at $200 an acre, $30,086. Portion of tract containing 294.53 acres. Foot of north-east slope of Cahill Ridge. Gently sloping, includes part of upper Crystal Springs Lake.

Map 4, parcel 47, of 49.25 acres, at $200 an acre, $9850. Portion of tract containing 70.75 acres. Two prominent knolls at foot of northeast slope of Cahill Ridge, sloping gently to Crystal Springs Lake.

Map 4, parcel 48, of 925.88 acres, at $175 an acre, $162,029. Part of tract containing 1161.78 acres. Large level knoll near top of Pulgas Ridge, and gentle west slope to upper Crystal Springs Lake on the southern end. On northerly end several prominent knolls with steep slope. Cottage near center on west slope. Elevation 300 to 700 feet.

352

Map 4, parcel 49, of 643.90 acres, at $125 an acre, $80,487.50. Portion of tract containing 659.80 acres. Northeast slope of Cahill Ridge, gently sloping at the top; level meadow land at the foot, but steep side hill with deep ravine between. Elevation 300 to 1800 feet.

Map 4, parcel 50, of 310.90 acres, at $200 per acre, $62,180. Portion of tract containing 481.80 acres. Level bottom land and foot of northeast slope of Cahill Ridge and part of upper Crystal Springs Lake. Elevation 300 to 600 feet.

Map 2, parcel 51, contains 17.52 acres, at $300 per acre, $5256. Bottom land at northerly end of San Andres Lake.

Map 2, parcel 52, contains 1.03 acres, at $200 an acre, $206. Mouth of ravine northerly slope of end of Sawyer Ridge, fronting on San Andres Lake. Gentle slope.

Map 2, parcel 53, contains 5.18 acres, at $300 an acre, $1554. Gentle slope on east side of north end of San Andres Lake.

Map 4, parcel 54, contains 64.32 acres, at $300 an acre, $19,296. Portion of tract containing 104.22 acres. On the westerly slope of Pulgas Ridge. Gently sloping at top, then steep to Crystal Springs Lake, which comprises one-third of the piece.

Map 4, parcel 55, of 74.24 acres, at $200 an acre, $14,848. Portion of a tract containing 98.94 acres. Bottom land on westerly side of southerly end of upper Crystal Springs Lake.

Map 3, parcel 59, of 6.18 acres, at $200 an acre, $1236. Portion of a parcel containing 15.68 acres. Steep easterly slope of southerly end of Sawyer Ridge. Includes part of Crystal Springs Lake.

Map 3, parcel 60, of 243.80 acres, at $40 an acre, $9752. Ox Hill with slope easterly and southerly. Elevation from 700 to 1600 feet.

Map 3, parcel 62, of 43.17 acres, at $150 an acre, $6475.50. Fronting on Crystal Springs road, leading to San Mateo. Northerly slope of north end of Pulgas Ridge and mouth of Alms House Canyon. Very steep. 353

Maps 3 and 4, parcel 68; there are a number of parcels there. No. 1 is 40 acres, at $40 an acre, $1600. This is on map 4. Northeasterly slope of Cahill Ridge. Steep. Elevation 500 to 1000 feet. No. 2 is 51.65 acres, at $70 an acre, $3615.50. It is at the foot of east slope of Cahill Ridge. It is not very steep. The next is 116.08 acres, at $60 an acre, 6964.80. It is a big ravine on east slope of Cahill Ridge. Steep slope. The rest of parcel 68 is what is left of the watershed lands of these other parcels, the balance contains 622.04 acres. They are the l pe of the Crystal Springs Lake, but are in scattered parcels. That is they are the remnants of the various portions of these other four tracts. I put them in at the uniform price of $125 an acre, $77,755. I have not the segregated amounts of those various parcels. Mr. Sharon gave me the total of what was left. I think they have that in the office; I have not got it. I do not think there is any material difference in the land. It is all about the same. Those that I value at $125 an acre would come a portion in No. 5, and a portion in No. 6. 354

The first parcel of 68, containing 40 acres, appears on map 4, almost in the middle of the map, and on that I have placed a valuation of $40 an acre. The next piece containing 51.65 acres, lies a quarter of a mile to the east, and on that I have placed a valuation of $70 an acre, and that runs down to the main road running from Burns' store. The third piece, containing 116.08 acres, is almost due north of the first piece containing 40 acres. It is at the junction of the Half Moon Bay road and the road that runs up to Redwood Park, the Ridge Road, and that I have valued at $60 an acre.

Next I have a piece containing 622.04 acres, made up of several different pieces. It comprises first, the piece on the map entitled

355 ''68'' with an acreage of 196 and some odd acres, a little to the north-east or about due north of the 116 acre piece. That 200 acres shown immediately to the north of the last mentioned piece is a mistake, and should not be on there. This is 562.22 acres, and it takes in the piece that is marked the 200 acres; that 200 acre piece is a mistake, and is really a part of the 562 acre tract. The 562 acre · tract appears in part on map 3. These properties lie to the north of the Half Moon Bay road, and on the easterly slope of the Crystal Springs reservoir; the northerly portion of the property is immediately across the way from the Crystal Springs dam.

Map 3, parcel 72, containing 8.80 acres, at $300 an acre, $2640. That is a portion of a tract containing 32.80 acres. Long strip at north end of Crystal Springs Lake.

Map 3, parcel 73, contains 276.45 acres, at $400 an acre, $110,580. Portion of a tract containing 284.55 acres. Westerly slope of Buri Buri Ridge. Steep slope much cut up with small ravines. Level on top.

Map 3, parcel 89, of 47.06 acres, at $200 an acre, $9412. The south end of Sawyer Ridge, steep slopes to the east and south.

Map 3, parcel 90, of 856.10 acres, at $400 an acre, $342,440. Part of tract containing 981.50 acres. Large part practically level on top 356 of Buri Buri Ridge, and the steep southwest slope to the Crystal Springs Lake, including part thereof, and very precipitous slope to San Mateo Creek.

Map 3, parcel 91, of 28.55 acres, at $150, $4282.50. The north slope of Pulgas Ridge, level on top, quite steep below.

Map 3, parcel 92, of 31.31 acres, at $200 an acre, $6262. Part of tract containing 80.01 acres. Foot of steep east l pe of Cahill Ridge, and gently sloping end of Sawyer Ridge, with Crystal Springs Lake in between.

Map 3, parcel 94, containing 4.95 acres, at $200 an acre, $990. Nearly all in Crystal Springs Lake. It is part of a tract containing 14.45 acres—nearly all in Crystal Springs Lake.

Map 4, parcel 96, 12.20 acres, at $200 an acre, $2440. Part of a tract containing 23.65 acres. Foot of steep east slope of Cahill Ridge and Crystal Springs Lake.

Map 3, parcel 97, containing 68.09 acres, at $150 an acre, $10,-213.50. Portion of the tract containing 86.79 acres. On the east slope of Sawyer Ridge, two prominent knolls with a ravine between. Includes part of Crystal Springs Lake.

Map 2, parcel 101, containing 240 acres, $25 an acre, $6,000. Top of Montara Mountains, very steep slopes.

Map 2, parcel 102, 160 acres at $40 an acre, $6,400. Top of the Fifield Ridge, with a spur to west. Very steep slope; elevation 700 to 1300 feet.

Map 2, parcel 104, 327.90 acres, at $50 an acre, $16,395. Junction of Whiting and Fifield Ridge. Very steep, rugged slopes to north and east. Steep slopes to southeast. Elevation 900 to 1400 feet.

Map 2, parcel 106, 295 acres, at $100 an acre, $29,590. Portion of a tract containing 320 acres. Southerly half of Spring Valley Ridge, with small part of the level top of Fifield Ridge. Precipitous slopes between. On the southwest slope of Spring Valley Ridge. Steep and rough to Pilarcitos Lake. Foot of steep slope of Montara Mountains in southwest corner of piece.   357

Map 3, parcel 101, 2.10 acres, at $200 an acre, $420. Portion of tract containing 3 acres. East slope of Sawyer Ridge. Upper half steep. Lower half not steep. Includes portion of Crystal Springs Lake.

Map 4, parcel 122, 117.48 acres, at $75 an acre, $8,811. It is a part of the tract containing 118.58 acres on the east 1 pe of Cahill Ridge. Steep. Elevation from 400 to 1100 feet.

Map 3, parcel 124, 165 acres, at $60 an acre, $9,900. East of Scarper Peak. Fine growth of firs. Ravine running northerly through east side of this peak. Elevation 800 to 1700 feet.

Map 3, parcel 128, 47.93 acres, at $30 an acre, $1,437.90. That is in two parcels; one of 40 acres south of Scarper Peak at the top of the ridge. Slopes to the east and west. The other is 7.93 acres near the top of Coral De Tierra. Not very steep.

Map 2, parcel 130, 390.04 acres, at $50 an acre, $19,502. At the north end of Sawyer Ridge. Slopes to northeast and somewhat cut up with many small ravines. Slopes to the west to San Mateo Creek. On the west side of this piece foot of slope of Fifield Ridge quite steep.

Map 4, parcel 132, 505.75 acres, at $70 an acre, $35,402.50. These are two pieces. One piece containing 340 acres, and the other piece containing 165.75 acres. The 340 acre piece is on the northeast slope of the Cahill Ridge. Side hill only. Elevation 500 to 1400 feet. The 165.75 acres piece is on the east slope of the Cahill Ridge, steep on northerly end, with a large ravine. South end not so   358 steep. Elevation 500 to 1000 feet. The same map, the same number, 160 acres, at $125 an acre, $20,000. Foot of east slope of Cahill Ridge. Prominent knoll, gently sloping, level at the bottom.

Map 4, parcel 134, 200.92 acres, at $70 an acre, $14,064.40. On northerly slope of Cahill Ridge. Gentle slope on top. Southern part steep. Elevation from 500 to 1300 feet.

Map 3, parcel 138, 320 acres at $30 an acre, $9,600. Top of spur from Ox Hill Ridge. I have only one piece there.

Map No. 2, parcel 144, containing 152.43 acres, at $250 an acre, $38,107.50. Ridge between Buri Buri and Sweeney Ridges. Gentle slopes on top and on each side. Elevation 500 to 700 feet.

Map 2, parcel 146, 15.89 acres, at $30 an acre, $476.70. On the southwest slope of Fifield Ridge. Elevation 800 to 1000 feet.

Map 2, parcel 153, 1066.11 acres, at $100 an acre, $106,611. Fifield Ridge gently sloping on top. East slope of ridge is very steep and cut up with very small ravines to San Mateo Creek. Sawyer Ridge slopes steeply to the west with three ravines. The east slope is very precipitous and rugged.

Map 5, parcel 164, 429.20 acres, at $175 an acre, $75,110. On the west slope of the Pulgas Ridge. Gently l ping on top with two or three prominent knolls. Steep side slopes and large flat below. Elevation 400 to 700 feet. Occasional oaks and other trees.

359   Map 3, parcel 182, 34.45 acres, at $150 an acre, $5167.50. Very steep east slope of Sawyer Ridge from the edge at the top to edge of lake.

Map 4, parcel 191, 449.19 acres, at $100 an acre, $44,919. Northeast slope of Cahill Ridge. Steep slopes, flat at bottom. Elevation 400 to 1700 feet.

Map 5, parcel 194, 1059.07 acres, at $125 an acre, $132,483.75. Northeast slope of Cahill Ridge. Very prominent point. Steep slopes, one-quarter of piece gently rolling at bottom. Second growth redwoods on westerly portion. Elevation 400 to 2000 feet.

Map 5, parcel 195, 503.30 acres, at $125 an acre, $62,912.50. Northeasterly slope of Cahill Ridge, gently sloping on top, then very steep to West Union Creek. Gently sloping from east side of creek. Pretty much the same as 194.

CROSS EXAMINATION BY MR. STEINHART.

I have not valued separately the portion in the West Union Watershed, as against the Crystal Springs watershed.

Map 2, parcel 196, 80 acres, at $40 an acre, $3200. Top of Fifield Ridge, very steep slopes to east and northeast and to the west.

Map 4, parcel 199, 50.53 acres, at $50 an acre, $2526.50. Those are triangular pieces on top of Cahill Ridge, gently sloping.

DIRECT EXAMINATION BY MR. OLNEY.

There are three such pieces, and I have lumped them.

Map 5, parcel 202, 92.73 acres, at $100 an acre, $9273. That is No. 2 on map 5, the southwest slope of Pulgas Ridge, prominent knoll
360   in center, gently l ping. The next is 153.16 acres, at $150 an acre, $22,974. That takes in the two pieces there combined, one piece of 92.75, and the other 60.43. I am not sure as to the 92.73 being the most southerly. I think there is a mistake on the map. The combined area of what is left is 153.16 acres, and I put it in at $150 an acre. That makes $22,974. The northerly one I put at $100 an acre; the two southerly pieces combined I put at $150 an acre.

Map 5, parcel 203, 32.54 acres, at $100 an acre, $3254. The description of that is the southwest slope of Pulgas Ridge, gently sloping. There is a bungalow on the property.

Map 5, parcel 205, 314.30 acres, at $150 an acre, $47,145.

DIRECT EXAMINATION BY MR. GREENE.

Parcel 204 I have here. It is the Polhemus Tract. I have the description here but it is eliminated from the watershed there.

The description of map 5, parcel 205, is northeast slope of Cahill 361
Ridge. Very steep. Prominent point and big ravine opening into West Union Creek, well wooded. Ground rises less steeply to the east from West Union Creek, then falls gently to flat below. Old vineyard on east slope.

Map 5, parcel 208, 156 acres, at $200 an acre, $31,200. Ridge fairly level on top. Slopes steeply to the west to West Union Creek, and gently to the east to the flat.

Map 5, parcel 210, 214 acres, at $150 an acre, $32,100. Steep slope northeasterly from top of Cahill Ridge, connected by a narrow strip to piece across West Union Creek, which slopes steeply to the west and the east. Old vineyard and winery on east slope.

Map 5, parcel 211, 346.10 acres, at $150 an acre, $51,915. Northeasterly slope of the Cahill Ridge. Deep ravine into West Union Creek. Ground rises steeply to ridge on the east of West Union Creek and then falls sharply to flat below. Well timbered on 1 pe toward creek. Old vineyard on easterly slopes.

Map 5, parcel 212, 10.23 acres, at $125 an acre, $1278.75. That 362
is a level piece of land at the intersection of the roads, leading north to the Half Moon Bay road, and the other road running west, which is known as Canada. It is right at the circle where the road diverges.

Map 2, parcel 218, 22.84 acres, at $300 an acre, $6852. Portion of a tract containing 34.74 acres on the southwest slope from Buri Buri Ridge. Big ravine flowing south, with prominent point to the west, then falling steeply to San Andres Lake, which comprises about half the piece.

Phelps Tract, 969.94 acres, at $125 an acre, $121,242.50.

(Discussion between counsel as to ownership of Phelps Tract, and of conditions surrounding option held by Spring Valley Water Co.)

Description of this property: it extends from the top of Pulgas 363
Ridge, westerly to near the center of the lower arm of upper Crystal Springs Reservoir, immediately south of parcel 48. Land rolling, with occasional groups of oak trees. Spring Valley Water Co. has option to purchase this property on basis of $100 per acre.

The Master here suggests that to supplement Mr. Baldwin's testimony, counsel for Plaintiff introduce this tabulation of values, and have him testify as to the correctness of the final totals.

DIRECT EXAMINATION BY MR. OLNEY.

363½ · I did not know that there are two totals, one excluding the Phelps Tract, $2,879,120.90, and the other including the Phelps Tract, $3,-000,363.40. My total valuation, excluding the Phelps Tract, is within 50 cents of the figure $2,879,120.90. That is as near as I can say. I don't know whether those additions are correct, or whether mine are, but it is one or the other, but the valuations set out in the table are a correct tabulation.

Offered in evidence, and marked "Plaintiff's Exhibit 18".

SEVENTH HEARING.   JULY 21, 1915.

Witness A. S. BALDWIN.

364-365 Telegrams introduced in evidence to show Geo. W. Reynolds deceased April 24, 1914. Decided not necessary to supplement this showing in order to use the testimony of Mr. Reynolds given in the 1903 case.

365-366 Objection to introduction of "Exhibit 12-bb" overruled, and the exhibit admitted in evidence.

Admission of "Exhibit 12-cc" to depend upon Mr. Metcalf's testimony.

Counsel for defendant does not object any further to Reynolds matter.

DIRECT EXAMINATION BY MR. OLNEY.

367 I have prepared a tabulation of the valuations which I have placed upon the watershed lands of the Crystal Springs, San Andres and Pilarcitos Reservoirs, in which these lands and various parcels have been segregated in accordance with the value per acre. That is a tabulation which you now show me.

Offered and received in evidence, and marked "Plaintiff's Ex-
368 hibit 19".

That summary includes the Phelps tract; the difference is the value of the Phelps tract, if it is to be eliminated, to come out of that.

The average value per acre of these watershed lands is $130.55 an acre, which includes the Phelps tract.

These watershed lands are more available for residential purposes I think, than for general farming or agriculture, except in certain places; there is a diversity of soil naturally throughout a large area, some bad, some not so bad, and some very good. The matter of soil, however, from my experience and observation, is not a very
369 essential feature or element in disposing of properties down the Peninsula. I do not suppose there is a tract of land being sold, or that has been sold from San Bruno to Woodside that would produce an income for any purpose on what is the intrinsic and salable value of

the property, with very few exceptions. Beyond Woodside is bottom land that is used for strawberries, vegetable purposes, that rents for $25 or $30 an acre, but even at that rental it would not pay interest on probably $400 or $500 an acre that might be obtained for it. The same is true of practically all of these 22,000 or 23,000 acres of the water company. I have had personal experience with a 1200 acre tract known as McDonough Ranch below Portola, that can hardly be made to pay expenses, eliminating the special use to which it has been put, the raising of thoroughbred horses, and yet the land could be sold, I think, very quickly for $150.00* an acre, or about $180.000. Even with the most careful farming there, I do not believe that any more than expenses could be made out of it; the land has outgrown in value the agricultural use, and is essentially a suburban residential proposition.

Referring to map, Plaintiff's exhibit 16, and Plaintiff's exhibit   370
17: I valued the land in the westerly portion of that property at very much lower rate per acre than on the easterly part of it. There are farms adjacent to all the land there in the westerly portion of the tract, used partly for stock and partly for agriculture; a large portion of that land on the top of what is known as Montara Mountain, would not be adaptable at the present time for anything except stock purposes. Land that we will say is worth $30 or $40 an acre; but that land by reason of its connection with the other tract, assuming that the tract was acquired as a whole, and developed, would naturally feel the influence of the development of that portion of the property that would be nearest to transportation, and nearest to the present line of development.

There are thousands of acres that have a very great value from   371
a scenic point of view, and practically all of it is within accessible distance by automobile transportation of San Francisco for suburban homes. The automobile has had the effect within the last ten years of bringing into the market, and increasing the value of all such properties very considerable. The adjoining lands on the east and south sides of this tract (watershed lands) are now, to a very large extent, in the hands of wealthy people who have built fine homes; that applies to the section west of Burlingame and San Mateo, and also to the southerly portion of this property, by reason of the development at Woodside.

There has not been as much development immediately around   372
Belmont as there has been down toward Woodside and in San Mateo; the Beresford Country Club, however, have a very fine building not far from Belmont, and that property comes up to within a very short distance of the Spring Valley property.

*This was stated in the testimony $150,000. Corrected in Court July 23, 1915. See page 438.

There has been development of the land about and adjoining Redwood City, but I do not think values are as high there, nor has the development been as great immediately around Redwood as higher up. There have been several very pretentious homes built in the Hooper tract. George Oxnard lives there, and also George Lent.

(Discussion between counsel and the Master as to Mr. Baldwin's valuation placed on lands outside of the watershed; also as to the inclusion of such lands as the Locks Creek Lands and Howard tract.)

375

Map showing certain pipe lines and lands of the Spring Valley Water Co., in the northern part of San Mateo County, offered in evidence, and marked "Plaintiff's Exhibit 20".

I made a valuation of the property designated No. 87, and which appears on map 9, of "Exhibit 8". It is a level piece of land, sandy soil in the northern part of San Mateo County, in the line of the Valencia Street branch of the Southern Pacific Railroad, and on the east side of the Junipero Serra Boulevard. It is mostly in San Mateo County, but with a narrow strip in San Francisco County. The market value of this property on December 31, 1913, was $3,000 per acre for the 7.72 acres, making $23,160. There is a spur track that runs through the property.

376

Questioned by Master.

My valuation included the little strip in San Francisco also. The spur track that crosses that property leads to the Ocean View pumping station, as I understand, and it is quite necessary in supplying fuel oil and material. The spur track which leaves the Southern Pacific line and runs across the property leads, as far as my knowledge of the matter is concerned, to the Ocean View pumping station on the westerly side of the Junipero Serra Boulevard, and I believe to the pumping station down near the lake.

377

Referring to parcels 118, 179 and 187, appearing on map 8, I valued the combined area in the three parcels, containing 1.471 acres at $3,000 per acre, making $4413. That is on the upper righthand corner of map 8, and is property that runs partly in San Francisco, and partly in San Mateo County, Hillcrest and Daly Hill Reservoir property. I have placed a valuation on parcel 168* on map 9. The tract contains 59.783 acres at $1500 per acre, $89,674. It is a level piece of land; the Southern Pacific Railroad runs along the westerly side of it; the county road runs through the center, and it is near South San Francisco, which is quite an industrial section.

378

Parcel 127, map 8, I placed a value upon. It is a strip between county road and Southern Pacific Railroad near Baden, 8.847 acres, at $1,000 per acre, $8847. It is a level piece of land lying between the county road and the Southern Pacific Railroad. The San Andres pipe line extends through the tract. The southerly portion of the

*This was written 188 in transcript. Corrected in Court July 23, 1915.

property is subject to overflow during some of the winter months, otherwise, the tract is valuable as a truck garden, and could doubtless be disposed of to Italian or Portuguese gardeners. The same may be said of parcels 214, 215 and 216, containing 3.84 acres, which I valued at $1500 per acre, $5,760. These tracts all have a frontage on the county road, also the railroad, and are near the tracks of the United Railroad.

(By counsel: Tract 127 is the tract appearing on exhibit 20 at the southeast corner of the map, and between the tracks of the United Railroads and the Southern Pacific, and crossed by the San Andres pipe line. Tracts 214, 215 and 216 comprise the property immediately to the northwest of 127, and they are all traversed by the pipe line, and are not used, so far as I have been informed, for water producing purposes, but they are included in the condemnation suit.†) 379

Map 9, parcel 32, lot 1, block 17, School House Extension Homestead, fronting 49 feet on Washington Street, and 139 feet on Hill Street. This property is just across the way from Colma Station, and close to the San Pedro Road, which gives it a somewhat more than normal value. The valuation placed on it by me is $1500.

Map 9, parcel 186, lot A, Castle tract, northeast corner of Price St. and County Road, fronting 129 ft. 9 in. on the county road, 104 ft. 4 in. on Price Street, and 70 ft. in depth on the north line. It has, in my opinion, a value of $20 per foot for the county road frontage, giving it a value of $2,595.

Map 9, parcel 192, portions of lots 11, 12, 13 and 14, block 2, Visitacion, 40 by 60 ft., $500. That size that I gave you of 40 by 60, should be 40 by 160. It is 40 ft. on a straight line, and 48 feet on the diagonal. 380

Parcel 35, map 8, of "Exhibit 8": The total valuation on all of the lots in the Abbey Homestead, is $2500, divided as follows: Lot 3, block 32, size 100 by 100, $600. Lot 3, block 156,* size 100 by 100, $250. Lot 8, block 171, size 100 by 100, $250. Lot 30 by 100 east of and adjoining block 8, lot 171, $75. Lot 70 by 100 in block 171, corner Lake and Linden, $175. Lot 5, block 177, size 100 by 100, $250. Lot 2, block 177, size 100 by 100, $250. Lot 8, in block 176, size 100 by 100, $250. Lot 2, block 185, size 100 by 100, $400. Total $2500.

Map 30, parcel 200, Diamond tract, lots. Strip 14 by 397 feet long, being 5,558 sq. ft., at 10 cts. sq. ft., $555.80. 381

Map 9, parcel 197, 25 foot strip north of Millbrae pump, about 320 ft. long, 19 one-hundredths of an acre, at $2000 per acre, $380.

Map 9, parcel 133, Millbrae Reservoir lots, 51.70 acres, at $1000 per acre, $51,710.

Map 9, parcel 131, Millbrae pump lot, 15.356 acres, at $1500 per acre, $23,034.

†Correction made in Court July 23, 1915, that pipe is not on 214, 215, 216.
*In transcript p. 380 Mr. Olney stated that 156 was off the pipe line and was not in use. Correction was made in Court July 23, 1915, that lot 156 is used for standpipe on San Andres pipe line.

Map 9, parcels 124 and 193, Silva tract, 146.251 acres, at $650 per acre, $95,063.15. It is a little level strip of land 320 feet long, used I presume as a right of way. The reservoir lot of 51.71 acres is on the westerly side of the county road; it rises from the level of the county road toward the westerly portion of the property, 75 or 100 feet, I presume. It is well situated and valuable for residence purposes; practically everything else is sub-divided down in that section. The other three tracts are also very well situated for residential purposes; I think they are all specially adaptable for those purposes. Referring to the pipe line running the length of the Silva tract, I have not studied the property with the purpose in view of ascertaining whether it would be possible to sub-divide and sell off that property and retain that right of way, and still keep the value of the land with the property sub-divided. I do not know. In a general way it would be quite remarkable if the pipe line was situated advantageously so that a street could be laid out to follow it; it would probably go rather awkwardly into the property in making a sub-division of it.

382

CROSS EXAMINATION BY MR. STEINHART.

I only know about this particular pipe line from the map.

DIRECT EXAMINATION BY MR. OLNEY.

Map 9, parcel 95, Belmont pump lot, 44.67 acres, at $750 per acre, $33,502.50. Map 9, parcel 158, Belmont Reservoir lot, 33.825 acres, at $500 per acre, $16,912.50. Map 9, parcel 206, San Carlos Park lot, 20 by 30 ft., $250, a total of $50,665. Parcel 95 is situated on the westerly side of the railroad, slopes gradually from the railroad up westerly, a very sightly tract, and I think, would be quite salable at that price for residential purposes as a whole. That is the tract that has the water tower and pumping plant on it.

383

Questioned by Master.

That blue extension from parcel 158 is a connection with the Ravenswood right of way. The company had a right of way extending from Ravenswood up to Redwood City, and that right of way connects with this parcel 158. I do not know whether it is in use at the present time or not.

DIRECT EXAMINATION BY MR. OLNEY.

That portion of the right of way in connection with parcel 158, I have valued, and that is included in the area, so I understand, of parcel 158, which is valued at $500 an acre.

CROSS EXAMINATION BY MR. STEINHART.

I have valued this parcel as a whole. At the time I valued it, I only knew it as a parcel of land. I did not know it was connected with the Ravenswood right of way, and I did not include the Ravenswood right of way in my valuation of this parcel. I valued that tract as an entirety, and incidentally it seemed to take in as a part of that, the right of way. I did not value it differently from other land owned in fee. 384

DIRECT EXAMINATION BY MR. OLNEY.

The little piece that runs off to the southwest in parcel 158, and which is apparently a part of 158, I valued upon the basis of the company owning the fee to it. It is a part of the 33 acres. The land included in 158 is a level piece of bottom land immediately across the way from the pumping station. The company owned an undivided one-half interest in a larger piece there, and made a partition with the owner, and got this—Livernash, I believe, owns the balance of it. 385

I have made a valuation of the Ravenswood land, appearing on map 7 of "Exhibit 8".

Map 7, parcel 157, marsh lands between bay and Ravenswood Creek, 1328.22 acres, at $50 an acre, $66,411. Map 7, parcel 156 marsh land lying north and east of the Frisbie tract, fronting on San Francisco Bay, 285.65 acres, at $50 per acre, $14,282.50. Map 7, parcel 155, marsh lands fronting on San Francisco Bay, north of San Francisquito Creek, 191.28 acres, at $50 per acre, $9564. Map 7, parcel 154, Frisbie tract, high land contiguous to marsh land, 40.85 acres, at $300 per acre, $12,255, making a total of $102,512.50. I have been thoroughly familiar with the property for a good many years. In 1902 I bought a large portion of the property for the company. In fact, I bought all of it, except parcel 155.

Referring to the tracts on the pipe line from Baden Junction to the Central pump, "Exhibit 20"; we bought all of the right of way, with the exception of a portion through the Flood lands, that portion was purchased by Mr. Schussler. I have appraised these, and all of my appraisements are as of December 31, 1913. 386

Map 8, parcel 152, known as the Burnett property, a strip 60 ft. wide, 450 ft. long, at $7 per foot, $3150. I do not know that I can answer as to what relation that valuation bears to the valuation of adjoining property, because there is no adjoining property that has been sold, so far as I know. I only know what we had to pay when we wanted to get it, and as it was a considerable cut through the Burnett property, we probably had to pay considerable more than the prevailing value per acre of adjacent property. We paid $3000 for it on April 2, 1906. I figured it by the lineal foot, at $7 a foot, making $3150. Acreage .62 acres.

Map 8, parcel 181, lots 1, 2, 3 and 4, block 7, School House Homestead, each 120 by 125, at $500 each, $2000. 387

Questioned by Master.

There are some other lots in that tract; lots 7 and portions of lot 2 and 8 of block 1, City Extension Homestead, $1600; then in the same section there is a strip on map 8, parcel 167, 16.3 ft. wide by 126.06 ft. long, and I put a value of $630.30—$5.00 per foot. We paid $500 for that strip on March 28, 1907, and we paid for lot 7, and portions of lots 2 and 8, of block 1, City Extension Homestead, being a portion of parcel 181, $2400, which I value at $1600. We had to pay more than the normal value of the property because it is part of a yard of Mr. Geilfuss, and this triangular piece was a part of his orchard, and he parted with it even at that price with considerable

388   objection. It could not be gotten now for that price.

Questioned by Master.

The 4 lots in 181 cost $1600. They were bought considerably before that time. Lot 1 was bought January 6, 1904; lots 2 and 3 January 6, 1904, and lot 4 June 17, 1904. We had to pay $800 for lot 4, and we only paid $400 for lots 2 and 3 and 1. They were all bought from different parties.

DIRECT EXAMINATION BY MR. OLNEY.

I have placed a valuation of $2000 on them now, although only $1600 was paid for them, as I think they are worth that from all the information I can get. That property is built up pretty well around; the Thornton home is right near it, and there are several cottages on both sides of it.

There is still another parcel in 181. There are three lots in the

389   Villa Homestead. These I valued at $8000. We paid $3000 on October 1, 1906, for lot 37, and on the same day, $5000 for lots 38 and 42, $8,000 for the property.

Questioned by Master.

Lot 37 is part of parcel 165 according to this map.

CROSS EXAMINATION BY MR. STEINHART.

Lot 37 on this map is the only lot in 165, and we paid $3000 for it, and I am now valuing it at the same price.

DIRECT EXAMINATION BY MR. OLNEY.

Referring to the long strip that runs through the Odd Fellows and Masonic Cemetery, and which forms a part of parcel 181, that is 7 acres, which I valued at $10,000 an acre, or $70,000. It is a strip

390   132 ft. wide, and 2312.2 ft. long.

CROSS EXAMINATION BY MR. STEINHART.

I valued this strip higher, by reason of the fact that it runs through a cemetery. I did not consider it an improvement, but I considered the fact that it was very difficult to get at that time, and you could not buy it now for anything like that price. I did not value that on the basis of neighboring land in the cemetery, for if I did, I would get it up to about $1.50 a sq. foot.

DIRECT EXAMINATION BY MR. OLNEY.

In 1904, when we started to acquire this right of way, we found in dealing with some of the property owners in the City Extension Homestead, of which this cemetery was a part, that there were other negotiations instituted by somebody. We found that we were bidding against somebody else. There were no cemeteries established at that time. Mr. Fred Bergen, who carried on these negotiations for us, reported difficulty in getting options. Somebody was offering more than he was for the property, and we finally ascertained that Colonel Patton, and several others were organizing a company to buy the property, and we also ascertained subsequently, from an interview with Colonel Patton what he wanted it for. We had an understanding with him that if he would give the water company a right of way through the lands that he was acquiring at cost, plus ten percent to cover expenses, we would turn over to him any lands that we got that were not required for the pipe line. During a period of two or three years the property was rounded up, some purchased by him, and some purchased by us for the water company, and an adjustment was made, I think, some time in 1907. The ultimate result was that we saved each other considerable money. He got his property without having to pay an exhorbitant price and we got the right of way at very much less than we would have had to pay for it if we were buying it from the cemetery. When it came to Cypress Lawn, we paid 15 cents a square foot for a portion of the property, and 12 cents a square foot for a portion. We made an adjustment of the various purchases, and I could not tell offhand the cost without going into the account; it could be done.

Subsequently the cemeteries were established there, and they are there now.

Questioned by Master.

Comparing the cost with my valuation, it did not cost anything like that. I can ascertain very closely on examination of the accounts what we got from him for the land we turned over, and what he paid us for the lands we turned over to him.

Map 8, parcel 180, through City Extension Homestead, 132 ft. wide, 1449.35 ft. long, 4.39 acres, at $3000 an acre, $13,170. That comes, I think, in the Patton arrangements.

Questioned by Master.

That is not in the cemetery. The cemetery is not extended up there. Mr. Tommingson sold me the other day some of the land that they had acquired, with the intention of putting it into the cemetery, and which they had not included and still owned, which is a part of the City Extension Homestead.

391

392

393   Map 8, parcel 160, that is a strip of land through Cypress Lawn Cemetery, 80 ft. wide, 1624 ft. long, 3.94 acres, at $10,000 per acre, $39,400. The cost of that I will have to get. My recollection is that it cost a little over $20,000. It was acquired through the influence of Mr. Borel, who was a director in the water company, and also in the Cemetery Association.

CROSS EXAMINATION BY MR. STEINHART.

Parcel 60, 3.94 acres, my recollection is, cost $20,153. There was another strip also bought from the Cypress Lawn Cemetery that runs along the cemetery line. That is in an easement 60 ft. wide, 1027.98 ft. long, 1.47 acres, at $2500 per acre, $3675. That is put at a very much lower rate, owing to the fact that it is at the extreme end of

394   the cemetery. I think that cost $1674. That is parcel 169.

(Counsel for Plaintiff advises that there will be no question in the record as to what property the Spring Valley Water Co. owns in fee, and what they have an easement to, as it is all stated in the inventory.)

Questioned by Master.

I would have to do a little guessing in valuing an easement. I am considering the damage to property more than anything else. That is the only way that I can arrive at the value. The difference between the value of the property, and also what injuries there might be to it. The company must have the absolute control over it, or otherwise I do not imagine they would have to pay $1674 for it. If it was an easement for all purposes, it is not very much different

395   from the fee.

Referring to parcels appearing on map 8 of Exhibit 8, and numbered 173, 174, 179, 184, 171, 172, 176 and 170, owned by the company on the pipe line from Baden Junction to College Hill,* those parcels are all 80 feet in width; a portion of the strip is 100 feet wide, that is the strip through the Baden Tract, the balance is 80 feet. My record shows that parcel 170 is 100 feet wide, and whether it is or not, the valuation is made by the acre. I placed the same value per acre upon all these parcels, including 177, $3000 per acre. The average cost of those parcels to the company, per acre, was $2763.58 net and exclusive of any commissions or extensions.

Questioned by the Master.

Parcel 177, which is a triangular lot at the intersection of the County Road and right of way, was purchased on May 20, 1907, for $500 from the Baden Company. There is .08 of an acre in it. On

396   the basis of $3000 an acre, makes the appraisement $240.

Parcel 170, containing 3.15 acres, was purchased on the same date for $10,000, appraised at $9450.

---

*This was corrected in Court to "Central Pumps" July 23, 1915.

Parcel 176 was purchased from Flood and Mackay, I think it was at the same time, contains 9.76 acres. The price was $19,500, at the rate of $2000 per acre, on the basis of $3000 per acre the value is $29,280.

Parcel 172, purchased on March 28, 1907, contains 1.37 acres, cost $6350, or $4635.03 per acre. On the basis of $3000 per acre, it figures $4110.

Parcel 171, containing 2.64 acres, was purchased on April 8, 1907, for $8500, which is at the rate of $3219.69 per acre; appraised at $7920 on the basis of $3000 per acre.

Parcels 173, 174, 178 and 184 contain 1.40 acres, costing on March 28, 1907, $6000, which is at the rate of $4285.71 per acre; appraised at $4200.

CROSS EXAMINATION BY MR. STEINHART.

I have not the cost of those separate parcels. It was all bought at the same time. They were bought from Mr. Brooks. I don't know why the map is made in separate parcels, unless it is owing to courses and distances. I have not any question but that we can explain them.

397

DIRECT EXAMINATION BY MR. OLNEY.

The account in Baldwin & Howell's office showed that we paid $6000 for the property. I think the reason that those are separate is that there were probably four of the Brooks family that made deeds; the property came from the heirs of Brooks, and the probability is that it took four deeds to convey the title. I have had a copy made of the record in our office, showing all properties purchased, the total cost, and the total amount of sales that were made, so as to show the net cost of the entire right of way from Baden to Merced. This is the tabulation so made.

This tabulation covers parcels 180, 181, 169, 173, 174, 178, 184, 171, 172, 176, 170, 177, 152, 167, 165, and it takes in all of the 181's, and also another lot which is on map 9, parcel 186; it includes the lot on Mission Road and Price St. This piece cost $1000. I appraised it $2595. The Clark piece, parcel 186, is marked Fountain purchase, $1000 October, 1906.

CROSS EXAMINATION BY MR. STEINHART.

I think you will find parcel 165 on there. One is $3000, and another one is $5000. A man named Bowle is the man as to the $3000 piece, and a man named Guisto as to the $5000 piece.

(The document referred to is as follows):

BADEN-MERCED RIGHT OF WAY.

January, 1904—

Joost purchase ....$	6,800.00
Rodolph purchase	5,500.00
Hawley purchase	300.00
Parkins purchase	750.00
Yearean purchase	650.00
Lagomarsino purchase	500.00
Schath purchase	400.00
Koerner purchase	500.00
Pierce purchase	400.00

February, 1904—

Geilfuss purchase	2,400.00

May, 1904—

Patton purchase	2,730.00
Patton purchase	500.00
Patton purchase	600.00

(These three purchases were made through Mr. Patton who had previously acquired the options from the original owners at the prices named.)

Masonic Cemetery purchase, right of way	8,755.20
I. O. O. F. Cemetery purchase, right of way	3,760.00

June, 1904—

Ulmer purchase	800.00

July, 1904—

Overton purchase	300.00

March, 1906—

Cypress Lawn Cemetery, purchase of right of way.....	20,152.11
Burnett purchase	3,000.00

October, 1906—

Thornton purchase	1,000.0

January, 1907—

Bole purchase	3,000.00
Guisto purchase	5,000.00

March, 1907—

Heirs of P. Brooks purchase	6,000.00
Arata and Lagomarsino purchase	6,350.00
Thornton additional purchase	500.00
Baden Co. (Burr)	10,000.00

April, 1907—

Hamlin purchase	8,500.00
Patton additional	1,039.70

(These two pieces were purchased from Mr. Patton as before, he having options on the property from the original owners at the prices named.)

May, 1907—
    Baden Co. (Burr), additional purchase 500.00
    Flood purchase, right of way 19,500.00
    Cypress Lawn Cemetery Association right of way
        additional 1,674.74
    Patton purchase (final strip to complete right of way)   5,701.78

       Total purchases $128,268.03

Sales, November, 1905—
    Sale to Patton ....$ 9,267.50
Sales, April, 1907—
    Sale to Patton 13,358.50

       Total sales 22,626.00

                               $105,642.03
    Add expense and commission 8,294.70

       Total cost $113,936.73

DIRECT EXAMINATION BY MR. OLNEY.

I have valued the parcels appearing on map 7 of "Exhibit 8",   400
and indicated by numbers 148, 183, 189, 163, 147, 145, 150, 149, 201
and 159. They constitute a strip or right of way for, I assume, a
pipe line. The strip varies in width. Some portions of it are 100
feet wide, some 150. A small part of it is only 30 feet in width, but
that portion of it is only .55 of an acre, and about 787 feet long.
    Parcel 148, 14.89 acres, strip 100 by 6475.40 feet.
    Parcel 183, 1.90 acre, strip 100 by 825.35 feet.
    Parcel 189, 2.35 acres, strip 100 by 1023.94 feet.
    Parcel 163, 8.36 acres, strip 100 by 4270.70 feet.
    Parcel 147, 6.35 acres, strip 100 by 3095.37 feet.
    Parcel 145, 10.59 acres, strip 100 by 4442.04 feet.
    Parcel 150, 14.59 acres, strip 100 by 6345.22 feet.
    Parcel 149, 6.25 acres, strip 100 by 2578.02 feet.
    Parcel 201, 1.45 acres, strip 150 by 470 feet.
    Parcel 201, 1.39 acres, strip 50 by 1200 feet.
    Parcel 201, .55 acre, strip 30 by 787 feet.
    Parcel 159, 4.69 acres, strip 30 by 5627.80 feet.*

(Conceded by counsel for plaintiff that there are no pipes on
that right of way.)

Total acreage, 73.36 acres, 37,140.84 feet owned in fee. Valuation $2 per lineal foot, $74,281.68.   401

*Correction made in Court July 23, 1915, that parcel 159 is occupied by
Alameda 36-inch pipe line.

Referring to parcel 917 of easements, map 7, it runs from the Carnduff property, through the lands of the University of California.

Questioned by Master.

It is that section of the strip between the colored portion marked 150 and the colored portion marked 149.

DIRECT EXAMINATION BY MR. OLNEY.

I placed a value on it of 50 cents a lineal foot, $4,100.58.

402   Map 9, parcels 139 and 197, I have described as follows: Right of way Tanforan to Baden Station, north of the County Road, 25 ft. wide, 412 ft. in length; south of the County Road 25 ft. wide, 2542 ft. in length; adjacent strip on the south 28.30 ft. wide, 3846 ft. in length; total 6800 feet. Total area in the right of way is 3.973 acres, at $2000 an acre, $7946. (Suggested by both Mr. Dockweiler and Mr. Baldwin that there has never been a pipe line on it, and that it

403   is not in use).

I have placed valuation of $1 a lineal foot upon the pipe line easement across private property on the Crystal Springs pipe line from the company's property immediately east of the Crystal Springs Reservoir to the San Francisco County line, containing 24,177.96 lineal feet.

Questioned by Master. Is that owned in fee, or is it only an easement?

Mr. Olney: That is an easement, and my question was so put. In many cases the easement has a specific width, but in some cases it has not, it is only an easement for a pipe line.

DIRECT EXAMINATION BY MR. OLNEY.

404   I placed a valuation of $1 per foot for the 13,177.3 ft. of right of way occupied by the San Andres pipe line from the San Andres Reservoir to the County line of the City and County of San Francisco, exclusive of any properties owned in fee, making $13,177.30.

Map 9, parcel 129; this is situated on the Crystal Springs road, adjacent to the Templeton Crocker home. To a certain extent it is within the grounds or boundaries of the home place, contains only .42 of an acre. By Crystal Springs road I mean the County Road from San Mateo to Half Moon Bay, which passes and runs across Crystal Springs. I put a valuation of $1260 on the lot, which is at the rate of $3000 an acre. It is about three-quarters of a mile, or a mile west of San Mateo. It is indicated on the map as San Mateo screen tank lot.

A tabulation of Mr. Baldwin's testimony in regard to these miscellaneous pieces and rights of way offered as "Plaintiff's Exhibit 21".

(Witness subject to further call on direct examination of this   406
valuation year by year. Also to make a separate value for the West
Union lands, and on the possibility of something having been
omitted in this examination.)

CROSS EXAMINATION BY MR. STEINHART.

In regard to lot 129, I put a valuation on it of $3000 an acre due
to the fact that the property, especially a small tract, could be sold
on that basis in that vicinity. If it were a larger one, I would have
put a smaller value per acre upon it. The two factors that partien-
larly enhance its value are that it is a small tract and that it is close to
San Mateo. Even if it were further from San Mateo, or if it were a   407
larger tract, it might, perhaps, have a greater value, because, perhaps,
I should have valued it just as a lot, or maybe by the foot. I valued it
at $3000 an acre as an acreage proposition for convenience more than
anything else. If it had been an acre tract, I probably would have
valued it the same, or if a two acre tract, I might have shaded it somewhat, as I increase the area. I would shade it if it were a bigger
piece, and think that that might account for part of the difference.

Map 9, parcel 168; I will read you the description that I have
of that parcel from my report made on the 12th of July. I did not   408
make the report on parcel 168 from notes taken on the ground. It
was just simply a mental note. I inspected the property several
times within the last six or seven months. The description of the
property is Southern Pacific Railroad Company is in operation immediately adjacent to westerly line of this property; County Road
runs through it; it is a level tract of land, partly subject to overflow
at high tide; its chief value is for industrial uses. I am informed
by Mr. W. J. Martin, Mgr. for the South San Francisco Land Co.,
that it is meeting with success in selling factory sites in South San
Francisco on the basis of $3000 per acre, and he tells me that he re-
gards $1500 per acre as a very conservative value for the property
mentioned. I did not discuss with Mr. Martin, nor am I familiar
with or aware of a sale to the Presto Light people. That is marsh   409
land, but I do not think it is covered with water all the year round.
I have been along there several times, and it was not covered with
water when I was over it. I don't think the County Road is shut
off and fenced in. It runs along near the pipe line trestle. I have no
recollection of a white fence built there, making it impossible to get
out from that road. I do not know whether it is though or not, as I
have not seen it for some months.

Map 8, parcel 214, 215 and 216; this is low land, sandy soil,
good vegetable land, and used for vegetable gardens. The water, at
certain seasons of the year, in the winter time, comes down, and may
effect the land to some extent. I do not think that those parcels   410

fill every year with the wash; I am quite sure they do not. I do not know what that land rents for. I should be surprised if it rents for as much as $30 to $40 per acre per year. I did not purchase the Ravenswood to Belmont pipe line right of way referred to on page 7. I am quite sure I bought those parcels 214, 215 and 216, but I don't remember any additional rights of way purchased by me outside of those. I have not purchased any other rights of way for any other public utility. I have had no experience in purchasing rights of way, outside of the rights of way that I have testified to, nor have

411 we acted as rights of way agents for anyone else. In valuing rights of way, in fee, I have considered to some extent the value of the land over which the rights of way extend, but I have not made the value of the right of way to correspond with the value of the land over which the right of way exists, for the simple reason that my experience and observation is that you cannot buy rights of way, especially for a pipe line, at anything like the actual value of the land over which it goes.

I increased the value over the mere acreage value that is contained in the right of way very much. I don't figure the percentages, because it does not strike me that that is the proper way to do it.

412 DIRECT EXAMINATION BY MR. OLNEY.

The Ravenswood right of way, valued at $2 a foot, figures about $1000 an acre. The only reason for doing that is the fact that a right of way was sold to the Sierra Light & Power Co., across marsh lands in March, 1910. The company paid $14,500 for the easement, and for a double power line across the Bowie Estate lands. The Pacific Gas & Electric Co., in February, 1913, paid $3500 for an easement across 2 1/3 acres which were part of the Laurelwood Farm, near Santa Clara. Those are the only two instances I am familiar with regarding easements. In this case, I know that a pipe line constructed on the right of way would have to be on a trestle over the marsh lands. I realize the fact that the lands are not worth $1000 an acre, but it seems to me that the injury to the property and the inconvenience that is caused by the construction of the pipe line on a trestle is a greater objection than would be a power line. No benefit can come to the property by reason of a pipe line and trestle. A power line furnishes power for pumping purposes and for other electric purposes, and it seems to me that if a power company has to pay at any such rate as that, which seems to be the case in the only two instances I know anything about, it is not unreasonable to

413 suppose that this line would be worth that much. I don't know what it cost. I have no information on that. I do not pretend to be an expert on that subject; I give it to you for what it is worth.

CROSS EXAMINATION BY MR. STEINHART.

It was a double power line that was included in that easement. I do not know that a person letting a power line go through his property, could use that power direct. Buildings could not be put immediately under the power line, but the land can be utilized.

I do not know that the San Francisco and Sierra Power Line Company had an agreed understanding that nobody along those lines was to have power. I have no recollection of ever having sold properties west of Pilarcitos, nor west of San Andres, or west of Crystal Springs. 414

I not only bought San Mateo Park, but sub-divided it, I think, along about 1901. I think there may be four or five lots in there unsold. It was put on the market 14 years ago.

Dingee Park came to us after it had been sub-divided by someone else. It was put on the market, I think, in 1907, and it was in 1907 or 1908 that we took hold of it, I think.

We have not sold anything north of the southerly end of the lake. 414½ I don't know of anything in there except what is owned by the water company. The El Cerito property I mentioned was adjoining San Mateo.

The Uplands, sold to Colonel Crocker, was sold in 1897 or 1898.

My experiences have been, I should say, from Redwood City to 415 Burlingame. I don't recall selling anything north of Burlingame, excepting 140 acres in the Silva tract, which we bought for the Spring Valley Water Co. some years ago. We have bought a good deal of property for the Spring Valley Water Co., and have been connected with them for a good many years in that way. The late firm of McAfee & Baldwin was not connected with them. I never heard of a map that the firm of McAfee & Baldwin put out, sub-dividing Lake Merced about 1889. In regard to these transactions in Burlingame, the one to which you have specially referred, the Colonel Crocker home for instance, I handled personally in 1897. I purchased San Mateo Park immediately adjacent to San Mateo, put on the market, I think, 416 very shortly after it was purchased in 1901. It would be pretty hard for me to recall at the moment the various transactions that I have handled personally.

Referring to map 3, parcel 124, it has a very fine growth of firs. There is a canyon, a ravine that runs east, particularly wooded. It is extremely steep. I do not recall in detail the character of the soil. 417 In a general way it might be called a rough tract of land. It has, as I recall it, particularly attractive features by reason of the growth of timber. I went on that parcel myself. That is, I think we were on the corners. They were pointed out to me by Mr. Lawrence. It is possible that we were at least from one-eighth to one-sixteenth of a mile away from it.

Map 3, parcel 60, valued at $40; I don't recall whether I was on that particular tract, but I went up very close to it, probably within a quarter of a mile. I think I went along the road that is in the next quarter section.

418   I do not recall the character of the soil, parcel 20. I think it is very rough; a good deal of rocks. I don't remember any ravines and gullies. There may be some. I have been over there twice. I think it was in April, 1914, that I was there for two or three days.

419   Map 3, parcel 6, $50 an acre; I think I might answer the question as to whether I went on that property myself, and maybe some others that you are going to ask, by saying that I did not walk over every one of those parcels of land. My examination was confined largely to the view that I would get going up in a machine and stopping at different places. The probability was that I was close enough to see it, and to get a general idea of it.

Parcel 6, valued at $50, parcel 60 at $40, parcel 124 at $60. There have been no sales made there so far as I know, and in making my valuation, I did not take into consideration any sales made immediately adjacent to these properties within the last seven years.

Parcel 138; I do not know of any sales in the immediate neighborhood of that parcel, and in making my appraisal, I did not consider any sales made immediately adjacent to that parcel within the last seven years.

420   I did not go upon that tract of land referred to as Parcel No. 92. I did not go to any extent upon any tracts of land in making my investigations, other than such tracts of land as were adjacent to the roads covered by automobiles. I walked over portions of the property; we would stop and get out of the machine and walk some little distance over the property; practically all of it is reasonably accessible by means of those roads. This tract to which you refer now is practically all in the reservoir. It is not very likely I would be on that. I put a value of $200 an acre on that portion of the land which is out of the reservoir. That property is inaccessable. I did not consider it necessary to go upon the land immediately adjacent to it, as it is in perfectly clear sight. It is probable that the portion immediately

421   adjacent is very difficult to get over, and rough in character, but that would not make any difference so far as my idea of the value of the land is concerned. I did not go there.

Map 5, parcel 212, $125 an acre; I do not know when that was purchased by the company. I know absolutely nothing about it.

Map 5, parcel 202, $100 an acre; there are two pieces, one at $100, and one at $150. I did not take into consideration, in making my valuation, a sale made to Finckler immediately adjacent to that

422   property, as I don't know of it at all.

Referring to the Phelps property; it is rolling land, and runs up to the top of the ridge. I went upon the property myself. There are gullies and ravines upon it, but not to any extent. There is a great deal of that land that is agricultural land. I do not think that the character of the country about there is extremely precipitous.

"Exhibit 14", parcel No. 9, valued at $1750. That parcel is a particularly well sheltered portion of the tract. It is on the west slope, and I think practically all of that is in vegetable gardens; some portions of it down towards the end is in a forest. I think the fact that it is in San Francisco County gives an added value to it, though there is some of the land adjoining it in San Mateo County that is just as good so far as the soil is concerned. The disadvantage of overlooking the ocean is that you are that much farther away from transportation; also the character of the soil is not nearly as good upon the ridge as it is down on those slopes. I did not value that for agricultural purposes. I do not consider that the fact that the lake is there adds very materially to it; it may. I did not value the property with a view of selling the tract in any such sub-division as that. I was simply using those methods of sub-division as a means of grading the value of the property as a whole.

I do not think that there was any property bought by Brickel in that neighborhood. There was a sale made to Brickel, I think, of 60 acres in San Mateo County, immediately southwest of parcel No. 9, and running down to the ocean. The selling price of that, I think, is about $30,000, I am not sure, being about $500 an acre.

I am familiar with the sale from Whitcomb Estate to Eyre. That is immediately adjacent to parcel No. 9, and sold at $1000 an acre. I valued parcel No. 9 as a part of the whole, at the rate of $1750 an acre. These sales have no bearing, in my opinion, on the value of the Merced property. They are cut off, isolated, and inaccessible, and are surrounded by this large holding. I consider Merced particularly accessible. Ingleside Terrace might be better, but it is quite accessible. The United Railroads, I know, have not discontinued the service to Ingleside Terrace and St. Francis Wood. I consider that the valuation of Merced is greater than the land covered by those two sales, because that property is a portion of the whole tract, and the tract as a whole is worth, I think, per acre, more than a couple of isolated tracts that were sold at particularly low prices.

I sub-divided to some extent the Sutro Forest purchase, which was made in the early part of 1912, 823 acres, at $2000 per acre. The three sales made by the syndicate of which I was a member, were made at $3000 an acre, being one tract of 82 acres, one tract of about 143 acres, and another tract of 173 acres, I think. The 173 acre tract is what is known as the St. Francis Wood. The 82 acres is what is known as the Forest Hill tract. They were sold practically at the same time that the other was bought, and the selling price was $3000 per acre. The St. Francis Wood tract was sold in April, and the deed was recorded in March or April, 1912, I am not sure.

427   Tract No. 3; outside of the fact that it faces on the Pacific Ocean,
it also has a frontage on Sloat Boulevard, and is at the extension of
the car line. It is covered with water to a large extent, and a great
deal of it is swampy, tule land. Ingleside Terrace was sold in 1911 for
$2700 an acre, being a tract of 140 acres. It is immediately opposite
parcel No. 5. I am not familiar with the price at which Ocean View
Park was sold. I do not know anything especially about Ocean View
Park. I know there is a tract of land there that has big signs on it,
428   saying that they are offering it for sale in sub-divisions. I do not think
it is any worse than Lake View, which is around Ingleside Terrace. It
may be true that those tracts which are opposite the parcel I valued
at $3000 were put on the market immediately after the fire, and
tenanted by refugees, and that there is not a house on those tracts,
that cost more than $600 to $1000. If it were not the case, this property, probably, would be worth more, but being the case, I consider
that the property is worth $3000 an acre. I do not place this valua-
tion on the land because of the fact that it is suitable for vegetable
gardening.

There have been no single sales along the Junipero Serra Boulevard opposite Lake Merced at a figure equal to $4000, $5000 or $6000,
because the property is all sub-divided, with the exception of this land
that may have been sold some years ago as a whole. I think the fact
that Lake Merced being in one ownership, a large unsettled and unsubdivided tract, would influence to some extent the value of surrounding
property, and would retard development to some extent. It did not
influence the Urban Realty Co. in attempting to put a high-class subdivision right opposite, but I think it has not accelerated it to any
great extent.

EIGHTH HEARING.   JULY 23, 1915.

Witness A. S. BALDWIN.

431-437   Discussion on reserved ruling brought up by question appearing
at page 318 of the record, and which was argued by the parties at
pages 330 and following, of the record. Objection was based on question to have witness, Baldwin, place a value upon the Lake Merced
lands, which he had valued on the supposition that the lake, as well
as the property valued, was not dedicated to a public use.

The answer of the witness was that if the lakes were not dedicated
to a public use, nor the property which was being valued, it would
add a 10% increase to the value of the said lands for the reason that
the lakes being private would be available to pleasure uses of the adjoining property, and possibly as a source of water supply.

Statement by the Master that when he should come to decide this
case, he is quite clear that he would not find his mind inclined to in-

crease this valuation 10% by reason of the fact that possibly the lake would be used as the witness suggests, and the result would be, that the objection to that question would be sustained.

After statement by Mr. Olney correcting certain misapprehensions in the mind of the Master, he decided to ponder over it further. Holds the ruling under reservation.

Certain corrections noted in the record. 437-440

CROSS EXAMINATION BY MR. STEINHART.

In relation to parcel 5-2, west of Pilarcitos, it contains 2852.82 acres, valued at $100 an acre; I did not make any segregation of this tract, but made a lump valuation, which includes the various grades and kinds of lands. I could not describe the different kinds of lands, 441 nor have I any idea as to how many gulches or ravines there are on it. I did not put any range of valuation on the different parts of that tract of land.

Referring to portions of this land, Tract 5-2, east of, and adjacent to parcels 7 and 28; I can show you on this big map where we went. We went on the road which runs southeast down the point between 442 the two arms of Pilarcitos Lake, and which runs on top of the Spring Valley Ridge and the Whiting Ridge. We went through No. 7, the other road runs along the top of the Montara Mountain Ridge. I did not get out of the automobile to go down into any of the ravines or gullies, nor could I tell you the time that I spent on that particular tract. I went over it two or three times, and probably went through the center of it, perhaps, as many as thirty or forty times on the road leading down to the stone dam. I have been over the upper portion of the tract, near the two tracts we mentioned, 7 and 28, four times. I could not describe the different parcels of land composing it; I only 443 know it in a general way. My recollection is that it is covered with brush and some small timber. Referring to the entire Tract 5-2, the land on both sides of the road running south from Pilarcitos dam down through the canyon slopes to the east and also to the west. The west slope is nearly all quite heavily timbered with firs, madrones, and manzanitas. I could not tell you the number of acres of flat land there are in that tract. Comparatively small portions of it are flat, and only from guess, perhaps, 10% of it is what you might call absolutely flat land, and that is down along the Pilarcitos Creek. Possibly the hill tops, and I think throughout the whole tract, that 10% of the entire tract is flat land. That would not alter my opinion or my judgment as to the average value of the tract. The portion that I testified 444 to as being flat land runs along the road down to stone dam, measured according to my memory, probably an average of several hundred, 200 or 250 feet. The road is apparently, from the map, about two miles long. I have never figured out the acreage, but I suppose it is somewhere in the neighborhood of 48 acres, but I am not positive as to the area. I have not valued any of this land as agricultural land. The hillsides and wooded surface are worth more for residential purposes than for agricultural land. I did not consider it important to grade it to see what portion of it was suitable for residential land and what for other purposes, as I am taking the whole 22,000 or 23,000 acres 445 and making a valuation of them as a whole. If this tract had been cut up into smaller pieces, I should have made a separate valuation upon each piece; but looking at it as an entirety, I regarded the value of it at $100 as being conservative.

Map 3, parcel 27, those are triangular pieces on the edge of the ridge, valued at $30 an acre. My reason for putting a nominal figure on those was simply because of the shape. In valuing it as a whole, I took into consideration that it had to be acquired in those shapes, and I think that in many instances the valuation of these pieces, by reason of their shapes, is not of advantage to the company, so far as establishing the value is concerned. I valued them separately, and that would apply to all of it; at the same time, it establishes the value of the whole tract, which value I consider a conservative value. I valued those lower separately than I would if they had been attached 446 to property adjoining and had been a part of it.

Parcel 5-2, valued higher than parcel 27 because it was in much more advantageous shape than those triangular pieces; if it were necessary to acquire this property on December 31, 1913, and you had to deal with these various owners at that time, the valuations that I have put on each tract is what I would consider a conservative price to pay for each particular tract, and in order to get the whole piece. If you are dealing with owners that have only a small piece of land like that, I do not think that the valuation should be as high as a tract that could be used to advantage. I valued that on the basis of what should be paid for it in acquiring the 22,000 or 23,000 acres. When I valued these parcels here, I did not value them at a higher price, because they were a part of a large acreage. Why should I? I do not think it would have been the proper way of valuing them. I looked at it this 447 way, that there were 22,000 acres of land there to be acquired from the various owners, assuming that they were in various ownerships, and then I considered what each one of those parties should receive for the property at that time, on December 31, 1913, and I consider the amount that should be paid—the value of that property as a whole—the value of the separate subdivisions.

Map 8, parcel No. 127, is valuable as a right of way, and could be used for that, but I did not give it an additional value due to that fact. I do not know of any other use that it could be put to. I do not mean to say that the property could not be used, except those portions of it here, which is the lower part here,—and that might be drained; the southerly portion is subject to more or less overflow in high water. Unless some provision was made for taking care of the water, it would be difficult to use the property for residential purposes. It is reasonable to assume that it could be used for that purpose. The value, $1,000 an acre, is quite consistent with the valuation which is placed on the right of way for the State Highway, which is adjacent to that, or very close to that, which was $1200 an acre. I am informed that was put on by surveyors and appraisers at the time the highway was built. It is higher ground, but especially considering the fact for which it was used, it seems to me that $1200 an acre is a pretty good price to pay to benefiting owners.

Parcel No. 127 has value for vegetable gardens and for living there. I do not see why it could not be used and utilized for the homes of those people who would have their places there, and that is so with reference to all of the lands in that section used for vegetable gardens. The rent paid for the vegetable gardens, I suppose, runs from $20 to $30 an acre. That is all that is paid as rental by the persons who use the land for vegetable gardens and living there, but people do not get 6% interest on what they hold their land for. The whole section there is practically vegetable gardens, chicken ranches and duck ranches, and there is no other use than for vegetable gardens. I have not added anything to the value of it by reason of its residential value, but come to think of it though, it might be used as a duck ranch.

Map 7, parcel No. 154, Frisbie land, the 40 odd acres is all high land. I went on it in 1902 when we bought it, and I was down there a little over a year ago. I did not go around every corner of it, but I know what we paid for it, and I know the difficulty we had in getting it. I do not think that at least 25 per cent of it is marsh land, but even if that were the fact, my idea of the value would not be changed.

Referring to easements, and also to the Ravenswood right of way, I do not pretend to be an expert on that question, except for the experience we have had in the purchase of the right of way from Baden, and also with the data that I have been able to obtain, and the fact that we did sell a right of way a short while ago. That is the limit of my experience. I have no recollection of ever having acquired any right of way other than the Baden-Merced right of way. I handled this Baden-Merced right of way in part, assisted by Colonel Fred Bergen. He worked absolutely under my direction. We worked together on it.

Parcel No. 152; at the time that parcel was purchased by me, the Burnett lands, I think, were used for vegetable gardens.

Parcel No. 181 is in three parcels, and is the parcel in which I had the dealings with Mr. Patton, in part, but not entirely. Referring to the portion in the lower left hand corner, south of No. 180, that land, as I recall it, was practically all used for vegetable gardens. The portion of that land in parcel 181, through the Geilfuss holding, is the portion north of 180, the triangular piece. The Geilfuss home was in existence at that time, and it ran through the orchard. The Fountains lived there for years. I did not say that the Fountain home had been built there. If I did, it was unintentional. I had no intention

448

449

450

451

452   of saying that the property had increased by reason of the construction of the Fountain home.

Map 8, parcel 173. All of the land from there down to Baden was all of the same character,—vegetable gardens. In fixing the value of this property, I did not establish it by reason of the value of the lands themselves—by reason of the balance of the tract. Put it this way: The value, $3000 per acre for this right of way from Baden to Cypress Lawn Cemetery, was arrived at largely by reason of the cost; that cost was about $2700 an acre net to the company, exclusive of any commissions or expenses that we were at, in 1907. I valued this largely by reason of the cost. I don't think the cost of the neighboring land

453   entered appreciably into the cost of the right of way, or was it a big factor with the owners. Not in that instance, because I think they regarded largely the injury it would be to their property. The property is still used as vegetable gardens, and I only increased that portion of it in value to any extent through the cemeteries.

453-456   Here ensued discussion between counsel as to what the increase in valuation, $80,000, referred to. Counsel for complainant wants it understood that it includes much more than these particular tracts about which witness is being examined, and that the witness' answers have been confined to speaking of the right of way from Cypress Lawn to Baden Junction, and that from Cypress Lawn Cemetery south this right of way had cost on an average $2700 an acre, exclusive of commissions and expenses.

457   Referring to the Crystal Springs pipe line, the only information that I have on that subject is that it consists of the right to lay and maintain a pipe line extending through these various tracts owned by private parties, and that the easements are of varying widths. I do not know anything about the conditions in those easements, but I assume that in all cases they are easements to lay the pipes under the ground. I do not know whether there are any other restrictions. I assume that in granting easements the company would have right of

458   access to them at all times. I consider that it is a very great detriment to the property of any one having a pipe line easement; it is objectionable in case of sale. (The last answer of witness was stricken out as not responsive to Counsel's question.)

Questioned by the Master.

I don't know what the conditions are, if there are any.

CROSS EXAMINATION BY MR. STEINHART.

In valuing my pipe line fee land, I assume that the company would have the right to lay the pipes either above or below the ground.

Map 7, of "Exhibit 8", parcels 148, 183, 189 and so forth, valued at $2 per foot, which is equivalent to about $1000 an acre, that is less than I have valued the right of way covered by parcels 173, 174, 178, 184, and so forth, being the Baden-Merced right of way. This I valued

459   by the acre, based upon what it cost. My reason for valuing one at

$6 per lineal foot, and the other at $2 per lineal foot, is because the Ravenswood right of way is over marsh land, and corresponds with the prices paid for rights of way by power companies. I don't know what this cost. I have no data on that. Mr. Sharon gave me one or two cases and I will say from memory, they were 147 or 149, costing about $1500 an acre. I think it was either 147 or 149, a strip 6.35 or 6.25, and another one that went up pretty high. He did not know what the whole was worth. He had only the data on four pieces. Another piece was about $200 an acre. The other piece, as I remember it, was the piece through the University lands, but I don't remember what it was; it seems to me it was 30 or 40 cents a foot. I do not recall sales there at $245 an acre, $214 an acre, and $180 an acre. I had no notes of those. It was such a small part of the right of way that I could not form any views upon the subject, and I thought that sales of rights of way to power companies were more in line. I do not know anything about what the Sierra Power Company's agreement exacts, but I do not think that that would cut any figure. I did not consider the $1500 an acre sale, because I thought, perhaps, they bought the other, and if they had one piece left, the man, perhaps, was a little grasping on it, and I didn't think it established the value. I did consider the Baden-Merced right of way a more valuable right of way than the Ravenswood-Belmont right of way. 460

Ravenswood-Belmont right of way runs as far as my information goes, along the marginal land between the marsh and the high land. The portion around 147 and 145 runs through Redwood City, and I think it is practically all marsh land. My valuation is not based on the character of the land, and is only governed by what other people have paid for rights of way, and taking into consideration to some extent the fact that the pipe would have to be on a trestle, which I think would be very objectionable. It might not be on a trestle through the Frank Tanning Co. land, and through Redwood City it will have to go underground, under the water, I think. 461

Refer to page 381 of testimony, map 9, parcel 193, in regard to the Silva tract.

(Counsel for Complainant here interjected that he was not referring to the Silva tract there.) 462

I should have, perhaps, qualified my statement (page 381 of testimony) by saying, that a great deal of the property in there, Lomita Park, close to it; there are unsubdivided tracts adjacent to that property. You get south of the Silva tract quite a distance before the property is sub-divided; when you come to Millbrae, you strike the Mills place, which is held in its entirety. If you have drawn the conclusion that my valuation was placed on this property because I thought everything else around had been sub-divided, that is not the case. 463

(Counsel for the Complainant here read from the testimony to show that the reservoir lot is parcel 133, and not the Silva tract.)

Taking the easterly side of the road, I am of the impression that the property opposite the reservoir lot has been sub-divided; also the property opposite the Silva tract. The Coleman property on the north has not been sub-divided, and the property adjacent to

464 it on the south has not been sub-divided. The tract south of, and contiguous to the Silva tract is the Bay Side Co., containing 337 acres, which is not sub-divided. The County map shows next to that the Millbrae Villa tract, and I don't think that has been sub-divided or built up. Next to that is the D. O. Mills land, 1100 acres, not sub-divided. North of that is the Coleman tract, 133 acres, not sub-divided. North of that is the Ludermans, used for a nursery. I presume that north of that is the Dealman and Buck tract; I have

465 not looked at it. North of that is the Cupertino Land Co., where there have been sales of $1000 an acre. This has an acreage of 484 acres. These frontages extend for probably about a mile.

(Counsel for Complainant stated according to the map one tract immediately north of the reservoir tract, C. P. Chesley, had been omitted. Counsel for Defendant claimed that to be the Bush tract unsubdivided.)

I don't know whether it has been sub-divided or not. I can give you some prices, if you would like to have them, on some of these lands.

466 Referring to the factors of difference going to make the valuation of $650 on the Silva tract, and $300 on the portion immediately on the other side of the ridge, I think this piece is worth more, owing to the fact that it has a frontage on the highway, it is worth at least twice as much as that piece on the top of the hill on the

467 west side of the ridge. I think that the east side of the ridge is more valuable than the west side. I do not know that the Beresford land has been found objectionable because of its windy character, but the land on the east slope of the ridge, I think, is protected from the wind, and I think all of the land on the east slope, all of the way up, is worth more than it is on the westerly slope. It does not always apply that the nearer you get to the state highway the more it is worth. I do think the Silva tract, having a frontage on the road there, taken as a whole, is worth more than the land on the

468 westerly l pe adjacent to it. If it had been near San Mateo or Burlingame, it would have been worth more. It happens to be near Millbrae, but I am not influenced in placing a valuation by reason of the fact that that is the case. I think the people who buy lands are the ones to speak of that factor, as to whether it is an advantage being close to Millbrae. If it were further south it would be worth more.

Mr. Olney asked you this question: "Let me ask this question, "Mr. Baldwin: In valuing these lands did you assume that the pur-"chaser of the land, for instance, would have the right to put down "wells?

"A. I do assume that. I assume that a man would have the
"right to do with that land just as he would do with any other land
"he was buying there.

"Q. And to the extent then to which the ownership of the   **469**
"land gave him the right to use the water for domestic purposes, or
"irrigation, or anything else on the land, you would assume that he
"would get whatever rights went with the land and in the nature
"of things the water? A. Yes."

It is my understanding, in speaking of the watershed lands,
that the owner has the full use of the land. Where the land borders
along a stream, I think the owner would have the right to use the
water in that stream. I presumed that in part on the westerly side,
a man would get his water there for pasturage and stock purposes
on the land. There are springs there in places. I am not prepared
to give you the location of all of them, nor have I any idea how   **470**
many springs there are there. I have no idea as to their location,
but am taking it for granted that there are some there. I don't
know whether there are any or whether there are not. I have not
examined it as a cattle proposition, and I did not say that it was a
stock proposition. I might have said that incidentally some of it
might be used for stock purposes, but I have regarded the entire
tract absolutely as a residential proposition. To the east of the San
Andres property is the Kohl place, not immediately adjacent to
Spring Valley land. I don't think there are any of the finer homes
immediately contiguous to San Andres property. To the east of
Crystal Springs, and west of Burlingame and San Mateo, the homes
that are there are large acreage tracts, and the rear of those tracts
is more or less contiguous to Spring Valley. The Carolan place is   **471**
pretty close; the Crocker place is not very far; the Poniatowski
place is a comparatively short distance.

The Kohl place is probably three-quarters of a mile from the
Spring Valley holdings.

Mrs. Carolan paid for the Carolan place, $310 an acre in 1912.
It is all on the east slope, and runs practically up to the top of the
ridge, and runs down quite a distance.

The Polhemus tract is not settled. There are homes within a
very short distance of it. It covers between 700 and 800 acres.   **471½**
Below that we get the Poor Farm. I do not know where the Finkler
home is.

The Carolan place is contiguous to the Spring Valley Parcel No.   **472**
90, map No. 3. It has an acreage of about 554 acres. The property
was bought some time prior to the deed—in October, 1912.

In regard to the Merced valuation, the highest value on the
acreage on any of the tracts is parcel No. 1, and to the south and
west values grade down. The factors that make toward that difference in valuation are that you are further away from the developed

135

section of that district, St. Francis Wood, and Ingleside Terraces. Ocean View Park and Vista Grande Park are more closely settled than Ingleside Terraces, and Forest Hill, but the character of the improvements is very different. The decrease in values to the west is due to the same reasons to some extent, but the value is less on that tract near the ocean because it was partly subject to the seepage water from the lake, which would have to be drained if it were used for residential purposes, or on the other hand, the waters might be of very considerable advantage if used for the purpose that I suggested. I am referring to parcel 3.

Forest Hill was very beautifully wooded, but I do not think the trees are of any very great advantage to that property in the quantity as they existed. They have been made use of in sub-divisions. Some of the trees have been left, but it has been a very expensive proposition clearing the land, even to the extent that it has been used.

St. Francis Wood was sold by us at $3000 an acre, and I valued parcel No. 9, which is opposite, at $6000 an acre in connection with the valuation of the whole. I did not increase the value, because I was valuing it as a whole. I did not make those sub-divisions with the idea of putting prices on those particular tracts, or of sub-dividing the property in that way. It was simply a proposition of grading the property, beginning at some point having a maximum value, and grading it from that point. Parcel 1, in my opinion, is the point of maximum value. St. Francis Wood, immediately opposite that, sold in 1912 for $3000.

Q. In 1912, yes. Now is the difference that you placed on that due to the fact that you were valuing parcel No. 1 in connection with all the rest of the land? A. I confess I do not get the standpoint of your question. The St. Francis Wood tract was 176 acres which was sold as a whole. Shortly after that an offer of $4000 an acre was offered for it and declined. Mr. Titus, who was one of the original purchasers wanted to sell at $4000 an acre, and the others did not want to sell, and they bought him out and paid him for his interest on a basis of $4000 an acre. Now, that was before any development had taken place in that section at all; it was in a raw state, and I therefore think that this property, of a limited area, being only a little more than 10% of the whole, and not taking in any of the high and remote land that the St. Francis Wood tract took in, should be worth that much per acre.

Ingleside Terraces was on the market in 1912. It was bought as a whole in 1911, and I think they had begun selling at that time. I do not think it a fact that practically the only sales there were made during the first year and a half it was on the market, which would run up to about 1912. They have sold over $800,000 worth of property at retail. There have been no movements since about

August 1, of last year. I don't know what they have been doing within the last year. I imagine that their property has been very much, as all real estate is, difficult to sell. I do not think that that movement stopped before December 31, 1913, in Ingleside Terraces. I am quite sure it did not. I valued a very small tract at $6000 an acre opposite St. Francis Wood, as compared with the other. I 476 might have thrown it into the whole tract, and made the other tract a little more, that is the adjoining tract No. 2. I would have raised tract No. 2 above $5000 if No. 1 were thrown into it. I should have made an increase proportionate to what this increase is on No. 1, and I would still have considered No. 1 worth $6000 an acre. I raised this piece $2000 above the figure of $4000, which Mr. Titus sold his interest opposite at, because it is a smaller piece, and also because it is worth more. I did not do the same in regard to my valuation of the watershed lands. On the contrary, many of the smaller pieces I have given smaller valuations, because they were not as useful, or not in as good shape as the larger pieces.

The value I placed on Merced is residential value. I don't know 477 that in my own office, land was offered at $2400 an acre, near the Park at "K" Street; I don't know the particular sale to which you refer. It might have been offered through my office. I am not familiar with all of the lots that we have for sale in my place.

Ingleside Terraces, I think I said, would have brought a better price had it not been for the surroundings. I considered these surroundings a detriment. It does not affect, perhaps, every foot of the property, but it does have an influence upon it. The property in Ingleside Terraces, on the whole, will not, and has not sold for anything near as much as it has in St. Francis Wood. It is not 478 desirable to have that class of property either directly to the south of you, when the line of travel is from the north to the south, or directly opposite to you, I do not know that I could draw any special distinction whether it was opposite, or whether it was south. People coming into Ingleside Terraces from San Francisco do not pass Ocean View Park. You could very easily conceal Ocean View Park in the property opposite Ingleside Terraces, the Merced tract, by planting trees. Junipero Serra Boulevard, at the present time, is a traveled road, and probably will always remain so, but the approach to this property is not restricted to that particular road. You do not have to go through Ocean View Park, or would not have to go by every time you went into it; that would not be the method that anybody would be likely to pursue in sub-dividing the property. It is directly opposite.

I have valued all property fronting on Junipero Serra Boulevard as being worth more than the property west of it, and I consider the property fronting there of an increased value, in arriving at the 479 value of the entire tract.

137

Ingleside Terraces sold for $2700 an acre in 1911. A portion of the property opposite Ingleside Terrace I have valued at $5000, and a portion at $3000. I think there is fully the difference in value, within that period, between $1300 an acre in 1907 for Ocean View Park, and $3000 an acre, at which I valued the portion in Merced opposite that tract. I have not graded parcel No. 6, because practically all of the tract within the 143 acres is level, or nearly so. I did not value the northerly part, nor the southerly part as worth more, and I did not make any difference between the northerly and southerly part. I valued the tract as a whole. That is as a part of the entire tract.

480   Referring to the distinction between the Brickell piece and parcel No. 9, my distinction takes place exactly at the county line. There is a difference between property in San Mateo and in San Francisco Counties. One in the city has at least the prospects of police protection, fire protection, water, gas and conveniences, and transportation.

Vista Grande tract, if opposite parcel 7, is in San Mateo County, and has, I imagine, rather limited police protection. I don't know whether it has water or electric light service. If the Pacific Gas & Electric Co. supplies electric light and power there, that might

481   perhaps increase the value of parcel No. 7.

The Brickell piece is a small piece pocketed by this ranch on the shores of the Pacific; that of itself is very considerable against the sale of it at any price approximating the Merced lands. It is about sixty acres in size, but only about one-half of it is available. The balance is precipitous. It is on the shores of the ocean, and slopes down very steeply. It is worse in character than parcel No. 10. In proportion, there is less level land in the Brickell piece than in parcel No. 10.

482   Parcel No. 4 sold for $1000 an acre (Whitcomb property), I think in 1911 or 12. Maybe it was sold in November 1913. The purchaser was Mr. Edward L. Eyre. I don't know whether he was buying it for himself or someone else. I assume that it was bought for someone else, but I understand that it was not bought for the

483   Spring Valley Water Co. I am quite sure that it was not. The Twin Peaks tunnel was authorized by a resolution, finally passed I think, in the latter part of 1912. The Twin Peaks tunnel increased values, in my opinion, about Merced, to the extent of the assessment. That would be a charge against the property. I did not say that an immediate increase had followed the passing of that resolution to the extent of the assessment, unless the assessment had been paid. At the time of December 31, 1913, the Twin Peaks tunnel had not increased the value of this land; the fact of this resolution having been passed, and the proceedings having been completed, had not, in my opinion, increased the value of this property

beyond any figure that I have put on it. My valuation did not   484
include any increase at all due to the Twin Peaks tunnel. I only
put a value on the property of what I considered it worth at that
time. The Twin Peaks tunnel project having reached a conclusion,
might have had some influence on values there, and I think it did.
I don't know what increased the prices; I won't say that it was
entirely due to that. I think to a certain extent, also, it was due
to the development that had taken place in 1912 and 1913 in Forest
Hill, St. Francis Wood, and Ingleside Terraces.

I think somewhere between 50 and 55 acres at St. Francis Wood
was sub-divided and put on the market. We have had nothing to
do with the development of that property, only incidentally. The
Mason-McDuffie Co. are the owners of the property, and we have
cooperated with them in a measure.

I did not attempt to give the valuation of Lake Merced according to the lines in which that property was acquired; I have not
seen any map that gives the property according to the acquisition.
I have based my value of Lake Merced entirely on the residential
possibility. I think on the lower portion of the property there is
an opportunity for industrial development. The Southern Pacific   485
Railroad line is close to it, as is also the Ocean Shore Railroad. I
think it highly probable that the southerly portion of the property
might be developed in that way, but I have not made any close study
of any plan of development. I valued this as a whole, by taking
the separate parcels here, placing the valuation upon them, and by
adding them together, got the valuation of the whole, and that is
my idea as to the market value of that property as of December 31,
1913. The meaning of market value is the price at which it could
be sold as a whole if it was available within, I should think, five or
six months. It might take that time to organize a syndicate. The
Residential Development Co. took about that time to organize. The
operations were suspended for quite awhile, owing to the fact that
some of the people backed out, and we had to buy the undivided
interests of the people who were selling the tract, from whom we
were purchasing. I was working on the proposition, off and on,   486
for about a year. It was a tract of about 820 odd acres.

I don't know anything about the Hooper tract. I am not
familiar with the property. I only know that the Lent and Oxnard
homes are there. I have had nothing to do with any sales. Some
portions of the margin of Lake Merced are broad and have an easy
slope; there is where the margin comes very close to the line, and   487
the banks are abrupt. I have put what I regarded as a nominal
value on the margin acres at $1000 an acre. That marginal strip
could be used in connection with the balance of the land for residence purposes, if it were permissable. There is a great deal of it
that is not steep land, particularly along tracts 9 and 10, and there

are many portions of it along the line of No. 2. It all borders on the lake. No difference was made in the valuation between the portions that overlook the lake and those that do not, as I have not considered the lake in any aspect whatever. I have gone on that land, and completely ignored the lake from a scenic standpoint.

488　　I should say that the way to make money out of this land, would be to sub-divide at least a portion of it, but if I were going to sell it in large tracts, I would not sell it in tracts of the shape such as I have graded it.

RE-DIRECT EXAMINATION BY MR. OLNEY.

Parcel 129, in San Mateo screen tank tract; there have not been any sales immediately adjacent to that particular lot that I know of, but within a comparatively short distance of it. We sold, in 1911, a portion of the Duncan Hayne property, containing 4.48 acres, to O. C. Pratt, Jr., at $3000 an acre. That property is probably three-quarters of a mile north of the screen tank lot, which is practically within the enclosure of the Crocker home place, and naturally there have been no sales immediately adjacent to it, but I think anybody would admit, from looking at the Pratt property, and looking at the portion of the Crocker home place adjacent to the screen tank lot, that that portion of the Crocker home tract is worth as

489　　much as the property we sold. I think the screen tank lot itself is as valuable as these adjacent portions of the Crocker home tract. The land in Highland Park, about one-half a mile east of this property, has sold at from $30 to $40 a foot, or as high as $5000 or $6000 an acre; that is within a very short distance of this property.

There have been some sales of what you would call rough land in the Howard sub-division, which is west of it, between this property and the Crystal Springs dam. Driscoll, I believe, paid about $1500 an acre for his property up in the Howard tract. That Howard sub-division is rather a scenic tract; it is hillside and steep, but that seems to add somewhat to the value of the property up there for home sites. It is probably three-quarters of a mile west of this particular piece of property. At the time it was purchased by Driscoll, I think the roads were graded, the sewers were either built, or agreed to be built, and water was available. The Duncan piece, I think, is a more recent sale in that tract, and I understand, sold at $2500 an acre, and consisted of four or five acres. In the early part

490　　of 1901 I purchased for the company the land referred to as parcels 214, 215 and 216, on map 8, for which I paid $700 an acre.

Referring to the right of way from Baden Junction to the Merced pump, I valued the portion immediately to the north, through the cemetery, on the basis of $10,000 an acre, or about 22½ cents a square foot. Taking into consideration what the company had to pay for the right of way through Cypress Lawn, the circumstances under which it was purchased, and also the fact that from interviews that I have had with the representatives of the two cemeteries, that the value that I put upon it was, in their opinion, below the value. For instance, I asked Mr. Tonningston, of the Masonic and Odd Fellows Cemeteries, if in case this right of way was abandoned, would the Cemetery Association buy it at that price; he said he thought they would be very glad to take it at that figure. The cemeteries were established subject to the purchase of the right of way, and have been gradually settled up. There has been no improvement in the way of residences and sub-divisions, or anything of that sort, on the rest of the right of way down there, but the highway has been constructed through it. The property is much more accessible, although I doubt if it could be sold for any more. I do not think there has been any material increase in valuation. I should say the property along this particular line has remained practically the same. Outside of the cemeteries, I think it would be more difficult now to purchase this right of way for this reason; at the time this was bought, Mr. Schussler thought that the right of way might be used as a boulevard or public highway, and while no direct promises were made, to any of these property owners, it was suggested that in time there was a possibility of its being used for that purpose. In the purchase from the Baden Co., of the southerly portion of the tract, they asked $15,000 for the right of way through their property, and reduced the price to $10,000, with the understanding that the strip could be used by them at any time, as a road, but whether it was or not, the privilege of using that as a road was one of the reasons for their reducing the price, and I think that now that the highway is there, to go and get a strip would be more difficult to do, because that argument and that incentive is gone. I see no reason why it would be, outside of that, more difficult to acquire that right of way now, or more costly than it was then.

In regard to the lands west of Pilarcitos, the westerly boundary line of the lands of the company run up to the top of the ridge, and it depends upon how far west you go, to what extent the lands on the west side of that ridge can be compared with the company's lands on the east side. When you get over to the coast, you get into a better class of land, so far as the soil is concerned, but on the westerly slope of the mountains the property is more exposed, and it is not as accessible as these tracts are, by reason of the roads which exist through the Spring Valley Water Co.'s property. Generally speaking, I do not think the other property is in the same class as property on the easterly side, because it has an entirely different environment.

Take the Pilarcitos land, tract 5.2, and the other lands which lie immediately west of Pilarcitos, and leaving out of consideration their value for watershed purposes, I have already said that I

491

492

493

494

141

thought the whole property was practically residential property, and the value is large in looking at it from that standpoint, and not from an agricultural or stock proposition. When I say residential properties, it does not mean lots, or one- and two-acre tracts. I mean more of suburban or country homes, such as exist around Woodside, Burlingame, Millbrae, back of Redwood and Menlo, and any of the foothill sections. It is valuable for country estates.

495

Tract 5.2, viewed from that point of view, is one of the most picturesque and valuable portions of the property, because it is in parts heavily wooded, running streams, plenty of water. Pilarcitos Canyon is one of the most beautiful places that I have ever been in. Trees extend to a very considerable distance up the hillside slopes. Tracts 3, 6, 124 and 60 are on the west side of the Pilarcitos Canyon, and all run into this canyon or ravine. Tract 124, I think, would naturally come in with tract 5.2. It is a very difficult matter to say just what tracts would be connected with other tracts, without any data as to sub-division. These tracts are not heavily wooded in the entirety. The ravines are wooded. I have walked along the flume indicated on map 3, which runs from Pilarcitos southerly and westerly to tract 5.2, and am acquainted with the character of the country, which is all heavily wooded, that lies on each side of it. In disposing of that property, or putting a value upon it, and assuming that it is all owned by one person, I would consider and value these particular tracts in conjunction with the rest of the property. If the thing was not sub-divided, and had not been acquired in that state, it would have gone into the valuation on a larger tract, and my values upon these various tracts was placed upon them in view of the fact that the property was in one ownership.

496

497

Tract 92 is clearly visible from across the lake. It can be seen from nearby, and I did not consider it was necessary to go over every foot of the land. It was possible to ascertain with accuracy and with certainty what its general character was for purposes of valuation, without actually going on it. I did not consider it necessary to go on that particular tract, or on a good many others, because I felt that my general knowledge of values in that section, and the examination I could make in the way I did make it, was sufficient to give me the information I was endeavoring to obtain. In going over a portion of this property in an automobile, I got out at a number of places; wherever we could not see clearly from the automobile, and where the automobile could not go, we got out, as frequently as I thought it was necessary. I don't remember how often it was, but maybe half a dozen times or more, and when we got out we would look at the property.

498

I should say that taking all of this country which lies to the west of the line drawn north-westerly and south-easterly, through the center of the San Andres Lake and down the San Andres Creek, then down

499

142

through the Crystal Springs Lake, and taking the land that lies west of that, that it has, to a very large extent, the same general character. It consists of ridges and valleys. There are some streams, particularly in the Pilarcitos Canyon, and in the San Mateo Creek. The tops of the ridges are generally free from timber. They are generally open, except in the north-westerly portion of the property, which is more or less covered with brush, and the tops of the ridges here are generally open, grassy land. I think it is the Cahill Ridge where the road runs for a large distance through timber. The Montara Mountains are not, it is open. Generally speaking, the canyons are wooded.

Omitting the West Union Creek lands of 1322 acres, at $125 an acre, it would leave an average value of the land on the westerly side of the hypothetical line drawn through San Andres and Crystal Springs, starting from the southerly end of the holdings on the Canada, up to the northerly line of San Andres, and taking in entirely that northerly piece, of about $101 an acre. I should have included parcel 144. In round numbers there are about 17,000 acres in that territory. A little over 300 acres to the east of this imaginary line, on the easterly slope, are watersheds. I think it is 16,700 and something. I shall have to get those figures. This acreage, which lies to the west of this imaginary line, could, I think, without any doubt, be disposed of at $100 an acre, and I think it would be a profitable real estate investment to buy them at that figure and then dispose of them. I don't think there would be the slightest difficulty in getting real estate men to engage in that enterprise.

My average value for the watershed lands which lie to the east of this imaginary line, describing them in general as running from this imaginary line up to the top of the Buri Buri Ridge, is about $255 an acre. I assume that these figures are correct, and will have a statement prepared. I think this tract could be sold as a whole at that rate, but I think the entire property could better be sold in the aggregate of the two, than either one separately. As an entirety it would be more salable, and would be a more satisfactory project to develop and handle. The figures which I have placed on it are not the highest market price of these lands. I have put a price which I regard as conservative, and which would leave, in my opinion, a very handsome profit to any syndicate that would buy the property and develop it.

I have a list of some of the transactions that we put through, and those which I personally handled in and around San Mateo and Burlingame, and that general region immediately to the east of this property. This list includes sales of acreage property, and also of sales in Burlingame, El Cerito, and other properties that are of smaller acreage. The list is not intended to be a list of all sales that we have made there. It does not include sales that we made of Burlingame property, for the reason that my record of those sales was destroyed. I have a record of the principal sales made since 1897. Referring to this list,

500

501

502

503   we have conducted sales of acreage property in an amount considerably over a million dollars. I should say that our sales within the last fifteen years have amounted to between a million and a half, and two million dollars. In the amount of acreage involved it would not be very much, because with very few exceptions, it was all high-priced

504   property. The largest piece in the whole that was sold was the Clark Tract near San Mateo, which is now San Mateo Park, amounting to 300 acres. I fixed the prices on all subdivision property. For instance, Burlingame, El Cerito, San Mateo Park, Dingee Park, Hayward Addition, Hayward Park, every subdivision that we had.

       Map 5, parcel 212; I did not know that that piece was purchased by the Spring Valley Water Co., in 1912, for $56 an acre, but if it had been, I should not have made any different valuation from the $125 an acre, which I put on it; that value, I think, is fully sustained by a sale that has just been made to Mr. George Holberton, of some 700 ·acres lying to the east of this property, and in the canyon on the road leading to Redwood. I do not think that property is as good as this.

505   The price obtained from the Holberton sale was $125 an acre. I had Mr. Pickering, of our office, interview Mr. Holberton, and that is what he told me he said. That is neither here nor there, though, because that sale had not been made at the time I made this valuation. The Holberton land lies immediately to the east of Tract 202.

       We sold 100 acres, known as the Maloney property, to Connolly, which is immediately south of parcel 208. It was sold in May, 1910, for $11,000. That is $110 an acre. In February, 1913, we offered Mr. Connolly $200 an acre for it, but he said that the property was not for sale. Subsequently, it was acquired by Mr. Oscar Beatty, and is now

506   owned by him; it is for sale at $250 an acre. This property was immediately south of parcel 208. It adjoins it. As between Tracts 208 and the Beatty land, I think it is about the same in character. I don't think 210 is quite as good as 208. I have placed a valuation of $125 an acre on Tracts 194, 195, 205, 211 and 208, which are in the West Union Creek watershed, and not within the watershed of Crystal Springs. (The broken lines through there is the watershed line. The land which lies to the west and south of that land is the land of the watershed of the West Union Creek, 1322 acres). 1322 acres, at a valuation of $125

507   an acre, will make $165,250.

       Map 3, Tract 90 (Howard Tract). The irregular line running across the south-easterly corner of the property northerly and southerly, is the line of the watershed between the Crystal Springs watershed and the watershed of San Mateo Creek below the dam. I placed a valuation upon that portion of the Howard Tract which is not within the Crystal Springs Reservoir watershed of $400 an acre, $83,664. The acreage in there is 209.16. Referring to Tracts 37 and 54, on map 4, and parcel 36 on map 3, which is immediately to the north of parcel 54, there are portions of these tracts where the water runs into San

Mateo Creek below the dam, and the acreage which is so within the watershed of San Mateo Creek below the dam, and not within the Crystal Springs Reservoir watershed, is 85.58 acres, valued at $300 an acre, total $25,674.

The following tabulation, which is a valuation by Mr. Baldwin, 508 placed on the Phelps Tract, and on these three pieces, without the watershed of Crystal Springs, was copied into the record:

COMPLAINANTS EXHIBIT No.

No. 1054
Spring Valley Water Company
Appraisal Dept.
July 22, 1915.
W. O. Jr.

Valuation of portions of
Phelps Tract, West Union
Creek Lands, Howard Tract,
etc., not within the Crystal
Springs Res. watershed.
A. S. Baldwin.

Valuation of A. S. Baldwin on Phelps Tract (option lands), and the portions of parcels 194, 195, 205, 211, 210 and 208 (West Union Creek Lands), and of Parcels 90 (Howard Tract), 37, 54 and 36, not within the watershed of Crystal Springs Reservoir.

Phelps Tract .... 969.94 acres at $125. per acre $121,242.50

The portions of Parcels 194, 195, 205, 211, 210 and 208 lying in the West Union Creek Watershed, and not within the Crystal Springs Reservoir Watershed ....1322. acres at $125. per acre $165,250.00

The portion of Parcel 90 (Howard Tract) lying east of, and not within the Crystal Springs Reservoir Watershed ...... 209.16 acres at $400. per acre $ 83,664.00   509

The portions of Parcels 37, 54 and 36 lying east of and not within the Crystal Springs Watershed .... 85.58 acres at $300. per acre $ 25,674.00

Map 9, parcels 133, 197, 131, 193 and 24; I based my value on those lands by sales in or near the vicinity of the property in question. The Silva tract—not the Spring Valley Silva tract, but another one on the county road north of it, about 132 acres, sold four years ago for $500 an acre, and resold about two and a half years ago at $800 an acre, and about a year ago resold at $900 an acre. That is the only sale of a large piece close to this property, with the exception of a sale that has recently taken place from Ansel M.

510   Easton, to Hale Bros. The land was taken in on a trade at $1100 an acre.

(Motion to strike this last statement out, on the grounds that it is immaterial, irrelevant and incompetent, granted.)

I got at my valuation from my general knowledge of values down there, and also the sale of this other property, which is the only one in the way of acreage which I know of immediately near that. I do not think that the Silva tract, 132 acres, is as good as any of this property here belonging to the water company.

NINTH HEARING.   JULY 26, 1915.

Witness: A. S. BALDWIN.

511-512   Referring to reserved ruling on question appearing on page 318 of the transcript, which was answered on the following page: Interpretation put upon it by the Master is that having given value for the lands in the Lake Merced properties, exclusive of the lakes themselves, Mr. Baldwin, in response to question objected to, says that if the lakes were included and the whole property sold, he would increase his valuation 10% of the amount he has already given. Objection is, therefore, overruled.

Exception noted by counsel for defendants. Not necessary as stipulation already made to cover.

Certain corrections noted on the face of the record.

513-514   CROSS EXAMINATION BY MR. STEINHART.

In placing my valuation on the Lake Merced lands, I did not assume, or give any consideration to development of water upon the property itself, but that water could be obtained when needed from the Spring Valley Water Co., just as it is being supplied to St. Francis Wood and the Ingleside Terraces.

The Whitcomb purchase was made by Mr. Eyre, who is a director of the Spring Valley Water Co., and is the piece indicated on "Plaintiff's Exhibit 14", which is the easterly portion of that tract.

514-515   In regard to rights of way which I have been instrumental in purchasing, I did not consider as an important factor the value of the neighboring lands, and that applies to all the rights of way that

146

I have valued. The only other right of way, except the easement, is the Ravenswood land.

(Mr. Olney here calls attention to the fact that the witness' answer is possibly misleading; that the lots in the Abbey Homestead, which are on the right of way of one of the pipe lines, he simply put the market value on, but the strips he valued in the manner in which he testified to.)

RE-DIRECT EXAMINATION BY MR. OLNEY.

A map showing in a general way the cities of San Mateo and Burlingame, and the region thereabouts, offered and received in evidence as "Plaintiff's Exhibit 22". Map entitled "Map of the City of San Mateo and the Town of Burlingame, and surrounding properties", dated 1906.

Witness indicates by a cross the approximate location of the San Mateo screen tank lot.

Witness indicates boundary line of tracts which he or his firm purchased and subdivided in that general neighborhood. It is marked "San Mateo Park", and consists of 295.61 acres, acquired in 1902. El Cerito Park we subdivided and sold. We disposed of it for the Howard & Goewey people; we placed the value on it. El Cerito was sold, I think, about 1898, and Highland Park, immediately adjoins the property marked "Crocker Heirs", and that is the tract in which this screen house tank lot is located. Highland Park was sold in about 1900. The Hayward Addition was bought in 1905, consisting of 20 acres, for which we paid $4000. The adjoining property we sold to the syndicate, that is the 109 acres. This is known as Hayward Park, and was sold for $200,000.

The tract immediately south of the lands marked "A. L. Brewer", containing 24.33 acres, was sold on February 20, 1912, for $1200 per acre. This property slopes gradually up towards the west. Not steep land. Three sales were made by us for Mr. Pillsbury, in parcel marked on the map "Burlingame Park". These were small tracts west of the Burlingame Club, on the same road. One sale made January 29, 1913, 2.35 acres, at $3300 an acre; another February 10, 1913, of 2.23 acres, at $3300 an acre; another of 2.30 acres, at $3300 an acre. These tracts are adjoining each other. (Mr. Olney: We do not claim that a value of $3300 an acre for property down here would stand as a comparison with the value of the property over in Crystal Springs.) I have already testified to a sale at $3000 an acre, which was nearer the screen tank property than these others are. It is marked "2" on this map, north of the land marked "Howard", and was a sale made to O. C. Pratt, Jr., on November 20, 1911. This property is really west of El Cerito Park. The whole district, I assume, is called that now.

The sale Carolan to Irwin, of 31.25 acres, was made on September 5, 1913, for $165,000, and was an improved place, marked in

516

517

518

519

pencil on the map "W. G. Irwin". It included the house, but no
furniture. The improvements, I don't think, were worth over $15,-
000 or $20,000.

520

The piece marked in pencil on the map "The Jennie Crocker-
Whitman piece", I have not the data as to that.

The Carolan piece marked in pencil 500 acres; I have never
been over it, but have seen it from the top of the hill. Some of it
is hilly, some of it is cut up, some is flat, some of it is good land, and
I presume some of it is bad land. It is somewhat rocky in some
portions, and is high, sloping up toward the ridge, which is the westerly line of the property. The Carolan's new house, I have seen
from the road, and from memory I should say it is not over 100 feet
below the summit in altitude, but it is probably a quarter, or a half
mile from the top of the hill. It is on top of a sort of a spur that

521

runs out from the east.

(Objected to as immaterial, irrelevant and incompetent, and as
misleading. Objection sustained.)

The Poniatowski Tract was known as the old Reddington Place.
It contained 509 acres, and was sold at the rate of about $132.61 an
acre in 1898, to Prince Poniatowski, for $67,500. I also made all of
the Burlingame sales adjacent to the Reddington Place, at about
$1000 an acre. The Poniatowski Place is very hilly, very steep, and
considerably cut up by ravines. It is a broken tract. The land that
sold for $1000 an acre, at about the same time, lies to the north of
it. Those sales were in small parcels. This was a big piece.

I have not been into the Crocker place since he built there. It
is on a portion of that property.

522

The actual average per acre of the watershed lands of the San
Andres, Pilarcitos and Crystal Springs watershed, west of the line
running approximately north and south, through the center of the
San Andres and Crystal Springs Reservoirs, is $101.98. The average
as to the lands east of the same line is $253.53.

Referring to the Merced lands: The Brickell Tract is quite steep
on the westerly 1 pe, broken by the cliffs on the shore line. The
easterly portion is comparatively level. It is on the top of the ridge,
and pitches off to the ocean on the westerly portion.

The Whitcomb Tract is partly on the ridge, and then slopes to
the east. The south-westerly corner is quite sandy. The Brickell
Tract contains a little more soil, and not so much shifting sand as
there is in the southwest corner of the Whitcomb Tract. I do not
think there is any material difference in the soil in the easterly por-

523

tion of the Brickell property from that of the watershed lands immediately south of it.

Tract 9, "Plaintiff's Exhibit 14", as compared with these two
tracts, is very much more sheltered, and slopes easier. It is not so
steep as the Whitcomb Tract. The Brickell Tract is comparatively

level on top. The chief objection to the Brickell property is the fact that there is a good deal of waste land on it. Also that it is, or was pocketed, and is isolated, difficult of access, and surrounded by the property of the Merced lands. I think that had a good deal to do with the matter of value, and perhaps the difficulty of sale. I had nothing to do with the sale, and know nothing more about it than from hearsay. Tract 9 has quite a number of scattered pines and cypress in the easterly or north-easterly portion of it. It is not a forest.

The Whitcomb land, I do not think, is worth as much per acre as Tract 9, and the Brickell property would only compare in value with the land immediately south of part of Tract 8. Tract 8 I valued in two ways. A portion of it is valued at $1500 an acre, and there are about 98 acres valued at $500 an acre. A portion of Tract 8   524 which lies immediately south of the Brickell piece, would come under the $500 an acre valuation, and a portion under the $1500 valnation. I do not know the exact area in that parcel. If there are 60 acres in the Brickell piece, there are probably 70 acres in the adjoining piece.

The fact that the Brickell and Whitcomb Tracts are surrounded by the Lake Merced Tracts of the Spring Valley Water Co., would affect their market value because they are not get-atable. The average person would not care to buy a piece of property entirely surrounded by a large tract, as the Brickell Tract is. Nothing but frontage on the ocean, and no way of reaching it. The same would apply to the Whitcomb property.   525

I do not know about any dealings with the Webber Tract, except that it was offered for sale some time ago.   526

The portions of Ocean View Park, and Vista Grande Park, immediately adjoining the Lake Merced lands, and immediately to the east of the Junipero Serra Boulevard, are not thickly settled, but the thickly settled portions of those tracts are some little distance further east. Referring to ''Plaintiff's Exhibit No. 7'' Ingleside Terrace adjoins the City Land Association, and what is known as Lake View. Lake View is perhaps a little bit better in the character of its improvements than the Ocean View Tract, but there is not much difference. The character of the improvements in the City Land   527 Association Tract have apparently not materially effected the improvements in the Ingleside Terrace Tract, as in this latter tract they are all of a high class. The presence of the cheaper districts has not prevented the construction of these better houses. There are several very excellent residences within a block of the City Land Association, and quite a number within one or two blocks of Lake View.

Tract D, which is the 142 acre tract forming part of the Sutro Tract, sold to Spring-Meyerstein by me in 1912, for $300 an acre, is not worth anything like as much per acre as Tract 1, of the Lake Merced lands, map ''Plaintiff's Exhibit 14'', because there is land

528

there that will be very expensive to develop, and I should think there are 15 or 18 acres which consist of the rocky hill which has been developed since the purchase for quarrying purposes. Those 15 or 18 acres are not worth as much per acre as the balance of the tract. The portion now known as Claremont Court, in the southwesterly corner of the tract, was cut up by a ravine, which made it quite expensive to develop.

It is a map of the 823 acres included in the Residential Development Company's deal, which is the property that I purchased from the Sutro heirs, and divided into large tracts after it was purchased. Tract D I sold to John H. Spring and A. L. Meyerstein. That constitutes West Portal Terrace, Claremont Court, and El Portal, but those tracts do not take in the whole 142 acres. They constitute a portion of it. Tract D constitutes the portion sold to the St. Francis Wood people. With reference to this map, Forest Hill is indicated

529

in Tract A. Later they bought the 23 acres adjoining to the north; which is really a part of Forest Hill now, and I think they have given it the name of Forest Hill Court.

Offered in evidence as "Plaintiff's Exhibit 23".

Map entitled "Topographical Map of the Forest Hill and San Miguel Ranch, showing lands owned by estate of Adolph Sutro, deceased", offered and admitted in evidence as "Plaintiff's Exhibit 24".

Referring to "Plaintiff's Exhibit 23", the tract marked "D" was sold to the St. Francis Wood people, and is land that slopes up to quite an elevation toward the east; nearly all of it is covered with a pretty heavy growth of pines and eucalyptus, which have been quite expensive to clear. It is a more expensive piece of property to develop than the Merced property, or the same area across the way. It was sold in April, 1912.

530

The Forest Hill Tract, or Tract B, was sold several months afterwards, or maybe a month afterwards. The interest of Mr. Titus in the St. Francis Wood Tract was purchased, I understand, only a few

531

months afterwards for $4000.

Discussion between counsels as to whether this purchase, made from Mr. Titus, was not of his shares of stock in that company, and whether or not it was a cash sale. Conceded by counsel for defendant that there is no question about the sale by Mr. Titus of his interest in the property being on the basis of $4000 per acre. Counsel for Plaintiff to get direct evidence as to the nature of the transaction.

The tract marked on map "Plaintiff's Exhibit 23" as Balboa Terrace, and adjoining St. Francis Wood, is the 15 acre tract formerly owned by the German Benevolent Society. It was purchased

532

by Baldwin and Howell for $80,000, at the rate of $5,333.33 an acre, in August, 1912. On "Plaintiff's Exhibit 14" it is across the way, immediately east of Tract 1, and is north of Ingelside Terraces, south

of St. Francis Wood, and is right across the street from Tract 1 of
the Merced lands. It was sold in August, 1912.   533

I think that tract A (Forest Hill district) as compared with tract
D (St. Francis Wood district), is practically the same as to general
availability for residential purposes. Tract A is very much steeper
than tract D, which, however, does not militate against its desirability
as a residential tract. Immediately north of tract A there was a 23
acre tract, owned by the City, and I think its value for residential
purposes is about the same as that of tract A. I understand they are
asking the same price, and getting the same rate per front foot for lots
in that tract that they are in tract A. The 23 acres immediately north   534
of tract A, on "Plaintiff's Exhibit 23 ", was sold at public auction on
July 17, 1913, for $120,000 cash, which is $5,217 per acre. On November 3, 1913, the City purchased from the Forest Hill Realty Company,
$8\frac{1}{2}$ acres southeast of, and adjoining the Alms House tract, fronting
on the Alms House road, being in the north-easterly corner of Tract
"B". It is the portion of tract B which lies northerly of the road
marked "Alms House Road", and I understand they paid $4,000 per
acre.

The character of the improvements, (street work, etc.,) in Forest
Hill and St. Francis Wood tracts, has been good. The character of   535
the street work differs somewhat in the two tracts. They have been
developed as high-class residence properties, and it cannot have anything but a good effect on the value of the Lake Merced properties.
The value of $1000 an acre on the marginal land surrounding Lake
Merced was placed on them in conjunction with the balance of the
property. The fact that these Lake Merced lands are a large and
compact body of land under one ownership, I think is a very decided
advantage. It is an advantage to be able to control the character of
the development, prevent the construction of objectionable improvements, and to be able to restrict, which of itself adds to the value of
property, and which is difficult to do in any other part of the city,
except in that portion which lies to the west of Twin Peaks, and
especially the acreage property. I think that Forest Hill tract and
St. Francis Wood are restricted districts, as is also Ingleside Ter-   536
races. The City Land Association, Lake View, and Ocean View, are
none of them restricted districts, as far as my knowledge goes.

(Explanation of the meaning of the word "restricted" as used.)

Sales in this general neighborhood were fairly good, as of August
1, 1914, but it was not as active as it had been in the latter part of
1912 and during 1913. That condition is not confined to that particular district. It is the same, I think, all over the city, and is simply
the general depression due to the war.

K Street is three blocks south of the Park, and 42nd Avenue is   537
about seven blocks from the Beach. There are no such improvements
there as are in Forest Hill, St. Francis Wood, or Ingleside Terraces.

I am not referring now to 42nd and K, but to the property to the north of it, where the streets have been graded. 42nd Avenue is not cut through more than half way between I and J, then you come to the sand hills, and there are no streets there at all, except on the map. 42nd and K Streets, as a matter of fact, is in the middle of drifting sand hills.

538

RE-CROSS EXAMINATION BY MR. STEINHART

The sale from the City to the north of Forest Hill is right at the terminus of the 9th Avenue car. I am not positive as to whether that car was in operation at that time or not. It is right next to what is now Windsor Terrace, which I do not think was in existence at that time.

I do not know anything about the relation of the piece purchased by the City for $4,000, to the City's water supply to the Alms House tract.

539 There was a piece to the north of that, of 32 acres, sold for $2500 an acre, from Wells-Fargo to the City. Referring to Stanford Heights, to the south of that, I do not know that Mr. Crittenden is offering that land on an acreage basis at about $2400 an acre.

The Callamoor piece is to the north, and is separated from the Wells-Fargo piece that the City bought, by a little piece owned by Mrs. Craig, of 20 acres. The Callamoor tract sold at less than $1000 an acre. I sold it.

I did not give Balboa Terrace any consideration in placing my price on tract 1. Baldwin & Howell bought that. It was the one piece not owned at the time of the purchase by the syndicate, (Referring to the original Sutro tract), and was immediately adjoining the West Gate Park tract. It was the one piece of property located in the Sutro tract that was not still held by the Residential Development Company, or by one of the companies that had bought from them for subdivision purposes.

I do not think that Mr. Howell had anything to do in regard to the purchase of that piece of property. I called on Mr. Max Schmidt, the President of the German Benevolent Society, in regard to it. I did not offer $20,000 for the piece. If an offer was made by anybody from Baldwin & Howell, of $20,000 for that property, it is news to me. I never offered any such price. If Mr. Howell did, it is entirely without my knowledge. I never heard of it.

Mr. Steinhart—Q. Is not this the history of the entire transaction: that Mr. Howell called upon them and offered them $20,000 for that piece of land; that eleven out of twelve of their board of directors were willing to accept that; that one of them called attention to the fact that they were the one piece cutting into the Sutro Forest tract and that they thereupon refused to sell it; that Baldwin & Howell thereafter offered $25,000; that they kept going up, and that you yourself finally met one of the directors of the German Benevolent Society on the street and objected to the fact that they were holding you up, and you finally said "will you take $80,000?" Now, is not that a fact? A. No.

Q. That is not a fact? A. No; none of those statements are facts; they wanted $100,000 for the property.   541

(Moved that that be stricken out. Decided by Master that that can come out in further re-direct examination of the witness.)

Tract No. 8 in the Merced Tract; there are about 22 or 23 acres of land in the westerly portion of it that is precipitous, somewhat like the Brickell property. About 70 acres that I would not say was waste land by any means, but there are swales. They are not exactly ravines, but they are not level, and that is along the easterly portion of the tract. This ravine does not run parallel to the shore of the lake. It runs southwest of it. I do not know how many acres there are in that portion there. (Marked with a pencil by counsel for Defendant on map) I should say from looking at it, and making a guess, that there might be 75 acres. I made an average value of $500   542 an acre for 98 acres. That would take about 75 acres, and about 23 acres here on the south-westerly portion of tract 8. The remainder, next to the Brickell piece would come in with the balance of the property, $1500 an acre. That valuation, of course you understand, is made as a part of the whole.

As far as my observation goes, the character of the buildings in Ingleside Terraces, adjacent or near the City Land Association, is good. I will not say that they are as expensive as most of the buildings that are constructed in other portions of it. There is no building in Ingleside Terraces, either near the City Land Associaton or Lake View, of a cheap character. Those residence, as far as I can see, run in value or cost from $6000 to $10,000.   543

In relation to the Ingleside Terrace, I do not know about the limit of the restrictions there, and that the districts that are the poorest and the cheapest, and that have very low building restrictions, are the districts next to Lake View and Ocean View tracts. St. Francis Wood slopes back from the boulevard, and the higher portions have a view of the ocean, but the views are very limited. The slope of the land, so far as the present subdivision is concerned, is so gradual that only occasional views of the ocean can be had from it. I do not know that higher prices have been obtained as to the land further back from the boulevard; my impression is that there is no material difference in the prices. (Mr. Steinhart: Just for your own information, Mr. Baldwin, I will state that I investigated that; my   544 impression is that there is no material difference in the prices).

According to that list, the only sale in 1913 that I made, is the   545 sale to Irwin, but there were other sales. I have another sale we made there on July 3, 1913, of the Dingee Park property, which is not on that list, and there may be some others. I don't think there are very many. We have not been actively handling any property there. I don't know that any acreage property has been for sale between Burlingame, or even Millbrae and south to Redwood, except those who have had exclusive selling rights. Dingee Park is not a subdivision proposition.

Pompanio Ranch, 2600 acres, at $1000, is a ranch near Pescadero and San Gregoria, and is one of three sales in 1912.

546   Counsel for Defendant here referred to list of properties introduced by witness, and which list was a list of the properties which witness had personally conducted the sale of. Stated it to be his wish to have a complete list of all sales made between 1897 and 1913 for purpose of showing the number of sales witness has made.

547   I want to correct that, however; I have no recollection of ever having mentioned anything about the Pompanio Ranch. It was a sale I had nothing to do with. It was made in the office. It was, in part, an exchange.

In speaking of the two sales in 1911, one in El Cerito Park, and the other near Woodside, if you are referring to the list of sales that I gave Mr. Olney, those are the only sales on that list. The sale in 1909, of the Boswick Ranch, San Mateo County, Mares and Saunders, to C. A. Hooper, was made by Mr. Pickering in conjunction with Mr. Tuxton, of Redwood. This was west of the original Hooper tract, and runs over to the Canada. The price for the tract of 729 acres was
548 $50,000, about $70 an acre, in 1909. It adjoins parcel 202, of map 5, on the south and east. If the only sale in 1908 was a lot in Highland Park, as the list appears, that is correct. There are no sales on this list in 1907. The only sale as appears on this list in 1906 was the
549 sale of 14 acres in Hayward Park. I have everything on that list that I have testified to. We have sold no acreage property, excepting those sales in Burlingame, and excepting what is on this list, if you exclude sales in subdivisions, and if you exclude all sales in Burlingame made prior to, maybe, 1900. I can give you a full list of sales in properties that had been subdivided in San Mateo Park, Hayward Park, and Hayward Addition. The Burlingame sales that we made were all in acreage. The El Cerito sales were all acreage. The San Mateo Park was in lots, but averaging, as I recall, about an acre each. Hayward Park and Hayward Addition sales were similar. The average size of sales of that sort in acreage subdivisions, as distinguished from lot subdivisions, run usually 1, 2, or 3 acres. When I spoke of the Urban Subdivision, I had not in contemplation then any idea of a subdivision into small areas like that, 1 or 2 acres. That
550 property might be sold in 100 or 200 acres; some only in 5 acres, and some in 10 acres. I cannot tell you what the average urban proposition is. You can go to Woodside and find them probably as high as 50 acres. I think Fleischacker's place is probably 30 or 35 acres.

The Driscoll property, which I compared with the San Mateo screen tank property, is in the Howard subdivision, and west of the Crocker home, and between it and the Crystal Springs Reservoir, on the south side of the map. I do not know exactly the location. It is a piece marked estate of William Howard. Driscoll has a piece there, and also a man by the name of Duncan has a piece. I can get the exact location, but I cannot locate it on the map.

In reference to a sale from Maloney to Connolly, in November, 1910, for about $100 an acre, I said we had an offer of $200 an acre, in February, 1913. I did not handle the re-sale to Beatty. We had   552 nothing to do with it. I don't know what the deal was. Connolly and Beatty were either co-executors, or they represented in a way, the Hooper estate. Connolly sold the property, as I understand it, to Mrs. Hooper afterwards. At any rate, when Mr. Pickering went to Connolly to buy the property, he having told him some time that he would sell it for $200 an acre, Connolly said that that is out of my hands now, and I cannot sell it. Mrs. Hooper has it. Mr. Pickering had a party who was willing to buy it, and would have bought it at $200 an acre. That was the offer, and that was the refusal of the offer that I spoke of. I know nothing more about it, other than what Mr. Pickering told me. That was Mrs. George W. Hooper. C. A. Hooper owns the property on the east side of the Canada, and this   553 tract now owned by Mr. Beatty is on the west side. The property I have been speaking of is the Beatty property, and is south and east of West Union Gulch. The Silva land, not the Spring Valley Silva land, is a little piece of 23 acres that we sold down near Portola or beyond Woodside. It is a piece we sold in February, 1912, to McDonough, who owned land on the east of it. It was at about $300 an acre.

RE-DIRECT EXAMINATION BY MR. OLNEY.

The Callamoor tract was sold in the latter part of 1912 for $34,000, for 36.59 acres. It was a probate sale, and came up for confirmation January 3, 1913, and at that time other parties appeared at the sale and raised the bid. The bidding continued until it got up to $39,500, at which time it was knocked down to the party who had   554 overbid the original purchaser. The price at which it was finally sold was $1079.53 an acre. It is on the westerly slope of Twin Peaks, quite steep and inaccessible, being hemmed in by other properties there. The 8½ acres at $4000 an acre, is a better buy than this property was at $1000 an acre. Taking the property in Stanford Heights, which lies to the east of the Hooper property, I don't know exactly what Mr. Steinhart referred to, unless it was the holdings of Wells-Fargo, and if such is the case, that property is subdivided. It is in blocks, streets running at right angles without regard to topography. The property·

is not protected by restrictions of any kind. A portion of it runs up to the top of Mt. Davidson. The balance is either near, or in the big canyon, which I think is generally known as the Glen Park Canyon, and probably is a portion of the land that the City has sought to acquire under condemnation for a reservoir. Generally speaking, the Stanford Heights property has had its value very seriously impaired by the mistake of subdividing hillside property into square blocks, running streets at right angles. Some of that property sold, 20 years ago, for more than it could be sold for today.

Questioned by Master.

The Wells-Fargo that I spoke of this morning, lies to the north of the 8½ acre piece. That is, I think, about 32 acres that the City bought; that property, I think, is better than the property on the south side of Corbett Road, which is, as I understand it, the property which Mr. Steinhart says can be had at $2400 an acre.

DIRECT EXAMINATION BY MR. OLNEY.

The City paid $2500 an acre for the last mentioned piece.

Questioned by Master.

That does not include the Twin Peaks, which were bought recently at, I think, about $1000 an acre.

DIRECT EXAMINATION BY MR. OLNEY.

In relation to the Balboa Tract, or 15 acres, purchased from the German Benevolent Society, the facts were simply that we were desirous of buying the property, if we could get it at what we thought it was worth, or what we thought we could afford to pay for it. We never anticipated getting it for any $15,000, and I know that Mr. Steinhart has been misinformed. I inquired the price, and they asked $100,000 for it. We tried to buy it for $50,000 but could not do it, and finally bought it for $80,000. I had a number of talks with Mr. Schmidt about it. As to offering or considering, or thinking for a moment that the property could be bought for $15,000 or $20,000, there is nothing in that. We should have been very glad to buy it at $15,000 or $20,000 if it was available, but no figure was ever given to me by any body, except $100,000, and that came from Mr. Schmidt, and Mr. Mueller, the Secretary of the Association. That was after we had disposed of tract D, the St. Francis Wood property. We have no interest in any property adjoining that 15 acres. Baldwin & Howell have a very small interest in the Residential Development Company. It amounts to a very small fraction of the general ownership. Baldwin & Howell bought the Balboa Terrace. I bought it personally.

CROSS EXAMINATION BY MR. STEINHART

Baldwin & Howell, or the Residential Development Company had a mortgage on tract D.

RE-DIRECT EXAMINATION BY MR. OLNEY.

I do not think the Boswick property is as good as tract 208, 214 and 202. It runs up on to the top of the hill, and connects with the other Hooper land to the east. Those particular tracts to which you refer are nearly all level, except that portion of it running back to the West Union Creek. There are not many trees on it. There are occasional oaks in a few of the creeks or gullies. As you get back from the Canada Road, going east into the hills, it is pretty rough and rocky on top. You will find some of it rough on the sides, and some of it otherwise. I do not think, taking the same distance back from the Canada either east or west, that there is very much difference; for instance, opposite 208, running back the same distance that that does, I do not know that I would consider the land on the east side of the road any less valuable than it is on the west. The Boswick tract went back to the top of the ridge on the east, but I have not been over it for say five or six years. As I remember it, it is somewhat rough and rocky. There is a good deal of lava rock on top of the Hooper tract up there. There are a number of acres that are covered with that hard lava; I suppose it is volcanic rock. Some of the Boswick property is, as I recall it, affected to that extent. 558

FURTHER RE-CROSS EXAMINATION BY MR. STEINHART

In regard to tract B, the Meyerstein & Spring purchase, I think at the time that $50,000 was paid. From memory I should say there has been paid at least one-half, and probably more than that. Tract D, the St. Francis Wood tract, was $50,000 cash, and the rest on terms. The mortgage ran to the Residential Development Company, in which Baldwin & Howell were interested to some extent. Forest Hill tract, I think, was $50,000 cash also, and the rest on time, which has been paid. We have co-operated with Mason-McDuffie in the St. Francis Wood proposition, but only as selling agents. We have no interest in the property at all. 559

DIRECT EXAMINATION BY MR. OLNEY.

The deferred payments in all of those cases drew interest.

FURTHER RE-CROSS EXAMINATION BY MR. STEINHART

I said that I thought if 208 was on the other side of the road, I would value it at about the same price as I would if it was on this side; I do not think there is any material difference. There might be $25.00 or $50.00 in some of those pieces. 560

Witness WALTER R. HOAG.

561   DIRECT EXAMINATION BY MR. GREENE.

I live in Burlingame, and have been in the real estate business for 24 years. I started in Berkeley, Alameda County, was employed by Charles A. Bailey, continued in business there about three or four years. From there I went to San Francisco as an employee of McAfee Bros. I became office manager of the firm about a year after going there, and continued in that capacity until 1904, when Mr. Lansdale and I purchased the interest of McAfee Bros., and conducted the business under the name of Hoag and Lansdale. We were associated for about seven years after that, or up to about 1911, and since that time my business has been conducted under the name of W. R. Hoag & Co.

562 As a part of our business, we have been engaged in the purchase and sale of real estate in the City and County of San Francisco, on a commission basis, and also purchasing tracts and subdividing them. Some of the tracts in the city that I have been interested in are tracts along Bakers Beach; the Presidio Line; different tracts along Golden Gate Park. I am not now thoroughly familiar with the real estate situation in San Francisco, but I used to be. About fifteen years ago I first became interested in real estate in San Mateo County, and I have had occasion to become familiar with the market value of real estate in the Peninsula. My interests have been largely in real estate in San Mateo County. I have bought and sold property there, and have been interested in the subdivision of property. Specific instances, Hillsborough Heights, Highland Park, El Cerito Park, a tract of land near the Holy Cross Cemetery, which we auctioned off when I was with McAfee Bros., and Burlingame Terrace. I was interested in the Hoag & Lansdale Subdivision, of San Mateo, but that is further down. I have handled Stanford Heights, a subdivision of the town of Menlo; Baywood Field; Stanford Park Annex. There are one or two other tracts around San Mateo and Burlingame that I cannot quite

563 remember. I have been employed by institutions to appraise the values of properties in San Mateo, but most of my appraisals have been for friends that I have had in the institutions. I have appraised for the Hibernia Bank, for the Bank of Italy, for the First National Bank of San Mateo, for the Bank of Burlingame, for the Crocker Bank, and · for several building and loan societies. The first sale I made on the Peninsula was in Redwood City. I should say about fifteen years ago. I have known the properties of the Spring Valley Water Co., surrounding Lakes Pilarcitos, San Andres and Crystal Springs for a great many years. For the first three or four years after that first purchase of fifteen years ago, my interests were confined largely to the

564 city, but since that time have been actively engaged in Peninsula real estate, and have been continually in touch with the situation there,

and had a knowledge of real estate values during that time. I know the properties of the Spring Valley Water Co. situated on the Peninsula, and known as the watershed property of the company, comprising some 22,000 or 23,000 acres. I began riding horseback over those properties about six or seven years ago, and my familiarity grew from that time until the last two or three years. At the instance of the Spring Valley Water Co., about a year ago, I think, I made a definite appraisal of the value of those properties. Since that time I have been on the property nearly every week. I ride over there every Sunday, and some times two or three times during the week. I have been noticing conditions from that time especially. Prior to making my detailed appraisal and examination, I rode principally through the property that is nearest my home in Burlingame, but I have been riding practically nearly over all the property at various   565
times, and after the time at which I was employed to make an appraisal, I have made a careful and thorough examination of the property and have been on it at different times and for different lengths of time. I should say I have been on the property between 20 and 30 times since I was employed, on horseback, in automobiles, and on foot, and have made a thorough examination of the different parts of the property, so that I feel thoroughly familiar with all of the different parcels of the property that are situated within that area. I have made an appraisal of the market value of that property as of December 31, 1913, but did not take into consideration any structures located upon the properties of the company. I did not take into consideration, or make any allowance for whatever value the properties may have for water producing purposes. I have reached a determination as to the fair market value of these properties as of Decem-   566
ber 31, 1913, and I think the property is more suitable for residential purposes, omitting the present use of it, than for any other. I am not taking into consideration that the lands are watershed lands, or that there are reservoirs on the property, and have not valued the land that is covered with water. My total valuation for the proper-   567
ties, excluding what is known as the Phelps Tract, is $2,801,940.30. Including the Phelps Tract, it is $2,923,182.80. In reaching this final valuation of the entire tract, I followed this method: I was given maps by the company. Upon these maps were shown various parcels. I valued the different parcels of land, and my total valuation is the sum-total of these different parcels. I did not value the property without taking into consideration the different separate parcels. The value which I have placed on each of these separate parcels represents the amount for which those parcels would have sold in the open market on December 31, 1913. I have made no allowance in my valuation for the fact that the reservoirs of the water company are at present where they are, and that they are filled with water.

Referring to detailed appraisement of these various properties   568 in San Mateo County, taking them up in the order in which the parcels are numbered, etc., first take up parcel 2, on maps 2 and 3.

My values are without considering the fact that the lake is there, but the lake being there, I would value it higher on that account.

569   Parcel on maps 2 and 3, 40 acres, on easterly slope of the saddle, between Fifield and Cahill Ridge; location of settling pond; most all of this piece is steep; portions finely timbered with oak and pine trees. It runs into Pilarcitos Lake, and has a watershed area of 20.40 acres. I have placed a value upon that of $75 per acre, total $1530.

Parcel 3, map 3, 41.75 acres of watershed, at $25 per acre, total $1043.75. On the easterly slope of Montara Mountains, east of Scarboro Peak, bottom of canyon steep and heavily timbered.

Parcel 4, map 3, 4 acres of watershed, portals of tunnels, $100 per acre, $400.

Parcel 5, map 3, 23.60 acres in the watershed, $75 per acre, total $1770. On the westerly slope of Cahill Ridge, northwest corner includes the most southerly point of the Spring Valley Ridge, balance on slope, steep except on top.

Parcel 5-1, map 3, 31.62 acres, includes saddle between Fifield and Cahill Ridges, runs to east frontage of Pilarcitos Lake, and takes in the southerly top of Fifield Ridge. 28.33 acres in the watershed; valued at $75 per acre, total $2124.75.

TENTH HEARING.   JULY 27, 1915.

Witness WALTER R. HOAG.

570   DIRECT EXAMINATION BY MR. GREENE.

I purchased Hillsboro Heights, 20 acres; Highland Park, 22 acres; Stanford Park, 87 acres; Baywood Field, 100 acres; Stanford Park Annex, 30 acres; and also the Hoag & Lansdale Subdivision of the

571   Town of Menlo of about 15 acres. I handled El Cerito Park, a tract of a little over 100 acres. These tracts I took and developed. I sold some of them off, and am attempting to sell some of them now. Mezes Tract, which is a large tract near Belmont, I had something to do with when I was with McAfee Bros. Most of these tracts are east of the lands of the Spring Valley Water Co., but are not contiguous thereto. I am familiar with the sales, both wholesale and retail, of real property in San Mateo County for about fifteen years.

572   The 23,000 acres of the Spring Valley Water Co., if it were purchased outright, could be used for residential sites for homes of wealthy men, large country estates. I think that would probably be the best way in which the property could be sold, and would be an attractive proposition from a real estate point of view.

The tract owned by Mr. Edward Howard, on the easterly slope, 186 acres, was turned over to me two months before his death for me to develop and subdivide it. My experience has been both as acreage property, and with subdivision property.

Parcel 5-2, maps 2 and 3; this includes the beautiful Pilarcitos 573 Creek and stone dam, takes in the east slope of Montara Mountains, and west slope of Cahill Ridge. Most southerly very steep and rugged, central portion around lake contains beautiful knolls and fine timber. Easterly slope of Montara Mountains in central portion covered with low brush, grease-wood, and bear-berry; some of this slope is farming land. Northerly end contains the valley of the west arm of Pilarcitos Lake, the Spring Valley Ridge and Valley, and runs to the top of the Fifield Ridge. There are 2921.32 acres. In the watershed there are 2852.82 acres. I value that property at $60 an acre, total $171,169.20.

Parcel 6, map 3, northerly slope of Ox Hill on top of Montara Mountain, very steep on the sides, more level in the center; has standing timber. 80 acres watershed, value $25 per acre, total $2,000.

Parcel 7, map 2, 160.40 acres in the watershed; on easterly end of Whiting Ridge; contains two draws of the valley at the head of the westerly arm of Pilarcitos Lake; balance pasture land; value $40 per acre; total $6416.

Parcel 8, map 2; on Whiting Ridge; both slopes very steep; 160 acres, $20 per acre, $3200.

Parcel 9, map 2, top of Montara Mountains, steep and rugged; has patches of farming land; 58.25 acres, $20 per acre, $1165.

Parcel 12, map 2, spur of Sweeney Ridge, running into San Andres Lake, forming circular knoll with rather steep slope covered with poor timber. 181.09 acres; watershed 102.79 acres, at $60 per acre, 574 total $6167.40.

CROSS EXAMINATION BY MR. STEINHART.

The acreages in and out of the watershed are given on information furnished me by the company.

DIRECT EXAMINATION BY MR. GREENE.

Parcel 13, map 2, triangular piece on easterly slope of Sweeney Ridge, extending to San Andres Lake, steep and brushy. Watershed 332.74 acres, $60 per acre, total $19,964.40.

Parcel 13, map 2, is in three pieces, gently sloping knoll on the westerly side of San Andres Lake; foot of east l pe of Sweeney Ridge; 59.95 acres; 27.41 acres in the watershed, $300 per acre, $8223.

Map 2, parcel 13, southerly end of spur between two northerly 575 arms of San Andres Lake; sloping piece, 15.15 acres in watershed, $300 per acre, $4545. I have valued three parcels there; the first 332.74 acres of watershed, at $19,964.40, the second containing 15.15 acres, at $545, and the third 27.41 acres, at $8223.

Map 2, parcel 14, easterly slope of north end of Sawyer Ridge, running to San Andres Lake; prominent knolls separated by steep ravine; 234.56 total; in watershed 155.26 acres, $60 per acre, $10,515.60.

Map 2, parcel 15, westerly slope at north end of Buri Buri Ridge; runs to San Andres Lake; gently 1 ping; total acres 153.75; watershed 143.35 acres, at $275 per acre, $39,421.25.

Map 2, parcel 16, on westerly slope of Buri Buri Ridge, running to lake; location of keeper's cottage; some meadow land; balance rather steep; 67.61 acres, at $275 per acre, $18,592.75.

Map 2, parcel 17, westerly slope of Buri Buri Ridge, running to San Andres Lake, 17.39 acres, at $275 per acre, $4782.25.

576   Map 2, parcel 18, located between the two northerly arms of San Andres Lake; gently 1 ping; 53.36 acres, $275 per acre, $14,674.

Map 2, parcel 18, westerly slope of Buri Buri Ridge, running to San Andres Lake, not steep; 30.19 acres, $275 per acre, $8302.25.

Questioned by Mr. McCutchen.

There are two parcels marked 18 on that map.

DIRECT EXAMINATION BY MR. GREENE.

Map 2, parcel 19, westerly slope of Buri Buri Ridge, to San Andres Lake; has cypress and eucalyptus trees; oak trees on projecting knoll, fine view north and south; portions command Bay view. 43.12 acres, $275 per acre, $11,858.

Map 2, parcel 20, westerly slope of Buri Buri Ridge to San Andres Lake; cypress trees in westerly part; watershed 16.90 acres, $275 per acre, $4647.50.

Map 2, parcel 21, top of Buri Buri Ridge, and steep westerly slope to San Andres Lake; gulch with oak trees; 20.72 acres, at $275 per acre, $5698.

Map 3, parcel 25, westerly slope of Cahill Ridge; steep side hill, low brush, part wooded, runs down to Pilarcitos Creek; 27.23 acres. $25 per acre, $680.75.

Map 3, parcel 27; six triangular pieces on westerly slope of Cahill Ridge. Very steep; 67.49 acres, $40 per acre, $2699.60.

Map 2, parcel 28, top of Montara Mountains, some land very rough and steep, but contains patches of farming land; 235.76 acres, $25 per acre, $5894.

Map 2, parcel 28, on Montara Mountains; high ridge running north-easterly; very badly cut up; 160.40 acres, $15 per acre, $2406.

577   Map 3, parcel 29, on westerly slope of Montara Mountains; steep hillside, low brush, pasture land; 824.56 acres, $20 per acre, $16,491.20.

Map 3, parcel 33, on westerly slope of Montara Mountains; pasture land; top has ridge with steep sides; most all rough land; 153.50 acres, at $20 per acre, $3070.

162

Map 2, parcel 34, top of Montara Mountains; rough pasture' land; steep and cut up; patches of farming land; 58.84 acres, at $30 an acre, $1765.20.

Map 3, parcel 36, constitutes spur at northerly end of Pulgas Ridge at Crystal Springs Dam; Crystal Springs Road runs through easterly portion; beautiful property; fine timber; slopes to north and west; steep and covered with timber; 103.14 acres, $500 per acre, $51,570.

Map 4, parcel 37, westerly slope of Pulgas Ridge to lake; fairly level on top and near lake; 350.43 acres, $175 per acre, $61,325.25.

Map 3, parcel 38, projecting knoll opposite Crystal Springs Dam; 23.82 acres, $500 per acre, $11,910.

Map 3, parcel 39, includes Sawyer Ridge and top of Cahill Ridge; takes in part of San Mateo Creek; westerly slope of Sawyer Ridge, steep in parts. Has some building sites. Easterly slope of Cahill Ridge very steep; finely timbered; top of northerly portion of Sawyer Ridge, farming lands; southerly portion of Sawyer Ridge covered with timber and brush. Of great scenic beauty. Top of Cahill Ridge farming land on easterly slope. Sawyer Ridge has some nice knolls fronting lake; 2094.05 acres, $100 per acre, $209,405.

Map 3, parcel 40, on easterly slope of Sawyer Ridge; fairly steep, some knolls; 9.33 acres, $250 per acre, $2332.50.

Map 3, parcel 41, on easterly slope of Sawyer Ridge, from top of ridge to Crystal Springs Lake. Flat on top. Fairly level at bottom, steep between, and timbered. 42.45 acres, $150 per acre, $6367.50.   578

Map 2, parcel 42, on westerly slope of Buri Buri, near San Andres Dam, adjoining property with cottage; runs down to creek. Has willow trees in bottom; oak and laurel on slope; 22.38 acres, at $275 per acre, $6154.50.

Map 2, parcel 43, three triangular pieces along northerly boundary line of Spring Valley property; small valley in center; balance very rugged and steep. Central triangle head waters of San Mateo Creek; 311.69 acres, $15 per acre, $4675.35.

There are two parcels numbered 43, and that is the first one.

Map 2, parcel 43, on westerly slope of Fifield Ridge; very steep; rough pasture land. 80 acres, $20 per acre, $1600.

Map 4, parcel 44, timbered island in Crystal Springs Lake, opposite cottage. Has meadow land; 9.46 acres, at $350 per acre, $3311.

Map 4, parcel 45, on westerly side of Crystal Springs Lake, Canada Road passes through it; open country; timbered with laurel, oak and Buckeye trees; 147.47 acres, $350 per acre, $51,614.50.

Map 4, parcel 46, on easterly slope of Cahill Ridge running to lake; some oak timber on northeasterly corner, balance bare rolling land rising from lake. 150.43 acres, $250 per acre, $37,607.50.

Map 4, parcel 47, on easterly slope of Cahill Ridge; two prominent knolls, divided by Crystal Springs Road at upper Crystal Springs Dam; 49.25 acres, $300 per acre, $14,775.

579 Map 4, parcel 48, westerly slope of Pulgas Ridge; property on westerly portion is meadow land with knolls; some timber in the southerly portion, but bare of timber along lake, except in ravines near Crystal Springs cottage; easterly portion high plateau, with prominent knoll; fine view. 925.88 acres, $175 per acre, $162,029.

Map 4, parcel 49, on easterly slope of Cahill Ridge; splendid, large oak trees on easterly portion in the valley; fairly good timber on the steep central 1 pe; farming land on ridge. 643.90 acres, $175 per acre, $112,682.50.

Map 4, parcel 50, Canada Road runs through the central portion; series of knolls covered with very fine, heavy timber. Fine oaks and laurels. Dips down on northerly frontage; valley on northerly boundary, with redwood trees. 310.90 acres, $350 per acre, $108,815.

Map 2, parcel 51, bottom land at head of east arm of San Andres Lake, 17.52 acres, $300 per acre, $5256.

Map 2, parcel 52, mouth of small creek on northerly slope of Sawyer Ridge, fronting on San Andres Lake, nearly level, 1.03 acres, $300 per acre, $309.

Map 2, parcel 53, gentle slope at head of east arm of San Andres Lake. 5.18 acres, $300 per acre, $1554.

Map 4, parcel 54, divided by Crystal Springs Road; nicely timbered; live oak trees; fairly level on top; rather steep up from lake; fine building sites; 64.32 acres, $400 per acre, $25,728.

Map 4, parcel 55, runs from Canada Road east to division line in lake; two knolls covered with heavy timber. 24.70 acres, $300 per acre, $7,410.

580 Map 3, parcel 59, on easterly slope of Sawyer Ridge, running to Crystal Springs Lake; nicely timbered. 6.18 acres at $350 per acre, $2163.

Map 3, parcel 60, top of Montara Mountains, takes in Ox Hill; low brush; some standing timber, 240 acres at $20 per acre, $4,800.

Map 3, parcel 60, on westerly slope Montara Mountains; pasture land; 3.80 acres at $20 per acre, $76.

Map 3, parcel 62, northerly slope Pulgas Ridge, running across San Mateo Creek; top fairly level; northerly and easterly slopes precipitous; heavily wooded; 43.17 acres at $150 per acre, $6,475.50.

Maps 3 and 4, parcel 68, on the easterly slope of Cahill Ridge; very steep; 40 acres at $25 per acre, $1,000.

Maps 3 and 4, parcel 68, on easterly slope of Cahill Ridge; very steep; 51.65 acres at $60 per acre, $3438.60.

(There are five pieces in the parcel numbered 68.)

Maps 3 and 4, parcel 68, on easterly slope of Cahill Ridge; bisected by Crystal Springs road; some farming land on top of ridge south of Crystal Springs road; balance steep and rocky. 116.08 acres at $35 per acre, $4062.80.

Maps 3 and 4, parcel 68; westerly line does not go to top of ridge; pretty steep to center, and then good to lake; south arm rocky; pasture land. 174.50 acres at $125 per acre, $21,812.50.

Maps 3 and 4, parcel 68, easterly slope of Cahill Ridge; very steep in central portion; some very pretty gently sloping knolls on Crystal Springs Lake; flat and bare on top; farming land. 441.88 acres at $150 per acre, $66,282.

(Here ensued a discussion as to what map the different parcels 581 68 are on. The small piece 5.66 acres is included in parcel 68 in the parcel that has 51.65 acres, and is on map 4. The piece of 116.08 acres is on map 4. The piece of 174.50 acres is on map 4, and shown as 196.80 acres. The piece of 441.88 acres is the remaining piece on maps 3 and 4, running between them. The remaining piece of 68 acres in pink on map 3 is not testified to for the reason that it is reservoir land, and is not in the watershed at all.)

Questioned by Mr. Searls and Mr. Steinhart.

I think that the 5.66 acre piece, running down from the second number 68 on map 4, must be the little rectangular piece running down to the lake, but it is included in parcel 68, and valued at $60. That is the piece immediately south of 45.

DIRECT EXAMINATION BY MR. GREENE. 582

Map 3, parcel 72, narrow strip of land at the northern end of Crystal Springs Lake; very pretty property. 8.80 acres at $500 per acre, $4400.

Map 3, parcel 73, on westerly slope of Buri Buri Ridge to Crystal Springs Lake; fine building knolls with pleasing timber; very accessible property. 276.45 acres at $500 per acre, $138,225.

Map 3, parcel 89, takes in portion of southerly end of Sawyer Ridge; heavily timbered on both slopes; commands fine scenic view. 47.06 acres at $350 per acre, $16,471.

Referring to parcels 59 and 89, I concluded that those numbers 583 were in this parcel marked in yellow; I valued them, as I remember it, exactly the same. I remember now that in valuing that I could not find the two separate parcels.

(Mr. Greene: It is my recollection that there should have been a division line. That is one of the errors in this map.)

Map 3, parcel 90, on westerly 1 pe of Buri Buri Ridge; fairly level on top; sloping to Crystal Springs Lake; very southerly portion nicely wooded; central portion jutting timbered knolls into the lake; northerly end wooded in the ravines; building sites near lake. 856.10 acres at $400 per acre, $342,440.

Map 3, parcel 91, on northerly slopes of Pulgas Ridge; level on top; slopes very steep and precipitous; heavily wooded. 28.55 acres at $150 per acre, $4282.50.

Map 3, parcel 92, southerly end of Sawyer Ridge; takes in part of lake arm of San Mateo Creek; runs across to easterly 1 pe of Cahill Ridge; prettily timbered; beautiful scenery. 31.31 acres, $450 per acre, $14,089.50.

Map 3, parcel 94, on easterly slope of Sawyer Ridge. 4.95 acres, at $300 per acre, $1485.

584   Map 4, parcel 96, on easterly slope of Cahill Ridge running to Crystal Springs Lake; nicely situated on lake; oaks, wild cherry and laurel trees; steep in westerly portion; 12.20 acres at $300 per acre, $3660.

Map 3, parcel 97, on easterly slope of Sawyer Ridge to lake; has draw from lake with two prominent knolls. 68.09 acres, at $250 an acre, $17,022.50.

Map 2, parcel 101, on the Montara Mountains; draw through this piece; very steep; rough pasture land. 240 acres at $15 per acre, $3,600.

Map 2, parcel 102, on Fifield Ridge, with westerly spur; steep and cut up. 160 acres at $25 per acre, $4,000.

Map 2, parcel 104, runs from easterly slope of Fifield Ridge to Whiting and Spring Valley Ridges, one-third of the south-westerly quarter farming lands; northwest quarter gulch; fairly good in bottom; balance pasture land. 327.90 acres at $40 per acre, $13,116.

Map 2, parcel 106, takes in the ridge and the valley of the two arms of Pilarcitos Lake, and easterly slope of Montara Mountains; runs almost to top of Fifield Ridge; south-westerly portion good soil; ridge is farming land; east slope of ridge good; west slope is fair; top soil good. 295.90 acres at $60 per acre, $17,754.

Map 3, parcel 110, on easterly slope of Sawyer Ridge. 2.10 acres at $250 per acre, $525.

Map 4, parcel 122, on easterly slope of Cahill Ridge; rolling land; has been farmed; has new growth of cypress and pine trees; flat in easterly portion. 117.48 acres at $75 per acre, $8811.

585   Map 3, parcel 124, on the easterly slope of Montara Mountains; part of canyon, brush and standing timber on sidehill. 165 acres, at $25 per acre, $4125.

Map 3, parcel 128, on westerly slope of Montara Mountains; flat on top, balance very steep. 40 acres at $20 per acre, $800.

Map 3, parcel 128, westerly 1 pe of Montara Mountains. 7.93 acres at $20 an acre, $158.60.

Map 2, parcel 130, northerly end of Sawyer Ridge; easterly portion takes in property near San Andres Lake; balance of this slope very steep; Fifield Valley in the southerly portion; said valley running westerly in the central portion to the central portion of parcel 43, farming lands. 390.04 acres at $60 per acre, $23,402.40.

Map 4, parcel 132, easterly slope of Cahill Ridge; brush running up into it, with fair timber. 340 acres at $50 per acre, $17,000.

Map 4, parcel 132, on easterly slope of Cahill Ridge; very steep and rugged; poor land. 165.75 acres at $20 per acre, $3,315.

Map 4, parcel 132, Canada road passes through the north-easterly corner; big gulch nicely timbered; cypress, laurel, oak, eucalyptus trees in the north-easterly corner; 160 acres at $125 per acre, $20,000.

Map 4, parcel 134, steep easterly slope of Cahill Ridge. 52 acres at $40 per acre, $2080.

Map 4, parcel 134, running from top of Cahill Ridge down on easterly slope; flat on top; good farming land. 148.92 acres at $40 per acre, $5956.80.

Map 3, parcel 138, on Montara Mountains; very steep and rough; flat on patch in southerly portion. 320 acres at $20 per acre, $6400.

Map 2, parcel 144, sloping ridge between two extended arms 586 of San Andres Lake; sheltered; flat on top; some valley land on the easterly boundary. 152.43 acres at $250 per acre, $38,107.50.

Map 2, parcel 146, westerly slope of Fifield Ridge running to bottom of canyon. 15.89 acres at $30 per acre, $476.70.

Map 2, parcel 163, Sawyer Ridge, Fifield Valley and Fifield Ridge; portion of Spring Valley Ridge; includes easterly slope; very steep and timbered. Sawyer Ridge farming land; flat on top; Fifield Valley farming land. 1066.11 acres at $75 per acre, $79,958.25.

Map 5, parcel 164, on westerly l pe of Pulgas Ridge; southerly portions series of prettily timbered knolls, with the exception of two high hills; fine view; northerly portion level with rising land on the east, with wooded ravines; has some valley in the easterly portion. 429.20 acres at $225 per acre, $96,570.

Map 3, parcel 182, easterly slope of Sawyer Ridge; timbered and sloping to lake; projecting knoll. 34.45 acres at $250 an acre, $8,612.50.

Map 4, parcel 190, on east slope Cahill Ridge; two valleys on north and south boundaries; pine knoll between; balance steep; slope on top one-fifth farming land. 449.19 acres at $125 per acre, $56,148.75.

Map 5, parcel 194, on easterly l pe of Cahill Ridge; fine timbered knolls on the easterly portion; central portion steep with low brush; westerly portion nicely timbered. 1059.87 acres at $150 per acre, $158,980.50.

Map 5, parcel 195, on easterly slope of Cahill Ridge; flat at Canada road; then series of beautifully timbered knolls commanding fine view; good timber on top of ridge. 503.30 acres at $175 per acre, $88,077.50.

Map 2, parcel 196, on Fifield Ridge, near northerly boundary 587 line; westerly portion pasture land; central portion farming land; east bare low brush. 80 acres at $30 per acre, $2400.

Map 4, parcel 199, on top of Cahill Ridge near Crystal Springs road; three pieces; the first piece is 44.10 acres, at $75 acre, $3,307.50.

The second piece is 4.96 at $75 per acre, $372.

The third piece is 1.47 acres at $75 per acre, $110.25.

Hoag

Map 5, parcel 202, on westerly slope of Pulgas Ridge; level and rolling in front, with valley running along southerly boundary line; this valley is wooded on its slopes; steep and rugged in rear. 92.73 acres at $160 per acre, $14,836.80.

Map 5, parcel 202, westerly slope of Pulgas Ridge to Canada road; rolling land in front; steep in rear; soil poor; with surface boulders; particularly bare of timber. 60.43 acres at $140 per acre, $8,460.20.

Map 5, parcel 203, the description is the same as 202. 32.54 acres at $125 per acre, $4067.50.

Map 5, parcel 202, on the westerly slope of Pulgas Ridge; gently rolling; surface boulders; farming land in rear; level plateau in center; few nice oaks in rear. 92.73 acres at $140 per acre, $12,982.20.

Map 5, parcel 205, on the easterly slope of Cahill Ridge; two small oak covered knolls at Canada road; this is beautiful property. 314.30 acres at $175 per acre, $55,002.50.

Map 5, parcel 208, southerly parcel on Canada Road; rolling hills, with few white oaks; westerly portion goes over ridge; dips down into West Union Creek; timbered on westerly end. 166 acres at $175 per acre, $27,300.

588

Map 5, parcel 210, easterly portion sloping toward Canada Road; was vineyard land; now nearly bare; has small creek in front near road, with willow trees; westerly portion crosses ridge and dips to West Union Creek; nicely timbered. 214 acres at $150 per acre, $32,100.

Map 5, parcel 211, easterly portion l ping to Canada Road; very pretty with new growth of timber; redwood trees; good timber on top of Cahill Ridge. 346.10 acres at $160 per acre, $55,376. Map 5, parcel 212; level; surface boulders, brush and few trees; almost at circle. 10.23 acres at $150 per acre, $1,534.50.

Map 2, parcel 218, westerly slope of Buri Buri Ridge; small valley; cypress trees; 22.84 acres at $275 per acre, $6,281.

I have valued the so called Phelps tract at $125 per acre, 969.94 acres, total $121,242.50.

The computations showing map, parcel number, acres, value per acre, total value, was made under my direction.

589

Offered and received in evidence as "Plaintiff's Exhibit 25".

(Mr. Greene: Subject to correction the average value per acre of the total of 22,982 acres is $127.27 including the Phelps tract and $127.28 excluding the Phelps tract.)

I have tabulated a table showing the different acreages by grouping together the lands which are appraised by me at $15, and those at $20, and so on, and this tabulation, to the best of my knowledge, is correct.

Offered and received in evidence as "Plaintiff's Exhibit 26".

The 22,982 acres I have valued at $2,939,352.55 and in my opinion, those properties could be sold as an entirety for that sum.

There is demand on the Peninsula for so-called wild lands. My experience has been that wealthy men are proud of owning large acreage, and even pay a fairly good price for land that intrinsically is not worth very much. It is my opinion that the back land, which we have just been considering, could be sold as a portion of country estates.

590

My remarks which have been made as to value are directed toward the value as of December 31, 1913.

The reporter here read the description covering parcel 46. Witness advised that the description so read is a correct description of that parcel, and that the island referred to, is an island in the south-easterly portion of it.

I am familiar with certain other properties of the Spring Valley Water Co. which I have examined, situate in the County of San Mateo. Have determined the market value of those properties as of December 31, 1913.

591

Map 9, parcel 87, old Ocean View pump lot; on easterly side of Junipero Boulevard, south of San Francisco city limits; adjacent to Southern Pacific Railroad; 7.72 acres, at $2500 per acre, $19,300.

Map 8, parcel 187, strip in Hillcrest Tract, partly in San Francisco and partly in San Mateo County; contains .221 of an acre at $2500 per acre, $552.50.

Map 8, parcel 118, Daly Hill Tract, partly in San Francisco and partly in San Mateo County. 1.25 acres at $2500 per acre, $3125.

Map 9, parcel 192, portions of lots 11, 12, 13 and 14, block 2, Visitacion, 40 x 60, $500.

Map 8, parcel 35, Abbey Homestead lots; lot 3, block 32, 100 x 100, $500.

592

Lot 3, block 156, 100 x 100, $225. Lot 8, block 171, 100 x 100, $225. Lot 30 x 100 ft. east of and adjoining lot 8, block 171, $100. Lot 70 x 100 ft., in block 171, corner Lake and Linden, $200. Lot 5 in block 177, size 100 x 100, $225. Lot 2, block 176, size 100 x 100, $225. Lot 8, block 176, size 100 x 100, $225. Lot 2, block 185, size 100 x 100, $350. Total $2275.

Map 9, parcel 186, lot "A", Castle Tract, northeast corner of Price St. and County Road, $2750.

Map 8, parcel 216, strip between County Road and Southern Pacific Railroad, near Baden; contains .45 of an acre, valued at $450.

Map 8, parcel 214 and 215, strip between County Road and S. P. Railroad and S. P. R. R., near Baden, 3.39 acres at $1000 an acre, $3390.

Map 8, parcel 127, strip between County Road and S. P. R. R., near Baden, 8.847 acres, at $1000 per acre, $8847.

Map 9, parcel 168, South San Francisco land, east of S. P. Co. right of way, lying on both sides of county road, 59.783 acres at $1250 per acre, $74,728.75.

Map 9, parcel 32, School House Association property, containing .234 of an acre, at $1250.

Map 9, parcel 133, of Millbrae lands; water tower lot, on county road near Millbrae pump lot, 51.71 acres at $1000 per acre, $51,710.

593   Map 9, parcel 131, Millbrae pump lot; lies between county road and S. P. Ry. tract and electric car line; has spur track leading into property. Suitable for small subdivisions. 15.356 acres at $1500 per acre, $23,034.

Map 9, parcels 24 and 193, Silva Tract; runs from county road to top of ridge; level in front portion; rather steep in rear. 146.251 acres at $600 per acre, $87,750.60.

Map 9, parcel 95, Belmont lands; Belmont pump lot, slopes westerly and upwards from the county road; timbered in rear; suitable for residential purposes. 44.67 acres at $500 per acre, $22,335.

Map 9, parcel 158, Belmont reservoir lot; a flat level piece of land, with the exception of a hill on the northerly boundary line, with some oak timber. 33.97 acres at $400 per acre, $13,588.

Map 7, parcel 157, Ravenswood lands; marsh lands between bay and Ravenswood Creek. 1328.22 acres at $50 per acre, $66,411.

Map 7, parcel 156, marsh lands lying north and east of Frisbie Tract, and fronting on San Francisco Bay. 285.65 acres at $50 an acre, $14,282.50.

Map 7, parcel 155, marsh lands fronting on San Francisco Bay, north of San Francisquito Creek. 191.20 acres at $50 per acre, $9,564.

Map 7, parcel 154, Frisbie Tract; high land contiguous to marsh land. 40.85 acres at $200, $8170.

Map 9, parcel 129, San Mateo Screen tank lot, fronting on Crystal Springs road; adjacent to Templeton Crocker home, "Uplands", size 100 x 200 ft., less 100 x 60 ft., containing .42 of an acre, at $2500 per acre, value $1050.

594   The total values of the properties I have appraised, so far as the miscellaneous lots and lands in the northern part of San Mateo County are concerned, is $415,063.35. (The segregation as to the properties in the northerly part of San Mateo County follows:)
"Miscellaneous Lots and Lands in Northern part of San

Mateo County	$117,168.25
Millbrae Lands	162,494.60
Belmont Lands	35,923.00
Ravenswood Lands	98,427.50
San Mateo Screen Tank Lot	1,050.00
Grand Total	$415,063.35''

That total is only directed toward the total of the properties to which I have just referred.

A table showing a summary of the outside lands in San Mateo   595
County, and testified to as correct by the witness, offered and admitted as "Plaintiff's Exhibit 27".

(Referring to parcels numbered 59 and 89, on map 3, counsel for Plaintiff explained that No. 89 represents an undivided three-quarters interest in the property outlined in yellow, and 59 represents an undivided one-quarter in the same property. The acreage of the total piece outlined in yellow will be the sum of those two, or 62.07 acres.)

I think the automobile has played a great factor in the last   596
few years in the development of Burlingame and surrounding territories. Property that was not accessible five or six years ago, is now considered very accessible. The values in the westerly portion of the Peninsula have risen. I can go further than that, and say that in some districts the property close in has decreased in value. The population in Burlingame and in the surrounding property has shown a very material increase right along, and as that growth has increased, it has been more largely to the west from the railroad.

Questioned by the Master.   597

In finding a value for this watershed property, I took the different parcels as shown on the map, bearing in mind, of course, the valuation of the property, and presuming they would not be sold as they are mapped out. The appraised value which I have given as a sale value, I presumed as of 1913. I think the lands could be sold just as they are, either to a single person, or a coterie of men, who would acquire the land, and I think either plan would be possible in 1913. My valuations are such that I consider it would take a reasonable time to find a market for these properties, and when I say reasonable, I mean taking into account the magnitude of the lands.

CROSS EXAMINATION BY MR. STEINHART.   598

Stanford Park is located on San Francisquito Creek, the southerly end of San Mateo County; Stanford Park Annex is adjoining property; Baywood Field is to the east of the Southern Pacific line in that same country. It is just east of property in the San Francisquito District, and is east of Stanford Park and Stanford Park Annex. I have not bought any other properties than those mentioned in that location since 1906. Hillsboro Heights I bought about a year ago; Highland Park I bought, I would say, seven or eight years ago, or perhaps longer than that. It is built up now altogether with homes and has all been sold off. El Cerito was put on the market about   599
1905. Stanford Park Annex within the last year or year and a half. Baywood Field I bought in 1906, and sold off as a whole. Stanford Park was never what I would really call put on the market until

171

about two years ago. These properties I subdivided into lots of different sizes. Stanford Park Annex into acre and half-acre lots; Stanford Park into 60, 70 and 80 foot frontage lots. Burlingame Terrace, Hillsboro Heights, and El Cerito are mostly from one to four acre properties.

DIRECT EXAMINATION BY MR. GREENE.

I did not subdivide Hayward Field. I sold that as a whole.

CROSS EXAMINATION BY MR. STEINHART.

I am not familiar with sales from Fanciola to Righetti, or from Bernali to Wolfe, or of a sale from Scarba to Granyer.

600   Map 2, parcel 28, I think, has 235 acres in which there are patches of farming land. I do not know how many acres all told.

Map 2, parcel 34; 58 acres, is of the same character. I do not know how many acres of farming land.

Map 4, parcel 45, takes in part of an island. It is not an island now. It is a knoll with meadow land around it.

601   Parcel 46; there is wind there; as you go north from 45 it becomes windier. There is a gap there where the fog and wind come in.

Map 3, No. 92; that piece is located on the southerly end of Sawyer Ridge. There would be two valleys on either side of the smaller portion. I will state frankly that that is my pet piece of the Spring Valley land. I picnicked there many times and the scenery is very beautiful. The southerly end of the ridge is covered with beautiful oak trees; there is quite an open glade on the property. The portion across from what I will say is the lake, is a timbered knoll, with a very beautiful growth of timber on it. I assumed in valuing the land that they were not arid lands, and took it for granted that the owner would have the right to sink wells and use the water in that way. My general method of valuation was the same as Mr. Baldwin's.

ELEVENTH HEARING.   JULY 28, 1915.

Gale   Witness C. A. GALE.

DIRECT EXAMINATION BY MR. GREENE.

603-604   Discussion of plan to have Defendant's testimony produced on the question of land values at the close of Complainant's case on that subject.

605-606   (Certain corrections noted on the face of the record.)

607   I live in the town of Pleasanton, Alameda County, California. Have lived there since 1882. My occupation is the practice of law and the real estate business. Have been in the real estate business for myself since November, 1905. Prior to 1905, the firm of Harris & Donohue was conducting a law and real estate business there. I was in touch with the real estate business they conducted at that time. In November, 1905, Judge Harris having retired from the firm, I went

172

into the real estate business as a partner with Mr. Donohue. In April, 1906, I became also his law partner. From November, 1905, to April, 1906, was acting as law clerk for Mr. Donohue. From that time till he went on the bench, we were associated in the real estate and law business in Pleasanton. Since Judge Donohue retired from that association, I have conducted the real estate business myself, and am familiar with the character of properties lying near the town of Pleasanton, and what is popularly known as Calaveras Valley, and around Sunol, the Arroyo Valle, the San Antonio Valley, and at Niles. Have bought and sold a great many of those properties. Some several times, and up until the last year every sale and transfer was made in my office; parties selling properties would come to the office to have deeds drawn, and I made it a particular point to ascertain the purchase and selling price, and all the facts concerning the sale in order to keep posted on properties in that locality. I know, I think, every foot of property surrounding Pleasanton, and a great deal about the properties in Calaveras, San Antonio, Sunol, and Arroyo Valle.

I have not bought or sold any properties in Calaveras, San Antonio or Arroyo Valle, but properties surrounding Pleasanton I have bought and sold, and also property running toward Sunol; not in the town of Sunol. Properties immediately surrounding Pleasanton are being used for beet raising, alfalfa, dairying, hay and grain, truck gardens.

Questioned by Master.

They were used for hops at one time. The hop fields were removed some three years ago. I believe they were removed about a year prior to the time of making this appraisement.

DIRECT EXAMINATION BY MR. GREENE.

I make all appraisements for the Bank of Pleasanton on properties upon which they intend making loans; also make all the appraisements for the Pleasanton Mutual Building & Loan Association; have represented for a number of years the lands known as the Dougherty Estate. Up until 1913 there were about between 13,000 and 15,000 acres in the Dougherty Estate; portions of it have been sold off at different times. When I took hold of the property there were about 15,000 acres, and all of the lands that have been sold since 1907 I made the sales of. At one time our office handled the Chabot land of 1100 acres, now the property of the Spring Valley Water Co.

Have handled the Neal Estate of some 200 odd acres since 1905, and aside from these properties, have sold land myself in and near Pleasanton.

I have here a rough memorandum of some of the properties I have sold. Not a complete list: 7500 acres of the Dougherty property to the Tassajero Land Co., 300 acres of the Dougherty property to Nissen, 60 odd acres of Dougherty property to Brown, about 170 acres of the Fergoda Estate to Bettencourt. Some 67 acres to Casterson. Some

608

609

610

173

256 acres to Camp. Some 200 acres of Dougherty property to Goulart; afterwards I handled a trade where that property was transferred to Oxsen. I sold some of the Dougherty property to Pine & Escobar. Some 57 odd acres belonging to the Coffin Estate to Nebbin Bros. 10 acres of Dougherty property to Neat. I sold some four or five small tracts there of 10 to 12 acres, to different parties. Some 143 acres to

611 J. J. Hanson. Some 143 acres to Jurgensen. Some 60 acres to Avila. I purchased for Mrs. Clement 193 acres from George Cobb. Some of the Harris & Donohue Tract—108 acres—to Oxsen, 73 acres to Krueger; 150 acres of same property—now property of Spring Valley Water Co.—known as the Morriwa Stock Farm, to the Alameda Sugar Co. Some 10.13 acres of property of Harris & Donohue to De Freitas. Sold some property of Lepitavich to Jones. Some 21 acres of the Lilienthal property to Philpot. I bought and sold the race track property two or three times. In addition to that, there were other sales that passed through my office, and with which I am perfectly familiar.

Roughly speaking, I would say that the aggregate amount of the sales of the property I have made in Pleasanton during the past five or six years, is about $1,000,000.

I have appraised the property of the Spring Valley Water Co. at Pleasanton, and consider myself very well informed as to those prop-

612 erties. My familiarity, extending over a period practically ever since I can remember. I have made a thorough examination of those properties for the purpose of appraising them, and have determined the market value as of December 31, 1913. I did not, in determining the value, include the valuation of structures of any kind. I simply valued the lands themselves. I made no allowance in my valuation because of the value which those lands may be to the company.

I took the properties as laid out upon the map furnished me by the Spring Valley Water Co., and went over each individual property, made a study of it, took into consideration the knowledge that I had of real estate values in and surrounding Pleasanton, and placed thereon what I deemed was a fair and conservative valuation.

Questioned by Master.

I put a value on them that I felt there would be no question of doubt that a willing purchaser would pay to a man who desired to sell the properties; a man who would be a willing seller.

613

DIRECT EXAMINATION BY MR. GREENE.

In placing my valuation, I took the properties as they now stand in their present condition, without any reference whatever to the placing of improvements upon them. I took the properties as they now stand.

CROSS EXAMINATION BY MR. STEINHART.

I did not ignore the roads that now exist; that would not be taking the preperties as they now stand.

DIRECT EXAMINATION BY MR. GREENE.

Map 10, parcel 239c; this property lies below County Road 2000   614
(30 acres) in what was formerly known as the Belza lands. The soil
is sediment loam, rather dark; excellent alfalfa land. An artesian
belt runs all through it. The land is very good. Some years ago that
section of the country was used for berries and truck gardens. The
Arroyo De Laguna Creek borders it on the west. It is rather an ir-
regularly shaped piece. My value is $500 per acre, total $15,000.

Parcel 239d, lies across the creek, and upon a sloping hillside adjacent to Mrs. Hearst's property; a very prettily wooded piece; excellently located for a home site. The agricultural value is not the
same as that of the other property shown on map 10, because it is rolling, and there is considerable brush on it in portions. 18.067 acres, at
$200 per acre, $3613.40.

Parcel 239e, lies in the flat; rich loam, produces alfalfa, vegetables. 1.53 acres at $500 per acre, $765.   615

Questioned by Master.

It is all the same character of land right through there.

DIRECT EXAMINATION BY MR. GREENE.

Parcel 239f, is a triangular piece; is the same character of land as
e-239 and c-239, h-239, and i-239, and those lands lying in there together. .52 of an acre at $500 per acre, total $260.   616

239g, small piece, containing 1.138 acres at $500 per acre, total
$569. Same character of land as the rest of the land surrounding it,
and capable of the same uses.

239-h is capable of the same uses, raising alfalfa, beets, truck garden and vegetables; is now used for alfalfa. 108.48 acres at $500 an
acre, total $54,240.

239-i, a portion of this property is similar to the other properties,
such as 239-h, but there is a large round hill in it. A portion of the
low lands is used for general agricultural purposes, such as alfalfa.
The hill is used for hay. There is also a small knoll on it. 92.501 acres
at $300 per acre, total $27,750.30.

239-j is similar to 239-h; used for alfalfa. 137½ acres at $500,
total $68,758.

Questioned by Master.

In placing these figures on these different subdivisions, I consider it as a part of the whole. I took several pieces, and appraised
them all at $500 an acre. They were all adjacent to each other, and
of the same character. Those small parcels, 239-f, containing .52 of   617
an acre, by itself, I don't know that it would be of a value of $500.
That is taking it by itself, but taking it in connection with the other
lands, it would be of that value.

DIRECT EXAMINATION BY MR. GREENE.

239-k; that is similar to the other lands which I have just appraised at $500. The uses are the same. It is level, rich bottom land, dark sediment loam. 159.28 acres at $500, total $79,640.

239-l lies north of County Road 2000. It is bottom land, sediment fill, dark loam, used for general agricultural purposes, vegetables, beets, alfalfa. Its most valuable use is alfalfa and truck gardening. 91.204 acres at $500, total $45,602.

239-m, practically the same as 239-l, lies adjacent to it, and is a smaller piece. 4 acres at $500, total $2,000. Same character of land as 239-l.

239-n, lies adjacent to 239-l and 239-m; is the same character of soil. 20 acres at $500 per acre, total $10,000.

618

239-o, practically the same character of land. The uses are the same. 51.35 acres at $500, total $25,675.

239-p lies back of 239-o, and is not facing on the county road. Practically the same as the other lands valued at $500. If I were to make a sale of those properties, instead of running the line through where it is, I would probably run it in just the opposite way. That is the reason I placed the value as I did. 54.69 acres at $500 per acre, total $27,345.

Questioned by Master.

239-p has a 30 or a 40 foot right of way to the county road on each side of 239-o.

DIRECT EXAMINATION BY MR. GREENE.

239-q lies south of County Road 2000. Its uses are for general agricultural purposes, alfalfa; rich dark sediment loam. In some spots there is some light soil. 28.37 acres at $500, total $14,185.

239-r, very similar to 239-q. Its uses are practically the same. 43.92 acres at $500, total $21,960.

239-s, a small tract, practically the same as the balance of the property surrounding it. 4 acres at $500, total $2000.

239-t is a long oblong strip, practically the same as the other lands. 10.88 acres at $500 per acre, total $5,440.

619

239-u, practically the same as the other land surrounding it, with the same uses. 10.12 acres at $500 an acre, total $5,060.

239-v, practically the same. 8.12 acres at $500 an acre, total $4060.

239-v, 239-q, 239-s, 239-k, 239-p, 239-u, 239-r, 239-j, 239-c, 239-h and 239-e all lie together, and are practically the same tract. They lie below the county road, and practically all of them, with the exception of one parcel on the opposite side of the creek, next to Mrs. Hearst's property, and the property that contains the large hill and knoll, are practically the same character of land; some parcels are not quite as good as others, but taken as a whole, they are practically the same character of land; the same uses and the same kind of soil.

241-G (yellow strip right across the road from 239-r) the uses are practically the same as the other parcels. The soil varies considerably, and is not as good as the soil on the opposite side of the road as 239-p and 239-o. It has some sandy spots in it, and a few hog wallows. 76 acres at $450 per acre, total $34,200.

268-O, this is the piece of property upon a portion of which the Pleasanton hop yards were originally located. Rich bottom land, rather sandy sediment soil. Its uses are beet growing, alfalfa— general agricultural purposes. Hops were very successful on a portion of it. About 150 acres would make very fine vegetable land. 299.74 acres at $500 per acre, total $149,870. I do not know what was paid for that.

Questioned by Master.

That is an old map that was put on there by Lilienthal several years ago. Those roads that appear on the map are still through the property, I think, with the exception of what is marked as "Rose Avenue". Black Avenue still runs through, and is being used, and I think Valley Avenue. Only a portion of the one marked Rose Avenue is running through the property. All of this property was mapped off, and the roads mapped on it, but excepting the roads that are used continually now, they have been discarded.

DIRECT EXAMINATION BY MR. GREENE.

268-P lies just across the bridge from the town of Pleasanton. Practically all subdivided into town lots, and its use is more valuable for town lots than for any other. It would sell very readily for that purpose. 11.64 acres at $1000 per acre, total $11,640.

268-Q, the soil is rich sandy loam. Its uses would be general agricultural purposes, beet raising and truck gardens. A portion of it would be salable in smaller parcels; lying right along the county road. 241.43 acres at $500 per acre, total $120,715.

268-R lies on the opposite side of the county road, just north of what is known as the Pleasanton Vegetable Garden. Rich bottom land, suitable for berries and vegetables, and fruits. One bad strip through this piece of property; rather gravelly, where an old creek bottom runs. 64.70 acres at $550 per acre, total $35,585.

268-S is bottom land, dark loam; has been used for beet raising; portions of it for alfalfa. At present time there are only some five or six acres in alfalfa. There are small stretches of alkali in it. 296.79 acres at $300 per acre, total $89,003.70.

268-T, long oblong piece of property, originally purchased by the Alameda Sugar Co. for the placing of a beet dump; a portion of it is in alfalfa; sandy, fertile loam, lying right along the railroad track. 3.78 acres at $350 per acre, total $1323.

620

621

622   268-U, the soil varies from a rich dark loam to a rather sandy loam. Its uses are beet growing. Some portions are growing alfalfa. 785 acres at $350 per acre, total $274,750. That is one of the purchases from the Alameda Sugar Company.

268-V, another piece of property that was purchased from the Alameda Sugar Co. Some excellent bottom land there; portions being rather a black loam, and others a sandy loam. Its uses would be for the growing of beets. Alfalfa could be grown upon it. Faces two sides of the county road. 338.01 acres at $250 per acre, total $84,502.50.

Parcel 271, known as the Bryan property; bottom land; dark loam; some alkali. Its uses are for general agricultural purposes, alfalfa; it is a fair dairy ranch. 63.78 acres at $300 per acre, total $19,134.

Parcel 272, is a portion purchased from Peach. It is rich loam. Its uses are alfalfa. 10 acres at $500 per acre, total $5,000.

Parcel 273 is the Anselmo property. Its uses would be alfalfa and beet raising, truck farming. 5 acres at $500 per acre, total $2500.

Parcel 274, a piece lying upon the county road leading from Santa Rita to Livermore. It is bottom land, but has an alkali streak in it. 10 acres at $250 an acre, total $2500.

623   Parcel 275, low bottom land, dark heavy loam, very well drained. The uses would be alfalfa. 40.61 acres at $450 per acre, total $18,274.50.

Parcel 277, purchased from Caton Lewis. Lies adjacent to the Peach property. Same kind of land as the Peach and Anselmo property, fine loam. 11 acres at $500 per acre, total $5,500.

Parcel 278, purchased from Davis; rich bottom land. Some portions have the dark loam, and others the sandy loam. The uses would be alfalfa, berries, truck gardens. A portion of it formerly in hops. 177.37 acres at $500 per acre, total $88,685.

Parcel 279, a purchase from Green; rather adobe in portions, but some loam. Streaked with alkali. The uses are general agricultural purposes. At one time had some alfalfa on it. 117.533 acres at $200 per acre, total $23,506.60.

Parcel 280, the Kruse purchase; has a rich bottom sediment fill loam. The uses would be truck gardening, alfalfa, beets, vegetables, orchard. 70 acres at $550 an acre, total $38,500.

Parcel 281, rich land, all level; dark sediment loam; alfalfa growing; other general agricultural purposes. Faces the county road. 50 acres at $500 per acre, total $25,000.

Parcel 282, there are several pieces in parcel 282. The piece
624   that has 38.93 acres in it is divided into two pieces; one containing 29.20 and the other about 10 acres; they do not lie adjacent to each other.

SPRING VALLEY WATER CO. VS. CITY AND COUNTY OF SAN FRANCISCO

CROSS EXAMINATION BY MR. STEINHART

The rectangular strip is included in the 10 acres. It is excellent farming land; rich dark loam; some light loam in it; exceptionally clean of foul growth; well fertilized. Its purposes are general agricultural purposes, truck garden, fruit. 38.93 acres at $450 an acre, total $17,518.50.

Referring to parcel containing 19.47 acres, a part of parcel 282; heavy dark loam bottom land; general agricultural purposes, beet raising; a little too high for alfalfa; truck gardening. 19.47 acres at $400 per acre, total $7,787. The property lies upon a small mound. It is a little too high for alfalfa without irrigation; with irrigation it would grow alfalfa very well.

Referring to the 10.13 acres piece; that was part of the De Freitas purchase. Low bottom land, dark heavy loam; suitable for alfalfa, excellent grazing. 10.13 acres at $400 an acre, total $4,052. It is the triangular strip in brown, the number is marked on the side.

DIRECT EXAMINATION BY MR. GREENE.   625

Parcel 283, made up of four parcels; referring to parcel 143.14 acres. This is a portion of Schween purchase; rich bottom land; dark sediment loam to the west of the railroad track, and light loam to the east. About 40 acres west of railroad track has been for years used for pasture land; the balance general farming land, beet raising. 143.14 acres at $525 per acre, total $75,148.50.

Referring to piece containing 101.05 acres; excellent piece of level land, all of rich loam, rather light in color but good soil, a little gravel across the east end, not enough to hurt the land. Uses, general agricultural purposes, beet raising and alfalfa. Valued at $425 an acre, total $42,946.25.

Referring to the 40 acre piece; bottom land, dark; general agricultural purposes, beet raising. Valued at $350 per acre, total $14,000.

Referring to 106.72 acre piece; this is very similar to the 101.05 acres lying immediately north and adjacent. The soil is a little bit better than the lower piece. All of the Schween property, particularly the 143 and a fraction acres, and these two pieces are exceptionally clean of foul growth. Valued at $450 per acre for 106.72 acres, total $48,024.

Parcel 284, Oxsen purchase; rich bottom land, dark sediment loam; uses alfalfa, beet raising, and other general agricultural purposes. 16.70 acres at $450 an acre, total $7515.

Parcel 286, purchased from Wenig; bottom land, dark in color,   626 suitable for dairy purposes—alfalfa, excellent grazing land. 17.28 acres at $500 per acre, total $8,640.

Parcel 288, purchase known as the Clark, Chabot & Bothin purchase, what is commonly known as the Chabot Ranch. The soil varies, some adobe, some alkali, and some rich bottom land. Some loam. Uses, beet raising and general agricultural purposes, alfalfa. Some dark clay also on this property. 1191.61 acres at $210 per acre, total $250,238.10. This tract has a county road, which is known as the Hop Yard road, running through it, and faces the county road leading from Dublin to Santa Rita. About 150 acres of it are of adobe nature, with some alkali in it. There are about 100 acres of fair bottom land; 300 acres of pretty rich bottom land. The balance, about 700 acres, is of rather a dark clay loam, but not very sticky. The tract overflows considerably in heavy winters. The canals that are through there, if properly taken care of, would drain the property fairly well, and they would not have trouble with it.

Parcel 289, the Ronan purchase; dark rich loam, principally used at the present time, and for several years past, for grazing pur-
627 poses. Alfalfa could be grown on it. A railroad track runs through it and divides it rather badly. 47.37 acres at $350 per acre, total $16,579.50.

Parcel 291, the Head-Hewitt purchase; bottom land, dark loam, sandy in spots; the lower end is sediment fill. Uses are general agricultural purposes. There are a couple of bad spots of about 20 acres each. 210.547 acres at $275 per acre, total $57,900.42. Sediment fill is a fill that is drawn in, or washed in there by the creeks and canals. It is not a detriment to the property. In most cases it is a benefit. That rich loam is brought down and deposited there.

Referring to map 11, beginning at the right-hand upper corner, I did not value No. 224. In A-239, I only valued that portion of it lying outside of the creek bottom, and within, in places, from 25 to 100 feet of the high-water mark of the creek. 229, in brown, the little square piece, I did value. 232, 225, 231, and 235, which seem to be joined together, I did not value. 263 I did not value. The four
628 small parcels marked 225 in the lefthand corner, I did value, then the remainder of the map, beginning with E-239, that portion lying above the highwater mark, and beginning within a reasonable distance thereof, I valued. The remainder in the creek bottom, I did not. I valued D-239 above the highwater mark. I did not value the creek bottom, or the land lying immediately adjacent thereto. 233 I did not value. B-239 I valued, excepting that portion lying in the creek bottom, and within a few feet of the highwater mark. C-239 I valued, excepting the portion lying in the creek bottom.

There are four parcels in No. 225, located in the town of Niles. Beginning with .0023 of an acre, this is a very small piece that lies adjacent to, and on the east side of the railroad track. I would judge that it was not much bigger than a portion of this table, but I appraised it in the same manner, and at the same rate that I appraised the other properties contained in this parcel, at the rate of

$1000 per acre, or $2.30 for the entire piece. The second parcel of No. 225, containing .416 of an acre, is a portion of level land that faces the county road, and also the S. P. right of way. The uses this piece could be put to would be either for a dwelling, or possibly for a warehouse. I figured it in as a dwelling site, valued at $1000 per acre, or $416 for the entire piece.

The next piece has 11.46 acres; lies to the north of the county road, and the railroad tracks leading from Niles toward Mission San Jose. It does not lie immediately adjacent to those properties, but within a couple of hundred feet of it. The county road through Niles Canyon passes over or through this property. It has several dwellings on it now, used by residents of Niles. The company, I believe, only owns the land. Valued at $1000 per acre, or a total of $11,460. The other parcel in 225 contains .699 of an acre, and lies just south of the county road leading from Niles toward Mission San Jose. It is a triangular piece, rather hard to get at. I appraised that piece at a total of $350.

Parcel 229, is the square piece in brown, and lies about a mile or a mile and a quarter from the town of Niles. It is on the west side of the creek, and west of the county road. Is 139 feet square, and would make an excellent residence site. I appraised it at $250 for the entire piece.

Parcel 237, lies across the creek from Niles; is a long oblong piece; lies on the hillside. About one-half of it is under cultivation; the other half very steep. A portion of the other half could be placed under cultivation. There are some buildings upon the property, which are not the property of the company. The portion under cultivation is used for early vegetables. Appraised at $200 an acre, total $2,130. I paid no particular attention to the improvements that were on any of this property.

239-A is what is known as the Mayborg property, lies on the west and south slopes of Niles Canyon; it is rather irregular in shape. The northerly portion runs close to the top of the ridge on west side. All the property is steep. Portions of it are heavily wooded. No farming land of any kind on the property. Could be used only for grazing purposes, or the entire piece could be sold for a building site. 71.45 acres is the total acreage, and I appraised the entire piece at $500. I deducted from that 20.45 acres for creek bottoms, and which I eliminated from my valuation.

239-B, this is the Mehrmann property; lies on both sides of the creek. All steep, wooded, very little good grazing land on it, except some on top of the ridges. A small portion, possibly 10 or 15 acres on south side of creek, is fairly level, and would make an excellent building site. I appraised this entire parcel at $3,000, eliminating the portion that was in the creek. The total acreage is 263.56. I eliminated 20.56 acres in the creek bottom.

239-C, contains 109 acres. Only a small portion lies in the creek bottom. I eliminated 5 acres for that portion. Appraised at $20 an acre, total $2,080. This property is steep and wooded; about 50 acres of open grazing land. Also, possibly 5 to 10 acres that are fairly level, and could be used for buildings.

239-D is only a small piece of property. There is a building site upon it. It is very wooded and steep. I eliminated practically only a quarter of an acre. I appraised the entire piece at $500.

239-E, is a piece containing 29.99 acres, from which I eliminated 10 acres for the portion that lies in the creek, and immediately adjacent thereto. Property is steep and wooded. There is a fair building site on it. I appraised the entire piece for $500.

632   The total amount at which I valued the Pleasanton properties, appearing on map 10, is $1,994,454.27, and contains in total acreage 5,490.909, and makes an average value per acre of $363.23. To explain the difference in values, ranging at from $400 to $500 and $550 on the different parcels, as to which I testified this morning; through all that Pleasanton country the land differs. There is a difference in the character of the soil. One portion might be richer than the other, one might be lower than the other. I took all those things into consideration when appraising the property. Some portions might be adaptable for the same purposes; one might raise a larger crop than the other. I took those things into consideration in placing

633   my value. The distance of a given piece of property from the heart of the town of Pleasanton in some instances may have played a part in my valuation, but not to any material extent. Of course, a piece of property lying immediately adjacent to the town, if the soil was of the same character as that of a piece that lies three miles away, may be a little more valuable because of its location, but the difference in the selling price of it would be but little.

The properties referred to on map 10 are within a radius of from 3 to 3½ miles of the town of Pleasanton.

Referring to map 12, the properties there delineated are around the town of Sunol, and I have known these properties off and on ever since I can remember.

Parcel 228, the larger portion of this property is open grazing land. There are about 40 acres of farming land on top of the ridge. A portion of the Western Pacific Picnic Grounds are situated on

634   the property; also the dam known as Sunol dam. Practically all of it lies on the south slope of the Alameda Creek, including the top of the ridge. There are 30 acres along the creek that is bench; fair farming land. 198.94 acres at $60 an acre, total $11,936.40.

Parcel 239-b, referring to the one that has 20.32 acres; lies very close to, and adjacent to what is known as the Nusbaumer tract, and is south of this tract. The S. P. right of way cuts through the property. About six acres of it can be farmed. Balance of it rather rough and wooded. I appraised it in conjunction with the Nusbaumer tract, No. 290, at $100 an acre, total $2,032. It could be used for a home site, and a portion of it could be farmed, the balance cleared off. The 5.82 acre piece, lying almost adjacent to it, I appraised at $100 an acre, total $582. This piece, as near as I could ascertain when visiting the ground, is rather badly cut by the Western Pacific in making their fill. If leveled off, it would make a nice dwelling site. There are some trees on it.   635

239-w, that is the Behrens property; rich soil; some sediment fill in it; orchard, vegetables. Faces the county road. 4.15 acres at $350 an acre, total $1,452.50.

239-F, lies in Niles Canyon, and is practically opposite Feusier's property. Runs only a short distance from the bank of the creek up to the slope. About 3 acres is in an old prune orchard; it is fairly level; the balance is steep and wooded. Valued at $75 per acre, total $735.75.

239-G, lies on county road from Pleasanton to Sunol. Has been used for vegetable purposes. At one time Mr. Wells, of Tesicana raised a pea crop in there. A small portion of the property lies in the creek bottom. Generally good for agricultural purposes. Vegetables can be raised there; also alfalfa. 22.25 acres at $250 an acre, total $5,562.50.

239-H, that is the Charles Stone piece. Entire property is of rolling hills. Some of it is steep. Small portions of it wooded; practically all grazing land. A portion of it could be farmed. E. C. Apperson has used it for grazing purposes for a good many years. Valued at $60 an acre, for 1172.16 acres, total $70,329.60.   636

239-I, 239-J, 239-K, all small portions lying on the road that leads along the railroad track at Sunol. Lies between the creek and S. P. R. R. track. The Western Pacific Railroad track cut it up pretty badly. Valued at $100 for each piece, or $300 for all three pieces. Could only be used for residences.

239-L, Charles Hadsell piece. Contains 2317.59 acres. 350 acres lie where the water temple at Sunol is, on the county road from Sunol to Py's Corner, and from Py's Corner to the Mission Bridge; along the southern boundary would be the creek, and the western boundary would be the creek. 100 acres of this property is in a walnut orchard. In 1913 the trees were three years old, I believe. Good land, and can be used for almost any agricultural purposes. Quite a nursery upon the property at the present time. That is the property upon which the water temple is, and those buildings that stretch up to the corner. Then there is the portion lying on the east side of the county road, leading from Mission San Jose, consisting of about 100 acres of poor land. The soil has some gravel in it, and is rather red in portions. It is very good, however. This property can be used for general agricultural purposes, for farming, hay   637 and grain. There are 900 acres also lying on that side of the county road leading from Livermore through the Vallecitas road to Mission San Jose, and through Py's Corner. A portion of it is farming land, some of it grazing, and some waste. It is fairly well watered. Has some large oak trees scattered over it. Good grazing and farming land. Another tract of 750 acres lies between the Vallecitas road and the road leading from Pleasanton to Sunol; all rolling, hilly, with red soil. Some waste land in it. Most of it is farmed. Its uses are general agricultural purposes and grazing. Another piece of about 150 acres lies on the east side of the railroad track, and on west side of the creek, and bounded on the south by the Alameda; rather a sandy loam, reddish in spots; some dark loam in it. General agricultural purposes, truck gardening. A portion of it has been used for the planting of peas.

638 In regard to the land that was well watered, I did not make any additional allowance in my valuation because of that fact, other than this: properties which have water upon them for cattle ranges and for farming purposes, are a little more valuable than properties that have not, but I only took into consideration the water for the use on the lands themselves, and by the party residing thereon, for the purpose of caring for his stock and so on. I took into consideration no water whatever in any of these lands, excepting the consideration that the man who owned the property, and was living on it, could use the water on the land, and for his stock. The entire piece of 2317.59 acres I valued at $150 per acre, or $347,638.50.

Parcel 239-N, known as the Whitmore-Nusbaumer property. Lies on north side of San Antonio Creek; all rolling; soil is reddish; portions on the flat and benches are dark and very good; almost entire property can be farmed for general agricultural purposes, hay and grain raising. Some of it would make excellent grape land. Exceptionally well adapted to cultivation. 764.86 acres at $60 per acre, total $45,891.61.

Parcel 239-O, practically all lies on the south side of the San Antonio Creek, or southwest side, and runs back into the hills quite a little ways. Contains considerable flat land. Soil on the flat is loam and clay, and rather poor, with some gravel in it in places; balance is reddish and good farming land. About 300 acres of the property is farmed. 100 acres being practically level, the balance steep gulches and rolling grazing land. 421 acres at $50 per acre, total $21,050.

639 Parcel 244, lies just south of Alameda Creek, and west of the county road from Sunol to Mission San Jose. 75 acres is rather rich dark soil, some sand in it. Balance is rolling to a small degree. Rather good soil. General agricultural purposes, hay and grain. 110 acres at $200 per acre, total $22,000.

184

Parcel 252, lies on the south bank of the Arroyo de Laguna Creek, near Sunol. A very poor piece of property. In a few years there will be no property there. It will be washed into the creek. I valued the entire piece at $100.

Parcel 261, lies just below the property owned by Mrs. Hearst. Formerly an apple orchard on portion of it. Rich reddish soil. Faces the county road. 15.25 acres at $300 per acre, total $4575.

Parcel 262, small piece, lies in between the county road and the railroad track. Could be used for vegetables and fruit. Character of the soil is such, however, as is not well adapted for those purposes. 4.45 acres at $200 per acre, total $850.

Parcel 267, 175.40 acres. Lies in Niles Canyon, and runs across the ridge to what is known as Roumiguiere Gulch. About 75 acres on top of the ridge on southerly side is open fair grazing ground. About 40 acres on south slope of creek is open and has large trees on it. Fairly level. About 30 acres of orchard and level space near the creek. 30 acres on the other side of it that is very heavily wooded and steep. About 70 acres of the property would make excellent building sites for country homes. The balance is fair grazing land, with the exception of the portions that are steep and heavily wooded. 175.04 acres, at $75 per acre, total $13,128.

Parcel 268-A, known as the Roumiguire property. Faces on the south bank of Alameda Creek, with bluffs. Lies on the west and south slope of Sunol Valley. The soil is rather a red clay, not very sticky; it is all rolling. 200 acres used for general agricultural purposes, such as hay and grain raising, about 60 acres of vineyard in only fair shape; also portion of it that is very steep and thickly wooded. 256.90 acres at $125 per acre, total $32,111.50.

(The acreage on the map was shown as 248.17, but the inventory, which is stipulated to be correct, shows 256.90 acres. Corrected on the face of the map by the Master.)

Parcel 268-B, faces the County Road on the west side, leading from Mission San Jose to Sunol, bounded on the west by the property of Roumiguiere. The soil in the northerly portion is dark loam running to the south, with red adobe and clay. The property lies on the north and west slope of the Sunol Valley. General agricultural purposes, hay and grain raising; balance grazing land with some wood. 250.78 acres at $150 per acre, total $37,617.

Parcel 290, this is the Nusbaumer piece, lying on the west side of the valley between Sunol and Pleasanton. The Arroyo de Laguna runs through it. The entire slope is somewhat wooded. Portions of it, however, are very open. The property lying upon the floor of the valley has very good soil. It is suitable for orchard and general agricultural purposes, such as hay raising, also grazing. It is so situated that it would make some beautiful home sites. The value of the entire piece containing 652.23 acres is $100 per acre, or $65,223.

(A correction was made on the Nusbaumer Tract, changing 656.59 to 652.23 acres.)

643   A general description of the San Antonio lands; all of these properties lying in the San Antonio are grazing lands. Some of them are heavily wooded. Some of them good, open country; some of them tillable. They are not all grazing lands. There are some portions of the pieces that are tillable and are farmed. I was thinking of Arroyo Valle, gentlemen, I made a mistake. This property in the San Antonio; a great portion of that property lying below S-239, T-239 is farming land. The property such as A-239, X-239, Z-239 and V-239, are grazing lands. In portions steep and wooded, and in other portions open. Good grazing lands. This piece of property, a-239, is located on the north slope of the San Antonio, and practically at the end of the company's property. There is another section which connects the San Antonio with the Arroyo del Valle, Section 23, marked Y-239 on map 14. This property is fairly open, although the north line contains some steep gulches, but on a whole is fair grazing ground. The south portion is also partly wooded in one of the extreme corners. I

644   priced this property, containing 480 acres at $15 an acre, total $7,200.

239-P, this is what is known as the Sunol property. It lies on the south slope of San Antonio Creek. It is mostly open, good, tillable land, rather dark in nature. Indian Creek runs through the northeast corner, just touching it. The south end of the property is very steep. There is some light soil through the property. $40 an acre, total $18,425.20, for 460.63 acres. 60 acres of it is rather steep pasture land. About half of the 60 is fair open pasture, and the balance is rather steep.

239-Q, lies on the south side of San Antonio Creek. A portion of it is good bench land. The land lying in the flat is rather gravelly, and not so good as the bench land. There are 253 acres of grazing land. A portion of it very good, and a portion with some brush on it, but fairly open and with large trees. It contains 453.37 acres, at $45 an acre, total $20,401.65.

239-R lies on both slopes of the creek, and is cut up somewhat by the creek. The property is practically all rolling. The soil is rather red on the hillside. In the creek bottom it is a little darker with some gravel in it. About 200 acres of it are rolling, grazing lands, but good, with large oaks scattered over it. Contains 397.53 acres, at $45 an acre, total $17,888.85. The property could be used for general agricultural purposes, including grazing, and the raising of hay and grain.

S-239 lies on both slopes of the creek. The creek about bisects

645   the land. A little over 200 acres farming land of a rolling nature. The balance lies on the slopes and the tops of the slopes. The south slope is wooded to a small extent. It is excellent grazing land. It

can be used for general agricultural purposes, farming, hay and grain, and grazing. It contains 893.15 acres at $25 an acre, total $22,328.75. Parcels Q and R both have some very good land upon them. Good farming land. The farming land on this parcel is not as good as on Q and R, and the ratio of the farming land to the total acreage is different. In S-239 there is only a little over 200 acres of farming land, and the balance is grazing land. There is a balance of some 690 odd acres. In R-239 there are about 200 acres of farming land, and only about 200 acres of grazing land.

239-T, this property also lies on both sides of the San Antonio. About half of it is good farming land and good grazing land. The balance is steep in portions, and some portions wooded, particularly on the south side. The farming land is of fair soil. On the north side there are about 200 acres good farming land; that is, good for that kind of land, and lands that are located in that district—and some good pasture land. The south side is practically all pasture. The uses of this property would be general agricultural purposes, farming, hay and grain and grazing. On the entire piece containing 1038.29 acres, I placed a value of $30 an acre, total $31,148.70. The north end 646 is not very steep. It runs practically up to what is known as the Lilienthal property. I see no reason why all the north end could not be farmed. A portion of it is now farmed, but apparently for the last two or three years, and during the time of this appraisement, they were using it for pasture. Why I do not know. Farmers are farming much steeper land than that particular portion is.

239-U lies over on the south ridge adjoining the San Antonio Valley, and runs down to Indian Creek on the west. The portion running into Indian Creek is very steep, and covered with chaparral and brush. For the most part the north and west ends of the property are rather poor. About one-third of it is good, open grazing ground. I placed a valuation on the entire piece of $10 an acre, 313.61 acres, total $3136.10. Indian Creek cuts along the west side. Going down into Indian Creek the land is very steep, covered with a good deal of brush.

239-V, is a fairly open property with good grazing. Only about 30 to 40 acres in the southeast corner is covered with heavy brush. There is also a small vineyard of about 5 acres on this property. Portion of the property could be farmed. It contains 229.25 acres, at $17.50 an acre, total $4011.87.

239-W, is a piece of property which has along the south end of it 647 a small portion that is covered with chaparral, other than that it is fairly open, but steep in portions. It is grazing ground. It contains 107.85 acres, at $17.50 an acre, total $1,187.37.

239-X, on the north side of this property there is fair pasture, but very steep, with some rock outcroppings. On the south side it is also steep with lots of brush. There are two very deep gulches on this property. Its only use would be for grazing purposes. Contains 640 acres, at $12.50 an acre, total $8000.

239-V is a piece of property which is rather irregular in shape. It has a long, narrow strip running up the north end of it to the east. There are about 100 acres running along the bench on the north side, and through this narrow strip. It is rather steep. The south is also rather steep. Not as steep as some other property surrounding it. As a whole it is fair grazing ground. There is not brush on it. It contains 364.65 acres, at $20 an acre, total $7,293 for the entire piece.

The properties on map 14 are the Arroyo del Valle properties.

Parcel 239-Y is a section of land which adjoins the property of the company in the San Antonio with the properties of the company in the Arroyo del Valle. It is the one which adjoins the three-quarter section, ~~A-299~~ on map 13. It is open rolling grazing land, with a very few steep portions. It contains 640 acres, at $20 an acre, or $12,800 for the entire piece.

243-A, lies on the north slope of the Arroyo del Valle, and slopes south towards the creek bottom. The land lying on the slope of the hill and the top thereof is fair open grazing land. The portion lying over the top of the ridge to the north is wooded and steep. The property contains two ridges of excellent grazing land, the gulches on it, however, are steep. There is practically no brush, except in the north portions. This piece of property contains 80 acres, at $25 an acre, total $2000 for the entire piece. In placing this value upon this piece, I took into consideration the fact of its connection with other properties lying in there, and placed a value on several pieces lying together there at practically the same figure. I assumed that this particular piece in, and of itself, is more valuable as a portion of the other lands surrounding it than it would be by itself, if it was a lone piece. All that property is grazing land. Practically the only purpose to which the property is put is for grazing purposes. A small piece of 80 acres up there for the raising of cattle, for grazing purposes, would be of little value to anyone. In appraising these lands I did not take into consideration at any time the water producing purposes. I know nothing concerning the value of the land for that purpose, and I did not take that into consideration at any time. At no time did I take into account in making the valuation upon these lands any purposes to which they could be put for water storing or for supplying in any way. I did not consider myself capable of appraising lands from that standpoint. In all the lands I appraised I took the position of appraising the lands simply for the use it could be put to by any private individual who would purchase them—to conduct a small ranch, or for grazing purposes, or something of that kind. I understand, of course, that all these properties have another use, and are used for water purposes. What the value of that use is I have no idea, and do not pretend to know.

648

649

243-B, lies in the Arroyo del Valle. The Arroyo del Valle practically bisects it. About 50 acres of farming land. Some brush upon it; rather steep in places; large trees. 640 acres at $25 per acre, total $16,000.

243-C, lies on west side of creek. Portion in creek bottom. More or less rough and wooded, but as a whole is fair grazing land. 120 acres at $25 per acre, total $3000.

650

243-D, lies on west side of the Arroyo del Valle slope; is wooded, has some sage brush; rather steep. Also deep ravine in north end. There is a little grazing land on it. 40 acres at $25 per acre, total $1000. That parcel by itself would not be worth $25 an acre. In valuing these properties I took into consideration the fact of connection with other parcels.

243-I, 160 acres lying on the south-west slope of the Arroyo del Valle. Some good grazing land on it; also some that is rather steep, with a good deal of woods. One very steep gulch. As a whole it is fair grazing land. 160 acres at $15 per acre, total $2400.

243-J, is very similar to 243-I; lies on same side of the slope; has some large timber on it; a steep gulch. 160 acres at $15 per acre, total $2400.

243-K, very similar to 243-I and 243-J, although this parcel has some excellent grazing land on a small portion of it; also some timber. 160 acres at $15 per acre, total $2400. I and K are on the sides of the canyon, and running up pretty close to the top of the ridge, giving on both some open grazing ground. They are both a little better property than J from a grazing standpoint. 243-J is, I should judge, about one-eighth of a mile above the road leading into the valley.

651

243-M, open grazing ground; some little brush, a few large trees, rather a steep draw in a portion of it. As a whole very fair grazing ground. 87.79 acres at $25 per acre, total $2,194.75. The draw that I refer to is a small tributary to the creek that runs down from that draw, which is the arm of the creek; the large point running up there is where the draw is.

243-N, lies on the east and north slopes. About 40 acres of it is rough lying in the southeast corner. These are steep and wooded, and with gulches; the balance is good, open grazing land, except about half of it, which is tillable. 237.81 acres at $25 per acre, total $5,945.25.

243-O, a small piece containing 23 acres, lying practically where the roads fork. Practically all level land. Some large trees on it, and considerable gravel through it, although a portion of it is excellent grazing land. All the soil has gravel in it lying pretty close to the creek bottom. 23 acres at $25 per acre, total $575.

652

243-P, lies on a bench or valley to the east of the creek; contains about 100 acres which is farmed for hay. The balance is open grazing land. The soil is rather red, portions of it have adobe through it. 160 acres at $25 per acre, total $4000.

243-Q, lies on both slopes of the creek. Considerable level land in the creek bottom. About the middle of the north half is a steep gulch on the east side. Poor and covered with brush. Balance is good, open grazing land. The west side is considerably wooded, but is fairly good grazing land. 661.80 acres at $15 per acre, total $9,927.

243-R, about two-thirds lies on east side of creek, and one-third on the west side. South portion of east side is rocky and steep, and covered with chaparral; the balance is fair open grazing land. West side somewhat wooded and steep. Has some fair grazing land. 640 acres at $15 per acre, total $9,600.

653   243-S, lies mostly on west slope of Arroyo del Valle Creek, about 20 acres are excellent farming land lying on the floor of the valley. West slope is wooded and steep in places. Entire property is fair grazing land. 324.10 acres at $15 per acre, total $4,861.50.

243-T, lies on both sides of the creek, about 25 acres on the east side, the balance on the west side. Steep and wooded. East side rocky; grazing none too good anywhere upon the property. 160 acres, at $5 an acre, total $800.

654   243-U, lies midway on the south-westerly slope of the creek. Heavily wooded; some open places, pretty fair grazing. 160 acres, at $6 an acre, total $960.

243-V, lies at the extreme southerly end of the property owned by the Spring Valley Water Co. in the Arroyo del Valle on both sides of the creek. Steep on both sides; some wood, some chaparral, small brush; some open grazing ground, very little. 640 acres at $5 per acre, total $3200. I am familiar with all these properties, and have been on all of them. Not only during the time that I was appraising them, but I have been hunting over these properties, practically ever since I was able to hold a gun. I know all these properties.

I have appraised parcel 247 and Parcel N-268, which are not included on that summary. N-268 is in the bottom of the creek, down near Schween's. A considerable distance below the bridge, leading from Livermore along the Ruby Vineyard Road. 214.87 acres at $150 per acre, for the entire piece, total valuation $32,527.50. The uses of

655   this property would be the gravel contained in it. It is practically all a gravel bed. Parcel 247 lies almost adjoining the property known as the Cresta Blanca property. The north end is steep, with a rough creek or ravine running through. Some brush and trees on the side of the ravine. Contains a large washout or cliff on the east side, very rough; wooded in spots; south portion steep and rocky and covered with chaparral and scrub. Entire property is rather rough. A good deal of good grazing land; the feed is what is known as early feed. About 90 acres of it is open. 164 acres at $15 per acre, total $2,460.

Map 15 contains a portion of the properties in the San Antonio just east of the mouth of the San Antonio, and also properties along the Alameda Creek, up to a little beyond Haynes Gulch.

239-M, lies east of Alameda Creek, includes the Alameda Creek, up to what is known as the Crocker Place. The east side lies along Apperson Creek, taking in a portion thereof. The southeast corner lies near Maguire Creek. The north line lies north of San Antonio Creek; the south line is just north of Haynes Gulch. The east side, l ping into Apperson Creek, is very steep and wooded to the top of the ridge. In the southwest portion there are 650 acres of rather steep, but good, open grazing land, with very little brush, and some large oaks; also in the 650 acres is a small valley of about 30 acres containing very good soil. The soil in this pasture is a dark adobe, with rock outcroppings at the top of the ridges. Just west of the pasture are about 200 acres of farming land, fairly level, the soil being a black adobe. The road getting into the 200 acre piece is very steep. The north portion of this property includes San Antonio Creek, about 300 acres, all of which is fair farming land, containing about 60 acres of waste; the soil is reddish, with some gravel.

Along the Alameda Creek are about 300 acres of farming land, and some 400 acres in the creek bottoms. Practically all the balance is rugged grazing land, with some undergrowth. The slope to the Alameda Creek is very steep and rocky. Some rocky points. Many small valleys, and the tops of the hills are usually rather level. Some parts are heavily wooded, large oaks and other trees. 3,314.04 acres at $50 per acre, total $165,702.

Parcel 250 lies on both slopes of the Alameda Creek; includes creek bottom and valley, about one-half lying on each side. Is steep and wooded; the north end being particularly steep and rough. Some portions contain some very good grazing land. About 75 acres of farming land fairly flat. About 50 acres of rolling hills, farming land. About 175 acres of fair pasture. Considerable rough country. The east side is the best. Containing small flats and valleys. 1448.03 acres at $25 per acre, total $36,200.75.

Parcel 264, lies on the west l pe of the Alameda Creek. About 25 acres along the creek bottom that is very good for that character of land; can be used for farming; is tillable; can be used for agricultural purposes. The balance can be used for grazing. Some rough steep land, but not a great deal. 82.13 acres at $50 per acre, total $4,106.50.

268-C, lies to the west of the Alameda Creek. None of it touches the creek, but it slopes toward it. About 30 acres of it is excellent bottom land for general agricultural purposes, such as hay and grain raising. The balance is rolling. About 200 acres of rolling farm land, red soil, fairly good. 200 acres of fairly good grazing. About 50 acres is brushy, with chaparral. 494.89 acres at $75 per acre, total $37,016.75.

By general agricultural purposes, I mean any purposes the ordinary farmer uses land of this kind for; I mean by that the raising of hay and grain; he may raise a few hogs on a portion of it, or something like that. He may have a little truck garden in back of his house.

DIRECT EXAMINATION BY MR. GREENE.

268-D, this property is known as the Mendoza piece. A small portion of it slopes into Alameda Creek, although the property in itself does not touch the creek. It is all rolling. About 50 acres rather steep and wooded. About 100 acres of it tillable. 150 acres is good grazing land. 298.91 acres at $30 an acre, total $8,967.30.

Parcel 285, known as the Dougherty property; slopes east to Alameda Creek, running practically to the high water mark. I think a little of the creek runs through it along the lower edge. 30 acres farming land, and about 65 acres near the top of the ridge that is good grazing land. The balance is wooded and steep. 137.33 acres at $50 per acre, total $6,866.50.

659 Map 16, parcel 223, slopes north into the Alameda, which runs through a portion of it. The portion sloping into the Alameda is very steep and wooded. The remainder of the property rather steep and a little rough; some excellent open grazing land. 440 acres at $15 an acre, total $6,600.

Parcel 225 lies in two different portions. There are 160 acres entirely removed from the main portion of the land. This property lies on both slopes of the north end of the Calaveras Valley. The west side heavily wooded; has some steep, deep gulches on it. It is grazing land; level, and with very little wood on it.

The piece that is isolated from the other, the south and west 40 acres, being 80 acres altogether, is open, but rough and rocky, while the other portion is very good grazing land. Upon both pieces together, 1720 acres, I placed a valuation of $30 an acre, total $51,600. The total includes both pieces.

241-A, half of this property lies in Alameda County, and the other half in Santa Clara County. It is all rolling hills, very little wooded. Practically bare. Some places are rather steep. In the steep gulches and the draws there is some wood. The southwest

660 corner faces the La Honda Creek; that portion is steep and wooded. 634.08 acres, at $20 per acre, total $12,681.60.

241-E, lies east of what is known as the Weller place. It slopes into Calaveras Valley; rough on the slope and heavily wooded, particularly in the gulches. On top of the hills there is good grazing land, which is very good. 240 acres at $25 per acre, total $6,000.

241-F, lies mostly on the southern slope of the Alameda Creek, a small portion on the northeast, the creek running through it.

It is fairly level. The portion in the creek is very gravelly. There is some woods on the property. 40 acres at $25 per acre, total $1000. By fairly level, I mean that it is not as steep and as badly cut up as some of the other portions. It is not level land by any means; it lies on the slope. Down in a country like around Pleasanton, it would be considered steep land.

Parcel 246, lies in what is known as section 18, it is an ell-shaped piece of property; very open and rolling; grazing land. I don't know what the elevation is, exactly, but all the property lying between the Alameda and the La Honda is at quite an elevation; the drop into the creeks is steep. It practically lies along the top of the ridge. The northeast quarter slopes into Alameda Creek, and is steep and wooded. 474.12 acres at $20 per acre, $9,482.40.

Parcel 251, the Alameda Creek flows through the northeast corner of this property; the slope into the Alameda Creek is rough, steep and wooded; other portions of the property are rough, steep and wooded. There are about 1000 acres of farming land upon the property. There is some very fair grazing land. 1062.95 acres at $25 an acre, total $26,573.75. This piece of property is reached by taking the road from Mission San Jose. A small portion in the middle of it is owned by Mr. Metcalf, I believe some 5 acres. The road from Mission San Jose is the easiest way of reaching it.

Parcel 258, lies on the south slope of the Alameda Creek. The portion sloping into the creek is very rough. The remainder is very good. The land that is grazing land upon that portion is very good. 151 acres at $15 per acre, total $2,265.

268-p, practically all lies on the top of what is known as Poverty Ridge. It is all open, good grazing land, 160 acres at $20 per acre, total $3200. There is a small portion of it sloping into La Honda that has a little brush on it, but it is a very small portion.

661

662

TWELFTH HEARING   JULY 29, 1915.

Witness C. A. GALE.

(Certain corrections noted in the transcript.)   663-664

DIRECT EXAMINATION BY MR. GREENE.

268-W, known as the Weller property, lies on the ridge and on the slope to the Calaveras on west side of the valley. Portions rather heavily wooded. Lots of it good open grazing ground. About 250 acres, tillable. One large, fine spring on it. 646.75 acres at $30 per acre, total $19,402.50.

268-X, this is the Santos property, lying on west slope and top of the ridge of Calaveras valley; open rolling grazing land. Portion on east side rather steep. The soil is fair. 396.64 acres at $30 per acre, total $11,899.20.   665

268-Y, rather steep in places and rough. Considerable wood,

SPRING VALLEY WATER CO. VS. CITY AND COUNTY OF SAN FRANCISCO

sage brush. The grazing land is none too good, although fair. 120 acres at $15 per acre, total $1800.

(The bench marks of the proposed reservoir, looking at this map, are indicated at the 800 foot line.)

Parcel 295, Jacobson property, slopes south into Alameda Creek, the creek running through the lower end of it. The property is open, about 50 acres tillable. The uses are grazing, and general agricultural purposes. 320 acres at $25 per acre, total $8,000.

Questioned by Master.

That is in what is called the Upper Alameda, it lies on the north slope.

DIRECT EXAMINATION BY MR. GREENE.

Parcel 320. The Calaveras and LaHonda Creeks fork on the northeast line on this property. 50 acres are good farming land; the balance is wooded in portions. About 20 acres of it very gravelly soil; about 60 acres lying on the west slope of the valley. 120 acres at $60 per acre, total $7,200.

666 Parcel 322, slopes east into the Calaveras Valley. One branch of the creek running through it. 60 acres fair farming land; 40 acres rolling and flat farming land; balance grazing land; some steep gulches. 160 acres at $75 per acre, total $12,000.

Parcel 323, 50 acres are hills, and heavily wooded. The floor of the valley is excellent farming land; soil sandy and black loam mixed. 200 acres at $150 per acre, total $30,000.

Parcel 324, known as the Harris property; about 60 acres lie on the west slope of the valley. All of the property can be farmed. The floor of the valley to the east of the road is exceptionally good land; the balance is hay land. 160 acres at $200 per acre, total $32,000.

Parcel 325; both the Calaveras and the LaHonda run through this property; about 15 acres in prune orchard. Creek bottoms are wide and gravelly. A portion lies upon the east slope of the valley, and some portions can only be used for grazing purposes. 800 acres at $55 an acre, total $44,000.

Questioned by Mr. McCutchen.

That was originally the Gaynes property.

DIRECT EXAMINATION BY MR. GREENE.

Parcel 327, Cedarbloom property, lies upon west slope of the 667 valley. The larger portion lies on a hill pointing out into the valley. Rather steep, grazing land, but very good. Some rough country in the northern portion, wooded; the balance is open; some large oak trees scattered through it. 80 acres at $30 an acre, total $2400.

Parcel 328, Rasmussen property; the LaHonda Creek runs through it; slopes north and south thereon; rough and wooded in

194

portions; fair grazing land as to the remainder. 200 acres at $12.50 per acre, total $2500.

Parcel 329, also known as the Rasmussen property; lies adjacent to, and is very similar to property in 328. 40 acres at $12.50 per acre, total $500.

Map 17, parcel 241-B; this is one of the Crocker & Dillon sections. Larger portion of it lies upon north slope of Arroyo LaHonda Creek; balance in creek and on south 1 pe. Rough, steep; portions heavily brushed; about 200 acres good grazing land. 640 acres at $10 per acre, total $6,400.

Parcel 268-e, known as the Beverson Tract, lies along the ridge between the Alameda Creek and the Arroyo Honda. Some portions steep, but as a whole fair grazing land. Very little wood upon it. 320 acres at $15 per acre, total $4800. 668

Parcel 268-q, lies in the upper portion of the north slope of the Arroyo Honda Creek; a portion rather rough and steep. Large rocky cliff lies upon section 28; I think only a very small portion of the cliff lies upon this piece of property. Not as good grazing as 268-r. 160 acres at $12 per acre, total $1,920.

268-r, lies immediately north of 268-q, near the top of north slope of Arroyo Honda Creek; rather steep and somewhat wooded. In placing a valuation upon both "r" and "q", I considered them as a whole, and placed a valuation upon 268-r in a like amount as I did on 268-q. 320 acres at $12 per acre, total $3,840.

(There is another 268-r, containing 160 acres, adjoining the first one.)

Parcel 268-r, lies in section 22. A portion lies upon top of the ridge. A portion slopes into Alameda Creek. The slope into Alameda Creek is steep and wooded. 160 acres at $10 per acre, total $1600.

268-s, lies north of Oak Ridge road, and slopes into Alameda Creek; steep, considerable wood, but has some open grazing spots that are very good. 80 acres at $10 per acre, total $800.

268-t, this is an irregular ell-shaped piece lying to the north 669 of Oak Ridge road; heavily wooded; rather steep in portions; other portions contain fair open grazing land. There is a small orchard of about one-quarter of an acre. 280 acres at $10 per acre, total $2,800.

268-u, slopes into the Alameda Creek, one of the tributaries of the Alameda running through it; steep and wooded; some open grazing land. I stated that on 268-t there was a small orchard; I believe that that orchard lies upon 268-u, and not upon 268-t. 160 acres at $10 per acre, total $1600.

268-E; there are three parcels of that, I believe. Taking the first parcel 320 acres, it lies upon the north slope, or just north of the Alameda Creek, sloping toward Alameda Creek; portions have some

195

wood on it. Some good open grazing land. The soil is not of very great depth, however. 320 acres at $17.50 per acre, total $5,600.

The next is the 140 acre piece. This is one of the Mendoza properties; lies on the north slope of the Alameda Creek. About 20 acres near the creek is farming land; balance is rough and wooded in spots, but fair grazing land. 140 acres at $17.50 per acre, total $2,450.

670

The next is the 160 acre piece. This is about 3 miles or 2½ miles remote from the other property of the company; lies on Pine Ridge, and is practically the highest point upon the ridge. The larger portion lies a little bit to the north of the ridge. The property is steep, rather rough; a small part of it is grazing land. It is very wooded. 160 acres at $3 per acre, total $480.

268-F; there are two parcels under that number. This is the Andrews and Hughes property. The piece containing 320 acres lies upon the north slope of Alameda Creek; it does not touch the creek. Contains 20 acres of farming land; the balance is fair grazing, some woods and sagebrush. 320 acres at $15 per acre, total $4,800.

The piece containing 20.20 acres is practically all flat land; there is a small orchard on it; it has been used for farming; for hay. 20.20 acres at $25 an acre, total $505.

In connection with this property marked 268-E, and 268-F, excepting on 268-E, containing 160 acres, in placing my valuation, I considered each piece as a part of the whole of those properties.

671

268-G, lies on both sides of Alameda Creek, the Alameda Creek running through it. A three-quarter section piece, ell-shaped, both sides are somewhat rough. Some wood on them. Some sagebrush, some fair grazing land. On this property I placed a valuation of $12.50 an acre, or a total of $6,000.

268-H, lies on the top of what is known as Oak Ridge. Highest point is about 2900 feet. Some small portions that are steep; the balance is excellent open grazing land. 320 acres at $18 an acre, total $5,760.

Map 18, 241-D, lies along the ridge between the Arroyo Honda and Calaveras Creeks. The Marsh Road passes through it. All open and good grazing land; small portion of it is heavily wooded. The property on this ridge is a little steeper than that upon Oak Ridge. 244.22 acres at $20 per acre, total $4,884.40.

268-a; this is the Brandt property, lying along the ridge upon which the Weller road runs, on the west side of Calaveras Valley. Practically all of it can be farmed, tilled; some rock outcroppings. 15 acres at $30 per acre, total $450.

268-b, Brandt-Hansen property. About 100 acres rolling farm land; very red soil; balance good open grazing country. Small portion on the south side is rocky. North edge is steep and rough.

672

197.31 acres at $65 per acre, total $12,825.15.

268-c, lies upon the west side of the Calaveras Valley, sloping into it. About half is farming land; the balance open grazing country, good. 155.42 acres at $60 an acre, total $9,325.20.

268-e, Beverson property. Slopes east to Calaveras Valley; open rolling land; some gravel; some wood; about 15 or 20 acres rather steep. 82.88 acres at $60 per acre, total $4,972.80.

268-f, known as the King property, lies right near the road leading into Calaveras, known as the Calaveras Road. Portions are very heavily wooded; other portions are tillable, although rather steep in portions. 85.63 acres at $60 per acre, total $5,137.80. 673

268-g, known as the Patton property. Open rolling land; practically all can be farmed. About 4 acres of mixed orchard. The soil is rather light. 160 acres at $65 per acre, total $10,400.

268-h, the White-Gabriel property; about 20 acres in the northwest corner is farming land; the balance heavily wooded in portions, and rough; some open land. 120 acres at $30 per acre, total $3600.

268-i, 185 acres of this land is farming land; the balance open grazing land; slopes east into Calaveras Valley; lies on both sides of the Sierra Road. That is at the southern portion of the Calaveras Valley. 273.24 acres at $50 per acre, total $13,662.

(The acreage on the above parcel was corrected to read 263.34, and the extension for the total valuation to $13,167. This correction was made on the face of the record.) 674

268-j, known as the Williams property. Lies on east side of the Calaveras Valley. About 60 acres of farming land. The balance is grazing. 80 acres at $60 per acre, total $4,800.

268-k, also known as the Williams property. Lies immediately adjacent to 268-j, but there is less farming land on this piece. 80 acres at $40 per acre, total $3,200.

268-l, lies upon the south-easterly slope of the valley, Calaveras Creek running through it. About 60 acres of farming land near the flat; about 60 acres is farming land on the ridge; about 100 acres is good, open grazing land, with some wood on it. About 100 acres rough and steep, with some gulches. 321.44 acres at $50 per acre, total $16,072.

268-m; this is the Garick property. Lies in two pieces connecting at the corner. The smaller portion contains, I believe, 20 acres, some farming land; balance wooded and rough; some good grazing land. 180 acres at $25 per acre, total $4,500. 675

268-n, this is the Fererra property. Open grazing land; some good vineyards surrounding this property. 58.25 acres at $30 per acre, total $1,747.50.

268-o, the E. B. & A. L. Stone piece; lies at the extreme southeasterly end of the Calaveras Valley. Lots of brush and trees on it. 9.06 acres at $10 per acre, total $90.60.

268-p, lies on south slope of the Arroyo Honda. Grazing land, some canyon. There are gulches in it; some portions steep and wooded.

676   The portion containing 480 acres, I valued at $20 per acre, and the portion containing 221.26 acres I valued at $20 per acre, or a total valuation for the entire 701.26 acres of $14,025.20. I placed an average value of $20 per acre on the combined pieces. The 480 acre piece slopes into the La Honda; a portion of it lying on the top of the ridge. There is a good deal of open grazing land upon it, but with some wood. The other portion of 221.26 acres, is practically open grazing land; steep in some portions.

268-y, lies on south l pe of the Arroyo Honda Creek; open grazing land, practically lies upon the ridge. More on the south slope of La Honda than upon the north slope of Calaveras. Open grazing land; some canyons in it; some little wood. 160 acres at $20 per acre, total $3,200.

677   268-Z, lies on the west slope of the Calaveras Valley. It is grazing land, steep in portions. Some wood and timber. 40 acres at $20 an acre, total $800.

321, about 140 acres lies in the valley. It is situated in the Calaveras Valley, and runs on both slopes of the valley, and entirely across it. About 217 acres upon the east slope, and about 135 acres on the west slope. The entire property is of fair soil. The property in the valley is of excellent soil. The property on the west slope can practically all be farmed. The east slope is not as good as the other, but is very fair grazing land. A portion of it is tillable. 492.90 acres at $100 per acre, total $49,290.

(The witness here corrected his statement that the 217 acres were on the east slope, to the effect that he should have said on the west slope, and the 135 acres on the east slope.)

678   330; this is the John Sherman property. Lies in the south end of the valley; about 100 acres of it is level; the balance is rolling land. Practically all can be farmed for general agricultural purposes; the bottom land is very good. 311 acres at $100 per acre, total $31,100.

331, this is the Sherman property; lies at the south end of the valley; about 70 acres in the valley, and about 70 acres on a gradual slope out of the valley; 20 acres rolling, and in this 20 acres is a steep gulch. 160 acres at $90 per acre, total $14,400.

345-A; the Calaveras Creek runs through this property, the forks joining. Considerable gravel; soil rather reddish. About 40 acres tillable. The creeks have considerable timber on them. North portion is

679   open, good grazing land. 79.33 acres at $45 per acre, total $3,569.85.

Map 18-A, 241-C; this is known as section 33. The Arroyo Honda runs diagonally through this property. The southwest slopes are steep and heavily wooded, but contain some open grazing land. North slope is very steep. This entire property, lying along on both slopes of La Honda, is steep and wooded. 640 acres at $6 per acre, total $3,840.

268-e; another piece of the Beverson property. Lies on top of the ridge between La Honda and Alameda. The highest point on this piece is 3,200 feet above the sea-level. Some of it, particularly the slope into Alameda Creek, is steep, rough, some wood and brush. From one-third to one-fourth is good, open grazing land. 640 acres at $12 per acre, total $7,680.

268-p, the first one is a piece containing 480 acres, section 10. There are about 300 acres of this section which slope into Arroyo Honda; that is steep and wooded. The balance of it is practically all good, open grazing country. A portion of it is a little bit rough. 480 acres at $10 per acre, total $4800 for the entire piece. (The list showed a valuation of $8 per acre on this piece, but was wrong in that respect; the proper valuation being $10 per acre.) 680

The other piece, known as section 4, the portion sloping into Arroyo Honda is very steep and wooded. About 50 acres in the northwest corner of this property, and about 200 other acres that is open grazing land, and with fair feed. 643.80 acres at $10 per acre, total $6,438.

268-r, 320 acres in section 34; lies south of the Oak Ridge Road, on top of the north slope of Arroyo Honda Creek; all rolling, but has some good, flat grazing land on it; portions of it wooded. 320 acres at $10 per acre, total $3,200.

268-v, there are two parcels in that. The smaller parcel, 150 acres, the La Honda Creek runs through; the slopes directly into La Honda are rather wooded and steep. 160 acres at $6 per acre, total $960.

The other portion, containing 480.24 acres, lies in the southeast corner of section 2. It is marked in yellow; there is a blue strip containing 160 acres lying just to the east of it. The forks of La Honda lie upon it; both sides are steep and wooded. 480.24 acres at $4 per acre, total $1920.96.

268-w, slopes into La Honda, and is known as the Russel property. Steep; some grazing on it; brushy. 160 acres at $5 per acre, total $800. 681

268-x, lies adjoining 268-v; if anything it is rougher and steeper than 268-v; it has more wood upon it possibly. 160.72 acres at $3 per acre, total $482.16.

To explain the reason for the varying amounts which I have named as the value of the properties primarily susceptible for grazing use, leaving out of consideration whatever value they may have for water purposes; some of the parcels are open, rolling grazing land. Others have the entire portion open, with very little wood on it; a few large trees; other portions are open grazing land in portions, and the larger portion of them may be heavily wooded and very steep, and running into the creeks. I also took into consideration, at the time of the appraisement, the feed that grows upon the property; also the amount of acreage which could be used, and the advantages for grazing. Of course, the entire acreage, even when there is brush upon it, can be used for grazing purposes, but the portions that have brush upon them are not as good as the portions that are open.

682   I have known the property in the Calaveras Valley, between the Alameda and La Honda, and between the Arroyo Honda and Calaveras, for a good many years. I have fished and hunted over all those properties. I have camped for a number of days on La Honda Creek. I know of sales, and have known of sales somewhat similar in nature to those lands and properties. I have made it a practice to keep in touch with the values wherever I have gone. From my general knowledge of lands and land values, and their uses, I made my valuation upon the properties. I have not sold land in Santa Clara County similar in character to this, but have sold lands in Alameda County that were somewhat similar, but of a higher value. I have known of lands that have been sold that are very similar in nature to these lands, and what the purchase and selling price were.

    Map 10, parcel 276, lies within the town limits of the town of Pleasanton, and immediately across Rose Avenue from the race track. Very fine piece of land. Practically a sediment fill from the wash of the creeks in years back. Practically no gravel whatever in it. The property surrounding it is being bought and sold for residence purposes. This property I valued at $750 an acre, or a total valuation for the entire piece, containing 16.44 acres at $12,330.

683   Parcel 270 lies west of the County Road leading from Pleasanton to Santa Rita. The character of the land is bottom land; rich; portions of it rather wet; a portion of it has been, and I believe now is in alfalfa. The remainder has been used as a pasture land for pasturing some of the race track horses on. 102.28 acres at $300 per acre, total $30,684.

    Owing to errors, the table will have to be revised. When it is presented it will be marked "Plaintiff's Exhibit No. 28".

684   I have been furnished, by the engineers of the company, with the proposed acreages which will be covered by water in the Calaveras Valley, and have segregated the values which I have already given for parcels which would lie in the reservoir. The values which I have put on the portion of each parcel, to which I have just referred, are the same values which I have already testified to.

    Referring to a tabulation containing various columns, the first being "The map", second "The parcel", third "Total acreage", fourth "Reservoir acres", fifth "Value per acre", sixth "Total", and the last column not being headed, but stating the general description of the properties; this was prepared by me, with the exception of the data as to acreage. The entire table, with the exception of column 4, was prepared by me. The amounts appearing in column 5 are the amounts that I placed per acre upon the acreage lying in the proposed reservoir site, and those appearing in columns 6 are the totals of the acreage, multiplied by the value per acre, making the total for the 685 entire acreage set forth in column four.

(Counsel for Plaintiff here stated that the reservoir acreage would be proved, either by Mr. Sharon, or one of the other engineers.)

In appraising these properties, I did not take into consideration their value as reservoir or water producing properties. I appraised them simply as lands to be used for general agricultural purposes, and their value to an individual purchaser.

Questioned by Master.

Where I have placed this valuation of this reservoir acreage here, it is not the value I have used for the whole of the parcels. It is naturally the best land in most cases, and I took and based my figures, given in this memorandum, on values which I placed upon those same lands in appraising the entire parcel.

686

DIRECT EXAMINATION BY MR. GREENE.

In the way I stated, I made special figures; I took practically the figures I used in appraising the entire parcel, where I had the subdivisions of the farming lands, and figured that as to how much of those lands that I appraised at a certain figure, were in this reservoir site, and used those figures.

The total value that I placed upon the lands lying within the reservoir acreage, was $188,525, and the total acreage within the proposed reservoir, as given me by the engineers, was 1,927.80 acres. Making a per acreage value of $97.83 per acre. Offered and marked "Plaintiff's Exhibit No. 29", subject to proof of the figures as to acreage.

I gave the lands, which will lie within the San Antonio Reservoir, the same treatment. The acreage as given me by the engineers, as lying in the proposed San Antonio site, is 656 acres. At the rate of $56.36 per acre, I find the value of $36,976. This table was prepared under my direction, with the exception of column 4, covering the reservoir acreages.

687

Offered in evidence and marked "Plaintiff's Exhibit 30".

The values which are shown on "Plaintiff's Exhibit 30" and "Plaintiff's Exhibit 29", in the fifth columns, respectively, correspond with my valuation, as given in my previous testimony, to this extent: In the previous testimony I valued the entire parcel, using the same figures that I used in this valuation to value the entire parcel.

(The following caption, appearing on "Plaintiff's Exhibit 29' and "Plaintiff's Exhibit 30", was stricken out at the request of counsel for Plaintiff; "This appraisement is made from values heretofore placed on properties lying therein in appraisement of entire subdivision, and only the value thereof is used".)

688

My testimony with respect to the Arroyo del Valle properties would be just the same as respecting these other exhibits. The total acreage given me was 630 acres. The total valuation that I placed thereon was $15,477, or $24.56 per acre.

201

Offered in evidence, and admitted, (Striking out the caption, as above) as "Plaintiff's Exhibit 31".

689   I have caused a segregation to be made of the properties which I valued yesterday; I took all the properties on map 10, and 268-N, and parcel 247 on map 14, and had them segregated, and the total amount at which I appraised them put in. That was the second segregation. The first segregation was all of the properties of the Arroyo del Valle, shown on map 14, excepting lots numbered 268-N and 247. Then I took all the upper portion of the Alameda and San Antonio, the Calaveras and Sunol; that would be shown on map 16, 17, 18, 18-a and 12, excepting that on map 12 I did not take in 267 and 239-F. I also took the parcels shown on map 11, including the property lying in the town of Niles, or adjacent thereto, and that long narrow strip, No. 237, that is used for agricultural purposes, and excepting the creek bottoms, which I testified that I did not appraise, and made a segregation of them. That makes four segregations.

690   On the Arroyo del Valle the total acreage is 4,344.50; total value $84,063.50; at the rate of $19.35 per acre. The properties included under that segregation could be sold at that price.

The Pleasanton properties, containing 5,988.499 acres, at a total valuation of $2,072,158.77, or $346 per acre, are the second segregation.

The third segregation, the Upper Alameda, San Antonio, Calaveras and the Sunol properties, excepting those parcels I mentioned, containing 37,149.49 acres; total value $1,651,506.96. or $44.45 per acre.

The other segregation is the property shown on map 11. I found, excepting those parcels I mentioned that I did not include, 642.4483 acres, of a total valuation $35,052.05. These valuations were made as of December 31, 1913, and when I put these values upon these different parcels, I meant that in my judgment, these properties could be sold by a willing seller to a willing purchaser, for the amount I have valued them at.

(Counsel for the Defendant here advised that he would stipulate that if any omissions were discovered in the examination, the plaintiff would be given an opportunity to fill them in.)

691   CROSS EXAMINATION BY MR. STEINHART.

I believe that my first trip into the Calaveras was about fifteen years ago, and since that time off and on I have been continually back and forth through those lands.

Map 18-A, parcel 268-p, consisting of two separate parcels, and valued at $10 an acre, can be used for grazing purposes. I have a record, I believe, as to the price the Spring Valley Water Co. paid for those properties, but in my appraisement of the properties, I did 692   not take that into consideration. I did not pay any attention to the prices that the Spring Valley Water Co. paid for the land in Calaveras, as I was told to go upon these properties, and appraise them for what I considered them worth, placing a conservative valuation thereon. The fact of a certain payment being made by the Spring Valley Water Co. for these lands, would not affect my idea of the value of them to any extent.

(Counsel for Defendant here stated that the Spring Valley paid for these properties, on April 1, 1911, $8.31 an acre, which figure was agreed to as correct by Counsel for the Plaintiff.)

I don't think that I ever saw the figures before, and now having 693 seen them, it makes no difference in my idea of the market value of these properties. I do not know the dates of the various purchases of the Spring Valley in the Calaveras. I could not tell you when Spring Valley first began to acquire land in the Calaveras, but I understand that they purchased some land in there in 1902, but they must have owned land there prior to 1902, because it was prior to that time that I first visited the Calaveras, and at that time, they owned some land or had some interest there. I obtained my information that Spring Valley owned land at that time in Calaveras, from a gentleman who told one of a party with whom I was camping on La Honda Creek, that he rented some land from the Spring Valley in that vicinity.

Where the Spring Valley Water Co. has paid more than prices that I have set upon the land, that does not make any difference in my valuation. I have represented the Spring Valley in purchases in 694 Pleasanton, but the fact that Spring Valley paid more than the prices I have placed on these lands, would not influence me in my market valuation, because I know nothing concerning the history of the purchases. I know nothing concerning what the purchase prices were, the acreage, or why the company wanted them, nor whether the owner of the property knew who wanted the land, and for that reason asked an increased amount. Judging from some sales that I have noticed, and know about, I think in some instances the Spring Valley have possibly paid more than the market value of the land. I do not say that that is their practice. My experience only is in the Pleasanton 695 properties. In some instances they purchased lands in the Pleasanton District at a very low figure; in other instances they paid more than the market value at the time of the purchase. I have not made a particular study of that phase of the question, and without so doing, and comparing the valuations, I would not be able to give an answer to that question.

I ignored all sales made in the Calaveras district to the Spring Valley. I never had the figures of the sales and the purchases, and the prices paid for that land. The term, market value, means what a willing purchaser will pay to a willing seller, and in my mind, the best test is what a willing purchaser will pay to a willing seller in the sale of land. The conditions of the sale, possibly the purposes for which the property was bought, would all be considerations I would want to look into before I would consider the sale of the land. The seller, if he was desirous of selling, would sell it at what he could get for it in the market. The best evidence of the market price of that land, a sale of the land itself not having been made, is the sales of other lands of similar character surrounding it. I paid no attention to any of the sales actually lying in the Calaveras, to the Spring Valley Water Co., and in valuing these lands around the Alameda Creek below Sunol, I excluded the river bottom.

You refer now to the lands on map 11; I also stated at that time that I excluded lands lying immediately adjacent to the highwater mark. Possibly back a distance of 20 feet in some places, and fifty feet in others. I was taking simply those lands which were adjacent to, and practically part of the creek, but did not necessarily include all level lands by the bed of the creek.

Referring to the character of the land along Alameda Creek from Sunol to Niles; the lands running from the dam down to Niles in places is very narrow, and the sides are steep; there may be an acre or two of a fairly level bench along the side of the hills; in other places the acreage is wider; there is some level land lying in the gorge. Take the property of Mr. Fusier, in Niles Canyon, it is practically all level land; there is a little roll to it; it is all on a slope, but is practically all level land. That does not appear upon the map. There is quite a stretch along the Fusier piece also, running down as far as Brightside. That is not a part of the Spring Valley land. Then as you cross at Brightside, there is quite a level space on the left hand side of the road, going from Sunol to Niles, and as you go all the way down, and round the first tunnel of the Western Pacific, there also lies in there a small stretch, the bulk of which is a narrow gorge, and the amount of level land is comparatively small.

So far as the lands of the company are concerned, there is practically no level land by the creek. That piece that I speak of, that lies just beyond the bridge at Brightside, is a portion of the Mehrmann property, and I should say, roughly, that there are possibly ten or twelve acres in there that is fairly level property; about five acres of it has been an orchard. In these valuations of lands there have been no other exceptions or deductions made than what I have testified to. I have not deducted from the total acreage of the parcels any portion of the land and left it out of my appraisement. I remember of no other parcels that I deducted anything from in the way of acreage. I deducted the creek bed in this location because at the time I was requested to make an appraisement of these properties, including the creek bed, on several pieces, which had long narrow strips in the creek bed, I realized, from an agricultural standpoint that it was almost impossible to make an appraisement of the properties, and that I had no knowledge sufficient to allow me to make an appraisement of these properties for any purpose whatever. The creek in itself was of no benefit to the balance of the land, owing to the fact that railroads and county roads, and rights of way shut it off in most cases from the rest of the land. When I explained the situation to the attorneys for the company, I asked them to allow me to appraise the lands without taking into consideration the creek bottoms, and they granted me that permission. I requested that at Alameda, but not where La Honda runs, or where the Calaveras runs, or the Arroyo del Valle. I considered it was an entirely different proposition facing me to value these lands including those streams. In the Alameda, in the 700 portion I deducted, I realized that there was another value to those streams other than I was capable of giving, such as any value that it might have for water purposes, or for right of way purposes.

I have made appraisements for the Bank of Pleasanton, and pass upon all loans made by that bank, and in doing so, seek to value the property at its market value. I did not pass upon the loan made by the Bank of Pleasanton to Coopman, but am familiar with the loan made to Mrs. Luther Dickson, which amounted to 701 $2,000 on, I think, considerably over 200 acres. I did not make any appraisement on that property, because at the time that Mr. Benedict, the Cashier of the Bank, spoke of renewing the loan, which had been a loan of long standing with the bank, he told me that the amount of it was about $2,000, and as it was so small on such a large tract of land, there was no appraisement made. Mr. Benedict is also very familiar with lands surrounding Pleasanton, and often times when there is not a question as to the valuation, he does not ask me to pass directly upon the loans.

Refering to parcel 239-L, which I valued at $500 an acre, for 702 alfalfa and gardening, I would say that the vegetable use was the highest use that I considered in that case. It was a higher use than the alfalfa use, but those lands are good vegetable lands, and can raise practically most of the vegetables that are raised in that 703 vicinity, including berries. I won't say that berries are a better use, but they are an ordinary use. Those lands are capable of growing any and all sorts of vegetables, but there are some vegetables, I presume, that they will not grow. I spoke of the lands as vegetable lands, meaning ordinary vegetables grown in a vegetable garden. They are capable of growing vegetables at all seasons of the year, according to the seasons that the vegetable is to be grown in.

I cannot say as to 239-L that I have ever seen vegetables grown on that particular land, but years ago there were several Chinese 704 garden men down below the County Road 2000 raising vegetables and berries. Mrs. Hearst, who owns the property immediately south of this portion, has, and has had a rather extensive vegetable garden and berry garden. As to whether she is growing them at the present time or not, I do not know, but I think she is. I know that for several years she did grow vegetables on them. They are not growing any vegetables on the Pleasanton lands of the company, except in small portions; a man renting a piece of property may have an acre in vegetables. Immediately adjacent to the company, and just across the bridge, in the town of Pleasanton, there is a vegetable garden; on the road to Livermore, about half a mile out of the town of Pleasanton, there is another vegetable garden; immediately across from the company's lands at Santa Rita there is another vegetable garden.

DIRECT EXAMINATION BY MR. McCUTCHEN.

They are growing vegetables on these places, and peddling them around through that country, running regular wagons, and selling the vegetables to housekeepers.

CROSS EXAMINATION BY MR. STEINHART.

705   I would not say that this land is inaccessible to the market. The train service through there is very good. We have four or five or six trains running both ways each day, and are only 28 and a fraction miles from Oakland. I presume the commission houses in San Francisco and Oakland would be the market, which is the same market that the vegetable land around Niles and down through Milpitas have.

I considered the highest use as to portions of it, was the vegetable use. Of course, there are other portions in which, owing to a certain condition of the soil, the higher use might be an alfalfa use. I consider it accessible to the market, and suitable for a high grade good vegetable.

I know that that land is adapted to an alfalfa use, from my general knowledge of lands, and the alfalfa that I have seen raised upon several pieces; practically all of that land lying beyond County Road 2000, has been in alfalfa at one time or another. The tract

706 purchased from the Davis people, No. 278 I believe, had seven crops of alfalfa taken off from it the year that the company purchased it in 1911 or 1912, averaging more than a ton to the acre for each crop. That is one of the best tracts around there, and is one of the tracts rented by Heath. He was getting alfalfa from that land the last time I knew of it, which was a short time ago, and he stated to me that he is getting very good crops. I could not say as to how many cuttings he gets; I know that he must get at least five, if not more. He has irrigated some, I believe, on a portion of it. Taking the Heath land, the highest use that I have considered the land

707 adapted to, is alfalfa and dairying purposes, and also I did not overlook the fact that it is suitable and adaptable for vegetables. I took all those matters into consideration, and placed a value on the property at what it would sell for. That land is also suitable

for hay, but I did not place a valuation of $500 on it because it was suitable for hay. The portion which is suitable for hay, and is also suitable for alfalfa and vegetables, is certainly worth more than if it were only suitable for the hay. In giving it a value of $500, I considered both factors. Mr. Heath got at least five cuttings from the Davis land last year. Most of those lands surrounding Pleasanton, and belonging to the Spring Valley Water Co., alfalfa can be raised upon. Portions of most all of them have actually grown alfalfa.

708

There is a strip of alfalfa in the Chabot field; also there was a strip of alfalfa on the Oxsen property, No. 284. Alfalfa has been grown on 271, and has been grown, and is growing on 275 at the present time; also on 270; and also on 281, and several other tracts through there. In some places they have been growing alfalfa for a number of years. The only place I think of that is possibly an experiment is the little strip of alfalfa in the Chabot field, and I stated that alfalfa had been grown on numerous pieces in these properties surrounding Pleasanton at different times. I did not purchase for the company parcels S-268, T-268, U-268 and V-268 on map 10, and I do not know, of my own knowledge, when they were purchased, nor the price that was paid for them. I have a recollection that those lands were purchased some time in 1911, and I understand, but do not know positively, that the purchase price was somewhere around $250 an acre. I do not know exactly what it was. Those were the purchases from the Alameda Sugar Company.

709

Referring to my valuation on S-268, at $300 an acre, on T of $350 an acre, on U of $350 an acre, and on V of $250 an acre, I did not consider the purchase price of those parcels at all, as I did not know what was paid for them. I don't think I knew the actual price paid; as I stated before, I understood, and have understood that the price was something near $250, and I presume that I understood that in 1911. I don't think that I ascertained that, or that anybody told me, and I did not have any knowledge of what the Alameda Sugar Co. sold for until I had completed the purchasing of land around Pleasanton, which lands I was purchasing in the latter part of 1911 for the Spring Valley Water Co. I was purchasing lands there at the request of James A. Clayton & Co. I did not know, when I first began the purchase of these lands, that they were for the Spring Valley Water Co., and I have no remembrance of them notifying me what the Alameda Sugar Co. got for their properties, in order to assist me in my purchase of lands for them. Our office purchased the Chabot piece for the company in the latter part of 1911, or the early part of 1912, and as I remember it, the price was $150 per acre. The number of that is 288. I think at the time that purchase was made, we figured the Chabot lands as 1172 acres, and my remembrance is that a portion of it was cash, and the rest was by mortgage, and it is my recollection that the price paid for it was $147

710

711

712

an acre, and a part of that purchase price was represented in a mortgage. I believe that that mortgage ran three or four years; possibly only two years, and possibly as much as five. I do not know whether the Chabot-Bothin people were the Chabot people of Oakland, Mr. Henry Bothin was the brother-in-law of Chabot, but I guess that was correct. (Mr. Olney: Mrs. Bothin, who was a Chabot, owned the property.)

713 The Head-Hewitt purchase, map 10, No. 291, was handled through our office in the early part of 1912. The price paid for it was $52,316.75. I have not figured it out per acre. At the time it was purchased it was used for general agricultural purposes; a portion of it was used for raising hay and grain. The lower portion of it was in beets. A portion of it is used now for hay and grain, and I believe a portion—a small portion at the lower end—is used for beets. It has practically the same use now as at the time of purchase. That land has a couple of bad spots of alkali, but not very large.

714 Referring to map 18, parcel 268-O; on 50 acres thereof I placed a valuation of $600 per acre, and on 100 acres thereof, a valuation of $500 per acre. The portion valued at $600 per acre lies in what I call the neck of that piece of property, close in to the town of Pleasanton, running along between the county road and the Arroyo del Valle, and down toward Black Avenue. I gave that an additional valuation, because I considered it a better piece of land. The small farmers living in Pleasanton are very anxious to get hold of that particular 50 acres. It is vegetable land, and would raise vegetables, but it has never been used for vegetables.

Referring to map 10, parcel 268-R; I valued this higher than $550 an acre because it lies adjacent to vegetable gardens in Pleasanton, which is very similar land; not quite as good as the vegetable garden land lying right next to this property. The owners of lands in Pleasanton are, and have been continually, exchanging their lands between themselves, and the average price on exchange is about $1000 an acre. I offered one man, for the Pacific Gas &
715 Electric, for a little less than an acre, right adjacent to this, $1000 in cash. This was not a case of liberality, but it was a case of placing a conservative value on the property. It is not quite as good as the property now in vegetables. I would not say that it was in vegetables now, or that it never has been in vegetables. My impression is that several years ago that piece was in asparagus; it might be ten or fifteen years ago.

268-U; there is some low land on this, but it has been practically well drained of late years. The canals have been fairly well cleaned out along that particular piece, and the drainage is better than it was several years ago. The marsh land is not as extensive as it was at one time. I mean by that, the size of the marsh land is decreasing, though there is some marsh land in the property. Some 12 or 15 years ago it was practically all marsh land. Along about 1905, 6 or 7, they put a system of canals in there that drained the property fairly well. Since the company purchased the property, it has been renting it to tenants, who, together with the company, have kept the ditches fairly well cleaned, and the property fairly well drained. During the time the Alameda Sugar Co. had it, they allowed it to become rather wet, and did not drain it properly for awhile. 716

Referring to map 10, parcel 282; I mean by the expression "It is exceptionally clean of foul growths" such things as mustard, and other detrimental weeds, had been thoroughly well cleaned off the property, exceptionally so, more so than the ordinary farmer does. There is considerable foul growth in that district. There is a considerable growth of morning glory through a portion of those lands, particularly south of County Road 2000. Referring to the second parcel of 282, containing 19.47 acres, practically all the alfalfa that is raised in this district is without irrigation, and I stated in regards to the Heath people that they irrigated some, but not to any great extent. It is the custom to raise alfalfa in this district without irrigation, and they usually get at least five cuttings. Mr. Davis, one year, got seven cuttings. 717

I valued these Pleasanton lands as a whole, and when I say as a whole, I mean this: that I valued the parcels of land, taking into consideration the ownership of other parcels; I did not value it as one whole tract, but the sum total of the values placed upon each individual tract would represent the value of the entire property set forth upon the map, and I sought to give them their market value. 718

In placing my value on these properties, I did not take into consideration, or think of selling the properties from a subdivision standpoint. They could be sold as a whole, and at the value I placed upon them, but my impression and belief is that they would sell more readily to several purchasers, although I did not figure selling them in any particular sized parcels; if a man came in and wanted 50 acres, you could sell him 50 acres; if he wanted 100 acres, you could sell him 100 acres; if he wanted 2000 acres, you could sell him 2000; I did not make any subdivisions, even in my mind, and say that I would put three or four plats together and would sell those plats at one time. 719

I believe I am as active in the business as any other real estate man in Pleasanton. In fact, I don't believe there is any other real estate man in the Pleasanton district at this time. I believe there is a young man in the bank who has had a little to do with real estate. I have been in the real estate business since November, 1905.

720   I made one sale, where the purchase price would aggregate more than $200,000, which was not cash. There was a mortgage given back on the property. It is not my understanding that the market value of land is always a cash transaction. Often times a seller is glad to allow a portion of the purchase price to remain as a mortgage upon the property. I have never known it to occur in any of the sales around Pleasanton, that where time is given, the price is higher than if cash is paid. I will answer that question in this way: often times the question has been asked, "How much will you deduct from the purchase price for cash",—and that after an agreement was made to a certain portion being paid in cash, and the balance on a mortgage, the seller has said, "I don't want the cash, I would rather have the mortgage". I didn't say that in my experience in the Pleasanton district a seller would have been willing to sell his property entirely on a mortgage. A seller naturally asks to have a reasonable percentage paid down, practically 40, and possibly 50 per-cent. I have

721   known property to sell there with only 30 per cent paid down.

I am pretty sure I have not, outside of those two sales to the Tassajero Land Co., made any other sales in excess of $200,000. Those two sales were at an acreage value of $60 an acre, and represented—I have forgotten just what the division was—but both sales did not aggregate 7500 acres. These two sales were to the same people at the same time, and under the same conditions. They were

722   not in the Tassajero Valley, but were sold in the high lands which divided what we call the Tassajero Valley from a portion of the San Ramon and Pleasanton Valleys.

Map 12, parcel 239-H; the Stone piece; I have not my segregation as to what value I put upon the farming portion of this property; the property has been under lease to Mr. Apperson for some years, and when I talked to him concerning it, I made my segregation, he telling me how many acres were farming land, and together with my own judgment of acreage and so forth, I arrived

723   at my figures as to the farming and grazing land. I do not remember the acreage as to farming land, and as to grazing land. Some of the property up on the hills can be farmed, and has been farmed, so I understand, but to my own knowledge, I do not know it. I see no reason in going over this land, and from my knowledge of lands that are farmed, why it could not be farmed.

Referring to the Hadsell piece, I graded this, and appraised the walnut orchard, 100 acres, at $500 per acre; 250 acres where the water temple is, at $400; 100 acres opposite the road leading from the Mission bridge to Py's Corner, at $250. This is used for general agricultural purposes, hay and grain raising; a portion of it can be used for vegetables. It is flat and pretty fair soil. Practically all

724   of it can be planted to vegetables; I would not say that all of it would make excellent vegetable land. I think the hay and grain

purposes would probably be better than the vegetable purpose on that particular piece, and that is a portion I valued at $250 an acre. I practically appraised that piece from a hay and grain standpoint. The remaining acreage; 1650 acres of rolling hills, is the greater portion of it farmed, and some of it waste land. I did not segregate these acres in any way. Those rolling hills are suitable for hay and grain. The waste land could be used for pasturage. The 1650 acres I valued as a whole at $65 an acre, and it is now grown to hay and grain. There are some portions of it which are summer-fallowed. The number of tons to the acre varies in different portions. I presume it would average between a ton and a ton and a half of hay and grain. This would not necessarily apply to the part that they summer-fallow. I presume it would produce from two to three tons in most places. I did not particularly take into consideration the portion that was summer-fallowed and the portion that was not. I took into consideration the general character of the land, and what I considered it would sell for for hay and grain purposes. I have not been connected with the hay and grain business in any way, and am not an expert upon the prices of hay and grain. My knowledge is not very extensive in hay and grain matters, but I believe some of the best hay sold last year at $11 a ton. I have not any remembrance of what hay was worth at the time I valued this land, December 31, 1913; if it had been worth $20 a ton at that time, and I was only going to take that year into consideration, I would have put a greater value upon the land.

Map 15, parcel 239-M; the Alameda Creek and San Antonio Creek flow through the property. The east side of the land lies along Apperson Creek. I believe there are about 200 acres of level land lying upon the Alameda Creek, and there is some portion lying up on San Antonio Creek that is good farming land. About 150 to 200 acres lying upon a bench that leads off the San Antonio, has rather an adobe soil, and is very good hay land. There are about 150 acres lying up through the Apperson Creek, a portion of which is fair farming land. There are about 600 acres of fairly good pasture land. There is some creek bottom. There are some steep hills; some wooded places, and some farming lands through the tops of the hills. I give 1164 acres as steep land to the tops of the hills, and valued that at $12.50 per acre. Some of this, however, is fairly good grazing land. There is 650 acres of fairly good pasture land, which I valued at $25 per acre. The steep land, valued at $12.50 an acre, has considerable good pasture land through it, grazing land. As to the remainder; about 400 acres of creek bottom, lying in both the San Antonio and the Alameda, which I value at $75 per acre, because of the gravel that lies through it, and some little islands and spots that are fairly good for truck gardening, farming, and a little plat of hay. That does not include all of the

land there, the rest of it, 150 acres, I valued at $30 per acre, and is suited for farming land, lying in the back portion of this property; there are the tops of hills that can be farmed. I have had no experi-
728   ence as a stock man.

Map 12, parcel 244. This is good for hay and grain, and has been planted to that. I do not know how many tons they got to the acre in any particular year. It lies just south of the Alameda Creek along the county road from Sunol to Mission San Jose; 75 acres of it is of rather a dark soil, some little sand in it; the balance is rolling. The 75 acres is fairly level. I am sure that in the back end of this piece of property, and lying along the creek bottom there, it is a little bit rough, but very little of it is of that nature. That land does not run back into the hills to any great distance.

Map 12, parcel 262; I believe I testified as to that that the property could be used for vegetables and fruit, but that the character of the soil is such that it is not exceptionally well adapted for
729   such purposes. That statement was made for the purpose of showing that the soil in that particular portion was not as good as some soil lying in the flat immediately near it, as there is some gravel running through it and some reddish soil. I only meant that comparatively.

Referring to parcel 262; I know what the nature of the soil is in that parcel, but it is not exactly the same character of soil as the land immediately surrounding it. It is a good deal similar to the soil that lies upon the hillside there, and yet has some soil in it similar to that lying in the flat. That is not the piece I testified to, as having the creek and the railroads run through. The creek runs along one end of it, and the railroad is around it, and it is between all three of them. The creek may cut one corner of it.

THIRTEENTH HEARING.   JULY 30, 1915.

Witnesses C. A. GALE and C. H. SCHWEEN.

730   (Certain corrections in transcript noted.)

Referring to Holberton contract, counsel for Defendant stated that it checked out at $109 an acre on time. Holberton to pay the principal of $85,000 any time before 1920, but does not pay any interest until February 1, 1917, at which time he pays the back interest.

731   CROSS EXAMINATION BY MR. STEINHART

A reasonable time for disposing of all these lands at the figure I have placed upon them, as of the year 1913, would have been at that time a year. Exclusive of the sales to the Spring Valley Water Co., the total value of sales that I have made, taking them as
732   a whole, would aggregate about $1,000,000, and would cover a period of about ten years' experience in the real estate business.

I am 33 years old.

Map 10, 101.05 acres of parcel 283; I valued this acreage at $425 an acre, and that in parcel 281 at $500 an acre. 281 is known as the Blacow property, and lies on the county road from Pleasanton to Santa Rita, a very good piece of land. At one time I made an offer to Mr. Blacow and Mr. German of some $22,000 for that property, and it was refused. The property was in alfalfa in December 31, 1913, and the soil is a little different than the No. 283 piece, containing 101.05 acres. That portion lies to the north of the county road, leading from Pleasanton to Livermore. The S. P. R. R. tracks, and the Western Pac. Ry. tracks lie between this piece of property and the county road. The east end of it contains some gravel. It is not quite as good a piece of property as No. 281, according to my judgment. I think that this states as concisely as I can the factors of difference between those parcels. All those elements enter into the different valuations. There is some material difference in the soil conditions between 281 and 283 other than the mere gravelly conditions. The soil in 283 is rather reddish in color in portions; some is sandy; also this piece is more of a hay and grain land. In 281 it is a dark sediment fill mostly. There is a knoll running through it, which is hardly a fill, but it is a dark loam. It has been used for alfalfa and dairying purposes.

There is not a great deal of difference between these parcels and the lands immediately below County Road 2000. 239-d, 239-e, and 239-l. There is somewhat of a difference in the soil. The properties in that cluster, I believe, are appraised at $500 an acre; the properties here I am appraising at $50 an acre. I know that is what the Spring Valley Water Co. paid to Mr. Schween for those properties, and within a year's time after that sale, Mr. C. H. and Will Schween both called at my office, and told me personally that if I could get the lands back for them, they would be willing to pay a bonus of $10,000 over what was paid to them. I do not consider that fact of any particular importance as bearing upon price. I appraised that property absolutely from the standpoint of what I thought was a fair valuation, and the price paid to the Schweens played no part in my mind.

I believe Mr. Schween is now in the employ of the Spring Valley Water Co. This offer that Mr. Schween made was prior to the time that he was in the employ of the company, and was also prior to the time that he was even contemplating getting into the employ of the company; it was a bona fide offer.

Map 12, parcel 268-A; my remembrance is that I did not make any difference in the value between the agricultural and the vineyard land in this piece. The vineyard was not, on December 31, 1913, in very good condition. It had been allowed to go to waste; I did not consider the vines of any particular increased valuation, excepting that I appraised the whole, taking the fact into consideration that

733

734

735   there was a vineyard upon the property. The agricultural uses were hay and grain raising. There is some waste acreage on that land, but it would hardly be called waste acreage in that locality. It can be used for grazing purposes. One steep gulch in the back of that land is wooded; I took that into consideration in placing my value, also. I cannot say that I made any particular deductions from my general valuation because of that tract. I took into consideration that if the best portion of this land was in one parcel by itself, that I probably would have appraised it by itself at a greater valuation, because it would have sold at a greater figure. I graded this pasture land at the time I made the valuation, but I have not that here, and do not know how much acreage I allowed for the waste, and how much for the pasturage. The waste or pasturage land is not any great amount of the property.

Questioned by Mr. Greene.

My valuation on that was $125 an acre.

Questioned by Mr. McCutchen.

That was the Roumiguiere property.

736   CROSS EXAMINATION BY MR. STEINHART

Map 13, parcel 239-P; I figured that about 60 acres of that land could be put to grazing, and valued it at $15 per acre. The land could also be used for general farming purposes. I valued 200 acres at $50; 200 acres at $40; a portion of it is level, and a portion of it is rolling. The south end is quite steep.

Referring to page 645 of the transcript, the following statement was made by witness in reference to 239-P:

"This property also lies on both sides of the San Antonio. "About half of it is good farming land and good grazing. The bal- "ance is steep in portions, and some portions wooded, particularly "on the south side. The farming land is of fair soil. On the north "side there are about 200 acres of good farming land, that is, good "for that kind of lands, and lands that are located in that district."

737   I meant by that statement, that the lands located in that district are entirely different from other lands which I testified to. That is a different and a poorer kind of land. You could not compare the lands in that particular portion with the Schween lands.

Map 13, 239-Y; this land can be devoted to grazing purposes, and that is what I appraised it at. A portion of it could be farmed. I did not go into the question of how much of it, but it would sell as readily for grazing purposes as it would for farming purposes in that particular portion.

I do not know what the rental is as paid for this land, nor for grazing lands in Calaveras, nor do I know the rentals paid for land in the San Antonio. These lands on map 14 were used prior to the

738   time of purchase by the Spring Valley, for grazing purposes, and some portions of them were farmed. Some of the neighboring lands

are now used for grazing purposes; some of them are farmed; some of them are very steep and rough. I did not particularly go into the section of the country lying east of these lands, because that is an entirely different country, and an entirely different character of lands, excepting that they are all grazing lands, and used for the same purpose. At the time the Spring Valley purchased these properties, they were, in many instances, being used by the owners, and in many instances, were being rented. I do not even know when the Spring Valley purchased these lands.

Map 15, 268-C; I graded that land in four different portions. One 30 acres; one 200 acres; one 200 acres; one 60 acres. I placed my values on those pieces upon uses for general agricultural and grazing purposes. For the different purposes, I placed the different valuations upon the different parcels as follows: 30 acres for general agricultural purposes at $200 an acre. For property immediately surrounding it they are asking $300 an acre; 200 acres rolling farming land that lies practically adjacent to the level land in the flat at $100 an acre; 200 acres used for grazing purposes—portions of it could be farmed, at $50 an acre. I placed that more from a grazing standpoint. 100 acres of it could be farmed if they endeavored to do so. That is on the hillside, but is not the steepest portion of the place. I figured that about 100 acres of it could be farmed, and 100 acres of it would be for grazing, and in making my valuation, I took the two facts into consideration, and placed my value that way. As to the balance, 50 acres, I placed a valuation of $20 an acre on it. It contains considerable brush; some chaparral on it, and is pretty steep. It could be used for grazing, and some portions of it is used for grazing purposes.

Map 16, 241-A; is not an extremely steep tract. A portion of it, running into La Honda, is steep. Some of the hills run up to a point. There are some ravines in it, but I could not say offhand just how many. I went over the tract, was on it, and studied it from every angle, and placed my value in that way, taking all those things into consideration.

Map 16, 241-E; section 23. It is suited for grazing lands, and has practically no other uses. In all these lands, where I testified to a grazing use, and you ask me if they have any other use, I will say, any lands could be put to other uses if people purchasing them desire to do so, but I have taken into consideration no other uses. Around the Mt. Diablo region I have seen some very rough lands that were tilled. This piece was not ever tilled, to my knowledge. 241-A is a little bit further removed from the floor of the valley, and is upon a higher elevation than 241-E, which practically adjoins farming lands, and could be used in connection with such lands lying in the floor of the valley, while 241-A is removed from the farming land. My experience is that grazing lands which could be used in connec-

739

740

741

tion with farming lands, and lying immediately adjacent thereto, are worth a little more than simply grazing lands which did not lie close to farming lands.

Map 16, parcel 320, containing 120 acres, I graded in this manner: about 50 acres level farming land at $100 per acre, and 20 acres lying in the creek at $50 per acre. The purposes for which I figured that property are that portions can be farmed, and it also can be used for pasturage purposes in conjunction with the same uses that those properties are generally put to in connection with farming property. The balance, 50 acres, is heavily wooded, and very poor. I valued it at $20 per acre. The factors necessary to make pasturage

742 or grazing land, are the feed upon it. All lands can be used for grazing. Some is poor grazing land, but even if heavily brushed, it can be used. The feed upon the land is one of the principal elements; the element of water for your stock is another one. All of those things enter into the value of grazing lands. The factors or elements entering into general agricultural lands, are what the land will raise. The elements necessary to permit land raising hay and grain, are soil conditions; that the property is so situate that it is possible to go upon it and plant and harvest your crop. I consider the best alfalfa land those which have rather a sandy loam or fill at the top, and as you go deeper into the soil, you find it a little heavier, and land that carries a sufficient amount of moisture. It needs more

743 moisture than general farming land.

Map 17, 268-G; this is rough; has some sagebrush on it; wooded; is neither good grazing land, nor is it awfully poor. 268-E, in yellow, adjoining 268-G, is a much more open country; speaking of the 140 acres, instead of being rough and having wood practically all over it, there are some open spots, and it is not a bad grazing portion. There are 20.20 acres cut out by parcel 268-F.

Map 18, 268-c; I am not familiar with the purchase price paid for this parcel by the Spring Valley Water Co., nor for any of these properties I testified to in Calaveras. The same answer applies to 268-e. The only lands I am really familiar with, as to the price paid, are the lands around Pleasanton.

744 (An understanding was reached here, between counsel, that the purchase price of these different lands will be put in evidence, both on a table, and also on a map.)

Map 18, 268-1; about 60 acres farming land near the flat at $100; about 60 acres farming land at $50; about 100 acres of grazing land, rough, and has some steep gulches in it, and some wood, at $20; 100

745 acres at $40, open grazing, with some wood on it. The 60 acres are located down near the flat. I presume it would take in a part of No. 3 on the map. The 60 acres of farming land at $50 an acre lies on the north side of Calaveras Creek, back of the slope of the hill. Referring to lot 2; there is a strip in there that is rather steep and wooded, not

very long, and practically divides the lower from the upper lands. It is the incline of the hill where the land jumps on to the ridge. The 100 acres at $20 represents the wooded portion; a part of it is along the Calaveras, and a part along the other tributary to the creek that runs through that parcel. The 100 acres do not all lie in one portion; I included the wood. I did not pay a great deal of attention to the exact location of any portion of it, but simply went over the lands, and tried to segregate one from the other. The 100 acres at $40 is good grazing land between the two tributaries to the creek. There is a small portion of grazing land in other portions.

 268-m, in section 5; I graded that parcel 60 acres at $40, and 120 acres at $20. The $40 piece I valued for farming purposes—it is farming land, agricultural land—and the remainder I valued for grazing purposes. There is a portion of the remainder that is wooded and rough. When I say ''60 acres'' in these segregations I have made, there might be 65 acres of farming land in that portion. I simply made a rough guess at the acreage which was farming land, basing it upon my knowledge of lands. I do not remember that the bulk of this tract was very rough, brushy, and full of sage-brush. In making my memorandum upon the condition and character of the land, I simply took rough notes on the ground, and then recopied them, and dictated them to my stenographer in my office, and had her write them up, and then I went back over the properties, wherever I found something that I thought was either of benefit or a detriment to the property that I did not have in my notes, and I then endeavored to place it in my notes.

 268-e, map 18, the Beverson place (called by counsel for Defendant the Dennis Cullen place); lies on the north-east slope of the Calaveras Valley. Mostly open rolling land; rather a dark soil; has two or three springs on it, and some twenty acres that are rather wooded and steep. Has running through it one or two gulches, I don't remember just how many.

 Referring to the factors of difference in values between parcels 270 and 281; parcel 270 has some low lands in it; is also cut by the railroad track, whereas, 281 is not. In the lower end of 270 is some tules. It is rather marshy, and there are about 20 acres in that piece which, owing to the marshy character of it, is practically of no use at the present time. If some one would take the time, it would not be a great deal of work to drain that portion of it. Some years ago I undertook to do it, and was succeeding fairly well, when we rented it out to some parties under a lease, and it was allowed to go back into a marshy shape again. Joe Bentonunes, a tenant, offered $250 an acre for the entire property. Another young fellow offered for a portion of it, $300 an acre. We refused both offers.

 I would say that there has been practically no material change in the values of any of these lands that I have testified to, outside of the

746

747

748

217

lands immediately surrounding Pleasanton, since 1907; as to those lands, I would say that I do not consider there has been any particular or material difference in valuation since 1910, although I have not given that phase of the question any particular study.

RE-DIRECT EXAMINATION BY MR. GREENE.

The Beverson piece, 268-e, on map 18, lies on the west side of the Calaveras Valley, and slopes practically northeast into the valley, and is at the southwest end of the valley.

I consider the purchase price paid for the Chabot piece in Pleasanton was less than the value. It was a matter that was spoken of quite a good deal around Pleasanton at the time of the purchase. If the Spring Valley Water Co. had not taken it, my partner and I would have been glad to have taken it at that price, because it was a good investment, and there was considerable money to be made out of it.

The vegetables that are grown at Pleasanton are all shipped, more or less, into Oakland and San Francisco; they also have a market for them amongst the residents of the town of Pleasanton, and the vicinity surrounding Pleasanton; I believe they have practically the only vegetable wagons running into Livermore. The vegetable business seems to be a profitable business for those who are engaged in it around Pleasanton, as the people always apparently have money, and considerable of it. When they buy a small home around Pleasanton, it does not take them very long to pay off any indebtedness they have on it.

In regard to irrigation (Heath place), I thought that it was for the purpose of giving moisture to the alfalfa, but it was done entirely for the purpose of drowning out the gophers and field mice that were in the property. As to those vegetable lands, I have been informed that several vegetable men in San Francisco have been very anxious to get hold of some of the land of the Spring Valley Water Co. at Pleasanton for the purpose of raising vegetables, and have offered as high as $40 per acre rental per year, providing they could get a lease of from ten to fifteen years.

Questioned by Master.

I did not take into consideration the prices at which the Spring Valley Water Co. rented these lands to tenants, in my valuation, because of their refusing to issue a lease for any great length of time, and also they will not erect upon the property buildings for the accommodation of their tenants, and for that reason they are not getting a rental which they would be getting otherwise. I did not take into consideration the price paid by the Spring Valley Water Co. for the lands purchased by them, because the Spring Valley Water Co. wanted these lands for a certain purpose, and if the man who was selling did not want to sell, he would demand a greater price than the actual value, and the Spring Valley would pay it because they wanted those lands for some purpose possibly worth more to them than what they purchased them for. The people who owned lands in the vicinity of the Spring Valley Water Co. know as a matter of general knowledge that they could obtain more money for them from a company like the Spring Valley Water Co. than they could for general farming or agricultural purposes. I will not say that the purchase prices were generally higher than the valuations which I have placed upon these lands. The Hewlett place I believe they received $300 an acre for. We paid Blacow for the entire 50 acres $25,000, just what it was appraised for, and in addition, granted him a lease for a year or two years, the consideration for the first year being $1, and for the next year a very nominal consideration. The Schween property I think I appraised for a little more, as a whole, than what the Spring Valley Water Co. paid for it. The Freitas property will average just about what the Spring Valley Water Co. paid for it. The number of this property is map 10, 282-A.

752

CROSS EXAMINATION BY MR. STEINHART.

The Kruse property, I think they paid a little more money for than what I appraised it for. In some of these places, where there were good buildings upon the properties, I took into consideration no improvements in appraising the land. The Kruse property has improvements on it that are probably worth, off-hand, somewhere around from $7,000 to $10,000. The Davis property, I don't remember just what the purchase price was. For the Caton Lewis property, the company paid $501 an acre, and I appraised that at $500 an acre. The Peach property they paid $500 an acre for. On that piece there were some improvements. There is also a life estate mixed up in the property, and we had to buy off the parties to whom the property went upon the death of the then holder, as well as the then holder of the property. The Lilienthal property, I understand the purchase price was something between $500 and $600, but I will say this in regard to the purchase price of all these properties, that I have a record of them in my office at home, and I could get the purchase price of each very quickly.

753

RE-DIRECT EXAMINATION BY MR. GREENE.

I would not consider the rentals which are being paid now, and that have been paid for the last year, a fair test of the value of the property.

In regard to my knowledge of the purchase from the Alameda Sugar Company, at the time I was effecting purchases for the water company, the situation was, so far as I can recall it, this: I acquired that knowledge during the time I was making the purchases, and the knowledge was acquired by me, from Mr. Donohue, and was not acquired by him from the company. He informed me that the Alameda Sugar Company had sold their property to the Spring Valley Water

Co. for something over $250 an acre. My impression is that he did give me the exact figure, or rather, an exact figure. What that figure was I do not remember. It has always been my impression that the purchase price was something between $250 and $260 an acre. I think it was stated yesterday that the purchase price was $263 an acre.

All of those lands of the company, taken as a whole, are practically as good for the raising of sugar beets as for the raising of alfalfa. There is now alfalfa standing in about 400 acres, or possibly 300, situated along and below County Road 2000; there is also some alfalfa standing on the upper side of the road in 239-L. In 268-O, Heath has a very fine stand of alfalfa at the present time. I could not say as to how many acres he has. The old Davis property has quite an alfalfa stand on it. Practically all of that is in alfalfa. Parcel 275 is in alfalfa at the present time, and parcel 281 has some alfalfa upon it at the present time. A great many of the other tracts around Pleasanton have been in alfalfa. The lands on which alfalfa is not grown now are probably lands of the company upon which they refuse to give a lease of more than one year. Also several of those lands are equally as good for beets as for alfalfa, and parties renting them would rather farm them to beets than alfalfa. Some of those lands, suitable for alfalfa purposes, the parties farming them would rather farm to hay and grain.

The weed morning glory has practically no ill effects on the alfalfa crop, because the alfalfa chokes it, and does not allow it to grow. As to vegetables, vegetable lands continually working, the morning glory is kept back. Around Alvarado, they are using lands for vegetable purposes, and don't think anything of the morning glories. Morning glory on good land is usually the rule, and not the exception. When it once gets started on good land, it likes to stay there, and usually on good lands all over the county you will find morning glories, and there is a good deal of it in Santa Clara Valley also.

By the term "level lands from Sunol to Niles", I did not mean level lands in the sense of the word that the lands on map 10, and surrounding Pleasanton are level lands, but I mean that through the Niles Canyon there are portions sufficiently level to enable a man to work them, or build a house, or other improvements on them. They have more or less slope—more of a bench than level land.

Map 12, parcel 244 is the Behan piece, I believe. That has been farmed for hay and grain purposes. A portion of it was summer-fallowed last year, and a portion of it this year. They summer-fallow a portion of it one year, and another portion of it the next year.

The purchase price of the properties immediately surrounding Pleasanton, and which I purchased for the company, had some weight in my appraisal of the properties of the company. I gave these purchase prices some consideration, but not to the extent that I would have given the sales, had those sales been made from one individual

SPRING VALLEY WATER CO. VS. CITY AND COUNTY OF SAN FRANCISCO

to another as to each parcel, and providing that no one individual was buying any great amount of those lands. In placing my valuation upon the properties, I endeavored to give a valuation which would be a conservative selling price from one individual to another, and not a valuation which would be the selling price from one individual to one corporation, particularly a public utility corporation.

239-M is not the Hadsell property. It is the De Saissett property. I made ten segregations of this property. 300 acres of farming land along the Alameda Creek I appraised at $200 an acre; 200 acres of farming land along the San Antonio Creek I appraised at $65 an acre; 50 acres along the San Antonio Creek appraised at $75 an acre; 100 acres of farming land near the mouth of the creek appraised at $100 an acre; 150 acres of farming land on top of the hill appraised at $70 an acre; 150 acres near Apperson Creek appraised at $40 an acre; 150 acres of farming land on the tops of the hills appraised at $30 an acre; 400 acres of creek bottom, including the San Antonio and Alameda Creek bottoms appraised at $75 an acre; 650 acres of pasture land used by Mr. Lial, and lying principally in the eastern portion of the land, and appraised at $25 an acre, and 1164 acres of other grazing lands which I appraised at $12.50 an acre.

759

RE-CROSS EXAMINATION BY MR. STEINHART

Mr. Steinhart: On page 710 of the transcript I asked you the following question: "Q. You did not consider the purchase price "at all at that time, did you? A. No, I did not".

In regard to the Calaveras purchases I asked you whether or not you paid any attention to the purchase price, and you said you did not. When did you change your mind, and what caused you to change your mind? A. I have not changed my mind as regards to those things, Mr. Steinhart; the Alameda Sugar Co. purchases, as I stated before, I had no particular record of it. I knew nothing concerning the agreement of sales, or the facts concerning the sale, and naturally I could not take that into consideration. True, I knew about what the purchase price was. As to the Calaveras country, I knew nothing concerning the price of those lands, and I do not at the present time. My testimony this afternoon is only regarding those lands I purchased for the company.

760

The only consideration that I gave any purchases was such weight as I might have given the purchase price paid for the lands purchased by myself. Referring to the Pleasanton lands, which I purchased, I will give them as I read them from the map. Beginning about in the middle of the map; piece No. 273 contained improvements consisting of two dwelling houses, a barn, and some small out buildings, which I believe are still on there. Apparently I have misplaced my record of what I paid for this piece. I don't think it was $1300. It may have averaged that including the improvements. They were

761

221

fair improvements, and my remembrance is that Joseph V. Anselmo told me that the improvements he had upon the property cost him something over $1300. This was for the dwelling house that he lived in. The other dwelling house was very similar, and I would judge, cost about as much. The barn possibly cost $150.

762   Parcel 272, did not have any improvements on it, and $500 was what was paid for it per acre.

Parcel 277, had improvements on it consisting of a dwelling house, a barn, some fences and out buildings. I am answering what the value of the improvements were worth without giving that any consideration, and at the present time I should say those improvements were worth from $1200 to $1500. The purchase price of that property ran about $600 an acre, or $8,000. Including the improvements it would run very close to $800 an acre.

Parcel 278, had improvements on it consisting of barns, mens' 763   houses, corrals and warehouse. I would not like to say what those improvements amount to without my record. These same improvements are still there. My figure for that piece is $147,244, or $830.16 an acre.

Parcel 275; no improvements upon that. It was purchased from Mr. Callan, who resided at the time in Danville, for a little over $300 an acre.

Parcel 282, had numerous improvements on it, consisting of dwelling houses, barns, and out buildings of a general character used by farmers, and those improvements are still there. On the 10.13 acres of this parcel there is one small cow barn; on the rectangular strip there were no improvements; on the other portion there was a 764   dwelling house, and on the 19.47 acres there were some improvements. There were two dwelling houses on this parcel 282, one on the piece containing 29.20 acres, and one on the piece containing 19.47 acres. It is rather a hard question to answer, as to how much those were worth, without having gone over them particularly. I believe there were two barns and a shed on the piece containing 29 and a fraction acres, which are worth something, as you have to pay for material and 765   labor when erecting them.

Parcel 283, contains barns, dwelling, sheds and other general buildings that are used upon farm property. This is Mr. Schween's property, and my remembrance is that upon the 106.72 acres there is one large dwelling house, one large barn, one hay barn, an implement shed, a tank house, and some other buildings, which were there the last I knew of them.

Parcel 274, contains dwelling, barn and some other small out buildings; purchased from Cline, who lived in the town of Pleasanton, and had the property under rent. Taking a guess at it, I should say the value of those improvements were possibly $500, $600 or $700.

SPRING VALLEY WATER CO. VS. CITY AND COUNTY OF SAN FRANCISCO

Parcel 279, contains a dwelling, barn, a granary, I believe an im-   766
plement shed and a tank house, which are still there, but are not worth
much as they were in poor condition.

Parcel 271, contains substantial improvements, consisting of a
dwelling house, a couple of barns, and these were of such substantial
nature that an ordinary farmer would never be willing to pay anywhere near what they cost, in purchasing the land.

Parcel 289, contains an old horse shed, and a fence around the
property.

Parcel 270, Harris & Donohue piece; a cabin upon that property
about 10 x 10; also a wind-mill frame. The wind-mill had been down
for several years. There was a fence around the property.

Map 15, 239-M; in this subdivision the 650 acres lie along the   767
eastern portion of the property. I do not mean by that the north-
easterly corner of the property, but absolutely up against the line; it
lies to the west of the San Antonio Creek, and runs up and in the back
end connects with the east line about at the southeast corner of 239-O.
That is grazing land.

FURTHER RE-DIRECT EXAMINATION BY MR. GREENE.

I have not made any examination or appraisal on any of the
improvements to which I have just referred. In appraising these
lands, I entirely ignored the improvements that were on them, as I
was instructed so to do. Whatever figures I have given as the value
of any improvements on these properties have been simply a guess,
without any particular thought as to what those improvements were
worth.   768

Witness C. H. SCHWEEN.

DIRECT EXAMINATION BY MR. GREENE.   Schween

I live in Pleasanton, and have lived there for 21 years. Prior to
that time I lived about four miles east of Pleasanton. I lived there
21 years. Was born near Haywards, somewhere near what they call
Tar Flat, and have spent a considerable time in Alameda County.
I am familiar with the town of Pleasanton, and also with the properties in what is known as the Arroyo del Valle. My experience extends as far as the town of Sunol, and I also know the San Antonio
Valley. I have been engaged in farming principally, with the exception of nine years, when I was in the butcher business. I started in
work on the ranch, I guess, when I was about seven or eight years old,   769
and I left the ranch nearly 21 years ago. I engaged in the butcher
business for nine years, and since that time I have been doing odds
and ends, devoting my time principally to farming, in which I am still
interested. During the time I was in the butcher business, I gained

familiarity with the raising of live stock, and also with the feed which live stock should have, and do get. I have been, for quite a long time, road foreman, and immediately after I quit the butcher business, I devoted my time to farming. We had several ranches at that time. I, or my family, have owned land in Alameda County. We owned some of the properties since sold to the Spring Valley, and still have one ranch about four miles east of Pleasanton. I am Vice-President of

770 the Bank of Pleasanton, and have occupied that position about four years or so. I have been director for the past four or five years, but not prior to that time. As an officer of the bank, I was brought into touch with real estate in Pleasanton, as the directors of the Bank of Pleasanton generally look over mortgages, and so on.

I own two parcels on the main street in Pleasanton, and am interested in land about four miles east of Pleasanton; something like 400 acres, part of which is under option at the present time, and the balance we still own. I have been interested in cattle. We used to have stock of our own while we were engaged in farming. I know the property in what is generally known as the Arroyo del Valle, and have

771 run over those properties perhaps for the last twenty or thirty years, or maybe longer. I have been quite familiar with them for the last three years, and have examined them carefully. I am now employed by the Spring Valley Water Co., having charge of the agricultural department under Mr. Roeding, but have not been employed by the Spring Valley Water Co. prior to this time. My duties are to look after the tenants, collect rents, and to lease property to different parties who wish to rent. I pass over the ground day by day. I also have to look after the squirrels and such things. I have been requested to determine the market value of the property of the company in what is known as the Arroyo del Valle, as of December 31, 1913, which I have done. I have been over the property every week since I was requested to make that appraisal. I have been over each portion of it at some time.

CROSS EXAMINATION BY MR. STEINHART.

772 Outside of these two pieces of land that I own in Pleasanton, I owned a parcel of land containing 9 and some odd acres about three miles east of Pleasanton. I bought that and sold it. It is grazing land, and part of it can be farmed. I bought another parcel of land about a mile, or a mile and a half east of Pleasanton, containing 56 acres; this land lying near the Arroyo Valle. The piece nearest Pleasanton is right on the Arroyo Valle, and is right near the brick-yard. I owned another piece of land located half-way between Pleasanton and Livermore, north of the Arroyo Valle.

773 ### DIRECT EXAMINATION BY MR. GREENE.

I have been familiar with the value of lands, and know in general the sales that have been made in and around Pleasanton. (Mr.

Greene here advised the Master that Mr. Schween will value the Arroyo Valle lands, the Pleasanton lands, lands from Pleasanton to Sunol, and the Sunol lands up as far as Calaveras, which includes the San Antonio.)

I valued this property in this way. Some years ago I had land very much similar to the Arroyo del Valle, and I sold it; judging by what I got for that, I placed a valuation on the lands along the Arroyo Valle.

Map 14, parcel 239-Y; lies at the top of the west slope of the Arroyo Valle, and could be appraised with land of the San Antonio property. It has lots of water. I put a valuation of $20 an acre on that. It is in section 23, contains 640 acres at $20 per acre, total $12,800.

774

243-A is in section 12, lies nearly at the top of the hill; is nearly all open land, with the exception of the northerly portion, which is covered with some very small, scrubby oak; it is accessible; there is a road leading up to it. About 50 or 60 acres, the bulk of it, can be farmed. 80 acres, at $18 per acre, total $1440.

243-B, is on both sides of the Arroyo Valle. Most of it open grazing land, with the exception of small portions that might be covered with brush. Some small gulches running through it. 640 acres at $25 per acre, total $16,000.

243-C, is in section 14, very much similar in character to the other land. The soil is of a reddish nature, a red gravelly soil. In spots it has an adobe loam, which they call mellow adobe; is considerably more brushy than the 80 acre tract on top of the ridge, and also section 13. 120 acres at $20 per acre, total $2400.

775

243-D; similar to the other land; more wooded, and perhaps somewhat rougher; is accessible. 40 acres at $20 per acre, total $800.

243-I, 243-J, and 243-K, I have appraised as a whole in section 24, containing 480 acres. This is not as good as the other. It is somewhat rougher. Do not think there is as much feed on it as on some of the other sections. I placed the valuation of $15 an acre on it, which for 243-I, would make a total valuation of $2400, and the same for J and K.

243-M, lies pretty close to the top of the ridge; is quite open. Part of it can be farmed. A gulch running through it, and I think that gulch is somewhat brushy. 87.79 acres at $20 per acre, total $1755.80.

243-N, in section 18; very much similar to the other portion, although I think somewhat better. Has more farming land, and is more open. 238 acres at $30 per acre, total $7,134.30.

243-O, is near the creek. 23 acres at $30 per acre, total $690.

243-P, in section 18, is quite open. Nearly all of it can be farmed. A creek running through it. Fairly good farming land. Character of soil somewhat dark. 160 acres at $35 per acre, total $5,600.

776

243-Q, in section 19, is on both sides of the Arroyo Valle, and is quite open, good grazing land. 661 acres at $17.50 per acre, total $11,581.50.

243-R, in section 29, quite steep. Lies on both sides of the Arroyo Valle. Rough; considerable waste land; some fairly good grazing land. 640 acres at $12.50 per acre, total $8000.

243-S, in section 30, considerably better than section 29. Small portion lies to the north of the Arroyo del Valle; balance on southerly slope; fairly good grazing. Some rough, rugged hills. 324 acres at $17.50 per acre, total $5,671.75.

243-T, and 243-U I have appraised together. They are in section 32; quite rough and steep. Not very good pasture land. 320 acres at $8 per acre, total $2560.

777

243-V, section 33, not as good as T and U. Quite rough and rugged; open parts in it, and good grazing; abundance of water; good springs for grazing purposes. 640 acres at $7.50 per acre, total $4,800.

Parcel 247, Cresta Blanca Tract, is isolated and very rough. Of no value, except for grazing purposes. 164 acres at $20 per acre, total $3,280.

268-N, lies in the bottom of the Arroyo del Valle Creek, with the exception of about three acres of prune orchard, and is of no value except for the gravel, and for grazing purposes. Schween Bros. sold that gravel bed for $150 per acre. The Schween Bros. gravel bed is west of this property; there is a county road between the properties. (This last was stricken out.) 214.87 acres, according to the map;

778

a total valuation of $32,230.50.

Map 10, parcel 239-p; this property all lies south of County Road 2000, and in what is known as the artesian well belt. Well situated for irrigation, with lots of water. The pumping station is located on this property. Well situated and suitable for subdivision purposes. Valuation of $500 per acre, total $15,000.

Parcel 239-d, lies on the hillside known as the Hearst property. Partly wooded; good for home sites. Total acreage 18.067 at $200 per acre, total valuation $3613.40.

779

239-e, that and the adjoining pieces are in what is called the artesian belt, and included in that designation at the rate of $500 an acre, are 239-c, e, f, g, h, j, k, q, s, t, u, v, r. I include nearly all those, with the exception of d, and i, between the railroad track and the creek, and below County Road 2000. These properties all lie south of County Road 2000, and are used for truck garden, alfalfa, hay and grain, berries and some fruit.

239-i, lies at the extreme end of the property of the Spring Valley Water Co. on the south of County Road 2000, and between the two railroad tracks; one large hill upon the property, which is of a red gravelly clay. One knoll of black gravelly loam. I put an appraised value of $250 per acre on this.

Questioned by Master.

That is good for vineyard and for hay and grain. You can raise vegetables, such as potatoes, which they have been doing for the past few years. Some parts of it can raise alfalfa, which they are doing at the present time.

780

DIRECT EXAMINATION BY MR. GREENE.

I make a difference in the value between that parcel and the others, which I lumped together, because this is not as good, the soil being of a reddish nature, and not as good as the black gravelly loam, and you could not raise vegetables on that red hill, and you could not very well do it on the black gravel knoll. The other is level, and this is hilly. Contains 92.501 acres, total value $23,125.25.

239-l, m, n, o, p; these properties lie on the north side of County Road 2000, and bounded on the north by Arroyo Valle. I valued them at $450 per acre. They are very much similar to the lands south of County Road 2000, and can be used for alfalfa, fruit, vegetables of all kinds, hay and grain. There is a pear orchard close by, peaches and some apples. I placed the value of $450 per acre on these lands, as against $500 on the other, because the soil is a trifle lighter, and there are light streaks of gravel running through parts of it; in one place in particular, there is what is called the Dry Creek, containing perhaps 5 or 10 acres that is not so valuable, except perhaps for hay and grain. You could not raise any vegetables on that particular portion.

781

241-G; it is rather sandy, getting continually better up to 239-l, containing a bad piece. 76 acres at $450 per acre, total $34,200.

268-O, is what is called the hop yard; very much similar to the other land, as far as the use is concerned. Can be used for vegetable purposes; well adapted to alfalfa; also hay and grain, and beets and fruit. 299.74 acres at $500 per acre, total $149,870. There is a big demand for land of that character.

268-P, known as the Northern Addition to the town of Pleasanton; can be sold as town lots; very fertile soil; is used for truck gardening and fruit. 11.64 acres at $1200 an acre, total $13,968. It is due north, and just on the outskirts of the town of Pleasanton. The boundary line across the creek Arroyo del Valle, two small parcels adjoin it.

782

268-Q, called the "Big Field" of the Lilienthal Ranch. 241.43 acres at $500 per acre, total $120,715. Principally has been used for farming until last year we planted about 15 acres in alfalfa, and this year we also planted about 15 acres as an experiment, together with raising beets. It is good vegetable land, but is somewhat higher than around 2000. It seems they always want to rent it if they possibly can for grain raising.

227

268-R, is the Lilienthal property, where the main house is located, on the west side. of the road. 64.70 acres, at $550 per acre, total $35,585.

Questioned by Master.

I put a valuation of $550 on that because it is north of a vegetable garden, and it looks to me as though it could be bought by the vegetable people; they would be willing to buy it, and pay that much money for it.

DIRECT EXAMINATION BY MR. GREENE.

783   268-S, is called the Alameda Sugar Co. land; east side of the road. Can be used for raising beets. This year it is in grain, barley, wheat and oats. 296.679 acres at $275 per acre, total $81,586.72.

268-T, is where the beet dump is—a station called Asco; a long narrow strip. 3.78 acres at $375 per acre, total $1417.50.

268-U, is the Alameda Sugar Co. property west of the hop yard; principal uses raising sugar beets. A small portion is farmed this year also. 785 acres at $325 per acre, total $255,125.

268-V, also Alameda Sugar Co. property; west side of road from Pleasanton to Santa Rita. 338.01 acres at $275 per acre, total $92,552.75.

Parcel 270, known as the Donohue property; west of county road leading to Santa Rita from Pleasanton. 102.28 acres, at $325 per acre, total $33,241.

Parcel 271; the Bryan property; east of the county road leading

784   to Santa Rita. 63.78 acres at $275 per acre, total $17,539.50.

Referring to parcel 270, at the present time it is pasture; grazing purposes; can also be used for raising potatoes, beets, and garden truck. Parcel 271 is not as good as 270. I hardly think you can raise beets in sufficient quantity to make it an object. The soil is not as fertile. Good pasture land. Can raise grain on it. Last year they had a crop of barley.

FOURTEENTH HEARING.   AUGUST 2, 1915.

Witness C. H. SCHWEEN.

DIRECT EXAMINATION BY MR. GREENE.

785-788   The Master here offered certain suggestions as a possible means of saving time.

788   (Certain corrections made in the transcript.)

789   The following stipulation was dictated by the Master: It is stipulated that whenever in the testimony of Mr. C. A. Gale the name "Swayne" appears it is intended to be "Schween." Do you stipulate to that, Mr. Steinhart?

Mr. Steinhart: Yes, your Honor.

Introduction of tabulation "Value of Alameda and Santa Clara Lands". It was prepared under my direction, and sets forth the lands valued by me. The last three columns correctly set forth the acreage, value per acre, and the total value as to each parcel.   790

Offered in evidence and received as "Plaintiff's Exhibit 32".

Parcel 272, map 10, is in alfalfa; is of rich sediment loam; can raise most anything on it in the line of vegetables and alfalfa, etc. The lands which appear on map 10 can be used for vegetables, fruit to a certain extent, alfalfa, hay, grain and berries, and are all actually used for one or the other of those purposes at the present time, including some portions in pasture.

Parcel 273; used for the same purpose as parcel 272. It is in vegetables this year, such as corn and potatoes. Rich, sediment   791 loam.

On the land to which I have just referred, generally two crops of the following variety can be grown in a season. For instance: on these lands some times the hay crop is planted along about January—some parts may be in December—and it is harvested in the latter part of March. Then they immediately plow the ground and prepare it for vegetables, and will continue the use of it for beets, and such like, until they seed the ground for their hay in the Spring.   792

Referring to 1915, regarding land which has been devoted exclusively to alfalfa, the first crop was harvested immediately after the rain ceased. They have been harvesting since, about a crop a month, and judging from what I can see, will probably harvest six crops this year. The last crop they generally cut along about the first of December. I have taken particular notice of the land leased to Heath, formerly called the Lilienthal Ranch; they start cutting green feed along about the first of March, and continue until nearly the first of the year. Last year they were cutting green feed for about nine months. It is hard to arrive at the number of crops. They cut six crops on an average, and they will do the same thing this year. The crop per acre this year, I think, will run for the first cutting, in the neighborhood of three tons, or possibly four; the second cutting will be about two. It grows a little less as the cut-   793 tings continue. It is rather difficult to determine what those crops aggregate per acre for the entire season, but I should judge all the way from eight, nine or ten for those lands that have been in alfalfa for a number of years, and more, especially in the late years, when they have been irrigating once in awhile to destroy the gophers and field mice. This irrigating might benefit the alfalfa a little in its growth in the Fall of the year, but not to any great extent. All of this low land on both sides of Road 2000; in fact all the land on map 10, is adapted to dairying purposes. The lands are not devoted to

794

dairying purposes, because there are no accommodations for the dairy ·people, and there are no buildings on these lands for dairy purposes. Parties ·who come out to consult me will say, ''We want suitable buildings for that purpose; will Spring Valley supply such buildings for us?'' All I can say, is, that I am not positive whether they will or not. That that is a matter to be taken up with the Spring Valley people at the main office. Otherwise, it is somewhat difficult for me to answer the question, ''why aren't there buildings on those lands for dairying purposes''.

To explain what I meant when I said there had been some alfalfa planted as an experiment, many parties raising alfalfa have asked me what variety of alfalfa is best adapted to this climate. I tell them that I will take the matter up with Mr. Roeding, and upon doing so he has sent different varieties of alfalfa to experiment with,

795

to see what variety was best adapted to the soil. The purpose was to see whether one variety was better adapted for growth in that particular place than another. To the best of my judgment, you can plant almost all of the land on map 10, with the exception of this red, gravelly hill south of County Road 2000, and the railroad tracks, in parcel 239-i. Alfalfa can be grown on these lands successfully without irrigation.

Questioned by Master.

That would cover all the Chabot property; the big piece below it, parcel 268-U, and the outlying land on the edge of the map, like parcels 274 and 268-S.

DIRECT EXAMINATION BY MR. GREENE.

796

Referring to these lands, adapted to the growth of alfalfa, portions of which I have valued at $500 or over, and other portions at $300 or $255; in those that I have valued less the soil is not as good, nor as fertile; in many instances it is of a heavy, adobe nature. The parts I have appraised higher are of a rich, sediment loam, and better adapted to alfalfa, as the land that contains richer soil affects the resulting crop, and it is easier to work. I have been trying out some of these heavier adobe lands with good results. This year I planted some as late as May; we have cut one crop already, and another is growing. By irrigating the first year, the alfalfa roots don't go into the ground, they stay on top; they are always looking for moisture, and with non-irrigation, the roots must go down in the ground for moisture, and in the second year you would have almost as good a crop as you would otherwise have on land that

797

has been planted maybe four or five years.

Parcel 274, is called the Kline property, and is situated on the road leading from Santa Rita to Livermore. It is somewhat of an adobe nature, which during the Summer is of a chocolate color, and in the Winter is of a darker nature. It has a little alkali in it in spots.

Parcel 275, is west of the road leading from Pleasanton to Santa Rita; is in pasture at the present time, and is well adapted to alfalfa; is good rich loam.

Parcel 276, called the Old Rose piece, lying on Rose avenue. Rich, bottom sediment loam, somewhat light in color; this is good for home sites, and could be sold in subdivisions. Good for all kinds of vegetables, and is planted to vegetables this season. Has generally been in beets. You can raise fruit—peaches, pears and some apples. There is a continued demand for vegetable lands in and around Pleasanton.

Questioned by Master.

I made that figure $650, as against the $500 for the Lilienthal piece, or the hop-yard piece across the arroyo, because I think that could be sold in small parcels, and would be worth that much money. It is a good fertile piece of land, and always produces well per acre. 798

DIRECT EXAMINATION BY MR. GREENE.

There is scarcely any difference in the soil between those two parcels, and furthermore, it is within the incorporated limits of the town of Pleasanton, which has some effect on the value of those lands.

Parcel 277; is a small parcel facing on Black Avenue, called the Anselmo property; is in vegetables; is the same as parcels 272 and 273. I have appraised those three pieces, together with parcel 278, at the same amount, as there is practically no difference.

Those who raise just a small amount of vegetables, such as a few potatoes, generally bring them to Livermore to be disposed of in the local market there. Any surplus, such as cabbages, lettuce, potatoes, onions, or corn, they generally ship to the city markets. By county road from Pleasanton to Oakland, by way of Dublin, the distance is about 28 miles.

Parcel 279; lies near Santa Rita, on the road between Santa Rita and Livermore. I cannot say whether it is quite as good as 799 the Kline property. A portion of it might be a little bit lower; a little of the higher land is perhaps a little bit better for grazing purposes, and that is what it is generally used for, because there is a great demand for land for that purpose; more so than for anything else. I appraised 274 at $250, and 279 at $225, because I think the other is a trifle better pasture, and 271 I appraised at $275 because that is still higher ground, and better adapted for pasture than the other. I mean by that that it grows more feed per acre.

Questioned by Master.

These lands can be farmed also, but at $250 or $275 an acre, they will pay good interest if used for pasturage.

DIRECT EXAMINATION BY MR. GREENE.

800
I am not positive as to the rentals we get for that land for pasturage purposes, as this land has been leased for three or four years, but I have not seen a copy of the lease. They pay me the rents quarterly, and I have not figured what the company gets per acre each year. The piece of land that belongs to the Schween Company, parcel 283, I have collected the rents for, and I know we have paid ourselves at the rate of $20 per acre. This land is used, 35 acres for pasturage at a yearly rental of $20 per acre, and I have been offered $26 for it for the next year. This parcel 283 is east of the county road, leading from Pleasanton to Santa Rita. It is a tract along there containing 35 acres; this piece of land, 283, is subdivided, and a part thereof is in pasture, and that belongs to the Spring Valley Water Co., and is the one to which I refer as being rented at

801
$20 an acre per annum for pasturage uses.

802
Parcels 282; there are three of them. The De Freitas property; one parcel contains 40 acres, and the other 20 acres. It is practically the same land as the Lilienthal land; there is not a great deal of difference in it, only that it is a little further away from the town of Pleasanton; is good sediment soil and very fertile; has been used for grain purposes for a good many years, and is still producing good barley. It has been cropped with grain for the last 25 years steady; perhaps during that time it may have been pastured one season, but not more than that. We consider an average crop in through there, from 30 to 40 bags per acre.

Questioned by Master.

The 10.15 acres are pastured at the present time; that is east of the county road leading from Pleasanton to Santa Rita, and the

803
other pieces north of the railroad are farming land.

DIRECT EXAMINATION BY MR. GREENE.

The land to which I have just referred as being in grain, produces crops during the dry season. For example, during 1912 and 1913, we had very little rain, and as near as I can remember, had about 20 bags to the acre. That is considered very good during a dry year. In dry years you realize twice as much for your crop, and the expense of harvesting is very much less, so a person often does as well in a season of that kind as he perhaps would in a favorable season.

Parcel 283, four pieces, purchased from the Schween Company, and nearly all used for grain raising. Very little distinction between the different parcels. The one containing 40 acres, I felt was not quite as good as the rest, and consequently put an appraised value at a somewhat less figure per acre on it. That is the parcel away

804
from the other land to the north. The parcel through which the

railroad track goes, I valued at $525, and the parcel containing 101 and a fraction acres, at $450. The difference is owing to the fact that the soil is a little bit heavier, and perhaps a little bit richer in nature.

Questioned by Master.

When we had it, we got better crops of grain on the 140 acre piece than in the field over further to the east.

DIRECT EXAMINATION BY MR. GREENE.

I kept a record on this 140 acre piece in 1910, I think, when we had a portion to oats and to wheat that season; the oats went something like 44 bags to the acre, which we sold at $2.25 per sack in the field. We baled the straw and sold it at 65 cts. per bale. The gross income was $100 per acre, I think, and our net profit was something like $80 per acre that year, on that portion of the land. It would figure the same with the portion we had in wheat. It went 28 bags to the acre; we were offered 2½ cents for the seed; it went 152 lbs. to the bag. We sold the straw at 75 cts. per bale. The seed was absolutely clean seed, free from oats or barley.

Parcel 284; lies between Santa Rita and Dublin; a very small tract, on the east side, very fertile, and is in beets at the present, with the exception of perhaps a couple of acres in pasture. It produces a very good beet crop. What we call a good crop is 20 or 25 tons. The gentleman who had the beets this year thought he would have 25 tons to the acre, and I think he will. Beets bring this year $5.50 f. o. b. Pleasanton, and have run in previous years about the same. The freight is 45 cts. a ton from Pleasanton to Asco, which is on piece 268-T. That is where they deliver the beets at the present time. Some of the beet growers have told me that they had beets for fifteen years steadily; my advice to them would be to change; to plant something else and let the land rest a season, which would be sufficient, and then they could start in with a crop of beets over again. They have cropped beets for a number of successive seasons on the Alameda Sugar Co.'s lands, and on what they call the Kruse lands. That is right near Pleasanton.

Parcel 286; Wenig property. There is a successful dairy located on this property at the present time. The surroundings are used for pasture. They had a crop of hay on part of it. It is somewhat difficult at the present time to give the proportion as to the amount of land for a given number of stock for dairy purposes in Pleasanton. I have not given that matter any thought. On the Heath dairy, I think, they have between 600 and 700 acres, and he informed me awhile ago that they had 1000 head of stock altogether, but during the spring he generally rents some other pasture for a short time.

Parcel 288; the Chabot piece. This season there are not beets on it. I have seen good crops growing there. Some seasons there are

805

806

233

807   300 acres of the entire tract in beets. It is of an adobe nature. Along about the first of April the ground gets pretty solid and stiff, and it is hard to prepare it for beets. Consequently, they have raised somewhat of a crop of barley. Not a good crop, because of the late rains, and the ground being so wet it was difficult to work. The bulk of the land has been in volunteer hay most of this season, with small parts of it in alfalfa. A good many of the tenants on the Chabot land wish to try and plant alfalfa instead of raising beets and grain. This land varies a little in parts. In the northeast portion is a streak of alkali; also along what they call the Alamo Canal there is a piece containing 50 or 60 acres with some alkali in it. It is somewhat low, and not quite as good as the rest. The northwest portion, adjoining the road leading from Santa Rita to Dublin is very fertile and well adapted for alfalfa. On the east side the soil is somewhat of an adobe nature. Part of that is what they call a sediment, which is deposited on the adobe and makes it a very fertile and rich land. I have seen very good results from that land in the line of raising barley and oats, but

808   owing to continual rains the lands were so wet that the farmers could not prepare them for crops, and consequently the bulk of it is in volunteer hay this season. A little drainage by means of ditches would help this land to a great extent, so far as agricultural purposes are concerned. There is scarcely any drainage on that land now. There is a drain along Road 2578 which comes from Pleasanton through the Spring Valley lands toward Dublin. The Alamo Canal is the next drainage, and there is a small drain also between what they call the Hewlett property, parcel 291, and the Chabot land.

  Parcel 291 is practically, taking it as a whole, the same land as parcel 288, with the exception possibly of certain parts. There is a small portion adjoining the road between Santa Rita and Dublin where there is some alkali, and then south of the S. P. R. R., going to Contra Costa County, there is 75 acres or so that are very fertile.

808½   Parcel 267-V; is practically the same lay of land as parcel 291, 809   which lies next to it. With regard to the land that we sold to the company, and the lands generally about it in the immediate neighborhood, I feel that we have a little the best land there, because it yields much more per acre than the land east of it.

  268-Q, the 241 acre piece; is called the Lilienthal Ranch, and is east of the county road going from Pleasanton to Santa Rita. It has been used for raising barley, oats, wheat and so on, up to the present time, and also this year, with the exception of a small portion which is planted to alfalfa. Something like 25 acres were planted last year in alfalfa, but it has been in grain so long, and there has been a good paying crop, that they still remain raising grain, because a grain farm is much easier than beet raising, the marketing of fruits, and so on, and because there are only some months of the year you have to work.

The Pleasanton lands, total acreage, 5,988.479; rate per acre $338.76; total valuation $2,028,651.01. There are included in that acreage, aside from properties which appear on map 10, parcels N-268 and 247, which appear on map 14. 810

The Arroyo Valle total acreage is 5,094.50 acres; rate per acre $17.26; total value $88,433.35. In my opinion, those properties could have been sold for that amount as of December 31, 1913, as could also the Pleasanton properties for the amount which I placed on them of $2,028,651.01.

Map 12, parcel 228; is located between what they call the Alameda Bridge, going toward the Mission, and directly west of that, over on a plateau, and also comes down to the creek there. It is of a reddish nature, most of it, somewhat lighter; rolling land; some of it a little steep. A small portion of it is in a vineyard. 811

Questioned by Master.

I should judge one-half of it, or perhaps a little more is cleared, and there is a part of it in vineyard, grain and hay.

DIRECT EXAMINATION BY MR. GREENE.

239-b, two parcels; lies along the creek a little south of the Nusbaumer property; good for raising hay on small parcels of it; perhaps could raise some vegetables on it.

239-W; a small parcel of land that lies between the Southern Pacific and the county road. The same character of land; at one time was in a prune orchard. It is a soil somewhat better; seems to be a black gravelly loam.

Questioned by Master.

I have given that a value of $350, as it is far better than 239-b. The piece which I have valued is the one through which the railroad did not run. I only placed a valuation on one portion of it; on both sides of the Western Pacific there are two small parcels. I only put the valuation on one parcel. 812

DIRECT EXAMINATION BY MR. GREENE.

F-239; lies in Alameda Creek below Sunol. A small orchard on it and quite a little flat. Good for home sites; part of it is steep, that is the southerly portion as you go up the hill a very small distance; quite a nice little flat there; an orchard on it. 813

239-G; very fertile piece of land; lies on the Sunol road leading towards Pleasanton, and is in corn this year, and is well adapted for beans and garden truck.

239-H; lies west or northwest of Sunol. It is nearly all, with the exception of perhaps 100 acres, in hay; balance all pasture land. Good open country, some of it quite steep, other portions rolling. Known as the Stone property.

239-I, 239-J, 239-K; very small parcels in Sunol. Appraised at

235

$100 per acre on the entire piece. (The Master: $100 a piece you put on them.)

239-L, Hadsell piece; 100 acres is a walnut orchard; 200 acres is what they call the water temple; it is in a crop of alfalfa this year; good strong sediment bottom; east of that road leading to the Alameda Bridge, what they call the Py's Field, 100 acres in farming land; 150 acres west of Sunol, the Sunol picnic grounds, also farming land; about 67½ acres in creek bottom, and about 1650 acres in the hills, that is hill farming land; the bottom land could be used for vegetable purposes. In fact, the 150 acres west of Sunol has been in corn and beans for a number of years, but this year has been put to a crop of barley; at the water temple it is in barley this year, part of it in alfalfa. This could be used for vegetable purposes as well, such as corn, squash, etc. They have been raising a good crop this year there, and I have put an average for the whole acreage of $155 an acre. About 70 acres is in alfalfa now.

Parcel N-239; 764 acres, nearly all farming land; of a reddish nature; is located east of the Hadsell property; has been used for a long term of years for agricultural purposes, such as hay and grain. A very good crop this year; in fact, every year. By good crop, I would say for summer-fallow, all the way from 3 to 4 tons an acre, and winter-sown, perhaps 1 ton or 1 and a half.

Questioned by Master.

It is located between the San Antonio and Vallecitos Road, with reference to the road from Calaveras into the valley of Alameda Creek.

DIRECT EXAMINATION BY MR. GREENE.

O-239; contains about 300 acres of farm land, 120 acres of pasture land. A small portion is very steep. The farm land could be, and has been put to both hay and grain, and is so put at present.

Parcel 244; is west after you leave the Alameda Creek Bridge; very good property; used for hay and grain raising. Nearly all level, but there is a small portion on the creek right opposite the house that is not level, and with the exception of that part, it is agricultural land. It has been used for that purpose for years. I think a vineyard would do well there, and also prunes, almonds, and maybe Bartlett pears.

Parcel 252; another small parcel of the Sunol lands, which I valued at $100 for the entire piece.

Parcel 261; at one time had a very good orchard, consisting principally of apples and potatoes, but of late years has been used for agricultural purposes, hay and such like. I think you could raise an excellent crop of corn there; also potatoes, garden truck, and berries also if the orchard was taken out. The soil in the portion adjoining the county road is of a reddish nature, and that portion toward the creek is a rich sediment.

Parcel 267; is bounded by the Alameda Creek between Sunol and

Niles, is somewhat steep and rough; parts of it can be farmed. Valued at $70 per acre.

Parcel 268-a; is a far better piece than this other piece; is not as steep, and the bulk of it can be farmed for hay and grain, and I think also it is quite well adapted for vineyards, the same as parcel 244. Perhaps we could use half or a little more than half of this parcel for hay, grain, and vineyard.

268-B; is a very good piece of land. It joins the Mission Road, and you generally see good crops; has been used for hay and grain purposes; the soil in the bottom adjoining the road is of a dark black loam, and more of a reddish nature as you go up toward the hill land; it is practically open, and there are one or two creeks. All of it could be used for agricultural purposes, and it has been used for hay and grain; the upper lands, I think, are well adapted for vineyard purposes. Perhaps you could raise almonds and prunes on it also.

Parcel 290; lies west of the Arroyo De Laguna, and slopes up to the top of the ridge; is practically open; has been used of late years for grazing purposes, and perhaps 70 or 80 acres is still farmed—used for agricultural purposes, such as hay and grain, but perhaps half of that land could be used for agricultural purposes. It has been used for pasture of late years; it is good for home sites and many other things, and is a beautiful spot. The class of homes is to be determined by those who wish to have homes out in the country. There are many choice spots there to select from, and you could get a good price for that land for home sites. 818

Referring to what are known as the Schween lands, and the other lands of the company, which are valued by me at an amount larger than I put on my own lands; the reason why I have done that is that the lands formerly owned by the Schween Co., and perhaps other lands right near by there, have always been used for grain purposes, and I think that my valuation would be a fair valuation. The other lands along Road 2000, and what they call the Lilienthal lands, that is north of the Arroyo Valle, I valued higher, because they have been used for vegetables, truck gardening, together with alfalfa. They also could have been used for other purposes, such as grain raising and hay. When I referred to our lands as being the best lands there, I had regard to the use of other lands for grain purposes, and I forgot to mention that alfalfa will also grow there. They can be used for both purposes. 819

Map 13, 239-a; lies on the slope of what is known as the San Antonio Creek. Some of the land is very fine. The balance is grazing land, quite well up in the San Antonio; there may be small parts that are brushy and a little steep, but nearly all is good and open grazing land. 820

239-P; more open, and used for farming purposes, such as hay and grain. Two-thirds of it can well be farmed. Some of the soil is of a red gravelly nature, and some is what is called mellow adobe. It is very fertile, when we have not had too severe a winter, and it is not too wet, the remaining one-third is used for pasturage. The land is not so very steep, and is good grazing land.

239-Q; the character of both the low land and the upland is practically the same as 239-P, and is susceptible of the same uses.

239-R; these three parcels are nearly the same. I divided them the same; practically the same amount of farming land, and the same character of soil. Some may have a little more gravel running along near the creek than others. I think 239-R is as level land as 239-P and 239-Q. There is very little gravel in the streams that pass through there.

239-S; more pasture land than the other. Some good farming land also. The greater portion of it has been used for pasture of late years. The south portion is somewhat steeper and used for grazing purposes; the north portion is somewhat steep also, and the bulk of it can be farmed. The land near the creek can be farmed, and I think a part of it is farmed this year. The land produces fairly good crops, being fairly good grain land. I could not tell you how much of that land on each side of the stream is reasonably flat.

239-T; both the south end and the north end, especially in the south end, there is considerable grazing land. It is somewhat steep and brushy in parts; quite open toward the center, covered with quite large oak trees in through there. This middle portion could all be farmed. I put a value of $32.50 on 239-T, and $27.50 on 239-S, because I think there is more land in the former that could be farmed than in the other. There is more flat land, although it is somewhat rolling. Quite a portion of the soil is a black gravelly soil, which I think would yield pretty well if it was farmed.

239-U; is quite rough, nearly all used for grazing purposes. Maybe a few acres here and there that could be used for agricultural purposes, on the south side. On the side that is rough, the land is quite steep.

239-V; much better than 239-U for grazing purposes. Quite open in many places, and has some steep places. A portion toward the north could be used for agricultural purposes. 15 acres or so could be farmed.

239-W; most of it rough. Compares favorably with 239-U, but is better, being more open, and I think is better grazing land.

239-X; section 21. The San Antonio Creek runs through this near the south-easterly corner and near the center. Quite a good deal of it is open. Perhaps 20 to 40 acres can be used for agricultural purposes. It is better than U and W.

239-Z; San Antonio Creek runs through this portion; some level land lying near the creek that could be used for farming or agricultural purposes; the balance is pasture.

238

Map 11, 4 pieces in parcel 225; the .0023 acres, a very small par-   824
cel, triangular in form, lies north of the Southern Pacific's right of
way. The 11.46 acres is east of Niles, but within the city limits. They
are building lots, and there are houses on this property which are
rented to different parties living in Niles. I have excluded whatever value the improvements may have in placing my values on these
different properties, because the improvements belong to the tenants.

Parcel 229; is a square piece lying on the hillside, and only good
for residences. It is on the county road running from Niles to Sunol;
consists of three-fifths of an acre, and I have placed a valuation of
$300 on the entire parcel.

Parcel 237; lies on northeast side of creek, and along the hillside.
Good for early vegetables which I have seen grow there.

239-A; 53 acres, excluding lands in creek. It is rough, steep, very
small amount of flat land in it. It would be good for home sites. The
entire piece valued at $750.

239-B; 243 acres. The entire piece valued, excluding the lands   825
in the creek, at $3500.

239-C; 105 acres, appraised at $2000. Can be used for home
sites.

239-D; 14 acres, appraised at $350. Along the creek is practically
the same. Rather steep and brushy; beautiful scenery.

239-E; 20 acres, appraised at $750. That property is the same
character as the others.

Map 15, parcel 239-M; contains 3314 acres, with some very excellent farming lands, some good grazing land, and some steep and
rocky land. 300 acres farming land along Alameda Creek, appraised
at $185 per acre; 200 acres farming land along the San Antonio, or at
San Antonio, $70 per acre; 50 acres along the San Antonio at $75 per
acre; 100 acres farming land mouth of creek $110 per acre; 150 acres
farming land on top of the hill $65 per acre; 150 acres farming land
west of the Apperson Ranch, $50 per acre; 150 acres farming land
top of hills $30 per acre; 400 acres creek bottom, $65 per acre; 1814
acres grazing land, $20 per acre. A number of parcels which I have   826
designated as farming land, I put different values upon, because it
depends a little on the location; also on the character of the soil. I
will go even further than that; the 300 acres of farming land along
the Alameda Creek, I appraised at $185 because it is well adapted to
early vegetables, such as peas, corn, beans, and so forth. At the present time it has been in grain and hay. If the season had been more
favorable, 100 acres or so might have been planted to peas last year,
but owing to unfavorable weather and rain, it was impossible to plant
them. I hardly think that you can raise more than one crop of vegetables per annum on that land. It is like all the lands sloping from
Niles toward Hayward; they generally figure on one crop a year. The
land along the creek is not sub-irrigated.

Parcel 250; formerly the property of Crocker and Dillon; contains 1448 acres, and lies on both sides of Alameda Creek; has about 150 acres of farming land, the bulk of which lies on the north side of
827 Alameda Creek, and a small portion on the south and southwest side. The balance is pasturage. I am satisfied that will raise the same sort of vegetables as the land just referred to.

Parcel 264; called the Harlan place. 25 acres of farming land; the balance grazing land, which is rather steep.

268-C; Bachman place. 30 acres of this land is excellent farming land; lies on the bottom before you get to the rise along the hillside. 200 acres of good rolling farming land; 200 acres of good grazing land; 50 acres of brush and chaparral.

268-D; lies on top of the hills west of Alameda Creek. About 150 acres could be farmed; the balance is pasture; some very steep and wooded.

Parcel 285; 30 acres of this is farming land; 65 acres excellent pasture land; balance wooded and steep.

Referring to the Sunol drainage lands; the total acreage is 17,-
828 372.95 acres; rate per acre $61.56; total value $1,069,435.83. This includes maps 12, 13 and 15. Those 17,000 odd acres could be sold, in my opinion, for $1,069,435.83. In reaching my values, I have just considered what the lands were worth if they were placed on the market, and have not considered the value of the lands as a portion of the properties of the Spring Valley Water Co.

Questioned by Master.

I base my valuation on the value of the lands for sale to an individual, or to individuals.

(Counsel for Defendant is advised by Master that he understands clearly that his objection went to all this line of testimony, on the same grounds as he had urged as to others, namely that it was a special value.)

DIRECT EXAMINATION BY MR. GREENE.

829 Introduction of table headed "Appraisal Arroyo Valle Reservoir Areas, Spring Valley Water Company"; that table was prepared under my direction, and the acreages in the fourth column, "Reservoir Acreages", I got from the engineer. Aside from that, the table is my own. The values in the fifth column, "Per Acre", are the values which I placed on the lands in my direct examination, and the total value is the multiplication of the areas by those values.

Offered and received in evidence as "Plaintiff's Exhibit 33".

The same is true of the second table, the San Antonio Reservoir site.

Offered and received in evidence as "Plaintiff's Exhibit 34".

The values which I have placed in each of these tables per acre, correspond with the value which I placed on the same acreage in my valuation of the entire parcel.

240

CROSS EXAMINATION BY MR. STEINHART. 830

What I have taken here is the general market value, and means what anybody would come along and pay the owner. It did not make any difference to me who it was that was buying it. 831

Map 14, parcel M-243; part of it can be farmed; that is, part of the southeast corner and also on the northerly boundary, but as to how much of it, I hardly think I could answer that question. Part of it is grazing land. The portion of this land that would be included in the reservoir site is further down in the south-westerly portion, and I think there is a small portion there that could be farmed, but I could not say as to how much of it can be farmed. As near as I can remember, the south-westerly portion is the better part of the land. 832

(Counsel for Plaintiff here brought out the fact that the witness had been laboring under a misapprehension, and really meant the south-easterly corner, and not the south-westerly, which is rough land.)

The south-westerly portion is the rough portion, and is lower than the south-easterly portion, but the south-easterly portion is the better portion of the land. The south-easterly portion is not in the reservoir. The lower lands are in the reservoir site. The northerly 833 portion of this (indicating a point on the map) is the highest, and the south-westerly portion is the lowest. The better portion would be the southeast corner; a very small portion of that could be farmed, and, I think, a small portion of the northerly part, also.

The stock that I ran belonged to the Pleasanton Meat Co., and I was interested in that company, but I did not run any stock in the Arroyo del Valle, or in the Mocho. I had run cattle on land at different places other than that we owned, which we used to rent. This generally would be over towards the Tassajero, and also during the summer months we would rent land near Pleasanton. The land in the Tassajero country was used for agricultural purposes.

Map 14, parcels 243-A, 243-B and 243-C; these parcels are some- 834 what uniform in character, but I think my valuations differ a trifle. The factors of difference: the upper quarter section, that 80 acre piece which lies north on top of the hill, is good open country, and good grazing land, but harder to get at than some of the other lands along the Arroyo del Valle. There is scarcely any difference between 243-B and 243-C. The Arroyo del Valle passes through both of these lands, and the difference of $5 must be due to the fact that the smaller parcel is somewhat steeper than the other. There is quite a little steep brush land running up the hillside in 243-C. I trusted a great deal to 835 memory as to the lay of the land in the Arroyo del Valle. I knew this C-243 going up that hillside. There was more brush, and one being a small parcel of land, while the other, the Arroyo del Valle passes through from the northwest corner to the southeast, or nearly so, and being good open land on both sides, I thought it would be worth a little more money than B-243. The fact that the Arroyo del Valle passed through it had nothing to do with the difference in valuation, but I thought by averaging up these parcels there was more value in B-243 than C-243. I took the location into consideration; if this land was sold in subdivisions, we could get more for 243-C than you could for the upper piece, because it is much harder to get to the small par-cel on top of the hill. The fact that these lands were being held as a whole, did not make any particular difference in my value of them. I took the sections, or part of the sections, into consideration, and simply placed a value on them.

Map 14, 243-I, 243-J and 243-K; all this land is on the west or southwest slope of the Arroyo del Valle, with the exception that "J" slopes pretty well down toward the Arroyo del Valle Creek, quite a distance; the entire three quarter sections are somewhat rough and brushy. I do not think there is much chaparral on I-243. There is other brush there which is pretty thick in places, but there are open places on the three parcels, but the amount of open spaces varies. I should judge it would perhaps take ten acres to a hoof on these three quarter sections. I think that 400 acres would carry 40 head of cattle throughout the year. My valuation is just about based upon the idea that it can carry that amount of cattle. J. J. Moy is now running cattle there.

Map 16, parcel 268-C; 30 acres of excellent farming, which I have segregated, and placed a total value on of $80 an acre on that entire parcel. My approximation of the different values is: 30 acres at $250 an acre, $7500; 200 acres at $150 an acre, $30,000; 200 acres at $25 an acre, $5,000; and 50 acres of this brush and chap-arral at $10 an acre. The 30 acres are south of the land owned by Mr. Andrade. It is a flat, fertile piece of land. The 200 acres is somewhat rolling hills; some a little bit steep, but can be farmed. Good farming land of an adobe nature. The 200 acres at $25 per acre is quite steep, and the 50 acres at $10 is very steep. The vege-tables that can be raised on the lands in Pleasanton consist princi-pally of potatoes, onions, corn, some beans, peas, in fact all garden truck. I think they compare favorably with the vegetables raised and delivered in the San Francisco market. I guess they are as good, because they ship them, whenever they have large quantities, to San Francisco.

Map 10, parcels 268-P and 268-R; I do not know what the com-pany paid for those lands, and I did not inquire.

Map 11, parcel 239-B; it was rather difficult to place a valua-tion on the lands between Sunol and Niles, and this was very steep, and I had been on it, on some parts of it I might say, near the Ala-meda Creek, and I simply took this particular piece from a scenic standpoint, and placed a valuation on it, and did not value it from an acreage standpoint at all. I would consider it most beautiful scenery; small trees, live oaks, and other varieties. I did not consider it from an agricultural standpoint at all, as I did not consider it had any agricultural use.

Map 11, parcel 237; lies on northeast side of creek, and along the hillside, and is only good for early vegetables. It is quite steep, but that is what you want for early vegetables. One-half or maybe a little over one-half, is in vegetables this season.

The reason for my difference in value between parcels 239-m, 239-n, 239-o, 239-p, valued at $450 an acre, and 239-e, 239-f, 239-g, and 239-h, all on map 10, valued at $500 an acre, is that there is a small creek, what they call a dry creek, running through there, and of course this can only be used for, perhaps a little hay. It would not even raise grain. That is why I valued the small strip where that dry creek runs through at $50 less.

Map 15, 239-M; that is the De Saissett. 300 acres farming land along the Alameda Creek; faces toward the west, which can be used for early vegetables, and valued at $185 per acre; the other 200 acres are farming lands along the San Antonio, some being north, and some south of the creek, I placed a valuation of $70 an acre on. Also 50 acres along there I thought a little better, and valued at $75 per acre; 100 acres farming land mouth of creek, at $110 per acre; 150 acres farming land, on top of the hill, at $65 per acre; 150 acres of farming land west of the Apperson place, or the easterly portion of the De Saissett ranch, a little steep in parts of it, very good farming land, at $50 an acre. The soil is of an adobe nature, good for agricultural purposes, but hard to get at. Quite a climb to get on top of the hill. That is why I valued that at so much less per acre. 150 acres of farming land on top of the hill, at $30 per acre; 400 acres of creek bottom at $65 per acre; and 1814 acres pasture land at $20 an acre. I made this segregation the first time I went over the property in 1913, and I have been over this land ever since that time. I did not compare my segregation with Mr. Gale's. He went with me, as a rule, but always took his course, and I took mine. We talked in regard to the acreage, and perhaps we might have the same.

Questioned by Master.

I do not know anything about Mr. Gale's values.

CROSS EXAMINATION BY MR. STEINHART.

The creek bottom there is farming land. There are about 400 acres of creek bottom which I valued at $65 per acre. There is quite a warm belt along there, and I have noticed the condition of the sycamore trees, which is due, perhaps, to the season. The foliage may start, the frost nip it, or there may be some kind of a blight like we had this year. You will find it all over the country where you

go, on the sycamore trees, but last year it went a little further, and
there seemed to be a blight on the live oak trees.

Questioned by Master.

That blasted appearance of the sycamore trees is due to late
frosts, but we had no late frosts this year.

This year it was simply a blight. There might have been snow
in the San Antonio Valley as late as May this year, for half an hour
or an hour, but we had absolutely no frost since April, that I
know of.

In valuing the parcels in map 11, I deducted a portion of the
land along the bed of the stream of my own accord, because I am
not an expert in appraising rights of way, or anything of that char-
843   acter. I did not deduct the stream bed of the Arroyo Valle, as the
stream bed does not amount to anything. The water is confined to
a very narrow channel in most places. It is somewhat similar along
the Niles Canyon, but in the Niles Canyon, where the stream runs,
it is absolutely bare, but up the other creek, here is a little island,
and there is a little island, and the stream runs on each side and so
on; you cannot make any reduction for the land that is used by the
stream. In some places the islands in the Arroyo Valle are quite
large. I would say in section 19, map 14, for instance. There may
be other places, but I never paid any particular attention to it. I
think that is the only reason that I included it.

I did not exclude the San Antonio Creek. There are no islands
in that, but the water is confined to a very narrow channel. I have
844   admitted that the water is confined to a very narrow channel, but
there is a railroad track on either side of the Niles Canyon, and I
did not want to put any valuation on the creek bed through there
because I am not familiar with that.

Questioned by Master.

I included the creek bed in the De Saissett place, because there
is a great portion of that land in the creek bottom, and that land is
worth considerable for grazing purposes alone. If I were buying
the Hadsell piece, or this piece here years ago, and they had the
same acreage, I would try to cut out altogether, and not buy it, the
amount of acreage in the creek, as I hardly think it would have been
of any use to me.

845   I would get my water for the stock from the springs that are
throughout all of that land. I did not include the springs in the
value of the land. To get water for grazing purposes you could
bore wells or improve where there are springs, or at least indications of springs, and if you try to develop them you will certainly

get water. I did include the water because it is on the land. On the Arroyo Valle, on the steep land, I think in all those places where they are steep there is water from springs. I did consider the presence of that spring water there. In nearly all the pasture lands there were springs. I took that for granted, and took it into consideration in giving my valuation.

Map 14, parcels 243-I, 243-J, and 243-K; I am not positive whether there are any springs there or not. I made no examination when I went over these lands in regards to the water, because a person naturally would think there was water there. If I wanted to buy it, I certainly would go over the land more carefully, and any buyer would do that, and see whether or not there was water there. I was not positive whether there was water there or not, but going over this land, I found water in all the gulches from time to time, and there are springs throughout this entire country. The water in the gulch generally comes from the springs; some times you find a spring right on top of the hill. When I refer to these gulches, I do not at all times refer to the water flowing at the bottom of the gulches in order to know that there is water there, because there are one hundred and one places maybe throughout here where you may see a spring right on top of the hill, it being a little developed, or properly developed, and they have watering troughs there; you will find them all over these hill lands.

I could not say positively how many head of cattle Mr. Moy is running now to the acre. Last Fall he told me he had 163 head, but he has told me since that during the Winter he has bought more. I do not know how many head of cattle anybody is running in Arroyo Valle to the acre. I could not say when I first conceived the notion of not valuing the creek bed at Niles. I did not have any conversation with anybody when I was told to appraise it. The only one I did speak to was Mr. Gale.

The lands valued on map 10 are all used for the purposes designated at the present time, namely, alfalfa, vegetables, etc. That was correct in 1913, 1912, and 1911.

The land that Mr. Heath was using for dairy purposes was land included in the Pleasanton district, and I know, as a matter of fact, he is feeding all of that cattle from crops grown upon his place, with the exception of a few dry stock which he some times gets a hill pasture for. He grows nearly all of his alfalfa on his own place—last year he bought a few hundred tons, and he told me this year that he thought he would raise enough for his own use. He has bought some feed up to the present time, for the reason that last year he seeded about 300 acres of alfalfa, and of course he would not expect to get much the first year. Judging by the banks of the creek, alfalfa roots must go down about 10 or 12 feet, and they get moisture there, as much as they need.

846

847

848

849

245

850   Parcel 275 is farmed. It is an entire piece in alfalfa. I am not familiar with the price that the Spring Valley paid for it. The fact that Spring Valley might have paid $305 for that land does not affect my value of $450. That matter is up to the Spring Valley. If they could buy it at that, well and good, but the land is worth more money in my judgment. The land belonged to a man named Callen, who was a section boss for the Southern Pacific. He resided somewhere out in Contra Costa County at the time. He did not reside on the land.

Parcel 276, map 10, has not been subdivided, but it could be. There is some alkali in spots in parcel 279. The factors of difference in value between parcel 274 and the neighboring piece, is that 274 is a trifle higher, and there is less alkali, or scarcely any alkali that I know of in that piece. The only piece that I referred to, when I 851   said that I preferred to leave out the creek bottom, was the land between Sunol and Niles, and speaking truthfully in regard to that, I really did not know the value of it, because I did not know whether there was much gravel in that creek or not, and I simply did not want to place a value on the creek lands between Sunol and Niles. I answered the Judge's question in regard to this De Saissett property, when he asked me if I preferred to leave out that 400 acres of creek bottom, and I said yes, if I could buy the rest without it. I have many reasons for saying that, for pasturage purposes, one reason is this: if you want to have it enclosed—the creek bottom— how could you do it during the Winter months? How could you keep any stock there? You could not keep them there in the Spring until just about now, because you could not put any fences up. 852   The water would wash the fences away. I did not mean to apply that to all the lands in general.

Questioned by Master.

If it were in the San Antonio Valley, for instance, I would certainly take the creek, because there is no danger of breaking the fences down there. You could put them up and they would be there forevermore, but there is a large distance across it in this portion, and there are lots of fences to build, and that is why I answered your question that way.

CROSS EXAMINATION BY MR. STEINHART.

I would prefer the portion in San Antonio Valley for pasturing, because I can put my fences there, and they would remain. In my valuation, I have considered land with water on it to some extent. I do not think I spoke of parcel 271 as being rented for $20 an acre. I 853   referred to the lands formerly owned by the Schween Company, halfway between Pleasanton and Santa Rita. There is a strip joining the county road, 35 acres. At the present time it is leased to Mr. Christian. His lease is for one year. He uses it just for pasturage. Natural grass grows there. He has been running in the neighborhood of, I should judge, an average of about 30 head since last Fall. He has 29 acres. There is a small portion in potatoes. Somebody else has the six acres leased for potatoes.

Parcel 282 was cultivated by Mr. J. M. DeFreitas. I did not say that it had been used for hay and grain only, because they raise vegetables there also. The property will average year after year 30 to 35 sacks. It has been averaging that for 15 or 20 years. The owner before Mr. De Freitas was a party from Livermore. I forget the name. They bought it for vegetable purposes. I did not keep records on my own land for any year other than 1910. I think I could refer back to the record for 1909. I will get it for you if I can. Of course, all that I can refer back to are my books for the total yield. I won't say positively that I can do it or not, but I will consult my brother. Perhaps he can give me some information. We have been farming the place since I have been able to walk. The piece I testified to this morning, near the county road leading from Pleasanton to Santa Rita, I am not able to get the records for the previous years on that, because we generally put all the different parcels together, and we never figured one parcel by itself, when we are harvesting our crop. This field may go 40 sacks, another 25 or 30, or even as high as 45 sacks an acre. They run somewhat uniform throughout, but you are not raising the same kind of a crop. You may be raising Chevalier barley in one field, and common in the next; oats in another one, and wheat still in another field; and perhaps still in another field adjoining that you may cut the crop for hay.

In parcel 283, of 143 acres, I do not think that I can get the figures for the previous years, but I have taken this for one year, because I cut the crop, or rather, harvested it myself. We have our books in this way: We put everything together. The reason I can recollect it so well, is because all this grain and straw was sold out in the field. It was not hauled out at all. As a rule you haul your grain and stuff to the warehouse where it is either sold or stored. It is not customary to sell it always in the same way from the field; some times you store your barley; some times you store it two years before you sell it. The storage and the insurance increase the expense.

In reference to the long strip running from Sunol to Niles, included in map 11, I spoke to Mr. Gale, and he said "What are you going to do about this"? and I said "I am going to do absolutely nothing, because I don't know how to get at it". Mr. Olney spoke to me about it one afternoon in the office, and he said "You can leave it out."

854

855

856

FIFTEENTH HEARING.   AUGUST 3, 1915.

Witnesses: C. H. SCHWEEN,
             W. J. MORTIMER,
             W. S. CLAYTON.

857   CROSS EXAMINATION BY MR. STEINHART.

In valuing this land along the Alameda Creek, I did not leave
out any land additional to that included in the creek bottom, but
perhaps I included some of the lands near the creek bottom; there
858   is a road leading along there. Referring to the creek bottom in Alameda Creek, below Sunol, I figured along the road leading up toward
Calaveras Creek, and west of that road I considered creek bottom. I
am now talking about land near Sunol. In other words, southeast of
859   Sunol along Alameda Creek. There are several pieces that I excluded
southeast of Niles going towards Sunol. Pieces 263, 224 and 225 on
map 11; I gave no valuation whatsoever to those lands. In valuing
other lands along the Alameda Creek, I excluded portions of the creek
bottom on parcels 239-A, 239-B, 239-C, 239-D, and 239-E on map 11.
I do not think that I excluded anything more than the creek bottom
860   in those parcels. I got my acreage from Mr. Olney, and in my opinion
the acreage that I valued excluded only the creek bottom, and I feel
that I am perfectly qualified to value the land along the side of the
creek.

That portion of the Schween Ranch that was seeded to oats, produced in 1910, 44 bags of oats to the acre. That is a usual crop, and
we have had five running crops like that. Some of our neighbors have
also had crops like that, but I do not think that is a usual crop
throughout the Livermore Valley, unless you included Pleasanton in
that valley. To a great extent it is a usual crop through the Pleasanton Valley. I am not familiar with the usual yield throughout
861   the state, nor throughout the Livermore Valley, except a portion on
the west side of the Livermore Valley. I am familiar with just a
small portion of the yield to the west of Livermore Valley, on the
land that my brother-in-law and my uncle owned, and that is the
only land the yield of which I am familiar with.

Counsel for Defendant read the following figures as presented
in a pamphlet published by the University of California, Circular
No. 121, entitled "Some Things the Prospective Settler Should
Know, by Forsyth Hunt, and other members of the Staff", giving
the average probable and possible yields for different products in
the State of California. Counsel asked the witness whether or not
he agreed with these figures, which were as follows:

Q. In so far as oats are concerned—the average yield per acre
is 10 sacks. In your experience, is that correct or not correct; A. I
think that must be correct.

SPRING VALLEY WATER CO. VS. CITY AND COUNTY OF SAN FRANCISCO

Q. A safe estimate for business purposes as to oats per acre is 15 sacks per acre: In your opinion is that correct? A. Yes.

Q. A good yield which competent men may hope to obtain is 20 sacks an acre. Is that, in your opinion, correct? A. That is right.

862

Q. A yield not infrequently obtained, under favorable conditions is 30 sacks an acre. In your opinion is that correct? A. Yes.

Q. Possible but extraordinary yield is 40 sacks an acre. Now, do you consider that a possible but extraordinary yield? A. No; it is neither possible nor extraordinary, because I have seen better; I have seen more.

My crop, which runs an even four sacks to the acre, higher than the highest possible and extraordinary yield they give, has done that for five successive years. My books, perhaps, would not show that, but may show the total amount of money that we have gotten for our crop for the season; maybe I could produce that. I would like to refer back; I know on one particular piece of 100 acres, what you call the brickyard piece, they had 165 bags of barley to the acre average; that was an average for the five years, or 31 sacks per acre per year. It is not a fact at all times that barley runs more sacks to the acre than oats, and therefore that 31 sacks of barley to the acre is not at all extraordinary.

Counsel for Plaintiff here interposed that if Counsel is referring to the yield on irrigated land, and under favorable conditions, that in fairness to the witness, he should tell him so. It is Counsel's opinion that in excess of 40 sacks of barley to the acre is an extraordinary yield on irrigated land.

863
864

Counsel for Defendant states his own witness advises him that that is not an extraordinary yield for those things, and that this is on all land, and that the pamphlet used refers to ordinary yield throughout the State of California.

Last year we sold our oats for $1.55, and a little later it went up to $1.80. The price is about 2 cts. per lb. on oats for seed, and when we sold this oats of ours for $2.25, we sold it to different parties that came out to the field and got it, but we thought that $2.25 a cental was a little high, so we gave it to those that came out for 2 cents, but I think that the sacks weighed 107, which made it $2.14 per sack; but we could have gotten $2.25 a cental. What we got will average that, because it is very heavy oats, and in my statement yesterday, I said that the gross income of that land was equal to $100 per acre, as near as I remember; it will exceed that a little bit if you will figure it up very closely. Straw is not worth as much as 65 cents per bale right now, but at the time we obtained 65 cents for it, it was worth that much; the market is fluctuating. 65 cents is not the usual price per bale for straw. We sometimes sell it at $1 a bale, and sometimes for less, perhaps as low as 35 cents per bale.

865

The weight of our wheat per bag was 152 lbs. average, with 28 bags to the acre. I think that six and a half sacks per acre, (figure as given in publication before referred to), is correct as an average throughout the state.

Q. A safe estimate for business purposes is 10 sacks per acre; is that about right? A. I guess so.

Q. A good yield which competent men may hope to obtain is about 12½ sacks per acre? A. A pretty good crop.

Q. A yield not infrequently obtained under favorable conditions is 20 sacks per acre: Is that about right? A. Yes.

866 Q. And a possible but extraordinary yield is 25 sacks to the acre?

(Discussion between Counsel as to whether this means on irrigated or non-irrigated land.)

Q. Now, I notice you run three sacks higher. How often did you do that? A. You see, Mr. Steinhart, we are not in the habit of raising wheat on that land; it is just by chance that we will try a little piece of wheat in order to get the seed for some of our other farm lands—we get clean seed; and also once in a great while we change the crop, not always have barley; we will run barley as high as 7 or 8 years in succession, and then we will change it to a crop of wheat or oats.

Q. How often do you grow wheat there? A. Perhaps nearly every season or every other season we raise a small piece of wheat, just enough to get the seed. I hardly think that it always ran this crop of 28 bags to the acre. I know that on several occasions it ran over 20 bags, how much I could not say.

867 It seems to me that along about February, 1915, there were two gentlemen at my house in regard to rights of way. One of the rights of way runs parallel with the Southern Pacific, and the other runs triangularly through one of the fields of our land. My recollection of my talk with these gentlemen was that we started at Niles, and went as far as Tracy, and were simply speaking about rights of way; I do not remember anything in regard to the value of the land surrounding Pleasanton. That valuation was a valuation of the Western Pacific right of way, which does not go through, but runs along the southerly line of my land parallel with the Southern Pacific. I am not positive that I gave them a valuation of the land formerly owned by me, but I did tell them that the lands above us were worth much less per acre than our lands that we owned at that time. I am positive that I did not give them a valuation on the 868 lands formerly owned by us. I am positive that we did not discuss the lands, other than the right of way land. They may have asked me the value of neighboring lands along the right of way, but I do not think I gave them the figure. I am positive I gave them no 869 figure whatever.

Q. You are positive you gave them no figure whatsoever?
A. Yes.

Mr. Greene: Just for my own information, will you tell me which right of way this is you are referring to?

Mr. Steinhart: The Western Pacific right of way. I will state very frankly, I do not want any misunderstanding about this, Mr. Schween gave a figure. This is my statement—Mr. Schween gave a figure; I asked the Interstate Commerce Commission to give me those figures, and they said to me, they telegraphed East and said they could not voluntarily release those figures, so it will be necessary for me to subpoena the men. The only other source of information I have is Mr. McDonald, in our employ, who was present, but he states he will not give me that figure unless the Western Pacific tells him he can; he spoke to Mr. White, and Mr. White said if Mr. Olney would let him give those figures, he would give them. Now, then, I have been rather diffident about asking Mr. Olney to give Mr. McDonald permission to give me those figures.

Mr. Greene: I should like to have this land exactly placed, if you can do it, from map 10. Can we do that?

Mr. Steinhart: Mr. Schween gave a valuation of the lands formerly owned by him and of lands through which the Western Pacific runs on Map 10; he also gave a valuation as to the other lands; but very frankly, I am going to ask Mr. Olney for permission to use those figures.

DIRECT EXAMINATION BY MR. GREENE.

The Western Pacific right of way, on that map, runs parallel to the Southern Pacific.

CROSS EXAMINATION BY MR. STEINHART.

870

I am quite positive that I did not give a figure.

Parcel 288, Chabot lands; during the past two seasons there has been water on them for a period of maybe a few days or a week at a time, but after that the water has all drained off; but two of the years, 1912 and 1913, there was absolutely no water on them.

The Winter sown crop, referring to the Hadsell piece, runs on an average about one to one ton and a half per year, and that is the uniform crop through the San Antone Valley. During 1914, those that had summer-fallow wheat hay, averaged 4 tons per acre. The red oat hay will hardly average that high, but the wheat hay will, and in many instances that is the usual summer-fallow crop for the wheat hay. Their main object in summer-fallowing in the San Antone Valley is to prepare the land in Spring for early seeding in the Fall of the year.

871

Map 15, parcel 239-M; the creek bottom I valued for gravel purposes, and for good Spring pasture; it grows an abundance of feed. I valued it at $65 an acre both for Spring pasturage, and gravel purposes. I do not know that that land is not fit for gravel purposes, owing to the presence of the great quantity of shale.

There have not been so very many tenants pasturing in the Arroyo del Valle during the last six years. During my time there has been one other tenant before Mr. Moy, who had pasture land, and his name is Beauchamp.

872   I have been in the employ of the Spring Valley Water Co. nearly three years. I do not think that you have ever asked me what Moy paid for his land. When Beauchamp was unable to pay the rent, the company took the fencing, watering trough, some hay and such things, as part payment, and all that was sold to Mr. Moy. He took that, and he bought that from the company, which later became of the property of the Spring Valley; these fences, as well as wires and posts, etc., at the rental of $850 per year. Besides what he paid for that, it seems to me he paid in addition $325, and I think he has a three years' lease on between 4,000 and 4,400 acres.

I do not know positively what Heath pays, because, for a portion of this land (Lilienthal land), for the first year he paid $12

873   per acre, and after that $20 per acre. It may have been $12 for the first three years, and $20 for the next seven, I won't say. That is for about 300 acres.

Map 12, parcel 228; the bulk of it is somewhat steep, with some level spots in it. Part of the east end of it could be cultivated, and also on top, which is accessible. We generally get into that piece from what they call the Mission Road, which is in the neighborhood of a mile, or a mile and a quarter from it.

874   Map 12, parcel 290; I think the northeast portion of that could be cultivated. There is quite a flat in there, and along the Arroyo de Laguna there is a lot of flat land; also the rolling hills slope from the west to northwest. Some years ago, I should judge half of the entire parcel was under cultivation at one time, and that is the portion that I speak of along the Laguna Creek to Bonita. I have placed my valuation on that from an agricultural standpoint, and I think I placed a valuation on the half that is capable of cultivation of about $350 or $400 per acre. Some of this land is east of the Arroyo de Laguna. There is quite a strip along there, and I

875   included all the flat land, and I guess I included the creek bottom. I placed a value of $50 or $60 on the portion that is not cultivatable. I could not say positively as to that. I valued that for grazing purposes, and home sites. Have had no experience whatever in the selling of home site lands.

Map 13, parcel 239-W; can be used for grazing purposes, and I am almost postive that there are springs on it.

Map 13, 239-X; can be used for agricultural purposes; small portions that you could perhaps farm. Practically about the same land as in 239-W.

239-V; is a little better land, a part of it, than the other. There is water there. The San Antonio runs through it, and there are some springs.

Map 14, 243-R; quite steep, the most of it; used principally for grazing purposes; a very little that you could raise hay on. The southwest quarter has quite a gulch running through it. Along the northwest it is quite brushy; not chaparral. It is a resemblance of chamisal, not very long. That is up on top of the hill. The northwest quarter is somewhat better. It is quite steep, and the southeast quarter is quite steep. There is a creek running through there, or a gulch.

243-V; very rough and brushy. I do not know whether there are any government lines run on that land.

(Counsel for Defendant states that the Government Surveyors have not been able to run the lines up there, as it is too rough to get at, and that there are no stakes for five miles.)

Map 14, A-243; can all be farmed, with the exception of from the top of the hill sloping towards the north. That portion is practically covered with small oak trees.

Referring to Cresta Blanca; I think there is less than half of that that is grazing land. I did not put a valuation on the half that is grazing land, and a value on the half that is not. I put an appraised value of $20 an acre on it. I have been on the land myself. Not on all the rough part, but over the top of the hill to get the boundaries.

When we sold our land to the Spring Valley Water Co., as near as I can remember, we knew before making the contract for sale, that it was for the Spring Valley Water Co., but still I will not be positive as to that. I asked Mr. Reed and Mr. Gale, the parties that were around buying, if it was for a purpose, and they said yes, but I did not know that they were agents for the Spring Valley.

RE-DIRECT EXAMINATION BY MR. GREENE.

I think it was a fact that Mr. Olney instructed me in appraising the lands from Sunol down to Niles, on Map 11, parcels 239-A, 239-B, 239-C, 239-D and 239-E, to leave a line of 50 or 75 feet roughly above the creek bed, and in my values placed on these lands, I omitted such a strip as that, as well as the creek bed. I have appraised all of these lands for agricultural purposes.

RE-CROSS EXAMINATION BY MR. STEINHART

I asked the agents, when I sold my land, whether they were buying it for a purpose, because if it was for a purpose other than farming or agricultural purposes, we would not sell at that time.

RE-DIRECT EXAMINATION BY MR. GREENE.

That conversation was before we signed our contract of sale. I will explain what I mean by, a purpose other than agricultural. When Mr. Reed and Mr. Gale came to the house and said "Schween, we want to buy your land", I said, "You cannot get it". They said "What will you take for it". I said, "It is not for sale", and walked away. They said "Come back here". Upon my going back, they said "Now, we want to buy your land". I said, "What do you want to do with it?" They said, "That is all right, we want to buy

881   it." I said, "Is it land for a purpose other than agriculture?", and they said "It is". I studied over the matter, and questioned them a little closer who this land was for, and finally I told them I would not sell the land, unless we were compelled to. They finally told me, and I took it up with my brothers and sisters, and we decided that it was much easier to divide money than it is lands; that is how we negotiated the sale finally.

Questioned by Master.

If some neighboring farmer had come along to buy the land at the same price, I would not have sold it to him.

RE-DIRECT EXAMINATION BY MR. GREENE.

The following year we tried to get this land back; we were willing to give them back their money, but they would not consider the proposition.

881-883   (Discussion between Counsel as to laying of foundation by Counsel for Defendant, in regard to Witness' statement that the Interstate Commerce Commission retains.

Conceded by Counsel for Plaintiff that foundation is laid. Counsel for Defendant then gave names of the men to whom Witness made the statement and when and where it was made.)

Mortimer   Witness: W. J. MORTIMER.

DIRECT EXAMINATION BY MR. GREENE.

I have lived in Berkeley about twenty years, and have been engaged in the real estate business a little over twenty years, with my office in Berkeley, and operating chiefly in Berkeley and California lands. I deal in city property and country farming lands, fruit lands and grain lands. During the past 20 years the volume

884   of my business in the property in Berkeley and Oakland, and surrounding Berkeley, suburban property, about 20 million; and country property about $700,000. I have dealt in lands that belonged to the Alameda Sugar Co., at Alvarado, some lands in Ala-

meda County, Contra Costa County, and several interior counties. I have a knowledge of, own farming lands, and have engaged in farming. I own lands in Alameda County, Contra Costa County, Santa Clara, Kern, Tulare, San Joaquin, and Placer Counties. I have been employed by the State as an appraiser of Berkeley property. The Board of Equalization employed me about six years ago to appraise about 100 pieces of property in Berkeley, for the purpose, I presume, of learning if it were properly assessed.

I am familiar with the properties of the Spring Valley Water Co., at Pleasanton, and have been over the properties probably thirty or forty times, and have known them for years. I have made a careful appraisal of the parcels of property situated at Pleasanton, 885 and have placed my value on those properties as of December 31, 1913. I am familiar with alfalfa land, and sub-irrigated alfalfa land is more valuable than land that you have to irrigate, because it makes better hay. You can produce seed from alfalfa on sub-irrigated land where you cannot if you have to irrigate it; you can produce seed on irrigated land, but not seed that they will buy for seeding purposes. Sub-irrigated alfalfa land is not plentiful in this state, and that fact appreciates its value naturally. The extent of sub-irrigated alfalfa land within 100 miles of San Francisco is lim- 886 ited. The only land that I know of that is sub-irrigated, is in the Pleasanton country, at Alvarado, at Newark, and Byron, Contra Costa County.

Memorandum introduced headed "Value of Pleasanton Lands, Alameda County, as of December 31, 1913"; first column has the map number, second the parcel number, the third the acreage, the fourth the value per acre, and the last, total value. The figures in the third column were derived from the company's maps. The fourth column sets forth my appraisal per acre, and the last column the total valuation. The value per acre, and the total value, as set forth there, is correct, to the best of my knowledge.

Offered and received in evidence as "Plaintiff's Exhibit 35".

Most of your Pleasanton land is alfalfa, that will raise alfalfa without irrigation. It is good for beets, potatoes, corn and beans; I should judge alfalfa would be the main product, and beets would 887 come second; those two crops in my judgment, would be the best. The land toward the Dublin road, lying east of the Santa Rita road, some of it is best fitted for grain, although it is a soil that is adapted for alfalfa by irrigation.

Map 10; the land lying south of the Arroyo del Valle is all alfalfa land, with the exception of a knoll on I-239. All the land lying south of the Arroyo del Valle, and north of the Arroyo del Valle, and west of the Santa Rita road,—running north on the road leading from Pleasanton to Dublin—over to and including Livermore road, thence west, all those parcels to my mind, would raise alfalfa and beets. Portions of 288 are too heavy for alfalfa, and the western portion of U-268 is heavy.

The land around, and immediately west of Pleasanton, and some portions north, has a rich dark loam which is well adapted for alfalfa. The northerly portion of the land being heavier, is not so good, although it will raise it, but it will raise better grain; barley will grow well on the heavier soil, where alfalfa will not. I have taken each piece separately, and put a value on it as the conditions warrant. I have appraised the land in its present condition as to boundaries. I have paid no attention to the houses which are at the present time on the land.

888

DIRECT EXAMINATION BY MR. MCCUTCHEN.

The average land throughout the interior yields on an average 10 to 12 sacks of barley. Land that would produce 34 sacks of barley to the acre, I would say was extraordinarily good land.

889

Questioned by Master.

By sub-irrigation, I mean a natural condition of irrigation below the surface.

CROSS EXAMINATION BY MR. STEINHART.

I know that the land in the Pleasanton district is sub-irrigated, by information, and by asking questions. I can notice also, in the canal in the early Spring that the water shows evidences of it. Evidence of water 4 or 5 feet below the level of the ground. I also see alfalfa growing without irrigation—that is evident. That does not apply to all of the land there. Some of the land lying east of the road leading from Pleasanton to Santa Rita, is higher ground. I should judge it would apply to all of the lands, with the exception of that red hill I spoke of, and the water may be a little too near the surface on the west side of the Chabot tract. I examined the land especially for that purpose in May, 1914. I was out there two weeks ago, all over the tract, and I have driven through it numerous times. I cannot state positively that I have seen alfalfa growing prior to 1914, for the reason that in driving through the country I had no reason for picking out any particular part. A purchaser of land would certainly want to know that fact. I have had considerable experience with alfalfa land.

890

I am valuing the land just as it stands, and do not figure the crop in. You pay more than $250 an acre for good alfalfa land, sub-irrigated. We sold some for a higher figure than that at Alvarado. I don't know anything about the alfalfa land along the Sacramento River, and do not know what it is selling for. The factor necessary in order to have sub-surface irrigated alfalfa land is that the water must be below 20 feet. That is the maximum depth. It is better to have it 12 and 15 feet. If the water plane sinks and rises, but does not sink below 20 feet, it is of use for sub-

891

surface alfalfa, but if it does sink below that point, then you need to irrigate. I am familiar with the cost of raising alfalfa, and with the plowing, levelling and cultivating of the land, it would be about $4 or $5 an acre; the cost of seeding is worth 15 cents a lb. Plowing and checking will cost about $5 an acre, providing there is no levelling necessary. Cutting will cost $1.35 or $1.50 a ton. The baling, raking and sacking, $1.35 to $1.75 a ton.   892

If you have sub-surface irrigation, you do not necessarily have to irrigate because of gophers. My method would be to poison them. My friends have done that on sub-surface irrigation lands in Byron, Contra Costa County. I asked a friend of mine if he would take $400 for his land there, and he said, no. That is not the land of the Balfour-Guthrie people. I could not give you the exact figures on the hauling cost, or cost of delivery, in Pleasanton; a man's time would be $30 or $35 a month; he can haul 2 tons to a load; it is just simply a matter of figuring it out, but I could not say exactly what the cost is. I have not grown alfalfa myself, and had no experience of my own in alfalfa growing. My experience in alfalfa land has been only this land at Alvarado, which I have sold, and the information I gained is through my brother, who is in the business, and my friends. They are not beginning to irrigate the land we sold, which is located south of the Alameda Creek, and southeast of Alvarado,—between the Pleasanton road and Alameda Creek. This land lies west about a mile or two of the Beard tract, and is similar land to it, along the banks of the Alameda, of the Beard land; the Beard land along the Centerville road is heavier, more of a free soil, whereas, the Alvarado lands are sandy and free soil. We sold it from $375 to $475 per acre. You cannot live on that land because it overflows in the Winter-time.   893   894

Mr. Harvey bought his land from us last year; I think he paid $325. He is right on the land we are handling. He is on the railroad, between the railroad and Centerville and San Jose road. He bought some of the poorest land in the tract. Mr. Harvey paid $250 per acre for 22.58 acres, $5,645. I do not know whether it is sub-irrigated or not, but I hardly think so. When I spoke of the scarcity of sub-surface irrigation alfalfa land, I did not include the land along the Sacramento River, as the question was asked concerning land within 100 miles of San Francisco, and I did not consider that within 100 miles. In placing my value on this land, I figured the market price of alfalfa at $8.50 to $10 f. o. b. Pleasanton. The first cutting is not worth so much. The average price per ton I took at $8.50.   895   896

(Counsel for Defendant stated the pamphlet issued by the University of California, before referred to, gives $8.00 per ton as the average, but upon question by Counsel for Plaintiff, was not sure as to whether that meant the average price at the shipping point all over the State of California.)

897   I saw alfalfa quoted the other day at $8.50. The difference between $250 an acre, and the value of $500 an acre, that I have placed on the Pleasanton lands, is due to the fact that his land does not compare with the Pleasanton lands. I sold some land practically adjoining his for $475 an acre in the same tract. Then, the Pleasanton land is a far better place to live. This land at Alvarado overflows in the Winter-time. You cannot build upon it as it is all under water more or less. His particular piece lies between the railroad and the county road, and if I am not mistaken, that is overflowed. Overflowed land is particularly rich land, but it destroys its value as a residential section. Outside of that district, I do not know of any alfalfa land that has sold as high as $500 an acre, and I claim to be familiar with alfalfa lands. The Harvey tract is 22.58 acres. I sold several pieces there; 5½ acres, the low-

898 est, to the Harvey piece, the largest.

    Map 10, parcel 279, at $250 an acre, and parcel 274 at $225 an acre; I put a lower valuation on parcel 274 because it is a long narrow strip, and is of a lower nature; not so good. It is narrow, which offsets its value, and I appraised the smaller piece lower because it was a smaller piece, and it is lower ground. The factor of difference between parcels 239-h, 239-n at $500 an acre (exception 239-i), and 239-o to 239-t at $275 an acre, is that the cheaper portion is more of a clay; it is a clay loam; and not as rich as the other. I went over that twice very carefully to distinguish the difference. I gave parcels 272 and 273 a value of $550 an acre because it was a rich dark loam, with no clay in it, and I valued them at a higher price than 239-e, f, g and h, which I valued at $500, be-

899 cause there is some land along the creek there. The fact that parcels 272 and 273 were small pieces, did not play any part in that case; that is good vegetable land and berry land. Parcel 273 was $50 more an acre than the other on account of this other being along the creek. Brush was growing over the land somewhat, and it had to be cleared along the banks of the Laguna Creek. That is my reason for that.

    239-h, about 2 acres, along a portion of the creek that would not be in land; I did not take off much for the presence of the creek. There are 108 acres in this parcel, and I figured about 2 acres in the creek, and I took into consideration the fact, in valuing that parcel, that a portion of it was in the creek. Those are about all the factors of difference that I took into consideration.

900   Parcel 277; particularly adapted to alfalfa; will grow beets and most any kind of garden truck. It will go in alfalfa in 1914, rich dark loam. I have nothing noted here to offset this value of $550 an acre, as between the value on 239-h. I do not know that it was

in alfalfa in December 31, 1913, so that that could not have made any difference in my valuations as of December 31, 1913. As to other factors of difference, outside of the fact that there are 2 acres of 239-h in the creek, I called one a rich dark loam, and the other a rich loam. That land along the creek is very good land. I probably called it $50 less than the land in the interior, but I have no other reason, except that parcel 277 is better adapted for a home than it is along that creek. That might have had some bearing at the time I valued it. I don't know the reason right now, but that might have been the reason.

268-R, valued at $575 an acre; I have my note like this, in regards to 268-R and 280; "268-R, $575 per acre, dark free soil, about 15 acres in alfalfa", and so on. As to 280, I say that this land would be worth more, $600 per acre, on a main road, but being on a side avenue, it detracts from its value. Its proximity to the town of Pleasanton increases its value. I have it only at $550. My point there is that it is not so close to the main road, and I have attached a certain importance as a residential section to all these Pleasanton properties. For instance, if I were to buy one or the other, and both lands being the same, I would pay more to be on the county road than I would to be on an inside avenue, notwithstanding that the distance is very small, and the fact that 280 fronts on an avenue. 901

I put a higher value on 268-R than 268-Q, because in my judgment I determined that 268-R has a higher water table than 268-Q, being better suited for alfalfa. 268-Q is higher and splendid ground, being some five or six feet higher, but not so good, in my mind. I do not know what the water table below the ground is, only by the growth of the alfalfa. I do not know how long the alfalfa in 268-Q has been growing. My notation as to that parcel is, "all in grain with the exception of about 20 acres in alfalfa". I cannot say that I used absolutely the appearance of that 20 acres of alfalfa in judging as to the water plane between 268-R and 268-Q. I judged the land. In my mind I think it would not be as good alfalfa land, and made my appraisement accordingly. I have grown no alfalfa myself. 902

In regard to 286 and 283; 283 is all level land, good stand of grain. My notation states that I consider the water table too low for probable growing of alfalfa without irrigation, and so I placed a value on that of $350, and on the other a value of $500. Referring to the 143 acre piece in parcel 283, that is $450. The pasture land being rather heavy, and the water table near the surface, makes it rather too heavy for other use than pasture, although it could be drained at very little cost; the balance of the land good for all general farming—alfalfa, grain, especially beets. That would need some work to make it good alfalfa land. The 17.28 acres of 286 I 903

259

valued at $500. That is natural feed pasture land. I learn around Pleasanton that that land is peculiarly adapted for stock men. I made several inquiries about it. I saw so many horses in the pasture, that I inquired what they got per head, and I was told that the average price was $5 per month, and learned that it would carry a little better than one head to the acre.

The factors of difference between 286 and 243, the 40 acre tract: I had that all level land, and a good stand of grain; water table too low for proper growing of alfalfa without irrigation. First-class grain land, $350 per acre, and I so valued it because of that fact, and that it could be grown in alfalfa with irrigation. My statistics as to the water

904   table I got by judging it by the condition, by the appearance, and information that I gained. You could see the water in some of those canals, which would speak for itself that the water table was not very low. I did not see any water table in the 40 acre piece in parcel 283, as that is higher ground.

The factors of difference between parcels 275 and 282, the 38 acre piece. 275, 40 acres; is first-class alfalfa land. The difference between 275 and 239-c: I have it here that that is particularly adaptable for vegetables. It has a sediment loam, and I gave that a vegetable value, and the other an alfalfa value. I have sold high-priced alfalfa land—100 acres near Alvarado—in addition to the sales in the Beard

905   Tract. I do not know that this Beard Tract land is grown to alfalfa now. The Beard Tract, I think, I sold about three years ago, to Benjamin Bangs, or the Suburban Water Co., I have forgotten now just which. That was a sale to the Spring Valley Water Co., but I am not sure whether the deed went to them or not. That is all of the high-priced alfalfa land that I have handled.

288, the Chabot piece; I did not examine that to determine

906   whether there was any alkali in it. I found no bare spots indicating black alkali. There might have been white alkali, and if the Government Reports say that the Chabot piece contained alkali, I would not say that those reports are incorrect. You can find alkali in most all lands. $225 is my appraisement for all of the Chabot piece, except 200 acres at $100. It is a heavier soil, and will not grow alfalfa so rapidly and so well as the black and rich loam that I appraised further down below Pleasanton.

RE-DIRECT EXAMINATION BY MR. GREENE.

907   The Alvarado lands, which I sold for alfalfa growing, ranged in price from $250 to $475 per acre.

Beard land; we paid Mrs. Beard $400 per acre; Josephs $525 per acre; Duarte $450 per acre; and Diablo $475 per acre. This is the same Beard land which the water company purchased. The land along by the creek, that I paid $525 for, is good alfalfa land; the Beard property along the road is not; it is heavier.

SPRING VALLEY WATER CO. VS. CITY AND COUNTY OF SAN FRANCISCO

RE-DIRECT EXAMINATION BY MR. McCUTCHEN.

I do not know anything about the prices at which land was sold in the West Sacramento Reclamation.

Witness: W. S. CLAYTON.

DIRECT EXAMINATION BY MR. McCUTCHEN.

I was born in San Jose on October the 10th, 1864; am 50 years of age, and at the present time am, and since May 1, 1907, have been President of the First National Bank of San Jose. Prior to that time I was in the real estate business; first with my father under the name of James A. Clayton from 1884 to the 1st of January, 1887; and the 1st of January, 1887, was taken into partnership with my brother and father, and we continued as such until my father's death, in 1896, and thereafter until the distribution of his estate in 1906. In 1906 we turned the business over to a corporation, and called it the James A. Clayton Company, composed of my brother and myself. My brother, who is now deceased, and myself, had full charge of the business, my father retiring on the first of January, 1887. From the time I went into the business with my father, up to the time I became President of the First National Bank of San Jose, my time was entirely devoted to the real estate business. I was operating in San Jose, Santa Clara County, and we went into the Counties of San Mateo, Santa Cruz, Monterey, San Benito, and Alameda. I have been engaged in particularly looking after the loans, and making the loans and collecting them, and keeping track of them, since I first went into the bookkeeping department of the office in 1884. I have been in the habit of appraising real estate for the purpose of making loans, since I became President of the First National Bank. I approve all the loans made by the bank, excepting those that are made during my vacation. The loans that are made at the present time, anything over $5,000, by James A. Clayton & Co., are submitted to me for approval before they are made.

Questioned by Master.

I am situated in this manner in regard to the real estate office of James A. Clayton & Co. I do not own the real estate office at the present time. In 1906 I sold out my interest in it to my brother. He died on August 28, 1908, about 18 months after I went into the bank. My mother and his widow became his heirs. I had no money interest in the business; neither my mother nor his wife were able to run the business, so I induced a young man by the name of Mr. Reed, to take a one-third interest in it, and to become the manager of it. They retain me as Secretary, not particularly for the official work, but simply as an officer to look over things. I require them not to loan any money without my knowing it.

Since the death of my brother I have kept in close touch with the business as the representative of my mother and sister-in-law, and pass on all loans where the amount is over $5,000. James A. Clayton & Co. loan more money than any bank, firm or corporation that has been in that county since 1870.

I have known the Calaveras Valley, and the lands about it, since I was a boy, and have made probably two or three visits a year to the Calaveras Valley during the past 15 or 20 years. I have made an appraisement of the land of the Spring Valley Water Co., in and about Calaveras Valley, and lying on the Arroyo Honda and Alameda Creek. I have made a typewritten memorandum setting forth the individual valuations, and the aggregate valuation.

911   Introduces a memorandum with a heading "Value Alameda and Santa Clara Lands, Appraised by W. S. Clayton". This contains the detail of my valuation, and also the aggregate of them. Offered and received in evidence, as "Plaintiff's Exhibit 36".

Calaveras Valley is a perfect little valley, surrounded by strong mountains on each side, and a very narrow outlet that is almost in solid rock. The accumulation of soil in the level portions has been from hills that had very fine soil; the body of the valley is very rich. There are springs coming out on each side of the valley as far as these lands go in both directions, that make it a paradise for cattle, and for agricultural purposes, and brings the valley full of moisture. It is almost unparalleled in an agricultural situation. There is hardly any square

912   mile but what has its springs accessible to cattle. There are many running streams through it.

I have set out orchards on speculation. I have had to hire all the work, and since 1884 I do not think I have ever been relieved of the care of but one or two of such orchards or properties, and by that I mean that I have had them in charge for clients of my office, as well as for my own account.

Proceeding with description of Calaveras: floor of valley wonderfully productive; produces in dry years, and not killed in wet years; should have been a prune orchard, or any other high productive plantation. The fact that it has been in the hands of cattle men who have confined the production to hay, has simply been their loss. The productivety of that valley for sugar beets, potatoes, fruit, is easily proven. The fact that it has not been put to more profitable crops has simply been a loss of that much money to the world. Ideally situated for walnuts in certain portions; perhaps the water comes too near the surface in certain portions for fruit trees that require a greater rooting depth. There are two orchards in the valley that have withstood the neglect of the years. One of them, of 15 acres, is planted with prunes, and scattering other trees. The other orchard, of about

25 acres, is principally prunes and pears. I have seen very fair crops 913 on those orchards; very sizeable fruit. The rating of the crop in prunes depends upon the size of the fruit. The price of prunes increases at the rate of $1 a point about the number 80. We have the four sizes, and number 80 is the middle of the four sizes; if they are 30s, that adds $50 more than the basis of 80. I am a prune orchardist myself. Other portions of the valley than that now planted to prunes is adaptable to prune growing. From the point in the northern half of the valley, and climbing up on the hills in the south end, there is a most wonderful chance for fruit in there; I have been told that it would run 1000 acres, but do not know whether it would or not; it certainly would run from about 150 acres north of the 25 acre orchard, to the hills on the south end of the valley; how much they would contain I do not know, but it is a fine big area.

I think this land is superior to any land in Santa Clara Valley 914 upon which prunes are grown successfully, excepting the land around Coyote Station. The hills come rather close together in the locality around Coyote, so as to hold the water back. There is a little spur of hills running across the valley there. The lands for a matter of four miles above those hills are very much sought after, excepting where the water is excessive. When I say four miles above, I mean four miles to the south of that acreage in the main Santa Clara Valley.

The good quality prune lands that are not set out to trees, are hard to get, but when you can find them, you will have to pay from 915 $300 to $500 per acre, largely dictated by location. I do not think you would find any land in the valley from the Sixteen Mile House— down the valley toward Gilroy—northward throughout the valley, for less than $300 an acre. You might find a few that could be purchased at $300, but the majority of them would be higher than that.

The valley lands in Calaveras Valley would produce 20 to 25 tons per acre of sugar beets, and the portions of it that are not too wet, nor too dry, would be productive of heavy crops of potatoes. Some of those Portuguese along those hills there get as high as $1,000 an arce once in awhile. I do not mean in the Calaveras, but around in that neighborhood. I refer to some hills on the west side of the range leading into the big valley. I do not mean that that means vast acres at 916 a time, because Portuguese do not farm that way. Of course all farming is a great gamble. A man might produce in one year and get $300 for his work per acre, and another year he might get $30. I know of one party in there, not very far from the Calaveras Valley, but on the Santa Clara side of the range, that got approximately $225 off about three-quarters of an acre of early potatoes this year. Those lands are adapted to raising hay, grain, vineyards, and alfalfa under certain conditions. There are acres of this valley which will produce luxuriant growths of alfalfa without irrigation, and there are other portions that would require to be irrigated. I think that alfalfa will grow on any kind of land, it is just a question of productivity, but that better crops will be produced on some lands than on others.

CROSS EXAMINATION BY MR. STEINHART.

917   I have never grown any alfalfa.

DIRECT EXAMINATION BY MR. MCCUTCHEN.

I have dealt in and loaned money to farmers for the purpose of improving alfalfa lands, and have also loaned money on alfalfa lands. On the good lands, where the water plane leaves sufficient feeding ground, I think these lands could produce as high as any alfalfa lands there are in the State of California for a fraction of the acreage. I imagine, and therefore do not state it as a positive proposition, that such crops would run about one and one-quarter tons per cutting. The number of cuttings per acre would largely depend upon the climatic conditions. Where they devote the land exclusively to alfalfa, there will be some years four cuttings, other years seven cuttings.

These lands are ideally located for dairying and for cattle raising. I do not think there is any spot of a similar number of acres anywhere equal to that valley and the surrounding hills as a cattle range.

918   The natural feed is there, and with the valley, in connection with that natural feed, there is an ideal combination. There is a constant inquiry for favorable cattle ranges, and it is almost impossible to satisfy that inquiry. The people who own such ranges will not sell them, they think so much of them. The investment of money is a very difficult proposition, and where a whole family may be employed profitably to themselves and make a profit, that is, make more money than the ordinary interest investment, such opportunities are really very much sought after, and they are very hard to find.

Land valued at $300 an acre would not be a good stock ranch if it was all $300 an acre land; it requires grazing land to make a satisfactory stock ranch. A range is composed of many things. It is not only grass, but brush on the range is some times just as valuable as the grass; also the different kinds of grasses that get ripe at different seasons of the year; what today would look to be waste land on a range, might in the month of January or December be the sustaining acres.

919   This land would subdivide into four cattle ranges perfectly. That is, to take the two ridges on the east side, and to take the western slope for the other two. Aside from the Pleasanton Valley, I do not know of any valley within 50 miles of San Francisco where conditions of soil and of sub-irrigation present themselves as they do in Calaveras Valley. The only two spots of that kind that occur to me are that land south of the Coyote Hills, across in Santa Clara Valley, and on the banks of San Felipe Creek, or Old Gilroy, east of Gilroy, both of them of limited areas, but they both have subterranean water-fed land. Conditions of that kind are very rare.

Map 16, parcel 223; 440 acres appraised at $10 per acre. That is a low appraisement for cattle grazing in conjunction with the other lands.

Map 16, parcel 225; that is the big north end of the Calaveras reservoir site; takes in both sides of the valley. All kinds of lands are in that. A fair valuation for the entire acreage would be $40 an acre. On the hillsides—a portion of that land—hay can be raised. A majority of the hillsides are devoted to pasture, and probably most suitable for that. A good deal of the bottom land is being injured by the building of the dam. To consider that before construction by the engineers, there were some very good spots there for hay, grain, berries and vegetables—not too great a proportion of that, however. Valuation $40 an acre. 920

Map 16, parcel 246; the south half, and the northeast quarter of section 18, called the north hillside; $17.50 an acre. That is pasturage; quite a fair amount of standing oak trees; very good grazing ground, in conjunction with other lands to make more acres to hold out a whole season.

Map 16, parcel 320, valuation $75 per acre; kind of an adobe hill on the west side of the valley. A part of it runs down into the creeks, where there is good property. A majority of the land being not of that rich bench land, I made an average valuation of $75 an acre on the whole 120 acres.

SIXTEENTH HEARING. AUGUST 5, 1915.

Witness: W. S. CLAYTON.

DIRECT EXAMINATION BY MR. McCUTCHEN. 921

(Certain corrections made by witness on his previous days' testimony. Parcel 225 corrected to $30 an acre, corrections made in some remarks also about the productions and prices per acre of yields.) 922

The Portuguese have got as high as $250 per acre on early potatoes. Those are not average yields, but are good yields. On early peas one party got $200 for an acre and a half. On similar land in the immediate vicinity, a farmer, by name Jim Hansen, got $461.50 from 17 lemon trees in 1913. Lemons can be very successfully grown in the Santa Clara Valley. The principal thing is water, and the Calaveras neighborhood has plenty of water. The Hansen place lays between the Laguna School, which is on the far end of the Hansen lands, and Air Point School House that is on the west side of the Hansen place. The Hansen lands are distant from the westerly point of the Calaveras lands about one mile, and from the body of the Calaveras Valley land, which would be subject to raising lemons, and such things as he raises on his place. It runs from one to three miles. I do not know the facts with reference to the temperature of Calaveras Valley, as compared with the point where Hansen's lemon orchard is, but the elevations are so similar that I would consider the westerly slopes of 923 the Calaveras Valley equal to his at present. His elevation is 600 feet, according to the Government map, and the Calaveras land runs around approximately 700 feet.

924   There are apricot orchards planted this year almost adjoining parcel c-268, and on i-268, remains the wreck of an orchard, and on g-268 there was quite an orchard. The apricot orchard lies not over forty acres from parcel c-268, just outside of section 2, and sold for $10,500 for 76 acres before it was planted to apricots. These apricots are one year old, and look very good. This is the Rouse property.

Questioned by Master.

925   It is near the road which goes from Milpitas into Calaveras. The north line runs very close to the Laguna School House, and the property is on the west of the crest. c-268 runs pretty near along the line of the summit, and is entirely on the easterly slope of the range.

CROSS EXAMINATION BY MR. STEINHART.

The Rouse piece is entirely on the westerly side.

DIRECT EXAMINATION BY MR. MCCUTCHEN.

The difference in elevation between the highest portion of c-268 and the Rouse land is not material; 50 to 75 feet.

DIRECT EXAMINATION BY MR. GREENE.

Between the highest portion of c-268 and the lowest portion of the Rouse land, there may be 150 to 200 feet.

Questioned by Master.

The southern slopes are the best for apricots. There would not be more heat on the westerly slope than on the easterly slope, as there is a cooler climate on the Santa Clara Valley slopes on account of the

926   winds from San Francisco Bay. c-268 would be comparatively warmer than the westerly slope on account of that throughout the summer, but through the winter it might be a little colder on account of the lack of the ocean breeze.

DIRECT EXAMINATION BY MR. MCCUTCHEN.

Apricots are second in series of blossoming; almonds are first. They come along in February in the valley portions. Apricots bloom in March in the valley. Prunes run from the 20th of March to the 20th of April, according to the spring. The Saratoga Blossom Festival Committee sets the date for the Prune Blossoming Festival one month after the apricots blossom, but that varies season by season.

Map 16, parcel 322; very rich piece of property; formerly houses upon it, and around those houses a few family orchard trees, with some walnut and fig trees still remaining on the lower portion. Half the

927   land is below the reservoir land, and all that below is exceptionally good land, capable of irrigation from the little creek that runs through

there, and a very desirable, quickly salable piece of land. Above that line, outside of a few acres, which might be too steep, or in brush, it is tillable. The entire place is very desirable. Valued at $100 an acre on the whole place. The portion which can be irrigated could be used for fruit, alfalfa, sugar beets and dairying. All the higher grades of agriculture now in common use in the Santa Clara Valley could be produced on that place. All the deciduous fruits, walnuts, prunes, and apricots, could be grown there successfully. Beautifully located for a lemon orchard. I put a price of $100 an acre on that, as against a higher figure, on account of its rolling nature. I found but two or three walnut trees on the place, and these had grown very large. I did not notice that there was any fruit on them.

Map 16, 323; valued at $200 per acre, taking all of it. I would consider, if I could purchase it for $200 per acre, that I could make a ready profit of 25% within a few years. It is very rich land. A portion of it now is overflowed for lack of drainage. Produces its own water, and is capable of flowing artesian wells anywhere you want to bore. There are some flowing artesian wells existing now. The wet portion could be readily drained. All the portions that are not too wet are excellently adapted for raising fruits of all the kinds that we are accustomed to raising, and yielding perhaps a larger average yield than a common orchard in the body of the Santa Clara Valley. The soil is very good, and the trees would find their own water without irrigation. 928

In the portions of Santa Clara Valley planted to fruit, artificial irrigation is resorted to quite generally where the subterranean water is available in sufficient quantity, and can be obtained by boring wells, which cost a lot of money in the first place, and then pumping the water, by steam power, gasoline, or electric power. Some of these wells will yield 200 gallons a minute. I have one on my place that will run 2200 a minute. Between those sizes you will find almost every quantity of yield. The ones that yield the least are the most expensive to put in. The water you get from them is the most expensive to get out, and the land as a general rule, needs it the most. The yields of 200 to 600 gallons a minute are generally found at about a 200 foot depth, and they will sink a pit from 80 to 125 feet to get a sufficiently low enough stand to put the pump upon, if they are using a centrifugal pump, that will be within the reach of its power of suction. It is quite a common practice for orchardists to develop and pump water for use upon their lands where it can be developed in that way. Many 10-acre orchards have $2000 invested in a pumping plant. My pumping plant cost $4400; it is one of the indispensable investments necessary to land that does not have sufficient subterranean irrigation near enough for the roots of trees to reach of their own accord. Lands that have that are rare, and very much more valuable than lands that you have to sink wells on, and operate at the expense that 929

267

930   is necessary. In irrigating land in the Santa Clara Valley, where water can be had in this way, the farmers are dictated, not so much by the necessity for the irrigation, as by their energy and the possible cost. Many farmers trust to luck that it will rain enough to save them irrigation, and they will not do it to the extreme necessities. A farmer who seeks to produce the best crops should irrigate three times.

The first thing one has to do, in making one of these irrigations, is to make small reservoirs around the trees to hold the water. Then they pump the water to these reservoirs. Another method prevails in sandier land, where percolation is readily absorbed by the land, by what they call the furrow method. In the Santa Clara Valley we use the check method, which is more expensive, but I think irrigates more uniformly. After the water has sufficiently soaked in, they have to knock down the checks or reservoirs, and cultivate the land briskly for awhile to retain the moisture which they put into it, as the land would

931   bake if they did not do that. All that is avoided on land that has sufficient sub-irrigation, and it is of very material advantage in having land that has the water plane within the reach of the roots, and yet not too near the surface to kill the roots. Different kinds of trees can grow in soils that have different depths. In the prune business we have the myrobolin roots, which we plant on lands containing water. Peach roots will not grow so well on land where the water is not near the surface.

324; very desirable, fine piece of property. On account of a lesser desirability on the west end, I have rated the whole land at $185 per acre, valuing the valley portion equal to any other in the valley, and the hillside portion—also very good—but by making proper allowance for perhaps a lesser valuation in the hillside portion, I think the average value could be reduced to $185 an acre. In arriving at this estimate I did not put figures upon separate portions of the parcel. Any person purchasing at $185 per acre can calculate on that piece from 25 to 50 percent profit on a re-sale.

Questioned by Master.

There has been very little change in those values within the last five years.

DIRECT EXAMINATION BY MR. MCCUTCHEN.

The irrigated fruit land in Santa Clara Valley has had a very

932   fair market during the past year. It was better in December, 1913. The slacking up of the demand has been, I think, more on account of world-wide and national conditions than of any local conditions. Notwithstanding that, fruit lands in Santa Clara County sell very freely when one reduces the price slightly below the customary prices. You can get $1000 an acre for it very nicely now. The last sale I remember was $925 an acre, for 20 acres, planted to apricots and prunes. That was about a month ago, and was in the neighborhood where they

have to go over 200 feet for water, and where the land requires irrigation.

There are two orchards of prune trees in Calaveras Valley on these lands. They have been shamefully abused, but probably have been plowed and cultivated a little. The man who purchased the crops for several years told me that last year he paid more than $6000, and the year before about $5000 for the prunes. This year's crop he estimated to be about 100 tons of dried fruit.

Map 16, parcel 325; the old Gaines' place, at the junction of the Calaveras and Arroyo Honda Creek; some very fine land; some hillside, and some land washed over by the creeks. Valued at an average of $50 an acre, or $40,000 on the whole place. The land along the Calaveras Creek is readily worth $300 an acre, as there is a very good orchard there of prunes and pears; some 25 acres, and there is still good land there, so that you could possibly run it out to make 100 acres of orchard. A hill projects into that, dividing those two creeks, and on that hill they run some hay; north of the Arroyo Honda is the south hillside; very good pasture there, but there is also a corner of that where the rocks and clay show through, and that cuts down the valuation. In the land that is covered with gravel, the gravel is very valuable, as the county will pay 20 to 25 cents a yard for it for road purposes. In this particular instance, it will only be available for the roads that were within reach.

Map 16, 327; called Adobe Hill; available for hay on the upper portions. The face of it is steep, and would only be available for pasture; the soil is good, and a little creek runs down through there. Around the place on the side of the gulch, where an old house stands, there are some hay lands, and it is a desirable place in conjunction with the adjoining lands. This piece would be very attractive to the owners of the valley lands. 80 acres at $40 an acre, $3200.

Map 16, 328; hard piece to appraise for agricultural purposes. It is largely the north hillside running down into the bed of the Arroyo Honda, covered with brush and wood. Its value lies in connection with the adjoining land, to give seasonal feed when the opens have been eaten off and possible feed is scarce. Added to any of the adjoining places it was worth $15 an acre, $3000.

Map 16, 329; little 40-acre tract adjoining the last piece; has water and a portion of it can be used. I have put $1000 for the 40 acres. My explanation for putting that at $25, and the other at $15, is that this piece faces the south, which makes a material difference in feeding, and this is right below section 19, which is a celebrated fine feeder. The fact that one of these pieces of land can be used in connection with other land, makes a material difference in the valuation. For instance, that 40 acres in 329, you cannot do anything with alone, but it is absolutely needed in conjunction with other pieces.

933

934

935

936

a-241; there are three sections that dominate that entire ridge; 19, 20 and 21. This is 19, and is the lower of these fine feed sections, and has a higher value than the one higher up the ridge, because it dominates them, and cattle feed on it longer. I put a valuation of $20 an acre on those. I have known two men to make moderate fortunes on those ownerships right in there.

E-241; 240 acres at $25 an acre; contains a small amount of the high-grade valley lands in that neighborhood. The soil is good, and there is a creek runs out of it. The upper reaches have very fine feed, making it a desirable piece for a cattle man.

p-268; a portion on Map 16, and a portion on Map 18; 160 acres rolling land, open fine feed; formerly part of the Castle ownership. It is the lower reaches of a ridge that runs back a number of miles.

937   I am talking now about that piece up in 30, on page 18, at the top in red color; and this in 32, and this down here in 4, all running up that Marsh road ridge; then this 221 acres is a little lower down; has more hay fields on it, and some barns, but in this grouping those two have been separated and put into 480 acres at $25, and 221 at $30; there is readily that much increased value in that lower piece, on account

938   of the location, accessibility, more acres of hay land and some improvements. Following those, you will find 160 acres, and 643 acres, under the same number which I have valued at $20 an acre; that constitutes the four pieces of the Castle holdings. The 160 acre piece is on both Maps 16 and 18, and you can see it by the section number 30.

Map 16, W-268; that is on the other side of the valley, and is known as the Weller place; has the largest spring around our valley hills, which would irrigate and make alfalfa available on quite a territory. I have been informed there is 180 to 200 acres tillable. There

939   is some very rich land. Many years ago I saw some Portuguese farmers have such a crop on one of those flats that they had to use relays of horses to make the mower travel fast enough for the sickle-bar to cut the hay; that indicates a very strong, heavy crop. The pasture lands are good. There is some brush land. It is a very salable place, and I have put a valuation of $35 an acre on the whole piece. You will find many purchasers at that figure. There is no portion of W-268 on Map 18-A.

Map 16, Y-268; only good for wood and pasture. It is steep. Very little is open, and very little is cultivable. $15 an acre, total $1800. Its usefulness would consist in being used by some of the adjoining tracts, where the cattle could feed at such times as the grass feed is short on the ranges. Pomeroy Creek runs down through it.

940   Map 18, 321; very nice; runs across the valley, but the hillsides make the ranch very desirable. Subdividing that according to this map, the valley itself is very rich. There is an orchard of about 15 acres on the bank of the creek, and back of that orchard is very rich hay land, capable of being an orchard. That is the most southerly

upper prune orchard, and is more neglected than the other one. It has a fair crop of prunes on it, but the trees look barky and scaley. In my opinion, 412 acres could be planted to fruit. I have got that down at ●●●● an acre, and that is too low. Describing it; the easterly end, where these two 40s run up into a kind of a chimney on the hillside, are pastures, but taking the ranch as an individual proposition, that is an advantage, then all the valley is very rich. It will raise anything that is raised in Santa Clara County, and probably would excell any land that could be found in that county, both for richness and for moisture. The subterreanean water is very good. Going west, the hay fields are very desirable, and very fine. They ought to sell for $125 an acre just as they are, irrespective of the adjoining lands. Going above that, near the top of the ridge, there is possibly 100 acres now used for pasture, of which a portion could be put into hay and grain and corn, beets and other crops of that nature. I valued the whole of that ranch at $125 an acre.   941

Map 18, 330; very fine piece of property. $200 an acre as an entirety. The valley lies between the reservoir lines. The hills above the level are very good; rolling land, not hilly; all tillable and raise the finest kind of crops. There is good stubble on it today. The crops never fail. This has been the means of making one or two fortunes. I valued this at $200 an acre, as against the 180 acres in 321 at $125 per acre, because the 180 acres are not the same variety of soils and usefulness as in 330, and that piece is not in the same class of land as this land. They took off the hay crop on this piece, and then planted it to corn, about the first two weeks of June, and this land is particularly desirable. As an orchard land proposition, I could almost assure   942 a sale at $300 an acre for the portions that would be in the level, and running up upon the rolling flats, from $150 to $200 an acre. That land will produce 25 tons of beets per acre, and beets this year are $6. Ordinarily they run from $4 to $5 per ton.

Map 18, 331; is rising land, not all level; does not have the same adobe nature, and is a little more of clay with fine gravel in it. The land is deep, and in the creek banks I noticed that the soil is good and deep. Good orchard land, but not the highest grade. Not as good as the land north of it. The entire 160 acres would be available for orchard purposes. That is as good land as in Santa Clara that is now in orchard, and that sells from $350 to $400 an acre when developed. I valued that piece at $175 per acre.

Map 17, 217-B, 640 acres; lies on north side of Arroyo Honda   943 Creek, and has a south slope; pasture land. The lower portions running down near the creek are brushy. South of the creek is brushy and steeper. I valued the whole place at $15 an acre. It would have to be taken in conjunction with the adjoining places to get the grazing necessary to run the whole year around.

Questioned by Master.

It joins the Castle property in section 32, which I valued at $20; and is on the upper corner of Map 18.

DIRECT EXAMINATION BY MR. McCUTCHEN.

Map 18-A, 241-C; many ravines; a great deal of brush and wood; heavily wooded. The falls of the Arroyo Honda are located on this piece. Taken in conjunction with the adjoining lands, I have valued it at $15 an acre. There is demand in Santa Clara County for properties for grazing purposes that cannot be supplied. I have not kept a record of actual sales of similar lands in Santa Clara County, but **944-945** I can mention the Henry place on the Llagas, sold to a man named Henry Bennetii; that bears no comparison whatever with this though, so far as quality is concerned, because it does not have the quality— that was at $25 an acre.

Questioned by Master.

It is located on the Llagas in Santa Clara County, just south of New Almaden.

DIRECT EXAMINATION BY MR. McCUTCHEN.

A tract of approximately 3000 acres on the rolling hills, between or west of Perry's Station, 15 miles south of San Jose, for $90,000. The only valley land on this piece was about 150 acres in a little canyon. That was cosidered a cheap price.

The sale of the Snell Ranch, in Hall's Valley, to Bob Morrow, for $75,000 for 5000 acres. That is rolling land, with only a percentage of acres of grain land. It is a fine ranch, and was a very cheap price; foreclosure of mortgage necessitated the man selling. If the floor of **946** the Calaveras Valley proper could be used by the cattle men, it would increase the number of head that could be run on these ranges very materially.

I think the Calaveras has a better rainfall than this land on the westerly side of the Santa Clara Valley; the 3000 acre ranch I have spoken of.

Map 18, 241-D; lies on both sides of the Marsh road; rolling hills; some canyons with brush in them, but the majority of the land is the tops of the hills. Very good feed; in conjunction with the adjoining places, I put a value of $30 an acre on that, guided by the quality of the feed and the amount of it, and the south hillside. Consists of 244.22 acres.

Map 18, 268-a; 15 acres; a little piece on the Weller road, valued at $35 an acre; too small to be much unless taken in conjunction with **947** some of the adjoining ranches. Adjoins a very good ranch, and I think the neighbors would pay $35 or $40 an acre for it to get it as pasturage, and for what they could get out of the level places.

Map 18, 268-b; fine piece of land; on top of the hills lying between the Laguna and Calaveras Valley. Has persistantly produced good crops. A portion of it lies south of the Calaveras road, but that is not cropped this year. The head of the canyon runs up in there.

The small piece, odd shaped, along the Calaveras road, above the Laguna School House, is taken in connection with that. On account of these two pieces, which are not of similar value, as the balance of it, I put a valuation of $75 per acre on that. The portion over here, between the road and 268-a, will sell for from $100 to $125 an acre; it is just a question of the proportionate areas of these less valuable carrying down the price, that I put it down at $75 an acre for the whole piece; that is a low valuation.

Map 18, 268-c; known as the Levy place. Rolling, hilly, not steep. A little valley by itself, and capable of being tilled for hay, grain and portions of it for beets, corn and potatoes, etc. A very fairly good quality of land, valued at $75 an acre. There are places 948 where the soil is of sufficient depth to sustain fruit trees, and could be used for fruit raising. There is about a quarter of a mile, or 40 acres between this piece and the young apricot orchard to which I referred.

Map 17, 268-e; there are three or four pieces in that parcel. The 320-acre piece is the crest of the ridge in section 20, where the feed is so fine. Valued at $25 an acre. One or two people have made fortunes in running cattle there.

The next piece in that parcel, 82.88 acres on Map 18, is good rolling land; nearly all of it plowed this year and cropped by tenants. It has good soil on it. In conjunction with that there is a little spot on the County Road that had to be bought in order to get a right of 949 way out; that represents an acre or two. I put that at a conservative price at $75 an acre. Can be used for beets, corn, hay, grain and dairying.

Map 18-A, 268-e; a full section, section 36; valued at $12 an acre because of the distance, and the crest to the north hillside being in brush. A portion of it is on both sides of the road on top of the ridge. The northern portion runs down into Alameda Creek, and is not quite so good. A place on the other side of Black Mountain in that vicinity, and which has no comparison whatever in value; harder to reach; very difficult to carry cattle all the year round, sold for $6 an acre.

Map 18, 268-f; 85.63 acres in section 36, known as Maggie King place; not too good. A ridge runs up the middle of it that is capable of being farmed. Two canyons that take up too much in proportion to the size of the land. Valued at $70 an acre. A good piece for the 950 adjoining places, more than its own individual valuation. I would say about one-third of it can be plowed. Two ridges, one along side the road, and one in the middle, have been plowed. The place has supported a family for a long time, with careful economizing and so on. It could readily be sold for $5000 as a family supporting home place.

Map 18, 268-g, containing 160 acres; rolling land, but not steep except in one place. There is nice running water. It is in Section 1, and has had some orchards upon it. The buildings have been removed, and the man that lived there supported his family and afterwards left with quite a little fortune. Capable of raising hay, grain, dairying, cattle and such things. Fruit can be grown there. There are two badly neglected orchards there now. Not of much value today, but which give evidence that the land will produce fruit. Valued at $75 an acre.

951   Map 18, 268-h, 120 acres; rolling land; spots in it that can raise hay, grain, vineyard and orchard. Appraised at $40 an acre. About one-third tillable.

Map 18, 268-i, 273.24 acres; a very nice ranch; a typical Portuguese ranch. They can raise everything there; rolling, but not steep. Comparatively level; some orchard trees in there now. They raise corn, and they can raise potatoes, hay and grain. They do dairying.

952   A very good place. Valued at $60 an acre.

Map 18, 268-j, 80 acres in Section 31; very good property; quite a percentage under hay cultivation. All of it can be except just a few acres. Valued at $85 an acre.

Map 18, 268-k, 80 acres; those two places go together, and are known as the William's place. They have the best improvements upon them today of the range. There was hay grown this year. Valued at $85 an acre.

Questioned by Master.

I have not included the improvements. They add a value to it, because of the fact that the barns can hold the hay.

DIRECT EXAMINATION BY MR. McCUTCHEN.

I have not put a valuation on the improvements.

Map 18, 268-e, 321.44 acres; the John Carrick property. Upper portion rolling land, on which there is a crop of hay this year; little more gravelly than in other parts of the lands appraised; ravines there and some wood. On account of the water it is a very good

953   cattle place. Valued at $75 an acre. About 40% of it tillable.

Map 18, 268-m, 180 acres; adjoins the last piece, and naturally goes with it. Taken in conjunction with it, it is valued at $50 an acre. By itself would be considered inaccessible, and not attractive. More or less steeply rolling; not over 20% of it has been in hay. I don't think that is the maximum, but it would be hard to till more. Valued at $50 an acre.

Map 18, 268-n, 58¼ acres, Section 8; called the Ferreria piece. A little piece near the top of the hills; has a value as hay land, cattle, dairying and fruit land to a lesser degree. Valued at $40 an acre.

Map 18, 268-o; a little irregular piece adjoining, which would not be considered of much value for agricultural purposes. Has a value which might be recognized, however, and that is, it is a poacher's paradise; a little piece of property set in there where Joseph D.

Grant has a fine protected quail and deer country on one side, and the Spring Valley has the same on the other. It is a spot anybody would like to shoot on, and would pay $300 or $400 for it just to have it to shoot on. Valued at $40 an acre, or about $360.

The Rouse property was sold in part trade. $5000 cash, and the house and lot taken in part trade, and that Bonetti place on the Llagas, 3,670 acres, about 150 acres under immediate cultivation, and 350 or possibly more, that was sold for $75,000 at one time, and $110,000 at another. The $75,000 was cash, with $41,000 mortgage, and the $110,000 was part trade.

Map 18-A, q-268, on the Arroyo Honda, just above the point where the water level of the dam will bring the water to; consists of a hillside there, with a good deal of timber on it. Valued at $12 per acre. We have an offer of $25 an acre for that for camping and hunting purposes.

Maps 17 and 18-A, r-268; referring to north half of Section 28, 320 acres, I valued that at $12 per acre. Some rock on it, but is grazing land almost exclusively. The half-section in the north half of Section 34 has a southern exposure; good grass; fairly open, although the lower portions run into the heads of the gulches. Appraised at $15 an acre.

The quarter section which is the southwest of 22, right on the line dividing the counties, has a portion that runs down to the road; quite steep; and some flats on the northern portion, with some hay standing. Appraised at $10 an acre.

Map 17, t-268, 280 acres in Section 26; runs along the highest parts of the ridge; is good grazing land, and a portion of it runs into a canyon; quite heavily wooded. Appraised at $10 an acre.

Map 18-A, v-268, 168 acres, on southwest quarter of Section 34; down in the Arroyo Honda Gorge; heavily covered with standing trees; has some rich little flats. There formerly was an orchard there. The same party made us an offer of $25 an acre on that for camping, hunting, etc. Valued at $15 an acre, and will have to be taken in conjunction with other properties adjoining to get at its value, as it is down in the bottom of the gulch, and kind of steep.

v-268, the 480-acre piece; a little further up creek; more broken with gulches. Appraised at $6 an acre. I put that down at the minimum that I think any of those lands ought to be appraised for.

Map 18-A, w-268; in the bottom of the Arroyo Honda; steep; lots of trees on it; brush; good hunting ground; also good for cattle; camping privileges other than cattle; some rocks. It has to be used in conjunction with other property. The same party offered $25 an acre for it for hunting grounds. I valued it at $15 an acre. There is feed on it.

Map 18-A, x-268, 160.72 acres, valued at $6 per acre; east half of the east half of Section 2; part of a cattle range.

Maps 18 and 16, X-268; the Santos, formerly the Sox place; those are the tops of the hills on the westerly side of Calaveras Valley; 75 to 100 acres cultivable; good feed and pasture country. Valued at $35 an acre.

957   Map 18, y-268, 160 acres; is up on the ridge on the southwest quarter of Section 32; rolling land, with heavy pasture grass; around corral near the road, and quite a percentage of it has been plowed to hay; very good pasture.

Map 17, H-268, 320 acres; the north half of 20. Part of it very superior grazing land, and assists the adjoining properties as a cattle running field. Appraised at $25 an acre.

Map 18, parcel Z-268; rolling land; some hay land; good pasture land, and I know that it supported a man there for a good many years. Valued at $35 an acre.

Map 18-A, 345, 79.32 acres; lies at the head of the valley; has not been cultivated for years, but there is a portion that can be cultivated. The soil is not as strong as the valley land proper. Valued at $55 an acre.

Map 17, s-268, 80 acres; south half of the southeast quarter of 22; is not so good; good grazing on it between the brush. A little steeper. Valued at $10 an acre.

Questioned by Master.

It is all in the Alameda Creek side below the crest. The road
958   runs pretty nearly to the top, but this place is reached by the other road that runs down through the blue. There is some hay field, a pretty good house and buildings that are occupied by the tenants.

DIRECT EXAMINATION BY MR. MCCUTCHEN.

This piece is reached direct from the Oak Ridge Road, which extends through r-268-blue-, and that is the easiest way to reach it. There might be others.

Map 17, n-268, 160 acres, and strictly a pasture property. It is quite heavily wooded on lower portion; cut up by the gulches. Not of much value by itself, but in conjunction with the other ranges, appraised at $10 an acre.

Map 17, E-268, 320 acres; I did not go to see that, as the best way to see it is through spy glasses. It is in the north half of Section 8. Has splendid feed, and a south exposure. The other pieces of E-268,
959   and of F-268 right beneath it, has had the grass reserved by the tenant, who is farming it for later feed. Very fine feed for that ridge; which is a controlling factor. When I referred to a spy glass being necessary to find it, I referred to the little parcel of E-268, in the northwest quarter of Section 12.

Questioned by Master.

I appraised that other 320-acre piece, the north half of Section 8, at $25 an acre. This small piece is isolated.

276

DIRECT EXAMINATION BY MR. McCUTCHEN.

The 140 acres in the northwest quarter of 16, I appraised at $25 an acre. Good feed, and has good range for the supporting of other places about it. Some buildings upon it, not now occupied. Well worth the price I put on it.

Map 17, f-268, two pieces; taking the 320-acre piece first, this is covered with strong feed; has a south exposure, and I valued it at $25 an acre. The 20-acre piece has an orchard on it, and an extensive little vineyard of very vigorous growth, and hay land, and is occupied now by young Mendoza, who rents these other lands. It has quite a little pond on it, three or four feet deep, and is pretty country for selling, and to add value to the adjoining places.

Map 17, G-268, 480 acres; east half of the southwest quarter of 16. The portion which has the south slope, and is on the north side of the Alameda Creek, is very good pasture; somewhat broken. Some oak wood on it which is possible to get at and out. The south side of Alameda Creek is not so accessible, and the wood is not so easily gulched out. Appraised at $15 an acre. When I say I appraised these lands at the figures which I have placed upon them, I mean in comparison with other properties they bear that relative value; they would sell for the prices I have appraised them at, and by what other means a person judges property to be worth anything, they are worth that money, actual, practical valuation, taken from knowledge of what people will pay for such property. 960

(Counsel for Defendant stated there would be no objection to Counsel for Plaintiff putting in a tabulation from Mr. Clayton's testimony of the prices and the aggregate values put by him on the lands which will be within the Calaveras Reservoir site.) 961

CROSS EXAMINATION BY MR. STEINHART.

Parcel 268-i, the Spring Valley paid $12,100 for that, as near as I can remember, or $46 an acre. It was bought within the last four years, and the Spring Valley supplied me with the purchase price. I paid no attention, whatever, to the fact that the Spring Valley only paid $46 an acre. I have the figures of the different purchasers here and I have not even considered them. I did not consider the value placed on the land by the people who sold to the Spring Valley. 962

Parcel 268-p; valued at $20 and $25. The Spring Valley paid $16,500 for the whole piece, which was very low indeed, and the party that we bought them from has considered that we robbed him. Clayton & Co. handled some of these matters for the Spring Valley. 963

268-n; I valued that at $40 an acre, and the Spring Valley paid $1265 for it, or $21.72 an acre. Clayton & Co. bought that. I don't know the exact year.

268-y; Clayton & Co. bought that, and paid $2500 for it, or $15.62 an acre.

964

268-u; Clayton & Co. bought that, and paid $1000; that is $6 and a fraction an acre. That was a case of good work.

268-t; Clayton & Co. bought that for $2125, or $7.59 an acre. When buying property like that, you have to accommodate yourself to several things. It is harder to buy it than to sell it. You have to do rapid work from one neighbor to another, so that they do not know what the others are getting. It is not usual for all the neighbors not to know the value of their lands, but there was unexcelled work done in the purchase of these properties, and they were kept absolutely in ignorance of the character of their properties. Referring to the fortunes that I mentioned as being made in that neighborhood, the pieces that you have brought up are not comparable, as they are sufficiently isolated so that the owners could not do as well as they could if they had the adjoining land.

268-r; Spring Valley paid $6500 for that, or $8.12 an acre.

965

268-s; adjacent, cost $700, or $8.75 an acre. Everyone of these people are non-residents of that district. We did not find them there. They rented them for nominal sums, and none excepting those who rented the whole range, could afford to range them. It is possible that one man may have rented more than one piece in Calaveras, but not as regards these places. The proposition in regard to that would be that it takes a large amount of money to stock the property. Cattle cost a lot of money, and unless they have extremely long leases, they

966

could not afford to put that much capital in there without positively knowing they could support them. They knew it was fine cattle country, and that they could support them if they had the property so strongly leased that it would warrant them in investing money under such propositions.

268-i, Map 18, Priesker place. The man who had worked the place had acquired it and bought it up, and died, leaving a wife with a family. The family had grown up and did not want to live there, so she was obliged to rent it, and commenced dealing with tenants who liked to make good bargains, which caused her to determine to sell out. We had a hard time getting the price down, but we finally got it down to $46, or something like that, and that is what we were

967

employed for.

Coyote Station district runs from the 12 mile house to the 16 mile house approximately. The belt of choice prune land I spoke of is in the district from the 16 mile house northward throughout

968

the valley. The portion that I wanted to exclude is the portion from 16 mile house to Gilroy. 16 mile house is about 14 miles from Gilroy, and I think about 5 miles north of Morgan Hill, and about 2 miles north of Madrone. I am acquainted with Mr. Fleming, the manager of Griffin-Skelley Co., but not with the land that he bought recently, nor do I know what he paid for it. I know a bookkeeper of Griffin-Skelley Co., but do not know his name, nor am I acquainted with the land he bought in the vicinity of Coyote, nor do I know what he paid for it. I am acquainted with the lands that were 969 owned by the Mary Murphy Colombat Estate, but I cannot recall what those lands sold for. I did not know. They sold for from $100 to $200 an acre for prune lands, but not recently. I don't think there is anything there that was sold for less than $200 an acre in four years. I am not acquainted with the sale made to Mr. Peppin, March 23rd, 1912. It is possible that some of these lands sold for from $100 to $125 an acre in 1912 and 1913, but it did not come to my knowledge. There is a big variation in values there. I have land that I will sell you right now, with a vineyard on it five or six years old, this side of Madrone, for $150 an acre. The Madrone district, and the southerly end of the Murphy Colombat Estate are very different. I don't think that the Colombat Estate land was 970 sold all together, but I am not familiar with the price of the Murphy-Colombat Estate on the State Highway. Opposite one portion of this estate is some land recently sold, called the Sharon Subdivision, at as high as $275 an acre. The Colombat Estate is not the best prune land. Mr. Fleming, manager of Griffin-Skelley, who are buyers of prunes, ought to be a good judge of prune lands. He might have purchased his property for speculation, under which conditions a person does not pay the same. I don't know what he bought, but I know it could not be the best land in that neighborhood.

Mr. Frank Holmes is the man who bought the prunes growing 971 in the Calaveras Valley that I spoke of. I did not inquire from him when those prunes in the Calaveras Valley ripened, and my conversation was very hurried, just before the train left this morning. Whether the prunes in the Calaveras Valley ripen earlier or later than the other prunes, I have never thought that of sufficient importance to inquire about. It would not make any material difference if those prunes ripened in October, and it was not possible to dry them in Calaveras Valley. It is not an advantage to have to haul over such a grade as you have to haul to get out of Calaveras, but that particular haul is not considered very strong. An ordinary hay-load of 50 bales would take a good many horses to 972 haul over that grade.

The shrinkage in prunes between their green and their dry state, runs all the way from $2\frac{1}{4}$ to 3. Therefore, if they have to be hauled in their green state, the weight to be hauled is just $2\frac{1}{4}$ or 3 times as much as in their dry state, so that if in their dry state there were 100 tons to be hauled, in their green state there would be 300 tons, and that would be somewhat of a disadvantage, if they were dried after hauling out of the Calaveras Valley. The elevation of the pass through which exit and entrance are made to the valley, I understand to be about 1100 feet.

279

973   Mr. Holmes did not tell me how the prunes ran last year, and
I do not know anything about the productivity of those prunes.
I know from looking at them, that they have produced heavily. It
is possible that a person might be deceived in judging prunes, as
prunes may appear to be running heavy, but when they dry out
their condition may be quite different. I do not know who cultivated that prune orchard, but Carson had them for a number of
years, and made quite a fortune out of his ability to make money
in that way. The men who made fortunes out of Calaveras out of
grazing properties, both owned lands and rented, but I do not know
974   what anybody paid for renting lands there.

When I spoke of Patton making quite a comfortable fortune
there, by a comfortable fortune I mean, between $15,000 and
$25,000. He was there as long as I can remember, about 15 or 17
years, and if he made $1,000 a year net, he did very well.

The southerly exposures for vegetables and fruit are better,
and the land, or hill that marks the westerly boundary line of the
Calaveras country, on the westerly side, has more or less of a south-
westerly exposure. On the Calaveras side, it has both north-easterly
975   and easterly exposure. The Portuguese are very careful about selecting a southerly slope to get early vegetables, but this land of
Hanson's goes right across the little valley, and considerable of it
I do not think has so much southerly exposure as it is easterly. I
knew the general location of the land he bought from Snell, and
have been over it, but not recently, and I think he paid $44,000 for
976   it. I loaned him the money to buy it, but I have forgotten the
details. I do not know what was on the place, nor how much an
acre he paid for it when he bought it. There is good hay land, and
good orchard on it, and there is pasture lands and Portuguese hillside land.

When I spoke of the land planted to prune orchards selling at
$300 an acre, that was without the orchards on it. The first few
fruits in a prune orchard come in four years in the Santa Clara
Valley, but we don't count on a crop, or to get your money back
before six years. When we are buying on speculation, we calculate
977   the first six crops to be the good ones. They have only been growing
prunes now since 1880, and long experience shows that you cannot
tell when the biggest crop is going to be. We count on getting the
cost of the work back, and perhaps a profit at six years, and beyond
six. Land worth $1000 an acre, is with a bearing orchard, and gen-
erally the improvements go with it, so I add about $600 or $700 an
acre for the improvements and the bearing crop.

Map 17, 268-u; is quite a distance from the valley. The road
is narrow and rough. The fact of its distance, and so forth, has a
depreciating value. The Coyote lands that I spoke about, is very
near the State Highway, which is along the railroad. I only know

the Colusa prune lands from hearsay, and my knowledge of the 978
prune business is, that the Santa Clara Valley prunes command a
premium over the Colusa prunes. I do not know what the Colusa
prune lands sell for. I am not surprised that one of the heaviest
prune packers states that he prefers to have the Colusa prunes
than the Santa Clara prunes, because anything you can buy for
$20 in one place, and sell at another place for $70 is preferable.
That is why he goes to Colusa to buy them and comes to Santa Clara
to sell them. They are not larger prunes. The range of prunes is
from 20's, which are quite rare, down to 130's, which are also not
too common. Santa Clara produces every one of those grades, from
the best to the poorest.

268-u; I did not go upon this parcel, but I went on 268-t, not
only on the road, but away from the road. We couldn't tell just
where we were. I cannot tell you just the day that trip was made,
but I have made a number of trips to refresh my memory on these
places within the past few weeks. I did not change my valuations,
however, within the last two weeks. I made my valuations from 979
my general knowledge of the lands, and then went over them to
prove that I was right, and I did not change the valuations on any
of those trips. I have taken half a day when I could get it, and I
have taken a whole day when I could get the time to spend on these
trips.

Map 18-A, 268-x; I didn't get in there, but you can see that
very nicely from the two sides that I did get into.

268-v; I did not go on that piece, but saw it from Section 3, 980
Section 34, and Section 35. It is very hard to get on that property,
on account of having to cross both those canyons.

268-r; I did go upon that piece. We crossed from the road
down through there, and the party I was with didn't look for any
trails. If he saw a rock he would jump for it. There is considerable rock in there, and the big slide terminates on that parcel. That
comes in best when the snow is on the ground. The steep sides there
warm up quickly. The grass comes up quickly, and the animals
come earlier in there than in other places, but of course they have
to be in the neighborhood to avail themselves of such warm spots.
In that neighborhood whenever it snows it snows all over. The
north half of Section 28 is considerably better land than that.

Questioned by Master. 981

That is the other 268-r on Map 17, and that is south slope also,
and there is good grazing in there too.

CROSS EXAMINATION BY MR. STEINHART.

I don't admit that the $12 land is better than the $15 land,
on account of the flat in the north half of 34. It is more open and
easier to reach. I cannot tell you where the flats are by looking at

the map, but there are flats there, and if I am not mistaken, it is
on the site of the old school house. I can see that one was better
land than the other, but I may have got those mixed up a little.
Calling my attention to them, as you do now, there is no question
but what the north half of 28 is better than the north half of 34,
on account of accessibility, if the two areas were equal. The north
982   half of 34 is not poor stuff in a grazing country. 268-r is not as
poor as 268-v, and just as steep. I went on 268-v, the 160 acre piece.

983   Map 18-A, ▓▓▓▓; I called that ridge the Marsh road district,
but am not acquainted with what the United States Government
has seen fit to designate it on the topographical map. One of the
good ridges in Santa Clara County they have designated Poverty
Ridge. I don't know where they got such a name. It is very
likely that this happens to be Poverty Ridge that we are talking
about now. I did not know that this one was called Poverty Ridge,
as that is a common name. Some of these places they call Starva-
tion Ridge. I don't know where Poverty Ridge is in this district,
and I went through those sections, and in my opinion, this is not
a bare and wind-swept country, and I disagree with the party who
has the opinion that this is some of the poorest land in the whole
Mt. Hamilton country. I don't think so.

984   Map 18-A, w-268; I went up the bottom of the creek into that,
and the trees were so tall, and the woods so heavy and thick, that
I could not say much about that. That is down in the bottom of
the Arroyo Honda. Outside of looking at it from the adjoining
places, I didn't get a very good impression of it by looking at it
down there. I took that in connection with the adjoining places,
and also the fact that it is a celebrated hunting grounds, and a beautiful camp.

Map 18-A, 241-C; I went on that, and crossed in and out of
there. There is a trail that runs through there, and you get a fine
view of the falls. I did not include in my values the view of the
falls. I took into consideration in valuing that at $15 that they
were pasture lands, and heavily wooded property. Wood is of
good value, and could be snaked out. San Jose buys a great deal
of wood, and although the cost of hauling is high, it means cash
to the people there as they sell it to farmers along the road; it does
not all reach town by any means.

985   241-C; there were ravines and canyons on this parcel, and also
a slide there down in the southeast quarter. While that slide is
very steep, it does not make a great deal of acreage. In including
bottom lands, I would go up to the point—as a general rule—as far
as the soil was deep; as the soil on the hills and the soil on the
valley is distinguishable. I would say that on the opposite side of
the valley, the line of demarcation is very slight, and the gradual
rise in the hills is pretty near as good as the valley, that is on the

westerly side of the valley, which is the side as you come in. The soil is very good, and it is deep. It runs up the hill very nicely, and is rich land. On the easterly side, some of the points that butt out there are steeper, indicating shallowness of soil, and they are not so good as on the other side. It is not difficult to determine what I valued and included as bottom land, if you are in the neighborhood you can kind of walk right up to it. The reservoir line there is a little above the bottom land line of demarcation, and its distance below the reservoir line would be different in each case. I cannot give the ranges from so many feet to so many feet, because if you look over in 327, you will find that 50 feet is all there should be between the reservoir line and the roadway, and the roadway runs along there about the line of good soil. In that 50 feet there is a jump, looking down upon which you would think was 100 feet, and looking up at it you would think it was about 60 or 75 feet. I have seen the white fence posts, showing the level of the reservoir line. This map shows the elevation there to be 800 feet. The Santa Clara Valley runs from nothing up to 321 feet, while the floor of the Calaveras, I estimated, was about 700 feet. I understand the dam is going to be 300 feet high, and as the water level must be the same, the lower portion of the valley will be 300 feet deep, and the extreme south end would peter out to nothing. I think that I mentioned in some of these places, between 321 and 330, on Map 18, the bottom, that land ran up as high as the contour line. I have understood the height of the outlet was 1100 feet, and the floor of the valley I estimated at 700. On 321 I ran my bottom land right up to the marking. In 330 I would consider that it was equally desirable up to the reservoir line. In 331 is a complete change of character of the soil. It is quite uniform up to, and beyond the reservoir line. That is a kind of clay soil, with lots of little fine gravel in it. I do not consider j-268 and k-268 the same character of soil. The fertility would diminish as you go up the hill. My remembrance of the soil in these last two parcels is that it is a kind of a lightish, grayish, gravelish mixture. The clay is the portion above 268-j, marked "2".

In the valuation I included almost all of parcel 324 as being equally valuable. The easterly three 40's are actually more cultivatable, and having more subterranean moisture under it, it would be more productive. There is a hill or two on the westerly side of 324, but not bad. It rises abruptly until you get into the gravelly part of 322, and then it seems to change the slope of the hills, and run southward to these adjoining places with a much more modified grade.

322 is the blue one right below 327. In that one, you will see the ravine runs up the hill quite a distance. As those hills disappear up that canyon on that side, they are all abrupt, and when

283

they come out on the other side, they are not so abrupt. The land in 322 is fine land. I presume you would not call it bottom land, because it does slope, but it is of a rich texture, and would carry a value in selling that would be indisputable without regard to the grade. The grade there is not sufficient to cause annoyance to a farmer, and it could be put under the irrigaton of that small stream with very little effort. The Potham piece is very steep, and a portion of that steepness may run into 322, but it would not be so high as to stop the taking of that water out on levels as high as one would want to go, to work the valuable portions, which I think the reservoir line there would indicate.

991   (Discussion between Counsel as to fairness to Witness in this line of questions.)

There may be some small ravines on parcel 322, besides the large ones. In valuing that property, I did not place much depreciation on the land that is too steep to be called anything but pasture. That is beautifully situated, and there is enough water there

992   to use it to the greatest degree of agricultural development.

Map 18, 268-b; fairly light colored soil. While it runs together when it gets wet, it is not of a character that bakes. It must have a sufficient amount of clay in it to be termed a clayey soil. It is fer-

993   tile and has good productivity. That is not a stiff clay, and there may be an outcropping or two of sandstone, but you cannot say it is all over. I know the place called Monument Peak, but it is not located on that section. It is 2 miles north of that. This is a nice clear field; nice stubble. Monument Peak is on Map 16, in Section 21.

(Mr. Steinhart: I will withdraw that question as to Monument

994   Peak; it is not a fair question.)

DIRECT EXAMINATION BY MR. MCCUTCHEN.

Monument Peak is at least 2½ miles, in fact 3 miles from this land.

CROSS EXAMINATION BY MR. STEINHART.

It is not a fact that that parcel has sandstone outcroppings right straight through that portion of it. This is a beauiful field, and in the lower portions there is a good picket fence around it. As, to the other portion, I cannot tell you how that fence is, but it is not a fact that the fence is a stone fence, composed entirely of stone taken off of that property. I do not say that all this land may not have any stone fence at all. It is possible that from the Calaveras road you can see a pile or two of gathered stones piled up in one or two spots. That is a fine field, nice, and clean and free from stones. There is not a noticeable peak on the land.

SPRING VALLEY WATER CO. VS. CITY AND COUNTY OF SAN FRANCISCO

(Witness advises he was talking entirely of parcel 268-b when   994-996
he was asked if there was a peak on the parcel, and that the portion
by the school house, across the Pueblo Ranch line, has a little rock
in it.

It developed that the witness was talking of land north of the
Calaveras road, whereas the Counsel for Defendant was referring
to the portion south of it.)

SEVENTEENTH HEARING.   AUGUST 6, 1915.

Witnesses: W. S. CLAYTON and WM. W. PARKS.

Certain corrections noted in the inventory and in the transcript.   997-999

CROSS EXAMINATION BY MR. STEINHART.   1000-1001

P-268; These parcels dominated the ridge, and without them
many lands would be affected in value; that is the people who live
above them would starve without the very qualities that these
places present. They cannot get all the year round feed for their
stock. Different seasons require these different elevations and the
changes in the character of the feed throughout the year. On the
higher places, the feed is excellent, at certain times of the year. At
other times, it would be non-profitable.

The feed is excellent in Poverty Ridge. On that entire ridge
it is excellent for the year. The cattle are not eating the grass
on these places at present, because they have eaten what they
wish in the Spring, and they will come back after that grass gets
soft. I cannot answer what season of the year that will be, but it
will be when it gets frosty. My experience with cattle has been in
lending money on them, and watching them very carefully. I have   1002
never been in the cattle business, but we loaned money to those
fellows in the business.

These ridges control the upper reaches to the east, and that is
why I gave them the additional value, but not only for that reason,
but also because the feed is better. It will carry more cattle.

Referring to Map 16, 268-Y; when I spoke of the other ranges,
in which the grass would be short, I meant the adjoining tracts,
where the grass grows in the brush, and they turn the cattle on
those lands when the hay and grain are growing. The hay and   1003
grain grows, speaking in broad terms, from the first of December
to the first of June, and they are liable to have cattle in there in
December, but my own impression would be that it would be from
the first of December through until Spring. That would apply to
the east side also on p-268, as they would have to turn their cattle
up there during that season, as you know feed is scant in Decem-

ber. Without personal knowledge of the month, however, I would say that December is a little too early, that it would be about along in the middle of February that they would turn their cattle into 268-p. Feed becomes short on the other ranges by nature, and by the number of cattle that eat it. I should say that with the stubble of the valley, they could run a bullock to about four acres, and without the stubble, they could not do it with less than 6 to 10 acres. I will not get on the subject of the running of cattle on land around Calaveras, because I do not know the history of the different herds. You have to take into consideration in describing this property, described as an ideal cattle range, that it has not been used to its capacity, and the people who have had the farming of the valley acreage, have not been the people who have been farming the ranges. Carson, a good farmer, was in there for a number of years. He had good horses and was a hay man and cattle man.

There is no sign that the cattle are very hard put for food on any of these tracts to which I have testified as being of a very fine nature cattle ranges.

W-268; The Portuguese farmers that I saw a good many years ago, using a relay of horses to make the cutter travel fast enough for the sickle-bar to cut the hay did not have the extra horses, owing to the steepness of the land. W-268 is the rolling tops of the hills of Mission Ridge. There are rocks projecting in a few places. Canyons run up in there, and you have to farm in between such physical conditions. That parcel is right up at what we call the top of the ridge.

Questioned by Master.

County Road 2518, shown on the map, is east of the crest, which is just about the limit of the brown line, and the line of the Rancho Tullarcitos is supposed to follow the crest. The Pueblo line San Jose is also supposed to follow the crest. Monument Peak is right near where it says "Santa Clara and Alameda County", in 21, and was chosen as the point to mark the county division line. Mission Peak is probably three-quarters of a mile or a mile further north.

CROSS EXAMINATION BY MR. STEINHART.

The crest line comes just a little east of the westerly line of W-268. The lands to the west of such parcels as p-268 have a sufficient value in themselves for other purposes than cattle, such as fruit and vegetables, and that would make the valley lands not dependent on the cattle ranges. The raising of cattle as an auxiliary to consume stubble, etc., would add quite a little income to the farmers of the valley, and for that reason, adjoining hillside would be very desirable. I have never mapped out those sections

1004

1005

1006

on the topographical map, and do not know the elevation of p-268, Map 18.　　　　1007

Parcel 321; Subterranean waters are evidenced there by the growth of vegetation at this time of year after other vegetation has　1008 dried up. I do not know anything about the plane of the subterranean waters there, but I do know that the valley demonstrates the permanency of that plane. Just north of 321 are places where there are natural water spots, and they have to drain the valley. The banks of the creek will demonstrate the depth of the soil, and they show it to be good clay, rich soil, more of an adobe nature in some places, but of the consistency that produces hard, heavy produce. I examined the little creeks in there to determine that. I think the portion where the land would have to be drained　1009 to make an orchard satisfactory, would be in 323, and not very far north of the line dividing 323 and 325. That and the south end of 325 seem to be the wettest place, but it showed very clearly that it was readily drainable.

I think there are about 17 forty-acre tracts in that good land portion of the valley, and to get those, I have taken two of them　1010 out of 325 just north of 323. By counting these 40's, it runs about 680 acres, instead of 1000 acres. There are approximately 100 acres out of parcel 325 that will come in under that description, and there are a few benches even north of that which I have not taken into consideration. The balance of 325 could grow orchard, but it would not be as fine a one as could be raised on the 100 acres. Where water would do damage, one wouldn't go into the fruit　1011 business. As to the depth of the water below that point south of it, I simply take the surface indications, and in a few places, from neglect of the farmer, there are indications showing water at the surface. I know that this condition does not apply very close to the surface, because the creek, itself, has not a large volume of water in it, and it did not appear to me to be a heavy flowing creek during the winter season, on account of the length and breadth of it. I presume it does overflow at times.

Map 17, F-268; I did not give any added value to the tillable portions of this piece nor any lesser value to the untillable portions. I took it all as an entirety. 320 acres at $25 an acre on account of the feeding qualities.　　　　1012

(The Master here stated that the table indicated that the 320 acre piece of this parcel is valued at $30, and the 20 acre piece at $25 per acre. Witness stated that $25 an acre should cover the 320 acres and $30 should cover the 20 acres.)

268-h; I do not know that there is a house there, nor that it is in a habitable condition. Parks lives in 268-j and 268-k. He grows hay, and I think I heard him state this year that he got about 10½, but I don't know how many acres he had, nor how many tons

1013   of hay he had. He has 1200 tons, but it is scattered over a great deal of land, and that contributes its share, when I speak of 10½ tons to the acre.

I have had acquaintance with growers of sugar beets in the Salinas Valley, the San Juan Valley, and the Santa Clara Valley. My experience varies from 15 tons to 25 and 30 tons to the acre, although I have never grown sugar beets myself, and have only had to do with them in connection with dealings with the farmers. I am not familiar with the Alvarado sugar beet country, and do not know how many tons of beets that runs to the acre. I am unacquainted with the Pleasanton country, and do not know how many sugar beets that runs to the acre. I do not know the

1014   Woodland country, nor how many tons to the acre that runs. I can give you an individual instance of a man named Flint, in San Juan, who had 25 tons to the acre some years ago. I have been interested in a number of different ranches that grew sugar beets, but I did not take a sufficient notation of the production to know just who ever did raise 25 tons to the acre, other than this man, Flint. Our interest in these ranches that I mention was simply loaning money on mortgages to people who had those lands. We have not dictated crops in any way, nor interfered with them. The Alvarado country is quite a distinct territory from Santa Clara Valley, and according to my own private opinion, I would not say that it is the best sugar beet country in the state. I gain my knowledge as to what sugar beets need in going through the. Salinas,

1015   San Juan, and Santa Clara Valleys. It is possible that you misinterpreted my remarks that the lands of Calaveras Valley would grow from 20 to 25 tons to the acre in these two sections. These two 80's have not quite as fertile conditions of soil as the bottom of the valley. I would not know how much they would produce per acre. In general terms, I do state, that new land will produce more than land which has been used before for the same purpose. The Alvarado country has been used for sugar beets enough to take off its cream. I don't know whether sugar beets were ever grown in the Calaveras Valley, or whether alfalfa was ever grown there. It does not bear evidence of alfalfa growing, as when an alfalfa field has been plowed up, there are always a few stumps that come back, and I don't see that in the Calaveras Valley.

1016   I do not know how old the Carson prune orchard is, but it bears evidence of age.

Map 18, parcel 330; I have seen grain and hay raised there.

There is a patch of corn growing in the parcel which runs alongside the county road, which I really believe is in parcel 330, although I cannot positively locate it. It is near the corner of

1017   the road. I could not state positively that it was not a volunteer crop, but the land does not bear evidence of its being volunteer.

Map 16, parcel 323. West of the creek, the soil is very rich, and clear of evidences of too much water. East of creek, there is a spot that contains a little wet spot. The balance of the land is very good. It runs up the hill a little ways. The easterly half is rather hilly, but not bad. In valuing this parcel, I considered the rich portions of the land so desirable that it would overcome any acreage of poor land, even if they should be of no value. There is quite a little acreage of hilly land to the east, but I considered myself justified in putting the valuation I did on that, notwithstanding the hilly acreage to the east holds up quite a few acres.

Parcel 324; The westerly portion slightly less desirable than the rest, because it has a slope instead of being perfectly level, and I made a slight reduction because of that fact.

1018

Parcel 328; is the north slope, and is not such bad land in regards to roughness, and is good cattle range. It would be of value to the lands behind it, such as p-268, and it is of more value in conjunction with other lands than it is individually. It is an entrance to the water from those places higher up the hill. When I valued the adjoining lands, I did not depreciate them because of the fact that they needed this adjoining land, and when I came to value p-268, I took into consideration solely its own feed. I remember about there being water on each section, and cattle will go to the nearest water. That does not necessarily mean that the nearest water from p-268 was in the creek in 328, for from whatever portion the cattle may come, if for instance, it would be easier to reach a spring going down hill than going up, they graze along, and do just as the circumstance would dictate to a human being.

1019

In regard to how much it is usual to add for a one-year orchard, it will cost from $50 to $75 an acre to plant an orchard, according to the price of trees the year you plant them. Trees will run 25 cents some years, and 50 cents other years. You plant about 100 trees to the acre. My experience has been we could never sell a one-year old orchard. The trees don't begin to show their value in the first year's growth. $100 ought to cover the cost.

1020

I am not familiar with the sale made opposite the Murphy-Colombat property by E. J. Sharon and McKillip Bros. I know it took place, and I know that it was partly in trade. I can give you the figures if you want them.

(Discussion between Counsel as to what Mr. Holmes told Mr. McDonald about the prune crop in Calaveras Valley not being harvested until October.)

1021

RE-DIRECT EXAMINATION BY MR. McCUTCHEN.

This is a normal season for prunes. Those are extraordinarily developed (referring to a box of prunes shown Witness), and are further along than any I have seen yet.

Mr. McCutchen: We will show later where these came from.

Mr. Steinhart: Oh, if you say that they came from Calaveras, Mr. McCutchen, we will admit it.

1022 I had a talk last night with Mr. Holmes, about the prunes purchased by him from the Calaveras land, and he said they were very good, but at times, when they bore an excessive crop, they appeared to be short in sugar, and did not run up so heavy in weight. The crop of 1914 appeared to run lighter than normal, and he thought they averaged 83 to the pound. The year before they ran 63 to the pound, and the crop of a nearby former year were the finest he 1023 had ever seen. He told me the prunes were delivered to him green, purely as a matter of convenience, and not because they could not be dried in Calaveras Valley. They were hauled six miles from Calaveras Valley to the Holmes Dryer, and he dried them for the Carson Bros. Mr. Holmes is a professional dryer, and a buyer of green prunes. We went through his receipts for the green fruit delivered to him by Carson Bros., and found the last two deliveries 1024 to have been made on December 22nd and 23rd.

September is the usual month for prune crops to be harvested in the Santa Clara Valley. I have sold my crop this year to be delivered a distance of six miles, and will deliver them with horse-drawn vehicles. It is customary to deliver wherever you get the best price. Some times we get a dollar more for delivery at a distance, but that is only used as a subterfuge by the buyer, when the buyer has agreed to pay a certain price. They want a crop that is particularly desirable, and will give the grower a dollar for delivering it. Sometimes they allow a dollar by way of a brokerage charge. It is simply a rise in the price. Milpitas, I think, is about six miles from Calaveras Valley, and it is just nine miles to the 1025 buildings around the dam. Milpitas is a controlling factor in the vegetable trade, and is one of the best markets in the State of California for what we call surface crops, the Portuguese market. Formerly it was the controlling factor in asparagus, but asparagus was found to grow better up in the islands, so it has no longer that market. The California Fruit Canners Association have considered that that territory was so good for their purposes, that they have erected a vegetable cannery there, and have rented many acres of land, all of which represent a total outlay of money by them in that neighborhood of $60,000 or $70,000. I know of freighting of farm produce by horse-drawn and gasoline trucks for a greater distance than six or nine miles. The market at Milpitas is so attractive that Oakland commission men send their trucks down there, and haul the produce to Oakland, or to San Francisco, and I would like to bring out this point, that the accessibility to market dominates the value and the price of land. The fact that the Milpitas and San Jose markets, both of which are virtually head centers for marketing, are there, gives a material advantage, and adds value to these Calaveras lands, as against lands at a greater distance. 1026

I never counted the number of persons that are living in and around that section at the time when the company began to make purchases in 1911. There was a family on the Weller place, W-268, and they are there yet. There was a family on the Santos place, X-268, and they are there yet; a family on the Jacobson place, parcel 295, and there is one there yet. On parcel F-268 there was a family— there is a different family there now. People who were living there in 1911 are pretty well scattered. Every one of these places, or 90 percent of them, show evidences of dwelling houses, and which now you only, find the remains of. The Spring Valley Water Co. has bought out and depopulated the country during a series of forty years, possibly, and it is hard for me to remember which ones have come out since 1911. There was formerly a school house in Calaveras Valley. I have noticed three depopulated school houses; one in Calaveras Valley, one at the Oak Ridge Road, and one down the creek a little ways. Also there are either one or 1027 two school houses up the Felker road on the Santa Clara County map, and called the Sierra road on this map. These are also vacated.

The prune crops in Colusa County do not bring as good a price as those produced in Santa Clara County. The market allows a differential of a quarter of a cent a pound on those produced in Santa Clara County.

Questioned by Master.

This is as against any other county. It is quoted in the papers that Santa Clara prunes are one-quarter of a cent extra. The trade rates them much different. The real fact is that the quality is much different.

RE-DIRECT EXAMINATION BY MR. MCCUTCHEN.

The rolling lands in Calaveras are partially possible of irrigation from the water supply on themselves or from the adjoining property. It would be a commercial possibility to pump water for the irrigation of these lands that are sufficiently level, to admit of irrigation. You cannot get a correct idea of the topography of these bench and bare lands which can be cultivated from an automobile or wagon, because, generally the roads are in the lower 1028 places. The best way is to get up on the hills. I have a photograph taken from the Priesker place, 268-i, which shows some of the 1028-1029 land that I was asked about yesterday, and asked whether it was not "abrupt". This photograph is looking northwest the length of the valley.

Photograph offered and received in evidence as "Plaintiff's Exhibit 37".

There is cattle on the range now where I stated that the cattle ate the feed to the grass roots, and they are in fine condition. The land on which the wet places are, could be drained at a very slight expense, and after being drained, I think the land is very finely adapted to growing fruit, and the fact that there are different depths to the water plane, makes it also desirable, because different varieties of fruit grow in different depths of the soil. Pears are a very profit-
1030   able proposition, and they like water near the surface. The Calaveras Valley, in times past, has produced as fine peaches as the canneries in San Jose could get. Prunes are a good staple crop. I don't think there is anything in the valley that mitigates against raising fruit to a very profitable degree.

The land of Mr. Fleming is in the Dougherty and Randall tract, south of the Murphy-Colombat tract. It had the reputation among the real estate agents in San Jose of being poor land, very hard to sell, low values.

RE-CROSS EXAMINATION BY MR. STEINHART.

In that case Mr. Fleming bought poor prune land; he must have just speculated. The Murphy-Colombat tract had some wonderfully nice land upon it, and also some poor land. I don't think the Sharon
1031   land is very superior.

Referring to the different depths of water planes in Calaveras: there are wet places there where water makes some big growths, and in the south end of the valley there is good evidence of lack of water. Between those two, I would infer that if one planted an orchard, they would have to look out for the depth of the water, although I never bored for it.

Referring to photograph of Calaveras Valley, introduced by Counsel for Defendant: these little buildings here look as if they were the men's camps and the dining room, and the hills against which these buildings rest, are the hills on the west side of the valley. I think it was taken from the Oak Ridge Road, as it leaves the valley. Marked "Defendant's Exhibit 38".

Parks   Witness: WM. W. PARKS.

DIRECT EXAMINATION BY MR. OLNEY.

1032   I live in Calaveras Valley, and went out there in 1881. I have been there ever since, and am acquainted with land around Calaveras Valley. I have lived on Section 26, Township 5 south, Range 2 east, which is about 7 miles due east of the valley, between Alameda Creek and Arroyo Honda. I lived there from 1881 until about 1903 or 1904, and have lived the rest of the time right in the Calaveras vicinity, at the place known as the Bayne Ranch, and the William's Place. The Bayne Place is less than half a mile from the dam site. The William's place is at the extreme south end of the valley. My occupation is cattle and farming. I have been carrying it on right in the Calaveras vicinity, and have had all the water company's lands east of the valley for seven years. Now I am renting the land west of the valley, and the valley also. I have been raising cattle, farming, buying and selling also. I think I am familiar with all of the Spring Valley Water Co.'s properties in that vicinity. I have all, except about 3000 acres, under lease now, and am very familiar with it. I know the ruling prices of lands of the character of Spring Valley Water Co.'s lands in that neighborhood, but only from sales. I don't know any of their sales other than hearsay. I am acquainted, in a general way, as to what can be done with this property for agricultural and stock purposes.   1033

Map 16, parcel 223, in Section 14; as you leave the valley at the dam site, going up the Sunol road, traveling north-westerly of the dam site, there are about 60 acres of farming land there. It has been farmed up to two years ago for 8 or 10 years, by Bill Carson.

Parcel 223 is almost directly north of the dam site, and there is   1034
very good pasture land in there; value being $30. The market value of this land would have been higher on December 31, 1913, for the cattle business, than it is today, but there is really no difference in the market value. This is simply grazing land, and beef was higher then than it is today. There has been pretty nearly a cent difference on beef between then and now, and that is what that land would be used for, for grazing. If beef was high, the land would be worth more money. In 1913 beef was higher by three-quarters of a cent than it is today. Referring to the 440 acres in section which includes the forks of the creek, I would not consider that there is a great deal of difference in the value of land on December 31, 1913, and today. I would value it just the same today, and I valued that at $30 an acre. I have paid $110 for three months of that land, to put steers on last year. That is what I valued the grazing at.

Parcel 258, northwest quarter of Section 18, known to me as the   1035
Miller property—by the Brannan property—the Rideout property, is rough, and there is some timber. Valuable for grazing purposes and wood. My valuation would be mostly for grazing, as it is all good for that. Valued at about $15. The Brannan place, marked Parcel 246, being the balance of Section 18, is very good grazing land. I have seen 100 acres of it farmed. The balance is very good grazing land, and I valued the 474 acres at $30.

Parcel 225, 1720 acres, containing portions of Sections 14 and 24. There is always a field at the dam site that could be plowed, before they commenced work on the dam. Some farming land in that piece,

1036   perhaps some 20 acres, and the rest is very good grazing land. The farming land is located just where the houses are built now to accommodate the men, or the officials. That used to be known as the Old Steamboat House to me.

I am very well acquainted with the county road which runs up by the little creek. That is the Sunol Road, and runs in at what we know as the Bayne place. There is more than 20 acres of farming land in there. There is that portion that they tore up for the pumping station. It runs clear across to the east, and takes in a part of that. Valued at $60 an acre. There are 60 acres there north of the road,

1037   just after you leave the dam, and start to Sunol. The farming land of which I speak was right north on the road from the houses at the dam site, which runs up the little canyon, and over the hill, down to Sunol. After you leave the camp site, you go up that canyon about a quarter of a mile, and get in to where Carson farmed up to the top of the hill; the farming land lying north of the road. Two years ago Carson cut a volunteer crop of 120 acres of hay. I put a valuation on these 60 acres of farming land of $60 an acre. There is no other farming land on that tract that I know of. The balance of the parcel is very good grazing land, and worth $30 an acre, including this part of 24, which lies east of the creek, and it goes into that one tract. The tract of 30 or 35 acres is inside of the reservoir site, but there is not over two or three acres, or four or five acres of the tillable land up to the road going to Sunol, that is in the reservoir site. The rest of the

1038   land in the reservoir site would be pasturage land.

W-268, 646 acres; Weller place. 200 acres of farming land, now farmed by Mr. Wool, who has been farming it for at least three or four years. Valued at $100 an acre on the farming land. The balance is fair land, all pasture, higher than the other. Valued at $25 an acre. Two years ago they had grain-barley on this Weller place, and harvested about 4000 sacks of barley, but I do not know at what it was sold, but it is easy to figure, as I know about what prices were along about that time. Those prices vary. Last year I could have bought feed barley for 90 cents, but before the season was over, I paid $1.86 for it. Barley from that country will run ordinarily from 108 to 112 lbs. to the sack.

1039   E-241; Crocker & Dillon piece, in the middle of Section 23. The extreme west side is very rough, and the entire piece contains about 240 acres. At least 100 acres of that is very rough, being right up in the canyon. I put a value of about $10 an acre on that rough stuff. The balance of 140 acres is pretty good feed land; good grazing land; which I valued at $25 an acre. The rough land lies above the reservoir, and it is the grazing land that is in the reservoir. There is a big bald hill at the northwest corner, very good grazing land. The very rough land lies at the southwest end of this property.

Parcel 320, Chapman Flat, is marked on the map as the Alameda Water Co., and contains 120 acres. 60 acres of fair farming land in the bottom. Land down in that section of country is lighter than it is in the valley, and really belongs in the valley farming. I do not consider that as good as the valley land. It is irrigable, and I put a valuation of $75 an acre on it. The balance is good grazing property, valued at $30 an acre. 1040

Questioned by Master.

60 acres at $75, and 60 acres at $30. The farming land in this parcel is below the white posts of the reservoir, and the reservoir contains all of the $75 land. Some of the rougher land is also inside the reservoir.

DIRECT EXAMINATION BY MR. OLNEY.

Parcel 327, Cedarbloom place; 80 acres immediately south of the Chapman piece. Some farming land on that, but has not been farmed for a number of years. A point in this piece was always considered Carson's place, and he used to put his young colts up there in order to wean them. About 30 acres of farm land in there, worth $60 an acre, is hilly land. The balance of 50 acres is good grazing land, being a warm place, which produces good feed. I valued that at $30. The 30 acres of farming land are above the reservoir line, so that all of the land in the reservoir site is the grazing land. You have to go up an old road to get up to the farming land. 1041

Parcel 325, Gaines' property; 124 acres of sub-irrigable land. There are two 40's, two 20's and a 12. Those five pieces of land are right in the bottom adjoining the orchard. The soil is a black loam adobe. I don't think there was ever any soil any better than that soil. Sub-irrigable land is described in this way: I cut my hay this year, and could not pick out over half of it, as the green stuff stood as high as this table. It was the moisture from the bottom rising all the time. As soon as you leave that territory of ground, you get into dryer ground, that I consider is not sub-irrigable. That is, the water does not rise up and cause the stuff to grow. I think, without any doubt, alfalfa could be raised on this land. It is as fine alfalfa land as ever was. On that particular piece of ground you could raise alfalfa without irrigation. There are ditches running all the way through it for drainage. That shows you what the water underneath the land must be. To farm that land, Carson put in many and many a cross ditch to get it dry enough. This year I had to haul the baled hay out in order to keep the bottoms of the bales from rotting out. I have 400 steers in that ground now. Before I could get the hay baled, and it has been baled now two weeks, there was as good a second crop as the first crop. It is good grass there too. Red Top and Jackass clover. You cannot handle that land unless you keep the ditches open. I consider that is sub-irrigable land. 30 acres, which lie east of the Rasmussen or Gaines house, is good level farming land. It is irrigable, 1042

1043

295

but not sub-irrigable. On the sub-irrigated land I put a valuation of $400, as I think anything on earth will grow on it, and on the 30-acre piece, not sub-irrigated, I put a value of $175 an acre. There is an orchard of pears and prunes on this property of about 25 acres. This orchard is irrigable land, but is really on sub-irrigated land. Leaving the orchard out of consideration, I would put a valuation of $400 on it, the same as I did on the other. The orchard was not included in that 132 acres. The acreage of sub-irrigated land is made up in detail of two 40's, one 20 and two 12's, which make the total of 124, instead of 132, as I gave it before.

1044

CROSS EXAMINATION BY MR. SEARLS.

There are 25 acres prunes and pears in the orchard.

DIRECT EXAMINATION BY MR. OLNEY.

I have seen that orchard recently, and there is a very good average crop on it. In this piece there is 124 acres of sub-irrigated land, 25 acres of orchard, which is also sub-irrigated land, and 30 acres of irrigable land. There is some hill farming land directly south of the 30 acres that run out from the house. There are about between 20 and 25 acres of that, valued at $100. The balance of the section is very good pasture land, valued at $30. All of the sub-irrigated land is in the reservoir, as is also the orchard, and the 30-acre tract of irrigable land. The 20 acres of farming hill land is mostly above the posts. There may be one-third of it below the posts, and the balance of the

1045 land would be the pasture land. To my knowledge there has never been a failure in the orchard, and the condition of the sub-irrigated land in dry years has been fine. I never saw a year where we did not have crops to feed in that locality, from Black Mountain to the Milpitas line. Two years ago, which was a very dry year, Mr. Carson baled 1800 tons of hay. California never suffered so much as it did two years ago. It was the toughest year we have ever had. Still we sold beef. I sold my hay for $23. Mr. Carson offered to sell 1500 tons of hay at that time for $24 a ton, and the buyer offered $22.50.

Parcel 322, Pomeroy place; I know it quite well. There is a 32-acre field lying right along Pomeroy Creek. 24 acres of it fine veget-

1046 able land. Mr. Carson, and Mr. Pomeroy grew vegetables there. It is as good vegetable land as anybody can find. There is a stream of water running alongside of it to irrigate from. 66 acres of farming land across the creek; the rest is pasture land. The balance of the 32-acre field is A-1 farming land. The 24-acre piece is irrigable land, and I valued it at $250 an acre. The 8 acres in the same field, I valued at $150. I estimated 66 acres of farming land, hilly, and not so good as some of the farming land adjoining it. I valued that at $75; the balance is very good pasture, valued at $30. The 24 acres of vegetable land lie inside the reservoir site, and there are about ten acres of the hill farming land, or possibly more, which lie in the reservoir site. The balance of the pasture land, and of the hill land, lies outside the reservoir site. Going by the white signs that mark the height of the water, and not according to the map, the 32-acre field practically lies all inside the reservoir site. The fence runs along in those gulches, or flat places in there, and lots of those sign boards have been torn down, which makes it rather hard to remember. All of the vegetable land is inside, and possibly half the 8 acres, and about 10 or 12 acres of the farming land on the other side of the creek.

1047

Parcels 323 and 324; the Ham and Harris pieces together, commonly known as the Harris, or Wells place; lies due south of the Pomeroy place and the Gaines place. 200 acres of A-1 sub-irrigable land in that tract, valued at about $400. On extreme west about 120 acres of hill land, is being farmed, and has been farmed for 30 years. Valued at $100. On the east side, I have seen as good potatoes grown many years ago, as I have ever seen grown in California. About 50 acres in that patch not included in the 200 acres of sub-irrigable land. This I valued at $150 in the condition it is in now. The balance is very good pasture land; valued at $30.

1048

Y-268; Popham piece; 120 acres, immediately west of the Pomeroy and Harris places. Very rough; grazing, wood and timber; second rate or third rate grazing ground. Pretty rough stuff, valued at about $15.

X-268; Santos place; immediately west of the Popham place, and south of the Weller place. Farming land and pasture land. At least 100 acres, or more, of farming land, which I valued at $100. The balance is very fair grazing land; valued at $25.

1049

Section 19; Crocker & Dillon property; 634 acres. Very good for grazing purposes. At least 80 acres have been farmed, but is now used for grazing purposes. I place a valuation of $30 on Section 19, A-241. I valued the whole section at $30 an acre, including 36 acres in the reservoir, and 598 acres in the watershed. I think the land in the reservoir site is about the same as that in the watershed.

1050

Map 17, parcels H-268 and e-268, Section 20; it is a very good section, and some times known as the Walker place. He raised hay there, and it contains at least 60 or 70 acres of farming land, used at the present for pasture. It is very good. I put a value of $30 on that.

Map 16, parcel 328 and 329; 240 acres, known as the Dave Jeffery place; I am familiar with that, and the character of the land is very rough. It is good for grazing, with some wood on it. Valued at $15. There is no difference between the watershed and the reservoir lands, and my valuation of $15 an acre will apply to both.

1051

Map 16, parcel p-268, the Jack Jeffery place, Section 30: I know it well. It is very good feed land. That is, grazing land, which I valued at $25 an acre.

E-268; Mendoza piece, north half of Section 8; very good feed land, but high up. Good open ground, and good land for that country. Valuable for grazing purposes. Valued at about $15.

1052

F-268, south half of the same section; the Hughes place. Not any clearer ground, but is in a warmer line. Just goes into the snow belt, and is a little better ground. Valued at $17.50.

Parcels E-268, F-268 and G-268, Section 16; altogether containing 640 acres. Rough grazing land at $15 on the entire section.

E-268, northwest quarter of Section 12, part of the Mendoza property; I have been on it many and many a year. It is high and cold; good for grazing purposes at certain times of the year. Worth about $6 an acre. That high ground is badly needed at times. For instance, in the lower country, our feed starts to dry up in the middle of May. The cattle have not finished feeding, and if they can follow the snow line, there is no snow there to speak of, but as it is colder up there, the grass is later, and as long as you can keep cattle on green stuff, they are going to do well and get fat. There are times of the

1053

year when that ground is valuable for finishing up the cattle.

B-241, Section 29; I am very well acquainted with that particular section. It is rough in character; not good for anything but pasture. The entire section is worth $15 an acre.

r-268 and q-268, Section 28, north half of the southwest quarter; fair grazing land; farmed only in spots, and amounts to nothing. I put a value of $20 an acre on 480 acres in that section.

r-268 and s-268, Section 22, the southwest quarter and the south half of the southeast quarter. Rough and high, and not useful for

1054

anything but pasturage. Valued at $10 per acre.

Section 26, the west half of the west half, the southeast quarter of the southwest quarter, the south half of the northeast quarter, and the southeast quarter, 440 acres; is fair grass land, but high. Not so rough, but pretty fair grazing. Valued at $10 an acre. I lived on the adjoining quarter for not less than 18 years of my life.

Map 18-A, parcel C-241, Section 33; fair grazing land for the height it is in. Valued at about $15 an acre.

Parcels r-268, v-268 and w-268, Section 34; part of that is fair, the other part rough. All grazing land; turns off lots of feed. I think I would subdivide it for the purpose of valuing the land. The northwest half $15, and the southeast half at $10.

Questioned by Master.

The high part of the section is the northwest half, but that is clear. The southwest half takes you down into the rough part. The northwest half is good feeding ground, but it is high; that is what

1055

holds the value down. You could call it the north half, and could indicate it by drawing a diagonal right through the center of the section as she lies.

DIRECT EXAMINATION BY MR. OLNEY.

The 320-acre piece, r-268; the north half I would value at $15, as it is all open, fine grazing land, but the south half runs down into Honda Creek, and becomes rough. I valued that at $10.

Parcel e-268, Section 36; high, but good grazing land of its kind. Valued at $8.

p-268, 640 acres in Section 4; the south half of that section clear, good feed, and grazing ground. The north half that tips toward Honda is not so good. The south half I value at $25 an acre, and the north half at $15.

Section 10, immediately to the southeast of Section 4, contains 480 acres, is clear and high, having no brush; is in the snow line. Value per acre $10.

v-268 and x-268, Section 2; very rough; valued at about $6 an acre.

Map 18, z-268; Brandt place; also known as the Pat Murray place. Contains 40 acres. About 12 acres of farming land on it, and the rest is pasture land. I put a valuation of $40 per acre for the entire quarter section.

Questioned by Master.

I valued the farming land at $60, and the pasture land at $30. I may have figured that a little wrong, but I valued the whole thing at $40 straight through. When I placed my valuation of $40 on it, I classified it by the farming land alongside of it.

DIRECT EXAMINATION BY MR. OLNEY.

Parcel 321, the Carson home piece, or the Campbell piece; beginning at the creek, and going west to the road; 15 acres of orchard, 80 acres of A-1 farming land, irrigable land; 42 acres of the same class of land between the ditch and the road. The 15 acres of orchard is very good, and has a good crop on it of prunes and a few apricots this year. The prunes are all commencing to color up nicely. The orchard land is irrigable, but is not sub-irrigated land. Leaving the orchard out of consideration, I put a valuation on that land of $200 per acre. The 80 acres of irrigable land I valued at the same price. The 42 acres I placed the same value on. Going still further west, you are running into hilly farming land. There are about 60 acres that lie west of the house that is good farming land, and about 80 acres lying south or southwest of the house, of hill farming land. Then about 100 acres in what is known as the Roderick place, on the west of the two described pieces of land, that is about half farming and about half pasture. The 60-acre piece is farming land, and has a crop on it today. I valued that at $100. The 80-acre piece is the same class of land, with the same value. That land is producing right now about a ton and a quarter to the acre. The 100 acres is fully 50 per-

1056

1057

1058

1059

299

cent farming land. The balance is very good pasture land, which I would value at $30 an acre. The farming land, I value at $75 an acre. There is about half and half. The land immediately east of the creek is farming land; 50 acres irrigable valley land. I put a value of $175 on that. The balance of the tract is pasture land at $30 an acre. Good open land. All the level land is in the reservoir site; that would be 1060 the 80, the 42, and the orchard. There is about 15 acres that is west of the road and below the water level, and that is made up of the $100 farming land. There are 60 acres on the east side all farming land that is in the reservoir.

Parcel 330, John Sherman place, 311 acres; it is divided into three fields. The valley field has 131 acres. West of the road the hill field has 120 acres; east of the road there are 60 acres, all farming land. The 131 acres of valley land can be irrigated. The soil is getting lighter there, and I valued that at $150 per acre. The 120 acres of hill land I value at $100.

(The witness here explained that when he was describing the 131-acre piece, he understood that he had been questioned about the 60-1061 acre piece, and described that, and not the 131-acre piece.)

The 131 acres which lie west of the creek is good land, flat, all level, and capable of irrigation. This I valued at $200 an acre. About 3 acres of the 60 acres of the $150 land on the east, do not lie in the reservoir site. About 85 acres lying on the west of the $100 land do not lie in the reservoir site. The remainder is in the reservoir site. I just estimated the amount of land to the west, and it may be 77 acres instead of 85, but it is made up of the land that I described as farming land, and valued at $100 an acre.

Parcel 331, the Sam Sherman piece; 160 acres. 90 acres of level ground, good soil, well located for irrigation. Valued at $200. 1062 There is about 60 acres of hill land, farming land, rather light soil, valued at $75. The balance of the section, about 10 acres made up of roughness. The corner that runs up to the Collins place, is very rough and brushy. The condition of the 10 acres, so far as water is concerned, is fine. A stream of water runs through there, and there is a good deal of wood which can be sold. Valued at about $25 an acre. The 10 acres is above the white posts which mark the water level, and is at the corner that runs up to the Beverson and Patton property. The entire 90 acres of the $200 land lies inside the reservoir site. The balance, outside of the 10 acres, is of the hill land, valued at $75 an acre; so that I would have, in the watershed, 10 acres of rough land, and 54 acres of farming land.

g-268, Patton place; 160 acres. That is light, and is all farming land with the exception of about 20 acres. It is hilly land. I 1063 farmed it for three years myself, and I value that hill farming land at $75. The 20 acres not farming land is grazing, wood and timber. It would not be of any use without that corner. There is a good deal of water there, and it has to come in conjunction with that land to make it right. I valued that at $30.

a-268, over against the Brandt-Hansen place on the west, I am not familiar with.

b-268; 197 acres. I am very well acquainted with that place. About 30 acres lies south of Calaveras road; 10 acres of that is rough; 20 acres of it good hill farming land.

Questioned by Master.

This will fix this piece—the Brandt-Hansen piece, about 30 acres down here. There is no number on that; that is south of the Calaveras road, in the extreme southeast corner of Section 35. 22 acres of this land lie above the hog-back the road passes through. The 30 acres in that piece have always been considered south of the road and below the road.

DIRECT EXAMINATION BY MR. OLNEY.

It actually lies below the road in altitude, but when you come over to the west, there is a piece containing 22 acres south of the road, which is actually above the road. The road is in the saddle of the hill and brings that 22 acres above the road. That is the piece that runs down to the Sierra School House, and is outside the watershed. Part of the water from there runs into Harrison Gulch, and empties toward Santa Clara Valley. The 22 acre piece is all farming land. It is farmed this year. I valued that at $75 an acre. Referring to the 30 acre piece, the 10 acres of rough land in that I valued at $15 an acre, and the 20 acres at $60 an acre; it lies off where it is a little colder. It is part of the Phoebe Brandt place still, and is farming land with some good springs. Three of the A-1 springs of the country are situated on this piece. It is all farming land, and there is a ravine through it. I value that at $75 an acre.

f-268, King piece; containing 85 acres; same type, but no where near as good land as the Brandt-Hansen property, because it is broken up too badly. There is a good deal of wood there, and some farming. Valued at about $30 an acre. There are 3½ acres in the reservoir, but there is no difference between the reservoir and farming land so far as the value goes. There is too large a ravine running through it.

e-268, Dennis Cullen place; 82 acres. 60 acres of farming land, being good hill farming land, which I valued at $80 an acre. The 22 acres that remain are grazing land, valued at about $30 an acre. A good deal of timber and water there. Lies right in the head of two canyons that corner there.

c-268, Levy piece; immediately west of the Dennis Cullen place, all farming land, excepting one broken end that lies over adjoining this parcel of land known as the Brandt-Hansen property; 140 acres of good farming land, valued at $75 an acre, and 15 acres of broken

1067   pasture land for grazing purposes, at $25 an acre. There has been an orchard just planted on what is known as the Ede property, which adjoins this on the west. They are planting some oranges and some apricots, mostly apricots on the Ede place. The Levy place is within the watershed.

i-268, Priesker place; there are 60 acres of land lying north of the Sierra road; 100 acres lying on the summit south of the road, and the balance against the Bolinger Ranch. Referring to the 60
1068   acres, two-thirds of that is farming land, and is farmed today; the balance has broken pieces of land through it. There are 40 acres of farming land in there, and I would value that at $70 an acre. The 20 acres I value at $20 an acre. The 100 acres that lie right on the summit is good farming land, and well worth $75 an acre. The balance of the land, against the Bolinger Ranch, becomes rough. It is farmed in the hollows and the hills. Not much over one-third of that farmed. Would be A-1 pasture land. I value that at about $40. It would outclass good grazing land by leaving in the farming land.

Parcel n-268, Ferrerra place; containing 58 acres, a short distance east of the Priesker place. It is good grazing land outside of the road running there; a little vineyard on it, but the vineyard has practically become dead. I valued that at $25 an acre.

Parcel o-268; the E. B. & A. L. Stone Ranch; containing 9 acres. I would give that the same valuation. It is all clear, and very good
1069   pasture ground.

EIGHTEENTH HEARING.   AUGUST 9, 1915.

Witnesses: W. W. PARKS and W. J. MARTIN.

1070   DIRECT EXAMINATION BY MR. OLNEY.

Referring to Maps 16 and 18, parcels 323 and 324; the 65 acres of watershed land on the west side was $100 farming land, and the
1071   20 acres watershed on the east side was $30 pasture land. There is a prune orchard on the south side of the valley near the top of the mountain, and near the Sierra road, and lying directly south of the Dennis Cullen place, and west of the Patton place. (Cullen place, e-268; and Patton place g-268.) This orchard is in good shape, being about 15 years old, and showing a very good growth. The land occupied by it is the same as the Patton, or Cullen place. It is hilly land, the balance being farming and orchard land. No other orchard of any size in that locality, outside of family orchards,
1072   such as on the Bolinger place, which contains probably 50 trees, which are in very good condition.

Map 18, D-241; northeast quarter and east half of the northwest quarter of Section 31; very good grazing land, valued at $30 an

302

acre. There is no distinction in this piece between the land which is below the white posts which mark the water level, and that which is above.

The John Sherman property, parcel 330, which is east of the road from Milpitas, as you get into the valley, is now planted to corn. The corn is in the adjoining field, from where the road turns   1073 directly north and is less than 200 feet to the corner of the corn. It was planted between the 20th of April and the 1st of May, by a boy named Manuel George, who is farming with me on shares. It has not been irrigated, is there now, and is a very good crop.

Questioned by Master.

This is the first year that corn has been planted, and it is just ready to pick now. It is wheat corn and very good corn.

DIRECT EXAMINATION BY MR. OLNEY.

The corn is harvesting now, and it will probably be three weeks before they get it all off. This corn is in the extreme south end of the valley, which is the poorest land for corn and vegetables, but this is a very good crop, so I am informed by corn men. I have raised other vegetables in the valley but they are on the southeast 1074-1075 side. I have some tomatoes that have been ripe about a week or ten days, and I have cucumbers and summer-squash. All of these I have irrigated.

Parcel j-268, Williams estate; 80 acres; 37 acres farming land, level; value $75 an acre; balance pasture or grazing land; value $30 an acre. The white line of the reservoir runs right at the base of the mountain, which is the farming land that lies on the level; the outer edge of the farming land is really the outer edge of the reser-   1076 voir site. All the 37 acres lie within the reservoir site. I live on the line of these two properties, within 100 feet of the line of j-268 and just inside of k-268, the Mary Williams property, about 150 feet from the line of the two properties.

Parcel k-268, Mary Williams place; 45 acres farming land, valued at $75 an acre. The balance is both grazing and farming, and valued at $35 an acre. I have farmed this property for five years, for hay, and have gotten from a ton and a quarter to a ton and a half per acre off from it.

Questioned by Master.

It was red oat hay and is on the ground now. I sold it to the San Jose Water Co. at $12 a ton. All the pasture land is without the reservoir site, leaving the reservoir site entirely made up of   1077 farming land.

DIRECT EXAMINATION BY MR. OLNEY.

Parcel A-345, Auctioneer-Bland place, 79.33 acres. 25 acres of very good farming land at $75. Balance is grazing land, valued at $25. The land within the reservoir is farming land, and is made up   1078 of $75 an acre land.

h-268, Patterson place; 25 acres good farming land, valued at $75 an acre. I have farmed it for three years; balance grazing land; rough, well timbered, with plenty of water; valued at $25 an acre.

l-268; 321 acres; old Carrick home; 70 acres of farming land, valued at $60 an acre; balance very good pasture land, at $30 an acre. The 70 acres of farming land, I have farmed myself.

m-268; 180 acres; a part of the Carrick place; 60 acres farming land, valued at $60 an acre; balance grazing land at $20 an acre. I have tilled the farming land in this tract.

1079   Parcel p-268, called the Billie Wright place. I am acquainted with this property, and all of it is very good grazing land, which I valued at $30 an acre.

Section 32, parcel p-268 and y-268, containing 640 acres; one is called the northeast half of Section 32, and known as the hog ranch; the northwest quarter is known as the Dixon Place. The

1080   southeast quarter is known as the Fennell property. The north half, which is very rough, I valued at $15 an acre, and on the south half, which is very good land, I placed a value of $30 an acre. I think that the land being in one piece, is worth as much, if not more, than what I have appraised it at parcel by parcel. To get at that valuation, I have appraised each parcel piece by piece. I am familiar with those parcels and have been for years. In placing a value upon this property, I have not considered the question of water supply at all, any more than the water for the use of the range. It would make an A-1 cow ranch, because it is made up of a country that practically lies all under the snow, and does not get cold enough to hurt cattle as long as you have feed. I value it very high, because of that valley being there for green feed in the Fall, and also to produce all the hay you need before the green feed is on

1081   the ranges. Also you have feed in the valley when the cows come off the ranges. A cow ranch without that insurance as to feed, would not be worth much, in my estimation, because you must have a place where you can carry hay over from one year to the other. If you have a dry year, hay will go up if feed is scarce. A man, one year after another, can cut hay enough to insure his cattle over any ordinary season that we ever have had in that country. If it is dry there, it is dry all over. My main experience with cow ranches has been right there. I have bought and sold cattle for the past 12 or 14 years. I have shipped cattle from Mexico; from several parts of Nevada, and from many parts of California in there. I have seen most of the cow ranches in California and know them very well. By making this particular property into smaller acreage, it could be subdivided, so as to make more than one good cattle ranch. There are about three grades of pasture land on that range of mountains. The extreme top land, up to Black Mountain, Mt. Lewis, or any of that high country, will take about nine acres to keep a bullock for a year. Down next to the valley I have fattened 584 steers on about 5½ acres this year. They came in on the ground last October, and have already gone to market. They have not cleaned up all the pasture, and I figure there is forty percent of that feed left this year. Other years, which have not been so strong, there probably would have been from twenty to twenty-five percent left, as I figure this was a 15% better year for grazing.

Questioned by Master.

When I said 5½ acres, I meant per steer, on the foothills adjoining the valley, which is the land that I have appraised as grazing land at $30 an acre.

DIRECT EXAMINATION BY MR. OLNEY.

The third grade of land is land that I have appraised at $15, $20, $22.50 and $17.50. This land you reach as you climb up the hill and get into the snow lines. It is worth about $6 or $8 an acre up in the rougher country. As you gradually drop down it gets to be worth more, as it produces more feed, and the grass is better.

Questioned by Master.

I figure that that would run about 6½ to 7 acres a steer; the poor lands from about 8 to 9 acres, according to our season.

DIRECT EXAMINATION BY MR. OLNEY.

There was some alfalfa grown 14 or 15 years ago on the property known as the Harris & Ham property. That is the only alfalfa that I ever have seen growing in the valley. I saw it, I suppose, two or three times, and I imagine that was within, say a year and a half. It was sub-irrigable land, and right in back of the house. Mr. Wells used to put the calves in there, and he raised the alfalfa without irrigation, as he never had any way of putting water on it. Alfalfa has not been raised on this land, simply because you cannot get a lease long enough to operate, as the leases are from year to year, and that is as long as they will issue them for. My lease runs from year to year, and there is a clause in it that provides that they can throw me out without any cause whatever in 60 days, and in 30 days if I violate any of the clauses in the lease. There is no waste land in the valley, but there is foul land there, because they would never allow anybody to put cattle in behind the crops, and naturally it grew up strong and went to seed before the farmer could get around to it again to take care of it. It is not foul land. The only trouble is you cannot use the land, as after you harvest your crop, this heavy stuff will grow up, and it is hard to get out. Cattle will clean that all out in two years' time, if they will allow you to pasture it. That has been the cause of the foul-

1082

1083

1084

ness of the valley. At the south end, where I have been for a number of years, and they did not hold any restrictions on my pasturing, the land was absolutely clean.

CROSS EXAMINATION BY MR. STEINHART.

1085   I have never figured the value of this ranch (Harris and Ham) as a whole. I have been on the San Ardo Ranch, which is just below Bradley, and also on the Santa Margharita Ranch, which is the J. H. Henry

1086   ranch. I do not know the Eureka Ranch. These prices that I have figured did not mean that the land would sell for that, as I figured only that it would pay interest on this money at a rate of from 6% to 7%. Those small parcels, I figured, were worth the amount I placed on them. That portion of the Wells place, being 200 acres at $400 an acre, would figure $80,000 for the whole portion. I have not heard of many ranches of 200 acres selling in Santa Clara County for $80,000, but I can tell you of a ranch sold at Eden-

1087   vale for $1000 an acre. I compare the Wells place with this Edenvale land, which was the Sheriff Estate, and was within a mile or a mile and a half from the state highway, and close to Edenvale. He bought it about five months ago with some small improvements on the place. I do not own any land, nor have I ever bought $80,000 worth of land in my life. I have been in and around the valley since 1881, and have had experience in running cattle on the Crocker-Dillon land, which I rented before I rented the Spring Val-

1088   ley land. I am carrying some Crocker-Dillon land now in partnership with S. D., but I could not tell you the acreage. I think there are some there within the neighborhood of from 4000 to 6000 acres. We pay about $165 or $170 a section. I rent about 11,000 acres from the Spring Valley Water Co. and Archie Parks is interested with me in the Spring Valley lease. The Crocker-Dillon land we have held under lease in the family, and Sam, my elder

1089   brother, is carrying it on today. I have been leasing from Spring Valley since 1907 or 1908, but none of my family had been leasing before that. The Sheriff place in Edenvale is 97 acres. My brother Sam is not interested in the Spring Valley lease. My brother Archie is the only one who is. Two years ago, I ran about 1200 head of cattle but that was before I took over this valley property. I started in with the Spring Valley people with 1340 acres, and each year I gained some property. The Crocker-Dillon land, which I

1090   had first, I got in the early nineties. Before I got the Carson place, I was renting 8000 acres from Spring Valley and in the Springtime, ran about 1200 head of cattle. This is the time when we are running the most cattle, and during that time we ran the Crocker-Dillon land and the Spring Valley land separated. Consequently, I could not say how much we did run in both together, but it was more than 1200.

I had about 4000 acres of the Crocker-Dillon place but I do   1091
not know how many of my own cattle I ran on the Crocker-Dillon
place and on the Spring Valley land, because the fences were poor
and the lands lie together.

The Carson lease, I got on December 15, 1914, but I have not
leased the portion covering the prune orchard. I cannot answer the
question as to how many cattle we ran throughout the year as an
average, but I told you we had about 1200 head. I do not know how   1092
many head we sold that year, and I will have to average what we
paid for three steady men that we had running cattle, because we
don't pay all men the same price. We get three men for $115 a
month, and we furnish them with board, horses, and saddles. The   1093
board is not included in the $115.

I think I commenced my lease with the Spring Valley Water
Co. on December 1, 1907, and have been paying them about 50 cents
per acre per year. I paid them $3,120 for a trifle over 8,000 acres
before I took over the Carson lease. The Crocker-Dillon lease runs
from year to year, but has no 60 day clause in it. I cannot answer
as to how many head of cattle we sell on an average a year. Last
year, to the best of my knowledge, we sold between 500 and 600
head. I have bought and sold cattle besides that. In one sale, I
sold 215 cows to a man named Lessier. The Patterson Bros., of
Alvarado, got 256 cows and calves at one sale. I will have to look   1094
in my books to tell how much we got for those cattle, but they were
all stock cows, sold from that range. I have never owned any
land individually, but only had an interest in an estate, which was
my father's home place on Section 26. I rent between 10,000 and
11,000 acres from the Spring Valley now, and I pay them $5,100
odd. This land is all under the 60 day clause, but you understand
that in the last lease of the valley, it is only for ten months.

I only know from hearsay what Carson paid for his place. We   1095
keep no cattle in the valley, only after we have harvested our crop.
When it starts to rain, we take the cattle out of the valley land
to our grazing land, but I have never taken any out of the Spring
Valley or Crocker-Dillon land on other land. We have land to
the west, land to the east, land to the south and land to the north
and it would therefore depend where we would take them. We do
not buy any outside feed at all.

Parcel 323; I paid $110 for that land for three months, in order
to put steers on it, but that was not in my lease. The feed was
down there, and I bought it to put some steers on until the feed
started in the Spring. These were some work oxen that I shipped
from Mexico up here.

k-268, Mary Williams place; I farmed that to hay and got from
a ton and a quarter to a ton and a half of red oat hay per acre off it.   1096

A-345, Auctioneer-Bland place; I farmed that, and got red oat hay there. It ran very good, and I figure that two years ago I cut on about 30 acres of farming land, 34 or 35 tons of hay.

h-268, Patterson place; I farmed this for three years, and it was good land. I could not tell how much I got from it. It is all there on the ground today. The baler is there and the hay, and they will start baling this morning. It all runs about the same, from a ton and a quarter to a ton and a half. There is poor land, and there is better land, in strips. The Williams piece was good farming land for that class of land there.

1097 Referring to parcel h-268, I could not tell you the rental I paid for it, as I am renting it as a whole, the entire tract of land. I have not seen the cattle eating the grass down to the roots this year on the westerly side of the valley, but I have seen that in past years. That occurred two years ago in the dry season, and is the sign of a short year.

1098 Parcel 258, Map 16; I think it was homesteaded by a man by the name of Miller, and thus became known as the Miller property. I do not know where he is now. This land has been used for grazing land. The Brannan's, referring to the Brannan place: They were a family that took up that property but what they did with it I could not say. Mr. Walker rented it in the very early part of the Nineties from the Brannan Estate, I suppose. He grew hay, but I do not know what he paid for the place.

1099 Parcel 225, Bayne place. They were people that owned a foundry here in San Francisco. They never used the land, except for summer outing; that is, in years gone by. They built this house a number of years ago and it got to be called the Bayne house. Afterwards, the property was called the Bayne place. A man by the name of Bouchard used to farm it to hay and they lived there afterwards, where the Bayne people built the house.

(The witness here corrected an answer he had made in regard to the Brannan place. He stated that on Section 18 he had seen a threshing machine once, and that he may have stated in his appraisal that they raised all hay there.)

1100 Parcel W-268, Weller piece. He was Justice of the Peace for many years at Milpitas, and belonged to one of the oldest and best known families in Santa Clara County. In former years, he lived on the Weller ranch, which he used to farm. That was before my time but I imagine he got fair crops, as three years ago they had a fine crop on that place. I cannot account for the fact that the Spring Valley Water Co., in 1911, got that land for $29 an acre, except in one light; that the people were getting tired of it, as they had picked up so much of this land that they had run the school houses out of there. There were four schools there at one time. Now there are not any children

1101 —in one there was only my children, and two others. From the Weller piece to the nearest school house is at least 2½ miles through

rough country, the nearest route you can take. It is west of the Hansen place, and the Hansen, Campbell, and Santos places are between the Weller place and the school house. I am speaking about the Air Point school house. It looks as though the people had been gradually dropping out of there simply on account of the schools.

There may have been considerable land in that valley not owned by the Spring Valley in 1911, but there were no people living on them to my knowledge. Patton moved out four or five years ago. Mr. Wool, who farmed part of that land, has a home in San Jose. I am not in a position to say who they rent their land from—there are three brothers of them—but I imagine they rent from the Spring Valley. The Weller place has been farmed by Portuguese. One of the Weller boys is farming with me. The father is dead.

Parcel 325, Gaines place; none of my hay on this place rotted particularly. It got stained. I consider it an advantage, at this time of year, on that land, to have the hay rot on it. In that valley land hay runs about 1½ tons to the acre—volunteer. The sowed hay beat it, running about 2 to 2¼ tons an acre. There was no sowed hay on the Gaines place. That was a volunteer crop. The Campbell property, parcel 321 and parcel 324 had sown hay on it, which ran from 2 tons to 2¼ tons an acre, because there was a late spring this year, and the hay rusts, and there is no weight in rusted hay. That is the reason why it ran light. Mr. Carson had it planted in previous years, and he has told me it ran as high as 3 tons to the acre. He figured that 2¼ to 2½ tons straight through on his land was a good crop, and he was there thirty years. I have never grown alfalfa myself. In regard to this land that there is corn on, there was never a previous crop of anything else on that land.

Parcel 322, Pomeroy place; Mr. Carson grew vegetables there; as good vegetables as anybody could find—not for the market, but for himself. This is as good vegetable land as we have in Pleasanton. I placed $250 an acre on this vegetable land, which is not the usual price for such land, for one particular reason, and that is you have to plant your vegetables late there. Ground that faces to the north a little, does not get the sun in the early part of the season. It is fine ground, and has a fine stream of water, but the condition of that land is what I based my value on, namely, that these vegetables would have to be grown later. The southerly exposure is the better exposure for vegetables. I have not bought nor sold any vegetable land. My interests are cattle and hay. I am not in any business outside of the stock business, and outside of the period when I owned the lease of a hotel in Milpitas, I have not been in any other business. I owned the hotel there for four years but did not run it. William Carson died, and Jim Carson is Superintendent of the Alms House now. Referring to parcels 323 and 324, being the Ham Harris and Wells place; N. R. Harris was a man that ran for sheriff some 25 years ago. Captain

1102

1103

1104

1105

1106

Ham owned some property, and had interest through the John Sherman property in Santa Clara County; Wells is one of the best known men that Santa Clara County has. They were all residents of Santa Clara County to the best of my knowledge. The Harris and Ham
1107 people owned their places, and the Wells people were renters. That land has been used for farming purposes, and some orchard. By farming purposes I mean either hay or grain, and vegetables such as potatoes. They grow potatoes for the market, and about 18 or 20 years ago I saw a big crop right east of Wells' house, and I have seen potatoes every year since, up till last year. William Carlson grew these potatoes for his own use. The only crop that I ever saw grown
1108 for the market was between 15 and 20 years ago, and the tenant at that time was Mr. D. Wells, who continued as a tenant for a number of years. After that he grew hay and grain and that place runs about 3 tons of hay to the acre. The average run would be about 2½ tons to the acre. The orchard on the Wells and Harris places was a family orchard, and the fruit was not grown for the market.

Y-268, Totten place. He was a blacksmith who lived in Milpitas, and I think got that land on a mortgage. He had cattle himself on the place.

X-268, Santos place; Joe Roderick, now living at Berryessa, farmed about 100 acres of that to hay. It ran along about the same as the hill land, about a ton and a quarter to a ton and a half. I could
1109 not say whether anybody is leasing it now or not.

p-268, Jack Jeffery place. He was a wood chopper who owned that piece and sold it at least 20 years ago to the Williams Estate. They used it for cattle, and sold it to I. N. Castle, who also used it for cattle. The Castle people were in the cattle business themselves, and they ran
1110 their own stock for about three years. They lived on the Mary Williams property where I am living. I. N. Castle is dead, but when he was running there, he was one of the A-1 cattle men of California. I would account for the fact that I. N. Castle sold his land to the Spring Valley Water Co. for $8.31 an acre by stating that he sold his ranch there and went down and rented the Malarin Ranch, which is one of the best cattle ranches in California today, because he could rent 52,000 acres down there for $18,000—the most valuable cow ranch in the State of California. He needed this money to go into the cow business and he absolutely went out to raise this money, to
1111 buy the Freitas cattle. I consider he made a considerable sacrifice there. I did not buy it, because I was not connected right to buy it at that time. That is, I did not have the money ready.

H-268, Map 17, Walker place, north half of Section 20; Beverson, a cattle man, who was engaged in running cattle on that place,
1112 owned it before the Spring Valley owned it. Mendoza owned a part of Section 8. Spring Valley bought from Hughes and Mendoza, I imagine, who were in the cattle business. They were running them

there, but they did not live on that property. I do not know the highest elevation of the land, nor could I say exactly the elevation of the top of the ridge.

r-268, north half of Section 28, southwest quarter of Section 22; these parcels were bought from Arnold. I think he was the home- 1113 steader of Section 22. There have been so many homers there, I could not tell you which one sold to Spring Valley. That was used for cattle before the Spring Valley bought it, and they raised what little hay they wanted to use around the house. No more of it was farmed than just for their private use. Arnold ran cattle there—a man by the name of Carry, and my Dad also ran cattle there. I could not say what any of these people paid as rental.

C-241, Map 18-A, Section 33; that is grazing land, fair for the height it is in. By that I mean, lies out to the south, and any pasture land that faces to the south, it don't matter if it was 4000, 5000 or 10,000 feet high in this range of mountains, is worth double what it is 1114 when it faces to the north, and when you get into the high country, it is not as good land as the low country.

Z-268; That is the Bland place. Bland is one of the professors in the Normal School at San Jose. It is also known as the Pat Murray place and I think he was the man that sold to Bland. Bland was the grantor to the Spring Valley. It was used for pasture and some little farming, and this man Bland had it done for him. I was acquainted 1115 with Beverson, who was a cattle man. I do not know what he bought that land for; that is, what he paid for it; referring to the north half of 20, I do not know what he paid for that, or how long he owned it before he sold it to the Spring Valley. His home place was north of San Jose and not inside of the city limits.

Parcel 321, Carson or Campbell place; I think Campbell was the owner Spring Valley bought from, but I don't know for a certainty. That land was used for hay, grain and orchard. The fruit was sold 1115½ and one of the orchards was prune. I could not say who had that piece before Carson had it. I have been on the Peach Tree range— 1116 Mr. Miller's land—located, I think, part of it in San Benito County and part of it in Fresno County.

DIRECT EXAMINATION BY MR. McCUTCHEN.

It is south of the Bitter Water Ranch, about 30 or 35 miles in through those hills. It is a ranch, large in area through that broken country, and pretty hard for me to tell what county it is in.

CROSS EXAMINATION BY MR. STEINHART.

I do not know how many cattle that will hold, nor how many it will feed. The Sargent Ranch is located south of Gilroy, but I do not know how many acres there are in it, nor the price that it was for

1117 sale for. I do not know the Nasienta Ranch. I know the J. H. Henry Ranch, but do not know what that sold for, nor how many acres there are in it, but I know it is a large area. I make a return each year to the assessor as to the cattle I own, and that is a correct statement to the best of my knowledge. I made a return for 200 head of my own individual cattle on the first of March, last year, and the year before last, I made a return on, I think, 300. This year was about like that. I spoke about having 1200 head on there, but there were 600 steers from the Clark people from October to July, and those cattle are still

1118 on there. They belong to the Western Meat Co. My brother takes care of all of the pasture cattle, and I pay no attention to the books. We put pasture cattle on the Spring Valley land but I do not know how many are on there. This is a good, strong, average year for feed. Two years ago we had somewhere around 1100 or 1200 head of cattle on there. That was pretty nearly during the entire year. Cattle go in and go out from day to day. I could not state the number, as my brother, who is there, takes care of that matter. Four years ago we had about 1100 head on there, 400 of which belong to the Arrows boys who have rented the Sargent Ranch. They came in in October, 1912, and went out in the Spring of 1914. There were 265 or 275 of the

1119 Sperry Flour Co.'s that were on there just about the same length of time, or possibly two years. Last year we sold between 500 or 600 head of our own cattle, which we bought. We had some of them on there possibly 60 days, some of them 8 or 10 months, and some of them 2 or 3 years. 500 head of the cattle which we sold were on there in the spring and summer. I think we sold the last lot to the Patterson boys some time in the fore part of August, but it is impossible for me to tell you how many cattle we had on that range after we sold these cattle in August. My return to the assessor was about 300 head, which would indicate that I owned in March, of my own individual cattle, 300 head, and the 500 I sold, must have been purchased

1120 by me between March and August. I bought these from Carllitas, in Mexico, along in March, I think, and my recollection is, I sold them in August. The average cow man figures 3½%, or 3½ cattle to a calf as a natural increase year in and year out. The average of loss depends upon the condition of the weather and upon the feed you have.

Parcel 321, Carson or Campbell place; The farming hill land southwest of the house, I valued at $100. There is a crop of red oat hay on that this year, grown by a man named Pico, which runs about

1121 a ton and a quarter. The Roderick place was used for farming purposes, hay and grain, barley, oats or wheat. That is good farming land; good for the hilly character of it, and runs about a ton and a quarter to the acre. I valued one-half of that at $75 an acre.

1122 Parcel 331, the Sam Sherman piece; 90 acres at $200 an acre; 60 acres at $75; and 10 acres at $25 an acre. The $75 land is hay ground, and is in hay now, running probably a ton off; that is, about a ton to the acre.

g-268, Patton place; I farmed that for three years; two years ago to oats, and last year to barley. I sold the barley, and it ran about a ton to the acre, to a man named Linc. Shaw.

b-268, Brandt-Hansen place; Charley Brandt has been raised there. He is the farmer. The Hansens are the road masters; they own property and live at Lemon Grove. They lived there, and are farming the land today to red oat hay.

f-268, Maggie King place; they were two old maids who are now living in San Francisco. They lived there for years, and used the place for farming, chickens, and raised a little feed for a few milch cows. They farmed the place for hay.

e-268, Dennis Cullen place; Cullen was an old Irishman, a bachelor. He was a farmer and a kind of an old cow man. He used to have cattle way in back of this land, we are appraising. He used to farm his place both to hay and grain. He died ten or twelve years ago, and his place was sold by his sisters, to Beverson. He farmed it also, and used it along the same lines. Beverson owned 80 acres other than that, which he bought as a speculation, and sold again, I think, to the Spring Valley. I have no idea what he got for it. It is a good piece of ground, and for hill farming it is an A-1 piece.

DIRECT EXAMINATION BY MR. McCUTCHEN.

It is right directly north of the prune orchard I spoke of this morning. It does not bound it exactly, but the place where the prune orchard is lies directly north and northwest.

CROSS EXAMINATION BY MR. STEINHART.

This prune orchard was there when Beverson owned the place, and I would state that the line to the prune orchard is less than half a mile from this place. The prune orchard is on some widow woman's land, but it is in my mind that the old lady is dead. Their name is Collins. It is not on the same side of the road, but is on the same slope that the Dennis Cullen place is. I could not say that the prune orchard was on the Jeffery Cullen place. (Mr. McCutchen: We are informed, Mr. Steinhart, that that was the name of the owner.) I do not know what Beverson sold to the Spring Valley for.

The Priesker place is being farmed by a boy named Manuel George, who is growing hay on it, and he told me two years ago that he cut better than a ton and a half to the acre. It was high and wet. I'd class that ground right along at a ton and a quarter. The Priesker place has a little southerly exposure but not much. It is right on the top of the summit. It is not a good exposure, because it has the different formations in the mountain; one part would be formed by the little round mountains. The southerly portion of that place is right

1123

1124

1125

1126

on top of the summit. The little round mountains are coming in there and in between them are 7 or 8 acres in each place. I had no particular object in my mind in mentioning the Bolinger place the other day, nor did I have anything in particular in my mind when I stated that I had ridden over the Priesker place thousands of times. I might have said that that property I valued at $40 an acre on the Priesker place, is bounded on the south by the Bolinger place.

1127   Parcel 324; 65 acres on the west side, was grown, and is now being grown to hay which runs about a ton and a quarter to the acre.

The Ballinger place is south of the Jeffery Cullen place, and the family orchard that is there contains a few peaches, apricots and a few

1128   apple trees. It is a family orchard now. I don't think there was enough so that it could ever be sold in the market.

h-268; I farmed that to hay, which runs fully a ton and a quarter. That is a very good piece of farming land, and I farmed it three years. I have no idea of what rental I paid, as the rental includes this land as well as the other land.

n-268, Section 5 and part of Section 6; I farmed 60 acres of that a year ago, and the year before that to oats, which ran about a ton to the acre. I have sold pretty nearly all the hay that I have raised, and whatever hay I kept I put in loose. I cut it as volunteer, I don't sow it; I have 1200 tons of hay out there, today. This volunteer hay

1129   is from parts of the farming land that I do not farm, and I feed it to my cattle. There is not a great deal of land in the State of California that will feed one steer to every 5½ acres as will some of this land. The Malarin Ranch will beat it a little. That is down in Monterey County. The Jimmie Dunne Ranch in Monterey County will do it, and I think the Sargent Ranch will also do it. I think the Webber Ranch right off of Madrone, Santa Clara County, will do it. I do not know the size of the Webber Ranch but I have handled cattle in

1130   and out of there. I do not know of any more. I have a restriction in my lease from the Crocker-Dillon people that I must not cut any timber, but nothing to be compared with those in the Spring Valley lease.

The Master: Q. You said you wanted to correct something in your testimony, Mr. Parks. A. Oh, yes, it was about the assessor. My brother Arch and I went into partnership on the first day of April, 1914. The assessment of this cattle, for which he keeps all the books. He can be called at any time and he will testify that I don't go into the books once in six months, he keeps the books; part of those cows that went off from there, he shipped in at Christmas time and they were his; so that on the first of April, if that is when they came in as company cattle—they were in his name, I was not assessed for them.

The assessment for that year was not in both my name and Archie Parks' name. For the previous year they ran straight to me. He was not there.

(Counsel for Defendant here corrected a misstatement made by him in relation to what Mr. McDonald told him in regard to prunes purchased by Mr. Holmes for drying.) 1131

When I spoke about the Jimmie Dunne Ranch, I meant the Donnelly & Dunne Ranch at San Felipe. The volunteer hay that I got and baled came from the valley part of the land that I did not farm this year. 1132

RE-DIRECT EXAMINATION BY MR. OLNEY.

I can give you four years of my separate sales of hay and you can average them. Four years ago it went to N. P. Perry, a hay man in San Jose, at $15.25 a ton. It was hauled by the Hansen teams. Two years ago I sold 221 tons to the Santa Clara Mill & Lumber Co., for $22 a ton; hauled by St. Clarence. (Witness stated that this was some 200 and odd tons, he could not say exactly.) Last year I sold to the San Jose Water Co., the Welshcol Wholesale Grocery Co., San Jose, and also to Mangrum & Otter, for $11 a ton. This covers practically all, excepting a few tons scattered around. This season, I got $12 for one lot of red oats hay, between 80 and 100 tons of it delivered. I have received $7 in the field for one lot of volunteer hay. I have received from Manuel George $8.50 in the field for one lot of red oat hay; then I have stained cow hay to go to the Western Meat Co., and from 350 to 700 tons at $6 a ton. 1133

Questioned by Master.

That is in the field. I sold also to the Spring Valley Water Co., in the field, for $9 this year, which they took down to the dam site.

RE-DIRECT EXAMINATION BY MR. OLNEY.

Some of this hay I sold for $12 a ton, and others for $8, but one was delivered while the other was in the field. Last year I sold it for $12. 1134

Questioned by Master.

That was delivered.

RE-DIRECT EXAMINATION BY MR. OLNEY.

The third season back, I sold for $22 a ton, delivered, and the season before that for $15.25 a ton, delivered. I figure the expense of raising and baling hay at about $5.50 a ton to the cars. I figure that as the outside, planting, harvesting, baling and delivering.

RE-CROSS EXAMINATION BY MR. STEINHART 1135

I sold hay at $8 a ton in the valley within the last two weeks, and some at $12, delivered at San Jose, within the last three weeks. I sold some last year at $12, delivered at San Jose, and the year

before last I sold some at $22, delivered, and I never expect to
see hay at that figure again. The year before that, I sold at $15.25
a ton, delivered at the cars at Milpitas.

1136   Questioned by Master.

My deliveries are all at Milpitas on board the cars.

RE-CROSS EXAMINATION BY MR. STEINHART

On the hill land, we very rarely plow. It is disked, and costs
about 50 cents an acre. We sow it, disc it and harrow it, and we
are done for the season, until we commence to harvest it. We
never plow it. It would produce a crop year after year without
plowing. We figure about $1 an acre on seed. On barley, about 90
lbs. of seed to the acre, and on oats about 80 lbs. Last year I bought
1137   seed at two different prices. I bought barley at 95 cents, and later
on I paid $1.91 a hundred pounds for the same barley. The price
for barley and oat seed is not the same. This refers to barley seed
only.

Barley was the highest last year that is known in history. Oats,
I think, I paid $1.51 or $1.61 for per hundred last year. I bought
them about this time of the year. I figure on sowing barley about
90 lbs. to the acre, and on decent sowing on hill land, 60 to 70
acres a day, with two horses and two men. I pay the man about
1138 $1.25 a day and board him, but I do not figure my own time at
all. The horses I own and keep all the time, and I hardly know
how to figure the expense of them, but I would figure that you can
take care of the two for 75 or 80 cents a day. I have never figured
out what it costs for the care of them; I know that a four-horse
harrow would cut three acres an hour right along, and working
about ten or ten and a half hours a day, that is about 30 to 35 acres
a day. We harrow only once over disked ground in the hill lands,
and on a harrow that will harrow 31 acres a day, I use four
1139   horses and one man. I do not lap any when I harrow, and I do
not roll it. We are using a 5½ foot mower, and have been mowing
about 12 acres a day, with two horses and one man. I pay the man
$1.25 a day. We do not stack at all. We bunch it, but that is all
owing to the roughness of the ground. A man with a good buncher
1140   will bunch at least 40 tons a day in good windrows behind a good
rake man. We pay a bunch man the same as the others, and board.
We only use one man to a buncher, and two horses. Baling is $1.25 a
ton for me on a big job. The wire I furnish. A bunch of it cost me
this year $1.10, and it bales 8 tons of hay on an average. I do not
1141   use any men in baling but only in this bucking to the trap. I bale with
a baling press that is contracted from Tony Brannan, of Milpitas, and
from Johnny Valencia. By that I mean I contract for the baling of
the hay at $1.25 a ton. I use two bunchers to bring the hay to the
press, and two or four horses, four on the hill land, and two on the

valley. Those two men I pay the same rate as the others. I have four horses on the hills to bring the bunches to the press, but we never use over two bucks at any time. The cost of delivery is a little less than $1. The average run of baling a day is about 40 tons, but that would be owing to how much the hay weighs. The cost of haul is less than a dollar, about 90 cents, and a five-horse team takes out 8 tons to Milpitas.

1142

Questioned by Master.

I have not done it, but they have asked me if I am going to do it on this lot of hay just already sold. Other people have been doing it.

RE-CROSS EXAMINATION BY MR. STEINHART

Mr. Hansen did it two years ago, and it ran about 5 horses to 8 tons of one load a day. They don't pull both wagons over the mountains at the same time. It is only 6½ miles from the field to the depot, so they only pull one wagon with 4½ tons to the top of the hill, and then they bring up the other wagon, and take the two wagons down hill to the train. They load about 4½ tons on the front wagon, and about 3½ on the rear wagon. What I mean is this; we take the 3½ tons and pull it to the top of the hill with five horses. We then take the horses back and use them on the next load. Then we use the five horses to take the two wagons which we couple up at the top of the hill, down to Milpitas. We have a roustabout boy to help load, and he is generally one of the steady men, getting about $30 a month. The driver we pay $1.50 a day and board him. He goes into Milpitas and back in from 7 to 8 hours. Sometimes we insure, and it costs, I think, $2.50 on the thousand for about three months. Maybe I have that wrong. Last year I insured 100 tons of hay in one particular barn, and it seems to me it was only $12.50 in the barn. I do not insure in the field at all. I insured the hay in the barn with the St. Paul Fire Insurance Co., James A. Clayton Co.

1143

1144

I own my own farm implements, but I did not figure the cost of my tools into the price that I have given. I would not dare to say, without going to the ranch and going over it, how much of an investment my mowers, harrows, bucks, sowing machines, wagons, rakes, horses, harnesses, etc., represents. I do not know what the upkeep of those utensils amounts to in a year, for the reason that you might have five runaways in one year. You might have none, or you might have twenty.

1145

I did not include interest on my investment when I gave $5.50 a ton as the entire total cost. I just gave you a rough estimate. I figure planting and harvesting in that. The $4.50 is for planting and harvesting, and the $5.50 includes delivery. The hay that I sold

1146

at $22 a ton, was delivered to Santa Clara, but the price was the same as all these prices, f. o. b. Milpitas. When I say delivered, I mean delivered f. o. b. at the cars. I could not state how many acres I had in hay without going back over the maps. The year before I had about the same number of acres that I had last year. This hay we sell as soon as it is baled, and we have never stored any hay yet. In the estimate of $4.50 a ton, which is an estimate in my mind of that land there that I am used to working, I did not include rent, taxes, nor interest on my investment, because I did not own it.

1147

1148
Martin

Witness: W. J. MARTIN.

DIRECT EXAMINATION BY MR. OLNEY.

I am a land agent and manager for the South San Francisco Land Improvement Co., and am, and have been since 1890, acquainted with the lands in South San Francisco and its immediate vicinity. I have been the land agent for the South San Francisco Land Co. since 1891, and am familiar with the values of land in and about South San Francisco. I am acquainted with the piece of land immediately south of the town of South San Francisco, belonging to the Spring Valley Water Co. There were 45.78 acres swamp land, and 4.27 of hard land, making 50.05 acres which I sold to the Spring Valley myself. (Map 9, parcel 168.) I have sold all the land that has been sold there, and in my judgment the market value of that property on December 31, 1913, was not less than $1500 an acre.

CROSS EXAMINATION BY MR. STEINHART.

1149

I sold the land to the Prestolight people for $2000 an acre, and that is located right across the track to the west of the Spring Valley piece. The county road running through there was closed about 60 days ago at the crossing, by the Railroad Commission.

NINETEENTH HEARING.   AUGUST 10, 1915.

Witnesses: GEO. C. HOLBERTON, FRED J. RODGERS and WALTER R. HOAG.

Holberton   DIRECT EXAMINATION BY MR. OLNEY.

1150   I have resided for four years just west of Redwood City, and am familiar with the lands of the Spring Valley Water Co., in and about the southern end of the Crystal Springs Reservoir. I have been familiar with these lands since 1906, and I own land in that vicinity, which is probably about half a mile from the Spring Valley land. I have a contract for the purchase of other lands adjoining mine, which go to the limit of the Spring Valley property. I reside about one-half or three-quarters of a mile from the Spring Valley land, and am fa- 1151 miliar with the going values of properties in that locality.

Referring to "Plaintiff's Exhibit 8", page 5, the lands which I own, and which I have under contract, are those that adjoin the plot marked 164 on the easterly side, and I would say, by and large, that the market value of that property, plot 164, on December 31, 1913, was $150 to $200 an acre. Parcel 202, which lies immediately south, is worth a little less than 164, and the parcel 202, that is marked 92 acres, and which lies still further south, is worth about the same as 164, and I would easily value it at $150 to $200 an acre. The parcel to the north, marked 202, containing some 90 acres, I would say was worth a little bit less, due to the character of the soil; there is considerable rock outcrop in that which does not exist in either of the other parcels, and it is also a trifle steeper. If 164, and the southerly 202 is worth from $150 to $200 an acre, the other is probably worth from $125 to $175 an acre, or $25 difference.   1152

Parcel 203 is the same as the southerly parcel 202. The land which I have under contract, and which adjoins parcel 164, is for about 300 yards to the east of 164 just the same as 164, and then that land drops off very steep on the easterly side of the ridge; approximately 300 yards east of the easterly line of lot 164 is the so-called top of the ridge, and the portion that lies east of the top of the ridge, is absolutely inaccessible. When I go on to the upper end of my place, I drive south of the little creek on the northerly portion of the northerly 202, and then go through Spring Valley lands in order to get up on to mine, and up to the ridge the land is just the same; from there down there is considerable of it that is almost valueless. The northerly border of 202 shows a curved line, which is a portion of a creek, a deep, steep ravine, and there is considerable property in there that has no market value, because it is waste land. You have to go down near the Parkinson place, one-eighth to a quarter of a mile further east, before you get any suitable land at all. In this land on the westerly side, which is a rolling country, the contours are easier. The ridge is just east of that easterly line; then here these contours are very abrupt, and they do not cease till they get down to a little triangular piece where the arrow is above the name Marchand, which is occupied by a party by the name of Parkinson. There is about 13 acres in there, and that is the beginning of the flat. The reason that 1153 this land is so much less valuable in 202, is the fact that it is so steep here.

SPRING VALLEY WATER CO. VS. CITY AND COUNTY OF SAN FRANCISCO

CROSS EXAMINATION BY MR. STEINHART.

The land I have under contract, runs from the easterly line of 164 down to the city limits of Redwood. I own four lots in the Johnson subdivision, for one of which I paid $550 an acre, for another $500 an acre, and for the others $450. The city limits are over on the other side of them. These lands are near the ridge beyond.

DIRECT EXAMINATION BY MR. OLNEY.

You go over a ridge, and then you get into this little valley, and as you come up the valley, the land is worth, perhaps, $500 an acre, but the land at the extreme westerly end is very low in value.

Map entitled "Map of the County of San Mateo compiled from the County Records by Davenport Bromfield" introduced and received as "Plaintiff's Exhibit 39".

CROSS EXAMINATION BY MR. STEINHART.

1154

I am mainly in the employ of the Pacific Gas & Electric Co. Approximately 50% of this land that I have under contract is steep, and possibly 33 1/3% of it I value at $500 an acre. The land referred to is under contract. That contract was given in consideration of work which I had done for the Allis-Chalmers Co. on the property during the first three or four years that I owned any land down there. They anticipated that it would take some time to dispose of that land, and gave me a contract, such that in their judgment the amount of money paid, plus the interest, that they had saved in the work that I had done, would let them out—somewhere near the option. I believe they got the land for a debt from Mr. Dingee. I understand from hearsay that he owed a certain sum of money for machinery delivered to the Davenport cement plant, and this land was taken. The land covered by this last contract is approximately 779 acres, or to be correct 779.34 acres. The purchase price was work already done, for which nothing had been received, and the sum of $85,000, plus interest which commenced January 1, 1915, at 6% for five years. The interest was to accumulate, and was to be paid, I think, on January 1, 1917, or 1916, I am not sure which. The contract provided that it was to be paid in full on January 1, 1920, and if not paid at that time, I had the right to extend from year to year by increasing the values of the remaining land. The property which the Allis-Chalmers people own, and near which I live, is situated in a canyon. Some time ago a man in the employ of Mr. Dingee built a dam across that canyon, undoubtedly for the purpose of getting gravel for construction purposes, and that was allowed to fill up with gravel, and not being removed, the water finally broke off to one side, washing out the entire road, and a great deal of their land. When I came there I put in teams and scrapers, and cleared the creek, thus diverting the water. We have been work-

1155

ing at it ever since to get it back where it belonged, so that the lower road could be constructed. That work cost, I would say, approximately $5,000. I do not know what Finkler paid for his land, but he bought the Marchand ranch.

Questioned by Mr. Olney.　　　　　　　　　　　　　　　　1156

The Finkler property is about what you might call the average of the other land. His land is not so steep as the westerly end of my land, and is not as good as the Spring Valley land. If you could find out what Mr. Finkler paid for his land, the land lying to the west of the ridge would be worth perhaps 50% more per acre.

CROSS EXAMINATION BY MR. STEINHART.

In figuring the rough land on my land, that lies immediately east of the ridge, I never figured that in as being fit for anything save possibly pasture. I have not figured that of any value, and do not think it will be for many years to come.

(Admitted by Counsel for Plaintiff that the date of the contract with Holberton was December 29, 1914.)

Witness: FRED J. RODGERS.　　　　　　　　　　　　　　Rodgers

DIRECT EXAMINATION BY MR. OLNEY.

I reside in San Francisco, and am manager of the Easton Estate. I have had to do with lands in the neighborhood of San Andres and　1157 Crystal Springs Reservoir, in connection with the Easton Estate, which is composed of Ansel M. Easton and Adeline M. Easton. Both of them have interests consisting of considerable land in that locality.

Questioned by Master.

It would all be indicated by these maps, and has been held for over 50 years.

DIRECT EXAMINATION BY MR. OLNEY.

The last eleven years we have sold about $2,000,000 of property for the Eastons, part of which adjoins the Spring Valley property near San Bruno, and between the lakes, and also adjoins Spring Valley parcels on both sides between the lakes. The Eastons and the　1158 Mills have only the watershed, and that goes through the property of the Spring Valley Water Co. I do not represent the Mills, but we worked closely together. Quite a little of the Easton property has been sold off in acreage, and some in lots and small acreage. I am fairly familiar with the values of property in that locality, and I have made a list of some of the larger transactions which have been made in that immediate locality, beginning up at our holdings at the north end, and also showing the figures we have refused for some of the property.

Referring to "Plaintiff's Exhibit 8", page 2, parcel 144; I have been on that property, and I have taken those parcels as one unit, beginning at 144, and coming down to 16-42, which includes parcels 144, 51, 53, 15, 18, 17, 218, 20, 19, 21, 16 and 42. Most of the original

1159   boundaries have been lost, and it is almost impossible to state just what is in one, and what in the other, but there is no great difference in the properties. I have been over the property both ways, and I have made a memorandum of where our properties abut on some of this. The parcel which I have mentioned is the parcel going up the northern end of the San Andres Reservoir, and includes the land lying along the east of that reservoir. I have not crossed the lake at all, not being so familiar with it there, and my transactions have been limited to this end. I came down to parcel 42, which is that small piece, they got from the Mills Estate. In valuing that, I have taken it as a whole, 614 acres. I have not regarded any of the land embraced in the lake, but have left that out because I knew nothing about it. The other part I put in at $475 an acre, and that is lower than we have sold at, and refused offers for. The land varies; some places it is better, and in some not so good, but it is considerably below what we have refused to sell our own for.

Questioned by Master.

This land, below which we have refused to sell our own land for, is adjoining; the back land adjoins parcels 144, 51, 53 and 15, and

1160   there is a piece belonging to Eastons, and a piece belonging to the Mills Estate in there. In 1912, we refused an offer for the Mills and Eastons jointly, because they would not take one without the other, of $1000 for the lower land, and $650 for the back land.

Questioned by Mr. Steinhart.

That offer was made through Mr. Boody, from a syndicate headed by Mr. Louis Titus.

DIRECT EXAMINATION BY MR. OLNEY.

Our land slopes toward the east, but the back is very rough, and through the north end the fences were destroyed, so that it is not easy to state where the boundaries are. The land of the Spring Valley Water Co. lies a little better, and the outlook is more pleasing toward the western hills, and the l pe is better. Further back, past the Capuchino lands, Scott told me he would not sell under $1000. This is the land that we have refused the offers for, this 275 marked "Ansel M. Easton", and this 386 marked "D. O. Mills". The 386 was put at $650 an acre, and the 400 acres in the front at

1161 $1000 an acre. Of the Easton land, about 20 acres would have come in at $1000 an acre, and about 255 acres would have been at $650. This is the Easton land that is southeast of the Mills Estate, and marked 275. When we refused that, Boody took a firm offer, and he turned it over. He offered this 413, Flood piece, at $750 an acre. That does not adjoin it, but it does help to put a value on that land. That also was refused. The next piece of land on the north, also adjoining parcel 15, is the Capuchino Land Co., which was at one time Easton land, and was left by Mr. Easton to his daughter, Jennie Easton Crocker, and which afterwards became the Capuchino Land Co. Mr. Scott told me that they would not sell under $1000 an acre for the whole thing. The back is very rough, and it is practically the poorest piece. I have been told the Colmans held this at $1000 an acre, and I know the Bayside Company did. This is the Taylor property. Then comes the Mills land, and ours; we are the only ones that cross into the watershed. Between the two lakes we have 300 acres, and the Mills Estate have about 275 acres, and that land the Spring Valley negotiated to purchase from us in the Summer of 1910, at $500 an acre, and the water right. We could not agree on the water, as we wanted 3 million gallons, and the Spring Valley wanted to cut us down. This 100 odd acres on the opposite side, with a road through, we are now preparing to cut up, and we are going to try to get within the next six months, $1500 an acre for it. That is subdivided into about acre pieces. We have built a road through here to a point where we have sold to Felton E. Elkins (21 acres), which piece we sold to him at $1250 an acre, away below the market. The house cost him $50,000 or $60,000, and we thought at the time, by getting him in, it would bring up our other property. That is approximately 600 to 1000 feet from the top of the ridge, and is a knoll just west of the ridge. 1162

Questioned by Master.

It is in what was formerly called the A. M. Easton place, and is marked on the map "560 acres".

Questioned by Mr. Steinhart.

That was not a part of the subdivision. It was back of the subdivision, which is some distance further east. 1163

DIRECT EXAMINATION BY MR. OLNEY.

The top of the knoll that Elkins bought, I should judge, may be 100 feet below the summit of the ridge. Further east and north, we sold to Mr. Kohl quite a piece at $2500 an acre, and we have since got rid of a good piece here, 498 acres, to the Panama Realty Co. We have taken in exchange some city property, on the basis that the property pays somewhere around 6 or 6½% on the valuation we have taken it for. (Testimony objected to as immaterial, irrelevant and incompetent, and Counsel for Plaintiff admits that the testimony is objectionable.)

The sale to Kohl throws light on the value of this land, because

1164

we sold there at $2500 an acre, and also a small piece in addition at $2000 an acre, which he wanted for a reservoir site. We have sold small acreages; the Harriet Stetson piece at $3500, which is situated in the A. M. Easton piece. The Stetson place was about 3½ or 4 acres, and is about half a mile from the top of the ridge, and comes closer to the Spring Valley land. We have sold quite a little small acreage in what we call the Burlingame Hills, and that runs from $4000 to $7000, and is in subdivision. That subdivision does not include the acreages in the streets. It is net. The lands of the Spring Valley Water Co., which lie to the east or that portion of the Crystal Springs reservoir, which lies north of San Mateo Creek, I have placed a valuation upon. That is parcels 73 and 90 on Plaintiff's Exhibit 8, page 3. I have taken all of parcel 73, leaving out any of the lake or submerged lands, which leaves 276.45 acres that is not submerged. Parcel 90, I have divided into two units; one unit of 655.94 acres adjoining 73. Those two pieces of 73 and 90, I have valued at $500 an acre. The remainder of parcel 90, some 209.16 acres, which is a portion of the Howard tract along Crystal Springs dam, and is rather rough, I have valued at $300. In getting at the values, I had to take into consideration what we had sold at ourselves, and what we had held out our own land at, and also the fact that the southerly end is really nearer the good improvements than the northerly end. By the northerly end, I mean the San Andres property. The Crystal Springs is closer to good improvements, to Carolan's and Crocker's, and it helps very much in increasing values to be close to improvements of that kind. I was inclined to appraise it at a higher figure, but would not go beyond the figure that we ourselves had put on our own property at the time, regardless of the water right. There are no other sales in that locality that I have personally made, that would throw any light on this. The Carolan sale was made at some $300 an acre, and I took the matter up with Mr. Carolan and Mr. Bowie, because it gave our land there a black eye, and we did not like that sale very much.

1165

1166

I based my information also upon the sale of the Hobart land. That was fairly close, and was at a fairly good price. I took all the sales that have been made into consideration. Walter Hobart sold to Charles W. Clarke 270 acres there at $750 an acre. That was in April, 1913. That land runs immediately southwest of the tract marked "San Mateo City Homestead", and it is marked "W. S. Hobart, 282 acres". I could not say whether the homestead property comes up to it or not, and cannot say that it does adjoin it, but it does adjoin the Parrot Estate. On this map it lies southwest of the City of San Mateo, and is marked "W. S. Hobart, 282.32 acres". It is very rough land, not quite as rough maybe as these 200 odd acres of the Spring Valley that I have put in at $300 an acre. I

1167

1168

think it is rougher than the balance of the Howard tract, parcel 90 and parcel 73.

Another sale is the Armitage Orphanage, which Mr. Antone Borel bought. That was about 24 acres, and it approximated gross over $2000 an acre. There was a building there, which I believe he had to tear down. This piece adjoins the Antone Borel piece of 144.39 acres, and is marked on the map "Armitage Orphanage".

I am familiar with the sale of Tevis to Whitman. Mrs. Whitman, who is a niece of Mr. Wm. H. Crocker, bought about 143 acres of the Tevis land, which ran about $1845 an acre. That land is further down, and is the piece marked "Mabel Tevis", consisting of 143.62 acres. It is about a mile easterly of parcels 73 and 90, adjoining where the boundary line comes in. It is lower on the easterly slope. I have no other information that I can think of at the moment.

1169

CROSS EXAMINATION BY MR. STEINHART.

This Tevis piece at one end is practically next to San Mateo Park, but I would not say exactly. The Armitage Orphanage piece seems to adjoin the City of San Mateo on this map.

Questioned by Mr. Olney.

I have a list of the specific sales of the Easton properties, and have borne in mind my valuations as of December 31, 1913.

1170

CROSS EXAMINATION BY MR. STEINHART.

The Hobart piece appears to adjoin the San Mateo City Homestead on this map, and is right in back of the W. A. Clarke place. The front of it is one of the show places down there. The Carolan place runs near to the Spring Valley lands which I have appraised. The Capuchino Land Co. fronts on the state highway, as does that adjacent to D. O. Mills piece, and the Ansel Easton piece, Huntington Park. The Easton subdivisions, which I have spoken of, and the sales made in those subdivisions, are not all in improved subdivisions. The small sales at from $3500 to $4000 or $7000 were in Burlingame Hills, except the Felton E. Elkins, and the Kohl places, which were outside. In Burlingame Hills, improvements consisted simply of an oiled road. The street car line does not go there, but goes to a point from which you can reach it. In those high-priced sales, the size of the sales ran all the way from ¾ of an acre to 2 and 3 acres.

1171

RE-DIRECT EXAMINATION BY MR. OLNEY.

The portions of the Easton and Mills tracts for which we were offered $650 an acre, toward the back, do not front on the highway. That is the rough back end, toward the San Andres Lake property

belonging to the Spring Valley Water Co. Toward the front, we
have made some sales of $1000 an acre, but that is some time ago,
in 1906 or 1907, and for subdivision. We sold Lomita Park in 1904,
1172 and that got us about $1250 an acre. D. O. Mills sold at that point,
100 acres at $1000 an acre on the county road. The automobile
has had a great influence upon the value of such lands as the Spring
Valley lands, and adjoining lands of that character somewhat removed from the railroad, as has also the development of the county
road. It has had an especial effect upon the lands that I have dealt
with, because we have taken a road to within probably 600 or 700
feet of the road that the Spring Valley have along their easterly
line at the top. If those roads were connected, and it would be
very easy to do it, the machines that now go up through the middle
of the A. M. Easton piece, could continue on and go through the
Spring Valley land, and it would really bring them in, especially as
we are considering extending our car line, and have made tentative
plans to the summit, to open up our own lands. In a general way,
the highway has resulted in probably 6000 or 7000 machines going
past our land, and some of them through it, according to the figures
the county officials have given me. That is why we are going to
1173 open our lands across the lake. Our experience seems to have been
that the demand for the back lands today is greater than the demand for the front. The people that buy the back lands are those
who have machines, and they can reach them now, whereas they
could not before.

RE-CROSS EXAMINATION BY MR. STEINHART

The Easton addition to Burlingame was really offered before
the earthquake, about in 1905. That is east of the highway. The
second addition of the Easton subdivision, was somewhere about
1174 December, 1905, and that was to the west of the highway, and fronting thereon. The third one was filed probably near the end of
1906, and also fronts on the highway, but with rather a narrower
frontage than No. 2. The only one of the Easton additions that
fronted the railroad, was the Easton addition to Burlingame, which
is not really numbered. The other tract is about five city blocks
back from the Southern Pacific and the United Railroads. Subdi-
1175 vision No. 4 was probably filed in March, 1907, and the state highway runs along the front of it. There is a very narrow frontage on
the highway. That is some distance from the Southern Pacific and
the United Railroads. The next one was the Easton addition to
Burlingame, No. 5, which was filed in 1911, and then withdrawn.
That has a very narrow frontage along the highway. The next one
was Easton addition No. 6, filed, I think, about 1912. We withdrew
that, so that it would not be necessary to put in improvements,
which we did not care to do at that time. The next one was possibly

326

in October, 1912, when we only offered several blocks to work back to the old land. There may be half a dozen or so houses on that, but I won't say, as we are still building. It is about 15 minutes' walk from the station at Easton. The last one was the Burlingame Hills, put on July 7, 1913, containing about 45 acres. Part of it overlooks San Francisco Bay. It is adjacent to the Easton residence, which is beyond, and somewhat to the south of addition 6 and 7. There is only one house there. The car line runs from the end of Easton addition No. 7. Easton addition No. 1 was 72.78 acres. I could not tell you how many houses are there. I could not tell you how many houses there are in Easton addition No. 2, nor could I say as to the number of houses in Easton addition No. 3. We stopped selling Easton addition No. 5 when we began to offer additions 6 and 7 for sale, and probably about the beginning of 1913. Easton addition No. 7 is building up in a very satisfactory manner.

FURTHER RE-DIRECT EXAMINATION BY MR. OLNEY.

The railroad which the Easton Estate operates goes to the upper end of the property which we sold to Mr. Kohl, and is within probably a little over a half a mile of the Elkins property, and about the same distance in another direction from the Stetson piece. I think a mile and a quarter would take it past the Carolan place. The Templeton Crocker place is some distance back from the state highway. It is on the Half Moon Bay road. The De Guigne place is back from the highway a considerable distance, and is nearer the Spring Valley lands. The Carolan place adjoins the Spring Valley lands, and the W. H. Crocker place is also back, and adjoins the Spring Valley lands. A great many of the fine places are back from the main highway, but not all of them. The Clarke place is not. The Kohls have gone back some little distance. The W. H. Crocker place is back; also the De Guigne place, and the Elkins place will be. There is a disposition to go in the hills which has been more noticeable the last four or five years.

FURTHER RE-CROSS EXAMINATION BY MR. STEINHART

The Easton and the Mills people have owned these properties for something like 50 years.

Burlingame Addition No. 1, 72.78 acres; Easton Addition No. 2, 97.87 acres; Easton Addition No. 3, 41.35 acres; Easton Addition No. 4, 45.27 acres; Easton Addition No. 5, 18.41 acres; Easton Addition No. 6, 10.35 acres; Easton Addition No. 7, 46.15 acres; and the Burlingame Hills, 45.89 acres.

Questioned by Mr. Olney.

The total acreage which we have sold, as near as I can figure it, is about 1260 acres. The total in figures is about $2,034,000. I

1176

1177

1178

1179

have heard that the land which the Eastons and the Mills bought did not cost them very much at the time. I don't think anybody, today, really knows. I imagine it did not cost very much. Of the
1180   1200 odd acres that we have sold, the first piece was put on in 1904, which includes Lomita, and includes the subdivisions and the large pieces.

Hoag   Witness: WALTER R. HOAG.

DIRECT EXAMINATION BY MR. GREENE.

I placed a valuation of $100 per acre for the 1322 acres out of the watershed on the West Union land.
1181   The parcel lying to the southeast of that dotted line, I valued as of December 31, 1913, at $250 per acre.

TWENTIETH HEARING.   AUGUST 16, 1915.

Witnesses: A. S. BALDWIN and C. E. GRUNSKY.

Baldwin   RECALLED FOR DIRECT EXAMINATION BY MR. OLNEY.

1186   With reference to the lands in San Mateo County, which I have valued, I have made no report as to differences in value of the various parcels of land between the different years involved in the suits. Deal-
1187   ing with those lands as a whole, I think it is fair to say that the values for the years 1912, 1913 and 1914 are about the same. The difference between the valuation for 1913 and 1911 is not greater than five per cent, so that a valuation for 1911 of 95 percent of the 1913 value would be somewhere in the neighborhood of what is right, if you apply it to all the lands. In the same way for the year 1910, the valuation would be at least 90 percent of the 1913 value, and for the years 1907, 1908 and 1909, it would be at least 85 percent of the 1913 valuation.
1187-1188   Counsel for Plaintiff here stated that it was understood that no testimony contrary to these percentages would be introduced, and that they may be taken as constituting the differences so far as the peninsula lands are concerned. This applies to all that Mr. Baldwin covered in his testimony, with the exception of the Lake Merced lands in San Francisco and San Mateo Counties.

Also understood that Counsel for Defendant is satisfied with Mr. Gale's testimony that there had been substantially no change in the valuations of the Alameda properties, with the exception of the Pleasanton lands, as to which he testified that a change had occurred in about 1910. The city may wish to contend, and offer testimony to the point that the change in the Pleasanton lands took place at a little later date. Also understood that no testimony will be put in in regards to the Alameda or the Santa Clara lands, and in case an agreement is not reached in the matter of the Pleasanton lands, it is to be understood that Counsel for Plaintiff will introduce testimony to substantiate the statement which Mr. Gale made.

1189
1190-1191

The stipulation reached is that Mr. Baldwin's statement covers all the lands of the company which have been valued in San Mateo County, or which will be valued in San Mateo County, with the exception of the Lake Merced tract, and also such lands, if any, that Mr. Baldwin may have valued in Santa Clara County. Mr. Gale's testimony is to cover the lands on the east side of the Bay in Santa Clara and Alameda Counties, and is to govern, with the exception of the Pleasanton lands, which are to be taken up further.

A list of all sales which Baldwin & Howell have made in San Mateo County is offered and received in evidence as "Plaintiff's Exhibit 40".

1192

The official map of San Mateo County is introduced, on which have been colored the properties sold by Baldwin & Howell in and around San Mateo. The terra cotta color indicates the property we have sold in that vicinity. The green indicates the lands still owned by such families as the Parrots, the Howards, the Bowie Estate, also the Brewer and the Doyle property. Those that are indicated in white are the greater portion of the lands which have changed hands since 1897, but which have not necessarily all been sold.

1193

Questioned by Mr. Steinhart.

This is an official map which I had colored, and which I checked up myself, and know it is correct.

DIRECT EXAMINATION BY MR. OLNEY.

All of the white has not been sold, but practically all of the property down west of the railroad has changed hands, until you get into town, where there have been comparatively few sales. The Spring Valley property, in relation to this map, is immediately west of it and adjoining it. West is approximately the top of the map.

Questioned by Mr. Steinhart.

The place marked "Poniatowski" has all been sold. This was originally the old Reddington Place, and was bought by Poniatowski through us in 1897 or 1898. The whole place, up to the boundary line of Grant's place, is now owned by Mr. Crocker.

Received as "Plaintiff's Exhibit 41".

The Carolan place goes right to the line of the Spring Valley property on the west. The white portion, "Harriet P. Carolan", covers the Carolan place of about 500 acres.

1194

DIRECT EXAMINATION BY MR. OLNEY.

The piece marked "Jennie C. Whitman" was bought from Tevis. The total amount of sales from 1897 to date in San Mateo County, as made through my office, is $3,713,814. The total amount of sales of acreage property is net $1,603,730.20. This covers the land alone, and with the improvements it would total $1,676,230.20. The total acreage, exclusive of marsh lands, is 6,632.896 acres. The marsh lands amount to 3,353.28 acres.

CROSS EXAMINATION BY MR. STEINHART.

1195

The marsh land sales are included in the list, and are principally the purchase of the Ravenswood lands, with the exception of the Brewer Ranch, which was sold about four years ago. The Ravenswood sale is on the third page, Hearst to Morrison, under date of January 17, 1902. They constitute now, a part of the Spring Valley holdings, as does also the next piece. This was all marsh land. The only other sale was that of July 23, 1902,—Frisbie tract—which, so far as I know, is practically all high land. It is not included in my average of marsh land sales. Another piece that is included is a sale of July 15, 1911, of 1800 acres, known as the Brewer Ranch. It appears on "Plaintiff's Exhibit 39", in Sections 22, 23, 24 and 26, Township 4 south, Range 4 west, and is marked Brewer & Tompkins. I did not handle all of these sales personally, but did handle a great many of them, while the others were handled by employees of our company.

1196

The Robert L. Coleman sale to the Spring Valley Water Co. is the present Millbrae Pumping Plant lot. The Poniatowski sale is a piece to the west of Spring Valley. I do not know the exact location of the

1197

sale from Page to Dickinson.

The sale of 15.50 acres, Poniatowski to Baldwin, is a portion of the present Crocker tract to the east.

The 2.85 acres, Flood & Mackay to Baldwin, is part of the strip between the county road and the railroad, which was purchased for the water company. The pipe line purchases, or rights of way purchases in this list, are the rights of way between Colma and Baden.

The next purchase is Charles H. Abbott to B. P. Oliver and J. Costa, of the Clark Ranch, and is known as the B. P. Oliver purchase.

The next is 3.93 acres on the Middlefield road, Menlo, Josephine Frank to W. B. Weir, $20,000. That is in Menlo Park, about two

1198

blocks from the station on the Middlefield road.

The next is 10.2 acres, near San Mateo, Bonestell to Barneson, located southwest of San Mateo, not far from the Beresford Country Club.

The next is 20 acres, San Mateo, estate of Alvinza Hayward, to E. J. De Sabla, which is immediately north of the old Hayward Home place, opposite the Frederick Kohl place.

The next is 84 acres, the portion of the Clark tract west of subdivision 2, San Mateo Park, Carmany to Borel, which is a portion of the property that was sold to Oliver and Costa, and is the westerly portion of what is now known as San Mateo Park.   1199

Johnson Ranch, 1159 acres, near Redwood City, is northwest thereof, and west of the railroad. It constitutes what is now known as White Oaks.

The Hayward tract, San Mateo, 109.08 acres, sold by Emma Rose to John Barneson. It is in the town of San Mateo, and lies south of Ninth Avenue, east of the county road. It includes what is now known as the Peninsula Hotel, and property to the south of it.

The next is Silva to Borel, 140 acres, which was purchased for the Spring Valley Water Co.

The next Claffey to Burgin, 451 acres, San Mateo County, was a purchase by the Water Company.

The next is 40 acres south of and adjoining Dingee Park—Dingee to Mrs. Pississ—and west of the county road, and within the present   1200 city limits of Redwood City. I handled that sale myself.

Besotti to Howell was a purchase for Spring Valley.

Scalmanini Ranch, 202 acres, was a purchase for Spring Valley.

Borel to Janes, 24.33 acres, San Mateo Park, west of subdivision 3.

The Pomponio Ranch is in the San Gregorio Country.

The next is 2.35 acres which was owned by Mr. Pillsbury, and was cut up into three lots. It is near the Burlingame Club. The 2.23 acres sold to Thomas B. Eastland was made up also of three sales.

The 98½ acres west of, and adjoining Dingee Park, sold to Geo. H. Irving, is not a part of the Johnson Ranch, but is a part of the   1200½ Dingee tract. It is the parcel marked W. H. Crocker, 110 acres, immediately to the southwest of Dingee Park. It is quite level, and   1201 slightly sloping to the west.

F. J. Carolan to Wm. G. Irwin, 31 acres, cross-ways, San Mateo County; that is an improved piece of property a short distance from the Burlingame Country Club, probably not more than half a mile.

Questioned by Mr. Olney.

It is in a northwest direction, marked "Carolan".

CROSS EXAMINATION BY MR. STEINHART.

It is the piece marked "Carolan" in Burlingame Park.

The 6½ acres, South San Francisco Land & Improvement Co., was high land. It is, I should say, northwest of the property marked "Western Meat Co."   1202

San Mateo Park is a subdivision as far as we had anything to do with what was originally known as the Clark Ranch, and included subdivisions 1, 2 and 3, but did not include the 24 acres which lies to the west. The total lot sales in Baldwin & Howell's Re-subdivision of San

Mateo Park was made of a re-subdivision of a portion of the original. The total lot sales in Hayward Addition, $159,130, was a subdivision of the 20 acres that were sold to De Sabla and others. In San Mateo Park the lots ranged from about one-half an acre to an acre. The Hayward Park and Hayward Addition lots were none under forty feet, with the exception of a few lots along the line of the railroad.

The Central Addition were 50 foot lots, and the Dingee Park lots were from 70 to 80 feet. These lots fronting on the street did not include the area of the street in making the sales.

1203   The sales in Subdivision No. 1, Burlingame, and Subdivision No. 1, El Cerrito Park, were in tracts of about an acre or a little more. These did not include the streets. The reason the total number of transactions excludes Subdivisions 1 of Burlingame and El Cerrito, is that I do not know exactly how many transactions were in each, but I do know the area.

The Bostwick sale is included in there, and I think you will find it in 1909 as 737 acres sold for $50,000.

The 6,632.896 acres only includes those I checked, and which have been sold as acres. Some of that acreage, in fact a large portion of it, was subdivided, but it is only counted in the original sale. It does not

1204   include the marsh land sales, but does include the Pomponio Ranch.

RE-DIRECT EXAMINATION BY MR. OLNEY.

The Pomponio Ranch is down near San Gregorio, and is southwest of anything shown on "Plaintiff's Exhibit 39". In 1904, when the land was sold to De Sabla, I do not think that that particular tract of land was within the city limits of San Mateo.

———————

Grunsky   Witness: C. E. GRUNSKY.

1205   ### DIRECT EXAMINATION BY MR. OLNEY.

I am a civil engineer, and have been since 1878. I received my education in the Polytechnic Institute at Stuttgart, Germany, from where I graduated in 1877. I then took up the practice of my profession in California by entering the employ of the State Engineer of California, being engaged on field surveys and river work. Subsequently I became Chief Assistant in the Engineering Department, and was connected with that department until 1888. My work had to do with water problems, and the supply of water. The problems that were under consideration by the State Engineer related to irrigation, to drainage, to the mining debris problem, and to flood control waters. It was in reference to those matters that I was active in the department. I was employed in the State Department until 1888, but after that entered private practice at Sacramento, and subsequently at San Francisco. I was again in the employ of the State in 1889 and 1890, as a member of the Examining Commission on Rivers and Harbors; the function of that Commission being to report upon the river problems connected with the Sacramento and San Joaquin Rivers. From 1894 to 1895 I was Consulting Engineer to the Commissioner of Public   1206 Works of California. In 1892 and 1893 I was a member of the Sewage Commission for the City of San Francisco. In 1899 I was engineer in charge, to design a sewer system for San Francisco. From 1900 to 1904 I was City Engineer of San Francisco. In 1904 I was appointed on the Isthmian Canal Commission, and was on that commission from 1904 to 1905. I was then made consulting engineer in the United States Reclamation Service, and was adviser to the Secretary of the Interior in connection with the United States Reclamation Service until 1907. Since 1907, I have been in private practice. My principal place of business has always been considered San Francisco, and although I maintained an office for a short time at New York, I have been back in San Francisco since 1910. I have been following that profession since that time, and have had occasion to concern myself with the reservoir properties of the Spring Valley Water Co. My first connection with these properties was as early as 1886, when I was called upon by Mr. Howard to act as an expert in connection with property that the Spring Valley Water Co. desired to acquire on San Mateo Creek. This property was located just south of the creek, and included a portion of the dam site of the Crystal Springs Reservoir. Several years later I was employed in valuing the Drinkhouse Tract   1207 in the Crystal Springs Reservoir site. As City Engineer of San Francisco, I made valuations of all of the properties of the Spring Valley Water Co., which included the reservoir sites owned, in use, and held for future use. I have kept in touch with the problem of supplying San Francisco with water, and as City Engineer, I was required to make an examination of all available sources of water, and I have, at various times since then, had problems in connection therewith presented, and have kept in touch with what has been going on in the matter of the water supply for San Francisco. In connection with my valuation of the properties, I valued the reservoir sites, and I rendered a number of appraisals of the property which were used in connection with rate fixing. I am familiar with the reservoir sites of the company, both on the peninsula and across the bay.

I have made a study, for the purpose of getting at the market value, on December 31, 1913, of these reservoir sites, and I have put the results of my study into the form of a memorandum relating to the problem of valuing reservoir sites, with my conclusions in the matter.   1209

MEMORANDUM

Relating to the Value of the Reservoir Lands of the Spring Valley
Water Company.

By C. E. Grunsky,
Aug. 7th, 1915.

SUMMARY OF CONCLUSIONS AND GENERAL STATEMENT OF THE
PROBLEMS:

The reservoir properties of the Spring Valley Water Co. consist
of the Peninsula system of reservoirs embracing the Crystal Springs,
the San Andreas and the Pilarcitos; of Lake Merced, and of the three
reservoir sites in the watershed of Alameda Creek, the Calaveras, the
San Antonio and the Arroyo Valle.

The aggregate area of the reservoir lands in the Peninsula system
as now in use, not including Lake Merced is about 2100 acres.

An additional area at Crystal Springs Reservoir of about 640
acres will be in this reservoir when the Crystal Springs dam is raised
so as to bring the ultimate high water to elevation 323 feet.

Lake Merced should be permanently controlled for water storage
and emergency use up to elevation 30 on the gage (elevation 15.7
above Crystal Springs datum). At this elevation its water surface
area is about 336 acres.

In the Calaveras Reservoir site there are about 1930 acres below
contour 800.

In the San Antonio Reservoir site there are about 656 acres below
elevation 450 feet and in the Arroyo Valle Reservoir site there are
about 630 acres below elevation 800 feet.

The problem of determining the market value of reservoir lands
is one of the most difficult that can be presented to the engineer.

No definite solution of the problem generally applicable has yet
been found. There is no recognized rule for determining the market
1210   value of a property which is adapted to some special use, such as
that of a reservoir which makes possible the development of a water
supply or which is necessary to hold water in reserve, for use in the
case of an emergency, such as may arise when the ordinary supply
is temporarily not available.

No other course is open in ascertaining the market value of such
reservoir sites than to determine the effect upon the market of a
knowledge of all the circumstances bearing upon each case. This
is particularly true when as in the present case some of the reservoir
sites whose values are to be determined are the only ones of their
character which are available for the particular purpose which they
fulfill.

If the necessity to use the property is an immediate one it may be proper to determine an upper limit of value by comparison with the next most available source of supply; but this limit is not market value, though it may be the measure of what the party desiring to use the property can afford to pay. There should always be a margin in favor of the party who actually uses the property for the purpose to which it is specially adapted.

Ordinarily when the value of land is to be determined the return which it produces in rents or otherwise, or which may reasonably be anticipated, and the sales of other similarly located property adapted to similar uses, can be used as an index of its market value. But in the case of land which is in use or that is available for use as a storage reservoir, there is usually no such standard of value than can be applied. It would be an unusual circumstance to find sales of recent date of similar property that would with any definiteness demonstrate value. Neither is the rental value of such property, for the use to which it has special adaptability, ascertainable even when already in use, because this is a special use generally more 1211 or less monopolistic in character. A reservoir may be a material factor in making possible certain net earnings resulting from the sale of water, but even when these net earnings can be ascertained with definiteness there will be much uncertainty in the matter of determining what part thereof should be assumed to result from the use of the reservoir land.

Nevertheless there are many circumstances which will have an effect upon the market value of reservoir properties, such as for example the time when the use of the site will be a necessity, and the time when the water supply commanded by the reservoir will be in full use; the availability of other equivalent storage sites or other equivalent sources of water; the location and all circumstances affecting cost of developing the storage and of effecting a delivery of the water, particularly when the reservoir site is not yet in use nor immediately requisite; also the extent to which the availability of any particular site has been demonstrated, and every circumstance relating to valuations that have been made by competent authority of the properties under consideration for rate fixing or for other purposes.

In the case of the reservoir sites now owned by the Spring Valley Water Company, consideration must be given,—

To the adaptability of the land for use as a reservoir site.

To the necessity of such use and the continuance thereof.

To the fact that the reservoir lands have been assembled at each site in one holding.

To the fact that in the case of the Peninsula reservoirs the adaptability of the several reservoir sites for use as reservoirs has 1212 been demonstrated by actual use.

To the cost of the lands and the increase of their value since the time of purchase.

To the valuations placed upon the reservoir lands by San Francisco for rate fixing purposes.

To the valuation as judicially determined in the rate case of 1903.

To the fact that San Francisco has declared the Peninsula reservoirs and Lake Merced necessary as a part of its ultimate water supply system.

To the fact that there are no other sites for water storage in large amount, near at hand, that could be used in place of the Peninsula reservoirs.

To the proximity of the reservoir sites to population centers and to regions in which population is increasing rapidly.

None of these factors taken separately leads to a determination of value which can be accepted without question. All of them should be brought under review. It is the consideration of all these factors which would influence a willing seller and a prudent purchaser in reaching conclusions relating to market value; and it is by such consideration that the values herein set forth have been determined.

The circumstances which affect the market value of the reservoir lands of the Spring Valley system are more fully discussed in the following pages.

GENERAL CONSIDERATION OF THE FACTORS WHICH AFFECT THE MARKET VALUE OF THE RESERVOIR LANDS.

COST OF THE RESERVOIR LANDS:

The records of the Spring Valley Water Company show the amounts which were paid for various tracts of land now owned as a part of the Peninsula reservoir system. The individual land purchases which covered lands partly within one or the other of the reservoir sites have been examined with a view to obtain some idea of the amount of the purchase price which may be assumed to have been applied to the acquisition of the reservoir lands. The preliminary assumption was made that an apportionment of total cost on the basis of ten times the per acre cost for reservoir lands as for watershed lands, would not be unreasonable, although it seems probable that this ratio of value may not have been approximated until after the lands were actually in use for reservoir purposes. On this assumption the results obtained appear sufficiently consistent to merit consideration.

In the Crystal Springs region 21 tracts of land, whose total acreage aggregates 8445 acres of which 1338 acres lie below eleva-

1213

tion, 288 within the reservoir site as shown in Table 1, were examined and it was found that the assumed apportionment of cost would indicate about $430 as the average per acre cost of these reservoir lands.

The prices paid for the reservoir lands of individual tracts when determined in this way range from a minimum of $77 per acre to a maximum of $1700.

Eight of the tracts show cost per acre in excess of the average and 13 show cost per acre less than the average. In three cases the indicated cost per acre exceeded $1000, and in one other case it was about $890 per acre.

The highest cost per acre is found in the case of the San Mateo Water Works whose properties to the extent of 980 acres were acquired for $396,645.83. This purchase is somewhat complicated by the fact that it included developed water rights, although these rights are apparently fully offset by the obligation to furnish an equivalent amount of water delivered at or near San Mateo free of cost.

The lands relating to which the purchase price has been thus examined were acquired in part about 1875 when the construction of the upper Crystal Springs reservoir had been decided upon and in part about 1887 just before work on the main Crystal Springs dam began.

1214

The following tracts of land of which some portion lies in Crystal Springs reservoir are not included among the selected tracts as listed in Table 1:

Tract No. 38. Original owner, Isaac Friedlander. Cost $37,500. This tract of 95.14 acres has 71.32 acres in the reservoir and 23.82 acres outside of same.

Tract No. 44. Original owner, Sam'l Theller et al. Cost $1867.50. This tract of 21.86 acres has 12.40 acres in the reservoir and 9.46 acres outside of same.

Tract No. 110. Original owner, E. C. Bowen. Cost $349.50. This tract of 3 acres has .90 acres in the reservoir and 2.10 acres in the watershed.

Tract No. 122. Original owner, B. McNamara. Cost $15,000. This tract of 118.58 acres has 1.10 acres in the reservoir and 117.48 acres outside of same.

If these tracts had been included the results noted at the bottom of the table would have shown:

Total area of the reservoir lands: 1423.64 acres.

Total area of watershed lands: 7259.56 acres.

Total cost: $935,724.30.

Mean indicated cost of reservoir lands: $435 per acre.

Mean indicated cost of watershed lands: $43.50 per acre.

1215   Although these additional tracts might properly have been included among the selected tracts enumerated in Table 1, they had been excluded in the original study for various reasons such as, the small proportion of reservoir land in a tract, or peculiar location, or uncertainty relating to the property acquired, and the small effect of their inclusion did not seem to warrant a reestimate of the results which are at best only approximations.

     Ten tracts of land of which each includes some of the San Andres Reservoir land as shown in Table 2, have an aggregate area of 1486 acres and were acquired at a total cost of $84,977.00. The area thereof in the reservoir is 440 acres and in the watershed of the reservoir 1046 acres. On the same ten to one assumption with reference to the cost of the reservoir lands in relation to the cost of the lands outside of the reservoir it was found that it would appear, though this is by no means conclusive, that these reservoir lands cost on an average $156.00 per acre and the watershed lands $15.60.

     Of the individual tracts 7 are indicated to have cost more than these average prices per acre and 3 less. The highest indicated cost is for a tract of 153.75 acres of which 10.40 acres lie within the reservoir. In this case the indicated cost per acre was $438.00 for the reservoir land and $43.00 for the watershed land. All of the 7 tracts on which the reservoir lands are thus estimated to have cost more than the average cost per acre show probable costs in excess of $200.00 per acre.

     The lowest indicated cost per acre of the reservoir lands of the San Andres system in the examined list of tracts is $67.00 and applies to a tract of 531.95 acres of which 156.65 acres lie within the reservoir.

     The lands in the San Andres reservoir were purchased in or about the year 1868.

1216   The following tracts of land of which some portion lies in San Andres Reservoir are not included in the list as enumerated in Table 2:

     Tract No. 43. Original owner, Edward Sweeney. Cost, $11,487.50.

     This tract of 392.69 acres has 1.00 acre in the reservoir and 391.69 acres outside the same.

     Tract No. 218. Original owner, R. L. Coleman. Cost unknown. This tract of 34.74 acres has 11.90 acres in the reservoir and 22.84 outside the same.

     If the Tract No. 43, which was omitted from the selected tracts owing to the small proportion of its area in the reservoir, had been included in the determination of average results these would have been:

Total area of reservoir lands: 441.45 acres.
Total area of watershed lands: 1,437.68 acres.
Total cost: $96,464.50.
Mean indicated cost of reservoir lands: $165 per acre.
Mean indicated cost of watershed lands: $16.50 per acre.

In the case of three tracts of land at the Pilarcitos Reservoir with an aggregate area of 3,273 acres of which 96 are reservoir lands, as shown in Table 3, the purchase price was $19,996.50.

On the same assumption, as in the case of the other reservoirs, of a ten to one ratio of the cost of reservoir lands when compared with the cost of watershed lands, it was found that this ratio indicated an average cost per acre of $48.50 for the reservoir lands and $4.85 for the watershed lands of the Pilarcitos system.

These lands were purchased in or about the year 1865.

The following tracts of land of which some portion lies in Pilarcitos Reservoir are not included among those listed in Table 3: 1217

Tract No. 2. Original owners, Pioche, Mezes and Arguello. Cost, $15,000.
This cost included rights of way and water rights which could not be segregated from the cost of the land. Of this tract of 40 acres 19.60 acres lie in the reservoir and 20.40 acres outside of the same.

Tract No. 5. Original owner, R. Roxby. The cost of this tract is included with other lands and could not be segregated. Of this tract of 40 acres 16.40 lie in the reservoir and 23.60 acres are outside the same.

Tract No. 27. Originally owned by Arguello, Pioche, Linden and Mezes. Cost $2,057.60. Of this tract of 67.99 acres .50 acres lie in the reservoir and the rest 6 separate parcels lie outside the same.

Tracts Nos. 2 and 5 were not included in the list given in Table 3 owing to lack of information relating to cost and No. 27 was not included owing to the small portion thereof in the reservoir.

Taking the reservoir land purchases of the Peninsula system in their entirety, without distinction as to the particular reservoir in which they lie, it is found that the 34 tracts of land which are listed in tables 1 to 3, have a combined area of 13,204 acres of which 1,874 acres are in the reservoirs as at present in use. The total cost of these selected tracts of land was $985,980.80. (See Table 4.)

The ten to one ratio of unit cost would indicate $328 as the average cost per acre of the reservoir lands and $32.80 as the average cost per acre of the watershed lands.

APPRECIATION OF REAL ESTATE IN THE SAN FRANCISCO BAY REGION AND IN CALIFORNIA.

(Objected to by Counsel for Defendant as calling for the opinion of the witness as a real estate expert, but allowed to go in subject to that weakness.)

1218
Since these reservoir lands were bought there has been a continning increase in the value of real estate. This appreciation can be determined approximately at least from the valuation of real estate for taxation purposes.

Confirmation of the increasing value will be found too in the fact that there has been a constantly increasing density of population in the Bay region (see Table 5) and a corresponding increase in the demand for land such as those in the various reservoir sites on the Peninsula which if not used for reservoir purposes would be available for country homes.

Some information is presented in Table 6 relating to the assessed valuation of real estate in the 4 counties—San Francisco, San Mateo, Santa Clara and Alameda.

Prior to 1900 no published records were found showing separately the assessed valuation of the improvements. The table therefore shows for these years the assessed value of the real estate together with improvements.

For the more recent years the assessed value of the land only could be given.

The information contained in Tables 5 and 6 is the basis for the percentages noted in Tables 7 and 8 for diagrams on sheets Nos. 1 to 5.

After these diagrams had been prepared some additional information relating to the assessed valuation of real estate including improvements in San Mateo County and of the assessed value of real estate, without inclusion of city and town lots, was obtained and is presented in Table 17 and on Sheet 6, supplementing the information presented in Table 6 and on Sheet 1.

1219
During the 40 years following 1870 the population growth of the State of California has been at the average rate per decade of about 44%, which is equivalent to 3.7 per cent per year. The average rate of growth of San Francisco has been about 30 per cent per decade during the same 4 decades or about at the rate of 2.7 per cent per year.

The population growth of Alameda County has been so largely due to the growth of its urban district and Alameda County is so remote from the location of the peninsula reservoirs that it may be left out of consideration as a factor influencing the increase of value of real estate on the peninsula. Nevertheless some figures will be presented to show in this county, too, the close relation between the increase of population and the increase in the value of real estate.

The population of Santa Clara County has increased from 26,246 in 1870 to 83,539 in 1910 or at an average rate of 34 per cent per decade. This is at the average rate of 3 per cent per year, and is at about the same rate of growth as maintained during the last decade, 1900 to 1910, for which records are available.

The population of San Mateo County increased from 3,214 in 1860 to 26,584 in 1910. It increased about 8.2 per cent per year in the decade 1900 to 1910. During the 20 years, 1880 to 1900, the growth of population was only between 1.5 and 2 per cent per year. The average annual population increase in the county since 1870 has been between 3 and 4 per cent.

In Table 7 is presented a comparison of the rate of increase in population and in the assessed value of real estate for the four counties, San Francisco, San Mateo, Santa Clara and Alameda.

While there has been a considerable irregularity in the rate of growth from decade to decade and the assessed value of the real estate shows fluctuations which are undoubtedly due in part to the vagaries of local assessors, the table is nevertheless a good index of the continually advancing value of land. It will be noted too that 1220 generally, particularly in the case of periods of 20 years or more, the increase in the assessed value of real estate exceeds somewhat the increase in the rate of population growth.

A further comparison of those rates of increase is given for the decade 1900-1910 for the same 4 counties, in Table 8.

The figures presented show for each of the counties the effect of the period of business depression, 1893 to 1898, which fell into the decade 1890 to 1900, upon the taxable value of real estate. Notwithstanding the resulting check which the increase of value received at that time the average rate of increase for Santa Clara County was almost 5 per cent per year for the 40 years, 1870 to 1910.

In San Mateo County, too, values remained practically stationary in the decade 1890 to 1900, but have increased rapidly since. The increase indicated by the tax valuation was 7.5 per cent per year from 1900 to 1910 and averaged over 7 per cent for the 40 years, 1870 to 1910. In this county, too, the increase of land value seems to have kept pace with the growth of population. The value of farm lands in San Mateo County is given in the U. S. Census reports as shown in Table 9. This table shows an average annual increase in the value of farm properties of about 4.5 per cent for the 40 years, 1870 to 1910, and 7.5 per cent for the ten years, 1900 to 1910, the increase being about the same for the recent 10-year period as the increase in the assessed valuation of all real estate in the county.

Due allowance should be made in making such comparisons as the foregoing to the uncertain and irregular ratio of the assessed

341

value of land to its actual market value; and also to the fact that some of the figures presented relate to land and improvements and not to land only. It is believed that if the market value of real estate could be ascertained with the same degree of accuracy as population that the ratios of increase would show a more dependable relation to each other than that indicated by the results presented in Tables 7 and 8.

In San Francisco, as shown in Tables 7 and 8, the assessors' valuations for the ten years, 1900 to 1910, appear to indicate a probable average increase of real estate values in the city of about 4 per cent per year, despite the fact that the fire of 1906 came in as a disturbing factor.

It is interesting to note that while the population of San Francisco increased from 149,473 in 1870 to 416,912 in 1910, or nearly three-fold, the assessed value of real estate and improvements grew from $75,145,700 to $433,000,000, or about six-fold. Here is an additional indication that in San Francisco the value of real estate is growing faster than the population, a double rate of growth appearing possible. On the assumption that the relative assessed value of land and of the improvements thereon has remained substantially the same these figures indicate an average increase of real estate value in San Francisco during the 40 years from 1870 to 1910 of about 4.5 per cent per year.

In Tables 13 to 16 data are presented relating to the population of California, the value of the farming lands of the State and the assessed valuation of real estate and improvements. The figures are taken from U. S. Census reports.

Considered by decades, the population of California has been increasing at average rates, since 1860, ranging from 2.1 to 4.9 per cent per year. The average rate of growth for the 50 years since 1860 covered by the records has been about 3.7 per cent per year.

During the same 50 years the aggregate value of farms in the State, including improvements on the farms, has increased at the average annual rate of 6.9 per cent or nearly twice as fast as the population.

During one decade, only, is information available relating to the value of farming land without the inclusion of buildings. This value, according to the census figures, increased 109 per cent in the 10 years, 1900 to 1910, or at the rate of 7.7 per cent per year. In the same decade the population increase was 4.9 per cent per year and the increase of the value of farm lands, including buildings, was 7.4 per cent.

These statistics confirm the fact indicated by the records for the South San Francisco Bay counties that the value of real estate grows somewhat faster than the population.

1221

1222

The information contained in Tables 13 to 15, relating to this statistical information concerning California, is shown diagramatically on Sheet 5.

The increase in the valuation for taxation purposes since 1870 as shown by Tables 7 and 8 averages:

In San Francisco, 4.5 per cent per year.

In San Mateo County, 7.3 per cent per year.

In Santa Clara County, 4.8 per cent per year.

In Alameda County, 7.6 per cent per year.

The increase in the value of farm properties in San Mateo County as reported by the U. S. Census since 1870 averages 4.6 per cent.

As shown in Tables 14 and 15 appended hereto the value of farm properties in the entire state has been increasing since 1870 at an average annual rate of 5.9 per cent and the assessed value of all real property in the state at 6.6 per cent.

THE PROBABLE APPRECIATION OF THE PENINSULA RESERVOIR LANDS: 1223

From such facts as presented it appears that the mean annual increase in the market value of real estate in such attractive spots as the valleys now occupied by the Peninsula Reservoirs for long time periods has probably been about 7 per cent.

The preliminary apportionment of the cost of the various tracts of land on the basis of ten times as much per acre for the reservoir land as for the land outside of the reservoir was made because of general knowledge that this ratio might be about right. It was sought to find a ratio which, though not necessarily resulting in a fair apportionment of the cost in the case of each tract, would nevertheless indicate a reasonable average apportionment on the basis of values as they obtained after the reservoir was in use.

The ten to one ratio was tried and comparisons were made with other results obtained by the use of other ratios, such as 5 to 1, 3 to 1, and 2 to 1.

From these comparisons the conclusion was reached that the 10 to 1 ratio, better than any lower ratio, would give a reasonable apportionment of the cost to reservoir and to watershed lands for use as basic values in estimating what the cost might have been at a later day.

The appropriateness of some such ratio as 10 to 1 is further indicated by the fact that this is the ratio which appears in the findings of the 1903 rate case.   1224

If the approximate acre cost of the reservoir lands as determined by use of the 10 to 1 ratio be used as a starting point and an average annual increase of value of real estate at 5 per cent instead of the probable rate of 7 per cent as above noted for the Peninsula Reservoir lands be made the basis of the calculation, land values in the reservoir if still held in individual tracts would be indicated for 1903 and 1913 as shown in Table 10.

These indicated values in round figures are, for the year 1903, Pilarcitos Reservoir lands, $310 per acre; San Andres, $860 per acre, and Crystal Springs, $1200 per acre. For the year 1913, Pilarcitos, $505 per acre; San Andres, $1400 per acre, and Crystal Springs $1950 per acre.

The indicated average value per acre of all the lands as in use in the three reservoirs for the year 1903 was $1070 per acre and for the year 1913 it was $1750 per acre.

COST AS AN INDEX OF VALUE HAS LIMITATIONS

A study of this kind, while it is interesting and instructive, can not be accepted as conclusive. Before the reservoirs were constructed a selection of sites was possible. The growing need for water could be met by varying the order in which the reservoirs were brought into use. The opportunity to develop water in each of the three sites did not acquire its full subsequent value so long as the time remained uncertain which would elapse before the use of each site was a necessity. The effect of this circumstance seems to be reflected in the purchase price of the reservoir lands, the first acquired were very much cheaper than those acquired at a later date.

1225   If the cost represents or is fairly proportional to the market value of these reservoir lands at the time of purchase then the figures as presented show a material increase in the value thereof during the period 1865 to 1889, in which this reservoir system was under development. Moreover the cost of the reservoir land acquired first can not be accepted as a good index of the market value of the land of the completed reservoir system, and for the same reason the mean indicated average value per acre as above noted for the entire reservoir system, which is affected by the early purchases made for the Pilarcitos and San Andres Reservoirs, is not the best indication of the value of the reservoir lands at the time of the completion of the entire reservoir system.

If the reservoir at each site had been valued separately at the time that the last of the reservoirs, the Crystal Springs reservoir was being constructed, there would, without doubt, a value have been found for the lands of the two other reservoirs, already in use, fully equal per acre to that of the new reservoir which was not yet fully demonstrated either as to feasibility or as to its yield.

The various tracts of land under consideration in this illustrative study were more or less improved. Information is lacking which would permit an estimate of the value of these improvements at the time of purchase. But whatever may have been the added cost of acquiring them due to the improvements this increment of cost was a part of the necessary outlay to secure the land. These improvements were of no value as a part of the reservoir. Their removal involved additional cost. In using cost as an indicator of value it is immaterial whether the lands were improved or not, because the resulting aggregate cost and the mean unit costs determined therefrom indicate a minimum, which at the time of purchase and before full demonstration of successful development, the purchaser considered these properties worth.　　1226

Furthermore the average cost per acre as indicated by the preliminary assumption results from a consideration of individual tracts each acquired separately. If this indicated cost even approximately represents the market value of these separate tracts at the time of purchase it would not represent the full value of the property when brought under one ownership, nor would it include the increment of value that results from the demonstration that the reservoir will hold water, nor yet the gradual increase of value due to the bringing of the property into use up to its capacity to supply water.

For confirmation of the fact that both Pilarcitos and San Andres Reservoir lands make a larger development of water per acre of water surface possible than the Crystal Springs Reservoir and at higher elevations, reference may be had to Table 11.

Furthermore the acquisition of each of the reservoir tracts was made while San Francisco was being supplied with water from sources that did not include the particular source of supply commanded by the reservoir site about to be acquired. Consequently the market value of the lands at the time of acquisition must have been somewhat less than the market value of the same lands would have been after demonstration of the feasibility of development by actual construction and actual utilization to the limit of capacity to produce water.

It is not surprising in view of these circumstances to find that the unit cost of the reservoir lands first acquired was less than that of the last purchases which were necessary to make the system complete.　　1227

ADDITIONAL CIRCUMSTANCES AFFECTING THE MARKET VALUE OF THE PENINSULA RESERVOIR LANDS:

The necessity of maintaining the reservoirs for all time as a part of the water works system of San Francisco is generally recognized.

The reservoir lands in connection with the other properties that make up the established system of water works have frequently been valued by San Francisco as a basis for the regulation of rates.

The value of these lands in 1903 for rate fixing purposes has been judicially determined.

It is a generally accepted fact that reservoir lands, whose availability for water supply purposes is recognized and whose utilization is proximate have special value due to these facts.

345

In the case of the Peninsula Reservoirs the fact that they can be depended on for a supply of about 18 million gallons per day has been demonstrated and these reservoirs were in full use long before 1903 and at all times thereafter.

Even though a large supply of water be brought into the Bay region from Sierra Nevada or other sources, the reservoirs will continue in use to safeguard uninterrupted service. This function will be retained by them even though the water supplied by the distant source is fully adequate to meet the requirements, in so far as the amount thereof is concerned, because they are the only available adequate nearby storage sites, and because of the fact that they are already in use as reservoirs.

For a number of years beginning in 1901 the valuation placed upon these reservoir lands, by the city to the extent that they were in use, was $1250. per acre.

Questioned by Mr. Steinhart.

I was City Engineer at that time, and that was my valuation.

1228   Lands that will be within the limits of the Crystal Springs Reservoir when the Crystal Springs dam is raised to its full height but which were not yet subject to submersion were valued by the city at $625. per acre.

The effect upon the market of the fact that the value of these lands for rate-fixing purposes applying to the year 1903 was determined by Judge Farrington at $1000. per acre for lands actually in use as reservoirs and $100. per acre for lands in the watersheds. The Court made no distinction in the value between the lands whose use as reservoir lands was prospective and those which are simply reservoir lands.

The undeveloped storage at the Crystal Springs Reservoir (about equivalent to present capacity) which can be realized by raising the dam, about 40 ft. is of minor importance in so far as increased yield of water is concerned. Its development would increase the yield of this source by only a small amount.

The increase of storage capacity will, however, be a valuable feature in connection with any large water supply from a more remote source such as Calaveras Creek or the Sierra Nevada Mountains. But the development of this storage, even for this purpose, cannot be regarded as an immediate essential requirement. In view of this fact the lands that are necessary to make the added storage possible do not have the same value as the lands already in actual use as reservoirs.

The raising of the Crystal Springs dam to the contemplated height of 328 feet with a water surface in the reservoir when full at 323 feet, will increase the storage capacity from about 22,000 million gallons to
1229   about 43,000 million gallons. The additional storage capacity will be at a higher elevation than that of the present reservoir. A conduit

adapted to the increased head and to all conditions of service will have a smaller diameter for the same required delivery than would a conduit planned for the reservoir as now in use.

Taking all of the circumstances into account which affect the market value of these reservoir lands and giving consideration to the fact that the Peninsula Reservoirs will continue in use even though the development of water from some other source should for a time make it unnecessary to draw upon them to their full yielding capacity, I consider the market value at the end of the year 1913, of the lands actually in use as reservoir lands, to have been at least $1400. per acre and the market value of the higher lying lands at the Crystal Springs Reservoir which will ultimately be in the reservoir, to have been at least $700. per acre.

LAKE MERCED.

Lake Merced is a source of water which has been in use for many years to supplement the other sources at the command of the Water Company. The lake is still in use. Its water, in so far as quality is concerned, is less desirable than water from other sources. The lake is but slightly above sea-level, consequently its water must be pumped to make it available for distribution. The lake, however, is located within the limits of San Francisco. The delivery of its water is effected through a short pipe line. Its water, when in use, is filtered to fit it for human consumption.

Whenever water is brought to San Francisco in large quantity from some new source, such as the Calaveras Reservoir or the Sierra Nevada Mountains, the use of Lake Merced as a source of continuous yield will be abandoned. The lake will thereafter be drawn upon only in the case of an emergency. When the emergency arises, as it did in 1906 when the various main pipe lines, leading into San Francisco from the Peninsula Reservoirs, were all thrown out of commission, the lake is available for a much larger amount of water than its ordinary yielding capacity. Under such conditions the city may become dependent almost entirely upon this lake for water for domestic use, and a large part of the city not yet commanded by the high pressure fire protection system will get its protection against fire mainly from this source.

1230

At the stage at which the lake will probably be permanently maintained when no longer used as an ordinary source of supply it contains about 2659 million gallons of water. This is about a 60 days' supply at the present rate of consumption without regard to the accession of water from springs that would result if the lake's water surface were materially lowered by pumping.

After the lake ceases to be of use as an ordinary source of supply and its water is to be furnished for domestic use at infrequent intervals upon occasions which are not to be expected oftener than once or twice in a century and which may never arise at all, the need of the same care as at present in preventing a possible contamination of the lake water will disappear. There will thereafter be no necessity of restricting the use of watershed lands. The quality of the supply, even though there should be a recognized possibility of contamination, will be amply safeguarded for the brief period of its use in an emergency by filtration and such treatment as may be found necessary to sterilize the water.

1231   It follows that the control of the Lake Merced watershed by ownership, will no longer be necessary after the lake ceases to be in use as an ordinary source of supply. It has been difficult heretofore to separate the value of the lake from the value of the lands of its watershed. The problem will be presented in a new aspect when these lands are released for subdivision and the lake, as a feature of the water works, is to be considered apart from the surrounding lands.

When this will occur is not definitely known. It must be in the near future because the developed supply of water, available for use in San Francisco, is at present inadequate and the bringing of an added supply from some source in an amount which would make further draft upon Lake Merced unnecessary can not be deferred many years.

Lake Merced as a source of water and as a container of water is compared with the Peninsula Reservoirs in Table 12.

When it is considered that the nearness of this supply and its dependability offset the need of pumping and filtering the water, then the yield per acre of water surface alone, as shown in this table would indicate a value per acre not greatly at variance with that of the Peninsula Reservoir sites. But the prospective abandonment of the use of the water has a depressing offset upon market value.

The maintenance of Lake Merced as a water body adds attractiveness to the surrounding lands. The lake, if permanently maintained together with its marginal lands, will become available as a place of recreation without losing value as an emergency source of water.

Under consideration of these and other circumstances affecting the value of the lake I consider its market value at the end of the year 1913 to have been at least $1000. per acre of water surface at gage reading 30. This does not include marginal lands whose market value depends upon uses other than water production.

1232   The lake as a part of the entire Lake Merced tract owned by the Water Company may have a value in excess of $1000. per acre but I have not given consideration to land values outside of the lake which would result from its assured continuance as a lake.

THE CALAVERAS RESERVOIR SITE.

At the close of 1913 a Calaveras Reservoir did not yet exist. The reservoir site was not yet in use as a reservoir. Nevertheless the lands of the site at that time had value due in part to the fact that their ownership would, at a conveniently located site, make possible the development of a large amount of water.

It would be possible to estimate this value with some degree of precision if it could be assumed to have been then known when the utilization of the site would become requisite, and when in the still more remote future the reservoir would be in use to its capacity, in supplying water.

Notwithstanding the fact that the availability of the site and the possibility of erecting a high dam at the Calaveras site has long been recognized and was generally accepted as sufficiently demonstrated in 1913, there could be no certainty at that time relating to when the construction of a dam would commence, nor yet with reference to the time when there would be a demand for all the water which the Calaveras Creek, when regulated by the reservoir can supply.

(Witness here stated that he desired to make a correction in this paragraph, because the construction of a dam in the sense of preparation and the expenditure of about $300,000 had commenced at the end of 1913.)

At that time no one could foretell whether the early development 1233 of a water supply from the Sierra Nevada Mountains, for use in the Bay region, would not postpone the requirement of a development on the Calaveras to an indefinite future. It was known then, as it is today, that both the East Bay region as well as San Francisco are in need of more water than is now available for delivery. This need of an increased supply was already pressing in 1913. But although this was the situation there could have been no assurance given to an outside owner if there had been such an owner of the Calaveras Reservoir site, that within two years the construction of the Calaveras dam would be well advanced and the reservoir would be ready for partial use. In fixing upon a market value at that time, consideration would have had to be given to the fact that by an early development of other sources of supply such as those of San Antonio and Del Valle Creeks, the development of the Calaveras supply could be deferred for a number of years. Conditions have changed since 1913, the construction of a dam being well advanced. The value at that date is not the present day value.

Under the circumstances, as explained, the Calaveras Reservoir land can not have had value greatly in excess of the value of similar lands not available for reservoir purposes. But there nevertheless was some excess value due to the location and elevation of the reservoir

349

site and the opportunity which it affords to develop a large amount of water for which there will some day be a market.

The water surface of the completed reservoir will be at elevation 790 feet. The top of the dam will be at elevation 800 feet. The reservoir will have a capacity of 46,315 million gallons. It will store 24 million gallons of water per acre of reservoir area. It will make possible the development and utilization of some 37,000,000 gallons per day of water, of which only a small portion is at present under control and available at Sunol.

Per acre of reservoir area the water production will be about 19,200 gallons per day.

There can be no doubt that in the light of these facts, particularly when consideration is given to the constant increase of population in the Bay region and to the growing demand for water, that the lands of the Calaveras Reservoir site had more than farming land value at the close of the year 1913.

As a water producing property the Calaveras Reservoir is expected to take higher rank than the Peninsula Reservoirs. Its full development will make possible the production of twice as much water per acre of land in the reservoir as is produced per acre of reservoir land on the Peninsula.

Its storage capacity per acre is also greater about 24 million gallons to be compared with 14.3 million gallons as the average for the Pilarcitos, San Andres and Crystal Springs Reservoirs. But the reservoir was not a constructed reservoir at the end of 1913 and there was at that time uncertainty, not alone with reference to the time when its use would be a necessity, but also with reference to the more remote date at which it will be in full use.

In view of these circumstances I consider the market value of this reservoir site at the end of the year 1913 to have been at least $200. per acre.

SAN ANTONIO AND ARROYO VALLE RESERVOIR SITES:

Both the San Antonio and the Arroyo Valle Reservoir sites are valuable features in the ultimate full development of the water of the Alameda Creek region.

Topographically both sites are favorable for the storage and the development of water. At neither site has any work of construction been done but the dam sites have been explored with satisfactory results.

Some facts relating to the water that can be stored in these contemplated reservoirs and their prospective yield is presented in Table 12.

It is uncertain when either of these reservoirs will be requisite as a feature of any water supply whether for San Francisco or any other community. It is uncertain too which reservoir will be required first and to what extent the completion of the Calaveras Reservoir, or the completion of either of these reservoirs will delay the construction of the other. The use of the San Antonio Reservoir site is a feature of the John R. Freeman plan for developing a water supply from Tuolumne River. Nevertheless it is recognized as possible that when water is brought into the Bay region from some Sierra Nevada source, the utilization of one or both of these sites for water storage may be long deferred.

Notwithstanding this fact the lands in each of these sites have some value due to the adaptability for reservoir use in excess of their value for farming and grazing purposes. This excess at the end of the year 1913 I consider to have been at least 25%.

SUMMARY.

In reaching conclusions as herein presented relating to the market value of reservoir properties the circumstances have been weighed which would effect an intelligent public or a prudent purchaser in determining market value. The seller of such properties, as well as the purchaser, would give consideration to every known fact relating thereto. Both would be influenced more or less in their conclusions by the various circumstances to which I have called attention and both would give consideration to the effect of all these circumstances upon the minds of an intelligent public, because it is this effect and the resulting attitude of the public which is the main factor that influences market value.

1236

On the basis of the areas as herein noted and the unit values found, the valuation of the reservoir properties would appear as follows:

Peninsula Reservoir System:
    Crystal Springs .....1493 acres
    San Andres .... 498 "
    Pilarcitos .... 109 "
                2100 acres at $1400. per ac. = $2,940,000.
Crystal Springs Reservoir land not yet in use
                640 acres at $700. per ac. = 448,000.

    Total Peninsula Reservoirs ....$3,388,000.
Lake Merced:
    336 acres of water surface at $1000...............$ 336,000.
Calaveras Reservoir Site:
    1930 acres at $200.............................$ 386,000.
San Antonio and Arroyo Valle Reservoir sites at
    125 per cent of value for ordinary uses.

Tables 1 to 17 and diagrams 1 to 6 herein referred to are appended.

Table 1.

CRYSTAL SPRINGS RESERVOIR.

Cost of Reservoir Lands.

On the assumption that Reservoir Lands cost ten times as much as Watershed Lands. Selected Tracts.

No. of Tract	Area Acr æ	Area in Res.	Area in Watershed	Total Cost	Approx. Cost Per Acre Res.	Approx. Cost Per Acre Watershed	Original Owner
72	32.80	24.00	8.80 }	$ 26,974.75	$ 445.00	$ 44.50	Home Mut. Ins. Co.
73	284.55	8.10	276.45 }				" " "
41	44.95	2.50	42.45	6,000.00	890.00	89.00	John Spaulding et al
40	13.23	3.90	9.33	5,500.00	1,140.00	100	R. Mauvais
94	14.45	9.50	4.95	10,248.55	1,025.00	102.50	Mary and J. A. Drinkhouse
97	86.79	18.70	68.09	7,500.00	294.00	29.40	Mary Craig
92	80.01	48.70	31.31	32,500.00	628.00	62.80	R. Sherwood et al
90	981.50	125.40	856.10	122,150.00	579.00	57.90	W. H. Howard et al
68	980.04	150.27	829.77	396,645.83	1,700.00	170.00	San Meo Wtr Works
36	135.24	32.10	103.14	8,150.00	192.00	19.20	Jas. Byrnes
39	2,162.25	68.20	2,094.05	38,624.35	139.00	13.90	Jas. D. Walker
96	23.65	11.45	12.20	6,500.00	513.00	51.30	Ellen Corey
54	104.22	39.90	64.32	5,000.00	108.00	10.80	Edwin A. Rowe
37	516.43	166.00	350.43	15,492.90	77.00	7.70	Gustave Touchard
47	70.75	21.50	49.25	15,000.00	567.00	56.70	Michael Dolan
46	294.53	144.10	150.43 }	40,250.00	223.00	22.30	James Byrnes
45	154.17	6.70	147.47 }				Al æ Cossell and G. F. Maynard
50	481.80	190	310.90	42,000.00	208.00	20.80	L. and J. C. Maynard
59	15.68	9.50	6.18	392.12 }	343.00	34.30	Louis æla (Und. Int.) Joliet J. C. C. & S. E.
89	47.06		47.06	4,706.00 }			Mezes (Und. Int.)
55	98.94	24.70	74.24	11,872.80	370.00	37.00	A. C. Webber and J. Claffey et al
49	659.80	15.90	643.90	15,500.00	193.00	19.30	Margaret O'Callahan et al
48	1,161.78	235.90	925.88	70,000.00	213.00	21.30	Chris. Bolinger
Totals and Means....	8,444.62	1,337.92	7,106.70	$881,007.30	$ 430.00	$ 43.00	

Table 2.

SAN ANDRES RESERVOIR.

Cost of Reservoir Lands.

On the assumption that Reservoir Lands cost ten times as much as Watershed Lands.

Selected Tracts.

No. of Tract	Area Acres	Area in Res.	Area in Watershed	Total Cost	Approx. Cost per Acre Res.	Approx. Cost per Acre Watershed	Original Owner
18	119.25	35.70	83.55	$10,965.00	$249.00	$24.90	F. Cunningham
15	153.75	10.40	143.35	10,762.00	438.00	43.80	A. I. Easton
13	531.95	156.65	375.30	13,000.00	67.00	6.70	D. S. Cook
12	181.09	78.30	102.79	12,000.00	135.00	13.50	Ge. Bement
17	31.69	14.30	17.39	3,802.00	237.00	23.70	A. Bollcoff et al
20	36.60	19.70	6.90	1,392.00	205.00	20.50	C. K. Garrison
19	66.92	23.80	43.12	8,030.40	286.00	28.60	Ed. Taylor
21	34.52	13.80	20.72	4,142.40	261.00	26.10	H. S. Jones et al
16	96.11	28.50	67.61	11,533.20	328.00	32.80	D. O. Mills
14	234.56	59.30	175.26	6,350.00	83.00	8.30	Tho. Leroy
Totals and Means..	1,486.44	440.45	1,045.99	$84,977.00	$156.00	$15.60	

Table 3.

PILARCITOS RESERVOIR.
Cost of Reservoir Lands.
On the assumption that Reservoir Lands cost ten times as much as Watershed Lands.
Selected Tracts.

No. of Tract	Area Acres	Area in Res.	Area in Watershed	Total Cost	Approx. Cost per Acre Res.	Approx. Cost per Acre Watershed	Original Owner
106	320.00	24.10	295.90	$3,200.00	$59.60	$5.96	A. A. Wallace
51	31.63	3.30	28.33	788.50	128.00	12.80	Pioche, Mezes and Arguella
52	2,921.32	68.50	2,852.82	16,008.00	45.30	4.53	Robt. Roxby
Totals and Means..	3,272.95	95.90	3,177.05	$19,996.50	$48.50	$4.85	

Table 4.

PENINSULA RESERVOIRS.

Cost of Reservoir Lands in the Three Reservoirs, Crystal Springs, San Andres and Pilarcitos.
On the assumption that Reservoir Lands cost ten times as much as Watershed Lands.
Selected Tracts.

Reservoir	Area Purchased Acres	In Reservoir Acres	In Watershed Acres	Total Cost	Approximate Cost per Acre Res.	Watershed
Crystal Springs	8,444.62	1,337.92	7,106.70	$881,007.30	$430.00	$43.00
San Andres	1,486.44	440.45	1,045.99	84,977.00	156.00	15.60
Pilarcitos	3,272.95	95.90	3,177.05	19,996.50	48.50	4.85
Combined	13,204.01	1,874.27	11,329.74	$985,980.80	$328.00	$32.80

Table 5.

POPULATION BY COUNTIES.

South San Francisco Bay Region.

Year	San Francisco		San Mateo		Santa Clara		Alameda	
	Population	Increase Percent since last Census	Population	Increase Percent since last Census	Population	Increase Percent since last Census	Population	Increase Percent since last Census
1860	56,802		3,214		11,912		8,927	
1870	149,473	163.1	6,635	106.4	26,246	120.3	24,237	171.5
1880	233,959	56.5	8,669	30.7	35,039	33.5	62,976	59.8
1890	298,997	27.8	10,087	16.4	48,005	37.0	93,864	49.0
1900	342,782	14.6	12,094	19.8	60,216	25.4	130,197	38.7
1910	416,912	21.6	26,585	119.8	83,539	38.7	246,131	89.0

Table 6.

ASSESSED VALUE OF REAL ESTATE.

South San Francisco Bay Counties.

Year	San Francisco Real Est. and Impts.	San Francisco Real Estate Only	San Mateo Real Est. and Impts.	San Mateo Real Est. Only	Santa Clara Real Est. and Impts.	Santa Clara Real Est. Only	Alameda Real Est. and Impts.	Alameda Real Est. Only
1860	$ 25,125,800		$ 996,400		$ 2,584,700		$ 2,290,700	
1870	75,146,000		1,533,450		8,733,900		9,621,700	
1880	165,024,000		5,520,800		21,451,800		40,314,500	
1890	235,362,000		12,332,500		45,852,600		69,649,500	
1900	288,531,000		11,902,400		46,027,100		75,028,100	
1900-01	288,531,000	$190,457,000	8,503,000			32,130,000		47,856,000
1901-02	289,682,000	192,7 00	8,554,000					
1902-03	288,436,000	191,804,500	8,633,000			31,894,500		50,006,000
1903-04	300,092,000	201,508,000	9,970,000					
1904-05	882,000	293,500,000	10,360,000			33,657,000		56,516,000
1905-06	066,000	304,136,185	10,917,000					
1906-07	887,000	237,083,000	11,981,000			35,199,500		61,526,500
1907-08	305,000	260,689,800	15,322,000					
1908-09	349,513,000	258,651,000	16,542,500			37,620,500		106,901,500
1909-10	406,144,000	283,169,000	17,256,500			42,285,000		120,278,000
1910-11	433,000,000	288,095,452	17,413,000			44,478,000		110,964,000
1911-12	427,828,000	288,653,700	19,020,000			42,969,000		110,309,000
1912-13	493,545,000	323,715,060	19,293,000			42,877,000		131,675,500
1913-14	506,292,000	326,305,105	19,600,000					
1914-15	519,832,000	326,057,234	19,979,220			43,041,000		146,022,000
1915-16	527,286,000	327,409,000						

Table 7.

COMPARISON OF THE GROWTH OF POPULATION WITH THE INCREASE OF THE ASSESSED VALUE
OF REAL ESTATE.

South San Francisco Bay Counties.

Average increase per year in percentage.

Period	San Francisco		San Mateo		Santa Clara		Alameda	
	Popul.	Real Estate Tax Value	Popul.	Real Estate Tax Value	Popul.	Real Estate Tax Value	Popul.	Real Estate Tax Value
1860-70*	10. %	11.6	7.5	4.5	8.2	13.0	10.5	15.4
1870-80*	4.5%	8.2	2.7	13.7	2.9	9.4	4.8	15.4
1880-90*	2.5%	3.6	1.5	8.3	3.2	6.5	4.1	5.5
1890-00*	1.4%	2.1	1.8	0.3	2.3	.0	3.3	.7
1900-10	2.0%	4.2	8.2	7.5	3.3	3.3	6.6	8.8

* For these periods the increase of the taxable value includes improvements.

Table 8.

COMPARISON OF THE GROWTH OF POPULATION WITH THE INCREASE
OF THE ASSESSMENT ROLL, 1900 TO 1910.

South San Francisco Bay Region.

Average increase per year.

County	Population Per Cent	Taxable Value of Real Estate Per Cent
San Francisco*..	2.0	4.2
San Mateo..	8.2	7.5
Santa Clara..	3.3	3.3
Alameda	6.6	8.8

* The fire in San Francisco in 1906 falling within the period covered by this
table has no doubt had a masterful effect upon both the rate of population growth
and the increase of real estate values.

Table 9.

VALUE OF FARM LAND AND BUILDINGS IN SAN MATEO COUNTY.

(U. S. Census)

Year	Value	Increase in Per Cent Since Last Census	Average Annual Increase Per Cent since last Census
1860................................	$ 1,907,687		
1870................................	3,397,701	78	6.0
1880................................	7,916,196	133	8.8
1890................................	11,509,540	45	3.8
1900................................	9,534,530	17	1.6
1910................................	19,454,985	105	7.5

1247

Table 10.

INDICATION OF THE VALUE OF RESERVOIR LANDS IN 1903 AND 1913.

On the assumption that original cost represents value at the time of purchase and
on the further assumption that the per acre cost of reservoir lands in
each tract acquired was ten times the per acre cost of
lands outside of the reservoir.

The increase of value has been estimated at 5 per cent per year.

Reservoir	Approx. Date of Purchase	Estimated Cost Per ·Acre	Indicated Value 1903	Indicated Value 1913
Crystal Springs..........	1882	$430.00	$1,200.00	$1,950.00
San Andres..................	1868	156.00	860.00	1,400.00
Pilarcitos	1865	48.50	310.00	505.00
Weighted average....			$1,070.00	$1,750.00

The results in this table are illustrative and apply to the several tracts of
land considered individually and not as assembled into one holding ready for use
as a reservoir.

1248

Table 11.

PENINSULA RESERVOIRS.

Storage Capacity and Water Yield.

	Crystal Springs	San Andres	Pilarcitos	Peninsula System
Area, Acres	1,493	498	109	2,100
Storage Capacity M. G.	22,360	6,230	1,083	29,673
Yield M. G. D.	9	6	3	18
Storage Cap. per Ac. M. G.	14.98	12.50	9.94	14.13
Yield per Ac. Gals. per day....	6,030	12,000	27,500	8,570
Elevation, Top of Dam............	288.85	449.5	698.75	
Elevation, Water Surface........	288	446.25	696.75	420

The elevations noted in this table are above Crystal Springs datum. Subtract
4.98 feet to reduce to elevations above City Base.

Table 12.

COMPARISON OF AREAS AND CAPACITIES OF RESERVOIRS, AND
RESERVOIR SITES.

	Peninsula System	Lake Merced	Calaveras Reservoir	San Antonio Reservoir	Del Valle Reservoir
Area, Acres....................	2,100	336	1,930	656	630
Storage Cap. M. G.....	29,673	2,659	46,315	11,674	13,800
Yield M. G. D.	18	3	37	*8.9	*15
Storage Cap. per Ac. M. G.	14.13	7.9	24.0	17.8	21.9
Yield per Ac. Gals. per Day	8,570	8,930	19,200	13,600	23,800
Elevation Top of Dam	†420	+20.7	800	450	800

*Estimates by the Spring Valley Water Co.
†Average.
+Elevation of water surface above Crystal Springs datum, at 30 feet on
the gage.
Note—The capacity of Lake Merced is generally given at 2500 M. G. This
would require the lake's surface to be maintained at gage reading 29 feet (Elev.
19.7 ft.). The ordinary elevation of the water surface is 20 to 22 feet on the
gage. When the draft upon the lake ceases the water can probably be maintained
at gage reading 30 feet or 20.7 feet (Crystal Springs datum).
(To reduce elevations above Crytal Springs to elevations above City Base sub-
stract 4.98 feet.)

Table 13.

California.

POPULATION.

From United States Census.

Year	Population	Increase Per Cent Since Last Census	Since Last Census	Since 1860	Since 1870	Since 1880
			—Increase in Percentage Per Year—			
1850......................	92,597					
1860......................	379,994	310.4				
1870......................	560,247	47.4	4.0	4.0		
1880......................	864,694	54.3	4.4	4.2	4.4	
1890......................	1,213,398	40.3	3.4	3.9	3.9	3.4
1900......................	1,485,053	22.4	2.1	3.5	3.3	2.8
1910......................	2,377,549	60.1	4.9	3.7	3.7	3.5

1251

Table 14.

California.

CASH VALUE OF FARMS (INCL. BUILDINGS).

From United States Census.

Year	Value of Farms Incl. Buildings	Increase Per Cent Since Last Census	—Increase in Percentage Per Year—			
			Since Last Census	Since 1860	Since 1870	Since 1880
1860	48,726,804					
1870	141,240,028	180.	10.8	10.8		
1880	262,051,282	85.	5.8	8.3	5.8	
1890	697,116,630	166.	10.3	9.0	8.0	10.3
1900	707,912,960	1.4	0.1	6.8	5.4	5.2
1910	1,450,601,488	105.	7.4	6.9	5.9	5.9
	Land Only					
1900	630,444,960					
1910	1,317,195,448	109.	7.7			

1252

Table 15.

California.

ASSESSED VALUATION OF REAL ESTATE AND IMPROVEMENTS.

From United States Census.

Year	Assessed Valuation	Increase Per Cent in 10 Years	—Increase in Percentage Per Year—			
			In Last 10 Years	Since 1860	Since 1870	Since 1880
1860	66,906,631					
1870	176,527,160	164.	10.2	10.2		
1880	466,273,585	164.	10.2	10.2	10.2	
1890	891,449,172	91.	6.8	9.1	8.5	6.8
1900	974,492,563	9.	0.9	7.0	6.0	3.9
1910	2,163,020,203	122.	8.4	7.3	6.6	5.4

SPRING VALLEY WATER CO. VS. CITY AND COUNTY OF SAN FRANCISCO

Table 16.

California.

ASSESSED VALUATION OF ALL PROPERTY IN CALIFORNIA.

From United States Census.

Year	Assessed Valution	Increase Per Cent In 10 Years	—Increase in Percentage Per Year—			
			In Last 10 Years	Since 1860	Since 1870	Since 1880
1860	139,654,667					
1870	269,644,068	93.	6.8	6.8		
1880	584,578,036	117.	8.0	7.4	8.0	
1890	1,101,136,431	89.	6.6	7.1	7.3	6.6
1900	1,290,238,964	17.	1.6	5.8	5.4	4.1
1910	2,921,277,451	126.	8.5	6.3	6.2	5.6

Table 17.

ASSESSED VALUATION OF REAL ESTATE IN SAN MATEO COUNTY, 1901 TO 1914.

Supplementing Information in Table No. 6.

Year	Real Estate Other Than —City and Town Lots—		—City and Town Lots—		Improvements by Tenants
	Land Only	Improvements	Land Only	Improvements	
1901	$ 6,916,210	$2,537,835	$1,637,845	$ 906,645	
1902	6,972,220	2,525,480	1,678,425	948,445	
1905	8,583,580	3,017,090	2,333,145	1,197,640	
1906	8,878,030	2,813,315	3,057,655	1,200,540	88,410
1907	10,908,940	3,139,445	4,413,210	1,535,565	17,250
1909	10,643,230	4,416,025	6,611,415	2,396,210	35,400
1910	10,875,500	4,454,310	6,542,870	2,664,790	36,950
1911	12,225,900	4,635,590	6,747,180	2,758,160	67,790
1912	12,385,750	4,745,590	6,895,680	2,818,610	74,850
1913	12,621,210	4,984,240	6,981,130	2,944,350	68,950
1914	12,742,450	5,178,890	7,167,770	3,008,600	67,700

Table 17 (Continued).

1255   ASSESSED VALUE OF REAL ESTATE, SAN MATEO COUNTY.

| Year | ———All Real Estate in County——— | |
	Land Only	Including Improvements
1900	$ 8,503,000	$11,902,500
1901	8,554,055	11,998,500
1902	8,633,000	12,217,000
1903	9,970,000	13,925,000
1904	10,360,000	14,333,000
1905	10,916,725	15,131,500
1906	11,981,000	16,102,500
1907	15,322,150	19,997,100
1908	16,542,500	21,824,000
1909	17,256,500	24,108,000
1910	17,413,000	24,532,000
1911	19,020,000	26,520,000
1912	19,293,000	26,912,485
1913	19,602,500	27,531,000
1914	19,910,000	28,097,000

(Pages Nos. 1256 to 1261 inclusive in Master's
copy cover Sheets 1 to 6 inclusive, "Comparison of
Population and Assessed Value of Real Estate",
etc.)

1256-1261

1262   DIRECT EXAMINATION BY MR. OLNEY.

I have had more or less experience in appraising real estate throughout my experience as a civil engineer. I have assisted in the acquisition of properties for various purposes. About 1892 the City of Vallejo acquired lands for reservoir purposes, which I was instrumental in bringing about the acquisition of.

As City Engineer I valued property to the amount of between eight and nine million dollars that was required for play-grounds, public parks, school houses, and for other public purposes. I was made arbitrator in the matter of the valuation of damages that resulted from the construction of the Bay Shore Cutoff of the Southern Pacific Railroad. There were, I think, some 800 individual property owners affected at that time. I was also in charge of the appraisal of benefits and damages relating to the construction of the Stockton Street Tunnel. As City Engineer, I made an investigation, in a general way, into the value of these very lands which I have been discussing. I did not attempt to value individual tracts at that time, but I made an investigation with considerable care, particularly in the matter of the Lake Merced lands, and I generally informed myself about the market value of the lands, at that time.

1263   (Counsel for Plaintiff states that Mr. Grunsky's figure—made at the time he was City Engineer—as to reservoir values, is put in as a fact which occurred in connection with the history of these properties, and was not put in with the idea that it constituted an admission on the part of the city which was binding upon the city in this case. There is no idea that it is binding here upon the city.)

1265   CROSS EXAMINATION BY MR. STEINHART.

I am familiar with the Spring Valley Reservoirs, and outside of the study that I gave when I was in the employ of the city, I have been on the ground a number of times since, and have quite recently informed myself with reference to the market value of these properties to the extent of knowing that the values which I found were in excess of the value which these lands might have if used otherwise. I made no special inquiry with reference to any particular tract of land east of San Andres, but made my inquiry generally with reference to lands in that vicinity.

1266   In determining the value of lands to the east of San Andres Lake, and bordering along the lake, I examined the figures which had been presented by Mr. Baldwin and Mr. Hoag as part of the information which I have in connection with this matter.

I did not value the land to the east of Crystal Springs Lake, and contiguous to Crystal Springs Lake. I placed no valuation upon any of the lands outside of the reservoir areas, and that applies to the lands to the west and contiguous to San Andres Lake, and to the west and contiguous to Crystal Springs Lake.

In the Calaveras region I did not reach any conclusion other than that the value which I placed upon the land was higher than the land values for ordinary uses. It is not my theory that the reservoir value must always be higher than the value of the land. 1267

Referring to the San Andres lands; I did not place any valuation upon those lands other than that they have a greater value than they have for the ordinary farming and grazing purposes, due to the fact that they are reservoir lands. The same thing applies to Arroyo Valle.

If I had found the lands surrounding Crystal Springs were worth $12.50 per acre, I do not think that I would have valued the Crystal Springs Reservoir differently than I did, and if I had found that the lands surrounding San Andres were worth $10 an acre, I do not think that I would have valued San Andres Reservoir any differently than I did. I would pre-suppose different values in that section from those which do exist there, and, therefore, I am unable to answer the question. The value of adjacent land is not necessarily the measure of the reservoir land values. 1268

I did not take any exhibited figure for a valuation of the Calaveras land, but I knew what the valuations were that had been placed upon it by Mr. Gale, Mr. Parks, and Mr. Clayton. I do not know Mr. Parks, and am accustomed in my scientific work, to take the word of a man I do not know, only to a certain extent.

I ascertained the cost of the different parcels of watershed lands in Crystal Springs Watershed from the records furnished to me. I did not know of that from other sources than the compiled record. The parcel numbers, as they are represented on the map of the Spring Valley Water Co., are the parcel numbers to which I referred in my memorandum. In getting at my valuations, I assumed a certain relationship between the neighboring land and the reservoir land for the purpose of determining to what extent the cost of the lands might confirm conclusions reached. I was endeavoring to secure every fact which a purchaser would make himself acquainted with, in connection with the value of these properties. In reaching my conclusions, I 1270 assumed a certain relation in value between reservoir lands and neighboring lands on the basis of the entire area. The comparison was made between cost per acre of the reservoir land with that of the watershed land. In reaching my conclusion, irrespective of cost, I did not assume any relationship between neighboring lands and reservoir lands. I do not recall any purchase of the Spring Valley Water Co. of reservoir lands where the price was $1000 per acre. I tried, in a general way, to get at the facts involved in the purchases that I examined.

1271   I did not examine the deed from the Drinkhouse people, but my recollection with reference to the Drinkhouse property is, that what was purchased after the condemnation proceedings was all classed as reservoir lands, and that of that entire tract that was acquired at that time, not all was in the reservoir below elevation 288. I did not examine the findings of fact, or the conclusions of law in the Drinkhouse case.

1272   (Counsel for the Defendant stated that the record in the Drinkhouse matter shows the following: the judgment was for $4667; the severance was $435.50; cost of suit $100, making a total judgment of $5,203. The testimony established $2,000 to $3,000 for the improvements.)

1273   In regard to the Drinkhouse matter, I did not go beyond ascertaining what the cost was that had been paid for these properties.

Parcel No. 50: Table 1, shows approximate cost per acre in the reservoir $208, and in the watershed $20.80.

(Counsel for Plaintiff advised that the judgment above referred to—in the Drinkhouse matter—was reversed in the 92 Cal., and the case was sent back for a new trial.)

Parcel No. 44; I did not include this in my Table No. 1, for the reason that it was a peculiarly located tract, crossing the island in the reservoir. If it had been included with the other tracts, and the entire area in the reservoir, and the adjacent watershed lands, as covered by the table, and by the other tracts which have some portions within the reservoir, it would have modified the result but slightly. That piece
1274   is not entirely within the reservoir. I had no particular reason for not including it, excepting that it appeared peculiarly located. The Spring Valley paid $1,867.50, or about $85 per acre for it. It is contiguous to, and immediately to the north of parcel 50.

The land in the reservoir was of a different character than the neighboring land, as most of it was nice, level land, and had improvements upon it. I was, to some extent, familiar with the land in the
1275   main Crystal Springs Reservoir before it was innundated, but not with the land in the upper Crystal Springs, which was already under water at the time I became acquainted with the country.

Questioned by Mr. Olney.

The Upper Crystal Springs Reservoir is that portion which lies to the south of the earthen dam, across which the road to Half Moon Bay runs, and was known as the Canada del Remunda.

CROSS EXAMINATION BY MR. STEINHART.

I was not familiar with the portion under the San Andres. The most careful examination that I made of the Crystal Springs land before water was held back by the Crystal Springs dam, was near the
1276   dam site, and outside of that, I did not study any portion of it closely

that I can recall. I was generally familiar with the character of the country. I made no estimate of the relative values of that land as land, and the neighboring lands.

Parcel 45: I do not want to be understood as stating that I put any valuation on the portion within the reservoir, and the portion without the reservoir, but I have, in Table 1, the apportionment of cost as $223 per acre to the land in the reservoir, and $22.30 to that in the watershed.

Parcel No. 55; apportioned at $370 per acre in the reservoir, and $37 in the watershed.

Parcel No. 46: That is given in the table in combination with parcel No. 45. 45 and 46 are given together. $223 per acre to the reservoir land, and $22.30 to the watershed land.

Questioned by Mr. Olney.

The apportionment is all on the ten to one basis.

CROSS EXAMINATION BY MR. STEINHART.

Parcel No. 38 is a tract of land that does not appear in Table No. 1, and I make it $509 per acre for the reservoir lands, and in round numbers, $50.90 per acre for the watershed lands.

Parcel No. 68: The apportionment of cost of the number of tracts included within this parcel was $1700 per acre in the reservoir, and $170 per acre in the watershed. That was the San Mateo water purchase with which I am familiar in a general way. There were included, in that purchase, some water rights, pumping works, and other property.

Parcel No. 92: $628 per acre in the reservoir, and $62.80 to land not in the reservoir.

Parcel No. 89: Parcels 89 and 59 were treated together, and the apportionment of cost on the same basis was $343 per acre in the reservoir, and $34.30 per acre in the watershed.

Calaveras is suited for reservoir purposes, and in placing my valuation upon reservoir sites, I have intended to place the market value thereon. Market value is the value which property would have in exchange. It is the amount which property would bring in the market if the owner were a willing seller and the purchaser were a prudent man, making necessary inquiries. I understand quite well the difference between cost theory and reproduction theory of valuation, but I know that neither of them represents value, and in making my valuation of reservoir sites, I have adopted neither theory. I have endeavored to obtain an idea of the effect of these various circumstances upon the market.

In the case of the properties on the east side of the bay, I have valued the reservoir on the basis of property that was available for such use, and intended to be used at some time. `In the case of prop-

1277

1278

1279

erties on the west side of the bay, I have valued them as properties available for the purpose, and ready to be used, and in full use immediately that they are acquired. I consider the facts as they are with the reservoirs having been used, and their values as reservoirs having been demonstrated, and having been developed to their full yielding capacity, and have then valued the land as naked land. I think that probably it would be a correct assumption to say that they had been used as reservoirs, because their availability for the purpose has actually been demonstrated, and has an effect upon the market value of the property, and that availability arises through the fact that they have actually been used as reservoir sites. When I come to a site whose availability has not been proven, in that it has not actually been

1280 used, I do not value it in the same way. There is no doubt in my mind as to the availability of Calaveras for reservoir purposes, but the fact has not been demonstrated, and in the market it would not have the same value as a reservoir that has already demonstrated its serviceability. I have valued these lands as though they might be owned by any party. Outside of the San Mateo Water Co. lands, which were acquired, none of the other lands acquired by the Spring Valley were used for reservoir purposes prior to their purchase.

1281 I did not assume any valuation for the reservoir land in Calaveras, other than for reservoir purposes. My value of the Calaveras lands is my judgment. I took all of these circumstances into account that would affect the value. I took into account also the fact that the city was urging the construction of the dam, and that the time was growing nearer when Calaveras would be required by somebody. I was very much in doubt whether the market value should not be placed somewhat higher than I finally concluded that it should be.

1282 The most recent purchases of which I have a note of land in Calaveras Valley, which land would be land in the reservoir, are the tracts marked f-268, k-268 and j-268. They were bought in 1911. j-268 contains 36.81 acres in the reservoir, and the total cost was $6000, or $75 an acre for the entire tract. k-268 contains 28 acres in the reservoir, and cost $75 an acre for the entire tract. In placing a valuation of $200 an acre on the portion in the reservoir in j-268, I get a value for that portion alone of $7,360. That is more than was paid for the entire tract of 80 acres. k-268; 28 acres in the reservoir, at $200, $5,600. That would give a valuation for the balance of 52 acres of

1283 $400. That balance I consider worth more than $8 an acre. These purchases were made in 1911, and the date of the valuation is 1913. It was known in Calaveras at that time that the Calaveras Valley was intended to be used as a reservoir site, and that would have affected, in some degree, the negotiations that went on between the seller and the purchaser.

To the best of our information at the present time Calaveras
1284 is adaptable for a reservoir site, and there is no question as to the

necessity for its immediate use. I want to qualify that, because the necessity for developing more water immediately, or in the near future, exists; I am putting myself back into 1913 in weighing the necessity for the immediate use, and at that time the development of other sources appeared possible. It was possible that water from the mountains might have been brought in within a reasonable time. There was some uncertainty about the time when Calaveras would be called requisite.

Beginning with the year 1907, I think you can carry that right forward to 1913, and say that there was no necessity for the immediate use of Calaveras, although the question as to the degree of necessity varies. A person selling the bare land with this question as to when it might be used, or as to whether it might ever be used, would consider that as a factor, and therefore would not get as high a price for his land because of that fact. He would also take into account that the probability of an early use was evident by the work which had been done as early as 1902 in exploring for dam sites, and the further fact that construction work in the nature of preparation for the dam, and the building of a concrete tunnel was well under way, and that some $300,000 had been expended there, at the close of 1913. Those are elements that would affect the market value.

The fact that the reservoir lands have been assembled at each site in one holding would affect the value at the time when these several parcels are all assembled into one holding, although the increase of value resulting from that assembling, may be greater for the reservoir that is to be used immediately than in the case of one whose use is far in the future. It is an added value after the reservoir has gotten into the hands of one holder. In my valuation, I have taken all these factors into consideration, and I have taken into account the fact that the reservoir lands have been assembled at each site into one holding.

In connection with the Peninsula reservoir system, I have considered the cost of the reservoir lands by taking the ratio of ten to one. I have given consideration to the cost of the land in the case of the Calaveras. In the case of the Arroyo Valle, and the San Antonio I have simply indicated a percentage increase of value due to the fact of their being reservoir lands, and therefore I did not analyze the cost of the land particularly.

The percentage increase was based both upon the theory that the lands have been assembled into a whole, and upon the theory that they had a reservoir value. My judgment was that that would be a reasonable allowance for their additional value. I felt that because, as City Engineer I had placed a valuation upon that ground, that it might have affected market value, and the valuation as judicially determined in the rate case of 1903 comes in the same category, and is referred to for the reason that that would have an undoubted, and a very material effect upon the market value. Regarding my statement that San Fran-

1285

1286

1287

cisco has declared the Peninsula reservoirs, and Lake Merced necessary as a part of its ultimate water supply system, I refer there to the
1288   well-known fact that the City has endeavored to make a purchase of these properties, and has thereby recognized the necessity of having the Peninsula as a feature safe-guarding the supply, and adding water to the system. That fact was established when the purchase of the Spring Valley properties was submitted to a vote of the people in 1909, and was rejected, and also more recently, when it was also rejected. Also the fact that there are no other sites at hand for the storage of water in large amounts. The San Miguel Reservoir is suitable for a reservoir site, but that is a small reservoir known as
1289   the Rock Creek Reservoir, and was suggested to the City of San Francisco in 1874, by Mr. Scowden.

The Calaveras, Arroyo Honda, and San Antonio reservoir sites command the flow of the Alameda Creek and its tributaries, and they are the sites which command quite well the water output from the Alameda Creek, supplemented by such amounts of water as can be obtained from the artesian wells at Pleasanton. There were other reservoir sites available in 1913, but they were more remote.

My statement in relation to the proximity of reservoir sites to population centers applies particularly to the reservoirs on the Peninsula, Crystal Springs, San Andres and Pilarcitos. It also applies with a great deal of force to Calaveras, which will be in a similar position in the course of time on the east side of the bay that we find these other reservoirs on the west side. Those are all factors going to make
1290   up the value of a reservoir site.

The principal difference between Calaveras reservoir site and the Peninsula reservoir site, lies in the fact that the former may not be in full use for a great many years, and that its serviceability has not yet been demonstrated. Also the further fact that the means of distributing the water are not yet there, and the water has not yet found a market, while the market exists for the reservoirs on the Peninsula side. Calaveras will supply about 37,000,000 gallons of water per day, and San Francisco is now using about 40,000,000 gallons per day, so that the capacity of the Calaveras developed will be an excess capacity to the capacity that will be needed for San Francisco for a time. In the meantime, the City will probably continue its work of bringing in water from the Sierra Nevada Mountains, and may postpone the time
1291   still further, when the full yield of Calaveras will be required.

In valuing the Calaveras as a reservoir proposition, I considered the possibility of competition by the City to that extent, namely, whether the City owns it or whether it is owned by the Spring Valley. If other water is brought in here, it may defer the time when it will be in full use. Some of the principle factors of difference between the Peninsula and Calaveras are, first, the fact that the Peninsula has been demonstrated to be adaptable for water for reservoir purposes, while Calaveras has not; second, the fact that in-as-much as the City is now using the reservoir water from the Peninsula, there is an immediate use, as against a not immediate use for Calaveras; third, the fact that Calaveras may, to a certain extent, be put out of business, as it were, to its full capacity by the City bringing in Hetch Hetchy water; and fourth, the distributing system is not yet constructed from Calaveras, whereas one exists from the Peninsula reservoirs. Also the population is larger on this side of the bay in immediate proximity to the reservoirs, and these reservoirs are of particular importance, due to the possibility of damage by earthquake, or possibly other matters that I do not think of right now.

In the last quake, the damage to the mains of Spring Valley occurred, just south of San Francisco, and between the city of San Francisco and Pilarcitos. These were the main lines bringing in the water from the Crystal Springs and the San Andres.

TWENTY-FIRST HEARING.   AUGUST 17, 1915.

Witnesses: C. E. GRUNSKY and HARRY THOMAS CORY.   1292

CROSS EXAMINATION BY MR. STEINHART.

Questioned by Mr. Olney.

There was a mistake made in Table 1 of my report. With reference to the division of 98.94 acres, known as Tract 55: In the table it appears that there are 24.70 acres in the reservoir, and 74.24 acres in the watershed. Those figures were transposed in the information that was given me, and as a result all figures that are dependent thereon are slightly modified. In Table 1, in the last line, "Totals   1293 and Means", the indicated cost of reservoir lands should be $421 instead of $430, and the watershed lands $42.10. For the particular tract, No. 55, the cost of reservoir lands would be $155, and of watershed lands $15.50. Also, the total area in the reservoir will appear as 1,387.46, and the total area in the watershed as 7,057.16.

In Table 4, on the line "Crystal Springs", the recapitulation in the last line of Table 1, and at the bottom of the table, the combined figures are 13,204.01 acres in both reservoir and watershed; 1923.81 acres of reservoir lands; 11,280.20 acres of watershed lands; total cost $985,980.80. The indicated cost per acre of reservoir lands, $323, and of watershed $32.30.

Table 10, the line "Crystal Springs", shows the approximate date of purchase 1882, and the estimated cost per acre $421. The indicated value, 1903, $1,170; the indicated value, 1913, $1,910; the weighted average at the bottom of the table for 1903, $1,056, and for 1913, $1,723.

1296   The City of San Francisco determined, in 1910, by vote to build Hetch Hetchy, and rejected the purchase of the Spring Valley Water Co., but, of course, in the rejection the question of price had something to do with it. They have never voted to the contrary. I drew up a plan for the construction of Hetch Hetchy, under instructions

1297 from the Board of Supervisors, and in the report I stated that the proper proceeding for San Francisco to pursue would be to first acquire the established waterworks, and use as much thereof as could be incorporated with the system. In that report I suggested a reservoir at Belmont, but the reservoir planned at that point was one of comparatively small capacity. My report stated that the Hetch Hetchy project could be carried out as an independent system by acquiring reservoirs at Altamont and Belmont, and excluding all reservoirs of the Spring Valley Water Co. It also stated that the reliability of service would be in favor of a system similar to that which is now established, with the large storage nearby. The water supply system which

1298 I proposed and recommended over my signature in that report, I still hold to be a feasible system.

    If, in valuing a reservoir site, I found that a recent sale of land had been made in that reservoir by a person having knowledge of the fact that it was a reservoir location, I should consider that sale entitled to consideration, but it is by no means certain that a sale of that kind is made with a full knowledge. It also makes a difference where the land is located, and what its character is, because the various parcels may have very different market values at the time of the sales. Of course, the greater number of sales of that character, the better the

1299 indication as to the market value at the time the sales were made. Such sales would be a matter for consideration in fixing what the market value was for reservoir use, as well as for other purposes. If all the lands in that reservoir have been sold by persons who knew the fact that they were to be used for reservoir purposes, then the sales were probably a good indication of the market value. If it is taken as a whole, and includes all of the land that is necessary for the development of the reservoir, the presumption is that it is market value at which these lands are sold. In valuing the reservoir site, I should

1300 only consider the sales of that kind as one of the factors to be considered in determining the value of reservoir lands. Some of the other factors are the availability of the reservoir site, the amount of water which it commands, the location of the reservoir site, and its proximity to population centers. Also any facts which are known with reference to the value of similar properties. If a seller did know these facts, I would not ignore them, and I would not ignore the price at which land was sold. If I had prices at which the land was sold I would assume it possible that the seller did not know these facts. He might know the advantages of his own land, but I should always consider it possible that he did not know them. The purchaser would have an advantage 1301 as a general rule over the seller, because of the seller's lack of knowledge as to the advantages that his own land possessed.

Referring to the rise in the assessed value of lands in San Mateo County, I made only such effort to find out how uniform this rise was · as is indicated in the tables which I have presented.

Questioned by Master.

I investigated generally assessed valuations of all property, and separately the assessed valuations of farming property. That is, real estate other than city and town lots, and for that given the assessed valuation of land, and then compared that with the valuation of land only in city and town lots.

CROSS EXAMINATION BY MR. STEINHART.

I differentiated the assessed valuations: On sheet No. 6 you will find, curves showing the assessed value of real estate, including im- 1302 provements, the assessed valuation of real estate and improvements, city and town lots omitted; the assessed value of real estate only, with city and town lots omitted. I got my assessed value of city and town lots from the Assessor's Office, and included whatever the Assessor had classed as city and town lots. That was compiled by my son, C. E. Grunsky, Jr. I differentiate between city and town lots and other land to this extent, that I gave the information for each of the classes separately. San Mateo County is given in Table 6 and in Table 17. The value of farm lands was also obtained from the U. S. Census, and 1303 is given in Table 9. That is not the assessed valuation, but it is the estimate upon the cash value of those properties as placed by the U. S. Census·officials.

The Spring Valley lands devoted to reservoirs are in the classification, real estate other than town and city lots. They are included in the farming lands and buildings, Table 9.

Parcel No. 44 is a peculiarly located tract in this: As I made my first selection of tracts which was for the purpose of endeavoring to obtain some idea of the cost of reservoir lands, that tract showed a small portion of watershed surrounded by the water of the lake or reservoir, and that peculiarity and the peculiar location of those watershed lands caused me to omit that from consideration when I prepared my table in the first place. The watershed land is the island on that tract, but the tract is not composed entirely of that island. 1304

Map 3, parcel No. 72 of "Plaintiff's Exhibit 8"; 24 acres in the reservoir, and 8.80 acres in the watershed. The essential difference between these lands within and outside of the reservoir is the location. The land is on the slope of the hill from the summit of the ridge easterly to the reservoir. (Witness here explained that for a moment he

1305　had been misled as to the piece indicated on the map, and that he now recognized 72 as a long, slender strip, in which there is very little difference between the land which is in the reservoir and the land that is on the hillside.)

Parcel 73: There may be some of that that extends over the top of the hill. It is supposed to follow the ridge. There is nothing on the map to indicate that the portion in the reservoir was any different from the portion outside. There is only the knowledge that the lower portion of that tract, the southwesterly corner, is lower down on the ridge, but there is no material difference besides the elevation. The 1306　slope of the lower portion may be flatter, and the location of that tract is from the summit of the ridge down into the reservoir, and near the lowest portion of the valley, only a small portion of it being below the contour 288. The portion below is substantially the same as that above the contour line.

Parcel 90; extends well down into the valley, and the land in the reservoir is flatter land than that over the reservoir line. There are ravines which cut down through the land from the east. This is the Howard tract, which includes a part of the summit of the ridge, and the northerly portion of the dam site, and extends along San Mateo Creek for some distance. The reservoir land to a considerable extent 1307　is valley land, and closely adjacent to the valley land, as I know from my knowledge of the situation there, and from my having been on the 1307-1309　ground.

(Discussion between Counsel in regards to statement by Witness in relation to lands under the reservoir being of a different character than the neighboring lands—page 1274 of transcript. Witness here explained that when he said different land, it had relation to the fact that when separated from the land in the valley, the back land would have a different value from what it would in combination with the valley land, and in that sense he referred to it as entirely different land.)

Its character is also different in the matter of much of it being brush covered, and less available for use than other lands. Most of 1310　the land that lies to the west of San Andres is brush covered, and is hill land. I do not think that I stated at any time that that land, as it continues into the reservoir, was of a different character the minute it struck the reservoir line. There was no immediate change at the reservoir line. In speaking of the value of the land, and the elements that affect value, I made a distinction. Referring to parcel No. 14; 1311　the portion under the reservoir line extends into the valley, and the portion above extends over the hill tops.

I have a knowledge of the land immediately south of that, and have traveled over it. It is a narrow valley, and I assume that the land above the dam was somewhat similar to the land below it.

Parcel No. 12: I made no assumption with reference to the sub-division of the individual tracts of the reservoir land and the hill land. The analysis which I made applies to these various parcels taken in the aggregate, and thus taken there was a certain amount of this land that was valley land, at comparatively low elevation, easily accessible, and land which added value to the other land that lies back of it. It is the division of the cost into those two parts which I attempted to make. The value of the reservoirs is of date 1913, but the sub-division of cost is of the date of the acquisition of the land. It would be substantially correct for 1913, and is about the ratio which would prevail at the present time. I have made no assumption with reference to residential values of the land in the reservoir in comparison with that on the slope.

    1312

I made a careful study of the assessed valuations in San Francisco, but I made no inquiry with reference to the various districts in San Francisco; I simply dealt with the aggregate figures. In making my valuation, and in building up my cost analysis, I examined, to some extent, the Spring Valley deeds and contracts in regard to the reservoir land. I do not recall finding any single deed or contract of sale wherein an owner charged Spring Valley ten times as much for the land in the reservoir as for that outside, unless it was the Drink-house sale.

    1313

    1313-1314

(Discussion between Counsel in regards to the Drinkhouse case.)

Apart from this Drinkhouse case, I do not know of any case wherein the seller knew concerning what portion of his land was to be used for reservoir purposes, and what portion was to be used for other purposes. I do not wish to be considered as familiar with all of the dealings of the Spring Valley Water Co.

    1315

In the case of the Arroyo Valle and San Antonio Reservoirs, I did not assume any fixed value for agricultural purposes. I figured that San Antonio and the Arroyo Valle would be worth less than the Calaveras. The cost of developing the storage at Arroyo Valle did not enter into consideration beyond the fact that the development of storage is a feasibility, and the same applies to San Antonio, but I should say that it was considered in a negative way, that the probability of an early development was remote. In comparison with other available storages and water developments, the early use of those sites is not probable. If a company acquires a reservoir site, and builds a reservoir and uses it, and another company acquires a reservoir site, and is not able to go ahead with it because it has no money, and assuming that all other circumstances are the same in the two cases, the reservoir which has been actually constructed would have the higher value. I took into consideration in regard to my reservoir sites the feasibility of the delivery of pure water, and I ranked all three of these reservoir sites about the same as regards feasibility for the delivery of pure water.

    1316

1317   Q. I am going to ask you whether you testified as follows in that
case and whether you have changed your opinion since giving that
testimony:

"Q. In your examination and investigation of the conditions
"surrounding the sources of supply of the Spring Valley Water Com-
"pany what did you find, if anything, which would tend to injuri-
"ously affect the water stored by that company for the purpose of
"supplying the inhabitants of San Francisco?

"A. Most of the water which the Spring Valley Water Company
"delivers to San Francisco is reservoir water. The water is collected
"in reservoirs from the catchment areas of comparatively small ex.
"tent; these catchment areas are not free from human activities;
"among these reservoirs is Lake Merced lying within the boundaries
"of San Francisco with a considerable population on the watershed
"area that is tributary to the lake. Although works have been con-
"structed for the interception of surface drainage in order that the
"water reaching the lake may be only that which percolates through
"the sands the lake cannot be regarded as furnishing a perfectly safe
"water. Water from such a source should be subjected to filtration
"before delivery to the inhabitants of the city. In the case of the
"Peninsula Reservoirs the watershed areas are low rolling hills and
"low mountain country, soil and brush covered and are of the char-
"acter from which it cannot be hoped to obtain water of the same high
"standard of excellence as would be obtained from such high moun-
"tain regions as those of the Sierra Nevada. Water obtained from
"such sources in order that it may be ranked as a high class water
1318   "should be filtered.

"Q. Is there any evidence of the fact that the water used in San
"Francisco is not of the highest excellence?

"A. Waters that are subject to contamination have a direct
"effect upon the healthfulness of the municipality in which they are
"used. It is often very difficult to connect the cause of any specific
"disease with the water, but it is the experience throughout the
"world that when water of a high standard of excellence is substi-
"tuted for water of doubtful purity the prevalence of certain dis-
"ease is materially reduced. This is notably true of typhoid fever,
"and the typhoid fever death-rate is therefore often referred to in
"determining whether or not a municipality is receiving first-class
"water.

"Q. If San Francisco were receiving a water that would be
"ranked of first quality what would be the expected death-rate from
"typhoid fever, in your opinion?

"A. The death-rate should be less than 10 per 100,000 inhabi-
"tants.

"Q. Do you know what the death-rate in San Francisco from
"typhoid fever has been for the last few years?

SPRING VALLEY WATER CO. VS. CITY AND COUNTY OF SAN FRANCISCO

"A. The death-rate in San Francisco from typhoid fever is "about 30 per 100,000 inhabitants."

My recollection is that I did testify that way in regard to the reservoir sites on the Peninsula, but in the course of the years that have elapsed since that testimony was given, I have changed my opinion to some extent. My criticism of those reservoir sites, due   1319
to the fact that they are low, rolling hills, and low mountain country soil, and brush covered, and of a character from which it cannot be hoped to obtain water of the same high standard of excellence, has not changed, but at the present time we know more about the effects of the storage of water for a considerable time in reservoirs upon the disease germs. It is also stated in there, with reference particu-   1320
larly to Lake Merced, and also to the watersheds of the other Peninsula reservoirs, that those areas are not entirely free from human activity. The fact that this is a low, rolling country, covered with shrubs, is to some extent a factor in derogation of the reservoir site when compared with water that would be obtained from a high mountain area. A reservoir site would have no value as a reservoir site if the water could not be marketed, or unless there is a profit in the delivery of the water. I mean by that, that the profit means a return in excess of interest on the investment and the cost of operation. In my valuation of these lands for reservoir purposes, they are valued as property used in connection with a public utility. At the time of the last earthquake the breaks that occurred in the mains occurred between the Peninsula reservoirs and San Francisco, and some of the breaks occurred on the fault, namely, the Pilarcitos   1321
pipe line. The San Andres gate house, which stands practically on the fault, was injured through the earthquake.

(Motion to strike out all of Mr. Grunsky's testimony denied.)   1321-1324

RE-DIRECT EXAMINATION BY MR. OLNEY.

With reference to the importance of the Peninsula reservoirs in connection with the supply of water to San Francisco: In the   1325
first place, these reservoirs store a very large amount of water, which is available within a comparatively short distance from San Francisco, so that it safeguards any large supply brought in from other sources. When connected with some supply from a remote source, the reservoirs will act as balancing reservoirs. They can be kept full, or nearly full of water, while the city is being supplied, so that practically at all times the large reserve will be available comparatively close at hand, and if an accident happens, it will take but a short time to restore the connections between the reservoirs and the city. Merced, as one of the bodies of water close at hand, is the reservoir which is particularly valuable in safeguarding the supply, and giving time in case of an accident for repairs.

Q. You have been questioned, Mr. Grunsky, about the vote of the people upon the acquisition of the Spring Valley properties; I will ask you if the responsible officials on behalf of the City have, from time to time, made declarations with regard to the importance of those Peninsula reservoir sites in connection with the water supply of the city.

1325-1328   (The above question was objected to as immaterial, incompetent and irrelevant, etc., and after discussion of the matter between Counsel and the Master, the objection was sustained.)

The San Miguel reservoir lies within the limits of San Francisco. It is a site in which water could be stored to the extent of about 500,000,000 gallons. Not a very favorable site, but would probably be feasible to carry out the storage of water in that site.

1329   It was first suggested by Mr. Scowden in about 1874. At the present rate of consumption, it would supply San Francisco for about twelve or thirteen days, whereas Lake Merced would supply the city for about sixty days. As compared with Crystal Springs, Pilarcitos, and the San Andres system, it is more in the nature of a service reservoir, rather than a storage reservoir. With the above system as developed, the reservoirs on the Peninsula would supply water for about 700 days.

The Belmont reservoir site, with which I am familiar, is a very much smaller reservoir site than the Crystal Springs. It is about in the neighborhood of 300 or 400 acres, but I am not sure of the figure in relation thereto. I have not the figures in mind as to what the cost of that reservoir site would be as compared with the valuation which I have put on these other reservoir sites, but I can prob-

1330   ably answer that question a little later. The Belmont reservoir, on account of the limited capacity and the low elevation, could not fully serve the purpose which is now served by the Crystal Springs, San Andres, and Pilarcitos reservoirs.

I think I did state in the report which I made to the Board of Supervisors and the Board of Public Works upon my plan of Hetch Hetchy development, that said project was made as an independent project, and that it involved the duplication of the pipe lines in San Francisco, and other portions of the established waterworks. Referring to the matter of a special market valuation on lands available for reservoir purposes; I know of the purchase which the City

1331   made of reservoir lands where a higher price was paid for lands simply because they were in the reservoir. The City bought the lands known as the Smith lands, a portion of which were in the Hetch Hetchy reservoir site, and the records seem to show that the City paid more than $200 an acre for those reservoir lands. There were included in the same purchase lands outside the reservoir site, and my recollection is that those lands were bought at $10 per acre, and the reservoir lands were $256 per acre. I give those figures subject to correction. My values were on property as an assembled whole, and this applies when the assembling has been consummated, but there is an added market value, increasing as the assembling progresses. The land comprised within a reservoir site, and valuable as a reservoir site, would have a greater value as an assembled whole than the aggregate of the values of separate tracts into which it might be divided. I think the value which would pertain to the assembled whole would gradually progress as the separate tracts came under a single ownership. When I testified that the population of Alameda County, in the neighborhood of Calaveras, was increasing rapidly, I meant by that the population on the east side of the bay, which might or would in the course of time have its water supply safeguarded more or less by such a reservoir as the Calaveras. It is the population that extends from San Jose northerly to Richmond. I did not mean in the immediate vicinity of the Calaveras reservoir.

1332

The estimated production of the Calaveras of 37,000,000 gallons daily, as appearing in my report, is my own estimate, and is lower than that which has been made by the engineers of the water company.

Map 2 "Plaintiff's Exhibit A", parcel 16 and 14: There is a reason for supposing a difference to exist between the land below the San Andres dam, which is not within the reservoir, and the land above the dam which is within the reservoir. The dam was put across the valley at its narrowest point, and at that point the hills coming closest together mark the proper spot for the dam. Above the same there is a spreading out of the valley, otherwise there would have been no such reservoir site there as the San Andres. The fall of the stream in the case of this reservoir is considerably greater below than it is above, the elevation of San Andres being nearly 500 feet as compared with the water surface elevation of about 288 in Crystal Springs.

1333

The fact of the earthquake, and the fact also of the breaking of the pipe line due to the earthquake, made more apparent than before the necessity of water storage in large amounts near San Francisco, and the importance too of a supply as near the city as possible.

1334

1335

In selecting a balancing reservoir on the Peninsula in connection with the scheme for bringing in the Hetch Hetchy water, I picked out the Belmont reservoir because that was the best site near at hand that I could find available, but it only became a balancing reservoir. It was to remain full at all times, and the discharge was to be into a full reservoir, and water drawn off from a full reservoir, the reservoir being at such an elevation that gravity flow into the city at a fair elevation to serve the low-lying districts would have been impossible from the outlet of the reservoir, if placed in

381

the bottom of the reservoir. The plan was that the water there stored, about three thousand million gallons, should in case of necessity be pumped into the city, so that there was a standby pump provided in connection with the Belmont reservoir. It was quite a different arrangement from the arrangement that exists, or would exist with the Peninsula reservoirs now owned by the Spring Valley Water Co., as a part of the water supply system. In the case of the Belmont reservoir, there is no possibility of utilizing the ordinary storage without pumping the supply into San Francisco; the water-

1336   shed that is tributary to the Belmont was only about 2½ square miles, and the yield of water was small. In the case of the Pilarcitos, San Andres and Crystal Springs, which are at a higher elevation, they have larger watersheds, and their storage capacity is very much greater. There would be about ten times the amount of storage in the reservoirs of the Peninsula system as now developed when compared with the Belmont reservoir. The water surface elevation of the Belmont as planned, in connection with the Hetch Hetchy project, was at elevation 177 feet above city base; the water surface of the Crystal Springs is about elevation 283 feet above city base, and the San Andres and Pilarcitos are both higher than Crystal Springs. The elevations that are referred to in the memorandum which I have submitted, are intended to be elevations above Crystal Springs datum, so far as the Peninsula system of reservoirs is concerned, and the elevations that I have just now mentioned are above city base. With an adequate balancing reservoir, the conduit across the bay could be kept smaller, because the irregularities in draft are overcome by the amount that can be stored in a reservoir,

1337   so that an adequate balancing reservoir will keep the main pipe line capacity at a minimum. It will be determined more nearly from the average requirement than it will be by the maximum requirement.

In my valuations I did not include anything for the dam that makes the reservoir possible. I simply valued the land. In regard to the San Mateo Water Co. purchase, I find that the land was acquired, and also certain water rights. The purchase included whatever was on the land, and certain rights were reserved by the seller to remove certain portions of the pipes and other material that might be useful elsewhere.

RE-CROSS EXAMINATION BY MR. STEINHART

1338   In relation to the Smith purchase, I was referring to a Mr. Smith who was owner of certain properties known as the hog ranch. and other lands, and of certain lands in the Hetch Hetchy Valley. I did not read the agreement of sale between Mr. Smith and the City, but I have an impression that there were about 1300 acres acquired from him. It was my impression that there was a segregation at the time of that purchase as to reservoir lands and other lands.

(Discussion between Counsel as to whether or not the price of 1338-1340
these lands was arrived at by a segregation between the reservoir
and outside lands. Counsel for Plaintiff contends that the Board
of Supervisors of the City and County of San Francisco segregated
it at the rate of $255 per acre for reservoir lands, and $10 an acre
for the other lands. Counsel for Defendant advised that there is
nothing in the agreement about the segregation, but that the purchase
price is a purchase price as a whole.)

The Belmont reservoir has a capacity of about three thousand
million gallons, and as the reservoir has a very small watershed, the
yielding capacity as far as water production is concerned, would be
very small. The reservoir would be more a storage reservoir than   1341
anything else. For that reason I compare it unfavorably with the
other reservoirs which have a larger watershed tributary to them.
In comparing the value of the two, I would consider that this is a
different type of reservoir, and fulfills a different function from the
other reservoirs, being more nearly of the character of simple storage
of water nearby. The additional character of the other reservoirs
is that they have a yielding capacity of about 18,000,000 gallons a
day, and I consider that as an item in the valuation of the Crystal
Springs reservoir, because the yielding capacity is an element of
value. It is the opportunity to develop that which is valued, and
not the water which is developed; it is the reservoir as a reservoir.
If that reservoir were merely a storage reservoir, with flat lands
all around it and no watersheds tributary to it, I would not value
it the same as I have valued it. When I recommended the Belmont
reservoir, I recommended it as the best that could be had, but it was 1342
not what I would have wanted in connection with the system. The
system would have been feasible for the City of San Francisco, but
with less reliability of service than desirability. I think you will
find in one of my reports in comparing the various projects, that
I gave the advantage of reliability of service to the Spring Valley
Water Co.'s works. The report in which I discussed the Belmont
reservoir was made after the progress report was made.   1343

I am familiar with the Arroyo Valle reservoir. The valley opens
out, it widens above the dam; the dam is in the narrow portion of the valley. The valley widens out possibly half a mile above
the site of the dam, widening a little almost immediately above the
dam.

Map No. 2, parcel 14; this parcel has its easterly portion in the   1344
reservoir site, and there is no indication on the map of the widening
out beyond the indicated water surface line, but the valley of the
reservoir almost immediately above that, at the water surface, is
considerably wider than it is at the dam site; it extends over from
parcel 14 into the parcels on the east side of the reservoir.

The San Andres Creek, which I am familiar with in a general

way, enters the reservoir at its upper, or northwesterly end, and it leaves the reservoir at the point where the dam has been constructed. It is the closing of this creek by the dam which has made the reservoir. The reservoir includes, and is on both sides of the San Andres Creek, which creek flows through the bed of the reservoir, and is practically parallel with the reservoir.

Cory   Witness: HARRY THOMAS CORY.

1345   DIRECT EXAMINATION BY MR. OLNEY.

I am a consulting engineer, and have followed that profession about 21 years. I graduated in civil and electrical engineering from Purdue University, and also took post-graduate courses in both civil and electrical engineering at Cornell University. In 1893 to 1900 I was professor of civil engineering in the University of Missouri, then I went as Dean of the University of Cincinnati, and retained my position there for three years. I then went into railroad work, becoming in June 1904 assistant to the general manager of the Southern Pacific Co., and in May 1905 assistant to the President of the Harriman lines in Arizona and Old Mexico, which latter position I held until 1911. In 1906 I was assigned, by Mr. Randolph, to act

1346   in co-operation with my brother, Professor C. L. Cory, of the University of California, to investigate commercial and engineering features of a large power project in Verdi River, and in April of 1906 there was added to my duties the work as general manager and chief engineer of the California Development Co., and its subsidiary Mexican Corporation, which formed the irrigation system in Imperial Valley. Shortly after the first of 1910, I came to San Francisco, and associated myself with my brother in the office of Consulting Engineer, and have been here ever since. My practice in San Francisco has been largely in hydraulic engineering, chiefly considered from the commercial side. By that I mean rather than designing and constructing systems, I have been valuing them and considering them as matters of investment, including their earning power and the elements of cost—the economic side of engineering, as distinguished from the constructive, and creative and designing side. I have frequently considered such matters as reservoir sites and the cost of their acquisition. The value of them for the purposes of watering cities and land, and as parts of complete projects, and as

1347   separate elements. I have made a very complete examination of reservoir sites in Alameda County. The first was in connection with a report made to the agent of Mr. Borax Smith, which involved the determining of the real assets of the properties of the Union Water Co. This company was one of the United Properties, and was the successor to first the Bay Cities Water Co., and next the Sierra Water Supply Co., which corporations were initiated by Mr. Tevis and Mr. Hanford, and finally the entire project, which resulted from the activities of those companies was merged into the United Properties Co. under the corporate entity of the Union Water Company.

The Union Water Co. proposed to serve water to the East Bay Cities in competition with the Peoples Water Co. They made an offer to the City of Oakland at one time to sell their property, and an election was held for a bond issue to take over their holdings, which election was defeated.

We were retained also by the reorganization committee of the Peoples Water Co. to value its properties and holdings, and we did that, completing our work last November. In that connection we had to consider and value the existing reservoir sites at Lake Chabot, and Temescal, and proposed possible sites at Upper San Leandro, San Pablo, Pinole, and Wildcat, and that valuation necessarily involved the consideration of other sources of supply which might be available both from the Sierra Mountains and from nearby sources. 1348

I am familiar with the reservoir properties of the Spring Valley Water Co. across the bay, and have made an examination to ascertain the market values of those particular properties. The results of my examination are in the shape of a report. 1350

The reasonable premises for judging of the market value of the reservoir lands in question as of December 31, 1913, are as follows

1. That all of the lands in each of the several reservoirs be considered as in one parcel and ownership.

2. That the real property and rights other than the reservoir site, necessary to utilize the latter, have been, or can be, secured.

3. That there was no legal obstacle to the sale to any purchaser, who on December 31, 1913, might have desired the lands for reservoir purposes.

4. That the availability of the property for reservoir purposes in relation to the water supply situation of the entire San Francisco— Oakland Metropolitan area was appreciated both by the owner and by the possible purchasers. 1351

GENERAL CONSIDERATIONS:

It is obvious that in general the market value of any piece of real property is determined by a consideration of the highest use to which it may be put. Generally speaking, the highest use of rural lands is for agricultural purposes, and the market value is determined by that use, while the highest use of urban lands is for other than agricultural purposes, such as residences, business buildings, etc., and their market values are determined by such uses.

Broadly speaking, almost every piece of land may be used for reservoir purposes—indeed, water storage is frequently created in level fields for use in connection with irrigation pumping plants, etc. In the majority of cases one or more essential elements are lacking to give even natural basins practical value for reservoir purposes. Such elements of importance are sufficient watersheds behind them; precipitation satisfactory in amount and character; practicable cost of structures; sufficient market for stored water; satisfactory character of geological formation, precluding excessive leakage losses, etc. In such cases the reservoir use of land is below the agricultural or urban use.

Since the market value of real estate is generally determined by its highest use, it follows that the absolute minimum market value of rural reservoir possibilities is the agricultural value, and of urban reservoir sites the residential or commercial values. In some cases they may govern.

Otherwise, agricultural, residence or commercial urban uses are lower than the use of collecting, storing or distributing water. In these cases the absolute maximum price which can be paid for these lands is measured by the return which can be secured from a project
1352 of which they are an essential part, together with the costs of all other elements of the system.

With reservoir lands, therefore, there are two limits—sometimes widely apart; the minimum being the value for agricultural or urban uses, the maximum being what the traffic will bear. At any given time the market value of such lands will be somewhere between the two extremes. With indifferent reservoir possibilities, the market values will closely approximate the lower limit; with excellent reservoir sites, when there are no alternatives, they will tend more toward the higher limit.

So many factors are involved that each particular reservoir or system of reservoirs must needs be considered separately. This will be done with each of the several reservoirs under consideration:

Calaveras Reservoir: On December 31, 1913, it was, and had been for nearly thirty years, a matter of common knowledge that the Calaveras Reservoir was an important factor in the water supply situation of the San Francisco Bay Region. It had been brought before the public mind through the reports of T. R. Scowden, Colonel Mendel, and others, as early as 1874. Within a few years after the city had rejected the so-called ''Calaveras Cow Pasture'' project in 1877, it was realized that a grave mistake had been made, and such realization has grown with the years.

(The last sentence was objected to and was stricken out by the
1353 Master.)

It was known that several examinations of the reservoir site had been made, and that it had been found to be geologically watertight; to have an excellent dam site; and to have a watershed with a precipitation insuring a large runoff. Through the application by the City of San Francisco for the so-called Hetch Hetchy permit, the reports required to be made in connection therewith, including that of the so-called Army Board, and the hearing held by Secretary Fisher in November, 1912, the common opinion was entirely confirmed that by the creation of the Calaveras Reservoir there would result a safe water yield of at least 40,000,000 gallons per day, which would be released into conduits at an average elevation exceeding 700 feet above sea level.

(The last sentence was objected to by Counsel for Defendant and by consent of Counsel for Plaintiff was permitted to go out.) 1355

On December 31, 1913, the Peoples Water Company on the East side of the Bay had just passed through a very severe drought, and by the narrowest possible margin escaped a water shortage disastrous not only to it, but to all the East Bay communities. The Union Water Company, which had aspired to be a competitor of the Peoples Water Company, had just abandoned its endeavors to develop enough underground water along the eastern bay coast to become an important factor in the water situation in the Bay Cities. A great deal of work had been done and plans were well advanced for bringing to a vote in the East Bay Cities the creation of a Municipal Water District. The requirements of the Spring Valley Water Company had reached its developed water supply.

In short, there certainly would have been at least three water companies and two sets of individuals deeply interested in, and perhaps even officially representing, one water district and one municipality, respectively, in active competition to secure this source of supply. There would doubtless have also been one or more syndi- 1356
cates of shrewd business men, who, appreciating the situation, would have endeavored to secure the reservoir site with the expectation of turning it over with a good profit to someone of these five interests.

The importance of the Calaveras source of supply can be appreciated by remembering that its safe yield is at least equal to, and doubtless in excess of, the total amount of water then consumed in the City of San Francisco; considerably in excess of the total supply which is controlled by the Peoples Water Company, both developed and possible of development; and considerably over twice as much as the quantity supplied to its consumers by the Peoples Water Company.

There is nothing else nearby comparable in availability. On the East side of the Bay, the undeveloped sources of the Peoples Water Company are far inferior, for several reasons. They cannot be made to yield half as much water; the cost will be materially greater per unit of capacity; the elevation of the points of delivery are lower; and the watersheds cannot be enough protected to obviate the necessity for filtration. On the San Francisco side, the developed resources were being utilized to their safe limit.

The Calaveras watershed is so sparsely inhabited, and the amount and time of storage so considerable, that the Calaveras waters will be more satisfactory without the filtration than either 1357 the developed or undeveloped supplies of the Peoples Water Company with filtration. In addition to this advantage of the Calaveras project, there are several others; the elevation of the intake, where the water surface will average about 700 feet; the earthen dam; and so far as the East side is concerned, the short length of pipe line. It is only 36 miles, by the pipe line route, to the Central Reservoir in Oakland, and over two-thirds of it follows closely the line of two railways. The estimated cost of the works, delivering 40,000,000 gallons daily to Oakland with a one-third excess pipe capacity, is only $10,000,000, or but $250,000 per million gallons daily, and to San Francisco about $16,000,000, or $400,000 per million gallons daily.

On the other hand, the Raker bill, granting certain rights in the Hetch Hetchy project, had just been signed by President Wilson, and in the minds of some people removed the necessity for developing the Calaveras source.

1358 However, there are very onerous conditions imposed upon San Francisco by the Raker bill—so onerous that it is by no means certain the project will ever be carried out. Warnings to this effect had been given wide publicity in September, when the bill passed the House, by a number of thoughtful citizens, among others, the two most earnest proponents of the project—ex-City Engineers Grunsky and Manson. Even assuming that work could have been begun at once, and vigorously prosecuted, it would have been so long before the Hetch Hetchy supply could be gotten into the Bay Cities, that the Calaveras supply simply had to be developed anyway and at once. That this was fully appreciated is made obvious by the fact that upon the insistence of the City of San Francisco in May of that year, work had actually been started on the Calaveras dam, has been continuously prosecuted ever since, and no one is more eager that this should continue than the city officials of San Francisco.

It was also a matter of common knowledge that San Francisco had a few years before paid as much as $255 per acre for reservoir lands away off in the Sierra Mountains; that the Peoples Water Company valued the Lake Chabot site at $1250 per acre; and that Judge Farrington had decided the Peninsula reservoir land to have the value of $1000 per acre over ten years before.

It was, furthermore, a matter of common knowledge that the development of this reservoir site was not only inevitable, but imminent, and that there would have been no doubt of the existence of an immediate demand for the land for reservoir purposes, either on the part of the owner, or of anyone contemplating their purchase.

Taking all these elements into consideration, it is my judgment that the holder of this reservoir site could, December 31, 1913, have sold it for at least $600,000, and might well have obtained a very much higher figure. I do not think any prudent owner would have opened negotiations for anything less than one million dollars, because even at the latter figure, the cost of the reservoir lands—absolutely vital to the project—is so small a percentage of the total cost, I do not think any prudent executive of anyone of the several interests mentioned would have risked much parleying.

Accordingly, I believe it is conservative to say that the market value of the Calaveras Reservoir site at the time in question was at least $600,000, and probably considerably more. Since it is proposed to flood 1928 acres, this is equivalent to $311.20 per acre. This is very much less than the figure at which it was possible to acquire anyone of the undeveloped reservoir possibilities of the Peoples Water Company, which are the only ones, other than San Antonio or Arroyo Valle, existing in the East Bay region.

The San Antonio Reservoir.

The San Antonio Reservoir would make possible a safe yield of only about one-sixth that from the Calaveras unit, which is so small, relative to the gross requirements of the region, that it may be many years before the site is utilized. It may well be that it will never be utilized. Its value for reservoir purposes is, therefore, somewhat speculative and remote. Under these circumstances, its market value will be largely controlled by the value of the land for agricultural purposes, and will not greatly exceed that value.

It is certain, however, that in view of the fact that it is known to be a good reservoir site, and generally recognized as such, and is included as a part of the Freeman Hetch Hetchy project, its market value as a unit was substantially in excess of its value for agricultural purposes. No owner of the land as a unit would sell the property for a price which did not take into consideration its availability for reservoir purposes, and, on the other hand, any person contemplating its purchase would be willing to pay more by reason of this fact.

I understand that the lands have been valued at between $50,000 and $60,000 for agricultural purposes. Under all the circumstances, I am convinced that a figure exceeding its agricultural value by at least one-third, or, on the basis of the property being worth for agricultural purposes $60,000, a figure of $80,000 is conservative, and that it had on the 31st of December, 1913, a market value of at least that sum.

ARROYO VALLE.

This is more of a regulating than a storage reservoir, and is even less essential to the urban communities than San Antonio. On the other hand, its construction would be an excellent thing for the entire Pleasanton Valley. All things considered, there would be just about the same excess of market value over agricultural value here as at San Antonio, namely, one-third. Since the agricultural value is about $35,-000, a figure of $50,000 is conservative, and it is my judgment that on December 31, 1913, its market value was at least that sum.

CROSS EXAMINATION BY MR. STEINHART.

1361   The fact that San Francisco a few years before paid as much as $255 per acre for lands away off in the Sierra Mountains appeared, as I remember it, in the newspapers at the time of the purchase. At any rate it has been a very well defined piece of information filed away in my mental catalogue. Perhaps we have a different definition of a matter of common knowledge. My understanding of the matter of common knowledge is something which has been published in the newspapers, and to the person who is interested in that particular kind of information. I do not remember what newspaper it was published in, but I discussed it with engineers numerous times.

    In regard to the Arroyo Valle, it is not a reservoir that you are going to draw from directly so much, but it is a reservoir the purpose of which is to insure the absorption by the Pleasanton gravels of the runoff from the watershed. That does make a difference in my opinion as to the value, because you are not actually getting the water out of
1362   the reservoir first-hand, as there is another step in the process.

    I have often noticed reservoir sites near the head waters of streams, and observed the fact that they were wonderfully formed, and yet they have no value because they have no watershed behind them to fill them. I have often noted beautiful reservoir sites with a very large watershed behind them, but it is in desert countries, where the precipitation is such that they are not really of any value. In this way, such elements of importance as sufficient watersheds and precipitation satisfactory in amount and character makes a difference.

    I do not remember what the Union Water Company paid for their reservoir site. The financial condition of that company, in 1913, was unsatisfactory. Its operating expenses were very much in excess of its receipts.

    The Peoples Water Company was in an unfortunate financial con-
1363   dition in 1913. The creation of a municipal district was voted on in June, 1914, but the vote would be considerably determined by the ability to get water in and make scrap value of the Peoples Water Company's plant. I do not know what the Peoples Water Company paid for its undeveloped reservoir lands.

RE-DIRECT EXAMINATION BY MR. OLNEY.

In my valuations, I have not included anything for water rights or for the structures.

RE-CROSS EXAMINATION BY MR. STEINHART.

I include something for the fact that there is a watershed in the neighborhood, for it is inconceivable that a reservoir site would have any value as a collecting and storage reservoir site, were it not for the watershed behind it. 1364

In valuing Lake Chabot Reservoir, I valued the reservoir land at $1250, and the real estate value of the reservoir site itself was appraised, I believe, by Mr. Woodward at $600 an acre. The outside lands' rapid decrease in value is the reason of my hesitation as to the value of the neighboring land. The Temescal Reservoir site, which I valued at $2000 an acre, is the nearest reservoir site of the Peoples Water Company to human habitation. In valuing it I valued it at its real estate value. It had no additional value at all, because its reservoir value was not in excess of its urban value, due to the fact that there were many other sites as available as that. It has little value 1365 as a collection reservoir. When I testified in regard to the value of Temescal Reservoir in the Peoples Water Company hearing, and testified as to its value not being in excess of its residential value, I stated that that is the only reason that is of importance, because the fact remains that there are a great many reservoir possibilites which cannot be afforded. The value of the land is too great, and you certainly could not afford to put a reservoir in that place, as there are other opportunities for reservoir locations elsewhere on cheaper ground. That was the objection of the Railroad Commission to the Claremont Reservoir. I do not know whether the Railroad Commission put any value on the Peoples Water Co. Reservoir in excess of the real estate value.

I do not place a higher valuation than $2000 on the Temescal Reservoir, because the real estate valuation is so great that if that reservoir were to be built again, it would not be built there. It would 1366 be built on other lands that are cheaper which would serve the purpose. I don't know that I could tell you exactly where I would put the Temescal Reservoir, but there are numerous places over on the hills of Berkeley where reservoirs may be placed. As a collection reservoir, you could not find a location where you could put another reservoir to take its place, but as a distribution reservoir, there are a great many places. It is at the present time a collection reservoir, collecting the small amount of 300,000 gallons a day, really negligible in quantity. I should say that within a distance of three miles north and three miles south you would probably find five reservoir sites that might be substituted for Temescal in holding that total quantity of

water, and probably be equally as good for further designing of the
system. I don't know that there are reservoir sites of similar type
as the Temescal Reservoir. There probably are not.

1367
1369

Mr. Olney, of Counsel for Plaintiff, read the following statement :

In 1907, Josephine O. Phelps was the owner of a large tract of
land in San Mateo County, which included a portion of the Crystal
Springs watershed. She contracted to sell it to one, John Partridge.
On June 10, 1907, Partridge leased to the Spring Valley Water Company the portion of the tract within the Crystal Springs watershed,
the land being described as 800 acres, more or less, and extending up
to the summit of the hills, so as to embrace all of the tract within the
watershed. I have got the original papers for that. The term of the
lease was seven years, and the rent therefore was $5,000 a year, the
water company paying the taxes. The lease also provided that the
water company should deliver to Partridge on the lands outside of the
watershed, which he had under contract from Mrs. Phelps, 100,000
gallons of water daily at the price of 15 cents per thousand gallons.
The lease further provided that at its expiration Partridge should
convey the leased land to the water company without further payment
other than the payment of $5,000 per year perpetually, and the con-

1370

tinued delivery of 100,000 gallons of water daily at the price of 15
cents per thousand gallons. The lease also provided that at any time
after the conveyance of the land, the water company must pay $100,-
000 and relieve itself of the $5,000 annual payment. At the same time
as the making of the lease by Partridge, the water company made an
agreement with Mrs. Phelps, the owner of the land, whereby she
agreed, in effect, that in case Partridge failed to perform his contract
of purchase from her so that the land came back to her, she would
lease the land to the water company upon the same terms as those of
the lease by Partridge, the term of the lease to be for 45 years. By
this agreement with Mrs. Phelps, Mrs. Phelps further agreed to convey the land to the water company at any time upon the payment of
$100,000. Partridge failed to complete his contract with Mrs. Phelps,
and on June 10, 1914, his rights ended. In the meantime, the land
had been surveyed, and it had been ascertained that there was, in fact,
some 969 acres in the watershed instead of about 800 acres, as supposed. Mrs. Phelps has now brought suit, which is now pending,
seeking to have it judicially determined that her agreement covers
800 acres only. I have looked these matters up; that is the situation,
if there is anything incorrect about that, you can state it.

(It was stipulated that the statement should be accepted for the
present, and if Counsel for the Defendant finds anything wrong with
it he can correct it.)

TWENTY-SECOND HEARING.   AUGUST 18, 1915.

Witnesses: J. F. Burgin and H. T. Cory.

DIRECT EXAMINATION BY MR. OLNEY.   1371

I am a resident of San Francisco, and have been since 1907. I was, and am acquainted with Elmer E. Smith, who owned certain lands on the floor of Hetch Hetchy Valley, and also outside the valley in the same vicinity. He sold those lands to the City and County of   1372 San Francisco.

(It is understood that the objection of Counsel for Defendant   1373 goes to all this line of testimony.)

The purchase price of the land was $150,000, plus 6% interest on deferred payments. I negotiated the sale of the property myself,   1374 as agent for Mr. Smith.

Questioned by Master.

I negotiated with Mr. Phelan, Mr. Manson, and the Mayor of the City of San Francisco, Mr. E. R. Taylor. I was a party to all the proceedings at that time, after bringing Mr. Smith and Mr. Manson, the City Engineer, and Mr. Phelan, a citizen, and the Mayor together.

DIRECT EXAMINATION BY MR. OLNEY.

Mr. Phelan acted as a citizen of San Francisco, I suppose, toward acquiring the Hetch Hetchy land for the city. The meetings were held at his office, and he was a party to arranging the first payment of $10,000. What other part he took in it I could not tell. He had   1375 been Mayor of the city, and I suppose, had been personally very much interested in the city acquiring water from Hetch Hetchy. The first negotiations I had regarding the property were with Mr. Manson, the City Engineer. In the beginning I made a verbal offer of the property to the city for $175,000. There was an offer made in writing, upon   1376 the basis of which the lands were finally purchased.

The transaction for the purchase of these lands was finally consumated upon the basis which is set out in this writing which I have here, according to my recollection.

(Discussion between Counsel and the Master upon the question 1376-1379 of whether this line of testimony is or is not properly admissable as evidence. The objection of Counsel for Defendant was overruled.)

The following was read into the record: "Oakland, California, September 3, 1907. Mr. Marsden Manson, San Francisco, California. My Dear Sir:—

"As you are representing San Francisco, and in compliance with your request, I make the following alternative propositions of sale of patented lands owned by me in Yosemite National Park. First, I offer

560 acres, more or less, in and adjacent to the floor of Hetch Hetchy Valley at the price of $125,000, of which $20,000 is to be paid upon the acceptance of this proposition by or on behalf of the city of San Francisco, and the remainder in three years at 6% on deferred payments.

1380

"Second, I offer 812 and 14/100 acres, more or less, in five separate tracts, one of which includes the tract included in the above offer. The others are in Tilltill Valley, 160 acres, more or less, Hog Ranch, 322 46/100 acres, more or less; Canyon Ranch, 160 acres, more or less; Middle Fork Homestead, 163 68/100 acres, more or less, for the sum of $150,000, of which $25,000 is to be paid in cash upon the acceptance of this offer by or on behalf of the City and County of San Francisco and the remainder upon the terms mentioned under this first offer. The offers will remain open until October 1, 1907. Yours very truly." Signed, "Elmer E. Smith."

The following portion of the agreement of sale was read into the record:

"MEMORANDUM OF AGREEMENT.

"This agreement, made and entered into this 14th day of December, 1908, by and between Elmer E. Smith of the County of Merced, State of California, party of the first part, and the City and County of San Francisco, a municipal corporation, the party of the second part.

"Witnesseth: Whereas, said party of the first part is the owner, through title derived by a patent from the United States, of all those certain lands situated in the Yosemite National Park, Tuolumne County, California, described as follows:

"First: Those certain lands situate, lying and being in and adjoining the floor of the Hetch Hetchy Valley, particularly described as follows:"

(Here follows description.)

1381

"Containing in the aggregate 560 acres, more or less. Said lands are hereinafter referred to as 'inside lands'.

"Second: Those certain lands situated within said Yosemite National Park, and adjacent reserves outside of and beyond the floor of said Hetch Hetchy Valley, particularly described as follows:"

(Here follows a particular description.)

"Containing in the aggregate 762 acres. Said lands last described are hereinafter referred to as 'outside lands' ".

Then the price is fixed by the contract at $150,800.

(Counsel for Defendant is willing to waive any objection to the testimony of Mr. Grunsky and Mr. Cory, so far as such objection might be based upon the fact that portions of their testimony had gone in by way of their reading from a written report, instead of by question and answer.)

SPRING VALLEY WATER CO. VS. CITY AND COUNTY OF SAN FRANCISCO

Witness: HARRY T. CORY.   1383

RE-CALLED FOR FURTHER CROSS EXAMINATION.

I have no satisfactory knowledge of the figures paid by the Peoples Water Company for its undeveloped reservoir sites, either as a whole or in separate pieces.

RE-DIRECT EXAMINATION BY MR. OLNEY.

Q. Were you not acquainted with the values which were placed upon the lands in the reservoirs at and about 1913?

(Objected to, and objection sustained.)

(Statements by Counsel as to the nature of the evidence which 1384-1387 they intend to introduce as following this.)

Mr. Olney: By the way, your Honor, so that you may be informed as to the result of this instrument that was put in this morning, those prices figure out $223 an acre approximately for the reservoir land of Hetch Hetchy, and $33 an acre for the outside lands.

INDEX

INDEX

Lightning Source UK Ltd.
Milton Keynes UK
UKHW010601110219
337000UK00006B/431/P